THE ECONOMICS OF EDUCATION

THE ECONOMICS OF EDUCATION

A COMPREHENSIVE OVERVIEW

SECOND EDITION

Edited by

STEVE BRADLEY

COLIN GREEN

ELSEVIER

ACADEMIC PRESS

An imprint of Elsevier

Academic Press is an imprint of Elsevier
125 London Wall, London EC2Y 5AS, United Kingdom
525 B Street, Suite 1650, San Diego, CA 92101, United States
50 Hampshire Street, 5th Floor, Cambridge, MA 02139, United States
The Boulevard, Langford Lane, Kidlington, Oxford OX5 1GB, United Kingdom

Notices

Knowledge and best practice in this field are constantly changing. As new research and experience broaden our understanding, changes in research methods, professional practices, or medical treatment may become necessary.

Practitioners and researchers must always rely on their own experience and knowledge in evaluating and using any information, methods, compounds, or experiments described herein. In using such information or methods they should be mindful of their own safety and the safety of others, including parties for whom they have a professional responsibility.

To the fullest extent of the law, neither the Publisher nor the authors, contributors, or editors, assume any liability for any injury and/or damage to persons or property as a matter of products liability, negligence or otherwise, or from any use or operation of any methods, products, instructions, or ideas contained in the material herein.

Library of Congress Cataloging-in-Publication Data
A catalog record for this book is available from the Library of Congress

British Library Cataloguing-in-Publication Data
A catalogue record for this book is available from the British Library

ISBN: 978-0-12-815391-8

For information on all Academic Press publications visit our website at
https://www.elsevier.com/books-and-journals

Publisher: Katey Birtcher
Acquisition Editor: Katey Birtcher
Editorial Project Manager: Michael Lutz
Production Project Manager: Surya Narayanan Jayachandran
Cover Designer: Matthew Limbert

Typeset by TNQ Technologies

Contents

Contributors xiii
Foreword xv

I

Overview

1. Empirical methods in the economics of education
GUIDO SCHWERDT AND LUDGER WOESSMANN

Introduction 3
From correlation to causation 3
Explicit randomization 5
    Randomized controlled experiments 5
    Lotteries of oversubscribed programs 7
Natural experiments 9
    Instrumental-variable approach 9
    Regression-discontinuity approach 10
Methods using panel data 13
    Difference-in-differences approach 13
    Fixed-effects approach 15
Conclusions 17
References 17

2. Behavioral economics and nudging in education: evidence from the field
METTE TRIER DAMGAARD AND HELENA SKYT NIELSEN

Behavioral economics of education 21
    Self-control 21
    Limited attention and cognitive ability 22
    Loss aversion 22
    Default bias 22
    Social preferences 23
    Biased beliefs 23
Education interventions involving nudging 23
    Defaults 25
    Framing 25

Peer group manipulations 26
Deadlines 26
Goal setting 27
Reminders 28
Informational nudges 28
Boosting skills to alleviate self-control problems 30
Social comparison nudges 30
Social belonging, identity activation and mindset
    nudges 31
Conclusion 32
References 32
Further reading 35

II

Private and social returns to education

3. Returns to education in developed countries
MORLEY GUNDERSON AND PHILIP OREOPOLOUS

Glossary of terms 39
Introduction 39
Estimating returns to education via schooling
    equations 40
    Basic schooling equation 40
    Hourly wages versus measures that include hours of
        work 41
    Measurement error in schooling 42
    Ability bias, omitted variables and selection bias 42
    Heterogeneous returns 45
    Annual returns, signaling, and sheepskin effects 46
    Non-pecuniary benefits and social benefits 47
Trends and some international evidence 48
Summary 49
References 49
Further reading 50

4. Returns to education in developing countries

HARRY ANTHONY PATRINOS AND GEORGE
PSACHAROPOULOS

Introduction   53
Estimation procedures   54
Global estimates   56
Low-income countries   56
Vocational education   57
Preschool   59
    Causality   60
    Cognitive ability   61
Conclusions and policy considerations   62
References   62
Further reading   63

5. Returns to education quality

MARK HOEKSTRA

Education quality and student outcomes   65
Assessing the causal returns to education quality   67
Benefits to attending more selective middle and high
    schools   68
Returns to college quality   70
References   71

6. Heterogeneity in the returns to higher education

IAN WALKER

Introduction   75
The economic value of degrees   78
    Estimating the college premium   79
    Student choice and heterogeneity in the returns to
        degrees   83
Conclusion   89
References   89

7. Parental education and children's health throughout life

MATHIAS HUEBENER

Glossary   91
Introduction   91
Theoretical considerations   93
    Immediate effects of education   93
    Intergenerational effects of education   93
Insights across children's lifecycle   94

Prenatal influences and health at birth   94
In childhood   95
In adolescence   96
In adulthood   97
In late life   98
Evidence from developing countries   99
Implications and outlook   100
References   101
Further reading   102

8. Education and civic engagement

T.S. DEE

The civic returns to educational attainment   103
Comparisons of public and private schools   105
Summary and future directions   107
See also   107
References   107
Further reading   108

9. Education and crime

LANCE LOCHNER

Introduction   109
The economics of education and crime   109
Evidence on education, school quality, and crime   110
    Effects of educational attainment on crime   110
    Effects of education on female crime   113
    Effects of school choice and quality on crime   113
    Contemporaneous schooling and crime   114
    Brief comment on measures of criminality   115
The effects of arrest and incarceration on education   115
Conclusions and policy lessons   116
References   116

10. Education and inequality

JO BLANDEN

Introduction   119
Inequalities in educational outcomes   119
    Inequalities by social background   119
    Inequalities by race, ethnicity and immigrant
        status   122
    Inequalities by gender   123
Education and economic outcomes   125
    Changes over time   128
Conclusions   130
References   130

11. Race earnings differentials
M. CARNOY

Glossary   133
Race and ethnic earnings differences in the United
    States   134
A model for explaining earnings differences   136
Explaining earnings differences with cross-section
    data   137
Earnings differences for minority women   139
Do ability/educational quality differences explain race/
    ethnic earnings differences?   140
What are the sources of the black/white test-score gap?
    142
Explaining changes in earnings differences over time   143
Comparing results for Brazil and Israel   145
See also   146
References   146

12. The economics of high school dropouts
RUSSELL W. RUMBERGER

Introduction   149
Who drops out of high school?   149
What are the consequences?   151
Why do students drop out?   152
    Individual factors   152
    Institutional factors   153
What can be done?   155
Conclusions   157
References   157
Further reading   157

III

Production, costs and financing

13. Education production functions
ERIC A. HANUSHEK

Glossary   161
Overview   161
Measuring skills and human capital   161
Basic production function estimates   163
    Measured school inputs   164
    Study quality   165
    More recent studies   166
Do teachers and schools matter?   167
Benefits and costs   168
Some conclusions and implications   168
References   169
Further reading   170

14. Education, knowledge capital, and economic growth
ERIC A. HANUSHEK AND LUDGER WOESSMANN

Early studies of schooling quantity and economic
    growth   172
Early evidence on the quality of education and economic
    growth   173
Recent evidence on the importance of cognitive skills for
    economic growth   174
Causality in brief   176
The interaction of educational quality with economic
    institutions   178
Simulating the impact of educational reform on economic
    growth   178
Summary   180
References   180

15. Education production functions: updated evidence from developing countries
PAUL GLEWWE, SYLVIE LAMBERT AND QIHUI CHEN

Introduction   183
Education in developing countries   183
The education production function   188
Estimation of education production functions   194
Evidence of policy impacts from developing
    countries   196
    Demand-side interventions   196
    Supply-side policies   203
Conclusions and suggestions for future research   210
References   211

16. Schooling inputs and behavioral responses by families
BIRGITTA RABE

Introduction   217
Conceptual framework: education production and input
    interactions   218
    Extensions   219
Methodological approaches to estimation   220
Empirical findings   221

Factors driving heterogeneous results   223
Multiple inputs and agents   224
Test score impacts   225
Conclusions   225
References   226

17. The economics of early childhood interventions
M. NORES

The economic rationale   229
Market failures   230
Equity and redistribution   230
Human capital formation   231
Types of early childhood interventions   231
Cognitive and academic outcomes   233
Noncognitive outcomes   234
Indirect effects: female labor supply   235
Economic returns   236
Conclusions   236
See also   236
References   237
Further reading   238

18. Parental socioeconomic status, child health, and human capital
J. CURRIE AND J. GOODMAN

Glossary   239
Introduction   239
Does parental socioeconomic status affect child health?   240
External benefits of parental SES   240
Evidence   240
Does child health affect future outcomes?   242
Possible channels   242
Evidence   243
Can health account for gaps in Children's educational outcomes?   247
See also   247
References   247
Further reading   248

19. Monetary and non-monetary incentives for educational attainment: design and effectiveness
H. SCHILDBERG-HÖRISCH AND V. WAGNER

Introduction   249
Monetary incentives   250
Sensitivity to cash size   250
Who should be rewarded?   252
Non-monetary incentives   253
Types of non-monetary incentives   253
Selection of non-monetary incentives   254
Effectiveness of non-monetary incentives   257
Non-monetary incentives for students   257
Non-monetary incentives for parents and teachers   263
Discussion and conclusion   264
Acknowledgments   266
References   266
Further reading   268

20. Educational mismatch in developing countries: A review of the existing evidence
H. BATTU AND K.A. BENDER

Introduction   269
Measurement issues   271
General findings   272
The degree of mismatch   273
Rates of overeducation and undereducation   273
Brazil   273
Russia (and post-communist transition economies)   273
India   274
China   274
Low-income countries   276
Explanations for mismatch   277
Introduction   277
Informality   278
Quality of education   280
Other factors   281
Consequences of mismatch   282
Brazil   282
Russia and post-communist countries   282
India   283
China   283
Low-income countries   283

Policy, conclusions and reflection　284
References　285

21. Peer effects in education: recent empirical evidence
ALFREDO R. PALOYO

Introduction　291
Recent empirical evidence　293
 Deliberate random assignment　293
 Regression-discontinuity design　295
 Instrumental variable　297
 Fixed effect　298
 Variance restriction　300
 Nonlinearity and heterogeneity　300
Conclusion　302
References　303

22. The role of teacher quality in education production
BJARNE STRØM AND TORBERG FALCH

Introduction　307
Estimating teacher quality　307
 The value added approach　308
 The between subject approach　310
What explains teacher quality variation?　311
 Individual teacher characteristics　311
 Teacher labor market variables　313
Use of teacher quality measures in pay and evaluation systems　315
Summary and the way forward　316
References　317

23. The economics of class size
D.W. SCHANZENBACH

Introduction　321
Why class size might matter　321
Empirical approaches to studying the impact of class size　322
Nonexperimental research　322
Experimental research　323
Checks for randomization　325
Achievement results　326
Additional caveats　328
Quasi-experimental research　329
Policy-induced variation　329
Discussion　330

See also　330
References　330
Further reading　331

24. School finance: an overview
JENNIFER KING RICE, DAVID MONK AND JIJUN ZHANG

Introduction　333
 School finance in context　333
 Raising revenue: multiple and evolving roles　335
Distributing resources: multiple and competing goals　337
 Mechanisms for distributing revenue across school districts　337
 Challenges to state funding systems　338
Utilization of resources: current policy issues for school finance　340
 Teacher compensation　340
 Expanding the scope of educational services　341
References　341

25. The economics of tuition and fees in American higher education
R.G. EHRENBERG

Glossary　345
Introduction　345
Tuition keeps rising in private higher education　347
Tuition keeps rising at public institutions　349
Graduate and professional program tuition and fees　350
Concluding remarks　351
References　351
Further reading　352

IV

Teacher labour markets

26. Teacher labor markets: An overview
JESSALYNN JAMES AND JAMES WYCKOFF

Introduction　355
Constrained teacher labor markets　356
Methodological challenges　359
Recruiting effective teachers　360
Retaining effective teachers　363
Developing an effective teacher workforce　365
Looking forward　366
References　366

27. Teachers in developing countries

PAUL GLEWWE, RONGJIA SHEN, BIXUAN SUN AND
SUZANNE WISNIEWSKI

Introduction to review of literature on teachers in
    developing countries   371
Methods for literature selection and categorization   372
Analysis of teacher interventions that increase time in
    school   372
    Impacts of teacher inputs on time in school   372
    Impacts of pedagogy interventions on time in
        school   373
    Impacts of teacher-related governance interventions on
        time in school   373
Analysis of teacher interventions that improve learning
    outcomes   374
    Impacts of teacher inputs on learning   374
    Impacts of pedagogy interventions on learning   378
    Impacts of teacher-related governance interventions on
        learning   381
Analysis of interventions that improve teacher
    outcomes   383
    School input interventions   384
    Pedagogy interventions   384
    Governance interventions   384
Conclusion   386
References   387

28. Teacher supply

PETER DOLTON

The labor market for teachers   391
The demand for teachers   394
    The supply of teachers   396
    Teachers' pay   399
Summary   401
References   402
Further reading   402

29. Economic approaches to teacher recruitment and retention

S. LOEB AND J. MYUNG

Introduction   403
The supply of teachers   404
Wages   404
Working conditions   404
Psychic benefits and costs   405
School location   405

Barriers to entry   406
The demand for teachers   406
Student enrollment and teacher retirement   406
Reduction in student-to-teacher ratios   407
Hiring processes   407
Institutional constraints   407
Recruitment and retention policies to date   408
Partnerships between districts and local colleges   408
Monetary incentives   408
Changes in entry requirements   409
Teacher induction and mentoring   409
Performance-based pay   410
Career differentiation through ladders   410
Improving hiring practices   411
Reform of due process   411
Conclusion   412
See Also   412
References   412
Further reading   414

30. Compensating differentials in teacher labor markets

LI FENG

Compensating wage differentials through empirical studies
    using hedonic wage regression   417
    Method   417
    Data   417
    Findings   417
Compensating wage differentials through empirical studies
    of teacher attrition and retention   423
Compensating wage differentials using policy
    interventions   423
Quasi-experimental evidence   424
Random assignment evidence   428
Findings and future directions   428
References   428

31. Teacher incentives   431

L. SANTIBAÑEZ

Background on incentive programs   432
Advantages of incentive programs   432
Individual incentives *Efficiency and productivity*   432
    Recruitment and retention of qualified teachers   435
Group incentives *Efficiency and productivity*   435
Summary of key findings   436
Disadvantages and criticisms   436

Adverse and unintended consequences of teacher incentive
   programs   439
Conclusions   439
See also   440
References   440
Further reading   441

V

Education markets, choice and incentives

32. The economic role of the state in education
   D.N. PLANK AND T.E. DAVIS

Glossary   445
Constructing education systems   446
Economics and the State's role   446
   Is education a public good?   446
Market failure in the market for education   447
   Externalities   447
   Information asymmetry   448
   Uncertainty and risk aversion   449
   Economies of scale   449
Equity and equal opportunity   449
Critique of state provision   450
Public choice and government failure   450
   Inefficiency in production   450
   Inequity in opportunities and outcomes   451
   Standardization and enforced mediocrity   451
   Rent-seeking and corruption   451
A role for the state?   451
Education and the shrinking state   452
See also   453
References   453

33. Quasi-markets in education: the case of England
   STEVE BRADLEY

Introduction   455
How could markets in education operate?   457
   Alternative approaches   457
   Quasi-markets in England   458
   Evaluating the effects of Quasi-markets on educational
      outcomes   462
   The effects of complementary and contradictory
      educational policies   465

Conclusions and future research   467
References   468

34. Tiebout sorting and competition
   THOMAS J. NECHYBA

Residential mobility, capitalization and household
   preferences for education   472
Tiebout sorting and the rationing of school inputs   472
Tiebout competition to enhance productive
   efficiency   475
A partial divorce between competition and tiebout   476
Conclusion   477
References   478

35. Economic approaches to school efficiency
   GERAINT JOHNES

Introduction   479
Models of efficiency   480
   Data envelopment analysis   480
   Stochastic frontier analysis   482
More advanced models   483
   Non-parametric models   483
   Parametric models   486
Conclusions   487
References   487

36. School competition and the quality of education
   FRANCESCA FOLIANO AND OLMO SILVA

Glossary   491
Introduction   491
Empirical evidence   496
   England   496
   US   499
   Sweden   501
Chile   503
Conclusions   504
References   505

37. The economics of catholic schools
   W. SANDER AND D. COHEN-ZADA

Glossary   509
Introduction   509
Overview   509
   History and enrollment   509

Teachers   510
Students   510
Location   510
Tuition and costs   511
Market served   511
School practices   511
Vouchers   511
Catholic schools in other countries   511
Demand   512
Effects   513
  Academic achievement and educational
    attainment   513
  Bad behavior   514
  Civic participation and altruism   515
  Economic effects   515
  Other effects   515
  The effect of catholic school attendance in other
    countries   515
Conclusions   516
See also   516
References   516
Further reading   517

38. Private schools: choice and effects
FRANCIS GREEN

Introduction   519
Theory   520
Evidence on choice   522
Evidence on effects   524
  Methods   524
  Findings   526
Conclusion   527
References   528

39. The economics of charter schools
ADAM KHO, RON ZIMMER AND RICHARD BUDDIN

Glossary   531
Introduction   531
Policy questions   532
What types of students do charter schools serve?   532
Are charter and traditional schools receiving comparable
  funding?   534
How do charter schools affect the performance of charter
  students?   535
Is charter school competition improving the performance of
  traditional public schools?   538

Conclusion   539
References   540

40. The economics of vocational training
SAMUEL MUEHLEMANN AND STEFAN C. WOLTER

Introduction   543
Costs and benefits of training investments for firms   544
  Why firms pay for general training   544
  Costs and benefits of apprenticeship training   545
  Cross-country comparisons   546
Benefits of apprenticeships for individuals   548
Fiscal returns to apprenticeship training   552
Conclusions   553
References   553

41. Student incentives
ERIC R. EIDE AND MARK H. SHOWALTER

Introduction   555
Student incentives in K-12 education   555
  Financial incentives   555
  Non-financial or mixed incentives   556
Incentives in developing countries   557
Teacher incentives in K-12 education   559
  Individual teacher incentives   559
  Group incentives for teachers   560
  Teacher-student aligned incentives   561
Higher education incentives   561
  Scholarships, grants, and cash awards   561
  Student loans   562
Conclusion   563
References   563
Further reading   564

42. The economics of school accountability
D.N. FIGLIO AND H.F. LADD

Glossary   567
The rationale for school-based accountability   568
Designing school accountability systems   569
The evidence on student achievement   571
Evidence on unintended consequences   572
References   573
Further reading   575

Index   577

Contributors

H. Battu University of Aberdeen, Aberdeen, Scotland

K.A. Bender University of Aberdeen, Aberdeen, Scotland

Jo Blanden Economics Department, University of Surrey and Centre for Economic Performance, London School of Economics, London, United Kingdom

Steve Bradley Department of Economics, Lancaster University Management School, Lancaster, England

Richard Buddin University of Virginia, Charlottesville, VA, USA

M. Carnoy Stanford University, Stanford, CA, United States

Qihui Chen College of Economics and Management, China Agricultural University, Beijing, China

D. Cohen-Zada Ben-Gurion University, Beer-Sheva, Israel

J. Currie Columbia University, New York, NY, United States

Mette Trier Damgaard Department of Economics and Business Economics, Fuglesangs Allé 4, DK8210 Aarhus V, Denmark

T.E. Davis University of Maryland, Baltimore, MD, United States

T.S. Dee Swarthmore College, Swarthmore, PA, United States

Peter Dolton Department of Economics, University of Sussex, Brighton, UK

R.G. Ehrenberg Cornell University, Ithaca, NY, United States

Eric R. Eide Brigham Young University, Provo, UT, United States

Torberg Falch Department of Teacher Education, Norwegian University of Science and Technology, Norway

Li Feng Department of Finance and Economics, McCoy College of Business, Texas State University, San Marcos, TX, United States

D.N. Figlio Northwestern University, Evanston, IL, United States

Francesca Foliano Institute of Education, University College London, London, United Kingdom

Paul Glewwe Department of Applied Economics, University of Minnesota, St. Paul, MN, United States

J. Goodman Harvard University, Cambridge, MA, United States

Francis Green UCL Institute of Education, London, United Kingdom

Morley Gunderson Professor at the Centre for Industrial Relations, Human Resources, The Department of Economics, The School of Public Policy and Governance, Toronto, ON, Canada; Research Associate of the Centre for International Studies, The Institute for Human Development, Life Course and Ageing, All at the University of Toronto

Eric A. Hanushek Hoover Institution, Stanford University, CESifo, IZA, and NBER, Stanford, CA, United States

Mark Hoekstra Department of Economics, Texas A&M University, College Station, TX, United States

Mathias Huebener Education and Family Department, German Institute for Economic Research (DIW Berlin), Berlin, Germany

Jessalynn James Annenberg Institute, Brown University, Providence, RI, United States

Geraint Johnes Lancaster University Management School, United Kingdom

Adam Kho University of Southern California, Los Angeles, CA, USA

H.F. Ladd Duke University, Durham, NC, United States

Sylvie Lambert Paris School of Economics, Paris, France

Lance Lochner Department of Economics, University of Western Ontario, London, ON, Canada

S. Loeb Stanford University, Stanford, CA, United States

David Monk The Pennsylvania State University, State College, PA, United States

Samuel Muehlemann LMU Munich, Munich, Germany; IZA Bonn, Bonn, Germany

J. Myung Stanford University, Stanford, CA, United States

Thomas J. Nechyba Duke University, Durham, NC, United States

Helena Skyt Nielsen Department of Economics and Business Economics, Fuglesangs Allé 4, DK8210 Aarhus V, Denmark

M. Nores NIEER, Rutgers University, New Brunswick, NJ, United States

Philip Oreopolous Professor in the Department of Economics, The School of Public Policy, Governance at the University of Toronto, Toronto, ON, Canada; Research Associate with the National Bureau of Economic Research

Alfredo R. Paloyo University of Wollongong, RWI - Leibniz-Institut fur Wirtschaftsforschung, Forschungsinstitut zur Zukunft der Arbeit (IZA), ARC Center of Excellence for Children and Families over the Life Course (ARC LCC), Global Labor Organization (GLO), Wollongong, NSW, Australia

Harry Anthony Patrinos Former World Bank, Washington DC, United States

D.N. Plank Stanford University, Stanford, CA, United States

George Psacharopoulos London School of Economics, World Bank

Birgitta Rabe Institute for Social and Economic Research, University of Essex, Colchester, Essex, United Kingdom

Jennifer King Rice University of Maryland, College Park, MD, United States

Russell W. Rumberger Gevirtz Graduate School of Education, University of California, Santa Barbara, CA, United States

W. Sander DePaul University, Chicago, IL, United States

L. Santibañez Fundación IDEA, México City, México

D.W. Schanzenbach University of Chicago, Chicago, IL, United States

H. Schildberg-Hörisch University of Düsseldorf, Düsseldorf, Germany

Guido Schwerdt University of Konstanz, Germany

Rongjia Shen Department of Applied Economics, University of Minnesota, St. Paul, MN, United States

Mark H. Showalter Brigham Young University, Provo, UT, United States

Olmo Silva Department of Geography and Environment and Centre for Economic Performance, London School of Economics, London, United Kingdom

Bjarne Strøm Department of Economics, Norwegiana University of Science and Technology, Norway

Bixuan Sun Department of Applied Economics, University of Minnesota, St. Paul, MN, United States

V. Wagner University of Mainz, Mainz, Germany

Ian Walker Department of Economics, Lancaster University Management School and IZA, Bonn, Germany

Suzanne Wisniewski University of St. Thomas, Saint Paul, MN, United States

Ludger Woessmann University of Munich, ifo Institute, CESifo and IZA, Munich, Germany

Stefan C. Wolter IZA Bonn, Bonn, Germany; University of Bern, Bern, Switzerland; CESifo Munich, Munich, Germany

James Wyckoff Curry School of Education, University of Virginia, Charlottesville, VA, United States

Jijun Zhang University of Maryland, College Park, MD, United States; American Institutes for Research, Washington, DC, United States

Ron Zimmer University of Kentucky, Lexington, KY, USA

Foreword

Economics is concerned with the efficient allocation of scarce resources in order to maximize productivity, output or more generally social outcomes. This is no less the case for the study of education, whether it be publically funded or privately funded. In addressing the overarching issue of making an efficient allocation of resources in education, economists and other academic disciplines, such as educationalists and sociologists have debated whether funding and provision should be separated. With this said, introducing market elements is becoming commonplace across the world and at all levels of education—primary, secondary and tertiary.

More specifically, in the previous edition of this volume, Brewer and McEwan (2010) highlight the development of the economic study of education from two initial analogies with economic production. First, the development of Human Capital Theory by Gary Becker and Jacob Mincer where individuals invest in their own education in a way that is analogous to physical capital, and in the same way, generates a stream of future returns. This initial work lead to a subsequent explosion in empirical work aimed at estimating rates of return to education across the world, and following that, a body of work aimed at honing-in on causal estimates of individual returns to schooling. At the same time, from the Coleman Report onwards, economists have endeavored to understand the determinants of test scores, focusing on how educational inputs (e.g., schools, families, policies) are transformed into educational outputs. Again, this has led to a voluminous body of research aimed at understanding what are the most critical educational inputs such as school expenditure, class size, teachers, and family inputs.

Since the publication of the first volume in 2010, the field of the economics of education has grown dramatically both in size and scope. The growth in empirical work in particular is notable. The study of education economics has been at heart of the so-called *identification revolution* and the current volume seeks to reflect this. While the book continues to cover the core issues of returns to education and determinants of test scores, there are additional sections aimed at reflecting developments in the behavioural economics of education and recent policy developments. The book is split into five parts.

Section 1: Methods and overview

The first two chapters seek to provide an overview of current empirical approaches in the economics of education (Schwerdt and Woessmann) and the key insights from behavioural approaches to the economics of education (Nielsen and Damgaard). These are important standalone chapters in their own rights, but also provide an overview of current approaches useful in reading many of the following chapters. They also highlight the development of econometric techniques to address the key questions in the economics of education.

Section 2: Private and social returns to education

Understanding the returns to education remains a core issue, both in developed economics (Gunderson and Oreopolous) and in developing economies (Patrinos and Psacharopolous). On a related theme, the rapid and ongoing expansion of higher education across a range of countries leads naturally to questions of the returns to a degree qualification (Walker). At the same time, there is a growing emphasis on the role of educational quality (Hoekstra). Similarly, the returns to education are wider than earnings alone, and cover areas such as children's health (Huebener), reduced crime (Lochner) and pro-civic behavior (Dee).

Insofar as the provision of, and investment in, schooling is not uniform across economics it has clear role in the development of societal inequality. Reflecting this, there are also clear roles for educational investment as determinants of intergenerational inequality (Blanden) and racial inequalities (Carnoy). A central aspect of educational decisions is the choice to quit schooling, and the consequences and social desirability of this decision (Rumberger).

Section 3: Production, costs and financing

How to distribute educational inputs and how these influence educational outputs is central to the development of efficient schooling and educational systems. An initial chapter provides an overview of the education production function approach to understanding this process (Hanushek), the relationship of educational attainment with economic growth (Woessmann and Hanushek), developing country evidence on the educational production (Glewwe, Lambert and Chen), how education is utilised in the labour market in developing countries (Battu and Bender), and the efficiency of educational production (Johnes).

The development of research on educational production has led to increased interest in specific inputs into the production function such as parental and family inputs (Currie and Goodman; Rabe), early childhood interventions (Nores), Class size (Schanzenbach), teacher quality (Strøm and Falch) and the role of peers (Paloyo). Recent research from the behavioural perspective highlights the role of both monetary and non-monetary incentives in the production of education (Wagner and Schildberg- Hörisch).

Finally, two chapters provide a discussion of educational financing. One in the form of an overview of issues in school financing (Rice), and another on tuition and fees (Ehrenberg).

Section 4: Teacher labour markets

Teachers provide the main labour input into the production of education and this naturally has led to a voluminous literature on teachers and teacher labour markets. This section starts with an overview of teacher labour markets (James and Wyckoff), with companion chapters that focus on the specifics of teachers in developing countries (Glewwe, Shen, Sun and Wisniewski) and issues of teacher labour supply (Dolton). Further chapters consider key issues such as recruitment and retention (Loeb), compensating wage differentials (Feng) and incentives for teachers (Santibanez).

Section 5: Education market, choice and incentives

The final section of the second edition, returns to the issue of the funding and provision of education, and examines the role of the state and the "market" in education. At the heart of much of this literature is the issue of to what extent the state funds and provides education (Plank and Davies). While a related question is whether and why firms provide vocational training, and how this affects individual outcomes (Muehle-mann and Wolter). More generally, a variety of different approaches to the broad issues of education provision and increasing efficiency have been tried, reflecting the different institutional settings in each country. Several themes have emerged in the literature, such as the role of parental choice vis-à-vis primary and secondary schools, and the impact, if any, of introducing competition between schools for pupils, whilst also addressing the question of school accountability, in an attempt to increase test scores (Figlio and Ladd; Bradley; Nechyba; Foliano and Silva). While a related question is what is the role and effect incentives aimed at improved educational performance (Eide and Showalter). The effects of private provision (Green), catholic school provision (Sander) and other models of provision such as charter schools (Kho) are also covered in this section.

Final comments

We hope that this volume introduces students, practitioners and policy makers to the subject matter of the economics of education, and does so in an accessible way for those who do not have any training in economics. We also hope that the volume builds on the first edition of this volume, whilst illustrating the rapidly developing nature of this field of academic endeavor.

Steve Bradley
Colin Green

PART I

Overview

1

Empirical methods in the economics of education

Guido Schwerdt[a], *Ludger Woessmann*[b]

[a]University of Konstanz, Germany; [b]University of Munich, and Ifo Institute, CESifo and IZA, Munich, Germany

Introduction

Empirical research in the economics of education often addresses causal questions. Does an educational policy or practice cause students' test scores to improve? Does more schooling lead to higher earnings? This article surveys the methods that economists have increasingly used over the past two decades to distinguish accidental association from causation.[1] The methods include research designs that exploit explicit randomization as well as quasi-experimental identification strategies based on observational data. All methods are illustrated with a range of selected example applications from the economics of education.

From correlation to causation

It is reasonably straightforward to establish whether there is an association between two variables using standard statistical methods.

Understanding whether such a statistical correlation can be interpreted as a causal effect of one variable, the *treatment*, on the other, the *outcome*, is, however, another question. The problem is that there may well be other reasons why this association comes about. One reason would be "reverse causality", which describes a situation where the outcome of interest asserts a causal effect on the treatment of interest. Another example of alternative reasons for the association is that of "omitted variables", where a third variable affects both treatment and outcome.

Whenever other reasons exist that give rise to a correlation between a treatment and an outcome, the overall correlation cannot be interpreted as a causal effect. This situation is commonly referred to as the *endogeneity problem*. The term originates from the idea that the treatment cannot be viewed as exogenous to the model determining the outcome, as it should be, but that it is rather endogenously determined within the model—depending on the outcome or being jointly determined with the outcome by a

---

[1] The exposition here is partly based on Schlotter, Schwerdt, and Woessmann (2011).

The Economics of Education, Second Edition
https://doi.org/10.1016/B978-0-12-815391-8.00001-X

third factor. Because of the problem of endoge-neity, simple estimates of the association be-tween treatment and outcome based on correlations will be biased estimates of the causal effect of treatment on outcome.[2]

Standard approaches such as multivariate regression models try to deal with this problem by observing other sources of a possible correla-tion and by taking out the difference in outcomes that can be attributed to these other observed dif-ferences. This allows estimating the association between treatment and outcome conditional on the effects of observed factors. The required assumption for the identification of a causal ef-fect in this case is often called *selection-on-observ-ables* assumption. It implies that the conditional estimate identifies the causal effect of interest if selection into treatment is sufficiently described by the observed variables included in the model. However, more often than not, one cannot observe all relevant and non-ignorable variables. But as long as part of the omitted variables stay unobserved, the estimated conditional associa-tion will not necessarily warrant a causal interpretation.

Over the past two decades, it has become increasingly apparent in the literature on the eco-nomics of education that there are myriad impor-tant factors that remain unobserved in our models of interest, often rendering the attempts to control for all relevant confounding factors in vain. Just think of such factors as innate ability of students, parental preferences for certain out-comes, the teaching aptitude of teachers, or the norms and values of peers and neighborhoods. Even if one manages to obtain observable

measures of certain dimensions of these factors, others—often important ones—will remain unob-served. Even more, controlling for observable fac-tors does not solve the endogeneity problem when it is due to plain reverse causality, in that the outcome causes the treatment. The only solu-tion is to search for variation in treatment that is not related with other factors that are correlated with the outcome.

The same caveats that apply to the traditional models also apply to other techniques that ulti-mately rely on a selection-on-observable assump-tion such as propensity score matching. The central idea of this technique is to find matching pairs of treated and untreated individuals who are as similar as possible in terms of observed (pre-treatment) characteristics. Under certain as-sumptions, this method can reduce the bias of the treatment effect. But as long as relevant factors remain unobserved, it cannot eliminate the bias (see, e.g., Becker and Ichino (2002)). In this sense, matching techniques cannot solve the endogene-ity problem and suffer as much from bias due to unobserved factors as traditional models.[3]

In this chapter, we turn to techniques, increas-ingly applied by economists, that aim to provide more convincing identification of causal effects in the face of unobservable confounding factors. In medical trials, only some patients get treated, and the assignment to the group of treated and non-treated patients is done in a randomized way to ensure that it is not confounded with other factors. The non-treated patients constitute a so-called *control group* to which the treated pa-tients are compared. The aim of the discussed techniques is to mimic this type of experimental

---

[2] Other sources of endogeneity can be self-selection (objects with different characteristics can choose whether to be treated or not) and simultaneity (treatment and outcome are choice variables that are jointly determined). Mea-surement error in the treatment variable gives rise to a particular form of association between treatment and outcome (one that in the case of classical measurement error biases the estimates toward finding no effect).

[3] Matching techniques can still improve on the formation of proper treatment and control groups when they are combined with one of the approaches discussed below, where the latter ensures exogeneity of treatment and thus causal interpretation.

design, often using data not generated by an explicitly experimental design. The techniques aim to form a treatment group (that is subject to the treatment) and a control group (that is not subject to the treatment) which are exactly the same. That is, they should not have been sub-divided into treatment and control group based on reasons that are correlated with the outcome of interest. Ideally, one would like to observe the same individuals at the same point in time both in the treated status and in the non-treated status. Of course, this is impossible, because the same individual cannot be in and out of treatment at once. Therefore, the key issue is estimating what would have happened in the *counterfactual*—which outcome a treated individual would have had if she had not been treated.

The central idea of these techniques is that if the separation of the population into treatment and control group is purely random and a sufficiently large number of individuals is observed, then randomness ensures that the two groups do not differ systematically on other dimensions. In effect, the mathematical law of large numbers makes sure that the characteristics of those in the treatment group will be the same as those in the control group. Thus, the causal effect of the treatment on the outcome can be directly observed by comparing the average outcomes of the treatment group and the control group, because the two groups differ only in terms of the treatment. The aim of the empirical methods discussed in this chapter is to generate such proper treatment and control groups and thus rule out that estimates of the treatment effect are biased by unobserved differences.

Explicit randomization

We start our discussion with two techniques that use explicit randomization to construct valid treatment and control groups that, on average, do not differ from one another in observed or unobserved dimensions.

Randomized controlled experiments

From a conceptual perspective, randomized controlled experiments—or randomized controlled trials (RCTs)—constitute an important benchmark with certain ideal features against which to judge the other techniques discussed in this chapter. Because of their desirable features, controlled experiments are sometimes being referred to as the most rigorous of all research designs or even as "gold standard" (e.g., Angrist (2004)). The most important feature is the random assignment of participants to treatment and control groups.

Suppose we are interested in evaluating whether a specific educational program has a causal effect on economic outcomes of individuals who participated in the intervention. Ideally, we would like to observe the same individuals in a counterfactual world and compare the two individuals' outcomes. As this is impossible, it is necessary to find research designs that provide good estimates of counterfactual outcomes. To this end, researchers typically try to build two groups that are "equivalent" to each other. One group (the treatment group) is assigned to the specific program, the other group (the control group) is not. As the groups consist of different individuals, creating two groups that are completely equal regarding all important aspects such as family background, social status, and the like is not possible. Thus, it becomes rather a question of probability in the sense that the task is to create two groups which should be on average equal with sufficiently high probability. This is possible by randomly drawing a sufficiently large number of individuals from a population and randomly assigning them to the treatment and the control group. Random assignment is of crucial importance in this context, because if the two groups are indeed on average identical apart from the assignment to the program, all observed differences in outcomes between the groups can be attributed to the average effect of the program.

A classic example of a controlled experiment is the Perry Preschool Program, which nicely illustrates the advantages, but also some limitations and caveats, of explicit experiments. The experiment was conducted in 1962 in Ypsilanti, Michigan, when school authorities recognized the low school performance of at-risk children from poor neighborhoods compared to better-off children. In order to improve the social and cognitive development of the children, they decided to test whether an intense intervention of high-quality early childhood education could help these children (see Barnett (1985)). The crucial feature of this program is that it was conducted as a controlled experiment. In particular, 123 at-risk children at ages 3–4 were randomly assigned to a treatment and a control group (see Belfield, Nores, Barnett, and Schweinhart (2006)). The 58 children in the treatment group received a high-quality preschool program for one or two (academic) years, including daily center-based care in small groups, home visiting each weekday, and group meetings of the parents. The 65 children in the control group did not receive these services. The members of both groups were followed until adulthood and have been surveyed several times. Ultimately, the study can document positive effects of the two-year preschool program on desirable outcomes in several dimensions. Among others, at the age of 40 the treated individuals had significantly higher earnings, higher probability of high-school completion, and fewer incidents of crime than the adults from the control group.

Research on several other topics in education has made use of RCTs. Another of the most well-known is the so-called Project STAR in the US state of Tennessee that randomly assigned students and teachers to classes of different size. This class-size experiment has been subjected

to extensive research (e.g., Finn and Achilles (1990)) that, among others, also takes into account incomplete randomization caused by later switching between classes due to behavioral problems of students and relocation of families (see Krueger (1999)).[4] Recent studies using the Project STAR experiment have investigated long-term impacts of classrooms and peers (Chetty et al., 2011; Bietenbeck, 2019).

RCTs are also increasingly being used to answer various other questions in the economics of education (see Fryer (2017) for a survey). For example, several RCTs have been implemented to study the effects of incentives for students on educational outcomes. Fryer (2011), Bettinger (2012), and Levitt, List, Neckermann, and Sadoff (2016) conduct a series of randomized field experiments on financial incentives and student achievement. The randomized treatments in separate experiments include financial rewards for performance on a test, for grades in core courses, for performance on a metric that includes attendance, behavior, and inputs to educational production functions chosen by schools, as well as offering students money to read books. In higher education, Bettinger, Long, Oreopoulos, and Sanbonmatsu (2012) implement an RCT to estimate the effect of application assistance and information on college decisions. Also on the classic question in the economics of education of how education affects labor-market outcomes, randomized controlled experiments have been implemented by sending out CVs with randomized education elements for application (e.g., Deming, Yuchtman, Abulafi, Goldin, and Katz (2016); Piopiunik, Schwerdt, Simon, and Woessmann (2018)).

Today, RCTs in schools are also extensively used in the context of developing countries. For example, Muralidharan and Sundararaman (2011) and De Ree, Muralidharan, Pradhan,

---

[4] However, substantial concerns remain with the implementation of the experiment which may compromise its evidence on the effects of class size on student achievement (see Hanushek (1999)).

and Rogers (2018) implement experiments on teacher pay in India and Indonesia.

Randomized controlled experiments are, however, not free of potential caveats and drawbacks. One important drawback of explicit experiments is that participants are often aware of their participation in an experiment.[5] Thus, they may change their behavior exactly because they know that they are observed. This so-called *Hawthorne effect* is an example of how evidence drawn from controlled experiments can be compromised. This should be especially the case if one result of the experiment appears more favorable to participants than the other result.

Another concern is that it is often not clear to which extent the results of an experiment can be generalized. In case of the Perry Preschool Program, for example, the choice of the underlying sample was explicitly targeted at at-risk children, limiting the *"external validity"* of the study to this sample. That is, the causal inference is limited to the specific group of African-American children from disadvantaged backgrounds. If the selection process had been completely random, effects might have differed. But generalized results that are valid for the whole population were not the aim of this specific experiment. Focusing on the effects for specific sub-groups is often more interesting and relevant from a policy point of view.

External validity may also be hampered by the fact that a full-scale implementation of a policy could generate general-equilibrium effects. If, for example, a small-scale experiment leads to more schooling and, therefore, increased earnings among treated participants, a full-scale intervention might not generate the same effects on earnings because a substantial increase in the supply of highly-educated workers may decrease the marginal returns to schooling in general equilibrium. In addition, there can be several factors that complicate both the random draw from the population and the random assignment to the groups. For example, Heckman, Moon, Pinto, Savelyev, and Adam (2010) show that the Perry Preschool Program did not fully reach random assignment, as treatment and control group individuals were reassigned afterward. More generally, controlled experiments often suffer from issues of non-perfect implementation, compromising the validity of their results.

Lotteries of oversubscribed programs

Researchers in the economics of education often use another form of explicitly controlled experiments as the basis of their empirical strategy. Sometimes, when an institution aims to implement a specific educational intervention, resources are not enough to finance participation for everybody who is interested. In such a setting, the assignment of an oversubscribed program is often handled by randomized lotteries, so that each applicant has the same chance of participation. Among those who apply for the program, this then boils down to being an explicitly randomized set-up. Lottery winners constitute the treatment group in this case, while lottery losers form the control group. For an empirical evaluation of the program, researchers then only need to collect data on outcomes and other characteristics of the two groups, preferably also before but in particular after implementation of the program.

A well-known example of randomized lotteries of oversubscribed programs is that of charter schools in the US. Compared to traditional public schools, charter schools are granted

---

[5] Ideally, participants should not be aware of the fact that they are part of an experiment. In their experiment analyzing the use of randomly distributed vouchers for adult training courses, Schwerdt, Messer, Woessmann, and Wolter (2012) created a setting in which both groups were completely unaware that they were investigated.

more autonomy to staff their own classrooms, choose their own curricula and manage their own budgets. Often, demand for seats in particular charter schools is so high that they must admit students by random lottery. This feature of the admission process has been exploited by several studies to investigate whether charter school attendance has a positive effect on student achievement (see Epple, Romano, and Zimmer (2016) and Chabrier, Cohodes, and Oreopoulos (2016) for recent surveys). The treatment group in these studies are students who won a place in a charter school, and the control group are those who did not win a place. Access to administrative data on student achievement then allows for a comparison of later outcomes of the two groups. This set-up allows to estimate both the effects of the offer of a place in a charter school (the "intention-to-treat" effect) and the effects of actually attending a charter school (the "treatment-on-the-treated" effect). Abdulkadiroğlu, Angrist, Dynarski, Kane, and Pathak (2011), for example, analyze student achievement in Boston's traditional public schools as well as in charter schools. Exploiting randomized admission lotteries, they find large positive effects of charter schools in this setting.

In a similar spirit to charter school evaluations, Deming, Hastings, Kane, and Staiger (2014) study whether school choice has an impact on postsecondary attainment exploiting a public school choice lottery in Charlotte-Mecklenburg. Angrist, Bettinger, and Kremer (2006) estimate the effects of school vouchers in Colombia exploiting a randomized lottery. A similar approach is also employed by Cullen, Jacob, and Levitt (2006) to estimate the effects of increased choice among specific public schools in Chicago. Bettinger and Slonim (2006) perform a laboratory experiment within the field setting of a voucher lottery in Toledo, Ohio, to estimate the effect of school vouchers on altruism.

An obvious key advantage of studies based on randomized lotteries of oversubscribed programs is that they do not require setting up a separate experiment, but rather build on the randomization that is implemented anyway. In addition, these programs tend to refer to field trials that are enacted in a real-world setting, rather than an artificial experimental setting. Similar to explicit experiments, evaluations of randomized lotteries of oversubscribed programs may be subject to Hawthorne effects and may miss general-equilibrium effects. In addition, motivating those who lost in the lottery to participate in subsequent surveys and tests may not be easy.

A key shortcoming of oversubscribed lotteries is that the very fact that specific schools or programs are oversubscribed may imply that their productivity is higher than that of other schools or programs that do not attract as many students. If parents and students vote with their feet, oversubscription status indicates preferred schools, so that average effects would be expected to be smaller than effects of oversubscribed schools. In fact, Abdulkadiroğlu et al. (2011) provide suggestive evidence that the effect of Boston charter schools that are not oversubscribed may be substantially smaller than the effect of the oversubscribed charter schools, thus limiting the external validity of results for oversubscribed schools.

Another potential drawback of the setting of randomized lotteries of oversubscribed programs is that the underlying population is just those individuals who applied for participation in the program. This will not necessarily be a random draw from the population at large. In particular, subjects who particularly like the program, who view a particular need for the intervention, or who place particular value on the outcome of the intervention may be more inclined to apply than the average population. In the context of charter school evaluations, this implies that lottery-based studies do not necessarily generalize to the vast number of students who do not wind up in admission lotteries. However, recent comparisons of results from other research designs that do not exploit admission lotteries find comparable results (e.g., Abdulkadiroğlu et al. (2011); Abdulkadiroğlu, Angrist, Hull, and Pathak (2016)).

Natural experiments

In the absence of intentional randomization, identifying causal effects is a challenging task. However, sometimes it is possible to exploit variation in observational data that stems from sources that are exogenous to the association of interest. In particular, two techniques try to mimic the random assignment of controlled experiments by building on incidents where nature or institutional rules give rise to exogenous variation. Such identification strategies are also referred to as *natural experiments* or *quasi-experiments*.

Instrumental-variable approach

The instrumental-variable (IV) approach is an identification strategy that tries to get close to the set-up of a controlled experiment using observational data. It aims to identify variation in the exposure to a certain education policy or practice that stems from a particular source that is not correlated with the outcome of interest.

The idea behind this approach is simple. Think of the treatment of interest as having two parts. One part is subject to the endogeneity problems discussed above. The other part does not suffer from endogeneity problems and can thus be used for causal identification. The IV approach aims to isolate the latter part of the variation in the treatment variable. This is achieved by using only that part of the variation in the treatment variable that can be attributed to an observed third variable (the *instrument*) which is not otherwise correlated with the outcome (or with omitted variables that are correlated with the outcome). Having information on such an instrument allows to isolate variation in treatment that is exogenous to the model

of interest and thus to obtain unbiased estimates of the causal effect of treatment on outcome.

The key to success of any IV approach is to find a convincing instrumental variable—one that is strongly associated with the treatment variable ("*instrument relevance*"), but is not correlated with the outcome apart from the possible indirect effect running through treatment ("*instrument exogeneity*"). If such an instrument can be found, it is possible to identify the treatment effect through a part of the variation in treatment that is triggered by variation in the instrumental variable, thereby overcoming problems such as reverse causality and omitted variables and achieving consistent estimation.

Changes in compulsory schooling laws constitute a good example that illustrates the use of an IV identification strategy in educational research. Several studies exploit arguably exogenous changes in the educational attainment of individuals caused by changes of the minimum school-leaving age as an instrument for actual education attainment (e.g., Oreopoulos (2006); Black, Devereux, and Salvanes (2008); Cygan-Rehm and Maeder (2013); Piopiunik (2014b); Fort, Schneeweis, and Winter-Ebmer (2016); Hanushek, Schwerdt, Wiederhold, and Woessmann (2015)). As a seminal study, Harmon and Walker (1995) estimate the returns to schooling on the labor market in the United Kingdom. To cope with the endogeneity of educational attainment, they use variables indicating changes in laws determining the minimum school-leaving age as an instrumental variable for years of schooling. This is possible as individuals in the sample (employed males aged 18–64) faced different minimum school-leaving ages during their youth because two legislative changes raised the minimum school-leaving age from 14 to 15 in 1947 and from 15 to 16 in 1971. The setup aims to meet the two key assumptions of IV. First, an increase in the minimum school-leaving age induces at least part of the population to stay in school longer. Second, this change in legislation should have no effect on individuals' earnings other than the indirect effect through increased schooling. The IV estimates of Harmon and Walker (1995) suggest that an additional year of schooling raises earnings by 15%—roughly three times the corresponding OLS estimate.[6]

However, IV estimates should always be interpreted carefully. Angrist, Imbens, and Rubin (1996) show that IV procedures estimate the effect of schooling only for that subgroup of the population that complies with the assignment, i.e., that actually changes the schooling decision because of a change in the instrument. Thus, one has to interpret the IV estimate as a so-called Local Average Treatment Effect (LATE), i.e., as applying only to the "local" sub-population that is affected by the instrument. In the example above, this suggests that the estimates reflect returns to schooling for those individuals with minimum schooling, whose schooling decisions are affected by the laws on minimum school-leaving ages. Thus, effects identified by IV estimation do not necessarily reflect average effects for the entire population, raising points of external validity in the same way as controlled experiments.

Several other studies in education rely on instruments for the identification of causal effects. Currie and Moretti (2003) use the availability of colleges in a woman's county in her 17th year as an instrument for maternal education in the United States and find that higher maternal education improves infant health. Machin and McNally (2008) exploit changes in the rules governing the funding of information and communication technology (ICT) across English school districts in an IV specification to estimate the effect of ICT spending on student performance. West and Woessmann (2010) exploit the historical pattern that countries with larger shares of Catholics in 1900 tend to have larger shares of privately operated schools even today. Using historical Catholic shares as an instrument for contemporary private competition, they investigate the effect of private competition on student achievement in a cross-country setting. Jackson, Johnson, and Persico (2016) study the effects of school spending on educational and economic outcomes and use the timing of the passage of court-mandated reforms and their associated type of funding formula change as source of variation in school spending in the United States.

These examples illustrate that IV approaches exploit arguably exogenous variation from very different sources. In practice, the "trick" of any IV approach is to find a good instrument. If a convincing instrument is found, causal effects can be well identified even with purely cross-sectional observational data. However, the main assumptions of IV—instrument relevance and exogeneity—must be carefully evaluated in any application.

A key advantage of such quasi-experimental analyses is that they circumvent some of the leading problems with RCTs, such as the facts that they are expensive, time-consuming, and difficult to explain to public officials whose cooperation is generally needed. In addition, quasi-experimental studies are not subject to Hawthorne effects because subjects are not aware that they are part of an experiment, and well-designed natural experiments can be able to capture general-equilibrium effects that RCTs usually cannot.

Regression-discontinuity approach

Another approach in the spirit of natural experiments is the regression-discontinuity (RD) approach. This approach is typically used in a specific setting where a treatment is determined by whether a subject falls above or below a

---

[6] Note, however, that Stephens and Yang (2014) find that similar results for the United States are not robust to allowing for differential year-of-birth effects across the four US census regions

certain cutoff value of a specified *assignment variable* (also called *running* or *forcing variable*).

The study by Papay, Murnane, and Willett (2016) nicely illustrates the use of the RD approach. They study whether performance labels in secondary school affect the college-going decisions of students. This is a challenging research question, because students typically receive good or bad performance labels for a reason. Thus, based on observational data it is difficult to disentangle the isolated effect of receiving a specific performance label from any effects that the underlying determinants of performance may have on future outcomes. Studying this question in the context of a controlled experiment is also unlikely to be an option, because it would be unethical to randomly assign actual performance labels to students for the purpose of an experiment.

Here RD can help. In the setting of Papay et al. (2016), students participating in state-mandated standardized tests receive a score between 200 and 280 as well as a label that summarizes their performance on these tests. In particular, students scoring more than 260 points on the tenth-grade mathematics test are labeled "advanced". The idea of the RD design then is to compare students in a sufficiently small range just above and below the cutoff value of 260, where those above form the treatment group and those below constitute the control group. Conditional on any continuous effects of the test score, students just above and just below the cutoff will in expectation not differ by more than the treatment (the label), because they are very similar in terms of the assignment variable (the test score). The comparison of units that are in a sufficiently small range below and above the threshold therefore comes close to an experimental setting with random assignment to treatment and control groups. Any jump or discontinuity in the outcome (the probability of attending college) that can be observed at the threshold can then be interpreted as the causal effect of receiving the performance label. In addition, the fact that the assignment to the treatment and control groups follows a non-linear pattern—the discontinuity at exactly the cutoff value—allows the RD approach to control for any smooth function of the variable determining eligibility. The assumption required for the RD approach to capture the causal effect (the identifying assumption) thus is that there are no other discontinuities around the cutoff.

A nice feature of the RD design is that is has a straightforward graphical depiction. When plotting the outcome of interest against the assignment variable, there should be a clear jump in the outcome at the assignment threshold that determines the treatment status of students (see Fig. 1.1). In the study by Papay et al. (2016), there is a jump in the probability of attending college at the threshold. To show that this jump is really caused by the performance label, they estimate local linear regression models controlling for test scores using only observations that fall within a small bandwidth (8 points in their preferred specification) on either side of the cutoff. Their results corroborate the graphical finding that receiving the "advanced" label on the tenth-grade mathematics test increases the probability that urban, low-income students enroll in college.

In similar setups, several recent studies apply RD designs to estimate the causal effects of grade retention on future outcomes (Jacob and Lefgren (2004; 2009); Eren, Depew, and Barnes (2017); Schwerdt, West, and Winters (2017)). Many US states have recently enacted policies requiring that students who do not meet minimum performance expectations on state-mandated standardized tests at the end of specific grades be retained and provided with remedial services. In this setting, scoring just below a threshold level induces a specific treatment. However, due to the availability of exemptions for students scoring below the promotion cutoff and voluntary retention of some higher-scoring students, the treatment in this case is not assigned deterministically by the assignment variable. Thus,

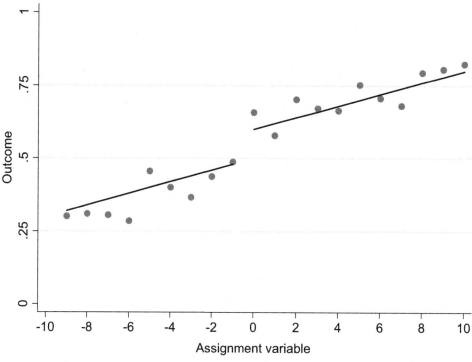

FIG. 1.1   Stylized exposition of the RD design.

in this case we rather expect to see a jump in the probability that students repeat the grade at the assignment threshold. In contrast to so-called sharp RD designs where the cutoff unequivocally divides observations into a treatment and a control group, such settings lead to so-called "fuzzy" RD designs. These designs exploit discontinuities in the probability of treatment and can be implemented as an instrumental-variable approach where the discontinuity acts as the instrument for treatment status.

Several other examples illustrate that there is a rich number of cases where educational policies and practices are implemented in a manner that involves a discontinuity which allows for evaluation through the RD approach. Prominent examples are studies exploiting discontinuities in average class size due to maximum class-size rules to study the effects of class size on various outcomes (e.g., Angrist and Lavy (1999);

Woessmann and West (2006); Fredriksson, Öckert, and Oosterbeek (2013); Leuven and Løkken (2018); Angrist, Lavy, Leder-Luis, and Shany (2018)). With maximum class-size rules, class sizes drop discontinuously whenever grade enrollment would lead to class sizes that exceed the maximum size determined by a specific rule. Other applications of the RD design use specified school-entry cutoff dates that lead to the effect that school entry ages vary due to the month of birth of the children (e.g., Bedard and Dhuey (2006); Mühlenweg and Puhani (2010); McCrary and Royer (2011)). Garibaldi, Giavazzi, Ichino, and Rettore (2012) study the effect of tuition fees on the probability of late graduation from university, exploiting the fact that tuition fees at Bocconi University in Milan are subject to discontinuous changes with respect to family income. Lavy (2010) uses a geographical RD approach that compares students in Tel Aviv that enacted free school choice to students in neighboring areas that were not subject to the treatment. Abdulkadiroğlu, Angrist, and Pathak (2014) exploit admission discontinuities to estimate the effect of elite schools on students' achievement. Kirkeboen, Leuven and Mogstad (2016) use cutoffs in the admission to different fields and locations of higher education in Norway to estimate the effect of field of study on earnings.

The most serious threat to identification in the context of RD designs is manipulation of the assignment variable around the cutoff. Individuals often have incentives to receive the treatment, or not. Thus, they might try to manipulate the assignment variable. Think, for example, of teachers who manipulate results on standardized tests to ensure that specific students get promoted to the next grade. Such behavior would give rise to selection bias and violate the core assumption of no sorting around the cutoff. A common robustness check in any RD study is, therefore, to plot all observable exogenous characteristics of observational units against the assignment variable. Ideally, this exercise reveals no jumps for a long list of relevant observable characteristics at the cutoff, which would strengthen the case that there are also no jumps in unobservables at the cutoff, supporting the core assumption of the RD approach. A related robustness check is to check for discontinuities in the density of the assignment variable at the cutoff (see McCrary (2008)). Ideally, inspecting the distribution of the assignment variable reveals no suspicious clustering of observational units on either side of the cutoff.

Other issues with implementing the RD design are the choice of bandwidth and of the functional relationship with the assignment variable included in the empirical model. As a best-practice way of dealing with these issues, researchers typically report results for a variety of bandwidths and functional forms. Finally, due to the local identification around the threshold, external validity is also an issue for estimates based on the RD approach.

Methods using panel data

The availability of panel data allows for the application of two methods that do not rely entirely on strong selection-on-observables assumptions. Panel datasets are characterized by the fact that observational units are observed at least twice. The methods described here can be applied as long as some observational units change their treatment status between two incidents of observation. Incidents usually refer to two points in time, but they may also refer to two other dimensions such as different grade levels or subjects. The two approaches attempt to implicitly control for unobserved variables that would bias regression estimates of the causal effect of interest based on cross-sectional data.

Difference-in-differences approach

Difference-in-differences (DiD) approaches are applied in situations when certain groups are exposed to a treatment and others are not. The logic of DiD is best explained with an example based on two groups and two periods. In the first period, none of the groups is exposed to treatment. In the second period, only one of the groups gets exposed to treatment, but not the other. To provide an illustration, suppose that there are two classes in a given school observed at the beginning and the end of a school year. During this school year, only students in one of these two classes have additional afternoon lessons. DiD estimation can then be used to estimate the effect of additional lessons in the afternoon on student achievement.

The DiD is implemented by taking two differences between group means in a specific way (illustrated in Fig. 1.2). The first difference is the difference in the mean of the outcome variable between the two periods for each of the groups. In the hypothetical example, the first difference simply corresponds to the change in average test scores for each group between the beginning and the end of the school year. The second difference is the difference between

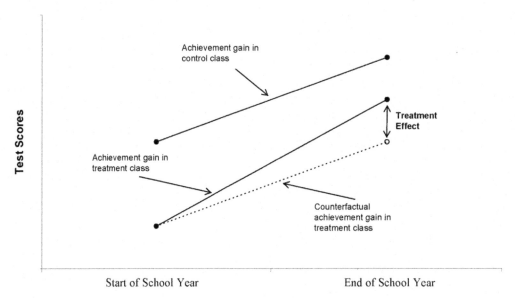

FIG. 1.2   Stylized exposition of identification in the DiD model.

the differences calculated for the two groups in the first stage (which is why the DiD method is sometimes also labeled "double differencing" strategy). This second difference measures how the change in outcome differs between the two groups, which is interpreted as the causal effect of the causing variable. Hence, in our example, the effect of afternoon lessons on student learning is identified by comparing the gains in average test scores over the school year between the two classes.

The idea behind the DiD identification strategy is simple. The two groups might be observationally different. That is, the group-specific means might differ in the absence of treatment. However, as long as this difference is constant over time (in the absence of treatment), it can be differenced out by deducting group-specific means of the outcome of interest. The remaining difference between these group-specific differences must then reflect the causal effect of interest.

The identification assumption of the DiD approach is that the group-specific trends in the outcome of interest would be identical in the absence of treatment. In terms of the hypothetical example, the identifying assumption is that both classes would have experienced the same increase in test scores over the school year in the absence of afternoon lessons. The assumption that the treatment class would have experienced a counterfactual achievement gain identical to the observed achievement gain in the control class is illustrated by the dotted line in Fig. 1.2. The plausibility of this identifying assumption depends on the specific setting to which DiD estimation is applied. If possible, researchers show that outcomes in the treatment and the control group prior to the treatment moved in parallel, which supports the assumption of parallel trends over the introduction of the treatment. In any case, the identifying assumption of the DiD approach is less restrictive than the assumption implicitly made in standard traditional methods, namely that the two groups are identical in terms of all relevant unobserved factors.

The DiD approach is particularly well-suited to estimate the causal effect of sharp changes in education policies or practices, providing policy-makers with vital information even in the absence of controlled or natural experiments. It has, therefore, been used extensively to study the impacts of various education reforms around the world. Examples include reforms of compulsory schooling and tracking (e.g., Meghir and Palme (2005), Pekkala Kerr, Pekkarinen, and Uusitalo (2013), Meghir, Palme, and Simeonova (2018)), education priority zones for disadvantaged schools (e.g., Bénabou, Kramarz, and Prost (2009)), subsidized child care (e.g., Havnes and Mogstad (2011)), and paid parental leave (e.g., Danzer and Lavy (2018)).

DiD estimation of the effects of education reforms is feasible if the entire sample population is not exposed to the reform at the same point in time. This could be the case, for example, because of a gradual implementation of the new system across a country or because the reform is targeted only at a specific part of the population or at specific regions. For example, Piopiunik (2014a) evaluates a school reform in the German federal state of Bavaria that moved the timing of tracking in low- and middle-track schools from grade 6 to grade 4, while students in high-track schools were not affected. The DiD identification in this case rests on the comparison of the change in average outcomes between pre- and post-reform of students in high-track schools with the change in average outcomes over the reform of students in low- or middle-track schools. A potential violation of this assumption would, for example, be the presence of a general trend in Germany in the selection of students attending high-track schools. To eliminate such Germany-wide trends, performance is furthermore compared between students in Bavaria and students in other German states, where the timing of tracking did not change, which effectively extends the approach to a difference-in-difference-in-differences ("triple diffs") approach.

However, a DiD strategy does not always have to include a time dimension. For example, Hanushek and Woessmann (2006) investigate whether educational tracking affects school performance and inequality in the school system. Their research design is based on comparing outcome differences between primary school (when no country uses tracking) and secondary school (when some countries use tracking and others do not) in countries with and without tracked school systems. Moreover, the usefulness of DiD approaches also extends to settings other than sharp changes in education policies or practices. For example, Hanushek, Schwerdt, Woessmann, and Zhang (2017) employ a difference-in-differences approach that compares employment rates across different ages for people with general and vocational education to test whether gains in youth employment associated with a vocational education may be offset by less adaptability and diminished employment later in life.

Fixed-effects approach

In recent years, extensive datasets have become available, in particular in many US states, which provide performance data for every student in the public school system and allow following each student over several years. Such extensive panel datasets allow an even more extensive treatment of cases where unobserved differences are constant over time than traditional DiD approaches. These more extensive panel-data techniques can be applied to the case where unobserved factors are heterogeneous across individuals (rather than groups).

Presumably the most prominent factor in educational research that is usually not observed by researchers is the innate ability of individuals. In many empirical applications, a possible "ability bias" is a typical challenge. Think of research investigating whether the attendance of private schools improves students' achievements. In this case, estimates are only reliable if one can exclude that they are driven by differences in innate ability between students that choose to attend private and public schools. In the absence of a clear measure for this factor and of a controlled or natural experiment, researchers sometimes try to circumvent this drawback by observing adequate proxy variables such as family background, parental education, and the like. This practical approach may help reducing the bias due to unobserved individual heterogeneity to some extent, but in most applications it presumably does not solve the problem completely.

While taking out fixed effects is also no panacea, it offers a solution to the problem in specific cases. As long as the factor that leads to unobserved heterogeneity—such as individual ability—has a constant impact on the outcome over time, it can be fixed by ignoring any variation in the level of outcomes across individuals and only focusing on changes over time. It is for this reason that panel data are needed that allow to observe the same individual at several points in time. In such a setting, the estimation can control for fixed effects of each individual in that it accounts for an indicator variable that takes out mean differences between individuals, so that only changes over time in inputs and outcomes are used to identify the effects of interest. This way, the estimation is able to control for unobserved but fixed heterogeneity across units of observation. In the most elaborate settings, such fixed effects can be introduced at the level of students, teachers, and schools.

An important special case of such models in the economics of education is the classical value-added approach that controls for previous outcomes of the same unit when estimating the effect of some input or intervention on current outcomes. In the special case of observing the same outcome (e.g., a test score) for a unit at two points in time, this approach estimates the effect of a specific education policy conditional on the previous outcome. This value-added approach is only a special case of more extensive models that use cross-sectional information of the same units (individuals, classes, schools) at several points in time in order to take out the effects of time-invariant factors.

Value-added models of educational production are most prominently used in the large literature investigating the contribution of teachers to educational achievements of students (see Hanushek and Rivkin (2012), Jackson, Rockoff, and Staiger (2014), and Koedel, Mihaly, and Rockoff (2015) for surveys). Estimating the effect of teacher characteristics on student performance is complicated because unobserved factors correlated with both teacher characteristics and student outcomes might bias estimates using non-experimental data. In this context, value-added models that focus on gains in student achievement help to eliminate the confounding impact of unobserved but fixed heterogeneity in student abilities across classes (Rockoff (2004); Rivkin, Hanushek, and Kain (2005); Aaronson, Barrow, and Sander (2007)). Very rich datasets covering multiple years of information for teachers even allow for estimating value-added models including a three-way fixed effects approach (student, teacher and school fixed effects). This provides the opportunity to link estimated teacher fixed effects with teacher characteristics or future outcomes of students (e.g., Chetty, Friedman, and Rockoff (2014); Cook and Mansfield (2016)). However, even in the most sophisticated models in this literature, extreme cases of non-random and dynamic sorting of teachers to students may give rise to remaining endogeneity concerns (e.g., Rothstein (2010)).

Fixed-effects panel approaches are not limited to the estimation of teacher effects or to exploiting individual-level treatments. For example, several studies on charter schools have employed student fixed effects approaches, which are not affected by the limitation of lottery studies of being restricted to oversubscribed schools (e.g., Imberman (2010), Booker, Sass, Gill, and Zimmer (2011), Baude, Casey, Hanushek, Phelan, and Rivkin (2018); see the survey by Epple et al. (2016)). Exploiting reforms of student assessment systems at the country level over time, Bergbauer, Hanushek, and Woessmann (2018) use country fixed effects to take out unobserved time-invariant country heterogeneity when estimating the effects of testing reforms in a cross-country analysis.

Using the time dimension is only one approach to take out fixed effects. Even without having observations for the same unit at several points in time, one can exclude fixed effects by using special datasets. Specific studies are able to use information on contemporaneously observed academic achievements in two subjects of the same individual, which allows them to take out fixed effects of a student that affect all subjects alike. Studies that use this approach include Dee (2005) on teacher-student matches, Schwerdt and Wuppermann (2011) on teaching methods, Metzler and Woessmann (2012) on teacher subject knowledge, Lavy (2015) on instruction time, and Falck, Mang, and Woessmann (2018) on computer use. Other approaches use data on siblings or twins to address unobserved heterogeneity (e.g., Black, Devereux, and Salvanes (2007); Kalil, Mogstad, Rege, and Votruba (2016)).

However, despite the substantial advancements made over recent years in the literature, it remains a fact that panel-data techniques can account for unobserved heterogeneity only inasmuch as the relevant unobserved characteristics do not differ systematically over the panel dimension. Unobserved interferences that are not constant over time (or subjects or twins) cannot be fixed by standard panel-data techniques alone and require the experimental methods discussed above.

Conclusions

This article has described empirical techniques that researchers have designed to allow for causal inference by overcoming the problem that unobserved confounding factors may give rise to spurious associations. The techniques described here are, however, by no means the only ones used in the economics of education literature to address causal questions. Also, the insight that experimental and quasi-experimental studies are best positioned to discern causal effects does not invalidate studies using more traditional techniques such as standard multivariate regressions. But the methods discussed in this article caution about possible limits to the causal interpretation of estimates and help to point out how more traditional research designs can yield results that do not capture causal effects.

References

Aaronson, D., Barrow, L., & Sander, W. (2007). Teachers and student achievement in the Chicago public high schools. *Journal of Labor Economics, 25*(1), 95–135.

Abdulkadiroğlu, A., Angrist, J., Dynarski, S., Kane, T. J., & Pathak, P. (2011). Accountability and flexibility in public schools: Evidence from Boston's charters and pilots. *Quarterly Journal of Economics, 126*(2), 699–748.

Abdulkadiroğlu, A., Angrist, J. D., Hull, P. D., & Pathak, P. A. (2016). Charters without lotteries: Testing takeovers in New Orleans and Boston. *The American Economic Review, 106*(7), 1878–1920.

Abdulkadiroğlu, A., Angrist, J., & Pathak, P. (2014). The elite illusion: Achievement effects at Boston and New York exam schools. *Econometrica, 82*(1), 137–196.

Angrist, J. D. (2004). American education research changes tack. *Oxford Review of Economic Policy, 20*(2), 198–212.

Angrist, J. D., Bettinger, E., & Kremer, M. (2006). Long-term educational consequences of secondary school vouchers: Evidence from administrative records in Colombia. *The American Economic Review, 96*(3), 847–862.

Angrist, J. D., Imbens, G. W., & Rubin, D. B. (1996). Identification of causal effects using instrumental variables. *Journal of the American Statistical Association, 91*(434), 444–455.

Angrist, J. D., & Lavy, V. (1999). Using Maimondides' rule to estimate the effect of class size on scholastic achievement. *Quarterly Journal of Economics, 114*(2), 533–575.

Angrist, J. D., Lavy, V., Leder-Luis, J., & Shany, A. (2018). *Maimonides rule Redux.* American Economic Review: Insights. Forthcoming.

Barnett, W. S. (1985). Benefit-cost analysis of the Perry preschool program and its policy implications. *Educational Evaluation and Policy Analysis, 7*(4), 333–342.

Baude, P. L., Casey, M., Hanushek, E. A., Phelan, G., & Rivkin, S. G. (2018). *The evolution of charter school quality.* Economica. forthcoming.

Becker, S., & Ichino, A. (2002). Estimation of average treatment effects based on propensity scores. *STATA Journal, 2*(4), 358–377.

Bedard, K., & Dhuey, E. (2006). The persistence of early childhood maturity: International evidence of long-run age effects. *Quarterly Journal of Economics, 121*(4), 1437–1472.

Belfield, C. R., Nores, M., Barnett, S. W., & Schweinhart, L. J. (2006). The high/scope Perry preschool program. *Journal of Human Resources, 41*(1), 162–190.

Bénabou, R., Kramarz, F., & Prost, C. (2009). The French zones d'éducation prioritaire: Much ado about nothing? *Economics of Education Review, 28*(3), 345–356.

Bergbauer, A. B., Hanushek, E. A., & Woessmann, L. (2018). *Testing*. NBER Working Paper 24836. Cambridge, MA: National Bureau of Economic Research.

Bettinger, E. P. (2012). Paying to learn: The effect of financial incentives on elementary school test scores. *The Review of Economics and Statistics, 94*, 686–698.

Bettinger, E. P., Long, B. T., Oreopoulos, P., & Sanbonmatsu, L. (2012). The role of application assistance and information in college decisions: Results from the H&R block Fafsa experiment. *Quarterly Journal of Economics, 127*(3), 1205–1242.

Bettinger, E., & Slonim, R. (2006). Using experimental economics to measure the effects of a natural educational experiment on altruism. *Journal of Public Economics, 90*(8–9), 1625–1648.

Bietenbeck, J. (2019). The long-term impacts of low-achieving childhood peers: Evidence from Project STAR. *Journal of the European Economic Association*, (in press).

Black, S. E., Devereux, P. J., & Salvanes, K. G. (2007). From the cradle to the labor market? The effect of birth weight on adult outcomes. *Quarterly Journal of Economics, 122*(1), 409–439.

Black, S. E., Devereux, P. J., & Salvanes, K. G. (2008). Staying in the classroom and out of the maternity ward? The effect of compulsory schooling laws on teenage births. *Economic Journal, 118*(530), 1025–1054.

Booker, K., Sass, T. R., Gill, B., & Zimmer, R. (2011). The effects of charter high schools on educational attainment. *Journal of Labor Economics, 29*(2), 377–415.

Chabrier, J., Cohodes, S., & Oreopoulos, P. (2016). What can we learn from charter school lotteries? *The Journal of Economic Perspectives, 30*(3), 57–84.

Chetty, R., Friedman, J. N., Hilger, N., Saez, E., Whitmore Schanzenbach, D., & Yagan, D. (2011). How does your kindergarten classroom affect your earnings? Evidence from project STAR. *Quarterly Journal of Economics, 126*(4), 1593–1660.

Chetty, R., Friedman, J. N., & Rockoff, J. E. (2014). Measuring the impacts of teachers II: Teacher value-added and student outcomes in adulthood. *The American Economic Review, 104*(9), 2633–2679.

Cook, J. B., & Mansfield, R. K. (2016). Task-specific experience and task-specific talent: Decomposing the productivity of high school teachers. *Journal of Public Economics, 140*, 51–72.

Cullen, J. B., Jacob, B. A., & Levitt, S. (2006). The effect of school choice on participants: Evidence from randomized lotteries. *Econometrica, 74*(5), 1191–1230.

Currie, J., & Moretti, E. (2003). Mother's education and the intergenerational transmission of human capital: Evidence from college openings. *Quarterly Journal of Economics, 118*(4), 1495–1532.

Cygan-Rehm, K., & Maeder, M. (2013). The effect of education on fertility: Evidence from a compulsory schooling reform. *Labour Economics, 25*, 35–48.

Danzer, N., & Lavy, V. (2018). Paid parental leave and children's schooling outcomes. *Economic Journal, 128*(608), 81–117.

De Ree, J., Muralidharan, K., Pradhan, M., & Rogers, H. (2018). Double for nothing? Experimental evidence on an unconditional teacher salary increase in Indonesia. *Quarterly Journal of Economics, 133*(2), 993–1039.

Dee, T. S. (2005). A teacher like me: Does race, ethnicity, or gender matter? *The American Economic Review, 95*(2), 158–165.

Deming, D. J., Hastings, J. S., Kane, T. J., & Staiger, D. O. (2014). School choice, school quality, and postsecondary attainment. *The American Economic Review, 104*(3), 991–1013.

Deming, D. J., Yuchtman, N., Abulafi, A., Goldin, C., & Katz, L. F. (2016). The value of postsecondary credentials in the labor market: An experimental study. *The American Economic Review, 106*(3), 778–806.

Epple, D., Romano, R., & Zimmer, R. (2016). Charter schools: A survey of research on their characteristics and effectiveness. In E. A. Hanushek, S. Machin, & L. Woessmann (Eds.), *Handbook of the economics of education* (pp. 139–208). Elsevier.

Eren, O., Briggs, D., & Barnes, S. (2017). Test-based promotion policies, dropping out, and juvenile crime. *Journal of Public Economics, 153*, 9–31.

Falck, O., Mang, C., & Woessmann, L. (2018). Virtually no effect? Different uses of classroom computers and their effect on student achievement. *Oxford Bulletin of Economics & Statistics, 80*(1), 1–38.

Finn, J. D., & Achilles, C. M. (1990). Answers and questions about class size: A statewide experiment. *American Educational Research Journal, 27*(3), 557–577.

Fort, M., Schneeweis, N., & Winter-Ebmer, R. (2016). Is education always reducing fertility? Evidence from compulsory schooling reforms. *Economic Journal, 126*(595), 1823–1855.

Fredriksson, P., Öckert, B., & Oosterbeek, H. (2013). Long-term effects of class size. *Quarterly Journal of Economics, 128*(1), 249–285.

Fryer, R. G. (2011). Financial incentives and student achievement: Evidence from randomized trials. *Quarterly Journal of Economics, 126*(4), 1755–1798.

Fryer, R. G. (2017). The production of human capital in developed countries: Evidence from 196 randomized field experiments. In A. V. Banerjee, & E. Duflo (Eds.), *Handbook of economic field experiments* (pp. 95–322). Amsterdam: North Holland.

Garibaldi, P., Giavazzi, F., Ichino, A., & Rettore, E. (2012). College cost and time to complete a degree: Evidence from tuition discontinuities. *The Review of Economics and Statistics, 94*(3), 699–711.

Hanushek, E. A. (1999). The evidence on class size. In S. E. Mayer, & P. E. Peterson (Eds.), *Earning and learning: How schools matter* (pp. 131–168). Washington, DC: Brookings Institution.

Hanushek, E. A., Guido, S., Simon, W., & Woessmann, L. (2015). Returns to skills around the world: Evidence from PIAAC. *European Economic Review, 73*, 103–130.

Hanushek, E. A., Guido, S., Woessmann, L., & Zhang, L. (2017). General education, vocational education, and labor-market outcomes over the lifecycle. *Journal of Human Resources, 52*(1), 48–87.

Hanushek, E. A., & Rivkin, S. G. (2012). The distribution of teacher quality and implications for policy. *Annual Review of Economics, 4*, 131–157.

Hanushek, E. A., & Woessmann, L. (2006). Does educational tracking affect performance and inequality? Differences-in-differences evidence across countries. *Economic Journal, 116*(510), C63–C76.

Harmon, C., & Walker, I. (1995). Estimates of the economic return to schooling for the United Kingdom. *The American Economic Review, 85*(5), 1278–1286.

Havnes, T., & Mogstad, M. (2011). No child left behind: Subsidized child care and children's long-run outcomes. *American Economic Journal: Economic Policy, 3*(2), 97–129.

Heckman, J., Moon, S. H., Pinto, R., Savelyev, P., & Adam, Y. (2010). Analyzing social experiments as implemented: A reexamination of the evidence from the HighScope Perry preschool program. *Journal of Quantitative Economics, 1*(1), 1–46.

Imberman, S. A. (2010). Achievement and behavior in charter schools: Drawing a more complete picture. *The Review of Economics and Statistics, 93*(2), 416–435.

Jackson, C. K., Johnson, R. C., & Claudia, P. (2016). The effects of school spending on educational and economic outcomes: Evidence from school finance reforms. *Quarterly Journal of Economics, 131*(1), 157–218.

Jackson, C. K., Rockoff, J. E., & Staiger, D. O. (2014). Teacher effects and teacher related policies. *Annual Review of Economics, 6*, 801–825.

Jacob, B. A., & Lefgren, L. (2004). Remedial education and student achievement: A regression-discontinuity analysis. *The Review of Economics and Statistics, 86*.

Jacob, B. A., & Lefgren, L. (2009). The effect of grade retention on high school completion. *American Economic Journal: Applied Economics, 1*(3), 33–58.

Kalil, A., Mogstad, M., Rege, M., & Votruba, M. E. (2016). Father presence and the intergenerational transmission of educational attainment. *Journal of Human Resources, 51*(4), 869–899.

Kirkeboen, L. J., Leuven, E., & Mogstad, M. (2016). Field of study, earnings, and self-selection. *Quarterly Journal of Economics, 131*(3), 1057–1111.

Koedel, C., Mihaly, K., & Rockoff, J. E. (2015). Value-added modeling: A review. *Economics of Education Review, 47*, 180–195.

Krueger, A. B. (1999). Experimental estimates of education production functions. *Quarterly Journal of Economics, 114*(2), 497–532.

Lavy, V. (2010). Effects of free choice among public schools. *The Review of Economic Studies, 77*(3), 1164–1191.

Lavy, V. (2015). Do differences in schools' instruction time explain international achievement gaps? Evidence from developed and developing countries. *Economic Journal, 125*(588), F397–F424.

Leuven, E., & Løkken, S. A. (2018). Long term impacts of class size in compulsory school. *Journal of Human Resources*, (in press).

Levitt, S. D., List, J. A., Neckermann, S., & Sadoff, S. (2016). The behavioralist goes to school: Leveraging behavioral economics to improve educational performance. *American Economic Journal: Economic Policy, 8*(4), 183–219.

Machin, S., & McNally, S. (2008). The literacy hour. *Journal of Public Economics, 92*(5–6), 1441–1462.

McCrary, J. (2008). Manipulation of the running variable in the regression discontinuity design: A density test. *Journal of Econometrics, 142*(2), 698–714.

McCrary, J., & Royer, H. (2011). The effect of female education on fertility and infant health: Evidence from school entry policies using exact date of birth. *The American Economic Review, 101*(1), 158–195.

Meghir, C., & Palme, M. (2005). Educational reform, ability, and family background. *The American Economic Review, 95*(1), 414–423.

Meghir, C., Palme, M., & Simeonova, E. (2018). Education and mortality: Evidence from a social experiment. *American Economic Journal: Applied Economics, 10*(2), 234–256.

Metzler, J., & Woessmann, L. (2012). The impact of teacher subject knowledge on student achievement: Evidence from within-teacher within-student variation. *Journal of Development Economics, 99*(2), 486–496.

Mühlenweg, A., & Puhani, P. (2010). The evolution of the school-entry age effect in a school tracking system. *Journal of Human Resources, 45*(2), 407–438.

Muralidharan, K., & Sundararaman, V. (2011). Teacher performance pay: Experimental evidence from India. *Journal of Political Economy, 119*(1), 39–77.

Oreopoulos, P. (2006). Estimating average and local average treatment effects of education when compulsory schooling laws really matter. *The American Economic Review, 96*(1), 152–175.

Papay, J. P., Murnane, R., & Willett, J. (2016). The impact of test score labels on human-capital investment decisions. *Journal of Human Resources, 51*(2), 357–388.

Piopiunik, M. (2014a). The effects of early tracking on student performance: Evidence from a school reform in Bavaria. *Economics of Education Review, 42*, 12–33.

Piopiunik, M. (2014b). Intergenerational transmission of education and mediating channels: Evidence from a compulsory schooling reform in Germany. *The Scandinavian Journal of Economics, 116*(3), 878–907.

Piopiunik, M., Guido, S., Simon, L., & Woessmann, L. (2018). Skills, signals, and employability: An experimental investigation. In *CESifo working Paper 6858*. *Munich: CESifo.*

Rivkin, S. G., Hanushek, E. A., & Kain, J. F. (2005). Teachers, schools, and academic achievement. *Econometrica, 73*(2), 417–458.

Rockoff, J. E. (2004). The impact of individual teachers on student achievement: Evidence from panel data. *The American Economic Review, 94*(2), 247–252.

Rothstein, J. (2010). Teacher quality in educational production: Tracking, decay, and student achievement. *Quarterly Journal of Economics, 125*(1), 175–214.

Schlotter, M., Guido, S., & Woessmann, L. (2011). Econometric methods for causal evaluation of education policies and practices: A non-technical guide. *Education Economics, 19*(2), 109–137.

Schwerdt, G., Messer, D., Woessmann, L., & Wolter, S. C. (2012). The impact of an adult education voucher program: Evidence from a randomized field experiment. *Journal of Public Economics, 96*(7), 569–583.

Schwerdt, G., West, M. R., & Winters, M. A. (2017). The effects of test-based retention on student outcomes over time: Regression discontinuity evidence from Florida. *Journal of Public Economics, 152*, 154–169.

Schwerdt, G., & Wuppermann, A. C. (2011). Is traditional teaching really all that bad? A within-student between-subject approach. *Economics of Education Review, 30*(2), 365–379.

Stephens, M., Jr., & Yang, D.-Y. (2014). Compulsory education and the benefits of schooling. *The American Economic Review, 104*(6), 1777–1792.

West, M. R., & Woessmann, L. (2010). Every Catholic child in a Catholic school': Historical resistance to state schooling, contemporary private competition and student achievement across countries. *Economic Journal, 120*(546), F229–F255.

Woessmann, L., & West, M. R. (2006). Class-size effects in school systems around the world: Evidence from between-grade variation in TIMSS. *European Economic Review, 50*(3), 695–736.

2

Behavioral economics and nudging in education: evidence from the field

Mette Trier Damgaard, Helena Skyt Nielsen

Department of Economics and Business Economics, Fuglesangs Allé 4, DK8210 Aarhus V, Denmark

Behavioral economics of education

Education is a core component of the human capital stock. Agents are thought to invest time, effort and money in education, which provides knowledge and characteristics enhancing productivity and, thus, lifetime earnings. At each stage in the education cycle, agents should in principle weigh the costs and benefits of education and decide whether to pursue further education. Considering the high estimated financial and non-financial returns, it remains puzzling why individuals drop out or perform poorly in education. Insights from behavioral economics provide some of the answers as students, parents and teachers are all potentially affected by behavioral barriers such as (1) self-control problems, (2) limited attention and cognitive ability, (3) loss aversion, (4) default bias, (5) social preferences, or (6) biased beliefs (Jabbar, 2011; Koch, Nafziger, & Nielsen, 2015).

Self-control

Decisions on education, like other investment decisions, have long-term consequences. Investing time and effort in studying or attending classes involves a trade-off between immediate costs (effort costs and foregone earnings) and future benefits (higher future income). When making these intertemporal trade-offs, students and their parents may be present-biased and hence put too much weight on the present costs (see e.g. Laibson, 1997). This may cause self-control problems where students do not properly regulate their own behavior to achieve long-term goals.

For example, students who start secondary school may clearly prefer graduating over dropping out, but they might fail on an everyday basis to resist the temptation to do something more enjoyable than studying or attending class. Students with self-control problems might also put off important decisions, such as what university to apply to.

In the context of education decisions, it is worth noting that children and adolescents are particularly likely to be influenced by self-control problems, because their brains and in particular their executive functions are less developed (Lavecchia, Lui, & Oreopoulos, 2016). Furthermore, self-control problems are correlated with socio-economic status (SES), meaning that both low-SES children and parents

The Economics of Education, Second Edition
https://doi.org/10.1016/B978-0-12-815391-8.00002-1

tend to lack self-control and parents may thus be unable to compensate for their children's lack of self-control. Moreover, students with self-control problems may lack non-cognitive skills, such as grit and perseverance.

Limited attention and cognitive ability

Cognitive and attentional limitations might pose an important barrier to good decision-making for complex choices such as education decisions. Standard economic theory assumes that individuals consider all of the relevant alternatives and all of the available and cost-free information when making decisions.

This implies that in theory, prospective students should consider all possible alternative colleges and fields, seek out all information about those alternatives and then make an informed choice about what to study and where. In practice, attention may, however, better be viewed as a scarce resource and as a result, some information may be overlooked or forgotten. In particular, there is evidence that students lack accurate information about the returns to education (Oreopoulos & Dunn, 2013), even though such information is freely available.

In the context of education decisions, the complexity of administrative processes such as college or aid applications may be a barrier to educational attainment and limited attention may make students forget to do tasks such as homework. Furthermore, people may adopt a number of heuristics to simplify the complex choice situations (DellaVigna, 2009) e.g. place excessive weight on the most salient information or option when making decisions. The overemphasis on salient information implies that decisions may be sensitive to provision and framing of information.

Loss aversion

People tend to evaluate outcomes relative to a reference point. Experimental evidence suggests that a loss relative to the reference point looms larger than an equal-sized gain, and this loss aversion leads to a strong aversion to downside risk (Kahneman & Tversky, 1979).

For example, suppose a student applies for financial aid and receives a study grant covering half of his tuition fees. If he had expected to get two-thirds of the costs covered, then such a grant will be disappointing. Conversely, if he had only expected to get one-third of their costs covered, the same grant would feel like a surprising gain.

In the context of education decisions, the typical investment involves some uncertainty with respect to the possible gains in terms of completion and wage gains. Consequently, students may underinvest in education to avoid possible losses and their decision-making may be sensitive to the relative salience of losses versus gains.

Default bias

A common empirical finding is that people tend to stick to the default (Kahneman, Knetsch, & Thaler, 1991). This is known as the default bias. Default bias relates to several of the concepts mentioned above. First, limited attention means that people do not pay adequate attention to other options, because the default is the most salient option. Second, loss aversion often leads to a default bias because the default serves as a natural reference point. Finally, present bias combined with immediate switching costs could make people stick to the default.

In the context of education, the default bias might help explain why some parents refrain from exploiting the opportunity to choose a primary school for their child, or why some students simply choose a career similar to one of their parents' careers. As people with low-SES are more likely to be influenced by present bias and attention limitations, they are also potentially more likely to be influenced by defaults.

Social preferences

People care about how they are perceived by others and by themselves and this might explain why some people apparently make choices in conflict with their own interests. Social identity and social belonging is closely related to such image concerns. People like having a sense of social belonging, and one means of achieving that is by using one's actions to signal information to others. Hence, actions may be motivated by the desire to shape one's image and social identity. In turn, this may lead to preferences (Akerlof & Kranton, 2002) and/or social pressure (DellaVigna, 2009) to follow the social norms in one's social comparison group.

In this line of reasoning, imagine a student who goes out drinking the night before an important exam. This behavior could either reflect a wish to conform to the social norm in his comparison group or it could reflect a wish to maintain a favourable self-image, as it would allow the student to attribute poor exam performance to being hungover rather than limited ability.

Social norms differ by groups. For example, in some social groups, it may be the norm *not* to exert effort, to skip classes or to drop out of secondary school. In other cases, the social norm may be conducive to education attainment, such as a norm to obtain a university degree or to enroll in a prestigious school. Therefore, from the perspective of the individual, social norms may in some cases lead to underinvestment in education and in others to overinvestment.

Biased beliefs

Evidence suggests that beliefs about probabilities are biased. For example, people tend to be overconfident about their own probability of succeeding and they tend to be influenced by projection bias, meaning that they overweight the probability that the future will be identical to the present (DellaVigna, 2009).

Student self-confidence in own ability is positively correlated with academic performance, but it may be biased leading to overconfidence or underconfidence. It is not obvious whether overconfidence in own ability has a negative or a positive causal effect on effort provision. If effort and ability are complementary, then overconfidence is predicted to increase effort provision (Benabou & Tirole, 2002). However, if effort and ability are better viewed as substitutes, as in the context of "pass/fail" exams, then overconfidence is predicted to have a negative causal effect on effort provision because students (wrongly) believe that their high ability can substitute for study effort. Opposite effects are predicted for underconfident students.

Students influenced by projection bias may not fully recognise that their life situation and needs will change over time, regardless of their education choices. Instead they may think that the current situation is a good predictor of the future. Hence, education choices (e.g. whether or not to move to a different part of the country to obtain a certain university degree) may be made given their current life situation and preferences and not taking their future life situation and preferences into account.

Education interventions involving nudging

The existence of behavioral barriers influencing decision-making motivates interventions that target these barriers and potentially try to remove them. Below we provide an overview of the use of *nudging* in field interventions in the education sector from pre-school through higher education. *Nudging* policies are aimed at *"alter[ing] people's behaviors in a predictable way without forbidding any options or significantly changing their economic incentives"* (Thaler & Sunstein, 2008).

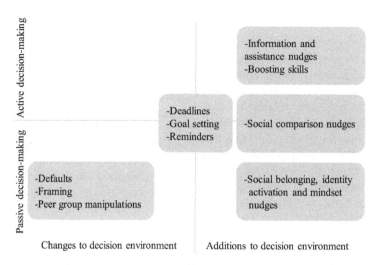

FIG. 2.1 Typology of nudging interventions. Note: Passive decision-making is sub-conscious, whereas active decision-making is conscious decision making.

Fig. 2.1 provides an overview of types of nudging interventions classified by two dimensions: (1) whether the interventions are likely to induce active or passive decision-making and (2) whether they involve changes or additions to the decision environment.

Defaults, framing and peer group manipulations are "pure" or "non-educational" nudges that target systematic biases in behavior through (small) changes to the decision environment that potentially work sub-consciously without promoting active decision-making.

Deadline, goal setting and reminder interventions induce people to utilise these behavioral tools in a specific situation where they may otherwise fail to use them sufficiently to self-regulate their own behavior. Such interventions therefore alter the decision environment by exogenously imposing use of already available tools and as a result may change behavior through better active or passive decision-making.

Information and assistance nudges are "educational" nudges that are thought to lead to better active decision-making by adding new information or basic assistance to the decision environment. However, like "pure" nudges, these

"educational" nudges may also influence behavior subconsciously, e.g. by making certain information more salient. *"Boost" interventions* are also sometimes referred to as "educate" interventions. They deliberately aim at improving active decision-making capabilities by teaching individuals about behavioral barriers and skills to tackle these barriers.

Social comparison nudges add social comparison information that consciously or subconsciously motivate individuals to change their behavior. The added motivation may or may not lead to more active decision-making.

Social belonging, identity activation and mindset nudges are brief psychological interventions that target students' mindsets and beliefs with the aim of creating a self-reinforcing but subconscious improvement in motivation and achievement.

Both brief psychological interventions and boost interventions are similar to many informational and social comparison nudges in the sense that they aim to de-bias behavior by adding specific and brief information to the decision environment. Furthermore, as the psychological interventions are brief there is a relatively short interaction with the target population and implementation costs (even at scale) are typically low as for "pure" nudging interventions. However, unlike "pure" nudges the goal of boost and brief psychological interventions is to influence behavior not only in the specific decision environment in which the information is provided but also in other contexts and long into the future. Below we describe the evidence for each type of education interventions. One caveat is that the evidence concerning interventions with nudging elements is relatively scarce and steeply increasing.

Defaults

One of the most well-known and powerful nudges is auto-enrolment. Because of default bias, people tend to choose the default option and as a result changing defaults is often a powerful policy tool. The results of two recent field interventions within the education sector suggest that defaults can positively influence student outcomes such as grades and earned course credits. This is consistent with the positive effects of default interventions found in other domains and suggests that default bias also influences education decisions.

For example, Marx and Turner (in press) provide a recent example of nudging with defaults in the education sector. Applicants accepted into a community college in the US were randomly assigned to treatment and control. Students in the treatment group received financial aid material with a nonzero loan offer in addition to an offer of a Federal Pell Grant whereas students in the control treatment received a $0 loan offer but the same Pell Grant offer. The change of default was a "pure" nudge as it did not influence eligibility for the loan nor did it require students to take the loan and students in both groups were given a link to an online loan request form where they could formally request a loan. Hence, the key treatment difference was whether taking out a nonzero loan was presented as the default choice. Marx and

Turner (in press) find that students who received the non-zero loan offer were more likely to borrow and more likely to borrow the default amount. In addition, there were positive effects on attempted and earned credits and the grade point average. The intervention did not influence enrollment and it is too soon to properly assess the effect on graduation.

Bergman and Rogers (2017) also study a default intervention but target different behavior and a different population. The intervention tested the impact of an opt-out versus an opt-in default for adoption of a text messaging service for parents of middle and high school children in the US The text messaging service provided information about their child's performance, missed classes and missed assignments. The study found a large difference in the share of parents adopting the technology with 7.8% adopting in the opt-in treatment and 96.5% adopting in the opt-out treatment. That is less than 4% of parents in the opt-out treatment, opted out at any point during the school year despite being given several opportunities to do so. The authors also found that parents who opt in were those who were already engaging more with the school and the parents of already high performing students. Hence, an opt-out default could reach a population of parents who were otherwise harder to reach. The authors also reported positive effects of the opt-out default on grades and the number of courses failed. This suggests that exposure to the messages translated into improved performance at school.

Framing

Framing interventions involve small deliberate changes to the choice environment that influence the salience or labeling of different aspects of already available information. Even small changes in the framing of information may change or de-bias behavior because of cognitive and attentional limitations. Framing interventions in the education sector differ in terms of the type of information — monetary or non-monetary - altered by the framing manipulation and results are highly mixed.

Framing of information about transfers with exact same monetary value have been studied in various contexts. For instance, Field (2009) exposed law students to two alternative financial aid packages: one involved tuition loans relieved if the student chose a low-paying public interest job after graduation, while the other consisted of tuition waivers that had to be repaid after graduation if the student chose a high-paying job not in public interest job. The different framings led to significant behavioral differences consistent with debt aversion, default bias and loss aversion because students behaved to minimize losses relative to the default. Similar positive effects are usually found in framing manipulations of monetary incentives provided that individuals are given sufficient time to allow them to meaningfully change behavior (Levitt, List, Neckermann, & Sadoff, 2016 provide an example with little time to adjust behavior and find no effects).

Framing of information on non-monetary payoff has been studied in the context of tests and grading. For example, studies have compared either a zero endowment of test points with the possibility to earn points by giving correct answers or alternatively they were given a positive endowment of test points from which points were deducted for wrong or omitted answers (loss frame). Results are mixed and heterogeneous, see e.g. Wagner (2017) or McEvoy (2016). Generally, framing interventions should only be expected to have effects if the framing manipulations are sufficiently different from trigger significantly different thought processes.

Peer group manipulations

Like framing interventions, peer group manipulations represent exogenous changes to the decision environment. Peer group manipulations involve a restructuring of the choice environment to facilitate peer interaction which may help improve the sense of social belonging, enforce or create social norms of effort provision or improve skill transfer through study partnerships.

Overall, peer group manipulations have not been particularly effective (Carrell, Sacerdote, & West, 2013; Rogers & Feller, 2016) unless combined with instructions or requirements to interact (Papay, Taylor, Tyler, & Laski, 2016). Non-interventional studies of peer effects in student housing have also found mixed effects on academic performance (Carrell, Fullerton, & West, 2009). It is apparently difficult to exogenously influence group identity.

Deadlines

Interim deadlines may serve as a commitment device for students with self-control problems who repeatedly procrastinate doing tasks such as homework, written assignments and exam preparation. Models with present-biased preferences predict that students benefit from such commitment devices and that sophisticates (who are aware of their self-control problems) will actively choose to use deadlines as a commitment device when given the choice.

The empirical evidence on the effectiveness of deadlines focuses on the impact on university students and is generally positive for grades but not when it comes to completion rates. An early and very influential paper documenting a deadline effect is Ariely and Wertenbroch (2002). They tested the effect in a setting with executive education students at the Massachussettes Institute of Technology who had to write three term papers for a course. They were assigned to one of two deadline treatments. In the first treatment, participants were given evenly spread deadlines, whereas the students set their own deadlines in the second one. In both treatments, there was a 1% grade penalty for each day of delay beyond the deadline.

Ariely and Wertenbroch (2002) found that grades were lower with self-imposed deadlines than externally imposed deadlines, suggesting that students did not set deadlines optimally. While these results indicate a positive effect of deadlines, they were obtained for a very specific sample of highly motivated students with strong incentives to complete the course (nonrefundable fees).

In the education context, tests and exams may be regarded as natural deadlines. There is some indication that increased test (and hence deadline) frequency affects performance positively. De Paola and Scoppa (2011) study a randomised trial where treated students had a mid-term and a final exam instead of just one exam covering all material. The students in the treatment group achieved higher grades and were more likely to pass the course. Low procrastinators (high ability students with good secondary school grades) benefitted most from the interim exam, and Tuckman (1998) find that such students benefit even more from extra homework assignments than from extra exams (in contrast to heavy procrastinators).

Overall, the initial positive effects on grades found by Ariely and Wertenbroch (2002) seem consistent with the positive grade effects of increasing exam frequency which is also found by De Paola and Scoppa (2011) and Tuckman (1998). Notably, a common feature of these environments is that the deadlines/exams involve (real) high stakes that motivate students to study. In addition, there is sufficient time to allow students to increase study effort and hence impact grades. In contrast, Levy and Ramim (2013) found faster completion but no effect on grades for students incentivized by time gains — possibly due to the short time scale in the experiment and the way deadline incentives were constructed. Burger, Charness, and Lynham (2011) studied deadlines in a less natural field setting which incentivized students to meet deadlines with monetary gains and found detrimental effects on study effort. This suggests that it may be

difficult to exogenously induce motivation to meet deadlines but variation in the level of motivation may be key to understanding the differential extensive margin results (i.e. task completion and pass rate results) with some evidence suggesting that positive extensive margin effects only arise if motivation is high but not so high that there is no room for improvement.

Goal setting

A number of recent studies have investigated another type of commitment device: goal setting. Theoretically, present-biased agents who invest too little effort in their education can benefit from self-set goals as internal commitment devices. Once set, goals become salient reference points that students (and parents) will be motivated to reach in order to avoid psychological costs (due to loss aversion) of not reaching the goals (Clark, Gill, Prowse, & Rush, 2017; Koch & Nafziger, 2011). Therefore, asking students, parents and teachers to set a *specific* goal for task completion or task performance may help alleviate self-control problems by subconsciously nudging individuals toward behavior that enables them to meet the goal. Later we discuss boost interventions which may improve *general* goal-setting skills.

Overall, the evidence on the effects of setting *specific* goals is somewhat mixed and it remains unclear whether task-based goals or performance-based goals are generally better at nudging behavior (see e.g. Clark et al. 2017 vs.; Lent & Souverijn, 2018). There is some evidence to suggest that goals *can* have positive effects on effort provision and student performance for types of tasks and individuals likely influenced by procrastination. For example, goals are effective for impatient parents (e.g. Mayer et al., in press) and low performing students (e.g. Lent & Souverijn, 2018) who are likely to also be high procrastinators. However, the evidence also suggests that care must be taken not to pressure individuals to set too high goals as suggestions of higher goals may have adverse effects (e.g. Lent & Souverijn, 2018).

Reminders

Due to attention limitations, there is a risk that people forget to make decisions they intended to make and fail to take actions they planned to take. Reminders target such problems by refocusing attention to the decision problem or task (e.g. Karlan, McConnell, Mullainathan, & Zinman, 2016). Moreover, reminders may have informational value, reminding people of already known information or providing easy access to new information. In addition, reminders may emphasise deadlines and tasks or the benefits of meeting deadlines and completing tasks. As a result they may mitigate self-control problems. In this section we focus on reminders that provide minimal new information and hence allow identification of a reminder effect. We discuss interventions targeting students, parents and teachers in turn.

Reminding students

At first glance, the results of studies using reminders targeted at students seem to be inconsistent. However, some patterns emerge. The effects of reminders on specific tasks such as completing college enrollment (Castleman & Page, 2015, 2017), aid applications (e.g. Bird, Castleman, Goodman, & Lamberton, 2017) or contributions posted in an online learning platform (Kizilcec, Schneider, Cohen, & McFarland, 2014) generally are positive with some indication that the largest effects arise among low-SES students. However, the effects mostly seem short-lived and the effect on outcomes which are more long-term and require ongoing effort (e.g. grades and earned course credits) are more mixed. Interestingly, Oreopoulos and Petronijevic (2018) contrasted their reminder treatment with a small-scale one-on-one coaching intervention on a similar study population. For the coaching intervention the authors reported much larger effects on earned

course credits and grades, suggesting that text message reminders are unable to substitute for coaching when it comes to ongoing effort provision at university.

Reminding parents and teachers

Overall, studies nudging parents with reminders have almost consistently found positive effects on parental involvement and student skills (e.g. Kraft & Monti-Nussbaum, 2017; Rogers & Feller, 2018). Additional studies targeting reminders at teachers are needed before conclusions can be made with respect to the effect of reminders for teachers.

Informational nudges

Attention limitations may also imply that students and parents do not acquire all of the relevant and important information when making decisions — even if the information is publicly available. By providing important information in an easily accessible manner, it may be possible to overcome attention limitations. In addition, choice architects can ensure that some information is more salient than other information. Consequently, informational nudges may target both attention limitations and other behavioral barriers. A large number of studies fall into this category, we structure our discussion around the type of information provided.

Parental information

Some informational nudges target parents and either (1) provide information relevant for education decisions influenced by parents or (2) provide information about child behavior. In the former category research support the beneficial effect of providing parents with information about school quality (Hastings & Weinstein, 2008) or benefits of specific high school courses (Harackiewicz, Rozek, Hulleman, & Hyde, 2012). In the latter category, studies are numerous. Interventions providing information on child behavior may de-bias beliefs about the child's behavior and thus alleviate possible negative effects of asymmetric information. Children are better informed about the effort that they exert than their parents. The asymmetric information problem is well-known, even in classical economic theory, and is not per se behavioral. However, some interventions to alleviate the problems are behavioral in the sense that they reduce information barriers by providing parents with easy access to standardised information.

Overall, with a few exceptions, the studies providing easy access to detailed information for parents have positive effects on student outcomes. Studies have documented positive effects on education outcomes of providing parents with detailed information about their child's missed assignments, classes attended or passed, or child performance via email, text messages or phone (e.g. Bergman, in press; Berlinski, Busso, Dinkelman, & Martinez, 2017). Moreover, there is indication that parents value the information as parents in Berlinski et al. (2017) indicated a positive willingness-to-pay to continue the messages. This is consistent with the findings of e.g. Bursztyn and Coffman (2012).

Information about behavior and ability

Students may also lack accurate information enabling them to assess their own ability and behavior. For example, students may (intentionally or not) lack information about what constitutes plagiarism. Moreover, students with self-control problems might find plagiarism an appealing alternative to hard work. Students may also lack information about the value of courses offered to them.

Overall, it appears that experiments providing information that make individuals reflect on whether current behavior is optimal are beneficial. A common feature of the interventions in Pistolesi (2017) and Bandiera, Larcinese, and Rasul (2015) is that they provide personalised information which may potentially de-bias beliefs about own ability or effort level, and therefore induce individuals to re-optimise

behavior (e.g. effort choices) and pathway (e.g. major choice).

Returns to schooling

Information may also be provided in an attempt at de-biasing beliefs about the returns to schooling. By making the benefits of schooling more salient, interventions providing information about the returns to schooling possibly also reduce self-control problems.

Oreopoulos and Dunn (2013) show that campaigns informing secondary school students about tuition costs and potential earnings can influence *beliefs* about the net returns to education but most research suggests that the change in beliefs does not necessarily translate into a change in behavior (e.g. Carrell & Sacerdote, 2017; Fryer, 2016). However, results are generally more positive for low-SES students (e.g. Peter & Zambre, 2017) and students in developing countries (e.g. Hastings, Neilson, & Zimmerman, 2015).

Overall, nudging with information about the returns to schooling has mostly had no effects on student outcomes in developed countries but positive effects in developing countries. It appears that effects are potentially larger for low-SES students, and there is some indication that the interventions providing information about the (financial or non-financial) returns to schooling are more likely to produce positive effects if done at young ages. Fryer (2016) and Jensen (2010) found positive effects for elementary or middle school children, while other studies involving secondary school and more mature students rarely found effects.

Financial aid and assistance

Several studies investigate the effects of providing information about financial aid. By bringing attention to available financial aid schemes, these interventions potentially lower the perceived immediate costs of continuing education and, hence, might indirectly reduce the effects of self-control problems. Overall, interventions providing financial aid information have mostly had no effects on student outcomes (e.g. Bettinger, Long, Oreopoulos, & Sanbonmatsu, 2012). There are a few exceptions where positive effects have been found for selective groups of high achieving students (e.g. Dinkelman & Martinez, 2014).

A possible reason for lack of effects is that recipients have limited attention and therefore may not pay attention to the information provided to them. Even if people do pay attention and want to act on the information, cognitive limitations and other behavioral barriers such as lack of self-control may imply that they are unable to do so. Basic one-on-one assistance (e.g. to fill out a form) might therefore be necessary to overcome the behavioral barriers.

Two US interventions have investigated this and found differing results. This may indicate that the provision of basic assistance on it's own may also not be sufficient to ensure better student outcomes. Bettinger et al. (2012) provided low-income individuals who had received assistance completing their tax returns with personal assistance to complete financial aid applications as well as aid estimates. The intervention potentially targeted several behavioral barriers, including limited attention, cognitive limitations and procrastination and led to an increase in aid applications and college enrollment in the treated families. Oreopoulos and Ford (2016) incorporated college application assistance into the curriculum for secondary school students in their final year. They found positive effects on college applications and enrollment in the first implementation when assistance was combined with application fee waivers and guidance in choosing eligible programs, but no effects when less guidance was given in second implementation.

Boosting skills to alleviate self-control problems

Recognizing that people may be unable to overcome the behavioral barriers they face (even if they are motivated to do so), an alternative to providing assistance, could be to teach students and parents skills that may enable them to do so. Boost policies teach people about possible behavioral barriers and general skills which may be used to mitigate the effects. For example, a number of recent interventions in education aim to boost skills alleviating self-control problems. The goal of these interventions is to promote more active (conscious) decision-making across a *broad* range of contexts. In contrast, specific deadlines and goals (discussed earlier) have a rather narrow focus on de-biasing choices in a *specific* context through better active (conscious) or passive (subconscious) decision-making.

Generally, the effects of interventions teaching students and parents' skills like grit, forward-looking behavior and goal setting have been positive (e.g. Alan, Boneva, & Seda, 2016; Morisano, Hirsh, Peterson, Pihl, & Shore, 2010) and some evidence suggests that the effects are largest for individuals with the greatest self-control problems (De Paola & Scoppa, 2015). However, recently Dobronyi et al. (in press) failed to find positive effects for a large scale intervention. This is possibly due to the use of a less selected sample with on average less motivation to improve skills. Lacking motivation may arguably undermine the effectiveness of boost policies.

Social comparison nudges

Nudges providing social comparison information are special cases of informational nudges. The nudges provide information that facilitates comparisons with others and in doing so may appeal to social preferences for adhering to the social norms and/or may create social pressure to adhere to the norms.

An example of a classical social information nudge in the education sector is provided by Coffman, Featherstone, and Kessler (2017). They study an intervention providing a random subset of high-achieving college graduates admitted to the Teach for America program with information about the percentage of people who accepted the job in the previous year. Teach for America recruits college graduates and professionals to teach for two years in public schools. Coffman et al. (2017) found that adding the line "Last year more than 84% of admitted applicants made the decision to join the corps, and I sincerely hope you join them" in the admissions letter significantly increased the likelihood of accepting the offer, starting to teach and returning to teach in the following year.

Overall, social comparison nudges in education have provided mixed and heterogeneous results with some studies reporting overall positive effects and others reporting no or even negative effects on student outcomes. Interventions providing relative performance information (in private or in public) may backfire because high-achieving students who perform better than the norm (who tend to have higher SES) reduce effort to adhere to the norm or because low-achieving students are demotivated by a high norm (e.g. Bursztyn & Jensen, 2015). It seems important that social comparison information is provided with enough time for students to adjust their effort level (Fischer & Wagner, 2017). Otherwise the information may also be demotivating. There is also some evidence that males respond more to social comparisons (e.g. Jalava, Joensen, & Pellas, 2015). In comparison, Coffman et al. (2017) studies an intervention that provides information about norms without providing *performance* feedback and find positive effects. This suggest that such nudges may be more effective, perhaps because they avoid some of the pitfalls that can make social comparison nudges backfire. Without the performance feedback, social comparison nudges in fact resemble social belonging nudges discussed below.

Social belonging, identity activation and mindset nudges

Student performance may also be inhibited by the students' underconfidence in their own ability or more broadly by biased or suboptimal self-

images. Interventions targeting students' mindsets and beliefs may thus potentially improve self-confidence, benefit students' self-image and ultimately improve student outcomes. A number of (brief psychological) interventions fall in this category.

Wilson and Linville (1982) is an example of an early small-scale intervention improving study outcome by influencing feelings of *social belonging*, where first-year students at a US university were informed that grades typically improve from the first year to later years. Similar favourable effects were obtained in large-scale studies by Yeager et al. (2016) and Kizilcec, Saltarelli, Reich, and Cohen (2017) in various contexts. In contrast, Broda et al. (2018) found no effects on any student outcomes. The authors argue that the lack of effects may be due to suboptimal adjustment of the treatment to the specific context.

Another set of interventions have tried to influence behavior through *identity activation* nudges. Lin-Siegler, Ahn, Chen, Fang, and Luna-Lucero (2016) provided ninth and 10th grade students in the US with information about the struggles of famous scientists, whereas Gehlbach et al. (2016) provided teachers and students with information about similarities in their values and interests. Both found favourable effects that match well with the results of non-experimental studies showing that minority students perform better when taught by teachers or instructors with similar ethnicity or race (e.g. Fairlie, Hoffmann, & Oreopoulos, 2014).

Students with a so-called *growth mindset* believe that intelligence can be developed. They understand that they become smarter with effort, and this way of thinking about intelligence as malleable is thought to be motivational, see Dweck (1986). Early small-scale interventions showed positive effects on academic behavior of such beliefs (e.g. Aronson, Fried, & Good, 2002; Blackwell, Trzesniewski, & Dweck, 2007). However, a recent meta-analysis indicates that interventions promoting growth mindsets are mainly effective in low performers and students from low SES families (Sisk, Burgoyne, Sun, Butler, & Macnamara, 2018). In addition, Bettinger, Ludvigsen, Rege, and Scolli (2018) and Andersen and Nielsen (2016) showed that positive effects mainly arose for students and parents who originally had a fixed mindset i.e. who viewed ability as fixed. In line with this, other studies suggest that effects prevail in specific subgroups with supposedly more fixed mindsets (Broda et al. 2018; Yeager et al. 2016). We interpret the literature as suggesting that positive effects of mindset interventions require a certain margin for behavioral change.

Overall, a long range of social belonging, identity activation and mindset interventions have almost all produced positive effects on student outcomes. However, in many cases there are only positive results for disadvantaged or minority students or other groups with some reasonable margin for behavioral change. A few studies result in non-positive effects and point to important learnings. First, the results of Broda et al. (2018) highlight a possible obstacle to scaling social-belonging interventions, namely the need to adjust the intervention to the local context using relevant quotes from local students. Second, the interventions by Bird et al. (2017) suggest that some priming interventions may be too small to produce effects. Finally, given the largely positive results, it would be natural to think that the interventions would be more effective in combination than separately. Existing evidence suggests that this is not true (e.g. Yeager et al. 2016).

Conclusion

In recent years, behavioral economics and nudging policies have rapidly made their way from research into policy design across a wide range of areas. Education policy is no exception. The characteristics of education decisions imply that education performance is potentially susceptible to suboptimal decision-making due to behavioral barriers such as self-control problems,

attentional and cognitive limitation, loss aversion, default bias, social preferences, or biased beliefs. Empirical tests of nudging interventions suggest that some nudging interventions can improve student outcomes and this lends support to the existence of behavioral barriers in educational decision-making. For example, nudging interventions providing decision-makers with information, assistance or skills often have positive effects suggesting that parents and students typically are motivated to improve decisions but may lack the capacity to do so.

However, not all nudging interventions have positive effects. Interventions that rely on passive decision making have the potential to provide broad and long-term effects on behavior, but if individuals can take actions to avoid the nudge as seen for peer group manipulations or if interventions are not substantial enough or do not allow enough time for people to adjust behavior, then they may be ineffective. Furthermore, social-comparison nudges may have no or negative overall effects with negative effects most likely arising for the best performers and positive effects arising for the worst performers. Other nudges such as reminders, deadlines and goal-setting have also shown heterogeneous effects and effects appear to depend on student motivation and exact implementation. In general, the empirical evidence suggests that beneficial effects are most likely for specific groups constrained by the behavior targeted by the nudge. This observation along with recent empirical evidence from other policy areas which suggests that it may be costly to be nudged (e.g. Allcott & Kessler, 2019) points to a need for well targeted rather than universal nudges.

References

Akerlof, A. G., & Kranton, R. E. (2002). Identity and schooling: Some lessons for the economics of education. *Journal of Economic Literature, 40*, 1167−1201.

Alan, S., Boneva, T., & Seda, E. (2016). *Ever failed, try again, succeed better: Results from a randomized educational intervention on grit* (Working Paper).

Allcott, H., & Kessler, J. (2019). The welfare effects of nudges: A case study of energy use social comparisons. *American Economic Journal: Applied Economics, 11*(1), 236–276.

Andersen, S. C., & Nielsen, H. S. (2016). Reading intervention with a growth mindset approach improves children's skills. *Proceedings of the National Academy of Sciences of the United States of America, 113*(43), 12111–12113.

Ariely, D., & Wertenbroch, K. (2002). Procrastination, deadlines, and performance: Self-control by precommitment. *Psychological Science, 13*(3), 219–224.

Aronson, J., Fried, C. B., & Good, C. (2002). Reducing stereotype threat and boosting academic achievement of African-American students: The role of conceptions of intelligence. *Journal of Experimental Social Psychology, 38*, 113–125.

Bandiera, O., Larcinese, V., & Rasul, I. (2015). Blissful ignorance? A natural experiment on the effect of feedback on students' performance. *Labour Economics, 34*, 13–25.

Benabou, R., & Tirole, J. (2002). Self-confidence and personal motivation. *Quarterly Journal of Economics, 117*(3), 871–915.

Bergman, P. (2019). Parent–child information frictions and human capital investment: Evidence from a field experiment. *Journal of Political Economy* (in press).

Bergman, P., & Rogers, T. (2017). *The impact of defaults on technology adoption, and its underappreciation by policymakers.* HKS Faculty Research Paper Working Paper Series RWP17-021.

Berlinski, S., Busso, M., Dinkelman, T., & Martinez, C. (2017). *Reducing parent-school information gaps and improving education outcomes: Evidence from high frequency text messaging in Chile* (Working Paper).

Bettinger, E. P., Long, B. T., Oreopoulos, P., & Sanbonmatsu, L. (2012). The role of application assistance and information in college decision: Results from the H&R block FAFSA experiment. *Quarterly Journal of Economics, 127*, 1205–1242.

Bettinger, E., Ludvigsen, S., Rege, M., & Scolli, I. F. (2018). Increasing perseverance in math: Evidence from a field experiment in Norway. *Journal of Economic Behavior & Organization, 146*, 1–15.

Bird, K. A., Castleman, B. L., Goodman, J., & Lamberton, C. (2017). *Nudging at a national scale: Experimental evidence from a FAFSA completion campaign.* EdPolicyWorks Working Paper Series No. 54.

Blackwell, L. S., Trzesniewski, K. H., & Dweck, C. S. (2007). Implicit theories of intelligence predict student achievement across adolescent transition: A longitudinal study and an intervention. *Child Development, 78*(1), 246–263.

Broda, M., Yun, J., Schneider, B., Yeager, D. S., Walton, G. M., & Diemer, M. (2018). Reducing inequality in academic success for incoming college students: A randomized trial of growth mindset and belonging interventions. 2018.

Journal of Research of Educational Effectiveness, 11(3), 317–338.

Burger, N., Charness, G., & Lynham, J. (2011). Field and online experiments on self-control. *Journal of Economic Behavior & Organization, 77*(3), 393–404.

Bursztyn, L., & Coffman, L. C. (2012). The schooling decision: Family preferences, intergenerational conflict, and moral hazard in the Brazilian Favelas. *Journal of Political Economy, 120*(3), 359–397.

Bursztyn, L., & Jensen, R. (2015). How does peer pressure affect educational investments? *Quarterly Journal of Economics, 130*(3), 1329–1367.

Carrell, S. E., Fullerton, R. L., & West, J. E. (2009). Does your cohort matter? Measuring peer effects in college achievement. *Journal of Labor Economics, 27*(3), 439–464.

Carrell, S., & Sacerdote, B. (2017). Why do college going interventions work? *American Economic Journal: Applied Economics, 9*(3), 124–151.

Carrell, S. E., Sacerdote, B. I., & West, J. E. (2013). From natural variation to optimal policy? The importance of endogenous peer group formation. *Econometrica, 81*(3), 855–882.

Castleman, B. L., & Page, L. C. (2015). Summer nudging: Can personalized text messages and peer mentor outreach increase college going among low-income high school graduates? *Journal of Economic Behavior & Organization, 115*, 144–160.

Castleman, B. L., & Page, L. C. (2017). Parental influences on postsecondary decision making: Evidence from a text messaging experiment. *Educational Evaluation and Policy Analysis, 39*(2), 361–377.

Clark, D., Gill, D., Prowse, V., & Rush, M. (2017). *Using goals to motivate college students: Theory and evidence from field experiments.* NBER Working Paper No. 23638.

Coffman, L. C., Featherstone, C. R., & Kessler, J. B. (2017). Can social information affect what job you choose and keep? *American Economic Journal: Applied Economics, 9*(1), 96–117.

De Paola, M., & Scoppa, V. (2011). Frequency of examinations and student achievement in a randomized experiment. *Economics of Education Review, 30*, 1416–1429.

De Paola, M., & Scoppa, V. (2015). Procrastination, academic success and the effectiveness of a remedial program. *Journal of Economic Behavior & Organization, 115*, 217–236.

DellaVigna, S. (2009). Psychology and economics: Evidence from the field. *Journal of Economic Literature, 47*(2), 315–372.

Dinkelman, T., & Martinez, C. A. (2014). Investing in schooling in Chile: The role of information about financial aid for higher education. *The Review of Economics and Statistics, 96*(2), 244–257.

Dobronyi, C. R., Oreopoulos, P., & Petronijevic, U. (2019). Goal setting, academic reminders, and college success:

A large-scale field experiment. *Journal of Research on Educational Effectiveness, 12*(1), 38–66.

Dweck, C. S. (1986). Motivational processes affecting learning. *American Psychologist, 41*, 1040–1048.

Fairlie, R. W., Hoffmann, F., & Oreopoulos, P. (2014). A community college instructor like me: Race and ethnicity interactions in the classroom. *The American Economic Review, 104*(8), 2567–2591.

Field, E. (2009). Educational debt burden and career choice: Evidence from a financial aid experiment at NYU law school. *American Economic Journal: Applied Economics, 1*(1), 1–21.

Fischer, M., & Wagner, V. (2017). *Effects of timing and reference frame of feedback: Evidence from a field experiment in secondary schools* (Working Paper).

Fryer, R. G. (2016). Information, non-financial incentives, and student achievement: Evidence from a text messaging experiment. *Journal of Public Economics, 144*, 109–121.

Gehlbach, H., et al. (2016). Creating birds of similar feathers: Leveraging similarity to improve teacher–student relationships and academic achievement. *Journal of Educational Psychology, 108*(3), 342–352.

Harackiewicz, J. M., Rozek, C. S., Hulleman, C. S., & Hyde, J. S. (2012). Helping parents to motivate adolescents in mathematics and science: An experimental test of a utility-value intervention. *Psychological Science, 23*(8), 899–906.

Hastings, J., Neilson, C. A., & Zimmerman, S. D. (2015). *The effects of earnings disclosure on college enrolment decisions.* NBER Working Paper No. 21300.

Hastings, J. S., & Weinstein, J. M. (2008). Information, school choice, and academic achievement: Evidence from two experiments. *Quarterly Journal of Economics, 123*, 1373–1414.

Jabbar, H. (2011). The behavioral economics of education: New directions for research. *Educational Researcher, 40*(9), 446–453.

Jalava, N., Joensen, J. S., & Pellas, E. (2015). Grades and rank: Impacts of non-financial incentives on test-performance. *Journal of Economic Behavior & Organization, 115*, 151–196.

Jensen, R. (2010). The (perceived) returns to education and the demand for schooling. *Quarterly Journal of Economics, 125*(2), 515–548.

Kahneman, D., Knetsch, J. L., & Thaler, R. H. (1991). Anomalies: The endowment effect, loss aversion, and status quo bias. *The Journal of Economic Perspectives, 5*(1), 193–206.

Kahneman, D., & Tversky, A. (1979). Prospect theory: An analysis of decision under risk. *Econometrica, 47*(2), 263–291.

Karlan, D., McConnell, M., Mullainathan, S., & Zinman, J. (2016). Getting to the top of mind: How reminders increase saving. *Management Science, 62*(12), 3393–3411.

Kizilcec, R. F., Saltarelli, A.,J., Reich, J., & Cohen, G. L. (2017). Closing global achievement gaps in MOOCs brief interventions address social identity threat at scale. *Science, 355*(6322), 251–252.

Kizilcec, R. F., Schneider, E., Cohen, G. L., & McFarland, D. A. (2014). Encouraging forum participation in online courses with collectivist, individualist and neutral motivational framings. *eLearning Papers, 37*, 13–22.

Koch, A., & Nafziger, J. (2011). Self-regulation through goal setting. *The Scandinavian Journal of Economics, 113*(1), 305–351.

Koch, A., Nafziger, J., & Nielsen, H. S. (2015). Behavioral economics of education. *Journal of Economic Behavior & Organization, 115*, 3–17.

Kraft, M. A., & Monti-Nussbaum, M. (2017). Can schools enable parents to prevent summer learning loss? A text messaging field experiment to promote literacy skills. *The Annals of the American Academy of Political and Social Science, 674*(1), 85–112.

Laibson, D. (1997). Golden eggs and hyperbolic discounting. *Quarterly Journal of Economics, 112*(2), 443–477.

Lavecchia, A. M., Lui, H., & Oreopoulos, P. (2016). Behavioral economics of education: Progress and possibilities. In E. A. Hanushek, S. Machin, & L. Woessmann (Eds.), *Handbook of the economics of education* (Vol. 5, pp. 1–74). Elsevier.

Lent, M. van, & Souverijn, M. (2018). *Goal setting and raising the bar: A field experiment.* Working paper Tinbergen Institute.

Levitt, S. D., List, J. A., Neckermann, S., & Sadoff, S. (2016). The behaviouralist goes to school: Leveraging behavioral economics to improve economic performance. *American Economic Journal: Applied Economics, 8*(4), 183–219.

Levy, Y., & Ramim, M. M. (2013). An experimental study of habit and time incentive in online-exam procrastination. In Y. Eshet-Alkalai, et al. (Eds.), *Proceedings of the Chais conference on instructional technologies research 2013: Learning in a technology era* (pp. 53–61). Raanana: the Open University of Israel.

Lin-Siegler, X., Ahn, J. N., Chen, J., Fang, F. A., & Luna-Lucero, M. (2016). Even Einstein struggled: Effects of learning about great scientists struggles on high school students' motivation to learn science. *Journal of Educational Psychology, 108*(3), 314–328.

Marx, B., & Turner, L. J. (2019). Student loan nudges: Experimental evidence on borrowing and educational attainment. *American Economic Journal: Economic Policy, 11*(2), 108–141.

Mayer, S. E., Kalil, A., Oreopoulos, P., & Gallegos, S. (2019). Using behavioral insights to increase parental engagement: The parents and children together (PACT) intervention. *Journal of Human Resources.* https://doi.org/10.3368/jhr.54.4.0617.8835R (in press).

McEvoy, D. M. (2016). Loss aversion and student achievement. *Economics Bulletin, 36*(3), 1762–1770.

Morisano, D., Hirsh, J. B., Peterson, J. B., Pihl, R. O., & Shore, B. M. (2010). Setting, elaborating, and reflecting on personal goals improves academic performance. *Journal of Applied Psychology, 93*(2), 255–264.

Oreopoulos, P., & Dunn, R. (2013). Information and college access: Evidence from a randomized field experiment. *The Scandinavian Journal of Economics, 115*(1), 3–26.

Oreopoulos, P., & Ford, R. (2016). *Keeping college options open: A field experiment to help all high school seniors through the college application process.* NBER Working Paper No. 22320.

Oreopoulos, P., & Petronijevic, U. (2018). Student coaching: How far can technology go? *Journal of Human Resources, 53*(2), 299–329.

Papay, J. P., Taylor, E. S., Tyler, J. H., & Laski, M. (2016). *Learning job skills from colleagues at work: Evidence from a field experiment using teacher performance data.* NBER Working Paper No. 21986.

Peter, F. H., & Zambre, V. (2017). Intended college enrollment and educational inequality: Do students lack information? *Economics of Education Review, 60*, 125–141.

Pistolesi, N. (2017). The effect of advising students at college entrance: Evidence from a French university reform. *Labour Economics, 44*, 106–121.

Rogers, T., & Feller, A. (2016). Discouraged by peer excellence: Exposure to exemplary peer performance causes quitting. *Psychological Science, 27*(3), 365–374.

Rogers, T., & Feller, A. (2018). Reducing student absences at scale by targeting parents' misbeliefs. *Nature Human Behaviour, 2*, 335–342.

Sisk, V. F., Burgoyne, A. P., Sun, J., Butler, J. L., & Macnamara, B. N. (2018). To what extent and under which circumstances are growth mind-sets important to academic achievement? Two meta-analyses. *Psychological Science, 29*(4), 549–571.

Thaler, R. H., & Sunstein, C. R. (2008). *Nudge improving decisions about health, wealth and happiness.* Yale University Press.

Tuckman, B. (1998). Using tests as an incentive to motivate procrastinators to study. *The Journal of Experimental Education, 66*, 141–147.

Wagner, V. (2017). *Seeking risk or answering smart? Heterogeneous effects of grading manipulations in elementary schools* (Working Paper).

Wilson, T. D., & Linville, P. W. (1982). Improving the academic performance of college freshmen: Attribution therapy revisited. *Journal of Personality and Social Psychology, 42*(2), 367–376.

Yeager, D. S., Walton, G. M., Brady, S. T., Akcinar, E. N., Paunesku, D., Keane, L., et al. (2016). Teaching a lay theory before college narrows achievement gaps at scale. *Proceedings of the National Academy of Sciences, 113*(24), E3341–E3348.

Further reading

Alan, S., & Ertac, S. (2018). Fostering patience in the classroom: Results from a randomized educational intervention. *Journal of Political Economy, 126*(5), 1865–1911.

Austen-Smith, D., & Fryer, R. G. (2005). An economic analysis of 'acting white'. *Quarterly Journal of Economics, 120*(2), 551–583.

Benabou, R., & Tirole, J. (2006). Incentives and prosocial behavior. *The American Economic Review, 96*(5), 1652–1678.

Benhassine, N., Devoto, F., Duflo, E., Dupas, P., & Pouliquen, V. (2015). Turning a shove into a nudge? A 'labelled cash transfer' for education. *American Economic Journal: Economic Policy, 7*(3), 86–125.

Cadena, B. C., & Keys, B. J. (2015). Human capital and lifetime costs of impatience. *American Economic Journal: Economic Policy, 7*(3), 126–156.

Damgaard, M. T., & Nielsen, H. S. (2018). Nudging in education. *Economics of Education Review, 64*, 313–342.

Madrian, B. C., & Shea, D. F. (2001). The power of suggestion: Inertia in 401(k) participation and savings behavior. *Quarterly Journal of Economics, 116*(4), 1149–1187.

Mischel, W., Shoda, Y., & Rodriguez, M. (1989). Delay of gratification in children. *Science, 244*(4907), 281–302.

Walton, G. M., & Cohen, G. L. (2011). A brief social-belonging intervention improves academic and health outcomes of minority students. *Science, 331*, 1447–4151.

PART II

Private and social returns to education

Returns to education in developed countries

Morley Gunderson[a,b], Philip Oreopolous[c,d]

[a]Professor at the Centre for Industrial Relations, Human Resources, The Department of Economics, The School of Public Policy and Governance, Toronto, ON, Canada; [b]Research Associate of the Centre for International Studies, The Institute for Human Development, Life Course and Ageing, All at the University of Toronto; [c]Professor in the Department of Economics, The School of Public Policy, Governance at the University of Toronto, Toronto, ON, Canada; [d]Research Associate with the National Bureau of Economic Research

Glossary of terms

Ability bias the bias to the returns to schooling that can result from the fact that people who acquire more education may have greater innate skills that would allow them to earn more even without additional schooling

Causal returns the returns to education that are induced or caused by additional education rather than simply correlated or associated with additional education

Endogenity of education the fact that education is a decision variable in that the amount of education acquired may be a function of such factors as ability, motivation, family background, income, proximity to school and compulsory school laws

Instrumental Variables in the context of education decision making, instrumental variables are variables that affect the amount of education acquired but that do not affect the education outcomes or the returns to education (examples include compulsory school laws or proximity to schools)

Measurement error the possibility that collected data like education may be measured with error since people may not accurately report their education

Regression discontinuity a procedure that approximates random assignment by comparing individuals just above and just below a threshold score with the difference being considered as the random luck of the draw

Returns to education the financial rate of return to investing in an additional year of schooling, obtained by comparing the additional earnings from an additional year of education with the cost of acquiring the additional education; shows how average earnings increase with added education

Selection bias in the context of returns to education, it is the bias that can be created by the fact that education may be a function of conventionally unobserved factors such as ability or motivation

Sheepskin effect the credential effect or additional return associated with the credential of completing key phases of education like graduating from high school or university (sheepskin was used historically to make the parchment for diplomas)

Social returns the returns or externalities that occur to third-parties over-and-above those that accrue to individuals who make the education decisions

Introduction

Understanding the causal relationship between education and the financial returns to such education is important for addressing a

The Economics of Education, Second Edition
https://doi.org/10.1016/B978-0-12-815391-8.00003-3

range of questions of practical and policy importance. What are the private returns that individuals can expect from investing in education? How do those returns vary by such factors as level of education, field of study and individual background characteristics? How have those returns varied over time and across different countries? Is there an extra effect from a year of education if that year provides the credential of completing a phase of study such as graduating from high school or university? If potential dropouts are compelled to stay in school longer by compulsory school laws do they receive returns that are higher or lower than the average returns? Are the returns higher or lower for marginal students, many of whom come from disadvantaged backgrounds? If so, what are the constraints that inhibit them from taking advantage of such higher returns? Are the returns the result of education enhancing the productivity and skills of individuals or are they the result of signaling of such conventionally unobserved factors such as ability, motivation and time management skills? Are there social returns or externalities that accrue to third-parties over-and-above the private returns that accrue to individuals making the education decision? What are the appropriate methodologies for estimating the returns to education, especially for dealing with such factors as measurement error, ability bias, credential effects and financial constraints?

The purpose of the article is to address these practical and methodological questions. The emphasis here is on the causal returns to education after controlling for other observable and unobservable factors like innate ability or motivation that may affect the outcomes associated with higher education. Understanding the

underlying causal relationship process is important for policy purposes so as to ascertain the effect of policy interventions, for example: to reallocate resources from fields of low returns to fields of high returns; to raise the age of compulsory schooling; to institute policies to deter dropping; or to provide information including in the application for financial aid. It can also be important for predicting future changes as the underlying causal factors change.

The article moves from the simple to the more complex. It starts with estimates of the return to education based on basic schooling equations where education is not exogenous but can be correlated with other factors that can affect outcomes. It then moves to a discussion of refinements to the basic model: the appropriate measure of earnings and the inclusion of non-wage benefits; measurement error in the schooling variable; and corrections for ability bias, omitted variables and selection bias; the possibility of heterogeneous returns, and credential or sheepskin effects.

Estimating returns to education via schooling equations

A wide range of methodological issues are associated with estimating the economic returns to education.[1] In this section, the main methodological issues are outlined in a non-technical fashion, generally referencing more technical treatments of the issues.

Basic schooling equation

Estimates of the private returns to education essentially build on the human capital earnings

---

[1] Reviews of many of these issues include Card (1999, 2001), Chamberlain (1977), Chamberlain and Griliches (1975), Griliches (1979) and Lemieux (2002). Heckman, Lochner and Todd (2006) provide a critical review of much of the literature, emphasizing the heterogeneous returns to education and the importance of psychic costs in explaining such heterogeneous returns. The procedure followed in our review is to cite articles that illustrate the issues and that contain references to related articles.

function of Mincer (1974) where the (natural) log of earnings is regressed on years of education and other control variables including years of labor market experience. The latter is often entered in a quadratic form to capture the non-linear relationship whereby earnings tend to advance rapidly for early years in the labor market, flatten in later years and decline slightly thereafter. Higher-order polynomial functions for experience have also been recommended so as to better capture the more rapid earnings growth early in an individual's career and the slower decline in wages later in an individual's career, albeit Heckman, Lochner and Todd (2006, p. 333) indicate that such higher order polynomials did not improve their estimates.

The estimated coefficient on the education variable in a log earnings equation has the convenient interpretation as the average percent increase in earnings from an additional year of schooling (e.g., a number like 0.10 or 10% which can be compared to the returns to other investments). For interpretation, Mincer and other social scientists often assume that tuition and psychological costs from schooling are negligible, that individuals do not work much while in school, and that schooling and years of experience have separate effects on earnings. Under these assumptions, the coefficient from the Mincer equation can be interpreted as the return to investing in the cost of an additional year of education and compared to alternative investments. In this case, the monetary benefits of an additional year of schooling are the additional earnings from such schooling, while the costs are the forgone income. Since both the benefits and the (opportunity) costs are in this way factored into the estimates of the earnings equation, the coefficient on the education variable

yields an internal rate of return to investments in education.[2] Since data sets often have different categories of highest level of education achieved, these are often entered in place of years of schooling so that the returns can vary by different categories of completed education.

Estimates from a basic Mincer schooling equation tends to yield estimates around 0.07 to 0.10, being slightly higher for females and lower for males. The returns are slightly higher for general academic streams compared to technical vocational streams, and they are higher in the more professional fields like engineering, medicine, business and sciences and lower in social sciences and humanities and especially in fields like fine arts, and they are increasing over time. These can be thought of as the simple benchmark returns to education against which to gauge the effect of the myriad of procedures (discussed subsequently) to improve on those estimates and to consider how returns differ across particular groups of individuals.

Hourly wages versus measures that include hours of work

The appropriate measure of earnings is one that approximates the hourly wage so as to reflect the productivity effects of education and to control for differences in hours worked given that higher educated persons tend to work longer hours. To the extent, however, that higher education leads individuals to work more hours, the additional time is an endogenous part of the returns to education. Measuring increased earnings per hour may therefore underestimate the true returns to education over a fixed period of work. Card (1999, p. 1809), for example,

---

[2] See Heckman, Lochner and Todd (2006) for a more detailed discussion on estimating internal rates of return from schooling and alternative approaches to assessing returns from education when the mentioned assumptions do not hold.

estimates that slightly more than two-thirds of the returns to education based on annual earnings in the US in the mid-1990s reflects higher wages while one-third reflects longer hours. More specifically, he estimated returns to education of about 10% for males and 11% for females based on hourly wages, and 14.2% for males and 16.5% for females based on annual earnings. The fact that the change was higher for females than for males highlights the fact that higher education is also associated with longer hours of work (both hours per week and weeks per year in his data) and that the effect on longer hours was greater for females than for males.

Measurement error in schooling

Returns to schooling are typically estimated from survey data where individuals report their highest level of schooling. This reported schooling can be subject to measurement error or misreporting of education. Estimates indicate that about 10% of individuals misreport their level of education, and this is true in administrative data as well as survey data.[3] If the misreporting is random or unrelated to the level of education, then such classical measurement error leads to a downward bias in the estimated returns to education. However, if the measurement error is systematically related to the level of education, then the bias can go in either direction. Persons with low levels of education may be prone to overstate their actual education and persons with higher education may be more accurate in their reporting, yielding an upward bias to the returns to education. But there is also the possibility of higher educated people having more opportunities to inflate their education given the multiplicity of different types of degree granting institutions. In essence, the biases from measurement error in schooling can go in either direction. Overall, based on his

assessment of the literature, Card (1999, p. 1834) concludes that measurement error in education leads to a downward bias in returns to education, with the estimated returns understating the true returns by about 10%. That is, if the estimated returns were 0.10, the true returns would be 0.11.

Ability bias, omitted variables and selection bias

The potentially most severe bias that can occur in estimating the causal returns to education occurs because educated people can have other characteristics that are associated with higher earnings and those other characteristics are not controlled for in the conventional estimating procedures. Indeed, models that attempt to explain differences in school attainment often do so by noting that costs and benefits from additional schooling are not the same for everyone. Individuals may differ by innate ability, motivation, organizational skills, entrepreneurship, time management skills and willingness to work hard. To the extent that these factors lead to higher earnings as well as higher education, and they are not accounted for in the statistical analysis, then omitting them from the estimating equation means that some of the higher returns to education may be reflecting the effect of these factors. That is, the estimated returns to education are biased because the higher education is capturing the economic returns to these omitted variables as well as the pure causal effect of education. Alternatively stated, higher educated people may be a select group in terms of not only observable characteristics that can be controlled for in the regression analysis, but also unobserved traits as indicated above that are not conventionally controlled for in the analysis. The returns to

---

[3] Misreporting is discussed, for example, in Ashenfelter and Rouse (1998) and Card (1999).

education can reflect a return to these traits as well as to education itself.

The literature on estimating the causal returns to education has been a growth industry in recent years based largely on devising ways to control for this ability or selection bias, often involving imaginative ways of obtaining exogenous variation in education that is independent of ability or selection bias. The following illustrate such procedures.

Include proxy measures of ability

A number of empirical studies have been able to include proxy measures of ability such as IQ scores or test scores designed to measure innate ability.[4] Such studies tend to find the ability bias to be small in that the estimated return to education drops only by about 10% (e.g., from 0.10 to 0.09) after controlling for the effect of ability.

Family characteristics such as the education of a parent or sibling are also sometimes included to control for factors that may help a person obtain more education and affect their earnings. Such studies[5] also generally find the return to education to drop very slightly (by around 0.01) after controlling for such family characteristics. Studies that have also examined how the return to education varies by the ability of the individual or their family background have yielded inconclusive results (Ashenfelter & Rouse, 1998 and the literature cited therein).

Twin studies

Another way to control for ability bias and perhaps some of the other potentially important omitted variables is to use twins since they presumably have the same natural ability (especially if they are identical twins from the same egg as opposed to fraternal twins from two different eggs). Differences in their education are assumed to occur for random reasons (a possibly questionable assumption) and in this way this procedure approaches the ideal random assignment procedure for estimating treatment effects (in this case the treatment being more education). Using same-sex twins also controls for the possibility that parents may favor one sex or the other in devoting family resources to them to improve their labor market outcomes.

Studies that utilize differences in education between twins[6] to identify education differences while controlling for ability and other differences generally lowers the return to education slightly (suggesting a slight upward ability bias) but this tends to be offset by the measurement error bias from mis-measuring education so that on net the true returns are about the same as those estimated in the conventional regression of earnings on education without controlling for ability bias or measurement error. Estimates of returns to schooling using US twins generally range between 0.06 and 0.12.

Natural experiments based mainly on features of the education system

A number of empirical studies have used institutional features of the education system or the environment to generate differences in education that arise for reasons beyond an individual's control and hence are considered as exogenous. A policy change that lowers the cost of college in one state, for example, affects some individuals but not others depending on when and where they are born. Using exogenous forces to estimate returns to schooling helps

---

[4] Studies that deal with test scores as a measure of ability are referenced in Card (1999, 2001) and Griliches (1977).

[5] Family background controls are used in Ashenfelter and Rouse (1998), Ashenfelter and Zimmerman (1997) and Card (1995).

[6] Earlier twin studies are reviewed in Griliches (1977, 1979) with more recent twin studies reviewed in Ashenfelter and Rouse (1998) and Miller, Mulvey, and Martin (2006).

address ability bias because differences in education that arise from exogenous forces are unlikely due to differences in individual ability. Returns to schooling estimates from this approach apply only to individuals affected by the exogenous force (e.g., policy change).[7]

- Geographic proximity to educational institutions can generate exogenous variation in education in that those close to a university are more likely to attend university and hence acquire more education than those who are far away from a university (e.g., Cameron & Taber, 2004; Card, 1995).
- Differences across regions or over time in financial costs to attending school (e.g. through tuition) can also lead to differences in education attainment (e.g. Chen, 2007; Kane & Rouse, 1995)
- The Vietnam draft lottery generated exogenous increases in schooling because many persons enrolled in school in order to defer military service (Angrist & Krueger, 1994).
- Local labor market earnings for persons at age 17 have been used to generate exogenous variation in education in that higher earnings may increase the opportunity cost of education and thereby induce dropping out (Cameron & Taber, 2004).
- The GI Bill in Canada gave rise to exogenous variation in education in that the cohort of males from English-speaking Ontario received additional education due to the GI bill and not to the decision, say, of higher ability people to acquire more education. The earnings of this treatment group were compared to the earnings of a control group from French-speaking Quebec who were less likely to have

served or to have taken advantage of the bill (e.g., Lemieux & Card, 2001).

- Compulsory school laws can compel some individuals to acquire more education because they cannot drop out until the compulsory age (e.g., Angrist & Krueger, 1991; Acemoglu & Angrist, 1991; Oreopoulos, 2006a, 2006b; but see Stevens & Yang, 2014 for a critique).
- Exogenous variation in education have also been obtained from situations where an additional year of schooling has been added or subtracted to the high school or university curriculum (e.g.,Krashinsky, 2014; Webbink, 2007).

Studies using the natural experiments from features of the education system or environment to obtain exogenous variation in education tend to find such causal returns to education to be in the neighborhood of 0.06–0.16 which are generally higher than the returns when conventional years of schooling are used. Heckman, Lochner and Todd (2006, p. 392) critique these studies and highlight that their effects are often imprecisely estimated. However, their own estimates are actually somewhat higher.

These high returns to education raise the issue of why more individuals do not acquire more education to take advantage of the high returns. Heckman, Lochner and Todd (2006) suggest that high psychic costs may inhibit those who find extreme disutility from the education process. Lack of information, credit constraints, risk aversion, debt aversion, poor peers, and financial constraints may also play a role.[8] These models suggest rational or economic barrier explanations for low attainment. On the other hand, behavior barriers, such as present-bias,

---

[7] Ashenfelter, Harmon and Oosterbeck (1999), Ashenfelter and Rouse (1998), Card (1999, 2001) and Carnoy (1997) review such studies. They are critically assessed in Heckman, Lochner and Todd (2006).

[8] Studies that emphasize many of these constraints include Hoxby and Turner (2015), Jensen (2010), Johnson (2013) and Scott-Clayton (2013).

negative mindsets, ambiguity, and lack of salience around productive actions may also play a role and imply sub-optimal long-term outcomes. (Lavecchia, Liu & Oreopoulos, 2016 for a review of that literature).

Regression discontinuity methods

Regression discontinuity (RD) procedures have more recently been used to estimate causal returns to education. The procedure generally involves comparing those who were just above a cut-off score for being accepted into university compared to a control group just below the cut-off and who did not get accepted. Such individuals just below and just above the cut-off are so close to each other in terms of getting the education treatment that receiving the treatment can be considered random luck of the draw and therefore approximating random assignment. Hoekstra (2009) uses such a procedure and finds that students in Florida who barely got into the top flagship university in that province earned 20% more than those who barely missed getting in, but who went to alternative pathways, mainly other universities in the state. Using an RD approach, Zimmerman (2014) finds similar large effects for marginal students who just got into the Florida state school system compared to those who did not get in. Canaan and Mouganie (2018) use an RD design to compare students who marginally pass and marginally fail the French high-school exit exams. They find that those who barely pass, enroll in higher quality institutions and STEM fields of study so that their earnings are increased by 12.5% relative to those who barely fail. Ost, Pan and Webber (2018) compare marginal students in the Ohio university system whose GPA is barely above the cut-off for being able to stay at their university with those whose GPA is barely below and who are dismissed. They find a return of 4.1% for being able to remain in university. Kirkeboen, Leuven and Mogstad (2016) use the discontinuities created by centralized admission cut-offs into different universities and fields of study in Norwegian universities to document large variation in the returns by field of study.

Heterogeneous returns

It is important to view returns to schooling as being individual and context specific, varying across different individuals (Carneiro, Heckman & Vytlacil, 2011). Gains from schooling depend upon the individual's background, motivation, and the quality and type of schooling. An individual's decision to take more schooling depends on both expected gains and costs. Estimates of returns to schooling using exogenous policy variation can often be interpreted as average returns to schooling among individuals affected by the policy variation. Sometimes the policy variation identifies particularly interesting parameters, like the average gains to schooling among those forced to stay on in school because of more restrictive compulsory schooling laws, or the average gains to schooling among those who entered college because tuition costs were lowered. As discussed in Card (1999, 2001), many of the natural experiments used to estimate returns to education identify average returns for more disadvantaged groups. The fact that increases in the education of such persons tend to generate higher than average returns suggests that increasing the education of such marginalized groups can have both desirable efficiency effects (high returns) as well as distributional effects (high returns to otherwise more disadvantaged groups). That is, they were not able to invest in the education to get the higher than average returns not because they lacked the ability, but rather they faced other constraint such as a lack if information or an inability to deal with the complexities of the application for financial aid. This suggests the viability of increasing the education of such groups through policy initiatives such as increases in the compulsory school age, funding assistance, expansion of accessibility (for example by facilitating transfers colleges to universities), campaigns against dropping out, and providing better information and perhaps assistance in the complex financial aid application procedure.

A number of recent studies have highlighted how small and low-cost interventions or "nudges" can improve the access of more disadvantaged students who otherwise do not take advantage of the high returns. Bettinger, Bridget, Oreopoulos and (2012), for example, provide evidence from a randomized experiment that small amounts of information and assistance in dealing with the complicated applications for financial aid in the US have large positive effects in their applying for and obtaining higher education. Jensen (2010) and Dunn and Oreopoulos (2013) provide evidence that a small amount of information on the returns to education can substantially foster perceptions of the benefits of education on the part of disadvantaged students who otherwise may be misinformed about the high returns.

A number of researchers have tried to model an individual's schooling decision by assuming more structure to the decision-making process (e.g., schooling only affects wealth, people have rational expectations, and discount the future geometrically). The models are simplified enough to allow estimation of a few unknown parameters, like an individual's time discount rate and return to schooling. A correctly specified model with enough structure permits estimation of a wide set of returns-to-schooling measures for individuals under different circumstances (e.g., faced with different costs or benefits or different schooling level decisions). The advantage of this approach is that it emphasizes the economic content of what is being estimated and offers a potential approach to measuring individual rates of return in situations where an experimental approach cannot. Studies using

this approach typically estimate returns around 0.04 to 0.07, which are lower than those from experimental approaches (Belzil, 2007 provides a review). If the assumptions of these models are incorrect, however, the returns to schooling estimates can be off significantly. Unfortunately, this is difficult to determine.

Annual returns, signaling, and sheepskin effects

An important issue to address is the extent to which the estimates of returns to schooling reflect not just the productivity enhancing effect of schooling but an effect on earnings of the underlying set of skills that schooling signals. There is a fundamental difficulty in unraveling the extent to which schooling is a signal of existing productivity as opposed to enhancing productivity: both theories are observationally equivalent—they both suggest that there is a positive correlation between earnings and schooling, but for very different reasons. If the rate at which employers learn an employee's correct set of skills is slow, or if early job placements influence long-term job opportunities, the effects of signaling can be long-lasting.

The empirical literature generally finds evidence of such signaling or sheepskin effects.[9] The returns to an additional year of education that involves completion of a stage (e.g., graduating from high school, or university) is higher than the return to a year of education that does not involve the credential of the completion of a phase. For example, based on the 1996 Canadian census, Ferrer and Riddell (2002) estimate rates of return to an additional year of schooling to be 6% for males and 9% for females. These are averages of both the credential effects associated with

---

[9] See Weiss (1995), Chatterji et al. (2003) for examples and reviews. Ferrer and Riddell (2002) provide estimates of the credential effects and review much of the earlier literature, as do Heckman, Lochner and Todd (2006).

milestones of completing various phases as well as the returns to years within the different phases. When the returns to completing the phases are calculated and annualized over the period of education necessary to complete the degree, the annual rates of return that are implied by completing university relative to high school are 9% for males and 11% for females.

While most researchers would agree that schooling affects earnings both by improving skills and by signaling skills, the relative importance of these effects is not well understood. A growing concern particularly among college students is the decline in study time and effort spent on courses. The amount of time college students spend studying has declined over the last 50 years. Between 1961 and 2004, the average study time of college students fell from 24 h a week to approximately 11 h per week. The percentage of students studying fewer than 5 h a week increased from 7% to 25% (Babcock & Marks, 2011). One possibility that students simply do not want to study more is because, conditional on being fairly certain of degree attainment, the high-effort strategy of going after high grades and learning a lot is not as attractive as settling for low average grades while having more free time (Oreopoulos et al., 2018). One paper estimates that the contribution of signaling to the returns to schooling is less than 25% (Lange, 2007). Understanding the relative importance of signaling in explaining returns to schooling remains an important area for further research.

Non-pecuniary benefits and social benefits

The previous discussion emphasized the private monetary returns to education to individuals making the education decision. However, education also can have non-pecuniary benefits to such individuals. Oreopoulos and Salvanes (2011) review the literature on such no-pecuniary benefits highlighting that education can lead to greater satisfaction with work, better decisions on health, marriage and parenting, and altering preferences toward being more patient and goal-oriented and less likely to engage in risky behavior. For some students, higher education can also confer consumption benefits, as evidenced by the title of one recent article: "College as a Country Club" (Jacob, McCall & Stange, 2018)

There is also a literature that estimates the social returns or externalities that occur to third-parties over-and-above the private returns that occur to individuals making the education decision. That evidence suggests that the third-party or social returns to schooling are in the neighborhood of 0.07–0.10, which is the same as the reasonable range of private returns, thereby effectively doubling the private returns. Reviews of that literature are given in Hout (2011), Riddell (2002) and Wolfe and Haveman (2001). Examples of some of the *mechanisms* for these third-party externalities are given below:

- Human capital, knowledge spillovers or externalities can arise as education on the part of one individual can affect the productivity of other individuals, for example, through positive neighborhood and peer effects (e.g., Duranton & Puga 2003; Moretti 2004a,b).
- Reduce negative externalities such as crime (e.g., Lochner 2004; Lochner & Moretti 2004).
- Positive externalities in such forms as increased participation in voting, volunteering and civic activities in general (e.g., Acemoglu & Angrist 2001; Milligan, Moretti & Oreopoulos 2003).
- Positive spillover effects on improve health, family planning, parenting skills and subsequent child outcomes that can have notable inter-generational effects (Currie & Moreitti, 2003; Lleras-Muney, 2005; Oreopoulos, Page & Stevens, 2006).
- Reduced social expenditures because of reductions in illness, unemployment and poverty (Oreopoulos, 2007)

Trends and some international evidence

Returns to education in the US have been increasing steadily in recent years likely reflecting the widening skill differential in wages (Card & Lemieux, 2001) in spite of the dramatic increases in education that would normally be expected to depress returns. In essence, the increased demand for skilled and educated labor associated with technological change and the computer revolution has more than offset the increased supply of educated persons (Acemoglu & Autor, 2011; Goldin & Katz, 2008; Oreopoulos & Petronijevic 2013).

International comparisons of the return to education are obviously difficult because of differences in the data sets and methodologies. In spite of this, reviews of the international evidence general find similar results as those in the US and Canada.[10] Psacharopoulos and Pat-

TABLE 3.1   Sample estimates of returns to education using alternative approaches.

Author	General method	Sample	Returns to education
Grilliches (1977)	Regress log median earnings of expected occupation at age 30 on schooling while using IQ score as additional proxy control for ability	17-27 year-old men in 1969 from U.S. National longitudinal survey for young men, using log median earnings of expected occupation at age 30	0.059 (0.003)
Ashenfelter and Rouse (1998)	Regress difference in log earnings between identical twins on difference in schooling	1991—93 Princeton twins survey of identical twins	0.102 (0.010)
Card (1995)	Use indicator for whether living near a 4year college as instrument for predicting schooling	U.S. National longitudinal survey for young men	0.132 (0.049)
Chen (2007)	Use average tuition fees at the local college in county as instruments for predicting schooling	25-42 year-old men in 1979—2000 from U.S. National longitudinal survey of youth, 1979	0.133 (0.028)
Oreopoulos (2007)	Use differences in state compulsory schooling laws as instruments for predicting schooling	25-64 year-old men and women in 1950—2000 U S. Censuses	0.142 (0.012)
Bezil and Hanson (2007)	Construct structural model on education attainment decisions and estimate model along with returns to schooling	White males from the U.S. National longitudinal survey of youth	0.069 (average between grade 10 −16)
Canaan and Mouganie. (2018)	Regression discontinuity comparing those who marginally pass and those who marginally fail French exit exams	Administrative data for France	0.125

[10] The international generalizations given here are based mainly on Psacharopoulos and Patrinos (2004, 2018) (earlier studies are cited therein). Similar generalizations for some of the issues are given in Trostel, Walker and Woolley (2002) with further international evidence provided in OECD (1998).

rinos (2018), for example, provide 1120 estimates from 139 countries and conclude that the returns to an additional year of education are around 9%, being slightly higher for females, and they are increasing over time for higher levels of education.

Summary

- Returns to education tend to be in the neighborhood of 10%, typically ranging from 6% to 15%. Table 3.1 illustrates the main approaches used to estimate these returns and their general findings.
- Returns to education tend to be in the 6% −10% range when based on OLS estimates from conventional schooling equations and the 10%−15% range (and sometimes higher) when based on instrumental variables (IV) and other procedures used to identify exogenous variation in education. As such, the 10% estimate is at the upper end of the OLS range and lower end of the IV range.
- The returns tend to be higher for
  - Females as opposed to males
  - Obtaining the credentials associated with completing phases like high school or university
  - General academic streams compared to technical vocational streams
  - Professional fields like engineering, medicine, business and sciences and lower in social sciences and humanities and especially fields like fine arts
- The returns tend to be increasing over time in spite of the large increases in the supply of educated persons, highlighting that the demands for education associated with the knowledge economy and the widening of the skilled-unskilled wage differential are outstripping the supply responses.
- These generalizations tend to apply on an international basis to a wide range of countries.

References

Angrist, J., & Krueger, A. (1991). Does compulsory school attendance affect schooling and earnings? *Quarterly Journal of Economics, 106*, 979−1014.

Angrist, J., & Krueger, A. (1994). Why do World War II veterans earn more than non-veterans? *Journal of Labor Economics, 12*, 74−97.

Ashenfelter, O., & Rouse, C. (1998). Income, schooling and ability: Evidence from a new sample of identical twins. *Quarterly Journal of Economics, 113*, 253−284.

Ashenfelter, O., & Zimmerman, D. (1997). Estimates of the return to schooling from sibling data. *The Review of Economics and Statistics, 79*, 1−9.

Belzil, C. (2007). The return to schooling in structural dynamic models: A survey. *European Economic Review, 51*(5), 1059−1105.

Cameron, S. V., & Taber, C. (2004). Estimation of educational borrowing constraints using returns to schooling. *Journal of Political Economy, 112*, 132−182.

Card, D. (1995). Using geographic variation in college proximity to estimate the return to schooling. In L. Christofides, K. Grant, & R. Swidinsky (Eds.), *Aspects of labour market behaviour: Essays in honour of John Vanderkamp* (pp. 201−222). Toronto: University of Toronto Press.

Card, D. (2001). Estimating the return to schooling: Progress on some persistent problems. *Econometrica, 69*, 1137−1160.

Card, D., & Lemieux, T. (2001). Can falling supply explain the rising return to college for younger men? A cohort-based analysis. *Quarterly Journal of Economics, 116*, 705−746.

Chamberlain, G. (1977). Omitted variable bias in panel data: Estimating the returns to schooling. *Annals de l'Insee, 30−31*, 49−82.

Chamberlain, G., & Griliches, Z. (1975). Unobservables with a variance components structure: Ability, schooling and the economic success of brothers. *International Economic Review, 16*, 422−449.

Chen, S. (2007). Estimating the variance of wages in the presence of selection and unobservable heterogeneity. *The Review of Economics and Statistics* (in press).

Ferrer, A., & Riddell, W. C. (2002). The role of credentials in the Canadian labor market. *Canadian Journal of Economics, 35*, 879−905.

Kane, T., & Rouse, C. (1995). Labor market returns to two-year and four-year college. *The American Economic Review, 85*, 600−614.

Krashinsky, H. (2014). How would one extra year of high school affect academic performance in university? Evidence from a unique policy change. *Canadian Journal of Economics, 47*, 70−97.

Lange, F. (2007). The speed of employer learning. *Journal of Labor Economics, 25*, 1−36.

Lemieux, T., & Card, D. (2001). Education, earnings and the "Canadian G.I. Bill,". *Canadian Journal of Economics, 34*, 313–344.

Miller, P., Mulvey, C., & Martin, N. (2006). The return to schooling: Estimates from a sample of young Australian twins. *Labour Economics, 13*, 571–587.

Oreopoulos, P. (2006a). The compelling effects of compulsory schooling: Evidence from Canada. *Canadian Journal of Economics, 39*, 22–52.

Oreopoulos, P. (2006b). Estimating average and local average treatment effects of education when compulsory schooling laws really matter. *The American Economic Review, 96*, 152–175.

Webbink, D. (2007). Returns to university education: Evidence from a Dutch institutional reform. *Economica, 74*, 13–134.

Weiss, A. (1995). Human capital vs. signalling explanations of wages. *The Journal of Economic Perspectives, 9*, 133–154.

Further reading

Acemoglu, D., & Angrist, J. (2001). How large are human capital externalities? Evidence from compulsory schooling laws. *NBER Macroeconomics Annual 2000*, 9–59.

Acemoglu, D., & Autor, D. (2012). What does human capital do? *Journal of Economic Literature, 50*, 426–463.

Ashenflelter, O., Harmon, C., & Oosterbeck, H. (1999). A review of estimates of the schooling/earnings relationship, with tests for publication bias. *Labour Economics, 6*, 453–470.

Babcock, P., & Marks, M. (2011). The falling time cost of college: Evidence from half a century of time use data. *The Review of Economics and Statistics, 93*, 468–478.

Belzil, C., & Hansen, J. (2007). A structural analysis of the correlated random coefficient wage regression model. *Journal of Econometrics, 140*, 827–848.

Bettinger, E. P., Long, B. T., Oreopoulos, P., & Sanbonmatsu, L. (2012). The role of application assistance and information in college decisions: Results from the H&R Block Fafsa experiment. *Quarterly Journal of Economics, 127*, 1205–1224.

Card, D. (1999). The causal effect of education on earnings. In O. Ashenfelter, & D. Card (Eds.), *Handbook of labor economics* (Vol. 3, pp. 1801–1863). Amsterdam: Elsevier Science.

Canaan, S., & Mouganie, P. (2018). Returns to education quality for low skilled students: Evidence from a discontinuity. *Journal of Labor Economics, 36*, 395–437.

Carneiro, P., Heckman, J. J., & Vytlacil, E. (2011). Estimating marginal returns to education. *The American Economic Review, 101*, 2754–2781.

Carnoy, M. (1997). Recent research on market returns to education. *Journal of Educational Research, 27*, 483–490.

Chatterji, M., Paul, S., & Singell, L. D., Jr. (2003). A test of the signalling hypothesis. *Oxford Economic Papers, 55*, 191–215.

Currie, J., and E. Moretti. Mother's education and the intergenerational transmission of human capital: Evidence from college openings, Quarterly Journal of Economics 118, 1495-1532

Duranton, G., & Puga, D. (2003). Micro-foundations of urban agglomeration economies. In J. Thiesse, & V. Henderson (Eds.), *Handbook of urban and regional economics*. North-Holland Elsevier.

Goldin, C., & Katz, L. F. (2008). *The race between education and technology*. Belknap Press.

Griliches, Z. (1977). Estimating the returns to schooling: Some econometric problems. *Econometrica, 45*, 1–22.

Griliches, Z. (1979). Sibling models and data in economics: Beginnings of a survey. *Journal of Political Economy, 87*, S37–S65.

Heckman, J., Lochner, L., & Todd, P. (2006). Earnings functions, rates of return and treatment effects: The Mincer equation and beyond. In E. Hanushek, & F. Welch (Eds.), *Handbook of the economics of education* (Vol. 1, pp. 306–458). Amsterdam: Elsevier Science.

Hoekstra, M. (2009). The effect of attending the flagship state university on earnings: A discontinuity-based approach. *The Review of Economics and Statistics, 91*, 717–724.

Hout, M. (2011). Social and economic returns to college in the United States. *Annual Review of Sociology, 38*, 379–400.

Hoxby, C., & Turner, S. (2015). What high-achieving low-income students know about college. *The American Economic Review, 105*, 514–517.

Jacob, B., McCall, B., & Kevin, S. (2018). College as a country club: Do colleges cater to students' preferences for consumption? *Journal of Labor Economics, 36*, 309–348.

Jensen, R. (2010). The perceived returns to education and the demand for schooling. *Quarterly Journal of Economics, 125*, 515–548.

Johnson, M. (2013). Borrowing constraints, college enrollment, and delayed entry. *Journal of Labor Economics, 31*, 669–725.

Kirkeboen, L., Leuven, E., & Mogstad, M. (2016). Field of study, earnings and self-selection. *Quarterly Journal of Economics, 131*, 1057–1111.

Lavecchia, A., Liu, H., & Oreopoulos, P. (2016). Behavioral economics of education. In E. Hanushek, S. Machin, & L. Woessmann (Eds.), *Vol. 5. Handbook of economics of education* (pp. 1–74). Elsevier.

Lemieux, T. (2002). The causal effects of education on earnings in Canada. In P. deBroucker, & A. Sweetman (Eds.), *Towards evidence-based policy for Canadian education* (pp. 105–116). Kingston: McGill-Queens University Press.

Lleras-Muney, A. (2005). The relationship between education and adult mortality in the United States. *The Review of Economic Studies, 72*, 89–221.

Lochner, L. (2004). Education, work and crime: Theory and evidence. *International Economic Review, 45*, 811–843.

Lochner, L., & Moretti, E. (2004). The effect of education on crime: Evidence from prison inmates, arrests and self-reports. *The American Economic Review, 94*, 155–189.

Milligan, K., Moretti, E., & Oreopoulos, P. (2004). Does education improve citizenship? Evidence from the U.S. And the U.K. *Journal of Public Economics, 88*, 1667–1695.

Mincer, J. (1974). *Schooling, experience and earnings*. New York: Columbia University Press.

Moretti, E. (2004a). Estimating the social returns to higher education: Evidence from longitudinal and repeated cross-sectional data. *Journal of Econometrics, 121*, 175–212.

Moretti, E. (2004b). Human capital externalities in cities. In J. Thiesse, & V. Henderson (Eds.), *Handbook of Urban and regional economics*. Amsterdam: Elsevier Press.

OECD. (1998). *Human capital investment: An international comparison*. Paris: Organisation for Economic Cooperation and Development.

Oreopoulos, P. (2007). Do dropouts drop out too soon? Wealth, health, and happiness from compulsory schooling. *Journal of Public Economics, 91*, 2213–2229.

Oreopoulos, P., & Dunn, R. (2013). Information and college access: Evidence from a randomized field experiment. *The Scandinavian Journal of Economics, 115*, 3–26.

Oreopoulos, P., & Salvanes, K. G. (2011). Priceless: The non-pecuniary benefits of schooling. *The Journal of Economic Perspectives, 25*, 159–184.

Oreopoulos, P., Page, M., & Stevens, A. H. (2006). The intergenerational effects of compulsory schooling. *Journal of Labor Economics, 24*, 729–760.

Oreopoulos, P., Patterson, R., Petronijevic, U., & Pope, N. (2018). *The disappointing impact of encouraging students to study more*. VOX CEPR Policy Portal. https://voxeu.org/article/disappointing-impact-encouraging-students-study-more.

Ost, B., Pan, W., & Douglas, W. (2018). The returns to college persistence for marginal students: Regression discontinuity evidence from university dismissal policies. *Journal of Labor Economics, 36*, 779–805.

Psacharopoulos, G., & Patrinos, H. (2004). Returns to investment in education: A further update. *Education Economics, 12*, 111–134.

Psacharopoulos, G., & Patrinos, H. (2018). *Returns to investment in education: A decennial review of the global literature*. Washington, DC: World Bank.

Riddell, W. C. (2002). Is there under- or over-investment in education? In P. de Broucker, & A. Sweetman (Eds.), *Towards evidence-based Policy for Canadian education* (pp. 473–496). Montreal and Kingston: McGill-Queen's University Press and John Deutsch Institute for Economic Policy.

Scott-Clayton, J. (2013). Information constraints and financial aid policy. In D. Heller, & C. Callender (Eds.), *Student financing of higher education: A comparative perspective*. Routledge Press.

Stevens, M., & Yang, D.-Y. (2014). Compulsory education and the benefits of schooling. *The American Economic Review, 104*, 1777–1792.

Trostel, P., Walker, I., & Paul, W. (2002). Estimates of the economic return to schooling in 28 countries. *Labour Economics, 9*, 1–16.

Wolfe, B., & Haveman, R. (2001). Accounting for the social and non-market benefits of education. In J. Helliwell (Ed.), *The contribution of human and social capital to sustained economic growth and well-being* (pp. 221–250). Vancouver: University of British Columbia Press.

Wolfe, B., & Zuvekis, S. (1997). Nonmarket outcomes of schooling. *International Journal of Educational Research, 27*, 491–502.

Zimmerman, S. (2014). The returns to college admission for academically marginal students. *Journal of Labor Economics, 32*, 711–754.

Returns to education in developing countries

Harry Anthony Patrinos[a], *George Psacharopoulos*[b]

[a]Former World Bank, Washington DC, United States; [b]London School of Economics, World Bank

Introduction

Earnings of workers classified by some dimension have been have been at the core of empirical economics since the dawn of the discipline. Up to the middle of the 20th century the main dimensions according to which earnings were classified were sector of economic activity, industry, occupation and formal versus informal sector in developing countries. From about 1960 onwards, following the human capital revolution in economic thought (Becker, 1964; Mincer 1974; Schultz 1961), the educational level of the worker was added as a classificatory variable.

Earnings differentials by level of education reflect the monetary incentives for someone to invest in education. Earnings differentials by education represent the intersection of supply and demand curves for educated labor. Differences in relative earnings between countries reflect a number of factors, e.g. the demand for skills in the labor market, minimum wage legislation, the strength of unions, collective agreements, the supply of workers with various levels of educational attainment, the work experience of workers with high and low levels of schooling,

the distribution of employment among occupations and the relative incidence of part-time and seasonal work (OECD, 2017).

The study of earnings by schooling has led to several empirical works testing hypotheses on a great variety of social issues. These include, for example, racial and ethnic discrimination (McNabb and Psacharopoulos 1981; Chiswick 1988; Psacharopoulos and Patrinos, 1994): gender discrimination (Psacharopoulos and Tzannatos 1992; Goldin and Polachek 1987); income distribution (Mincer 1958; Marin and Psacharopoulos 1976); and the determinants of the demand for education (Freeman 1976; Psacharopoulos and Soumelis, 1979; Psacharopoulos 1982). Under certain assumptions, earnings differentials by level of education have been used to identify the sources of economic growth (for example, Denison 1967; Psacharopoulos 1972). But perhaps the application *par excellence* that has used earnings by level of education is the estimation of the rate of return to investment in schooling.

In what follows we give a taste of the returns to education with emphasis on developing countries and compare them to those in advanced industrial countries. Section Global estimates provides a review of the returns to education for developing countries. Empirical estimates of the returns to education date from the late 1950s to the beginning of the 21st century. As the number of empirical studies increase, compilations of the rate of returns to education start to emerge in the early 1970s (Psacharopoulos 1973) and have continued to the present (Psacharopoulos and Patrinos, 2018).

Estimation procedures

It is a universal fact that, in all countries of the world, the more education one has the higher his/her earnings. Age-earnings profiles by level of education behave as predicted by the seminal theoretical and empirical work of Mincer (1974), taking the general shape depicted in Fig. 4.1.

Fig. 4.2 shows an actual age-earnings profile for Indonesia.

Based on such data, along with the direct cost of schooling, two types of returns are usually

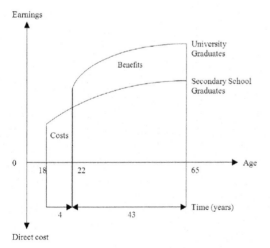

FIG. 4.1   Typical age-earnings profiles by level of education.

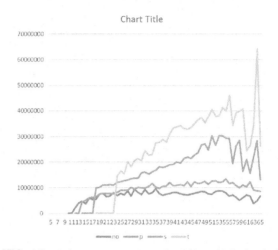

FIG. 4.2   Indonesia age-earnings (*rupiah*) profile by level of education. *Source: Based on Indonesia National Socio-Economic Survey (SUSENAS) 2010.*

estimated, each answering a different question: First, the private rate of return, that compares the costs and benefits of education as incurred by and realized by the individual student who undertakes the investment. Second, the social rate of return that compares costs and benefits from the country-as-a-whole or society's point of view.

The main computational difference between private and social rates of return is that, for a social rate of return calculation, the costs include the state's or society's at large spending on education. Hence, the cost would include the rental of buildings and professorial salaries. Gross earnings (that is, before taxes and other deductions) are used in a social rate of return calculation, and such earnings should also include income in kind where this information is available.

There exists some confusion in the literature regarding the "social" adjective attached to rates of return to investment in education. It has been the tradition in the mainstream economics of education literature to mean by a "social" rate, a private rate adjusted for the full cost of schooling, rather than just what the individual pays for his or her education. However, a "social" rate should include externalities, that is, benefits beyond those captured by the individual investor, such as lower fertility or lives saved because of improved sanitation conditions followed by a more educated woman who may never participate in the formal labor market.

Traditional social returns to education are called "narrow-social," and returns that include externalities "wide-social." The distinction between narrow and wide social returns is more than theoretical. By adding externalities to the narrow-social returns, one can reach diametrically opposite policy conclusions, for example, if primary and tertiary education have differential externalities, by considering the latter the ranking of profitable education investments could be changed.

Using an appropriate methodology, the above earnings differentials can be used to estimate the returns to investment in education. Most published estimates of the rate of return to schooling rely on the Mincerian earnings function (Mincer, 1974), the most widely used estimation in economics (for a review of the Mincerian earnings function see Heckman, Lochner and Todd 2006; Patrinos, 2016). However, the most correct methodology is what is known as "the full discounting method" that is based on the actual shape of the age-earnings profiles, rather than be smoothed out by an earnings function (Psacharopoulos and Mattson, 1998).

Computationally, there are two main estimation procedures:

(a) The earnings function method

This method, also known as Mincerian, involves the fitting of a function of log-wages (LnY), using years of schooling (S), years of labor market experience (EX) and its square as independent variables. This is called a "basic earnings function." In the semi-log specification, the coefficient on years of schooling can be interpreted as the average private rate of return to one additional year of schooling, regardless of the educational level this year of schooling refers to.

The basic Mincerian earnings function takes the form:

$$\ln Y_i = \alpha + \beta S_i + \gamma_1 EX_i + \gamma_2 EX_i^2$$

Since $\beta = \frac{\partial \ln W}{\partial S} = r$, this is the relative increase in wages following an increase in S, or the rate of return to the marginal year of schooling.

The only costs involved in this case is foregone earnings, so this method estimates only private returns to education.

(B) The full discounting method

The social rate of return to investment in a given level of education is estimated by finding the rate of discount (r) that equalizes the stream of discounted benefits (Y) over time (t) to the stream of costs (C) at a given point in time. For example, in the case of university education lasting four years and a working life of 42 years, the formula is:

$$\sum_{t=1}^{42} \frac{(Y_u - Y_s)_t}{(1+r)^t} = \sum_{t=1}^{4} (Y_s + C_u)_t (1+r)^t$$

where $(Y_u - Y_s)_t$ is the earnings differential between a university graduate (subscript u) and a secondary school graduate (subscript s, the control group) at time t. C_u represents the direct resource cost of university education (buildings, salaries, etc.), and Y_s denotes the student's foregone earnings or indirect costs.

A key assumption in a social rate of return calculation is that observed wages are a good proxy for the marginal product of labor. This is not necessarily the case when the sample includes civils servants. Hence, the earnings function could be fitted to a sub-sample of workers in the private sector of the economy where wages are more likely to relate to productivity.

Global estimates

The numbers in Table 4.1 are based on a meta-analysis of over 1000 rate of return estimates in over 100 countries. Based on the social calculation, primary education exhibits the highest returns, followed by secondary and higher education.

Since the costs are higher in a social rate of return calculation relative to the one from the private point of view, social returns are typically lower than a private rate of return. The difference between the private and the social rate of return reflects the degree of public subsidization of education. Hence, public subsidy to education is shown to be regressive.

The size of the economic rate of return to investment in education is inversely related to the level of education. Primary education should have been a priority in countries where the coverage at this level is not universal, next comes secondary education and university.

Across world regions, the returns are higher in countries with low educational attainment measured by the mean years of schooling (Table 4.2).

The stylized patterns reported here have been corroborated and reinforced by using the same household survey dataset and Mincerian specification in 139 countries to produce 819

TABLE 4.1 Returns by educational level (%).

Educational level	Private	Social
Primary	25.4	17.5
Secondary	15.1	11.8
Higher	15.8	10.5
Average	18.8	13.3

Source: Psacharopoulos and Patrinos (2018).

TABLE 4.2 Private Returns to schooling by region.

Region	Overall rate of return (%)	Mean years of schooling
Latin America and Caribbean	11.0	7.3
Sub-Saharan Africa	10.5	5.2
East Asia and Pacific	8.7	6.9
South Asia	8.1	4.9
Advanced economies	8.0	9.5
Europe and Central Asia	7.3	9.1
Middle East and North Africa	5.7	7.5
World average	8.8	8.0

Source: Psacharopoulos and Patrinos (2018).

comparable private rate of return estimates (Montenegro and Patrinos, 2014). The returns to schooling are more concentrated around their respective means than previously thought, and the basic Mincerian model used is more stable than may have been expected (Patrinos, 2016).

Low-income countries

Using the database compiled by Psacharopoulos and Patrinos (2018, online Annex 2), we focused on 68 rate of return estimates of a panel of 17 low-income countries between 1965 and 2012.[1]

The average number of years of schooling in low-income countries is 5 years and the overall Mincerian private rate of return 9.3% that is one-half percentage points higher relative to the global average of 8.8%.

Using the full discounting method to estimate the returns to education by educational level, the returns are significantly higher than the global

[1] The countries are Burkina Faso, Burundi, Cambodia, Ethiopia, Eritrea, Gambia, Ghana, Guyana, Madagascar, Malawi, Nepal, Mali, Niger, Rwanda, Sierra Leone, Somalia and Tanzania.

averages, and so is the degree of subsidization of higher education (Tables 4.3—4.5).

As expected, returns are higher in lower income countries where the quantity of schooling is scarcer. The low returns to primary education in upper middle-income countries can be explained by the fact primary education has reached most of the population and there is not a sufficient number of illiterates to serve as control group. It may also mean that given near universal coverage of primary education in these countries there is no much room to further

TABLE 4.3 Returns to education in low-income countries (%).

Educational level	Private	Social
Primary	25.4	22.1
Secondary	18.7	18.1
Higher	26.8	13.2
Average	23.6	17.8

Note: Based on the full discounting method.
Source: Psacharopoulos and Patrinos, 2018

TABLE 4.4 Returns by gender and sector of employment in low-income countries (%).

Gender	Males	8.4
	Females	9.2
Sector of employment	Private	10.7
	Public	9.1

Note: Based on the Mincerian method.

TABLE 4.5 Social returns to investment in upper secondary school streams, Tanzania.

Curriculum type	Rate of return (%)
Academic	6.3
Technical	1.7

*Source: Data from Psacharopoulos, George; Loxley, William; Psacharopoulos, George*Loxley, William. 1985. Diversified secondary education and development: evidence from Colombia and Tanzania (English). A World Bank publication. Baltimore, MD: The Johns Hopkins University Press. http://documents.worldbank.org/curated/en/243621468241777497/ Diversified-secondary-education-and-development-evidence-from-Colombia-and-Tanzania*

expand this level of schooling. It might instead make sense to increase investment in the quality of primary schooling (Figs. 4.3—4.5).

The returns for those working in the private sector of the economy are higher than for those working in the public sector. The finding lends credibility that, where productivity matters, education is recognized (Psacharopoulos, 1983; Harmon, Oosterbeek and Walker, 2003).

In terms of social returns, these are higher than any plausible social discount rate though lower than private, across all income groups. The social returns to higher education are particularly high, but these are driven by returns in Africa, where the social returns to higher education are 35% in Malawi (Chirwa and Matita, 2009) and 22% in South Africa (Salisbury, 2015) — this of course implies that private returns to higher education are even higher.

Vocational education

Within levels of education, and counter to any intuitive thought, general secondary education is more profitable than vocational education. The reason is that whereas general and vocational secondary school graduates have more-or-less equal earnings after graduation, the vocational track of secondary schools costs about twice that of the general track (see Psacharopoulos, 1987; Psacharopoulos and Loxley, 1985).

In many countries, the wage returns to academic qualifications are significantly higher than the returns to vocational qualifications, government training programs and adult skills training (Blundell, Dearden and Sianesi, 2005; Carneiro and Heckman, 2003; Dearden et al., 2002; Dickerson, 2005).

In a large World Bank follow-up study of students in the technical-vocational curriculum stream of secondary education in Colombia and Tanzania, it was found that the graduates

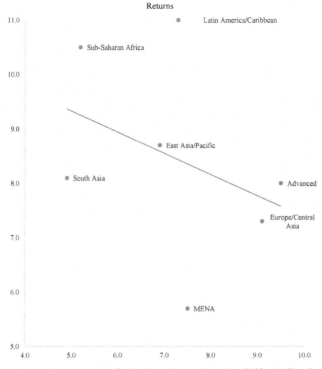

FIG. 4.3 Returns to education and mean years of schooling. *Source: Based on Table 4.2 (Psacharopoulos and Patrinos, 2018).*

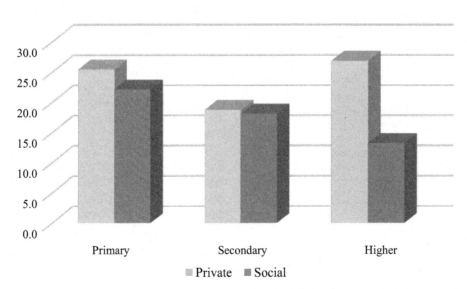

FIG. 4.4 Returns to education in low-income countries (%). Based on the full discounting method. *Source: Psacharopoulos and Patrinos, 2018.*

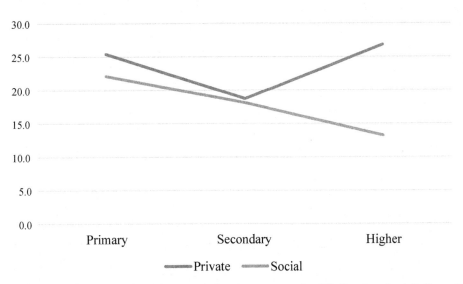

FIG. 4.5 The structure of private and social returns in low-income countries (%). Based on the full discounting method. *Source: Psacharopoulos and Patrinos, 2018*

did not seek or find employment in the sector they studied (Psacharopoulos and Loxley, 1985). It was such finding that made the World Bank change its lending portfolio as late as the 1990s away from secondary vocational schools, an activity the institution had been engaged nearly exclusively since its inception.

Beyond the formal school system, a very robust research finding is that retraining programs for the unemployed are ineffective (Heckman et al., 1999). The costs of such programs grossly exceed the benefits, the latter being measured by the length of time needed for a graduate of these programs to find a job, and by the earnings differential of those who graduated from the program relative to those who did not (Ashenfelter 1986; Ashenfelter and Card 1985; Ashenfelter and Lalonde 1997; Heckman and Hotz 1989).

Preschool

There have been many cost-benefit studies on the effect of preschool on eventual educational

attainment, adult earnings and other externalities. A World Bank study documented a long list of benefits associated with preschool education in Brazil, with an estimate of 12.5–15.0% return on the investment. On cost-benefit grounds, preschool is a better investment relative to the Bank's industrial and agricultural projects (World Bank 2001).

An experimental study with a 20-year follow-up of participants in a preschool program in Jamaica found that a preschool intervention increased the average earnings of participants by 42% relative to the control group (Gertler at al. 2013).

Preschool is most effective when targeted to the most vulnerable groups. In an early childhood development project in Indonesia, preschool had an impact on reducing achievement gaps between richer and poorer students (Jung and Hasan, 2014).

A major policy concern, therefore, is the relatively lower returns to education for women at the primary education level in developing economies. It is a major concern because families in poor countries may decide to send sons rather than daughters to school. The lower returns to females at the primary level in developing countries is puzzling given the fact that the rate of return to years of schooling is two percentage points greater for females than for males in developing countries, as well as transition countries. Dougherty (2005) considers various explanations. The most important involves the detrimental impact of discrimination and other factors that cause women to accept wage offers that undervalue their characteristics. It is hypothesized that the better educated is a woman, the more able and willing she is to overcome the sex handicaps and compete with men in the labor market. He also considers the possibility that part of the differential could be attributable to male-female differences in the quality of educational attainment. Also, women may choose to work in sectors where education is relatively highly valued. The lower return to primary education in developing economies may be evidence of discrimination — such that women need to achieve more schooling in order to garner sufficient wages — or the option value of schooling — that is, since women are likely to perform better, stay in school longer, and experience higher returns for each year of schooling, then the most able go beyond primary schooling, thus depressing the returns at that level.

Turning to the broader picture, the rate of return to education has fallen over the decades, while average years of schooling have risen. The returns to different educational attainments have fluctuated over the years, but it is also clear that amid the fluctuations, there has been a downward trend since the 1980s. The proportions of the population that are secondary educated and university educated have all risen markedly over the decades while the proportion of the population that is primary educated has declined slightly. The rate of return to primary education has fluctuated over the decades. For secondary education, the rate of return has risen until the 1980s. For university education, the private rate of return has declined as the proportion that is university educated increases (Patrinos and Psacharopoulos, 2007).

Causality

It is also worth noting that estimates of the returns on education based on advanced econometric techniques that control for different characteristics come to an average rate of return that is very similar to the global average presented in reviews: 10%. To estimate the true effect of education on earnings, some authors have employed instrumental variables (IV) estimates. A useful instrument should be correlated with schooling, but uncorrelated with unexplained variation in earnings. Various variables on family background are frequently used. However, they are not expected to meet the requirement that they are uncorrelated with earnings (among other possible reasons, due to inter-generational effects).

Recently, information on the costs of schooling and supply-side sources of identifying information, such as various types of education reform, are increasingly sought after as instruments. Costs are important because people make decisions about investing in schooling on perceived costs and benefits. Therefore, loan policies, tuition changes, and distance are possible sources of instruments. Institutional constraints are also important. Therefore, supply-side changes, such as the extension of compulsory school laws or making education facilities more accessible by reducing the distance to school, provide the researcher with the sort of "natural experiment" that allows one to say that the instrument is correlated with schooling but not earnings. One could argue for example that extending compulsory school age results in more people enrolling in school because of the legal change rather than because of their individual ability to generate more earnings. Such instruments will fail if they are corrected with earnings — as is sometimes the case with family background variables; in other words, the approach will fail when the researcher chooses bad instruments.

The IV estimates are often higher than Ordinary Least Squares estimates, although it is unclear to what extent this is due to measurement error or inadequate instrumentation (see Trostel et al., 2002). There are very few studies for developing countries dealing with the issues surrounding the endogeneity of education and the implications of estimating returns to education from IV. The rate of return estimates from IV are not only different from OLS, they are generally higher. Since the IV estimate is supposed to be the true return, this contradicts the standard ability bias intuition: OLS should be upward biased if higher ability individuals have more schooling. This approach uses sources for exogenous variation in educational attainment, such as institutional changes in the schooling system in the form of changes in compulsory schooling laws (Patrinos and Sakellariou, 2006) and reducing the distance to school (such as school construction projects; see Duflo, 2001) affecting the schooling decision, to estimate a causal return to education. The interpretation (Card, 2001) is that the returns to schooling vary across individuals. Institutional changes affect the schooling decision of a subset of individuals who, otherwise, would not have pursued a higher level of education and not the average individual. Furthermore, individuals affected by such reforms tend to have a higher return to education than the average individual. There is a distribution of returns, and OLS and IV correspond to different weighted averages of this distribution, and OLS can be below IV (see also Heckman & Li 2004; Arabsheibani & Mussurav, 2007; and Sakellariou, 2006).

Cognitive ability

Beyond the returns to increasing the quantity of schooling, recent research has thrown light on the returns to improving the quality of schooling, the latter being measured by the cognitive skill of the student or graduate. Ability, or school quality, matter for earnings attainment (Leuven et al., 2004). Table 4.6 summarizes research results to increasing cognitive skills.

Several important papers over the last decade on establishing causation between education and earnings have made the case for schooling as an investment. It is also clear that there is a need for more evidence on the impact of education on earnings using quasi-, and where

TABLE 4.6 Estimated returns to a standard deviation increase in cognitive skills.

Country	Estimated effect	Source
Chile	0.17	Patrinos & Sakellariou, 2007
Ghana	0.14—0.30	Glewwe, 1996
Ghana	0.05—0.07	Jolliffe, 1998
Kenya	0.19—0.22	Boissiere, Knight, & Sabot, 1985; Knight & Sabot, 1990
Pakistan	0.12—0.28	Alderman, Behrman, Ross, & Sabot, 1996
Pakistan	0.25	Behrman et al., 2008
South Africa	0.34—0.48	Moll, 1998
Tanzania	0.07—0.13	Boissiere et al. 1985; Knight & Sabot, 1990
Average	**0.17—0.22**	

possible, experimental design. Evaluation techniques are usefully applied in analyzing education and earnings, and providing evidence on the effectiveness of projects, programs and reforms. Thus, more research along the lines of Oreopoulos (2006) and others analysis changes in compulsory schooling laws and other reforms is warranted. Such analyses allow one to provide estimates not only for those likely affected by reforms (that is, the local average treatment effect, or LATE), but also estimates that come close to population average treatment effects (or ATE).

Recent research shows that skills — ability and learning outcomes — matter for earnings attainment. Overall, in several countries, a one standard deviation increase in school performance results in about a 12 to 15 increase in earnings. Though more work is needed in this area, clearly learning outcomes are important determinants of earnings. Therefore, a policy priority is to establish empirically which policies and programs lead to learning outcome gains.

Evidence of heterogeneity in the returns to education exists. From the evidence available, in most high-income and middle-income countries, higher returns at the upper ends of the wage distribution have been observed. Overall, in low income countries the returns tend to be higher at the lower ends of the wage distribution. Though more research is needed, such differences between countries could be due to: more job mobility in developed countries allowing individuals to improve their position by changing jobs; scarcity of skills; differential exposure to market forces and the link between pay and productivity; or differential access to quality education or distribution of quality outcomes. What is clear is that average returns to the average individual will not suffice for policy purposes. We need to know more about which interventions are more likely to affect which parts of the distribution, and to establish at the same causality. In the above review, we noted that a major policy concern is the relatively low private rate of return to primary education for women in developing economies.

Conclusions and policy considerations

The empirical returns to schooling literature has proven to be a useful standard. The global average rate of return to schooling, estimated at about 9%, is used as a global benchmark. Empirical evidence on returns on investment in education are a useful indicator of the productivity of education, and they serve as an incentive for individuals to invest in their own human capital.

More research is needed, however, on estimating the social benefits of schooling. After all these years it is still an underdeveloped theme in the literature and remains a research priority. Still, existing evidence suggests that social returns and externalities are likely high.

Disclaimer

The views expressed here are those of the author and should not be attributed to the World Bank Group.

References

Alderman, H., Behrman, J. R., Ross, D. R., & Sabot, R. (1996). The returns to endogenous human capital in Pakistan's rural wage labor market. *Oxford Bulletin of Economics and Statistics, 58,* 29–55.

Arabsheibani, G. R., & Mussurav, A. (2007). Returns to schooling in Kazakhstan: OLS and instrumental variables approach. *Economics of Transition, 15*(2), 341–364.

Becker, G. S. (1964). *Human capital.* Chicago: Columbia University Press.

Behrman, J. R., Ross, D., & Sabot, R. (2008). Improving the quality versus increasing the quantity of schooling: Estimates of rates of return from rural Pakistan. *Journal of Development Economics, 85*(1-2), 94–104.

Boissiere, M. X., Knight, J. B., & Sabot, R. H. (1985). Earnings, schooling, ability, and cognitive skills. *American Economic Review, 75*(5), 1016–1030.

Card, D. (2001). "Estimating the return on schooling: Progress on some persistent econometric problems." *Econometrica, 69*(5), 1127–1160.

Further reading

Chiswick, B. R. (1988). "Differences in education and earnings across racial and ethnic groups: Tastes, discrimination, and investments in child quality." *Quarterly Journal of Economics, 103*(3), 571–597.

Denison, E. F. (1967). *Why growth rates differ?* Washington, DC: The Brookings Institution.

Dougherty, C. R. S., & Jimenez, E. (1991). The specification of earnings functions: Tests and implications. *Economics of Education Review, 10*(2), 85–98.

Dougherty, C. (2005). Why are returns to schooling higher for women than for men? *Journal of Human Resources, 40*(4), 969–988.

Duflo, E. (2001). Schooling and labor market consequences of school construction in Indonesia: Evidence from an unusual policy experiment. *American Economic Review, 91*(4), 795–813.

Freeman, R. B. (1976). *The overeducated American.* Basic Books.

Glewwe, P. (1996). The relevance of standard estimates of rates of return to schooling for education policy: A critical assessment. *Journal of Development Economics, 51*, 267–290.

Goldin, C., & Polachek, S. (1987). Residual differences by sex: Perspectives on the gender gap in earnings. *American Economic Review, 77*(2), 143–151.

Griliches, Z. (1977). Estimating the returns to schooling: Some econometric problems. *Econometrica, 45*(1), 1–22.

Hawley, J. D. (2004). Changing returns to education in times of prosperity and crisis, Thailand 1985–1998. *Economics of Education Review, 23*, 273–286.

Heckman, J. J., & Li, X. (2004). Selection bias, comparative advantage and heterogeneous returns to education: Evidence from China in 2000. *Pacific Economic Review, 9*(3), 155–171.

Heckman, J. J., Lochner, L. J., & Todd, P. E. (2006). "Earnings functions, rates of return, and treatment effects: The Mincer equation and beyond,". In E. Hanushek, & F. Welch (Eds.), *Handbook of the economics of education.* North Holland: Elsevier.

Jolliffe, D. (1998). Skills, schooling, and household income in Ghana. *World Bank Economic Review, 12*, 81–104.

Knight, J. B., & Sabot, R. H. (1990). *Education, productivity, and inequality: The East African natural experiment.* Oxford University Press.

Kurian, R. (1999). "Women's work in changing labour markets: The case of Thailand in the 1980s,". In H. Afshar, & S. Barrientos (Eds.), *Women, globalisation and fragmentation in the developing world.* New York: St. Martin's Press.

Layard, R., & George, P. (1974). The screening hypothesis and the returns to education. *Journal of Political Economy, 82*(5), 985–998.

Leuven, E., Oosterbeek, H., & van Ophem, H. (2004). "Explaining international differences in male skill wage differentials by differences in demand and supply of skills. *Economic Journal, 114*, 466–486.

Marin, A., & Psacharopoulos, G. (1976). Schooling and income distribution. *The Review of Economics and Statistics, 58*(3), 332–338.

McNabb, R., & Psacharopoulos, G. (1981). Racial earnings differentials in the U.K. *Oxford Economic Papers, 33*(3), 413–425.

Mincer, J. (1958). Investment in human capital and personal income distribution. *Journal of Political Economy, 66*(4), 281–302.

Mincer, J. (1974). *Schooling, experience, and earnings.* New York: National Bureau of Economic Research.

Moll, P. G. (1998). Primary schooling, cognitive skills, and wage in South Africa. *Economica, 65*, 263–284.

Montenegro, C. E., & Patrinos, H. A. (2014). *Comparable estimates of returns to schooling around the world.* Policy Research Working Paper No. 7020.

OECD. (2017). *Education at a glance 2017.* OECD.

Oreopoulos, P. (2006). Estimating average and local average treatment effects when compulsory schooling laws really matter. *American Economic Review, 96*(1), 152–175.

Patrinos, H. A. (2016). *Estimating the return to schooling using the Mincer equation.* IZA World of Labor.

Patrinos, H. A., & Metzger, S. (2007). *Returns to education in Mexico: An update.* World Bank (processed).

Patrinos, H. A., & Sakellariou, C. (2006). Economic volatility and returns to education in Venezuela: 1992–2002. *Applied Economics, 38*, 1991–2005.

Patrinos, H. A., & Sakellariou, C. (2007). *"Quality of schooling, returns to schooling and the 1981 vouchers reform in Chile."* World Bank (processed).

Phananiramai, M. (1996). "Changes in women's economic role in Thailand,". In S. Horton (Ed.), *Women and industrialization in Asia.* London: Routledge.

Psacharopoulos, G. (1972). The marginal contribution of education to economic growth. *Economic Development and Cultural Change, 20*(4), 641–658.

Psacharopoulos, G. (1973). *Returns to education: An international comparison.* Amsterdam: Elsevier. San Francisco: Jossey-Bass.

Psacharopoulos, G., & Soumelis, C. (1979). A quantitative analysis of the demand for higher education. *Higher Education, 8*(2), 159–177.

Psacharopoulos, G. (1982). An analysis of the determinants of the social demand for upper secondary education in Portugal. *Economics of Education Review, 2*(3), 233–251.

Psacharopoulos, G., & Loxley, W. (1985). *Diversified secondary education and development: Evidence from Colombia and Tanzania.* Baltimore: Johns Hopkins University Press.

Psacharopoulos, G. (1987). Earnings functions. In P. George (Ed.), *Economics of education: Research and studies* (pp. 218–223). Oxford: Pergamon Press.

Psacharopoulos, G. (1987). The cost-benefit model. In P. George (Ed.), *Economics of education: Research and studies* (pp. 342–347). Oxford: Pergamon Press.

Psacharopoulos, G., & Layard, R. (1979). Human capital and earnings: British evidence and a critique. *Review of Economic Studies, 46*(3), 485–503.

Psacharopoulos, G., & Chu Ng, Y. (1992). *"Earnings and education in Latin America: Assessing priorities for schooling investments," policy research working papers WPS 1056*. World Bank.

Psacharopoulos, G., & Tzannatos, Z. (1992). *Women's employment and pay in Latin America: Overview and methodology*. Washington, DC: The World Bank.

Psacharopoulos, G., & Mattson, R. (1998). Estimating the returns to education: A sensitivity analysis of concepts and methods. *Journal of Educational Planning and Administration, 12*(3), 271–287.

Psacharopoulos, G., & Patrinos, H. A. (2004). Returns to investment in education: A further update. *Education Economics, 12*(2), 111–134.

Psacharopoulos, G., & Patrinos, H. A. (Eds.). (1994). *Indigenous people and poverty in Latin America: An empirical analysis*. Washington, DC: World Bank.

Psacharopoulos, G., & Patrinos, H. A. (2018). Returns to investment in education: A decennial review of the global literature. *Education Economics, 26*(5), 445–458.

Sakellariou, C. (2006). Education policy reform, local average treatment effect and returns to schooling from instrumental variables in the Philippines. *Applied Economics, 38*, 473–481.

Schultz, T. P. (1988). Education investment and returns. In H. Chenery, & T. N. Srinivasan (Eds.), *Handbook of development economics* (Vol. 1, pp. 543–630). Amsterdam: North Holland.

Schultz, T. P. (2004). Evidence of returns to schooling in Africa from household surveys: Monitoring and restructuring the market for education. *Journal of African Economies, 13*(2), 95–148.

Schultz, T. W. (1961). Investment in human capital. *American Economic Review, 51*, 1.

Trostel, P., Walker, I., & Woolley, P. (2002). Estimates of the economic return to schooling for 28 countries. *Labour Economics, 9*, 1–16.

Weisbrod, B. (1964). *External benefits of public education and economic analysis*. Princeton: Industrial Relations Section Paper.

Schultz, T. P. (2003). *Evidence of returns to schooling in Africa from household surveys: Monitoring and restructuring the market for education*. Yale University Economic Growth Center. Discussion Paper 875.

Spence, M. (1973). Job market signaling. *Quarterly Journal of Economics, 87*(3), 355–374.

Weiss, A. (1995). Human capital vs. Signalling explanations of wages. *Journal of Economic Perspectives, 9*(4), 133–154.

Willis, R. J. (1986). Wage determinants: A survey and reinterpretation of human capital earnings functions. In O. Ashenfelter, & Layard (Eds.), *Handbook of labour economics*. Amsterdam: North Holland.

Returns to education quality

Mark Hoekstra

Department of Economics, Texas A&M University, College Station, TX, United States

While economists have traditionally considered the role of education quantity in increasing productivity and generating private and perhaps social returns, in the last decade or so the focus has turned to the role of education quality. This emphasis reflects the fact that at any given level of schooling, there are significant differences across schools with respect to peer quality and other important inputs into education production. Moreover, it is clear that parents and students perceive large differences in school quality, as reflected by the efforts taken to attend more selective schools. Understanding whether these schools generate improved cognitive and labor market outcomes is important for several reasons. First, identifying the types of schools that generate benefits is critical for policymakers who must allocate resources to and incentivize attendance across many different types of schools. In addition, understanding the relative effectiveness across schools can speak to the relative importance of the underlying inputs that generate education production such as peer quality and teacher quality, as these factors often vary across schools. Finally, because there is significant sorting of parents and students across schools of different quality, understanding the effects of attending these schools has direct implications for inequality of outcomes later in life.

This article surveys the research on the academic and labor market benefits from attending more selective schools. It does so by first examining the mechanisms through which attending more selective schools can affect cognitive and labor market outcomes. It then discusses the identification problem faced by researchers attempting to estimate causal returns in this literature, as well as the quasi-experimental techniques used in an attempt to demonstrate causality. Finally, it discusses the research on the academic and labor market benefits from attending more selective schools.

Education quality and student outcomes

There are several dimensions of school quality that can lead to improved cognitive and labor market outcomes, including peer quality, teacher quality, class size, and others. Differences in peer quality arise because schools perceived as higher quality attract higher quality peers. The presence of these peers can lead to improved performance directly through peer-to-peer interactions, or indirectly by enabling teachers to teach more effectively and hold students to higher standards. Peer quality is easily quantified in most contexts, and as a result is often used by

The Economics of Education, Second Edition
https://doi.org/10.1016/B978-0-12-815391-8.00005-7

TABLE 5.1 Quasi-experimental evidence on the labor market returns to school quality.

Paper title	Journal (Year)	Author(s)	Research design	Sample	Treatment	Return to school quality
The effect of attending the flagship state university on earnings: A discontinuity-based approach	The Review of Economics and Statistics (2009)	Mark Hoekstra	RD (running variable = SAT)	Applicants to an unnamed flagship university in a large state in the U.S.	Attending a flagship university that had better peers (5%, or 60–95 points higher on SAT) and somewhat higher per-pupil spending (6%)	20% higher earnings for white men
Returns to education quality for low-Skilled students: Evidence from a discontinuity	Journal of labor Economics (2014)	Serena Canaan, Pierre Mouganie	RD (running variable = exit exam score)	Low-skilled French high schoolers	Attending a more selective college that had better peers (13–14% better baccalaureate scores) and more STEM majors (19-23 pp, 54%)	12.5% increase in earnings; no effect on years of schooling
The Learning and early labor market effects of college quality: A regression discontinuity Analysis	Unpublished (2009)	Juan Esteban Saavedra	RD (running variable = college entry exam)	Columbian college applicants	Attending a college with 0.5 standard deviation better peers, 40% more spending, and twice the fraction of Ph.D. faculty	16% higher employment rates; 20% higher earnings; 0.2 standard deviations higher college exit scores
The returns to college admission for academically marginal students	Journal of labor Economics (2014)	Seth Zimmerman	RD(running variable = SAT)	Florida college applicants	Admission to Florida International university; 0.38 year reduction in attendance at community college	22% higher earnings
Elite colleges and upward mobility to top jobs and top incomes	American Economic Review (2019)	Seth Zimmerman	RD (running variable = index of admissions tests outcomes and grades)	Chilean college applicants	Admission to highly-selective, business focused degree programs at the two elite universities in Santiago, Chile	44% increase in leadership positions held and a 51% increase in the probability of attaining a top 0.1% income; effects driven entirely by males from high-tuition private high schools
Black movement: Using discontinuities in admissions to study the effects of college quality and affirmative action	Journal of Development Economics (2018)	Andrew Francis-Tan and Maria Tannuri-Pianto	RD (running variable = entrance exam score)	Brazilian college applicants	Attending university of Brasilia	35 and 18% increases in earnings for male quota and non-quota applicants, respectively
The long-run effects of attending an elite school: Evidence from the United Kingdom	American Economic Journal: Applied Economics (2016)	Damon Clark and Emilia Del Bono	Regression Kink design (running variable = score from end of primary school tests)	Secondary school students from Aberdeen, Scotland in the 1960s	Attending an elite secondary school with peers whose assignment scores are 1.6 standard deviations higher	17% marginally significant increase in earnings for women; 20% reduction in fertility for women

researchers as a proxy for school quality or, more precisely, school selectivity. However, this reliance on peer quality as a proxy for education quality should not be mistaken for the only, or even the primary, mechanism through which school quality can matter. More selective schools also typically employ higher quality teachers, who can improve students' performance. In addition, more selective schools can also differ in other ways, such as having smaller classes, more capable administrators, or better infrastructure.

These differences across schools can lead to increases in human capital formation that are reflected in both cognitive and non-cognitive outcomes. In addition, in higher education there are additional mechanisms through which school quality can affect labor market outcomes. This includes signaling, in which students signal their ability and motivation by attending more selective universities (Spence, 1973). Indeed, a natural consequence of rising college graduation rates in recent decades may well be for employers to use college quality as a signal of ability, rather than years (i.e., quantity) of education. Attending more selective universities can also result in increased access to professional networks, which can help improve labor market outcomes. We note, however, that while there has been some progress in sorting out the importance of these alternative mechanism, most research has focused on estimating reduced-form effects that are causal under plausible assumptions.

Assessing the causal returns to education quality

Estimating the benefits from attending more selective, higher quality schools is difficult because the students who do so also differ in other ways. In lower education in the United States, these differences arise largely due to attendance zones, where students attend schools with other children from their neighborhood. Outside the United States, there is also selection due to tracking and school admission policies that allocate slots in more selective schools on the basis of test performance. In higher education, selection into more selective schools occurs at the application, admission, and enrollment stage of the college selection decision. As a result, it is difficult to distinguish between the effect of enrolling at a more selective university from being the type of student who is likely to do so.

To overcome the potential bias due to selection into better, more selective schools, researchers have used a variety of strategies. While some research used structural modeling (e.g., Brewer, Eide, & Ehrenberg, 1999), much of the early research used a selection-on-observables approach that aimed to control for as many confounding characteristics as possible or used propensity score matching to compare individuals who had similar observed characteristics. Other studies took this approach one step farther by comparing twins (Behrman, Rosenzweig, & Taubman, 1996) or by including controls for either applicant behavior or admission judgments by schools in an effort to control for other factors (Berkowitz & Hoekstra, 2011; Dale & Krueger, 2002, 2014).

However, most recent studies have used quasi-experimental research designs that exploit as-good-as-random variation in enrollment decisions driven by external factors, rather than choices made by students or their parents. The most common of these approaches is a regression discontinuity design. This design uses the fact that many schools use admission cutoffs to determine admission. Under certain conditions, applicants on either side of the cutoff are expected to be similar in all ways except that those just above the cutoff are more likely to enroll at the more selective school. Consequently, many of these studies effectively compare students who barely gained admission to more selective and arguably higher quality schools than those who were barely rejected. In addition, some studies make use of lotteries that are used to allocate students to open slots in oversubscribed schools. These studies relate closely to the literatures on school choice and charter schools.

Benefits to attending more selective middle and high schools

The existing evidence on middle and high school quality focuses almost exclusively on pre-labor market outcomes, such as test scores and college enrollment. Overall, the quasi-experimental evidence on this question is mixed. In particular, results from the United States provide limited evidence of positive benefits from attending more selective schools. Some evidence comes from Chicago, where lotteries were used to determine admission to academically advanced but oversubscribed schools. Cullen and Jacob (2007) and Cullen, Jacob, and Levitt (2006) find no evidence that lottery winners who attended elementary schools or high schools with better performing peers resulted in any systematic improvements in academic performance, though they did find winners at the high school level reported fewer disciplinary incidents and arrests. Regression discontinuity evidence on the effect of attending elite exam schools is provided by Abdulkadiroglu, Angrist, and Pathak (2014) for New York City and Boston schools, and by Dobbie and Fryer (2014) for New York City schools. Abdulkardiroglu, Angrist, and Pathak (2014) report little evidence of an average increase in seventh and eighth grade test scores or PSAT and SAT scores, and both studies report no positive average effects on college enrollment, college quality, or college graduation despite increases in peer quality of 0.2–0.5 standard deviations. Shi (2019) uses cutoffs from a quota-based admission procedure in North Carolina that induces barely-admitted students to study with peers who score nearly one standard deviation higher in math. She

also finds little evidence of an increase in SAT scores. However, she does find that those who attended the better schools went to colleges that awarded a larger share of STEM degrees, a result driven by students who attended lower quality sending schools. Deming, Hastings, Kane, and Staiger (2014) use a school lottery in Charlotte-Mecklenburg schools to look at the effect of attending one's first-choice school. They find a significant increase in college attainment for those who do, and show that gains are concentrated among those whose neighborhood schools were of low quality.

The most closely related research from a developed country outside the US is Clark (2010), who uses a regression discontinuity design to study the benefits from attending selective high schools in the UK He finds that any subsequent increases in test scores are small at best, though he does show some positive effects on university enrollment.

Much of the evidence on the benefits from attending more selective middle and high schools comes from developing countries. In Mexico, Fabregas (2017) studies the effects of attending better middle schools with higher achieving peers and a higher fraction of teachers in an incentive plan using assignment based on the outcome of a placement exam. She finds this leads students to improve their Spanish standardized test scores. However, she also finds that these students have lower GPAs, are less likely to earn a middle school completion certificate, score lower on indices of perseverance and college aspiration, and are more likely to enter a vocational track. This finding echoes the finding of DeJanvry, Dustan, and Sadoulet (2017), who look at the effects of elite high school attendance in Mexico. They show that winning admission to an elite school increases test scores by 0.12 standard deviations but increases the risk of high school dropout by 7.7% points. Duflo, Dupas, and Kremer (2011) show that primary school students in Kenya who were barely assigned to classrooms with high-achieving peers had no better performance on math and literacy tests than those who barely missed assignment to those classrooms. Similarly, Lucas and Mbiti (2014) show that despite attending elite schools in Kenya in which peers scored one-half of a standard deviation higher on tests, students do not seem to benefit with respect to test scores.

There is also considerable evidence from China, where admission to more selective schools is typically determined by exam scores, which generates the discontinuities that can be used to identify causal effects. Park, Shi, Hsieh, and An (2015) show regression discontinuity evidence that attending the most selective high school increases college entrance exam scores by 0.21 standard deviations. Zhang (2016) uses data from a lottery that determined admission to elite middle schools in a Chinese city and finds no effects on academic performance. Hoekstra, Mouganie, and Wang (2018) find mixed regression discontinuity evidence across different tiers of school quality, finding positive effects on college entrance exam scores for the most selective Tier I schools but not for other schools.

An important consideration in considering the evidence on whether returns to quality are positive is whether admission to more selective schools results in behavioral changes by students or parents. Pop-Eleches and Urquiola (2013) use a regression discontinuity design to show that attending more selective high schools and tracks within Romanian high schools—which is associated with a 0.1 standard deviation increase in peer quality—leads to a 0.05 standard deviation increase in performance on the Baccalaureate exam. They also show significant behavioral responses. Even within school, teachers with higher certification sort into classrooms and tracks with better students such that the marginal student does not have a better teacher. They also show that students barely admitted to the better schools or tracks receive less homework-related help from their parents and perceive themselves as weaker than their peers.

One pattern seen throughout many but not all studies in this area is that females attending more selective schools seem to benefit more relative to males. This pattern has been shown to be true across a range of contexts including China (Hoekstra et al., 2018), North Carolina (Deming et al., 2014), Mexico (Fabrega, 2017), Trinidad & Tobago (Jackson, 2010), India (Dasgupta, Mani, Sharma, & Singhal, 2017), and the United Kingdom (Clark & Del Bono, 2016). This suggests that girls respond more to the improved inputs at more selective schools than boys do.

Given the mixed findings on whether attending more selective schools leads to improved performance on standardized tests and college entrance exams, it is important to consider that these schools can be different with respect to peer quality, teacher quality, administration quality, class size, and other attributes. Differences in these inputs across different admission thresholds can potentially explain the mixed findings. A subset of these studies offer insights into which inputs seem to generate positive returns, and which do not. For example, Jackson (2013) estimates both the benefit from attending more selective schools and the impact of higher quality peers in the same setting of Trinidad & Tobago. He shows that increased peer quality can account for only 10% of the average improvement in high school graduation exam scores across the cutoff. Similarly, Hoekstra et al. (2018) show within a district in China that while there are significant discontinuities in peer quality across several school cutoffs, the only increases in exam exit exam scores occur when there are also significant discontinuities in teacher quality at those cutoffs. This echoes findings by Lai, Sadoulet, and De Janvry (2011), who use a preference-based random assignment of students in Beijing schools to show that estimates of school quality are highly correlated with measures of teacher quality in China. Combined with the other evidence suggesting that attending schools with better peers may not lead to improved outcomes, this suggests that peer quality seems unlikely to be the primary driver of returns to school quality at the primary and secondary levels. Thus, while peer quality has been and remains the most easily measured school characteristic that varies across admission thresholds, the overall pattern of findings in this literature seem to suggest that other inputs are likely central in generating any positive cognitive benefits from attending more selective schools.

Finally, estimates of the long-run benefits of attending more selective high schools comes from Clark and Del Bono (2016) and Estrada and Gignoux (2017). Clark and Del Bono (2016) used variation induced by the school assignment formula in the UK to show that elite high school attendance led to a significant increase in completed education, though they only find a positive effect on income for females. They also show that elite school attendance reduced female fertility. Estrada and Gignoux (2017) find stronger evidence of positive returns to elite high school in Mexico. Using a similar regression discontinuity design, they demonstrate elite school admission increased future earnings.

Returns to college quality

While most of the literature on the benefits from attending more selective primary and secondary schools examines cognitive outcomes such as standardized tests, the literature on college quality has focused primarily on labor market outcomes. Papers using selection-on-observables approaches find mixed evidence. Dale and Krueger (2002, 2014) use a design that makes use of two comparisons. The first is to compare students who are admitted to similarly selective institutions, but choose to enroll at institutions of different selectivity. The second is to compare students who choose to apply to similar types of institutions, but who enroll at institutions of differing quality. Using these

approaches, they find little evidence of positive labor market returns for men across the range of relatively selective institutions examined (mean SAT = 1180), though they do find effects for those who come from low-income families. In contrast, Black and Smith (2004, 2006) use matching and other selection-on-observables techniques and find evidence of positive college quality effects. Andrews, Li, and Lovenheim (2016) use a selection-on-observables approach in which they control for observed student characteristics such as race, Title I status, English proficiency, free/reduced price lunch status, high school test scores, relative rank within high school, and other high school characteristics. They estimate that graduating from Texas A&M and UT-Austin increases earnings by 21.2 and 11.5%, respectively, compared to attending non-flagship institutions. They find that returns to attending UT-Austin increase across the earnings distribution, while returns fall across the earnings distribution for Texas A&M graduates.

By comparison to the selection-on-observables literature, quasi-experimental research has consistently found positive and significant returns to college quality. These studies are summarized in Table 5.1. Hoekstra (2009) uses an admissions cutoff at a large unnamed flagship state university and estimates that men who (barely) attended the flagship earned approximately 20% more than those who just fell short of the admission cutoff. Relative to the flagship, the next-most-selective state universities had median SAT scores 65 to 90 points lower. Zimmerman (2014) also estimates large returns for students at the margin of entering four-year institutions. Using an admission discontinuity for the least selective four-year university in Florida, he estimates that four-year enrollment generates returns of 22% at ages 26 to 32. This large return can be explained in part by other regression discontinuity evidence that access to four-year versus two-year college results in higher 4-year graduation rates (Goodman, Hurwitz, & Smith, 2017).

Quasi-experimental evidence from outside the United States also indicates positive returns to college quality. Saavedra (2009) uses a regression discontinuity approach in Colombia to show that applicants who were barely admitted to a top-ranked college were 16% more likely to be employed one year after college, with the strongest effects for low-income applicants. Canaan and Mouganie (2018) examine returns to college and program quality by comparing students in France who barely passed and failed a high school exit exam. They show that barely passing was associated with no change in education quantity, but resulted in an increase in college quality and in the probability of a STEM major, as well as a 12.5% increase in earnings at the age of 27–29. This finding of positive returns for those near the margin of four-year university echoes the finding of Zimmerman (2014) who found similarly positive effects in the United States. Zimmerman (2018) uses a regression discontinuity design to show that admission to elite business-focused degree programs in Chile increases the number of leadership positions held in top firms by 44% and the probability of attaining a top 0.1% income by 51%. He further shows that all of these gains are driven by male applicants from high-tuition private high schools, along with further evidence suggesting some of these gains could be due to peer ties formed between college classmates from similar backgrounds. Finally, Francis-Tan and Tannuri-Pianto (2018) use a regression discontinuity in admissions to look at the effect of admission to a top university on years of education, college completion, and earnings four years after graduation. They estimate that admission increased earnings by 10%.

There is also evidence that college quality nets a return on the so-called marriage market. Kaufmann, Mesner, and Solis (2013) use a regression discontinuity design to show that attending a higher-ranked university program in Chile leads to an increase in partner quality.

While the quasi-experimental evidence from the United States and elsewhere indicates that there are large returns to college quality, it is less clear whether these effects are driven by increased human capital formation, signaling value, or access to professional networks. There is some evidence of increased human capital; Saavedra (2009) finds that applicants just above the cutoff for a top-ranked college in Colombia score 0.2 standard deviations higher on a college exit test. On the other hand, as noted above, Zimmerman (2018) finds evidence that social networks may be an important mechanism in Chile. Finally, MacLeod, Riehl, Saavedra, and Urquiola (2017) show using quasi-experimental evidence in Colombia that the introduction of a new measure of individual skill reduces the return to college reputation. As a result, while there is some evidence in favor of each mechanism, much work remains in assessing the relative importance of human capital, signaling, and networks in generating positive labor market returns to school quality.

In addition, while researchers have made significant progress in estimating the private returns to education quality, less is known about how the market for school quality interacts with larger issues such as income inequality and intergenerational mobility. Yet these are critical societal issues in which school quality likely plays an important role. Additional research can promote a better understanding of important factors that can increase or diminish mobility, and perpetuate or reduce income disparities.

References

Abdulkadiroğlu, A., Angrist, J., & Pathak, P. (2014). The elite illusion: Achievement effects at Boston and New York exam schools. *Econometrica, 82*(1), 1137–1196.

Andrews, R. J., Jing, L., & Lovenheim, M. F. (2016). Quantile treatment effects of college quality on earnings: Evidence from administrative data in Texas. *Journal of Human Resources, 51*(1), 200–238.

Behrman, J. R., Rosenzweig, M. R., & Paul, T. (1996). College choice and wages: Estimates using data on female twins. *The Review of Economics and Statistics, 78*(4), 672–685.

Berkowitz, D., & Hoekstra, M. (2011). Does high school quality matter? Evidence from admissions data. *Economics of Education Review, 30*(2), 280–288.

Black, D. A., & Smith, J. A. (2004). How robust is the evidence on the effects of college quality? Evidence from matching. *Journal of Econometrics, 121*(1–2), 99–124.

Black, D. A., & Smith, J. A. (2006). Estimating the returns to college quality with multiple proxies for quality. *Journal of Labor Economics, 24*(3), 701–728.

Brewer, D. J., Eide, E. R., & Ehrenberg, R. G. (1999). Does it pay to attend an elite private college? Cross-cohort evidence on the effects of college type on earnings. *Journal of Human Resources, 34*(1), 104–123.

Canaan, S., & Mouganie, P. (2018). Returns to education quality for low-skilled students: Evidence from a discontinuity. *Journal of Labor Economics, 36*(2), 395–436.

Clark, D. (2010). Selective schools and academic achievement. *The B.E. Journal of Economic Analysis & Policy, 10*(1), 1–40.

Clark, D., & Del Bono, E. (2016). The long-run effects of attending an elite school: Evidence from the United Kingdom. *American Economic Journal: Applied Economics, 8*(1), 150–176.

Cullen, J. B., & Jacob, B. A. (2007). Is gaining access to selective elementary schools gaining ground? Evidence from randomized lotteries. In *The problems of disadvantaged youth: An economic perspective* (pp. 43–84). University of Chicago Press.

Cullen, J. B., Jacob, B. A., & Levitt, S. (2006). The effect of school choice on participants: Evidence from randomized lotteries. *Econometrica, 74*(5), 1191–1230.

Dale, S. B., & Krueger, A. B. (2002). Estimating the payoff to attending a more selective college: An application of selection on observables and unobservables. *Quarterly Journal of Economics, 117*(4), 1491–1527.

Dale, S. B., & Krueger, A. B. (2014). Estimating the effects of college characteristics over the career using administrative earnings data. *Journal of Human Resources, 49*(2), 323–358.

Dasgupta, U., Mani, S., Shartma, S., & Singhal, S. (2017). *Cognitive socioemotional, and behavioral returns to college quality.* Working paper.

De Janvry, Alain, A. D., & Sadoulet, E. (2017). Flourish or fail? The risky reward of elite high school admission in Mexico city. *Journal of Human Resources, 52*(3), 756–799.

Deming, D. J., Hastings, J. S., Kane, T. J., & Staiger, D. O. (2014). School choice, school quality, and postsecondary attainment. *The American Economic Review, 104*(3), 991–1013.

Dobbie, W., & Fryer, R. G., Jr. (2014). The impact of attending a school with high-achieving peers: Evidence from the New York City exam schools. *American Economic Journal: Applied Economics, 6*(3), 58–75.

Duflo, E., Dupas, P., & Kremer, M. (2011). Peer effects, teacher incentives, and the impact of tracking: Evidence from a randomized evaluation in Kenya. *The American Economic Review, 101*(5), 1739–1774.

Estrada, R., & Gignoux, J. (2017). Benefits to elite schools and the expected returns to education: Evidence from Mexico City. *European Economic Review, 95*, 168–194.

Fabregas, R. (2017). *A better school but a worse position? The effects of marginal middle school admissions in Mexico city.* Working paper.

Francis-Tan, A., & Tannuri-Pianto, M. (2018). Black Movement: Using discontinuities in admissions to study the effects of college quality and affirmative action. *Journal of Development Economics, 135*, 97–116.

Goodman, J., Hurwitz, M., & Smith, J. (2017). Access to 4-year public colleges and degree completion. *Journal of Labor Economics, 35*(3), 829–867.

Hoekstra, M. (2009). The effect of attending the flagship state university on earnings: A discontinuity-based approach. *The Review of Economics and Statistics, 91*(4), 717–724.

Hoekstra, M., Mouganie, P., & Wang, Y. (2018). Peer quality and the academic benefits to attending better schools. *Journal of Labor Economics, 36*(4), 841–884.

Jackson, C., & Kirabo. (2010). Do students benefit from attending better schools? Evidence from rule-based student assignments in Trinidad and Tobago. *Economic Journal, 120*(549), 1399–1429.

Jackson, C., & Kirabo. (2013). Can higher-achieving peers explain the benefits to attending selective schools? Evidence from Trinidad and Tobago. *Journal of Public Economics, 108*, 63–77.

Kaufmann, K., Maria, M., Messner, M., & Solis, A. (2013). *Returns to elite higher education in the marriage market: Evidence from Chile.* Working Paper.

Lai, F., Sadoulet, E., & De Janvry, A. (2011). The contributions of school quality and teacher qualifications to student performance evidence from a natural experiment in Beijing middle schools. *Journal of Human Resources, 46*(1), 123–153.

Lucas, A. M., & Mbiti, I. M. (2014). Effects of school quality on student achievement: Discontinuity evidence from Kenya. *American Economic Journal: Applied Economics, 6*(3), 234–263.

MacLeod, W. B., Riehl, E., Saavedra, J. E., & Urquiola, M. (2017). The Big Sort: College reputation and labor market outcomes. *American Economic Journal: Applied Economics, 9*(3), 223–261.

Park, A., Shi, X., Hsieh, C.-tai, & An, X. (2015). Magnet high schools and academic performance in China: A regression discontinuity design. *Journal of Comparative Economics, 43*(4), 825–843.

Pop-Eleches, C., & Urquiola, M. (2013). Going to a better school: Effects and behavioral responses. *The American Economic Review, 103*(4), 1289–1324.

Saavedra, J. E. (2009). *The learning and early labor market effects of college quality: A regression discontinuity analysis.* Working paper.

Shi, Y.. 2019Forthcoming. (in press)"Who benefits from selective education? Evidence from elite boarding school admissions." Economics of Education Review, https://www.sciencedirect.com/science/article/pii/S0272775719300901.

Spence, M. (1973). Job market signaling. *Quarterly Journal of Economics, 87*(3), 355–374.

Zhang, H. (2016). Identification of treatment effects under imperfect matching with an application to Chinese elite schools. *Journal of Public Economics, 142*, 56–82.

Zimmerman, S. D. (2014). The returns to college admission for academically marginal students. *Journal of Labor Economics, 32*(4), 711–754.

Zimmerman, S. D. (2018). Elite colleges and upward mobility to top jobs and top incomes. *The American Economic Review, 109*(1), 1–47.

6

Heterogeneity in the returns to higher education

Ian Walker

Department of Economics, Lancaster University Management School and IZA, Bonn, Germany

Introduction

There is considerable research on the returns to education. In recent ears some progress has been made in estimating the returns to particular types of education — in particular higher education (HE). Several contributions have attempted to estimate heterogeneity across higher education subjects (ie by major) and even by institution (HEI). This chapter reviews work on the returns to HE, and contributes to the UK strand of this literature.

In the UK context, heterogeneity in returns is of particular interest because of the nature of the student loan system. This now takes the form of an income contingent loan with forgiveness. There are three elements of subsidy inherent in the system: no debt is collected until earnings hit a threshold; the interest rate is, at least on average, below market rates; and after 30 years any unpaid debt is forgiven. The operation of this implies that courses which provide modest returns will attract larger subsidies than subjects that offer high returns. Personal debt arising from student loans has steadily risen in recent years in the UK (although less so in Scotland which has retained zero up-front fees), and in much of the English-speaking world.[1] The most recent graduating college cohort in the UK (excluding Scotland) has incurred approximately £28,000 of student debt associated with their tuition fees, plus up to

---

[1] The USA has always charged "college" fees and these fees have risen markedly in recent years especially for the most academically selective institutions (see, for example, Hoxby, 2019). UK HEI fees (excluding Scotland) have risen more recently. Australia and New Zealand also have income contingent loan systems although neither country experienced the Great Financial Crisis to the same degree as most other countries. Australia has a large threshold before repayment starts but no forgiveness. New Zealand has a modest repayment income threshold and has, very recently, abolished fees for some part of HE. Ireland abolished HE fees some time ago. No EU countries (with the exception of Hungary) have economically significant fees or charges for HE — indeed, some have extensive provision of grants to cover subsistence costs. See Barr et al. (2019) for further details of international comparisons and developments.

£18,000 associated with their subsistence expenses (that arguably might have been incurred in the absence of attending university). In the US recent graduates average roughly US$30,000 of debt — although fees (or at least the sticker price) vary considerable across institutions, and the national total exceeds $1.4 trillion, a figure that some claim (FT April 9, 2017) represents an economic bubble which could have substantial negative effects for future generations. Particular concern has been expressed over US default rates (estimated to be 18%). An important difference between the US and elsewhere is that the US debt is typically mortgage style (known as time based repayment loans, TBRL) — the debt is repaid monthly at a constant rate until it is fully repaid, usually in 10 years. Most of the concern in the US is over former students being able to meet these payments. Elsewhere, loans are income contingent and collected via the tax system.

In addition to concerns over the public finances and their macroeconomic implications,[2] these numbers beg an important microeconomic question: is taking on substantial student loan debt to (possibly) obtain a college degree a sound financial investment? Although this is a simple question it has a complicated answer which depends on a variety of factors, such as the student's major, the HEI attended, ability, probability of dropping out, among many others. This paper aims to outline the evidence around these factors. Thus, this paper is concerned with a range of issues surrounding the effects of, and funding of, Higher Education with a focus on the UK.

HE in the UK is usually pursued from age 18, or soon thereafter, at over 150 Higher Education Institutions (HEIs), some very small and specialized, which are collectively referred to as universities. Higher education participation rates are over 40% of the cohort and this has grown dramatically in the last three decades. The old funding model was that central government provided extensive direct funding to HEIs, there were no tuition fees, and students received maintenance grants to support themselves during studies (although these were subject to extensive means testing against parental incomes). Course fees in England (less so in Wales and Northern Ireland where the devolved administrations have pursued their freedom over spending to impose lower fees, and Scotland have chosen to have zero fees) have been dramatically increased (and public funding has almost been eliminated) since 2010. This was part of a post-recession austerity drive, but was accompanied by a comprehensive, sophisticated, and highly subsidized, student loan program that supports access, especially for low parental income students. Take-up of these loans is high and repayments are income contingent with the balance after 30 years being written off. As a result, demand for university is relatively tuition fee inelastic, and there is little evidence that fees have resulted in any fall in participation—either overall or for low SES students (see Murphy et al., 2017), and this has not been the case in Scotland where low SES participation has fallen relative to higher SES participation.

The UK offers a convenient laboratory for HE research since UG study is highly concentrated, throughout the duration of study, on a single major. Courses are usually specialized where a single narrow major is often pursued exclusively. Dropping-out is relatively scarce (around 8% across the sector). HEIs in England, (and

---

[2] The ONS in the UK has recently recommended that the treatment of student debt in public finances should be changed. Previously, student debt did not appear in national accounts until the forgiveness point had been reached - so, to date, no student debt has reached this maturity. Now, the debt is to be counted as part of national debt as it accrues. It remains to be seen whether money markets had already priced-in the anticipated debt.

Wales and Northern Ireland) offer undergraduate courses that are typically 3 years duration (Scotland has many 4 year courses), studied mostly on a full-time basis and mostly straight from senior high school.[3] Although the UK is small, and so proximity to university is much higher than in many other countries, the majority of students move away from their parental homes to study HE, and most of those that do will form (or join) households elsewhere when they graduate and start work. Unlike the US, UK undergraduate professional courses such as law, medicine, and management are available across most HEIs.

The UK HE sector is much less homogeneous that the HE sector in the US The UK equivalent of the US Ivy League is the so-called "Russell Group" (RG) of HEIs — 25 institutions including ancient ones such as Oxford and Cambridge, many of the top London institutions, as well as the major provincial "redbrick" HEIs (named for the appearance of their largely Victorian architecture). These are research intensive institutions, they are large, they offer a full range of subjects, and they attract students from all over the UK and many from outside the UK The "Old" non_Russell HEIs are often refereed to ask "Pre-92", and comprise another 25 institutions that were founded before 1992 — the date when the former Polytechnics became able to grant their own degrees and could refer to themselves as universities. These are also full function HEIs but are not as focused on a research mission; many are old but not ancient and they include the HEIs that were founded in the 1960's. The "New" HEIs are former Polytechnics and, together with newer entrants, comprise approximately one hundred institutions that vary considerably in size and range of functions. Some are small and specialized — for example on music or other performing/creative arts.

HEIs are independent of government. Government has no control over the curriculum, and has, since 2014, exercised no control over student numbers across the sector, by course type, or by HEI. HEIs have also been free to set their fees within a range from £6000 to £9000 per annum (figures that have increased modestly since 2014 when they were set). While, the Minister for Universities has stated that he expected £9000 to be exceptional, in fact almost all institutions were immediately attracted to the £9000 focal point for almost all majors. Discounts on the sticker price are available but are usually both means tested and contingent on high school achievement. There is considerable obfuscation over the extent to which actual tuition costs vary by major differ considerable and firm figures are hard to find - it is thought that the costs of running most Arts, Social Science, and Management courses are below the £6000 lower bound for annual fees; while costs for most STEM subjects are likely to be well above the upper bound for fees; and those for medical, veterinary and dentistry courses are likely to be considerable higher than that (and these courses are invariably 5 years duration). The implication of the choice, by all universities, to engage in widespread cross-subsidization is that the large number of STEM (and the small number of medical/dental) students are being cross-subsidized by the larger number of low-cost students. The current government fees review has (so far) been largely silent on this and the regulator, the Office for Students, has not considered the fairness of a situation where low-cost students are subsidizing high cost ones who are, on average, going to enjoy higher levels of lifetime income. Indeed, the biggest cross-subsidies go from the successful upper tail of Arts students (who earn sufficient to not enjoy large subsidies) to the less successful lower tail STEM students

---

[3] This has become more likely to be true since mature students were disadvantaged in the student loan scheme.

II. Private and social returns to education

who do badly in their studies and may not earn sufficient to make loan repayments early enough to completely repay their loans.[4] In the meantime: institutions who have a small proportion of STEM and medical students can be extremely profitable; while others are experiencing financial difficulties in the face of competition for students from more prestigious institutions at the same time as English cohort sizes are falling; and political change makes the UK a less attractive destination for EU students and even for those from further afield.

The economic value of degrees

HE costs and private returns are central to associated funding issues. The common perception is that costs are tuition fees and the benefits are the earnings differential for having a degree relative to not. However, this is only a partial view — the opportunity cost of studying for a degree is the earnings that one could have earned otherwise and such opportunity costs would probably considerably exceed the actual tuition fees for most English students, even at minimum wage. Moreover, the benefits to the student is not just the pecuniary effect of HE on the individual student's earnings, but also includes any non-pecuniary benefits. Some of these are private benefits that are enjoyed immediately— the consumption value of a stimulating and engaging course. Others will be discounted future benefits. For example, there is a well documented effect of education on health (although there is little evidence that directly relates to higher education in particular). We know almost nothing about these non-financial effects: but it seems likely that they might vary by subject studied (major) and the quality of teaching, and by student aptitudes and preferences which

will vary by prior teaching quality, and parental background. The potential for quantitatively significant non-pecuniary benefits to be an important driver of student course choice is suggested by the (albeit, limited) available evidence that we have from research on the determinants of student choices.

However, it is difficult to put a lot of weight on the student choice literature for four reasons. First, the pecuniary returns occur in the future across the working lifecycle and these might be (heavily) discounted, while the opportunity costs of foregone earnings are borne early in the working life, giving rise to a net present value that might be lower than the raw earnings data might suggest. A weak financial private rate of return might be reinforced by credit market imperfections associated with debt incurred to finance human capital being inherently unsecured. It might be further weakened by the potential for young people to be time inconsistent in their decision-making. There is now an increasing volume of empirical research that points to young people being "hyperbolic" rather than "exponential" discounters leading them to make decisions that they ultimately regret. Secondly, the non-pecuniary benefits might be associated with the consumption value arising from the challenge of higher level learning, and the enjoyment of spending a few formative years in a safe environment surrounded by like-minded people. These are enjoyed in the moment and their value is therefore not affected by heavy discounting. The third argument, is that the benefits are uncertain and there is very little information that students can rely on to inform them. Higher education institutions will point to their successes amongst their graduate output and not to the long-left tail of their graduates' earnings. The little quantitative data that is out there refers to the mean outcomes

---

[4] Almost all medical/dental students are successful at university and almost invariably they pursue careers in medicine/dentistry.

and say nothing about differences associated with observable variation in the treatment (for example, across majors and across institutions which themselves exhibit a wide variation in student selectivity and in their own productivity) and in the treated (the students themselves are likely to vary in their degree of college readiness and their own non-cognitive skills and traits that might complement cognitive skills that a degree might offer, especially majors that are vocational in nature or offer high demand skills). In contrast, the costs are probably substantially less uncertain. In England (although not in the US) the sticker price is highly correlated with the actual price paid since discounts are smaller and less commonplace than in the US where alumni finance is often used to drive a large wedge between sticker and final prices. Given the large unexplained variance in private returns (i.e. wage rates) the role of attitudes to risk also play a role.

Importantly, the income contingent nature of the loan scheme insures students against the financial risks they face surrounding the match component of returns — in particular, how well they will do in their chosen course. Moreover, the loan scheme provides the largest subsidies to human capital investments that offer the lowest mean return. This tips the balance further in favor of majors that offer low private financial returns, as well as being high risk (for example, creative arts degrees). The income contingent nature of fees, which might well have encouraged low SES students to access HE, might also have encouraged students to take lower return subjects than would previously the case.

In addition, UK degrees are "classified" into "first class, upper second, lower second, third,

and pass" and there are large labor market wage differentials associated with better quality outcomes.[5] Since, within a course, there is relatively little variation in the quality of students on entry, the variation in quality on exit is largely due to the extent of individual engagement with studying. Students might now be less inclined to make the effort to excel in their studies because the highest loan subsidies are available to the lowest earning, and so weakest outcome, students. It would appear, from the size of wage differentials associated with degree class that there are large returns to student effort. Of course, the cost of effort is also endured in the moment so the hyperbolic nature of discounting will not affect this source of disutility.

The literature on the returns to HE (which is referred to in the US literature as "the college premium") is driven entirely by the "private benefits" of HE associated with the higher wage rates or earnings of graduates versus non-graduates. It ignores aspects of costs that could be very important, it ignores non-pecuniary private returns, and it ignores "social" costs and benefits. Moreover, it offers only a very narrow view on what is a very precise concept — the net present value calculation of private net (of tax, welfare, and loan subsidy) financial returns. Nonetheless, even this narrow view is itself very difficult to measure.

Estimating the college premium

The ingredients of a measure of the college premium is the wages (or earnings) of graduates and of non-graduates. Such data is readily available in many countries — for example, a great deal of research has been done on the US Current

---

[5] Walker and Zhu (2019) provide estimates from LFS data that differentials by degree class have proved, on average, to be stable in the face of the large HE expansion that occurred in the 80's and 90's even though, over this period grades themselves rose on average. This is surprising, since the expansion will have lowered the average quality of students entering the system. It would appear that the students and/or their teachers have increased their productivity and outcomes, in terms of markes skills, are actually better.

Population Survey (CPS) and the American Community Surveys (ACSs); while in the UK extensive use has been made of the Labor Force Survey (LFS).

An early example of LFS UK research is Walker and Zhu (2008). This work looks at the returns to UG (and PG) and reports estimates of the UK "college premium" for young graduates across successive cohorts from large cross-section datasets for the UK pooled from 1994 to 2006—a period when the higher education participation rate increased dramatically. The modest growth in relative labor demand over this period suggests that graduate supply considerably outstripped demand which ought to imply a fall in the college premium. However, the data showed no statistically significant fall for men (and a statistically insignificant rise for women). Quantile regression results revealed a fall in the premium only for men in the bottom quartile of the distribution of unobserved skills — a fall that was not statistically significant. This work was followed-up in Walker and Zhu

(2013), a report to the Department of Business Innovation and Skills — then the government department responsible for universities. The additional data that was available for the BIS Report resulted in more precise estimates but they were not substantially different from those reported in the earlier paper.

The most recent UK example is Blundell, Green, and Jin (2016) which is also focused on how the average college premium have changed across cohorts. HE participation rates have grown rapidly in recent years, especially the mid 80's to mid '90s, but more slowly from the mid '60s before that. Fig. 6.1 reproduces their headline finding in Blundell et al. (2016) and underlines the puzzle — that the college premium does not, at face value, appear to respond to a large shift in supply of graduates. The figure shows the familiar fact that earnings of graduates rise strongly across the lifecycle relative to that of non-graduates. It also shows that this phenomenon has NOT changed across cohorts despite the huge increase in the supply of

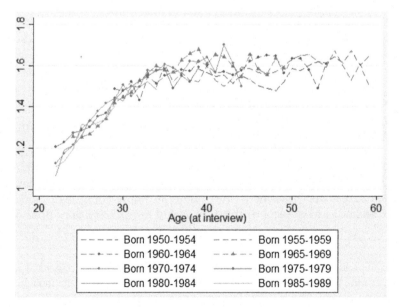

FIG. 6.1 The college premium (ratio of graduate to non-graduate earnings) by age across UK birth cohorts. *Source: Blundell et al. (2016).*

graduates — the age-earnings profiles for each cohort group overlap considerably. In particular, the first three cohort groups were 18 before the big expansion and the last three groups were 18 after the expansion. Yet in their 30's, where the lifecycles of these two groups overlap, the earnings for the pre and post expansion cohorts are very close to one another.

Moreover, across the lifecycle the college premium suggested in this figure is, in present value terms, worth over £250 k. This is consistent with previous estimates of the college premium in the UK that, in simple specifications, report estimates between 25% and 35% where the control group is those that report having A-levels (as in the Walker/Zhu work), and between 35% and 45% where the control group is all those that did not attend HE (as in Blundell et al., 2016). In almost all cases, research finds that the returns to HE for men is lower than that for women - reflecting to poorer opportunities in the labor market for non-graduate women compare to non-graduate men.

It is well known that OLS estimates, such as those in the Walker/Zhu and Blundell et al. work, may suffer from bias. In one direction, it may suffer from bias associated with omitted "ability". This is traditionally thought of as biasing the college premium coefficient upwards. In the simplest version of the traditional ability bias story, earnings (w) and schooling are determined (C) by: $w = \beta C + \alpha A + \varepsilon$, and $C = \gamma A + \zeta$, where w is the (log) wage rate, $C = 1$ if the individual has a "college" degree and 0 otherwise, A is unobserved "ability", ε is uncorrelated with C and with A, and ζ is uncorrelated with ε. That is, ζ and w are correlated only through their joint dependence on A. However, A is unobservable so least squares estimates of β in $w = \beta C + v$, where $v = \alpha A + \varepsilon$, will be biased such that plim $(\beta_{OLS}) = \beta + \alpha$ (σ_{AC}/σ_C^2) where σ_C^2 in the variance in C and σ_{AC} is the covariance between C and A - which is not recorded in the data because A is unobservable. If, as seems reasonable, $\gamma > 0$ and $\sigma_{AS} > 0$,

and if $\alpha > 0$, as also seems reasonable, then $\beta_{OLS} > \beta$. That is, OLS estimates of β capture the effects of both C and of any unobservables that are correlated with both C and w, such as A.

The expansion of HE is likely to result in σ_{AS} falling since HE institutions would then be accepting individuals with lower unobserved skills, A. This results in a fall in the estimate of β_{OLS} even if β were constant - that is, we would expect the anticipated fall in the OLS estimate of the college premium (β_{OLS}), in response to the supply of college graduates, to appear to be even larger than the fall in the true effect (β). The only way to reconcile the rise in college graduate supply with the absence of a fall in the OLS estimate of the college premium is if α were also rising. Of course, α, the return to unobserved skill, may not be constant. Indeed, much of the existing literature suggests that α has been rising as well as β. Thus, available OLS estimates are consistent with the view that the return to unobserved skill has been rising in the UK.

There is some suggestion in the literature that such ability, or "selection", bias approximately cancels out the bias associated with measurement error in schooling. The latter is indubitably downwards, in data where education is self-reported and so prone to mis-measurement, because of attenuation. But there is a worry, in this context, that one or both of these sources of bias may be changing over time in ways that are hard to sign on both theoretical and statistical grounds. For example, work is becoming remunerated in more complicated ways and it seems likely that the traditional hourly pay recorded in our data is less good at capturing actual remuneration. Ultimately it is an empirical issue that will be difficult to resolve without additional administrative data.

One approach to dealing with the problem of differential unobserved ability between graduates and non-graduates is to uncover some exogenous variation in the probability having a degree and use this to estimate the effect of a degree. It is unclear how one would be able to do that with the data that is currently available for the UK[6] A second methodology is provided by identical twins — who are (arguably) identical in terms of those unobservables that affect earnings. The twins research compares the earnings within (identical) twin pairs and so differences out the (common) unobserved ability factor. Unfortunately, there is only one UK twins study (see Bonjour et al, 2003), which is based on a very small sample of female only twins. This work finds that the effects of (a year of) education is to raise wages by approximately 8% (which might, heroically, be extrapolated to approximately 25% for a three-year degree). Their figure of 8% is identical to what they obtain by applying least squares to the raw twin data, rather than looking at within-twin differences. This might suggest that the extent of ability bias may be modest. On the other hand since is uses *differences* in self-reported education then measurement error bias might be large and the true return might be larger than this. A third methodology is to attempt to control for a rich set of observable characteristics. Altonji, Elder, and Taber (2005) bases a method for backing out the selection bias on the ability bias argument above (and, 2017, has developed this test). This is relatively straightforward: estimate an earnings premium (Altoni et al. considered the premium to having a college diploma using the US NLSY dataset) either unconditionally or controlling only for basic demographic characteristics, and compare this estimate with the premium one estimates while controlling for ability and factors which might drive selection (test scores, mother's education, etc.). The difference between the two earnings premia is an estimate of the degree of self-selection. Blundell et al. (2004) does something similar to this (as well as exploiting matching and instrumental variable methods) using the 1958 English birth cohort in the NCDS data. This study finds that

least squares provides a relatively tight bound on the earnings effect of a degree. Thus, there are some grounds, based on existing research, for thinking that least squares estimates are a reasonably good guide to the true causal effects of a first degree — at least at this broad level of computing a simple college premium.

Indeed, the report by Belfield et al. (2018) employs the newly available *Longitudinal Education Opportunities* (LEO) dataset, formed from merging the schooling history of all children (NPD) with their HE records (HESA), and their income tax (HMRC) records. Unlike the LFS research where almost no educational attainment information is available apart from higher education, the idea in the LEO data is to exploit the "pre-treatment" schooling cognitive achievements, as recorded by test scores, to better control for, at least, cognitive ability differences across individuals to attempt to drive out selection by ability into HE through reducing the covariance between higher educational attainment and the unobservables. Since the data is administrative it is likely that measurement error in the control variables is minimal so selection bias is the only source of bias that needs to be resolved. This LEO project report does this by exploring the role of control variables on the estimated effect of a bachelor degree on earnings. The LEO cohorts are relatively young and, as Fig. 6.1 suggests, the college premium is lower at young ages relative to higher ages. The definitive change in their estimates, reported below in Table 6.1, indeed occurs when prior attainment controls are added to the model — they find that then the return falls, for men, from 0.22 log points to 0.04, and for women from 0.46 to 0.23. In addition to adding cognitive skill controls, Belfield et al. (2018) also weight the data using estimated inverse probability (of having a degree) in its regression analysis. This IPWRA method is designed to ensure that the "treated"

[6] See Kirkeboen et al. (2016).

TABLE 6.1 LEO estimate of the overall returns to HE at age 29.

	(1)	(2)	(3)	(4)	(5)
Men	0.19***	0.25***	0.22***	0.04***	0.06***
	(0.00)	(0.00)	(0.00)	(0.01)	(0.00)
No. of observations	*2,183,120*	*2,183,120*	*2,183,120*	*2,183,120*	*2,183,120*
No. of individuals	*629,138*	*629,138*	*629,138*	*629,138*	*629,138*
Women	0.44***	0.50***	0.46***	0.23***	0.23***
	(0.00)	(0.00)	(0.00)	(0.00)	(0.00)
No. of observations	*2,619,982*	*2,619,982*	*2,619,982*	*2,619,982*	*2,619,982*
No. of individuals	*731,200*	*731,200*	*731,200*	*731,200*	*731,200*
Cohort/Age start controls	No	Yes	Yes	Yes	Yes
Background characteristics	No	No	Yes	Yes	Yes
Prior attainment	No	No	No	Yes	Yes
IPWRA weight	No	No	No	No	Yes

Note: Table reports derived estimates of the overall impact of HE on annual earnings at age 29 based on the 2002–07 GCSE cohorts, conditional on at least five A*-C GCSEs and on being in sustained employment. Table sequentially adds age, background and prior attainment controls, and finally IPWRA weights. Estimates are in log points, which can be converted into percentage points using the transformation $100 * (e^x - 1)$, where x is the log points estimate.
Source: Belfield et al. (2018) Table 7.

observations with a degree who are a closer match to those that do not have a degree are giving greater weight in the regression. This is an additional method for attempting to control for differences between the treated and controls. While the method only controls for observed variables in all likelihood the observables that determine treatment are correlated with unobservable determinants so it should contribute to the reduction in selection bias.

In the event, using IPWRA has no significant effect on the results for either men or women. One might argue that these estimates themselves fail to control for remaining unobservables and selection bias is not entirely removed. In particular, one might be concerned that there are important non-cognitive abilities that remain in the unobservables and these are correlated with C and with $w|C$. This idea is pursued in Buchmueller and Walker (2019) who use the

age 25 information on earnings (so even earlier than the LEO data), on whether individuals have a degree, and various non-cognitive skills that are recorded in the LSYPE dataset. Table 6.2 shows that adding non-cognitive abilities to the specification does reduce the estimated returns to college but by a much smaller extent than adding cognitive skills controls did in Table 6.1. The fall for men is just 0.002 log points and for women it is 0.005 — neither of which are statistically significant.

Student choice and heterogeneity in the returns to degrees

All of the above does not allow for heterogeneity in the estimate of the college premium. Blundell, Dearden, and Sianesi (2005) was an early attempt to allow for heterogeneity in

TABLE 6.2   LSYPE estimate of the returns to HE at age 25 and non-cognitive skills.

	OLS					
	Pooled		Men		Women	
	(1)	(2)	(1)	(2)	(1)	(2)
Degree	0.115***	0.112***	0.101***	0.099***	0.132	0.127***
	(0.016)	(0.016)	(0.024)	(0.024)	(0.022)	(0.022)
Locus of control		0.023***		0.025***		0.021***
		(0.005)		(0.007)		(0.006)
Conscientiousness		−0.008		−0.025		0.008
		(0.011)		(0.016)		(0.015)
Self-esteem		−0.001		0.001		-0.003
		(0.004)		(0.008)		(0.004)
R-sqr	0.074	0.083	0.071	0.084	0.067	0.076
N	4133	4133	1879	1879	2254	2254

Note: The dependent variable is log of gross hourly wage. Specification (1) does not control for non-cognitive skills, while specification (2) does. Non-cognitive skills included are: Locus of control, a proxy for conscientiousness, and a proxy for self-esteem where the higher the score the more non-cognitive skills the individual has. All specifications include the following additional controls: gender, ethnicity as well as regional dummies. OLS specifications further control for missing values in the sample for degree-observations as well as non-cognitive skill observations (see Section 3). PSM obtains the average treatment effect on treated. All observations are weighted by the most recent LSYPE sample weights. *Source: Buchmueller and Walker (2019).*

returns which contrasted estimates obtained using matching methods with those that relied on instrumental variables. Subsequent work by Walker and Zhu (2008, 2011, and 2013) explored heterogeneity by subject of degree at various levels of aggregation as the LFS data allowed. The 2008 and 2011 paper allowed only for differences by broad group of subjects (STEM, LEM (Law/Economics/Management), Social Studies, and Arts) while the 2013 report allowed for 30 majors. Since this work was based on LFS, unlike Belfield et al. 2018, there was no possibility of controlling for pre-treatment ability controls in any detail, leaving open the possibility of biased estimates. Moreover, the selection issue is now (much) more complicated since students can select into a wide variety of different majors across a wide range if institutions. Selection into each subject (and HEI) might be differently

correlated with unobservable determinants of wages there is no grounds for thinking that LFS research is able to come to a view about the ranking of returns across subject. Ignoring such reservations for the moment, such research does show that STEM and LEM are more strongly correlated with wages than Social Studies; and that Arts degrees have very little correlation with wages, relative to a control with no degree at all. The 2013 report gives a more nuanced view since the accumulation of LFS data meant that cells sizes at the level of 30 subjects were sufficient to provide more detail. For example, within LEM, Economics had by far the highest correlation with wages.

Buchmueller and Walker (2019) also estimate the returns to degrees by subject groups (and by Russell Group HEIs compared to the rest) and compare results that include non-cognitive skill

TABLE 6.3 Returns to Degrees by Subject Group and HEI type.

	OLS						IPWRA					
	All HEIs		Russell group		Other HEI		All HEIs		Russell group		Other HEI	
	(1)	(2)	(1)	(2)	(1)	(2)	(1)	(2)	(1)	(2)	(1)	(2)
All subjects	0.115***	0.112***	0.217***	0.213***	0.063***	0.061**	0.093***	0.087***	0.170***	0.152***	0.038	0.019
	(0.016)	(0.016)	(0.026)	(0.026)	(0.018)	(0.018)	(0.018)	(0.020)	(0.032)	(0.038)	(0.027)	(0.034)
STEM	0.147***	0.143***	0.264***	0.260***	0.104***	0.100***	0.111***	0.103***	0.192***	0.179***	0.087**	0.070*
	(0.022)	(0.022)	(0.038)	(0.038)	(0.024)	(0.024)	(0.022)	(0.024)	(0.041)	(0.044)	(0.031)	(0.036)
Social sciences	0.144***	0.142***	0.228***	0.221***	0.110***	0.111***	0.112***	0.106***	0.175**	0.139*	0.076	0.060
	(0.026)	(0.026)	(0.044)	(0.044)	(0.030)	(0.030)	(0.026)	(0.028)	(0.060)	(0.064)	(0.039)	(0.043)
Arts & humanities	0.021	0.019	0.142***	0.139***	−0.026	−0.027	−0.017	−0.022	0.072	0.048	−0.079*	−0.087*
	(0.024)	(0.024)	(0.042)	(0.042)	(0.026)	(0.026)	(0.027)	(0.028)	(0.049)	(0.048)	(0.039)	(0.039)

Note: The dependent variable is log of gross hourly wage. Specification (1) does not include non-cognitive skills, while specification (2) does. Non-cognitive skills included are: Locus of control, a proxy for conscientiousness, and a proxy for self-esteem (where the higher the score the more non-cognitive skills the individual has). All specifications include the following additional controls: gender, ethnicity as well as regional dummies. OLS specifications further control for missing values in the sample for degree-observations as well as non-cognitive skill observations (for reasoning see Section 3). IPWRA obtains the average treatment effect on treated. All observations are weighted by the most recent LSYPE sample weights.

control variables with results that do not. The IPWRA results are based on a multi-nominal logit model of the probabilities of attending a RG HEI versus the rest, and having a major in the STEM, Social Science and Arts & Humanities groups - based primarily on the individuals A-level (senior high school) subjects studied and attainment in them. It uses the LSYPE cohort who report their earnings at age 25. Table 6.3 below presents the headline results by subject group. Controlling for non-cognitive skills makes little difference to the results (compare cols 1 and 2) except for IPWRA results for RG graduates where the inclusion of non-cognitive skills reduces returns by approximately 0.03 for each subject group. Using IPWRA compared to OLS reduces estimated returns by around 2pp. RG degrees command much higher wages than those from the other mission groups. STEM returns are higher than Social Science, and Arts

offer insignificantly positive returns for RG graduates and large negative returns (both relative to the omitted category of non-graduates).

Recent US research by Altonji, Blom, and Meghir (2012) and Webber (2014) has focused on the ACS which has more detail on the nature of individual experiences of HE since it records detailed major. This work shows similar results as equivalent UK research. A notable advance over the UK LFS, and similar US, research is Britton, Dearden, Shephard, and Vignoles (2016) which uses SLC data merged to HMRC income tax records. SLC records major and HEI for a large majority of UK students. The ingenious feature in this paper was to use the average A-level scores of students by course, obtained from HESA data, to provide, at least at the course level, a control for average student prior ability. Fig. 6.2 shows the highlights of the results — the dots near the horizontal axis are

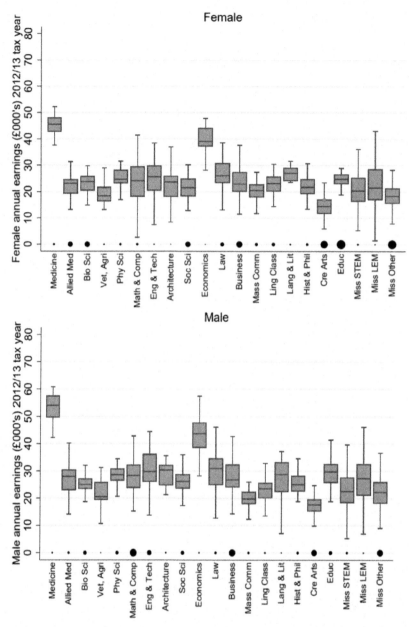

FIG. 6.2 Graduate earnings by subject, controlling for course level selectivity. Notes: Miss = Miscellaneous. The box represents the interquartile range, with the median shown as he horizontal divider. The size of the blobs above the horizontal axis show relative cell sizes. *Source: Britton et al. (2016).*

TABLE 6.4 IPWRA estimates of the college premium by subject group and HEI mission group controlling for course level selectivity.

	IPWRA average treatment effects			OLS		
	Men	Women	Pooled	Men	Women	Pooled
	(1)	(2)	(3)	(4)	(5)	(6)
New	0.075***	−0.071**	−0.007	0.007	0.010	0.003
Social science	(0.029)	(0.031)	(0.025)	(0.020)	(0.023)	(0.015)
New	−0.010	−0.050	−0.040	−0.155***	−0.065***	−0.106***
Arts & humanities	(0.036)	(0.035)	(0.030)	(0.025)	(0.024)	(0.017)
Old	0.161***	−0.047	0.054*	0.038*	−0.053*	−0.001
STEM	(0.031)	(0.037)	(0.028)	(0.022)	(0.028)	(0.017)
Old	0.133***	−0.036	0.045	0.085***	0.032	0.055***
Social science	(0.036)	(0.033)	(0.028)	(0.028)	(0.028)	(0.020)
Old	0.003	−0.156***	−0.077***	−0.090***	−0.121***	−0.110***
Arts & humanities	(0.037)	(0.033)	(0.028)	(0.031)	(0.030)	(0.021)
RG	0.153***	0.039	0.102***	0.115***	0.071***	0.092***
STEM	(0.033)	(0.041)	(0.030)	(0.023)	(0.027)	(0.017)
RG	0.196***	0.049	0.108***	0.109***	0.070**	0.086***
Social science	(0.041)	(0.038)	(0.031)	(0.027)	(0.029)	(0.020)
RG	0.027	−0.119***	−0.065**	−0.104***	−0.072***	−0.084***
Arts & humanities	(0.039)	(0.038)	(0.032)	(0.030)	(0.028)	(0.020)
Female						−0.131***
						(0.009)
Selectivity				0.071***	0.123***	0.097***
				(0.014)	(0.014)	(0.010)
Observations	3950	4083	8138	4072	4089	8161
R^2				0.404	0.355	0.391

IPWRA stands for inverse probability weighted regression adjustment. Robust SE in parentheses, *$p < 0.1$, **$p < 0.05$, ***$p < 0.01$. The observations which are off common support are excluded from the treatment effect models. Other controls include age, age squared, nonwhite, dummies for decade of birth, survey years, and regions. PG and good degree dummies only enter the outcome (wage) equations but not the treatment (selection) equations in the IPWRA specifications. We do not report the coefficients for selectivity in the 1PWRA estimates because there is one coefficient for each potential outcome - too many to report. The same applies to the female dummy.
Source: Walker and Zhu (2018).

proportional to cell sizes — Economics and Medicine have the highest median returns but are very small cells — each representing less than 2% of overall student numbers, while Maths/ Computing, Management, and the Creative Arts each represent more than 15% of overall male number; and Business, Creative Arts, and Education each represent more than 15% of

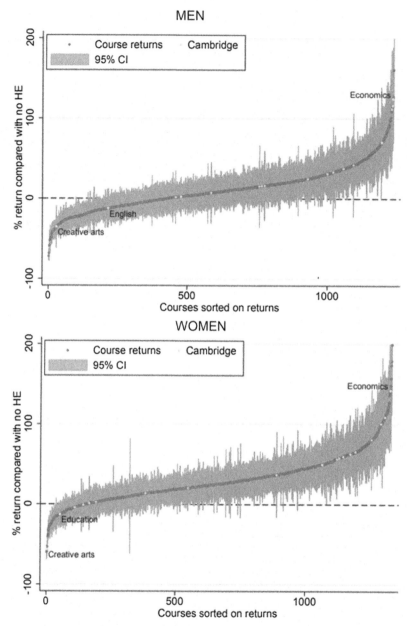

FIG. 6.3 LEO Returns to UG Degree Courses - IPWRA estimates. *Source: Belfield et al. (2018).*

female students. The highest earnings are associated with Medicine and Economics students — subjects which are studied by a very small proportion of students; while Creative Arts, in particular, offer earnings that, for females, are close to full-time minimum wage work, and little better for males, and yet large numbers of students study them.

In the UK, recent work has exploited the more extensive HE information being collected in LFS datasets which, from 2005 onwards, contain the major of study, and contains both major studied and HEI attended, from 2011 onwards. The idea of controlling for selectivity at the course level was also pursued in Walker and Zhu (2018) using LFS data, exploiting both subject studies and HEI attended. The use of the LFS data allows a longer run of cohorts that did the SLC data in Britton et al. (2016), and this paper also adopted to IPWRA method to improve the comparability of treatment and controls. The wage effects of institution and subject types in Table 6.4 suggest that OLS substantially underestimates the effect of attending the more prestigious HEIs for men. The effects of Old and RG STEM are not significantly different from each other, but they are approximately 15% greater than New-STEM. Using OLS for men we find no significant effect of Old-STEM relative to New-STEM and a somewhat smaller effect of RG-STEM For women, Old and RG STEM are not significantly different than New-STEM. There appear to be no significant Arts and Humanities effects for men in RG or Old relative to New. Although, for men, RG-SocSci is large and significantly different from Old-SocSci, which in turn is significantly greater than New-SocSci. The same is true for OLS estimates although these are again considerably underestimated relative to IPWRA.

The most definitive UK research is the recent work by Belfield et al. (2018) using the LEO data. This is based on administrative data on around 7 million students and so allowed much more granular analysis than the LFS does. This LEO work uses IPWRA estimation, much like the Walker and Zhu (2018) work. Fig. 6.3 visualizes the most disaggregated estimates which are ordered by returns from lowest on the left. These estimates are computed at age 29 — and early point in the lifecycle when we expect college premia to be low. The red dots are the point estimate course fixed effects and the gray bars are confidence intervals. The height of the red dots show the returns relative to nongraduates. For men only 60% of the approximately 1200 courses for which estimation is possible (the HMRC impose a minimum cell size of 50 to preserve confidentiality) show positive returns and only 20% show significantly positive returns. For women approximately 50% are significantly positive. Subjects available for Cambridge (an elite UK HEI) are highlighted in yellow and some examples are labeled. Even elite HEIs offer Creative arts courses that yield negative returns.

Conclusion

The evidence that the returns to higher education in both the UK and the US differs greatly by HEI and by subject is overwhelming. These findings have important implications for the implications of the effects of income contingent student loans that have, hitherto, gone unexplored. These differences are so large it is unclear what supports such differentials and why student choices do not respond to reduce them to more plausible levels. This is an important issue for further research.

Acknowledgments

I am indebted to collaborators on the LEO project and to my long time collaborator in education research, Yu Zhu, whose joint work I rely on here.

References

Altonji, J. G., Blom, E., & Meghir, C. (2012). Heterogeneity in human capital investments: High school curriculum, college major, and careers. *Annual Review of Economics, 4*, 185–223.

Altonji, J. G., Elder, T. E., & Taber, C. R. (2005). Selection on observed and unobserved variables: Assessing the effectiveness of catholic schools. *Journal of Political Economy, 113*, 151–184.

Barr, N., Chapman, B., Dearden, L., & Dynarski, S. (2018). *Reflections on the US college loans system: Lessons from*

Australia and England. Centre for applied macroeconomic analysis, Working Paper 29. Crawford School of Public Policy, Australian National University.

Barr, N., Chapman, B., Dearden, L., & Dynarski, S. (2019). The US college loans system: Lessons from Australia and England. *Economics of Education Review, 71,* 32–48.

Belfield, C., Britton, J., Buscha, F., Dearden, L., Dickson, M., van der Erve, L., et al. (2018). *The impact of undergraduate degrees on early-career earnings.* Department of Education Research Report. https://assets.publishing.service.gov. uk/government/uploads/system/uploads/attachment data/file/759278/Theimpactofundergraduatedegreeson early-careerearnings.pdf.

Blundell, R., Dearden, L., & Sianesi, B. (2004). *Evaluating the impact of education on earnings in the uk: models, methods and results from the ncds.* IFS Working Paper, WP03/20.

Blundell, R., Dearden, L., & Sianesi, B. (2005). Evaluating the effect of education on earnings: Models, methods and results from the national child development survey. *Journal of the Royal Statistical Society: Series A, 168,* 473–512.

Blundell, R. W., Green, D. A., & Jin, W. (2016). *The UK wage premium puzzle: How did a large increase in university graduates leave the education premium unchanged?.* IFS Working Paper 2016/1.

Bonjour, D., Cherkas, L. F., Haskel, J. E., Hawkes, D. D., & Spector, T. D. (2003). Returns to Education: Evidence from U.K. Twins. *American Economic Review, 93*(5), 1799–1812.

Britton, J., Dearden, L., Shephard, N., & Vignoles, A. (2016). *How English domiciled graduate earnings vary with gender, institution attended, subject and socio-economic background.* Technical report. Institute for Fiscal Studies WP1606.

Buchmueller, G., & Walker, I. (2019). *Non-cognitive skills and the return to higher education.* mimeo.

Hoxby, C. (2019). The productivity of u.s. post-secondary institutions forthcoming. In C. Hoxby, & K. Strange (Eds.), *Productivity in Higher Education.* University of Chicago Press.

Kirkeboen, L., Leuven, E., & Mogstad, M. (2016). Field of Study, Earnings, and Self-Selection. *Quarterly Journal of Economics, 131*(3), 1057–1111.

Murphy, R., Scott-Clayton, J., & Wyness, G. (2017). Lessons from the end of free college in England. *Brookings Economic Studies, Evidence Speaks Reports, 2,* 13.

Oster, E. (2019). Unobservable selection and coefficient stability: Theory and evidence. *Journal of Business & Economic Statistics, 37*(2), 187–204.

Walker, I., & Zhu, Y. (2008). The college wage premium and the expansion of higher education in the UK. *The Scandinavian Journal of Economics, 110,* 695–709.

Walker, I., & Zhu, Y. (2011). Differences by degree: Evidence of the net financial rates of return to undergraduate study for England and Wales. *Economics of Education Review, 30,* 1177–1186.

Walker, I., & Zhu, Y. (2013). *The impact of university degrees on the lifecycle of earnings: Some further analysis.* Department for Business, Innovation and Skills Research Report.

Walker, I., & Zhu, Y. (2018). University selectivity and the relative returns to higher education: Evidence from the UK. *Labour Economics, 53,* 230–249.

Walker, I., & Zhu, Y. (2019). *Wage differential by undergraduate degree class and grade inflation at college.* mimeo.

Webber, D. A. (2014). The lifetime earnings premia of different majors: Correcting for selection based on cognitive, noncognitive, and unobserved factors. *Labour Economics, 28,* 14–23.

Parental education and children's health throughout life

Mathias Huebener

Education and Family Department, German Institute for Economic Research (DIW Berlin),
Berlin, Germany

Glossary

Dynamic complementarities A higher stock of skills or health increases the productivity of further investments in skills or health in later periods

Exogenous variation The change in the variable of interest, e.g. parental education, is determined outside individuals' choices, and it is independent of other individual characteristics. It ensures that third unobserved factors are not spuriously driving the relationship between the variable of interest and the outcome

Grossman model An economic model on the production of health and the demand for health-related inputs outlined by Michael Grossman

Lifecycle perspective Dynamic perspective on how the variable of interest, e.g. parental education, can impact the outcome across the lifecycle. Any early changes can generate own effects on the outcome in later periods. The lifecycle perspective contrasts a static model in which the variable of interest can affect the outcome only in one period

Non-monetary returns Returns to investments, e.g. into education, on other dimensions than wages, such as health, life satisfaction, civic engagement

Quasi-experiment A research design that resembles an actual experiment in that the allocation of the observational unit to treatment and control group is, under specific conditions, as good as random. Examples for quasi-experimental designs are difference-in-differences designs, regression discontinuity designs and instrumental variable designs

Self-productivity A higher stock of skills or health in an earlier period increases skills or health in subsequent periods

Introduction

Less and better-educated individuals differ substantially in their health conditions and in their life expectancy—a phenomenon observed across countries that even seems to grow over time (e.g. Meara, Richards, & Cutler, 2008). For example, better-educated individuals are typically less likely to suffer from asthma, lung cancer, high blood pressure, diabetes and allergies. At the same time, better-educated individuals show better health-related behaviors: They exercise more, smoke less frequently and follow a healthier diet. The health-related behaviors that show important educational gradients are also associated with leading risk factors of premature death in developed and developing countries. The World Health Organization (2009) suggests that more than 50% of premature deaths can be attributed to the use of tobacco, high blood pressure, and overweight.

The Economics of Education, Second Edition
https://doi.org/10.1016/B978-0-12-815391-8.00007-0

Socio-economic differences in health and health-related behaviors, for example by education, can be pivotal to understand socio-economic inequalities in education and labor market outcomes. Health is increasingly recognized as a very important dimension of human capital, next to individuals' cognitive and non-cognitive skills. Already in school, unhealthy individuals can be impaired in their ability to learn, or they are absent from school more frequently, with consequences for their educational attainments. In the labor market, unhealthy individuals work fewer hours, have longer absences, and they may be less able to participate in continued training programs, impairing their ability to adjust to changing labor markets. With a lower productivity, they earn lower wages. Health thereby has a direct impact on the human capital stock and productivity of an economy (e.g. Goldin, 2016). Impaired health is also an important determinant of individuals' well-being and life satisfaction.

Can educational policies improve individuals' health, and that of society, in the long-run? Is the relationship between education and health causal? These are widely debated and actively researched questions. Still, the findings are mixed and far from being conclusive (e.g. Galama, Lleras-Muney, & van Kippersluis, 2018; Grossman, 2015). This large literature mainly focuses on the immediate effects of educational reforms on targeted individuals. An aspect that received much less research attention is the question whether *parental education* affects children's health, i.e. whether education also affects health *intergenerationally*.

The role of family background and conditions in early childhood in shaping future outcomes receives increased research attention. It is an almost universal fact that children from families with a low socio-economic status have lower birth weights and are more likely to be born prematurely (e.g. Currie & Moretti, 2003). At school entry, these children show a lower school readiness (e.g. Bradbury, Corak, Waldfogel, & Washbrook, 2015; Huebener, Kuehnle, & Spiess, 2019). Later in life, they obtain less education, earn less, are more likely to be unemployed, are less healthy, and have a lower life expectancy (e.g. Cunha & Heckman, 2007; Huebener, 2019). Consequently, children's own socio-economic status later in life correlates strongly with their parents' status, thereby perpetuating inequality. The education of parents is an important, if not the most important, characteristic to describe children's socio-economic background. A significant part of the intergenerational transmission of socio-economic status may work through the impact of parental education on children's health (e.g. Case, Lubotsky, & Paxson, 2002).

The health returns of children are important non-monetary returns to education. In a standard model of educational investment decisions, where individuals weigh their costs and benefits from attending school, such spillover effects on the next generation are externalities that individuals would not take into account. As a result, they invest less in education than would be optimal from a societal perspective. If their children are healthier, public health insurances are relieved. If children smoke less, they generate fewer negative externalities on people around them. These effects strengthen the argument for public investments in education.

This chapter provides an overview of the literature on effects of parental education on children's health. It first summarizes theoretical arguments on how parental education may affect children's health. It then discusses the empirical evidence, focusing on studies that use arguably exogenous variation (e.g. from changes in educational policies) to estimate causal effects of parental education. The chapter answers questions like: Does parental education impact children's health? Is it the mother's or the father's education that matters for children's health? At what age of children does parental education matter? What are potential transmission mechanisms? The article focuses mainly on studies from developed countries, as the mechanisms through which parental education affects children's health likely differ substantially between developed and developing countries. One section summarizes the scarce evidence from developing countries.

Theoretical considerations

Immediate effects of education

The literature on the link between education and health has been advanced substantially by Grossman (1972, 2000). Grossman suggests a theory in which health is part of individuals' human capital. Health is produced by a production technology and a variety of input factors. Education can essentially impact health through two channels. First, better-educated individuals have a better cognition to acquire and process health-related information. They spend available resources *better* with respect to their health. For example, better-educated individuals are more aware of the negative consequences of alcohol consumption or smoking, and they obtain better information about qualified doctors and

treatments. Second, better-educated individuals have higher incomes, and can therefore spend *more* resources on health-related inputs. Higher incomes can allow living in safer neighborhoods, buying healthier food or affording higher quality medical treatments. Better jobs may provide a healthier work environment or a better health insurance.

Intergenerational effects of education

Grossman's model also provides insights on how *parental* education can affect child health. In the intergenerational perspective, parental education can affect child health at various stages in the lifecycle. To structure the possible mechanisms, we assume a model in which children's health - as one dimension of their human capital - is formed in a dynamic process spanning children's lifecycle. The model is depicted in Fig. 7.1 (own illustration, based on Conti & Heckman, 2014). It describes how the stock of health evolves throughout life, considering environmental factors and investments.

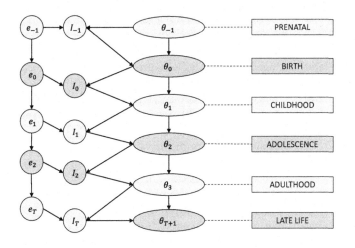

θ_t: Health at T
I_T: Investment at T
e_T: Environment at time T
$\theta_{T+1} = f_T(\theta_T, I_T, h_T)$

FIG. 7.1 Selected mechanisms for how parental education can impact children's health across the lifecycle.

Children's initial health endowments (θ_{-1}) are determined at conception. These initial endowments and environmental factors (e_{-1}), such as the family environment and parental education, determine prenatal investments (I_{-1}) and the stock of human capital at birth (θ_0). In subsequent periods, the stock of human capital (θ) at time $t + 1$ results from investments (I), environmental factors (e), and the stock of human capital at time t. Investments can be made by, for example, parents or policy-makers. Environmental factors include the family and peer environment of children, and the institutional environment, such as the structure of the education or health care system. Parental education can affect health preferences, the amount of resources parents can invest in children's health, and what parents do with the available resources.

The model has two important features. First, due to the multidimensionality of human capital, individuals can achieve each outcome by various combinations of different dimensions of human capital. Second, the model takes a lifecycle perspective and separates the human capital formation process into multiple stages. Consequently, a higher stock of health in an earlier period increases the health in subsequent periods (*self-productivity*), and it increases the productivity of health-related investments in later periods (*dynamic complementarity*). We now discuss the role of parental education at each of these stages.

Insights across children's lifecycle

Prenatal influences and health at birth

Already before conception, better-educated parents typically plan a baby more consciously. On average, they are more likely to be in stable relationships, finish professional training or university first, are older and more established in the labor market. Better-educated women work in jobs that are less physically demanding. In some countries, a better job comes with better health insurance that allows receiving better prenatal care. With more education, parents are better able to acquire and understand information about risk factors during pregnancy, and follow a healthier diet, as well as smoke and drink less (e.g. Aizer & Currie, 2014; Carneiro, Meghir, & Parey, 2013).

Many studies show that maternal schooling is related to neonatal health of children. At the same time, there are substantial differences in the health behavior of better and less-educated parents. Once studies control for differences in how parents' treat health inputs, the association between children's health and parental education becomes very small. This suggests that behavioral factors are important to explain these differences in children's birth outcomes. Several studies analyze the effects of schooling on economic conditions surrounding childbirth. For example, Black, Devereux, and Salvanes (2008) study effects of compulsory schooling reforms in the US and Norway, and find that teenage childbearing decreases in both countries with an increase in years of schooling. As teenagers giving birth often have not yet completed education and are in economically dependent or unstable conditions, a reduction in teenage childbearing suggests an improvement in economic conditions surrounding childbirth.

What about causal effects of parental education on child health at birth? Some studies explicitly estimate effects on children's birth weight, or severe health conditions that can be observed in administrative health data. A prominent study for the US by Currie and Moretti (2003) studies effects of maternal education on children's birth weight and gestational age. The study argues that US white women in counties with more college places are more likely to attend college. Using the college availability as an instrument, the study finds that maternal education improves children's health at birth; the increase in maternal education between the 1950s and

1980s accounts for 12% of the decline in low birth weights in that period. The study also finds that better-educated mothers are more likely to be married, they use more prenatal care, and reduce smoking during pregnancy. Carneiro et al. (2013) use rich data from the National Longitudinal Survey of Youth (NLSY79) and different sources of variation in schooling costs as instruments for maternal education (such as local tuition, wages, unemployment and grandparental schooling). They find no evidence for effects on low birth weights, but they report that mothers are on average older. They are more likely to be married and have a higher household income, i.e. their economic situation can be described as more stable at the time of birth. They also find evidence for a lower incidence of smoking during pregnancy for better-educated mothers.

McCrary and Royer (2011) use age-at-school entry policies to study effects of maternal schooling on children's low birth weights and probability of infant death. The idea is that "potential mothers" born the day after the school entry cut-off will enter school almost one year later, and by the time they reach the minimum school leaving age, they are allowed to leave school. In consequence, some "potential mothers" born just after the cut-off will have received less schooling. While McCrary and Royer observe differences in maternal education near the school entry cut-off, they find little evidence for differences in infant health outcomes. They caution that school entry policies affect fertility and infant health probably heterogeneously, and that their methodological approach captures mainly the effects of women at high risk of dropping out of school.

Lindeboom, Llena-Nozal, and van der Klaauw (2009) analyze the effects of a national increase in the minimum school leaving age in the UK on child health of new-borns, at age seven, eleven and 16 years. With respect to birth weight and whether the child suffers from an illness in the first week of life, there is little evidence for an effect of increased schooling of parents. However, the increase in education has a positive effect on living standards and reduces households' financial difficulties.

Overall, several other studies show that parental education improves the economic conditions of families which children are born into. The evidence on children's health around birth is mixed. However, the outcomes (low birth weights and severe health conditions) often reflect margins of severe health impairments; they may not fully capture more subtle dimensions of newborns' human capital that may improve their health in the course of life. Moreover, studies that rely on cut-offs and discontinuities for the estimation of effects, as they are employed in, e.g., McCrary and Royer (2011) and Lindeboom et al. (2009) may not capture the full causal effects as they cannot take into account any spillovers that materialize further away from the cut-off (Lochner, 2011).

In childhood

As children grow older, the number of possible channels for the link between parental schooling and children's health grows as well. The economic literature on the effects of parental education can now also build on richer measures of children's health. Following Fig. 7.1, any effects of parental schooling on children's health may now not only result from changes in children's early environment (e_0) or investments (I_0) due to changes in parental schooling, but also from health improvements at birth (θ_0).

Changes in children's early environment are, for example, safer neighborhoods with better facilities (e.g. playgrounds) and cleaner air. Parents may also serve as more health-oriented role models (encouraging regular teeth-brushing, body care, and exercising), they may better prevent children from family stress situations (money worries, professional worries), or use childcare earlier, which may affect children's immune system, for example.

Examples for changes in investments include longer breastfeeding, more post-natal support by a midwife, a more regular use of preventive medical check-ups for children, the prevention of behavioral risks (e.g. correction of posture, damage to the jaw due to excessive pacification), or providing healthier food. Better-educated parents also spend more quality time with their children, i.e. time on age-appropriate activities that support child development.

A large number of studies shows strong correlations between parental education and these changes in children's environment and early childhood investments. Other studies show that these conditions are associated with children's health in childhood. However, we know relatively little about the causal effects of parental education on these environmental conditions and investments in early and later childhood. Carneiro et al. (2013) are one of the few exceptions who try to estimate the causal effects of maternal schooling on child investments and environmental factors. They show that better-educated mothers breastfeed the child longer, and young children are more likely to be in formal child care. However, they also find a small negative effect on a motor and social development score of children below age one. They attribute it to an effect of maternal education on employment early after childbirth. More generally, the literature on the effects of maternal employment on child development suggests that mainly full-time employment shortly after childbirth can be harmful for child development. Employment after the first six months, especially part-time employment, shows no relevant effects on child development (e.g. Brooks-Gunn, Han, & Waldfogel, 2010). When children are seven to eight years old, Carneiro et al. (2013) consistently find improvements in children's overweight that are also substantial in size. However, the effects are only imprecisely estimated.

Lindeboom et al. (2009) study the intergenerational effects of the minimum school leaving age increase in England, and find no substantial causal effect of increased parental education on health in later childhood (ages seven, eleven and 16). The measures are based on parental reports on children's record of illnesses, psychological problems, accidents and hospitalizations, and on medical examinations performed by a physician. However, they find improvements in the economic conditions of the household.

In adolescence

In adolescence, better-educated parents may invest more time and resources to inform children better about the risks of smoking, drug use and alcohol consumption, or provide a better sex education on contraception and unwanted teenage pregnancies. With respect to the home environment, they may impose home smoking rules. Moreover, the exposure to the home environment becomes less relevant in adolescence, and the exposure to environments outside the parental home becomes more important.

Hence, the focus shifts more to the question of how parents affect environments outside the parental home that children are exposed to. One important channel can be that better-educated parents improve children's school and peer environment. There are at least two reasons for this: First, better-educated parents may change their preferences for educational investments into their children, and they may have a better endowment with resources allowing them to send their children to better schools. Second, improvements in childhood health can improve children's ability to follow the school curriculum and attend school more regularly, which then allows benefiting more from education and earning higher educational degrees.

If children attend better schools, they can also experience a better peer environment at an age at which important health-related habits are shaped. For example, smoking is typically initiated in the teen years, when children are still in school. Independent of the peer environment, increased educational attainments of children improve their earnings prospects and may even alter children's discount rates and risk aversion such that initiating unhealthy behaviors becomes more costly (Becker & Mulligan, 1997; Fuchs, 1982).

By now, there exists a significant number of papers studying the transmission of parental schooling onto children's schooling and cognitive ability. While earlier studies could not find evidence for a causal relationship (Black, Devereux, & Salvanes, 2005), other studies estimate compellingly robust effects (Carneiro et al., 2013; Dickson, Gregg, & Robinson, 2016; Lundborg, Nilsson, & Rooth, 2014; Oreopoulos, Page, & Stevens, 2006). For example, Piopiunik (2014) and Huebener (2018) find that an increase in compulsory schooling in Germany increases the probability that children of affected mothers attend a higher school track. The school tracking system in Germany not only shows substantial differences in teacher qualifications, instruction hours and the curriculum across school types, but also in smoking and overweight rates of peers. Even if increases in the minimum school leaving age do not show effects on selected health outcomes on children in their early adolescence (Lindeboom et al., 2009), other papers propose that such reforms increase children's educational attainment (Dickson et al. 2016). This implies that there may still be scope for long-term effects of parental schooling on children's health, even if health effects on children at birth or in childhood are small.

Huebener (2018) then examines the effects on children's smoking behavior, and finds evidence for a substantial reduction in smoking initiation of adolescents if mothers attend school for one year longer. Lundborg et al. (2014) estimate effects of a Swedish compulsory schooling reform in military register data, containing several measures of health. They find evidence that mothers', but not fathers' education has an effect on a global measure of health and boys' cognitive ability at age 18. They attribute their findings to increases in maternal income, as the reform only had effects on maternal but not paternal labor market outcomes. Whether this is the dominant underlying channel remains speculative, as several other explanations that cannot be observed in administrative data may explain effects on children. Other papers show that the link between income and children's health is much smaller if parenting skills and the home environment are considered.

Huebener (2018) also presents evidence that children's incidence of overweight declines in their teenage years because of increases in mothers' compulsory schooling. Improvements in dietary habits and a healthier body weight earlier in life may be one explanation, improvements in the school peer environment may be another. The data does not allow investigating the channels further, but other studies show that peers in adolescence can also impact children's weight problems, or determine the propensity to exercise. Carneiro et al. (2013) find no effect of maternal education on the frequency of taking joint meals at age 12–14, but it may still affect the quality of food provided.

Another mechanism for children's improvements in health-related behaviors and health in adolescence can stem from a higher family stability that several studies document for better-educated individuals. Living with both parents can lower the risk that adolescents initiate smoking (e.g. Francesconi, Jenkins, & Siedler, 2010).

In adulthood

Improvements in dietary habits, smoking or overweight in childhood and adolescence can carry over into adulthood. Any improvements in health-related behaviors in earlier phases of life may now materialize in terms of improvements in health, and a reduction in chronic conditions. For example, smoking is related to several severe health conditions, such as asthma and cancer. Preventing children from smoking initiation in adolescence can have a lasting positive effect on children's health in the further course of life.

Based on the preceding changes in children's environments, investments and accumulated health, some new mechanisms can also be at work during the phase of adulthood. If children improved on their cognitive skills and educational attainments, they may be more likely to work in jobs that are imposing lower risks on health or that are less physically demanding. In countries without universal health care coverage, better jobs may also lead to a significant improvement in health insurances. Moreover, better-educated parents may themselves work in better jobs and advise children in their professional careers. Such intergenerational links in parents' and children's occupations are well documented across countries (Black & Devereux, 2011).

The further one advances in children's lifecycle, the less is known empirically about the impact of parental education on children's long-term health. Only one study considered children's health outcomes in adulthood. Huebener (2018) traces the effects of a compulsory schooling increase in Germany into the adulthood of the children of treated individuals and finds evidence that they are still less likely to smoke, have a lower BMI and a lower incidence of overweight. Children's incidence of asthma declines, and they report a better general health status.

Despite the scarce evidence on the effects of parental education on children's long-term health, we may wonder what is known about the long-term effects of improvements in early life conditions. A related literature analyzes the long-term impact of improvements in prenatal conditions and health at birth, for which we have seen some evidence that maternal education can improve these outcomes. One strand of the literature links children's birth weight to their long-term outcomes. Many of these studies compare siblings or twins to hold the family context constant. They conclude that the sibling with the lower birth weight achieves lower levels of education, has a higher probability to live in a deprived neighborhood, experience lower earnings and worse health (Currie & Moretti, 2007). Several studies show long-term negative effects on body height and cognitive ability (Black, Devereux, & Salvanes, 2007).

Another strand of studies demonstrates that early life shocks, e.g. due to wars, famines, or epidemics, can have lasting effects on long-term labor market and health outcomes (such as suffering from diabetes or strokes, e.g. Almond, 2006; Almond, Edlund, & Palme, 2009). This evidence, however, is based on extreme circumstances, and it remains an open question how representative these findings are for less extreme situations and to what extent it can speak to improvements in early conditions that are observed for increased parental education.

In late life

Direct effects of parental education on old-aged children's environment and health-related investments (i.e. e and I in Fig. 7.1) now likely play a smaller role. Instead, changes in environmental factors or investments likely result from effects of parental education on earlier stages in life. If children of better-educated individuals had better jobs and higher earnings, they may receive higher pensions, live in better housing, or benefit from better health insurance, for example. They may afford more regular health screenings, and may engage in a more active life as higher financial resources increase the chances to participate in social life. Toward the end of life, the health capital that individuals have accumulated over the course of life plays an increasingly important role. The incidence of chronic conditions, which often result from un-healthy behaviors, increases with age. Improvements in health-related behaviors earlier in life, such as a better diet or no smoking, can lower the risk of suffering from cardiovascular diseases, type 2 diabetes, or cancer.

To date, there exists no causal evidence of the *effects* of parental education on children's late-life health or mortality. Still, a small number of studies for Germany (Huebener, 2019), Norway (Kravdal, 2008; Strand & Kunst, 2006) and the US (Lawrence, Rogers, & Zajacova, 2016) relate maternal and paternal education to children's mortality and life expectancy. Across all studies, maternal education correlates strongly with children's life expectancy, in Norway, fathers' education additionally explains differences in life expectancy. If studies include children's health and health-related behaviors in the analysis, the relationship between mortality and parental education falls. This suggests that the lasting impact of parental education on children's health and health-related behaviors can be an important pathway. While the existing studies cannot claim that the relationship is causal, they still complement the causal evidence on earlier stages of children's life.

Evidence from developing countries

The chapter so far focused on developed countries. In developing countries, education is undoubtedly of high importance. The World Bank campaigned in the 1990s that "there is no investment more effective for achieving development goals than educating girls." With respect to the effects of education on offspring health, the mechanisms can differ greatly between developing and developed countries. For example, if education increases earnings in developing countries, parents may be able to move to neighborhoods with fresh water and sanitary installations—a channel that is probably non-existent in the developed world. The education

margin in developing countries differs as well: While studies in developed countries consider education beyond eight years or more, in developing countries education reforms often enable individuals to visit school at all, or to increase schooling from very low levels where children receive the opportunity to learn basic skills in reading and writing.

This section briefly summarizes insights from developing countries. Almost all studies focus on fertility decisions and conditions surrounding childbirth, most studies look at effects of maternal education only. Breierova and Duflo (2004) study effects of a primary school construction program in Indonesia starting in 1973; Osili and Long (2008) study the provision of tuition-free primary education of a 1976 nationwide program in Nigeria. These two programs increased the number of primary schools at differential rates across regions, which is used in the estimation of causal effects. Keats (2018) examines a national reform abolishing primary school fees in Uganda in 1997 which increased schooling of children by about one year. All of these studies conclude that increased maternal education delays fertility, and, if examined, reduces completed fertility. One reason is that better-educated women are more likely to employ contraceptive measures and they are older when they get married. Duflo, Dupas, and Kremer (2015) provide experimental evidence from a program that subsidized the costs of education for upper primary school students by providing two free school uniforms over the last three years of primary school. The education subsidy increased primary school completion and delayed girls' first birth. The teen pregnancy rate fell from 16% to 13%. Following the hypothesis of a quantity-quality trade-off (Becker, 1960; Becker & Lewis, 1973), parents with fewer children can invest more per child and thereby improve their outcomes.

With respect to children's health, Breierova and Duflo (2004) find for the school construction program in Indonesia that both maternal and paternal schooling reduce infant mortality. Keats (2018) finds that primary school fee abolition in Kenya increased women's probability to give birth with a trained health provider. Their children are more likely to receive vaccinations by age one, and less likely to be chronically malnourished. Children are taller for their age and less likely to be stunted. However, there are no differences in mortality rates up to the age of five.

Going beyond primary school education, Chou, Liu and Grossman (2010) evaluate a substantial increase in compulsory education from six to nine years in Taiwan. The program was accompanied by the opening of new junior high schools, and some regions and cohorts were more affected by the educational expansion. The increase in both maternal and paternal schooling lowered the incidence of low birth weights and infant mortality. Ozier (2018) employs eligibility discontinuities in the admission to Kenya's government secondary schools, finding that secondary schooling also reduces teenage pregnancies.

Beyond birth and the very early years of childhood, there exists no empirical evidence on the effects of parental education on children's health outcomes from developing countries, but the strong effects on child health at birth promise substantial improvements in children's health also in later stages of life.

Implications and outlook

Parental education can affect children's health and health-related behaviors through numerous pathways across children's lifecycle. It is helpful to distinguish between environmental conditions and investments into children that better-educated parents can shape at the different stages in children's life. The existing convincing evidence proposes an important effect of parents' education at different stages. Increased parental education substantially changes the environment in which children grow up, it changes the investments into children, and these

changes start to happen early in children's life, some of them before children are born. The effect of parental education on children's health solidifies as children age. The arrival and impact of chronic conditions manifests later in life. The majority of studies conclude that maternal schooling causes better health of the offspring. A significant part of the intergenerational transmission of socio-economic status may therefore work through the impact of parental education on children's health.

Still, the causal evidence on the effects of parental education on children's health is relatively scarce. The few existing studies that exist exploit natural experiments in which policies manipulated the age at which parents could enter school or exit school, or policies that altered the opportunities to pursue college education. These experiments change the schooling of parents in different parts of the educational distribution, and they study outcomes of children at different ages. Many questions remain to be answered.

For example, most of the evidence relates to increased education at the lower end of the education spectrum. While returns to children's health may be highest there, it is still worthwhile investigating whether further increases in education can improve the health of the next generation. Moreover, more needs to be learned about the impact of fathers. In the analysis of intergenerational effects, both mothers and fathers can impact children's health. Some studies only look at the effects of maternal schooling. Studies that also consider the fathers find little evidence for effects on children. This may be related to the role that fathers play in raising children in the cohorts studied. It is also possible that the fathers' impact varies over the lifecycle or is only smaller for the health outcomes considered. The effect of fathers may also change over time as social norms and fathers' role in raising children change across countries. Finally, health has many dimensions, such as physical and mental health. To date, we know very little about the effects on children's mental health, probably because only few data sets satisfy the high requirements that analyzes of the causal effects of parental education need. We also know little about cumulative and interactive effects of health limitations.

Research suggests that environmental factors and investments are highly predictive of later life outcomes in families with a low socio-economic status—while genes are not. Only in families with a higher socio-economic status, genes have some explanatory power for later life outcomes (Rutter, 2006). Parental education is important to shape children's environment and health-related investments. Despite many open questions, intergenerational effects of education on health already prove to be substantial and important. Effects can be found in countries with generous social security systems and universal health care, as well as in countries with less generous systems. As health is increasingly acknowledged as an important dimension of human capital, more research on its socio-demographic determinants and the role of parents promises to be insightful, also to better understand intergenerational transmissions of socio-economic status.

References

Aizer, A., & Currie, J. (2014). The intergenerational transmission of inequality: Maternal disadvantage and health at birth. *Science, 344*(6186), 856–861.

Almond, D. (2006). Is the 1918 influenza pandemic over? Long-term effects of in utero influenza exposure in the post-1940 US population. *Journal of Political Economy, 114*(4), 672–712.

Almond, D., Edlund, L., & Palme, M. (2009). Chernobyl's subclinical legacy: Prenatal exposure to radioactive fallout and school outcomes in Sweden. *Quarterly Journal of Economics, 124*, 1729–1772.

Becker, G. S. (1960). An economic analysis of fertility. In *Demographic and economic change in developed countries* (pp. 209–240). New York: Columbia University Press.

Becker, G. S., & Lewis, H. G. (1973). On the interaction between the quantity and quality of children. *Journal of Political Economy, 81*(2), S279–S288.

Becker, G. S., & Mulligan, C. B. (1997). The endogenous determination of time preference. *Quarterly Journal of Economics, 112*(3), 729–758.

Black, S. E., & Devereux, P. J. (2011). Recent developments in intergenerational mobility. In O. Ashenfelter, & D. Card (Eds.), *Handbook of labor economics* (Vol. 4B, pp. 1487–1541). Amsterdam: North Holland.

Black, S. E., Devereux, P. J., & Salvanes, K. G. (2005). Why the apple doesn't fall far: Understanding intergenerational transmission of human capital. *The American Economic Review, 95*(1), 437–449.

Black, S. E., Devereux, P. J., & Salvanes, K. G. (2007). From the cradle to the labor market? The effect of birth weight on adult outcomes. *Quarterly Journal of Economics, 122*(1), 409–439.

Black, S. E., Devereux, P. J., & Salvanes, K. G. (2008). Staying in the classroom and out of the maternity ward? The effect of compulsory schooling laws on teenage births. *Economic Journal, 118*(530), 1025–1054.

Bradbury, B., Corak, M., Waldfogel, J., & Washbrook, E. (2015). *Too many children left behind: The US achievement gap in comparative perspective*. Russell Sage Foundation.

Breierova, L., & Duflo, E. (2004). *The impact of education on fertility and child mortality: Do fathers really matter less than mothers?*. NBER Working Papers, No. 10513.

Brooks-Gunn, J., Han, W.-J., & Waldfogel, J. (2010). First-year maternal employment and child development in the first seven years. *Monographs of the Society for Research in Child Development, 75*, 1–147.

Carneiro, P., Meghir, C., & Parey, M. (2013). Maternal education, home environments, and the development of children and adolescents. *Journal of the European Economic Association, 11*, 123–160.

Case, A., Lubotsky, M., & Paxson, C. (2002). Economic status and health in childhood: The origins of the gradient. *The American Economic Review, 92*, 1308–1334.

Chou, S.-Y., Liu, J.-T., Grossman, M., & Joyce, T. (2010). Parental education and child health: Evidence from a natural experiment in Taiwan. *American Economic Journal: Applied Economics, 2*(1), 33–61.

Conti, G., & Heckman, J. J. (2014). Economics of child well-being. In A. Ben-Arieh, F. Casas, I. Frønes, & J. E. Korbin (Eds.), *Handbook of child well-being* (pp. 363–401). Dordrecht: Springer Netherlands.

Cunha, F., & Heckman, J. J. (2007). The technology of skill formation. *The American Economic Review, 97*(2), 31–47.

Currie, J., & Moretti, E. (2003). Mother's education and the intergenerational transmission of human capital: Evidence from college openings. *Quarterly Journal of Economics, 118*(4), 1495–1532.

Currie, J., & Moretti, E. (2007). Biology as destiny? Short and long-run determinants of intergenerational transmission of birth weight. *Journal of Labor Economics, 25*(2), 231–264.

Dickson, M., Gregg, P., & Robinson, H. (2016). Early, late or never? When does parental education impact child outcomes? *Economic Journal, 126*(596), F184–F231.

Duflo, E., Dupas, P., & Kremer, M. (2015). Education, HIV, and early fertility: Experimental evidence from Kenya. *The American Economic Review, 105*(9), 2757–2797.

Francesconi, M., Jenkins, S. P., & Siedler, T. (2010). The effect of lone motherhood on the smoking behavior of young adults. *Health Economics, 19*(11), 1377–1384.

Fuchs, V. R. (1982). Time preference and health: An exploratory study. In V. Fuchs (Ed.), *Economic aspects of health* (pp. 93–120). Chicago: University of Chicago Press.

Galama, T., Lleras-Muney, A., & van Kippersluis, H. (2018). The effect of education on health and mortality: A review of experimental and quasi-experimental evidence. In *Oxford research encyclopedia of economics and finance*. Oxford: Oxford University Press.

Goldin, C. (2016). Human capital. In C. Diebolt, & M. Haupert (Eds.), *Handbook of cliometrics* (pp. 55–86). Berlin, Heidelberg: Springer-Verlag.

Grossman, M. (1972). On the concept of health capital and the demand for health. *Journal of Political Economy, 80*(2), 223–255.

Grossman, M. (2000). The human capital model. In A. J. Culyer, & J. P. Newhouse (Eds.), *Handbook of health economics* (Vol. 1A, pp. 347–408). Amsterdam: North-Holland, Elsevier Science.

Grossman, M. (2015). The relationship between health and schooling. *Nordic Journal of Health Economics, 3*(1), 7–17.

Huebener, M. (2018). *The effects of education on health: An intergenerational perspective.* IZA Discussion Paper Series, No. 11795.

Huebener, M. (2019). Life expectancy and parental education. *Social Science & Medicine, 232*, 351–365. https://doi.org/10.1016/j.socscimed.2019.04.034.

Huebener, M., Kuehnle, D., & Spiess, C. K. (2019). Parental leave policies and socio-economic gaps in child development: Evidence from a substantial benefit reform using administrative data. *Labour Economics, 61*, 101754. https://doi.org/10.1016/j.labeco.2019.101754.

Keats, A. (2018). Women's schooling, fertility, and child health outcomes: Evidence from Uganda's free primary education program. *Journal of Development Economics, 135*(C), 142–159.

Kravdal, Ø. (2008). A broader perspective on education and mortality: Are we influenced by other people's education? *Social Science & Medicine, 66*(3), 620–636.

Lawrence, E. M., Rogers, R. G., & Zajacova, A. (2016). Educational attainment and mortality in the United States: Effects of degrees, years of schooling, and certification. *Population Research and Policy Review, 35*(4), 501–525.

Lindeboom, M., Llena-Nozal, A., & van der Klaauw, B. (2009). Parental education and child health: Evidence from a schooling reform. *Journal of Health Economics, 28*(1), 109–131.

Lochner, L. J. (2011). Nonproduction benefits of education: Crime, health, and good citizenship. In E. A. Hanushek, S. Machin, & L. Woessmann (Eds.), *Handbook of the economics of education* (Vol. 4, pp. 182–262). Amsterdam: North Holland.

Lundborg, P., Nilsson, A., & Rooth, D.-O. (2014). Parental education and offspring outcomes: Evidence from the Swedish compulsory school reform. *American Economic Journal: Applied Economics, 6*(1 A), 253–278.

McCrary, J., & Royer, H. (2011). The effect of female education on fertility and infant health: Evidence from school entry policies using exact date of birth. *The American Economic Review, 101*(1), 158–195.

Meara, E. R., Richards, S., & Cutler, D. M. (2008). The gap gets bigger: Changes in mortality and life expectancy, by education, 1981–2000. *Health Affairs, 27*(2), 350–360.

Oreopoulos, P., Page, M. E., & Stevens, A. H. (2006). The intergenerational effects of compulsory schooling. *Journal of Labor Economics, 24*(4), 729–760.

Osili, U. O., & Long, B. T. (2008). Does female schooling reduce fertility? Evidence from Nigeria. *Journal of Development Economics, 87*(1), 57–75.

Ozier, O. (2018). The impact of secondary schooling in Kenya. *Journal of Human Resources, 53*(1), 157–188.

Piopiunik, M. (2014). Intergenerational transmission of education and mediating channels: Evidence from a compulsory schooling reform in Germany. *The Scandinavian Journal of Economics, 116*(3), 878–907.

Rutter, M. (2006). *Genes and behavior: Nature-nurture interplay explained.* Oxford: Blackwell.

Strand, B. H., & Kunst, A. (2006). Childhood socioeconomic position and cause-specific mortality in early adulthood. *American Journal of Epidemiology, 165*(1), 85–93.

World Health Organization. (2009). Global health risks: Mortality and burden of disease attributable to selected major risks. *Bulletin of the World Health Organization, 87*, 646.

Further reading

Almond, D., Currie, C., & Duque, V. (2019). Childhood circumstances and adult outcomes: Act II. *Journal of Economic Literature* (in press).

Björklund, A., & Salvanes, K. G. (2011). Education and family background: Mechanisms and policies. In E. A. Hanushek, S. Machin, & L. Woessmann (Eds.), *Handbook of the economics of education* (Vol. 3, pp. 201–247). Amsterdam: North Holland.

Currie, J., & Stabile, M. (2003). Socioeconomic status and child health: Why is the relationship stronger for older children? *The American Economic Review, 93*(5), 1813–1823.

Education and civic engagement

T.S. Dee

Swarthmore College, Swarthmore, PA, United States

One of the most fundamental and recurring questions in economics involves how we should understand the proper division of human activity across the public and the private sectors. The field of education is certainly no exception. Public-sector involvement in virtually all forms of formal educational activity is both diverse and extensive. Correspondingly, the intellectual justifications for education-related public policies and institutions reflect a broad variety of distinct normative concerns. However, a conjecture that is central to claims about the importance of government involvement in education is the substantive role that educational investments are thought to play in the formation of an engaged and enlightened citizenry. For example, the claim that widespread education is critical for a stable, functioning democracy was a key motivation for the dramatic growth in access to formal schooling in the United States during the nineteenth century. More recently, the putative civic benefits of investments in education have motivated arguments for private-school vouchers as well as for the Great Society investments in higher education.

From an economic perspective, the basic argument is that individual investments in education may generate a positive externality through improvements in civic engagement that effectively benefit the entire society. This article provides a critical overview of the available evidence that has examined the effects of schooling on subsequent measures of civic engagement. The available evidence is largely, although not exclusively, based on data from the United States. However, it is also important to note that, while the existence of a civic externality from schooling can motivate government intervention in education, it does not have unambiguously clear implications for the exact form of that intervention. The existence of civic externalities from schooling also does not speak directly to the important question of how public and private schools compare with regard to promoting subsequent civic engagement. This article also discusses the more limited and recent evidence that touches on these issues and concludes with some promising directions for future research.

The civic returns to educational attainment

Civic engagement refers to a diverse set of behaviors, attitudes, and knowledge that constitute effective citizenship.

For example, one particularly prominent dimension of civic engagement involves the allocation of time: participation in voting, volunteering, membership in civic organizations, and engagement with elected representatives. A second key component of civic engagement is a belief in the validity and desirability of democratic, pluralistic institutions, and related values such as tolerance and respect. A third dimension involves having both the requisite cognitive skills and an awareness of current events that make an informed deliberation on complex social and technological issues possible.

Investments in education are widely thought to be a critical determinant of all dimensions of civic engagement, and, by implication, of maintaining a stable, well-functioning democracy. In particular, increases in educational attainment are thought to promote civic engagement both by inculcating students with a sense of civic responsibility and by providing them with the skills and knowledge that allow them to make informed decisions. However, basic economic theory suggests a number of other, potentially contrary ways in which additional schooling may shape civic engagement. For example, the well-documented effect of schooling on wages implies that educational attainment increases the opportunity cost of time. This increase should reduce the willingness to invest time in civic activities such as voting and volunteering. This effect may be particularly relevant for volunteering, which, relative to voting, implies a more intensive and sustained commitment of time. Additional schooling could also reduce voter participation if it makes voters more aware of the paradox of voting. More specifically, additional school could encourage voters to view voting as a largely expressive and meaningless act rather than an instrumental one with a nontrivial likelihood of directly influencing an election's outcome. Finally, it should be noted that the effects of additional schooling on civic responsibility may work through the changes in peer-groups and social norms rather than through the effects of schooling per se.

A large number of older, empirical studies, mostly from the field of political science, have examined the effects of educational attainment on dimensions of civic engagement in the United States (Converse, 1972; Nie, Junn, & Stehlik-Barry, 1996; Putnam, 2001; Wolflnger & Rosenstone, 1980). These studies generally find that, conditional on several observable traits, higher levels of educational attainment are associated with substantial increases in multiple dimensions of adult civic engagement. In fact, several authors have stressed the central role that education seems to have among all determinants of civic engagement (Converse, 1972; Putnam, 2001). The apparent gains from increases in educational attainment appear to exist at both the secondary and the postsecondary levels. Furthermore, the strong partial correlations between educational attainment and civic engagement also appear to exist internationally (e.g., Franklin, 1996).

However, several recent studies on this topic have been motivated by the concern that the partial correlations between levels of schooling and civic engagement may be misleading. The basic concern is these correlations could, quite plausibly and to an unknown degree, reflect inherently unobservable individual, family, and community traits that influence both educational attainment and subsequent civic engagement. For example, families and communities that foster and encourage educational success may also be more likely to promote the development of civic virtue. One recent study addressed this potential source of bias by conducting comparisons within 85 pairs of monozygotic twins from New Zealand and found that an additional year of schooling appeared to lower the likelihood of volunteering by roughly 12.5% (Gibson, 2001). This contrarian finding is consistent with the effects of schooling on the opportunity cost of time.

Two other recent studies have examined the causal effects of additional schooling on more diverse measures of civic engagement by exploiting the credibly independent variation in educational attainment generated by teen exposure to child labor and compulsory schooling laws (Dee, 2004; Milligan, Morettl, & Oreopolous, 2004). Using different data sets of respondents from the United States, these studies find that increases in educational attainment do appear to generate substantial increases in the likelihood of voting. Furthermore, these studies present evidence that additional schooling increases the quality of civic participation both in the United States and in the United Kingdom as measured by awareness of public affairs and support for free speech (Dee, 2004; Milligan et al., 2004).

Additional evidence has focused on the civic returns from additional schooling at the postsecondary margin in the United States, using geographic access to 2-year and community colleges as a natural experiment (Dee, 2004). The evidence from this approach indicates that college attendance leads to substantial increases in rates of subsequent voter participation. However, the estimated effects of college attendance on volunteering in adulthood were negative and statistically imprecize. Furthermore, this study did not address the effects of college attendance on other dimensions of civic engagement (e.g., civic knowledge and values) because of the apparent lack of a data set that simultaneously accommodates the use of a credible natural experiment and includes the requisite outcome variables.

Comparisons of public and private schools

The available empirical evidence indicates that increases in educational attainment lead to substantial increases in several measures of civic engagement in adulthood, with the possible and notable exception of volunteering. In other words, the widely held view that investments in schooling generate some meaningful and positive civic externalities appears to be valid. These results imply that schools and classrooms are an important and highly effective setting for the development of civic engagement. However, the effects of additional schooling on civic engagement are often used to motivate continued or additional financial support for publicly managed elementary and secondary schools. From an economic standpoint, this policy interpretation is not clearly justified. Narrowly interpreted, the existence of these civic externalities argues only for the existence of corrective financial subsidies that encourage individuals to acquire additional schooling. More specifically, a subsidy equal to the value society places on the civic engagement created by additional schooling could encourage individuals to choose the socially optimal level of schooling (i.e., a level that reflects both the internal and external benefits of schooling). In fact, the seminal argument for private-school vouchers appealed to the existence of civic externalities as an important justification (Friedman, 1955).

A more compelling economic argument for an extensive and publicly managed system of elementary and secondary schools, similar to that observed in the United States, would turn on evidence that the public sector is more effective than the private sector at promoting the development of civic engagement. There are a number of reasons to suspect that, even with regulation, private schools will not promote a socially desirable level of civic engagement. For example, because private schools are largely accountable only to the parents of their students, they may place more emphasis on skills and knowledge with clear individual benefits and less emphasis on outcomes with larger external benefits. Furthermore, the sectarian and, sometimes, segregated nature of many private schools may also harm key dimensions of civic engagement. However, there are at least two ways in which private schools could be more effective at promoting the development of civic engagement. First, private schools may be more successful at developing civically relevant cognitive skills. Second, private schools may be more effective at increasing student exposure to social capital (i.e., shared norms and trust), which, in turn, promotes the development of civic engagement.

Despite the importance of these issues, the comparative effects of public and private schools in promoting civic engagement have been the subject of surprisingly little empirical study. However, the limited evidence that is available uniformly suggests that private schools are actually more effective than public schools. For example, two recent studies based on nationally representative survey data found that attending a Catholic high school instead of a public high school was associated with improvements in civic participation, knowledge, and attitudes (Campbell, 2001; Greene, 1998). Another study based on data from college students in Texas also found a correlation between measures of political tolerance and private-school attendance (Wolf, Greene, Kleitz, & Thalhammer, 2001). However, as with the strong correlations between increased schooling and civic engagement, this evidence could merely reflect selection biases. In other words, the students who attend private, instead of public, schools may experience unobserved family and community environmental traits that promote higher civic engagement in adulthood.

A recent study based on detailed data from the High School and Beyond longitudinal study examined the effects of attending a Catholic high school on several forms of civic participation, using specifications that addressed the potential influence of selection bias (Dee, 2005). In particular, this study used residence in a county with a Catholic high school as a kind of natural experiment (i.e., an instrumental variable) for attending a Catholic high school. The results of this approach suggested that attending a Catholic high school significantly increased the likelihood of voting in adulthood. However, the estimated effects of Catholic school attendance on volunteering were smaller and statistically insignificant.

A critical assumption implicit in this analysis was that the geographic distribution of Catholic schools is unrelated to the unobserved propensities for civic engagement in adulthood. The fact that the presence of Catholic high schools was driven in large part by patterns of immigration in the late 19th and early 20th centuries is consistent with this approach. Furthermore, a confounding bias would occur if communities with Catholic high schools also tended to have higher levels of civic engagement. However, Dee (2005) found that counties with Catholic high schools actually have lower voter-turnout rates. Nonetheless, Dee (2005) also estimated the degree of potential bias directly by assessing how the instrumental variable influenced the adult civic outcomes among students for whom the presence of Catholic high schools was largely irrelevant (e.g., those attending public school for eighth grade). The results provided no evidence of statistically significant bias from this approach. However, at least two other caveats with regard to this study are relevant. First, due to data constraints, this study did not provide any evidence on how Catholic schools influenced other key civic outcomes, such as tolerance and support for democratic values. Second, it is not clear whether the apparent civic advantage of Catholic high schools generalizes to other types of private schools.

Nonetheless, this evidence indicates that public schools are not as effective as they could be with regard to fostering voter participation in adulthood. Interestingly, the relative ineffectiveness of public schools does not appear to be due solely to being less effective at promoting educational attainment. More specifically, the estimated effectiveness of Catholic schools in promoting high school completion combined with the estimated effects of completing high school on civic outcomes explains less than half of the apparent Catholic school advantage (Dee, 2005). These effect-size comparisons imply that other factors, such as social capital within school communities and instructional practices, play an important role in the relative success of Catholic schools in increasing subsequent voter turnout.

This discussion has focused on how public and private schools promote the civic development of the students they serve. However, it should also be noted that a provocative recent study has argued that public schools play a critical role in sustaining and promoting civic engagement among adults in their communities (Fischel, 2006). More specifically, this study argues that local public schools provide an important complement to local social capital by facilitating connections among parents that, in turn, lower the transaction costs involved in a variety of civic activities. Some descriptive empirical evidence, such as the correlation between the levels of social capital and the presence of smaller school districts, is consistent with this claim (Fischel, 2006). This study also suggests that the extensive use of private-school vouchers would harm the production of social capital and civic engagement by dispersing students from their communities and increasing the social isolation of neighboring parents.

Summary and future directions

Investments in schooling appear to lead to substantial increases in voter participation and civic awareness, although not necessarily in volunteering. As it is not clear how to monetize improvements in civic engagement, the exact implications of these results for the social rate of return to education are not clear. Nonetheless, these results confirm the conventional wisdom that what occurs within schools and classrooms plays a vitally important role in the civic development of students. Furthermore, the existence of some civic externalities provides an important motivation for policies designed to promote high school completion and to expand access to higher education.

However, the limited evidence that is available also suggests that public schools are inferior to Catholic schools with respect to promoting adult voter participation and, possibly, other dimensions of civic engagement. These comparative results imply that public schools are, on average, underperforming with regard to one of their core goals. Therefore, the identification of educational policies and practices that are effective at promoting civic engagement will undoubtedly address an important policy need. One prominent way in which schools have been increasingly embracing their civic missions is through the encouragement of volunteer activity among students. A key argument made in support of promoting or requiring community service among students is that early engagement with volunteering may create lifelong volunteers. However, there is little in the way of credible evidence that these efforts have actually been effective in promoting sustained civic engagement. In particular, the evidence on college-level initiatives to promote volunteering and service learning is largely descriptive (Dee, 2008). Furthermore, a recent study examined the effect of Maryland's mandatory community-service requirement for high school graduates and found that it influenced only the timing, and not the overall level, of volunteering (Helms, 2007).

See also

Human Capital; The External Benefits of Education; The Economics of Catholic Schools; The Efficacy of Educational Vouchers.

References

Campbell, D. E. (2001). Making democratic education work. In P. E. Peterson, & D. E. Campbell (Eds.), *Charters, vouchers, and public education* (pp. 241–267). Washington, DC: Brookings Institution Press.

Converse, P. E. (1972). Change in the American electorate. In A. Campbell, & P. E. Converse (Eds.), *The human meaning of social change* (pp. 263–331). New York: Russell Sage.

Dee, T. S. (2004). Are there civic returns to education? *Journal of Public Economics, 88*(9), 1697–1720.

Dee, T. S. (2005). The effects of Catholic schooling on civic participation. *International Tax and Public Finance, 12*(5), 605–625.

Dee, T. S. (2008). Assessing the college contribution to civic engagement. In M. S. McPherson, & M. O. Schapiro (Eds.), *Succeeding in college: What it means and how to make it happen*. New York: College Board.

Fischel, W. A. (2006). Why voters veto vouchers: Public schools and community-specific social capital. *Economics of Governance, 7*, 109–132.

Franklin, M. N. (1996). Electoral participation. In L. LeDuc, R. G. Niemi, & P. Norris (Eds.), *Comparing democracies: Elections and voting in global perspectives* (pp. 216–235). London: Sage.

Friedman, M. (1955). The role of government in education. In R. A. Solo (Ed.), *Economics and the public interest* (pp. 127–134). New Brunswick, NJ: Rutgers University Press.

Gibson, J. (2001). Unobservable family effects and the apparent external benefits of education. *Economics of Education Review, 20*(3), 225–233.

Greene, J. P. (1998). Civic values in public and private schools. In P. E. Petersen, & B. C. Hassel (Eds.), *Learning from school choice* (pp. 83–106). Washington, DC: Brookings Institution Press.

Helms, S. E. (2007). *Involuntary volunteering: The impact of mandated service in public schools, mimeo.* University of Alabama at Birmingham.

Milligan, K., Morettl, E., & Oreopolous, P. (2004). Does education improve citizenship? Evidence from the United States and the United Kingdom. *Journal of Public Economics, 88*(9), 1667–1695.

Nie, N. H., Junn, J., & Stehlik-Barry, K. (1996). *Education and democratic citizenship in America*. Chicago, IL: University of Chicago Press.

Putnam, R. D. (2001). Tuning in, tuning out: The strange disappearance of social capital in America. In R. G. Niemi, & H. F. Weisberg (Eds.), *Controversies in voting behavior* (pp. 38–68). Washington, DC: CQ Press.

Wolf, P. J., Greene, J. P., Kleitz, B., & Thalhammer, K. (2001). Private schooling and political tolerance. In P. E. Peterson, & D. E. Campbell (Eds.), *Charters, vouchers, and public education* (pp. 268–289). Washington, DC: Brookings Institution Press.

Wolflnger, R. E., & Rosenstone, S. J. (1980). *Who votes?* New Haven, CT: Yale University Press.

Further reading

Courant, P. N., McPherson, M. S., & Resch, A. M. (2006). The public role in higher education. *National Tax Journal, 59*(2), 291–318.

Glaeser, E. L., Ponzetto, G., & Shleifer, A. (2007). Why does democracy need education? *Journal of Economic Growth, 12*(2), 77–99.

Haveman, R. H., & Wolfe, B. L. (1984). Schooling and economic well-being: The role of nonmarket effects. *Journal of Human Resources, 19*(3), 377–407.

Lange, F., & Topel, R. (2006). The social value of education. In E. Hanushek, & F. Welch (Eds.), *Handbook of the economics of education* (Vol. 1, pp. 459–509). Amsterdam: North-Holland/Elsevier.

Markus, G. B., Howard, J. P. F., & King, D. C. (1993). Integrating community service and classroom instruction enhances learning: Results from an experiment. *Educational Evaluation and Policy Analysis, 15*, 410–419.

Poterba, J. M. (1996). Government intervention in the markets for education and health care: how and why? In V. R. Fuchs (Ed.), *Individual and social responsibility: child care, education, medical care and long-term Care in America* (pp. 277–308). Chicago, IL: University of Chicago Press.

Taylor, L. L. (1999). Government's role in primary and secondary education. *Federal Reserve Bank of Dallas Economic Review, 1999*, 15–24.

Wolfe, B. L. (1994). External benefits of education. In T. Husen, & T. N. Postlethwaite (Eds.), *International encyclopedia of education* (pp. 2208–2212). Oxford: Pergamon Press.

Education and crime

Lance Lochner

Department of Economics, University of Western Ontario, London, ON, Canada

Introduction

There is a strong connection between education and crime. In the US, 75% of state and 59% of federal prison inmates in 1997 did not have a high school diploma (Harlow, 2003). Similar patterns have been documented in other periods and in countries around the world (Buonanno & Leonida, 2009; Machin, Marie, and Vujic 2011; Hjalmarsson, Holmlund, and Lindquist, 2015).

This article begins with a brief discussion of the relationship between education and crime from an economic perspective. It then surveys recent evidence on the impacts of educational attainment and school quality on adult crime, including analyses of the contemporaneous effects of school attendance on crime. Studies on the effects of juvenile arrest and incarceration on schooling behavior are also discussed. Finally, this article concludes with a number of policy lessons related to education and its potential role as a crime-fighting strategy.

The economics of education and crime

Why does education reduce crime, and which types of crime are likely to be most sensitive to education policies? An economic perspective provides several useful insights on these questions.

Lochner (2004) emphasizes the role of education as a human capital investment that increases future legitimate work opportunities, which discourages participation in crime. This is consistent with numerous studies documenting that higher wages reduce crime (e.g. Gould, Mustard, & Weinberg, 2002; Grogger, 1998; Machin & Meghir, 2004) and decades of research in labor economics showing that education increases wage rates (see, e.g., Heckman, Lochner, & Todd, 2006, chap. 12). If human capital raises the marginal returns from work more than crime, then human capital investment and schooling should reduce crime. Thus, policies that increase schooling (or the efficiency of schooling) should reduce most types of street crime among adults; however, certain types of white collar crime (e.g. embezzlement, fraud) may increase with education if they sufficiently reward skills learned in school.

Education may also teach individuals to be more patient (Becker & Mulligan, 1997). This would discourage crime, since forward-looking individuals place greater weight on any expected future punishment associated with their criminal activities. To the extent that time preferences are affected by schooling, crimes associated with long prison sentences (or other long-term consequences) should be most affected. Education may also affect preferences toward risk. If schooling makes individuals more risk averse, it should discourage crime with its greatest effects on offenses that entail considerable uncertainty in returns or punishment. Finally, schooling may affect who individuals interact with on a daily basis at home, school, work, or their neighborhoods. Due to assortative mating (Becker, 1991), more educated men tend to marry more educated women. This can affect family resources, fertility behavior, and family stability, which can all impact decisions to engage in crime. More generally, if more educated people interact more with other educated people who are less inclined to engage in crime, this is likely to compound any reductions in crime associated with schooling. In most cases, mechanisms related to changes in preferences or social interactions suggest that educational attainment is likely to reduce most types of crime among adults.

Evidence on education, school quality, and crime

There is growing evidence from around the world on the effects of educational attainment on subsequent criminal outcomes. A similar picture - that more education leads to less crime - emerges from most of these studies. A few studies also examine the effects of school choice and quality on criminal behavior; however, there is less consensus here. Finally, several recent papers analyze the contemporaneous relationship between school attendance and crime. These studies reveal a complex relationship that depends critically on context. This section briefly summarizes the current state of evidence on these issues. Lochner (2010, chap. 10, 2011, chap. 2) and Hjalmarsson and Lochner (2012) provide more comprehensive surveys.

Effects of educational attainment on crime

Early studies of the relationship between education and crime focused on their correlation conditional on measured individual and family characteristics using standard regression methods (Ehrlich, 1975, chap. 12; Witte, 1997, chap. 7). These studies must be interpreted with caution, since a negative cross-sectional correlation between education and crime, even after controlling for measured family background and neighborhood characteristics, does not necessarily imply that education reduces crime. First, unobserved individual characteristics like patience or risk aversion are likely to directly affect both schooling and criminal decisions. Individuals who choose more schooling (even after conditioning on observable characteristics) might also choose less crime regardless of their education level, in which case regression-based estimates do not identify a causal effect. Second, using variation in crime and education across states or local communities may also produce biased estimates. Governments may face a choice between funding police or good public schools, producing a spurious positive correlation between education and crime. Alternatively, unobserved characteristics about communities may directly affect the costs or benefits of both education and crime. Third, reverse causality is another important concern. Individuals who plan to heavily engage in crime (e.g. because they are particularly good at it, enjoy it, or live in areas with plenty of illicit opportunities) are likely to choose to leave school at a young age (Lochner, 2004). Arrests or incarceration associated with juvenile crime may also cause some youth to drop out of school early (Aizer & Doyle, 2015; Hjalmarsson, 2008).

Recent empirical studies generally estimate the effects of educational attainment on arrest, conviction, or incarceration rates. To address concerns with endogeneity and unobserved heterogeneity, researchers have typically exploited exogenous changes in state or national rules that affect schooling decisions, examining the effects of these policies on subsequent crime. This ensures that estimates reflect causal effects of education on crime and not simply spurious correlations.

Lochner and Moretti (2004) examine state-level male arrest rates by criminal offense and age from the FBI's Uniform Crime Reports (UCRs) for the US in 1960, 1970, 1980, and 1990. These data is linked to 1960-90 decennial US Census data on educational attainment and race. The main methodological contribution of Lochner and Moretti (2004) is the use of changes in state-specific compulsory schooling laws over time as instrumental variables for schooling. Intuitively, this strategy measures the extent to which an increase in a state's compulsory schooling age leads to an immediate increase in educational attainment and reductions in subsequent crime rates for affected cohorts. Because the laws only affect schooling at low levels (mainly grades 8−12), their instrumental variable (IV) estimates reflect the impact of an additional year of high school on crime.

Lochner and Moretti (2004) find that, for men, a one-year increase in average education levels in a state reduces state-level arrest rates by 11% or more. These estimated effects are very similar to the predicted effects derived from multiplying the estimated increase in wages associated with an additional year of school by the estimated effects of higher wage rates on crime (from Gould et al. 2002), which suggests that much of the effect of schooling on male crime may come through increased wage rates and opportunity costs. Given the strong relationship between high school completion and incarceration, Lochner and Moretti (2004) also estimate specifications using the high school completion rate as a measure of schooling. These estimates suggest that a ten percentage point increase in high school graduation rates would reduce arrest rates by 7−9%.

Lochner and Moretti (2004) also use ordinary least squares (OLSs) to estimate separate effects of education for different types of crime. These results suggest similar effects across the broad categories of violent (murder, rape, robbery, and assault) and property (burglary, larceny, motor vehicle theft, and arson) crime - a one year increase in average years of schooling reduces both property and violent crime by about 11−12%. However, the effects vary considerably within these categories. A one-year increase in average years of schooling reduces murder and assault by almost 30%, motor vehicle theft by 20%, arson by 13%, and burglary and larceny by about 6%. Estimated effects on robbery are negligible, while those for rape are significantly positive. Additional specifications suggest similar effects for a 10−20% point increase in high school graduation rates. Following a similar approach, Lochner (2004) estimates positive, though statistically insignificant, effects of schooling on arrest rates for white collar crimes (forgery and counterfeiting, fraud, and embezzlement).

Lochner and Moretti (2004) also use individual-level data on incarceration and schooling from the 1960, 1970, and 1980 U.S. Censuses to estimate the effects of educational attainment on the probability of imprisonment separately for black and white men (ages 20−60). Their estimates control for age of the respondent, state of birth, state of residence, cohort of birth, and state-specific year effects. Analogous to their analysis of state-level arrest rates, they use state-level changes in compulsory schooling ages as an instrument for educational attainment. That is, identification comes from the fact that in any given state and year, different age cohorts faced different compulsory schooling laws during their high school years, causing them to acquire different levels of schooling and to commit crime at different rates. Both OLS and IV estimates are very similar and suggest that, on average, an extra year of education reduces the probability of imprisonment by slightly more than 0.1% point for whites and by about 0.4% points for blacks. Given average incarceration rates for dropouts, this translates into a 10–15% reduction in incarceration rates for both white and black males associated with an extra year of completed schooling. These estimated effects are comparable to those for arrest rates described earlier. OLS results suggest that completion of the 12th grade causes the greatest drop in incarceration, while there is little effect of schooling beyond high school.

Machin, Marie, and Vujić (2011) exploit a 1972–73 increase in the minimum schooling age (from age 15 to 16) in England and Wales to estimate the effects of schooling on criminal convictions for property and violent crimes over the period 1972–96. Using both IV and regression discontinuity methods, identification effectively comes from cohort-level changes in schooling attainment and crime for cohorts turning 15 immediately before and after the law change. Among men, they estimate that a one-year increase in average schooling levels reduces conviction rates for property crime by 20–30% and violent crime by roughly one-third to one-half as much, although the latter estimates are statistically insignificant. Compared to estimates for the US by Lochner and Moretti (2004), the impacts of education on property crime appear to be greater in the United Kingdom, while the effects on violent crime are weaker.

Hjalmarsson, Holmlund, and Lindquist (2015) use administrative micro-data and Swedish schooling reforms to identify the causal effect of education on crime. The Swedish reforms primarily extended compulsory schooling from seven to nine years and were implemented at different times across municipalities during the 1950s and 1960s. As such, Hjalmarsson, et al. (2015) compare individuals who were exposed to two different school systems, but who were from the same birth cohort and worked in the same labor market. Exposure to the reforms significantly increased average educational attainment by 0.33 years for males and 0.20 years for females. Estimated effects on female crime

are imprecize; however, estimates for males suggest that one additional year of schooling reduces the likelihood of criminal conviction by 7% and the likelihood of incarceration by 16%. Looking across offense categories, an additional year of schooling decreases the likelihood of a property crime conviction by 14%, a violent crime conviction by 10%, and a conviction of other types of crime by 6% - similar in magnitude to estimates for the US (Lochner & Moretti, 2004).

Meghir, Palme, and Schnabel (2014) show that the Swedish schooling reform also affected the criminal activity of the next generation. Their estimates suggest that the reform led to a 0.8% point reduction in criminal conviction rates (about one-third of baseline rates) among the sons of fathers exposed to the schooling reform. Impacts were mostly concentrated among violent crime, serious traffic crimes, and fraud (including tax evasion). By contrast, they find no effect of the reform on conviction rates among the sons of women exposed to the reform, despite similar effects on their schooling.

Buonanno and Leonida (2009) estimate the effects of educational attainment on crime rates using a panel of 20 Italian regions 1980 to 1995. Using OLS, they control for region and time fixed effects, along with region-specific quadratic time trends, and a rich set of time-varying region-specific covariates. Their estimates suggest that a ten percentage point increase in high school graduation rates would reduce property crime rates by 4% and total crime rates by about 3%. (Effects on property crime are statistically significant, while effects on total crime are not.) They find no evidence to suggest that university completion reduces crime.

A final study examines the effects of an explicit education subsidy on youth burglary rates in England. Between 1999 and 2002, England piloted Educational Maintenance Allowances (EMAs), which provided subsidies of up to £40 per week (plus bonuses for completion of course-work) for low-income 16—18 year old youth to attend school. The program was administered in 15 local areas with low schooling participation rates. During the same time period, the Reducing Burglary Initiative (RBI) funded 63 different local burglary reduction schemes as a separate pilot project. Roughly half of all EMA pilot areas were also selected for the RBI. Sabates and Feinstein (2008) use a differences-in-differences strategy to identify the effects of each pilot program as well as the combination of the two on burglary. Their findings suggest that the combination of both the EMA and RBI significantly reduced burglary rates by about 5.5% relative to 'matched' comparison areas. Effects of the EMA alone were slightly lower but still significant.

Effects of education on female crime

Much of the literature has focused on males given their much higher crime rates. Cano-Urbina and Lochner (2019) provide some of the first evidence that educational attainment can reduce female crime. Using a similar IV approach (and data) to that of Lochner and Moretti (2004), they show that an additional year of schooling reduces the probability of incarceration by 0.05—0.09 percentage points among white American women (from 1960 to 1980), while a one-year increase in average schooling levels reduces female arrest rates for both violent and property crime by more than 50% (from 1960 to 1990). There is little impact of additional schooling on white collar crime.

Analogous IV estimates of the impact of an additional year of schooling on the probability of incarceration are about four times higher for men than women, while baseline incarceration rates are roughly 20 times higher for low-educated men versus women. Thus, the impact of education on imprisonment is much stronger for women in percentage terms. This is also true for arrests.

As discussed above, most of the effect of education on crime among men can be explained by increases in wages and greater labor market participation. Cano-Urbina and Lochner (2019) show that this is unlikely to be the case for women (at least for 1960—80), since they estimate little effect of schooling on female labor supply behavior. Instead, education appears to improve the marital prospects of women. The accompanying increases in marriage likely reduce crime by strengthening family bonds, while increases in spousal education and family resources may limit the incentives for women to turn to crime in order to support their families. Still, education reduces female incarceration even when conditioning on marital status, so other channels are also important. Cano-Urbina and Lochner (2019) estimate that increased schooling also causes women to have more children, which may discourage crime by raising the personal costs of time in prison and strengthening family/social bonds. Of course, the channels through which education impacts female crime may have changed in more recent decades as women have increasingly entered the labor market, reduced their time at home, and raised fewer children.

Effects of school choice and quality on crime

A few studies suggest that improvements in school quality may lead to reductions in criminal activity during early adulthood. Using randomized school admission lotteries, Cullen, Jacob, and Levitt (2006) and Deming (2011) find that students who 'win' the opportunity to attend better-performing public schools do not necessarily perform better academically, but they commit significantly less crime during school and the first few years after leaving school. Weiner, Lutz, and Ludwig (2009) show that desegregation initiatives in some US states led to substantial improvements in school quality for blacks. Among blacks experiencing desegregation, high school graduation rates increased by a few percentage points and homicide arrest rates declined by one-third at ages 15–19.

By contrast, the analysis of Cano-Urbina and Lochner (2019) offers mixed evidence regarding the effects of school quality (as measured by pupil-teacher ratios, term length, and teacher wage rates) on female crime. In particular, estimated direct effects of school quality improvements (holding educational attainment fixed) are inconsistent across measures of both quality and crime. Because school quality improvements lead to increases in educational attainment and the estimated effects of schooling attainment on crime are strong, the indirect effects of quality improvements (on both arrests and incarceration) through increased schooling are positive, though modest, for all observed quality measures.

Contemporaneous schooling and crime

There are three main ways in which altering youths' schooling attendance is likely to affect their contemporaneous engagement in crime. First, school may have an incapacitation effect - youth cannot be in two places at once, and many criminal opportunities are more limited in school than on the streets. This effect depends, in part, on the ease with which youth can engage in crime during non-school hours. Second, longer periods of school attendance should increase labor market skills and improve future employment prospects as emphasized above. This should make juvenile arrests and long periods of detention more costly, reducing incentives to engage in crime while enrolled in school. Third, schools bring hundreds of adolescents together for the day. The social interactions from this could lead to altercations and more general group-based delinquency. The incapacitation and human capital effects are likely to imply negative effects of school attendance on

crime, while the social interaction effect could be positive or negative.

A few studies shed light on these effects by estimating the impacts of different 'interventions' that directly affect youth schooling attendance. Anderson (2014) and Brilli and Tonello (2018) examine the effect of increasing compulsory schooling ages (i.e. forcing some youth to stay in school), while Jacob and Lefgren (2003) and Luallen (2006) study the effect of extra days off from school due to teacher in-service days or teacher strikes (i.e. keeping all youth out of school). These interventions differ in two important respects. First, increases in compulsory schooling ages typically 'require' that students stay in school at least one additional year and sometimes more, whereas teacher in-service days and strikes are of very short duration. Second, while teacher strikes and in-service days release all students from school, changes in compulsory schooling laws typically affect a small set of marginal students. All three potential effects of school attendance on crime are likely to be relevant to changes in compulsory schooling, while the effects of in-service days and teacher strikes are likely to be limited to incapacitation and social interactions. Social interaction effects are likely to be magnified in the latter cases due to the universal nature of the 'policies'.

Anderson (2014) estimates that increases in US state compulsory schooling ages from 16 to 18 significantly reduce arrests at the affected ages by about 17%, with similar impacts on both violent and property crime. (Effects are similar, though statistically insignificant, for drug crimes.) Using Italian administrative data on offending rates by age, year, and province, Brilli and Tonello (2018) study the effects of increasing the minimum schooling age from 14 to 15 years in 1999. While school enrollment increased by about 4% points at ages 14–17, offending rates declined by about 2 incidents per 1000 youth at age 14 only. They estimate no evidence of displacement to other times of the day/year when school was not in session; however, there did appear to be an increase in the probability violent crime victimization while at school. These results suggest a combination of general incapacitation effects (reducing crime outside of school) and social interaction effects leading to additional violent crime during school.

Additional support for conflicting incapacitation and interaction effects of school attendance is provided by Jacob and Lefgren (2003) and Luallen (2006), who estimate mixed effects of extra days off from school on crime due to teacher in-service days or strikes. Their estimates suggest that in urban areas an additional day of school reduces juvenile property crime by 15–30%; however, it increases violent crime by roughly 30%. Furthermore, Luallen (2006) finds that the impacts of an extra school day are insignificant in rural and suburban areas, suggesting that the incapacitation and social interaction effects of school attendance are particularly strong in urban areas and negligible (or offsetting) elsewhere.

Brief comment on measures of criminality

One potential concern with most of these studies is their reliance on arrest, conviction, and incarceration as measures of crime. It is possible that education improves the chances that someone evades arrest or conviction or that judges tend to give more educated defendants lighter prison sentences. While there is little direct evidence on these issues, Mustard (2001) finds negligible effects of defendant education levels on the sentence lengths they receive. Furthermore, results using self-reported measures of criminal activity in the National Longitudinal Survey of Youth support the case that education reduces actual violent and property crime, not just the probability of arrest or incarceration conditional on crime (Lochner, 2004; Lochner & Moretti, 2004).

The effects of arrest and incarceration on education

Two studies reach similar conclusions about the effects of youth arrest and incarceration on educational outcomes.

Studying the US, Hjalmarsson (2008) estimates the effects of juvenile incarceration on high school completion controlling for youth cognitive achievement, criminal and arrest records, and family background. She also considers specifications that account for state or family fixed effects to account for differences in state-level juvenile enforcement and education policies as well as differences in family (and, therefore, neighborhood) environments. Her regression-based estimates suggest that youth who become incarcerated, holding their juvenile criminal activity and arrest rates constant, are roughly 25 percentage points less likely to complete high school. Incarceration has its greatest effects on high school graduation when the sentence overlaps with the school year; however, the length of the sentence does not affect the graduation probability. Finally, she finds that incarceration has substantially larger effects on high school completion in states that require the justice system to notify schools of an arrest, suggesting that teachers and/or administrators may treat students differently if they are known to have been incarcerated. Juvenile incarceration may carry a negative stigma in schools, just as it does in the labor market.

Aizer and Doyle (2015) address concerns about unobserved factors that may affect both schooling and crime/arrest/detention using a novel natural experiment: the random assignment of case judges within the Chicago juvenile court system. Exploiting the variation across judges in the likelihood that they assign youth to detention (conditional on their criminal record, background, etc.), Aizer and Doyle (2015) estimate that juvenile incarceration reduces high school graduation by 13 percentage points and increases adult incarceration by 23 percentage points. Despite the fact that most youth only spend a few months in detention, very few ever return to school afterward.

Conclusions and policy lessons

Current evidence provides several important policy lessons regarding education and crime.

First, school-based policies can yield sizable social benefits from crime reduction. Lochner and Moretti (2004) calculate that the social savings of a one percentage point increase in male US high school graduation rates (from reduced crime alone) in 1990 would have amounted to more than $2 billion. This represents more than $3000 in annual savings per additional male graduate. In the UK, Machin et al. (2011) estimate a social savings of over £10,000 per additional student qualification (similar to high school completion in the US) from reductions in property crime alone.

Second, policies that encourage high school completion seem to be most promising in terms of their impacts on crime. Crime rates are already quite low among high school graduates, so policies that encourage post-secondary attendance or completion are likely to yield much smaller social benefits from crime reduction.

Third, policies designed to encourage schooling among more crime-prone groups are likely to produce the greatest benefits from crime reduction. Deming (2011) estimates that improved school choice for middle and high school students leads to significant reductions in arrests for high-risk youth but not for others. Consistent with this, the school-age Fast Track program appears to have reduced juvenile crime only among very high-risk children, showing little impact on even moderately high-risk children (CPPRG 2007, 2010).

Fourth, education policies can reduce both property and violent crime. In both the US and Sweden, the estimated effects of educational attainment or school enrollment on property and violent offenses are similar in percentage terms (Anderson, 2014; Hjalmarsson et al. 2015; Lochner & Moretti, 2004). Even murder appears to be quite responsive (Lochner & Moretti, 2004; Weiner et al. 2009).

Fifth, the effects of education on crime for men can be largely explained by improvements in wages and labor market opportunities; however, this is not the case for women.

References

Aizer, A., & Doyle, J., Jr. (2015). Juvenile incarceration, human capital, and future crime: Evidence from randomly assigned judges. *The Quarterly Journal of Economics, 130*(2), 759–803.

Anderson, D. M. (2014). In school and out of trouble? The minimum dropout age and juvenile crime. *Review of Economics and Statistics, 96*(2), 318–331.

Becker, G. S. (1991). *A treatise on the family* (enlarged ed.). Harvard University Press.

Becker, G., & Mulligan, C. (1997). The endogenous determination of time preference. *Quarterly Journal of Economics, 112*, 729–758.

Brilli, Y., & Tonello, M. (2018). Does increasing compulsory education decrease or displace adolescent crime? New evidence from administrative and victimization data. *CESifo Economic Studies, 64*(1), 15–49.

Buonanno, P., & Leonida, L. (2009). Non-market effects of education on crime: evidence from Italian regions. *Economics of Education Review, 28*(1), 11–17.

Cano-Urbina, J., & Lochner, L. (2019). The effect of education and school quality on female crime. *Journal of Human Capital, 13*(2), 188–235.

Conduct Problems Prevention Research Group. (2007). Fast Track randomized controlled trial to prevent externalizing psychiatric disorders: Findings from grades 3 to 9. *Journal of the American Academy of Child and Adolescent Psychiatry, 46*, 1250–1262.

Conduct Problems Prevention Research Group. (2010). Fast Track intervention effects on youth arrests and delinquency. *Journal of Experimental Criminology, 6*(2), 131–157.

Cullen, J., Jacob, B., & Levitt, S. (2006). The effect of school choice on participants: Evidence from randomized lotteries. *Econometrica, 74*, 1191–1230.

Deming, D. (2011). Better schools, less crime? *Quarterly Journal of Economics, 126*, 2063–2115.

Ehrlich, I. (1975). On the relation between education and crime. In F. T. Juster (Ed.), *Education, income, and human behavior*. New York: McGraw-Hill Book Co.

Gould, E., Mustard, D., & Weinberg, B. (2002). Crime rates and local labor market opportunities in the United States: 1977–1997. *Review of Economics and Statistics, 84*, 45–61.

Grogger, J. (1998). Market wages and youth crime. *Journal of Labor Economics, 16*, 756–791.

Harlow, C. (2003). Education and Correctional Populations. U.S. Department of Justice, Bureau of Justice Statistics Special Report, NCJ 195670, Washington DC.

Heckman, J. J., Lochner, L., & Todd, P. (2006). Earnings functions, rates of return and treatment effects: The Mincer equation and beyond. In E. Hanushek, & F. Welch (Eds.), *Handbook of the economics of education* (Vol. 1, pp. 307–458). Amsterdam: Elsevier.

Hjalmarsson, R. (2008). Criminal justice involvement and high school completion. *Journal of Urban Economics, 63*(2), 613–630.

Hjalmarsson, R., Holmlund, H., & Lindquist, M. J. (2015). The effect of education on criminal convictions and incarceration: Causal evidence from micro-data. *Economic Journal, 125*(587), 1290–1326.

Hjalmarsson, R., & Lochner, L. (2012). The impact of education on crime: International evidence. *CESifo DICE Report, 10*(2), 49.

Jacob, B., & Lefgren, L. (2003). Are idle hands the devil's workshop? Incapacitation, concentration, and juvenile crime. *American Economic Review, 93*, 1560–1577.

Lochner, L. (2004). Education, work, and crime: A human capital approach. *International Economic Review, 45*(3), 811–843.

Lochner, L. (2010). Education policy and crime. In P. Cook, J. Ludwig, & J. McCrary (Eds.), *Controlling crime: Strategies and tradeoffs* (pp. 465–515). Chicago: University of Chicago Press.

Lochner, L. (2011). Nonproduction benefits of education: Crime, health, and good citizenship. In E. Hanushek, S. Machin, & L. Woessmann (Eds.), *Handbook of the economics of education* (Vol. 4, pp. 183–282). Elsevier.

Lochner, L., & Moretti, E. (2004). The effect of education on crime: Evidence from prison inmates, arrests, and self-reports. *American Economic Review, 94*(1), 155–189.

Luallen, J. (2006). School's out forever: A study of juvenile crime, at-risk youths and teacher strikes. *Journal of Urban Economics, 59*, 75–103.

Machin, S., Marie, O., & Vujić, S. (2011). The crime reducing effect of education. *Economic Journal, 121*(552), 463–484.

Machin, S., & Meghir, C. (2004). Crime and economic incentives. *Journal of Human Resources, 39*, 958–979.

Meghir, C., Palme, M., & Schnabel, M. (2014). *The effect of education policy on crime: An intergenerational perspective*. Working Paper.

Mustard, D. (2001). Racial, ethnic and gender disparities in sentencing: Evidence from the US federal courts. *Journal of Law and Economics, 44*(1), 285–314.

Sabates, R., & Feinstein, L. (2008). Effects of government initiatives on youth crime. *Oxford Economic Papers, 60*(3), 462–483.

Weiner, D., Lutz, B., & Ludwig, J. (2009). *The effects of school desegregation on crime*. NBER Working Paper Paper No. 15380.

Witte, A. D. (1997). Crime. In J. Behrman, & N. Stacey (Eds.), *The social benefits of education*. Ann Arbor: University of Michigan Press.

Education and inequality

Jo Blanden

Economics Department, University of Surrey and Centre for Economic Performance, London School of Economics, London, United Kingdom

Introduction

This chapter considers the interplay between education and inequality. We have structured this into two, related, parts. First we consider the extent to which educational achievement is unequally spread through the population. Second, we look at the implications of inequalities in education for economic and social wellbeing. The analysis we present studies several dimensions of inequality in educational experiences and achievement: social background; ethnicity and immigrant status; and gender. In doing so, we gauge the magnitudes of these inequalities at different educational levels in the main industrialized countries and comment, as far as possible, on their changes over time.

Attainment gaps are so important because education is crucial in determining individuals' prospects and life chances. Even the attainment of low-level qualifications can substantially reduce the probability of unemployment or worklessness (a major cause of poverty) and higher level qualifications increase individuals' earning power. The second part of the chapter will review the size of these "returns" to education, and once again consider their evolution over time. We also briefly note the importance of education for individuals' non-economic wellbeing; low education levels are closely linked to poorer health outcomes, a higher likelihood of committing crime and even an earlier death.

Inequalities in educational outcomes

Inequalities by social background

The observation that children from poorer backgrounds do worse in terms of educational outcomes has a long history, for example being highlighted by Rowntree's investigation into poverty in York, England at the turn of the 20th century (Rowntree, 1901). Gaps in educational attainment between children from richer and poorer backgrounds continue to be marked more than a century later.

A large literature indicates that gaps in attainment emerge very early in children's lives. Substantial gaps in test score attainment are found by family background before children start school. Gaps at school entry are observed in the UK, US, Australia and Canada (Bradbury, Corak, Waldfogel, & Washbrook, 2015) with the largest gaps observed in the US, where the gap in the resources available for children from better and worse educated backgrounds are also the starkest (Corak, 2013, presents an enlightening comparison of the US and Canada).

Recent international surveys that test school-age children enable comparisons to be made of the strength of the influence of family background on achievement across many countries. For example, Fig. 10.1 shows family background effects on reading test scores, using cross-country data from PISA 2015 so that estimates are internationally comparable. In all countries the family background effect (in this

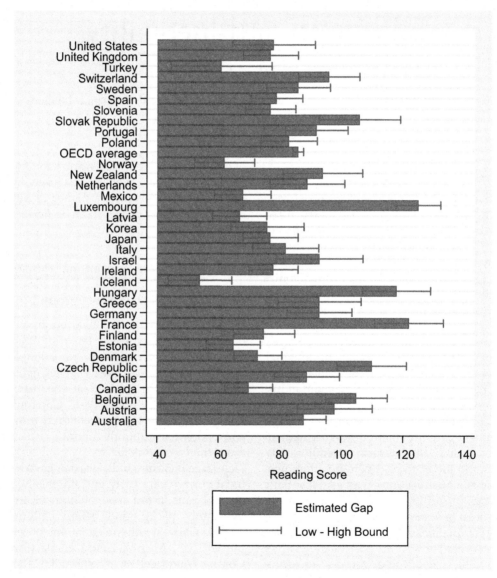

FIG. 10.1   Estimated effects of family background. On students' test scores across countries. *Source: OECD (2016). Data from PISA. Low-High bound are 95% confidence intervals. Note: the mean performance across all countries is 493 with a standard deviation of 96 points.*

study measured by comparing test scores of those in the top and bottom fifth of an index based on a number of family background indicators) is statistically significant and the implied gaps in test scores are extremely large in some countries.

These substantial gaps in test scores lead to inequality in final educational attainments. This includes a higher probability of dropping out of school and lower qualification attainment. Indeed there is evidence that inequalities grow as children age so that parental background influences final educational outcomes even once earlier achievements are taken into account.

Fig. 10.2 shows the proportion of young people from high educated v lower educated backgrounds who obtain degrees, ordered by the size of the gap between these proportions. All

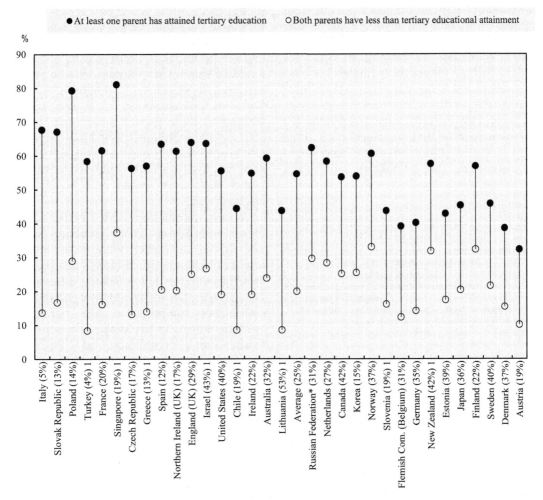

FIG. 10.2 Share of 30–44 year olds completing tertiary education by parents' educational attainment. *Source: OECD (2017). Data is from Program for the International Assessment of Adult Competencies (PIACC) 2012 or 2015. 30–44 year old non-students.*

are substantial, ranging from 20 to 50 percentage points.

Reardon (2011) has called attention to large and growing achievement gaps between low and high income children in the US but Jerrim (2012) using data from PISA 2000—9 indicates that gaps have narrowed in other countries. Indeed, Table 10.1 shows that updating Jerrim's work with information from PISA 2015 provides some evidence that the situation in the US may also have improved in very recent years. The finding of an improvement in the socio-economic gap in England is consistent with data from national assessments as discussed in Blanden and Macmillan (2016), this picture is confirmed by the data in Figs. 10.1 and 10.2 which no longer show England as having a particularly large gap internationally in contrast to the picture in our previous Encyclopedia entry. However, Blanden and Macmillan (2016) demonstrate that socio-economic gaps at high levels of attainment have been much more stubborn in England. Although educational attainment has risen overall, those who obtain the very best results at school and progress to post-graduate education are still highly likely to have parents in the highest income group.

Inequalities by race, ethnicity and immigrant status

Gaps in educational performance by ethnicity, race or immigration status are of interest because of the inequalities observed between different groups in the labor market. In the US, the focus of this debate has tended to be around differences in performance between blacks and whites (and to a lesser extent Hispanics), with our previous Encyclopedia entry highlighting the importance of differences in early test scores in leading to these gaps (Cameron & Heckman, 2001; Jencks & Phillips, 1998). However Rearden (2011) notes that the black-white gap has become relatively less important compared to the gap between those from richer and poorer income backgrounds.

A very recent paper by Chetty, Hendren, Jones, and Porter (2018) combines concerns with racial inequality with those about the impact of income on children's life chances by looking at the extent to which different racial groups in the US are able to move up the income distribution compared to their parents. This work demonstrates that despite the convergence in test scores between blacks and whites between the 1960s and 1980s (Card & Rothstein, 2007) blacks are less likely to be upwardly mobile than whites, and this seems strongly connected with the neighbourhoods they grow up in. The picture is more positive for Hispanics who have relatively high rates of income mobility. The tax data used by Chetty et al. does not allow the role of children's education to be directly considered as a mechanism, but this work indicates that racial inequalities in the US are still important.

TABLE 10.1 Comparing family background gaps in test scores over time in PISA.

	Estimated socio-economic gradient in children's test scores				
	2003	2009	2015	Change 2003—09	Change 2015—03
Australia	88	92	88	4	-4
Canada	70	67	70	3	-3
England	98	93	75	-5	-18
Finland	53	52	93	-1	41
Germany	91	89	77	-2	-8
US	—	106	78	—	-28
OECD	83	87	86	-4	1

Source: Jerrim (2012) and author's update from PISA 2015. The socio-economic gradient is the difference in mean test scores between children with parents in the top quintile of the HISEI index and the bottom quintile. The HISEI index is based on parental occupation.

Generally, the debate on the educational differences between whites and minorities tends to reach rather country-specific conclusions, depending on the groups involved and the historical patterns of migration experienced.

Platt (2007) finds substantial differences in educational attainment among the UK's 16–24 year olds in 2001, with young people from Chinese and Indian backgrounds exceeding the performance of whites. Black young people perform more poorly than whites, although the gaps are not as stark as between whites and Bangladeshi and Pakistani groups. Evidence from Strand (2015) using administrative data show similar patterns, with those from Chinese and Indian backgrounds extending their advantage since 2004, while blacks close the gaps with whites.

Given the diversity of the racial and ethnic dimensions pertinent in different countries, it is difficult to provide a concise summary across countries. Fig. 10.3 attempts this by considering the differences between mathematics test scores in PISA between both first-generation immigrants and native students. In most countries natives are outperforming immigrant groups at age 13. Dustmann, Frattini, and Lanzara (2012) highlight that difference in education performance among second-generation immigrants is strongly linked to the educational background of the foreign-born parents. Countries with historical patterns of immigration from rich countries have second generation immigrants who do as well as or better than native children.

Inequalities by gender

The relative performance of women compared to men in terms of qualifications gained has improved across the world in the past three or four decades. For example in 1970, 42% of all US college undergraduates were women, whereas by 2000 this had risen to

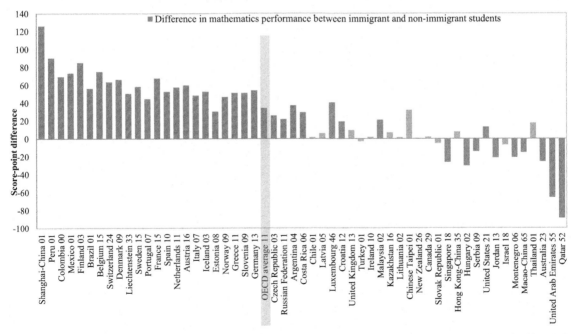

FIG. 10.3 Gaps in mathematics performance across countries: PISA 2012. *Note: Source OECD (2013). Paler colored bars indicate that differences between immigrants and natives are not significant. Note: the mathematics scores are scaled so that in the original 2003 survey the mean was 500 and the standard deviation was 100.*

II. Private and social returns to education

60% (Bae, Choy, Geddes, Sable, & Snyder, 2000). In 2014 women also outnumbered men on prestigious four year courses (Boston Globe, https://www.bostonglobe.com/metro/2016/03/28/look-how-women-outnumber-men-college-campuses-nationwide/YROqwfCPSlKPtSMAzpWloK/story.html).

Figures from the OECD Education at a Glance show women's relative improvement in terms of higher education is widespread internationally by comparing education rates for men and women in different age groups. Fig. 10.4 shows a large gain in the graduation rates of women when comparing the 25–34 age group with those aged 45–54. In all but two of the countries presented, in 2012 more young women attended tertiary education than young men.

Data from PISA 2012 shown in Fig. 10.5 reveals strong evidence that girls out-perform boys in reading. Evidence on maths and science is more mixed, with boys outperforming girls in maths and to a lesser extent science; especially in those countries where the gap in reading scores is smaller. However, compared to the evidence from Dustmann (2005) reviewed in our earlier entry there is evidence in several more countries that girls are outperforming boys across all three PISA domains.

Moss and Washbrook (2016) find that early differences are important in explaining gender differences in achievement by age 11 in the UK. Boys have lower levels of language and attention at age 5 and this is an important explanation of why they lag behind at age 11. As a result of these trends, policy attention is increasingly asking how boys can be helped in education, although their emerging disadvantage in this

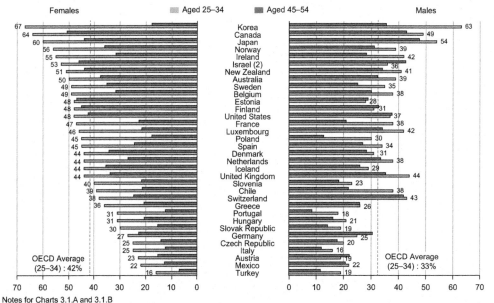

Notes for Charts 3.1.A and 3.1.B
Countries ranked in descending order of female educational attainment for the age group 35-34
1 Excluding ISCED 3C short programmes.
2 The data for Israel are supplied by and under the responsibility of the relevant Israeli authorities. The use of such data by the OECD is without prejudice to the status of the Golan Heights, East Jerusalem and Israeli settlements in the West Bank under the terms of international law.

FIG. 10.4 Chart CO3.1.B percentage of population that has attained tertiary education, by gender and age group, 2012. *Source: OECD Education database, v Sep 2014.*

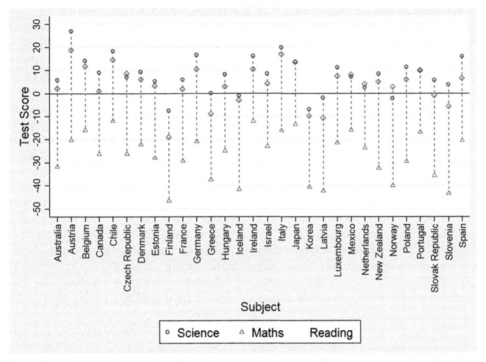

FIG. 10.5 Boys mean score − girls mean score across subjects in PISA 2012. *Notes: Data from OECD (2016).*

area has not yet fed through to women outperforming men in the adult labor market.

To summarize this section on the dimensions of inequalities in education, we can say that inequalities by family background are large and persistent. While they have shown some signs of reducing at some levels of education, they tend to reassert themselves when we consider the very highest level of attainment. The picture for race/ethnicity and gender is more positive, at least in some countries.

Education and economic outcomes

Higher levels of educational attainment are strongly associated with higher earnings and better employment prospects. Much of the empirical work studying the labor market impact of education has its roots in the work done in the economics of education field by American economists in the 1960s. In particular Jacob Mincer (1958) popularized the earnings function that relates wages to the number of years of schooling:

$$\log w = a + bS + {}_{c1}X + {}_{c2}X^2 + u$$

where w is earnings, S measures schooling, X denotes years of experience and u is a random error term. Psacharopoulos and co-authors have written numerous papers comparing the coefficient b across the world and have found evidence that earnings returns to schooling are widespread and tend to be higher for primary education, for girls and in countries with lower levels of development (see Psarcharopoulos & Patrinos, 2018 for the latest work). It is also notable that returns to higher education have grown in recent decades while the overall return to education has remained quite steady at around 9 percent for each additional year of education. This is despite a continuing steep growth in enrollment in HE, a point we shall return to below.

Fig. 10.6 shows OECD evidence on educational wage differentials that accrue to people with tertiary education levels relative to post-secondary non-tertiary levels in fifteen countries and for post-secondary education relative to below this level. The existence of sizable gaps in earnings is seen for all countries. According to these earnings differentials, acquisition of more education leads to significantly higher earnings.

As well as having higher earnings, workers with educational qualifications also tend to have improved employment probabilities. This is another effect of the increased productivity associated with education, as those with productivity below the effective minimum wage will not be employed. Fig. 10.7 compares the employment rates of those who do not complete upper secondary schools (equivalent to US high school) with employment rates for those who have high school but no college education. It is very clear from these statistics that obtaining at least the typical level of education increases employment probabilities.

Much research time has been devoted to understanding whether those who are more highly educated earn more and are more employable *because* they are educated, or because they are more able and motivated and would have done better in the labor market anyway. The consensus from a variety of techniques is that in most instances much of the higher earnings observed among the better educated is a consequence of their education (Card, 1999, Woessmann, 2016).

Recent work has moved the discussion beyond the quantity of education measured by

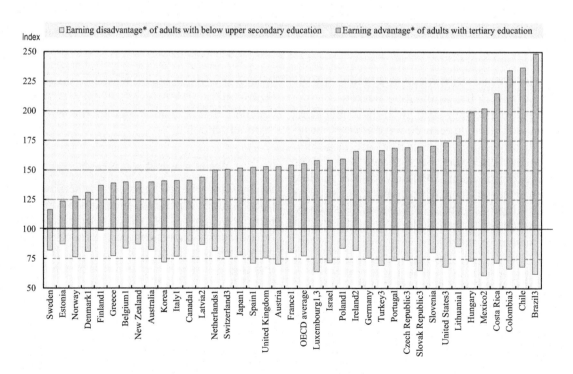

FIG. 10.6   Earnings by Educational Attainment. *Source OECD (2016). Note: For adults with upper secondary education, relative earnings are 100 and earnings (dis)advantage is 0.*

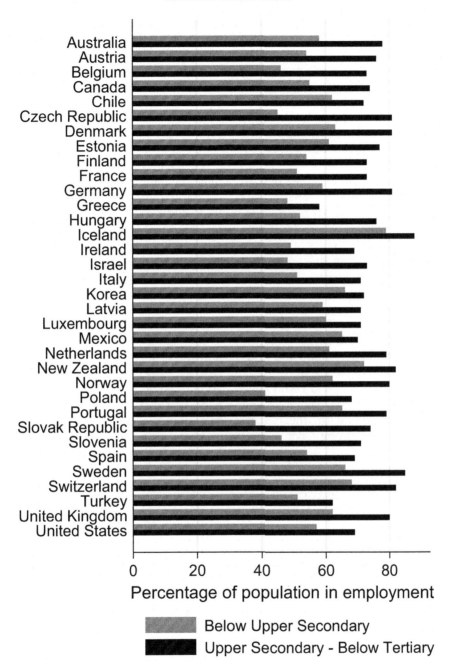

FIG. 10.7 Percentage of adults in employment by education level. *Source: OECD (2017). Note: Based on population of 25–64 year olds in 2016.*

years of education and degrees obtained to look at the quality of education; e.g. the type of education and specific skills workers have. The importance of skills has been considered using the internationally comparable PIAAC data which directly measures adult skills across three areas, literacy, numeracy and problem solving. Results show a good deal of variation in the returns to skill across countries, but strong evidence of the importance of numeracy.

Research on returns to different types of education has looked at differences between subject studied (Kirkeboan, Leuvin, & Mogstad, 2016; Webber, 2014) and college type (generally measured by the selectivity of entry, as in Dale & Krueger, 2014). Results seem to suggest that there is considerable heterogeneity in returns from different college degrees and universities, although evidence on whether the impact of institution is causal is less clear. Recent evidence from the UK (Belfield et al., 2018) assesses the impact of both subject and institution and finds important effects from both. Note that the highest returns are found for Science and Technology degrees as well as those in Law, Economics and Management; this chimes with the results mentioned above that find strong labor market benefits from numerical skills.

Social science researchers have considered the wider benefits of education by studying connections between education and a broader range of outcomes than just the labor market. These are often thought of as picking up "social returns" to education and include health, crime, civic engagement and intergenerational effects on children's outcomes (Oreopolous & Salvanes, 2011). From this work, there is evidence of important externalities, in that education significantly improves health outcomes and reduces early death (Lleras-Muney, 2005; van Kippersluis, O'Donnell, & van Doorslaer, 2011), is associated with lower crime levels (Lochner & Moretti, 2004; Machin, Marie and Vujic, 2011) and enhances the extent of civic engagement and participation (Brehm & Rahn, 1997; Bynner & Egerton, 2001; Dee, 2004).

Moreover, there are important intergenerational effects in that more education reduces the chances of early childbirth (Black, Devereux, & Salvanes, 2008) as well as increasing educational outcomes among the next generation. (Black, Devereux, & Salvanes, 2005).

Changes over time

We have so far reviewed the evidence that differential educational attainments can lead to substantial differences in earnings, employment probabilities and other outcomes that matter for individuals' welfare. It is clear that employers are prepared to pay higher wages to more educated workers; this reflects in part their scarcity value. Simple demand and supply analysis indicates that ceteris paribus as more workers become highly educated the earnings returns to being educated will decline.

Fig. 10.8 shows the proportion of the population aged 25−34 with tertiary education in 2005, 2010 and 2015. It shows that the proportion of young people in the labor market with higher education qualifications increased in all countries over the decade up to 2015. If demand had remained steady we would expect this to have resulted in a fall in earnings (and indeed employment) differentials over time. However, the newest survey by Psarcharopoulos and Patrinos (2018) reveals that while returns to each additional year of education have remained steady, worldwide the returns to higher education have continued to increase.

An increase in the supply of educated workers will lead to a decline in the wage premium they receive unless employer's demand for them increases by more. This seems to have been what has happened in practice. Large increases in the demand for graduates have occurred meaning that wage differentials related to education have stayed constant or increased in the face of the expansion of tertiary education in many countries. In both the US and UK wage premia have risen despite a massive expansion in the supply of graduates

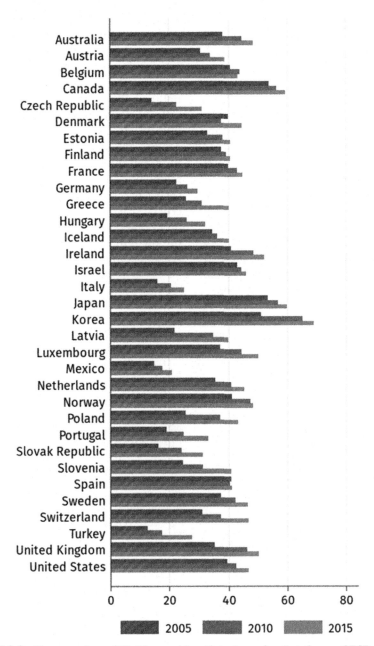

FIG. 10.8 The percentage of 25–34 year olds with tertiary education. Source: OECD (2017)

with a tertiary education and researchers have sought to understand what lies behind the implied increase in the demand for educated workers.

The skill-biased technical change (SBTC) hypothesis has received substantial empirical support (see the survey of Machin & Van Reenen, 2006). Through the 1980s and 1990s the data were well explained by a model of the supply and demand of skilled and unskilled workers where the demand for skilled workers grew in response to changes in technology. This interpretation was supported by evidence that linked the demand for skilled workers (measured by their share in the wage bill) to technology. The fact that similar industries were affected across the world made other competing explanations (like increased international trade) less convincing (see Berman, Bound, & Machin, 1998, or Machin & Van Reenen, 1998, for international evidence in line with this).

However in recent years the predictions of the "canonical" supply and demand model of SBTC fits the data more poorly than in the past and several new trends have emerged. These are explained by a more sophisticated version of the SBTC hypothesis known as Task-biased technical change (Acemoglu & Autor, 2011). In this model goods are produced by a combination of tasks which can be classified according to whether they are substitutable by technology. Tasks can be carried out by workers of any level of skill but skilled workers are most productive in abstract tasks that cannot be substituted by technology. These aspects of the model allow it to explain why the spread of technology is leading to a fall in wages and employment among some groups, especially those traditionally in the middle of the wage distribution whose routine non-manual tasks are easily substituted by technology.

Conclusions

Education and inequality are closely related. It is evident that education acquisition is related to family background and that different demographic groups acquire different levels of education. Since education yields a private return in the labor market and there are social returns to education, it is clear that the uneven patterns of education acquisition have the potential to generate inequalities in economic and social outcomes. Our summary reveals that gaps in educational achievement by family background remain strong and are likely a barrier to social mobility. However, the picture for women and ethnic minorities is rosier. It seems clear that education will continue to play a crucial role in shaping individuals economic and non-economic wellbeing and that its distribution remains critical for shaping overall inequalities in society.

References

Acemoglu, D., & Autor, D. (2011). Skills, tasks and technologies: Implications for employment and earnings. In D. Card, & Ashefelter (Eds.), *Handbook of Labor Economics* Vol. 4. Part B,. Amsterdam: North Holland.

Bae, Y., Choy, S., Geddes, C., Sable, J., & Snyder, T. (2000), *Educational equity for girls and women U.S. Department of education.* Washington, D.C.: U.S. Government Printing Office.

Belfield, C., Britton, J., Buscha, F., Dearden, L., Dickson, M., van der Erve, L., Sibieta, L., Vignoles, A., Walker, I., & Zhu, Y. (2018). *The relative labour market return to different degrees.* Department for Education Research Report No. 787.

Berman, E., Bound, J., & Machin, S. (1998). Implications of skill-biased technological change: International evidence. *Quarterly Journal of Economics, 113,* 1245.

Black, S., Devereux, P., & Salvanes, K. (2005). Why the apple doesn't fall far: Understanding the intergenerational transmission of education. *The American Economic Review, 95,* 437–449.

Black, S., Devereux, P., & Salvanes, K. (2008). Staying in the classroom and out of the maternity ward? The effect of compulsory schooling laws on teenage births? *The Economic Journal, 118*(530), 1025–1054.

Blanden, J., & Macmillan, L. (2016). Educational inequality, educational expansion and intergenerational mobility. *Journal of Social Policy, 45*(4), 589–614.

Bradbury, B., Corak, M., Waldfogel, J., & Washbrook, E. (2015). *Too many children left behind: The US achievement gap in comparative perspective.* New York: Russell Sage Foundation.

Brehm, J., & Rahn, W. (1997). Individual-level evidence for the causes and consequences of social capital. *American Journal of Political Science, 41*, 999—1023.

Bynner, J., & Egerton, M. (2001). *The wider benefits of higher education*. London: Higher Education Funding Council For England.

Cameron, S., & Heckman, J. (2001). The dynamics of educational attainment for black, Hispanic and white males. *Journal of Political Economy, 109*, 455—499.

Card, D. (1999). The causal effect of education on earnings. In O. Ashenfelter, & D. Card (Eds.), *Handbook of Labor Economics* (Vol. 3). North Holland: Elsevier.

Card, D., & Rothstein, J. (2007). Racial segregation and the black-white test score gap. *Journal of Public Economics, 91*, 2158—2184.

Chetty, R., Hendren, N., Jones, M., & Porter, S. (2018). *Race and economic opportunity in the United States: An intergenerational perspective*. NBER Working Paper 2444.

Corak, M. (2013). Income inequality, equality of opportunity and intergenerational mobility. *The Journal of Economic Perspectives, 27*(3), 79—102.

Dale, S., & Krueger, A. (2014). Estimating the effects of college characteristics over the career using administrative earnings data. *Journal of Human Resources, 49*(2), 323—358.

Dee, T. (2004). Are there civic returns to education? *Journal of Public Economics, 88*, 1697—1720.

Dustmann, C. (2005). The assessment: Gender and the life cycle. *Oxford Review of Economic Policy, 21*, 325—339.

Dustmann, C. T., Frattini, & Lanzara, G. (2012). Educational achievement of second-generation immigrants: An international comparison. *Economic Policy, 27*(69), 143—185.

Jencks, C., & Phillips, M. (1998). *The black-white test score gap*. Washington DC: Brookings Institution Press.

Jerrim, J. (2012). The socio-economic gradient in teenagers' reading skills: How does England compare with other countries? *Fiscal Studies, 33*(2), 159—184.

van Kippersluis, H., O'Donnell, O., & van Doorslaer, E. (2011). Long-run returns to education does schooling lead to an extended old age? *Journal of Human Resources, 46*(4), 695—721.

Kirkeboan, L., Leuvin, E., & Mogstad, M. (2016). Field of study, earnings and self-selection. *Quarterly Journal of Economics, 131*(3), 1057—1111.

Lleras-Muney, A. (2005). The relationship between education and adult mortality in the United States. *The Review of Economic Studies, 72*, 189—221.

Lochner, L., & Moretti, E. (2004). The effect of education on criminal activity: Evidence from prison inmates, arrests and self-reports. *The American Economic Review, 94*, 155—189.

Machin, S., Marie, O., & Vujić, S. (2011). The crime reducing effect of education. *The Economic Journal, 121*(May), 463—484.

Machin, S., & Van Reenen, J. (1998). Technology and changes in skill structure: Evidence from seven OECD countries. *Quarterly Journal of Economics, 113*, 1215—1244.

Machin, S., & Van Reenen, J. (2006). *Changes in wage inequality*, New Palgrave Dictionary of E conomics.

Mincer, J. (1958). Investment in human capital and personal income distribution. *Journal of Political Economy, 66*(4), 281—302.

Moss, G., & Washbrook, E. (2016). *Understanding the gender gap in literary and language development*. University of Bristol Graduate School of Education Working Paper 1/2016.

OECD. (2013). *PISA 2012 results: Excellence through equity (Volume II): Giving every student the chance to succeed*. Paris: OECD Publishing.

OECD. (2016). *PISA 2015 results: Excellence and equity in education (Volume I)*. Paris: OECD Publishing.

OECD. (2017). *Education at a glance 2017: OECD indicators*. Paris: OECD Publishing. https://doi.org/10.1787/eag-2017-en.

Oreopolous, P., & Salvanes, K. (2011). Priceless: The nonpecuniary benefits of schooling. *The Journal of Economic Perspectives, 25*(1), 159—184.

Platt, L. (2007). Making education count: The effects of ethnicity and qualifications on intergenerational social class mobility. *Sociological Review, 55*, 485—508.

Psarcharopoulos, G., & Patrinos, H. (2018). *Returns to investment in education: A decennial review of the global literature*. World Bank Policy Research Working Paper No. 8402.

Reardon, S. (2011). The widening academic achievement gap between the rich and the poor: New evidence and possible explanations. In G. Duncan, & R. Murnane (Eds.), *Whither opportunity? Rising inequality, schools, and children's life chances*. New York: Russell Sage Foundation.

Rowntree, B. S. (1901). Poverty: A study of town life (centennial ed.). Bristol: Policy Press.

Strand, S. (2015). *Ethnicity, deprivation and educational achievement at age 16 in England: Trends over time*. Department for Education Research Report 439B.

Webber, D. A. (2014). The lifetime earnings premia of different majors: Correcting for selection based on cognitive, noncognitive, and unobserved factors. *Labour Economics, 28*, 14—23.

Woessmann, L. (2016). The economic case for education. *Education Economics, 24*(1), 3—32.

11

Race earnings differentials

M. Carnoy

Stanford University, Stanford, CA, United States

Glossary

Ability differences Refer to innate ability differences as measured by tests before children enter school, but in most economics literature is usually the measured test performance differences among individuals on a school-based test

AFQT Armed Forces Qualifying Test—a test developed to screen individuals for service in the military

Cognitive skills Mental skills that are used in the process of acquiring knowledge, such as attention, memory, reasoning, symbolic thinking, perception, and self regulation

Cross-section data Data collected at one point in time on a sample of individuals

Educational quality Refer to the quantity of schooling inputs per student, the quality of inputs per student, such as teacher content knowledge or teacher experience, or the measured outputs of schooling, such as test score gains from year to year

Ethnic group A group of people that shares a self-identity, which can be based on language, national heritage, culture (often mixed with religion), and usually a combination of all these

Labor market discrimination Differences among race, ethnic, and gender groups in employment, wages, and promotion due to differential treatment of individual characteristics associated with productivity, such as education, experience, and measured ability

Longitudinal data Data collected on a sample of a cohort of individuals over a number of years in a series of follow-up questionnaires

Noncognitive skills Skills such as persistence, reliability, self-discipline, the ability to work with others, and the capacity to listen

Racial group Although controversial for scientific and political reasons, this usually means a category of individuals based on heritable characteristics such as skin color and facial features, but also on self-identification and social construct

Test score gap Refers to the difference in average performance on national tests by identifiable social class, gender, ethnic, and race groups

Earnings differentials between racial or ethnic groups exist in most societies. To the extent that they persist over rime in democratic political conditions, they are of considerable concern, since they suggest that different groups are not getting either equal access to human capital investment opportunities or equal treatment in labor markets, or both.

The literature on such earnings differences (and more generally, unequal economic and educational opportunities) have been of interest to economists for almost 70 years, especially in the United States, where, in 1944, a Swedish economist, Gunnar Myrdal, published the path-breaking *An American Dilemma: The Negro Problem and Modern Democracy*, and where the civil rights movement in the 1950s and 1960s continued to draw attention to the unequal education and income of African-Americans and Latinos. The pressure exerted by the movement enabled the collection of detailed census statistics that helped researchers estimate the existence of wage and schooling differences and to posit explanations for them. In other countries where such data are collected, the results also show distinct differences in economic performance between ethnic and race groups, suggesting that discovering differences is largely a function of data-collection politics.

More recently, in the 1990s, a major debate was held over whether racial/ethnic discrimination in labor markets has disappeared, and whether the main problem is that African-Americans and Latinos earn lower incomes for a given level of education because their academic achievement is lower. This then raises the issue of why different race/ethnic groups achieve differently in school (e.g., the Black–White test-score gap), and how important those differences are in explaining earnings differences.

Although the discussion in this article focuses on the United States, this is primarily because of the richness of the data available and the highly developed debate about the explanation of differences. The methodology is applicable to other economies with minor changes of local conditions. Such a comparison is made with Brazil, with a large Black and mulatto population, and Israel, where European immigrants and those of Afro-Asian origin differ considerably in education and cultural background, and a large minority of Israeli Arabs, representing 19% of the population, that faces major barriers to entry into private and public sector jobs and are discriminated against for ideological reasons.

Race and ethnic earnings differences in the United States

Data on race, ethnicity, and earnings in the United States are available for the period 1939–2006, and can be analyzed by native- and foreign-born percentage (see Chiswick, 1984 for the 1970 census breakdown). It is important to analyze the data by gender since earnings differ by gender across groups, and female labor force participation rates also differ among groups and over time.

The data suggest that certain ethnic groups, regardless of race, earn more than average and more than the dominant White Anglo (non-Latino) majority. Therefore, for example, Japanese Americans, Chinese-Americans, and Jewish-Americans all earn more than Anglo-Whites and this has been the case since at least the 1960s. African- Americans, Latinos, Filipinos, and Native-Americans are all examples of groups that earn considerably less, on average, than Anglo-Whites and have done so for as long as data have been available on such differences. Among Latinos there is also variation, with Mexican and Puerto Rican Latinos earning much less than those of Cuban origin.

Table 11.1 presents earnings data for the period 1939–2006 according to ethnic group, race group, and gender group. The Asian-American and Latino groupings are broad and contain distinct subgroups that earn significantly more or significantly less than the group average. Estimates of earnings of Latinos of Mexican origin, Puerto Rican origin, and Cuban origin show that Cuban-origin Latinos earn more on an average, than Latinos of Mexican or Puerto Rican origin. Part of the subgroup variation is due to large differences in the socioeconomic origins of different national groups that immigrated to the United States. For example, the first wave of Cuban Americans who came to Florida in the late 1950s and early 1960s were professionals leaving Castro's Cuba. That group of immigrants was markedly different from the unskilled laborers from Mexico who immigrated throughout the same period, and especially after immigration laws changed in 1965.

Yet, despite this variation within broad groups, Table 11.1 suggests that: (1) there are important and persistent ethnic/race differences in earnings in the United States labor market, (2) these differences cut across gender, and (3) they are subject to historical change. In the period

TABLE 11.1   United States: Annual median earnings by education, race/ethnic group, and gender, 1939—2006 (full-time workers, current dollars, and percent).

Category	Year 1939	1949	1959	1969	1979	1989	1999	2006
All schooling (males, 25—34 years)								
White	1356	3001	5438	8633	17,389	28,578	35,603	40,964
Black	42	55	58	63	70	71	78	77
Latino	62	71	72	76	70	67	62	66
Asian-American	65	76	86	101	96	98	–	124
High school graduate (males, 25—34 years)								
White	1353	3026	5241	8082	14,830	22,288	30,496	34,387
Black	58	73	69	73	80	80	88	88
Latino	88	83	82	85	89	85	73	79
Asian-American	75	85	99	100	86	89	–	93
College graduates (males, 25—34 years)								
White	2719	3760	6788	10,549	18,394	31,279	42,173	50,471
Black	59	72	67	68	82	70	87	80
Latino	99	66	78	76	88	83	90	88
Asian-American	73	85	85	110	91	100	–	112
All schooling (females 25—34 years)								
White	816	2038	3032	4956	10,226	18,613	27,296	34,034
Black	39	57	63	77	91	90	84	81
Latino	61	87	75	90	87	82	76	77
Asian-American	83	89	99	113	109	109	–	119
High school graduate (females, 25—34 years)								
White	935	2212	3470	5121	9523	15,421	20,655	25,058
Black	51	75	73	84	95	90	88	88
Latino	94	103	95	103	93	95	91	92
Asian-American	85	69	100	94	92	119	–	–
College graduates (females, 25—34 years)								
White	1128	2491	4378	6336	12,228	23,732	34,377	40,614
Black	67	89	71	101	95	94	90	91
Latino	–	–	–	99	94	98	94	92
Asian-American	–	–	–	104	110	106	–	109

From US Department of Commerce, Bureau of the Census, Public Use Census Sample, 1940, 1950, 1960, 1970, 1980, 1990, 1996, and 2007.

1939−79, non-Anglo men and women made large gains relative to Anglos, and after 1979, these gains leveled off, with some notable continued gains (Black male high school graduates), and notable reversals for Black and Latina women. Even with the large gains over four decades, African-Americans and Latinos have remained at a lower level of median income than either Anglos or Asian-Americans. It also should be noted that these data are reported for full-time, full-year workers, so they do not reflect the higher rates of unemployment among minority workers, and that, in real terms (adjusted for inflation), the average earnings reported for White male high school and college graduates, 25−34 years old declined, from US$14 830 in 1979 to US$12 369 in 2006 in the case of high school graduates, and from US$18 394 in 1979 to US$18 155 in 2006 for college graduates. Female high school graduates also had a 12% decline in real earnings in this period. Thus, except in the case of Black male high school graduates, after the 1970s, Blacks and Latinos generally maintained a constant or declining share of declining real earnings. It is also fairly evident from Table 11.1 that once education and age are accounted for, Latinos earn relatively more than African-Americans with a college education, but males earn less at the high school graduate level.

The two important questions that the literature has addressed about these earnings differences, logically, are:

(1) Why do some groups do better or worse than others?
(2) What causes them to change over time?

A model for explaining earnings differences

The human capital model has typically been used to understand race and ethnic differences in earnings (Becker, 1957; Chiswick, 1984; Freeman, 1973, 1976; Hanushek, 1981; Welch,

1973). This model characterizes individual earnings as a function of education and experience in the labor force. The premise is that earnings of various groups would be explained largely, if not entirely, by their average education and experience. This still leaves the issue of why average education differs among different groups. Is the difference voluntary, or the result of discrimination in the supply of educational services? However, leaving this issue aside, if the human capital model is a correct representation of the market for labor, then race or ethnicity should play no significant role once the human capital of individuals is controlled for, that is, the coefficients of education and experience in the earnings function should be equal of all ethnic groups. The model is as follows:

$$\ln Y_i = a + b_j \sum_{j=1}^{m} S_{ij} + C_k \sum_{k=m+1}^{n} E_{ik} + e_i$$

where Y_i = income of the individual i; S_{ij} = dummy for schooling level j; E_{ik} = dummy for experience level k; and e_i = unexplained variance.

Other models are more elaborate, including the possibility that earnings for different groups vary because of employment in different industries (with significantly lower or higher pay), in public versus private employment, different parts of the country, and because of differences in civil status, and in native versus foreign parentage, which could represent English-language skill differences (Bean & Tienda, 1988; Carnoy et al., 1976, 1990; Farley, 1986). Time worked per week or per year is also an important potential factor affecting earnings differences, since some groups may have higher average levels of voluntary unemployment and part-time employment than others.

Most recently, in the 1990s, the argument on race/ethnic earnings differences focused on the achievement score differences between these groups even when they have the same number of years of schooling and similar experience in the labor force (Herrnstein & Murray, 1994; Murnane, Willet, & Levy, 1995; Neal & Johnson, 1996; Thernstrom & Thernstrom, 1997). Such achievement differences can reflect varying initial endowments, varying family and community investments in children's academic ability, and possible differences in the quality of schooling available to different race/ethnic groups. Some analysts are persuaded that the Black-White and Latino- White test gaps are the main obstruction to Black and Latino economic progress. In their view, the test gap indicates that the cognitive ability of many Blacks and Latinos is weak and therefore the main reason their wages and income lag behind whites. In the human capital explanation, academic ability among those with the same number of years of schooling needs to be added to the model to measure human capital more fully.

We take these arguments step by step; first, we use cross-section data over a long period of time to estimate how much school attainment and other variables (not including academic ability) may contribute to earnings differences between race/ethnic groups. Then we look at studies that use longitudinal data to test the contribution of ability differences to these earnings differences. We also comment on how the contribution of various factors to earnings differences may be changing over time.

Explaining earnings differences with cross-section data

Empirical results of cross-sectional studies in a single year show that schooling level attained is a significant correlate of earnings differences among groups. African-Americans, Latinos, and Native-Americans take significantly less schooling than Anglo Whites and, particularly less than, Asian-Americans. The importance of education in explaining differences in income between various ethnic/gender groups can be simulated with log income equations, estimating

how much equalizing education differences would equalize income between groups. For each year and each ethnic/gender group shown in Table 11.2, the figure in the table represents the percentage point increase in average income the group would have had if its education were equal to that of White males in the same year. For example, in 1939, Black males would have had 27% points higher income if their education were equal to White males', taking account of age differences. White females, on the contrary, would have had 9% points lower income if their education were equal to White males', implying that that working White females were more educated than males in the 1930s. Adding work-experience differences changes these percentages marginally, except for Latinos in the 1970s, when the Latino labor force became significantly younger than other groups. The additional effect of Latino experience decreased sharply in the 1980s.

Observable factors other than the quantity of schooling and age may explain part of the gap in the earnings of Black and Latino workers compared to Whites. Some of these factors are industry and region worked in, English-language limitation (foreign birth/language spoken at home), and the quality of education taken by different groups, including differential investment in education at home.

Excluding measures of ability differences, which are not available in the census cross-section census samples, the graphs in Fig. 1 show the percentage points of income difference remaining when all the observable factors (school attainment, work experience, region of work, marital status, foreign/native birth, and industry of work) of each group are equalized by simulation to that of White full-time employed adult males (see Oaxaca (1973), Carnoy et al. (1990), and Carnoy (1994), for the standard model of such a simulation). This residual fell significantly for full-time-employed Black males between 1939 and 1982 and for Latino and Asian-American males between 1939 and 1969. The residual

TABLE 11.2   Percentage points of income gain that would result from equalizing minority education to White male education, by ethnicity and gender, full-time employed, 1939–89.[a]

Year	Latino males	Latina females	Black males	Black females	White females
1939	29	18	27	22	-9
1949	17	12	18	11	-8
1959	15	10	15	9	-2
1969	12	9	14	7	0
1973	16	9	12	5	0
1979	16	8	11	6	2
1982	15	10	11	6	2
1985	15	10	11	6	2
1987	15	8	10	6	1
1989	20	14	10	7	0

From Department of Commerce, United States Census, Public Use Sample. 1940, 1950, 1960, 1970, 1980 and Current Population Survey, 1974, 1983, 1986, 1988, 1990.

[a] *The education variable is measured in 1940, 1950, 1960, 1970, 1974, 1980, 1983, 1986, 1988, and 1990; incomes refer to the previous year - hence, the years in the table refer to the income year. The education gap is estimated from a simulation using a regression equation with human capital variables (years of schooling, labor-force experience, and, in census years, native or foreign born). The percentages in the table should be read as the number of percentage points that a given group would have gained just from getting the same distribution of education in its labor force as White males. A negative sign means that White females would receive lower incomes, all other variables equal, were education equalized with that of White males (White females in the labor market in those years had higher education than White males).*

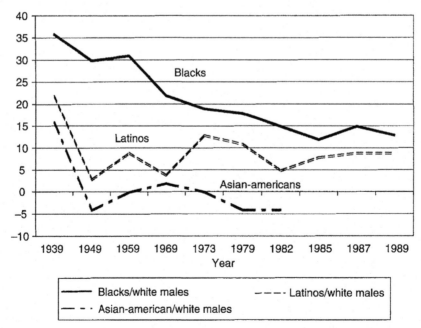

FIG. 1   Minority-White income gap explained by wage discrimination (does not include adjustment for ability differences), 1939–89.

shown in Fig. 1 is measured as percentage points of the earnings gap for each group that is not explained when minorities are made to look like White males educationally and in terms of experience and of place of work. In the 1980s, the residual rose for all three groups. The residual was essentially zero by the end of the 1940s for Asian-Americans, and has been, until the new Latino immigration after 1965, much lower for Latinos than for Blacks. In the 1980s, it represented about 16% points of White male income for Blacks and 13% points for Latinos. It is probable that the residual continued to rise for Latinos and may have fallen for Blacks between 1989 and 2006 (see Table 11.1). Part of the residual for Latinos is associated with foreign birth, and this, in turn, may be a function of English-language capability. When Latinos of Mexican origin are separated into native- and foreign-born, the corresponding residuals for the native-born are 3% points in 1960, 3 in 1970, and 6 in 1980, and for foreign-born, 27% points in 1960, 14 in 1970, and 14 in 1980 (Carnoy et al., 1990). The low residuals for native-born Latinos of Mexican origin suggests that the main explanation of lower incomes for Latinos, once English-language capacity is accounted for, is observable differences in educational attainment, experience, and place and type of work.

The residual can be interpreted as reflecting lower-quality education taken by minorities (Welch, 1973; Card & Krueger, 1992a, 1992b), lower returns to experience, such as in the choice of or access to jobs that have a smaller training component, hence flatter experience-earnings profiles, and possibly a strong interaction between the quality of schooling and access to training in jobs. The differences in quality of education received may not only reflect differences in the quality of schools attended by different groups, but also the amount invested in them by their families and the interaction between family background and school performance, which is discussed in detail below. Eliminating

discriminatory practices in school access does not necessarily equalize outcomes (the quality of an individual's education) because of the cumulative nature of learning before and during school and also because of interaction effects. Differences in returns to education and in access to jobs with more training for different groups may also simply be the result of discriminatory practices in the labor market.

Why labor market discrimination occurs has been the subject of considerable controversy. In his pioneering work on racial discrimination, Myrdal (1944) argued that it was historically institutionalized in the fabric of society and required public intervention to change.

Becker's (1957) model of discrimination focused on the taste for discrimination on the part of White workers and consumers, which drives the earnings of Black workers down relative to White workers. Reich (1982) refutes the claim by Becker that White workers profit when there is discrimination, showing that the lowest White earnings are in those states where the greatest discrimination exists. He argues that labor-market discrimination serves owners of capital, since it keeps all workers' wages lower.

Earnings differences for minority women

Racial and ethnic earnings differentials vary by gender. Table 11.1 suggests that full-time-employed minority women in the United States had, by the late 1960s/early 1970s, come to earn approximately the same income as full-time- employed White women when the level of schooling was the same, and, on an hourly basis, may actually have earned more than White women (Chiswick, 1987). By 2006, Black male high school and college graduates earned about 90% and 80% of the annual income of Whites, and Black women graduates earned about 90% of full-time White female incomes at both levels of schooling. Latino men high school graduates earned a much lower fraction of White male incomes than did Latina women relative to White women, but only slightly lower at the college graduate level - this is the opposite of the pattern for Blacks.

If Black women and Latinas are subject to the same race/ethnic discrimination as men, why should they earn higher relative incomes with compared to their White gender counterparts? The answer lies partly in the gender segregation of the labor market and the willingness of White male employers to group minority and White women in the same category of labor. This was not always the case, and, recently, differences in pay are beginning to emerge again in favor of White women, perhaps for somewhat different reasons than in the past. Black (but not Latina) female earnings were much lower than those of Whites in the 1940s and 1950s, when Black women were highly concentrated in domestic service. As Black women moved into manufacturing and clerical jobs and received much more schooling, the differences between White and Black female earnings tended to disappear, at least until the 1970s. After that time, with the steady increase in the labor-force participation of White women, the ratio of Black and Latina women's earnings to White female earning has gradually declined. Even so, Neal (2004) argues that the measured wage gap between Black and White women continues to be too small because of the failure to correct for differential labor-force participation.

Besides the continued gender segregation of the labor market, one reason that Black women may continue to earn a higher ratio of White salaries than Black men, particularly among college graduates, is that a higher fraction of college graduate Black women work in the public sector, where female salaries are much higher than in the private sector. Public sector employment was especially important in the late 1960s and in the 1970s, when such employment was at its peak.

Do ability/educational quality differences explain race/ethnic earnings differences?

The most recent debates center on whether discrimination has been eliminated or still exists in US labor markets (see, for example, Thernstrom & Thernstrom, 1997 vs.; Brown et al., 2003). The discussion centers in part on whether earnings differences not explained by education and experience differences are the result of continued discrimination or of race/ethnic differences in ability as measured by test-score differences (Neal & Johnson, 1996) - in part such test-score gaps are the result of family education differences (initial endowments) and, in part, of differences in the quality of schooling taken by Blacks/Latinos and Whites.

Estimates of the contribution of higher ability, as measured by scores on mathematics tests taken in high school, to individual earnings later in life suggest that its value is significant even when years of schooling are accounted for (Murnane et al., 1995), and that the return to academic skills may have increased in the 1980s (Blackburn & Neumark, 1993; Murnane et al., 1995). (However, this is not a universally held view. Some economists, such as Samuel Bowles and Herbert Gintis have long argued that cognitive skills explain relatively little of the variance of earnings and productivity (Bowles, Gintis, & Osborne, 2001; Bowles & Gintis, 1975).

Those estimates paid little attention to the role of race/ethnicity, but Carnoy and DeAngelis (1999) used the National Longitudinal Survey of Youth (NLSY) and High School and Beyond data to estimate the role of mathematics achievement and race/ethnicity in wages by gender group for the 1972 and 1982 high school senior cohorts in various years after graduation. They made these estimates separately for high school graduates, those who had completed some college, and for college graduates. They found that in the 1972 cohort, mathematics test score in high school had little direct effect on the wages of high school male graduates. Being Hispanic had no significant effect on earnings, but being Black had a strong negative effect; about 20—25% lower wages when education, mathematics achievement, and work experience were controlled for. The race effect was somewhat smaller but significant for those with some college, but was negligible for college graduates, whereas one standard deviation higher mathematics test score was worth 31% for those males with some college and 8—9% higher wages for college graduates. Higher mathematics score had a similar size effect for female college graduates, but neither race nor ethnicity had a significant relationship to wages.

For the 1982 cohort, only annual earnings (not wages) were available as the dependent variable. For male high school graduates, mathematics score is related to earnings in the 1991 follow-up, but so is race (being Black), although less so (10—18% lower earnings) than for the 1972 cohort. For those males with college education, race is unrelated to earnings when education and mathematics score is accounted for, but math score is related to earnings for college graduates to about the same degree as in the 1972 cohort. For females with college education, mathematics score is related to higher earnings, but race is generally not.

This analysis suggests that the labor market for high school graduates placed relatively less value on ability differences in the 1970s and 1980s and paid Black males considerably less even when all these human capital variables were accounted for. This did not appear to be the case for Hispanics with high school degrees or Hispanic/Black college graduates even in the 1970s, and by the 1980s and early 1990s, was not the case for even those males with some college. For females, race and ethnicity do not seem to have been correlated with wages or earnings even in the 1970s.

Thus, race discrimination for Blacks seems to have been important in the labor market for males with lower levels of schooling even in the 1980s and early 1990s, whereas it seems to have

played little role in the labor market for college-educated males by the late 1980s and for females with both high school and college education.

For the latter groups, mathematics ability was related to earnings; so if Blacks and Latinos had lower mathematics ability, they would have received somewhat lower earnings (about 10% lower earnings for one standard deviation difference in mathematics test score). If we extrapolated these results to the earnings differences in Table 11.1, most of the differences observed in Black/White male high school graduate earnings in 1989 and 1999 could be attributed to racial discrimination, and most of the observed Black/White differences in college graduate earnings for males and females, to mathematics achievement differences.

An analysis of yet another data set, the NLSY, which includes the armed forces qualifying test (AFQT) as a measure of ability among a sample of 16—23-year-olds in 1979, Carneiro, Heckman, and Masterov (2005) explores wage differences between Blacks and Whites and Hispanic and Whites, males and females, in that sample followed over the period 1991—2000. When the AFQT scores are corrected for the level of schooling attained by the test taker in order to get a purer ability effect, one standard deviation higher AFQT score is associated with 9—10% higher male wages whereas being a Black male is associated with 14—19% percent lower wages than White males. Once AFQT scores are taken into account, Hispanic and White males do not have significantly different wages. Being a Black woman is associated with 7—8%) lower wages than White women earn when ability is taken into account, and being a Hispanic woman is associated with a wage premium of 7—14% compared to White women. The payoff to ability is somewhat higher than for men, about 9—13% for one standard deviation higher AFQT score. These results are generally consistent with the results for the High School and Beyond Survey, but the test-score effect is somewhat larger in the NLSY, and being Black seems to have a negative effect on men and women's wages, although the coefficient is not large for women.

What are the sources of the black/white test-score gap?

Although it is beyond the scope of this article to provide a comprehensive review of the literature on the Black/White test-score gap, the overall question of race/ethnic difference in earnings merits at least some discussion of whether Blacks and Hispanics choose to invest less in themselves academically, hence achieve less, or whether the schools they attend and the society around them are the main source of their lower achievement - hence, it is the civil society and state that makes them less productive (this would be akin to the discrimination argument in labor markets).

Earlier Jencks and Phillips (1998) and more recently Rothstein (2004) summarized the empirical research on this issue. Rothstein argues that much of the achievement gap between Blacks and Whites exists at age 5 years when children enter kindergarten. His main point is that the achievement gap is largely the result of differences in the social context in which most Blacks and Latinos live in the United States and that the potential for schools to overcome achievement gaps is relatively limited. Thus, he concludes that a more productive strategy to reduce the achievement gap would be improving minorities' social conditions - nutrition, healthcare, and sense of being full participants in American society.

Part of those conditions is also the degree to which Blacks feel discriminated against in labor markets. A number of opinion surveys suggest that Whites believe that the United States is free of racial discrimination, and Blacks believe that despite great improvement in race relations over the past 40 years, racial discrimination is still a major feature of their lives (Brown et al., 2003). This could influence their desire to perform well in school and their test performance (Steele, 1997).

Evidence from national- and state-level data on whether the Black—White test score changes during schooling is contradictory:

Data from [longitudinal] ECLS-K and SEC-CYD suggest the gap is large at the start of kindergarten, and grows in the early elementary grades (particularly from first to third grade in ECLS-K), though the patterns differ somewhat depending on the gap metric used. Data from NAEP suggests that the gap continues to grow from age 9 to 13 (fourth to eighth grades, roughly), but [longitudinal] state-level data from Texas and North Carolina seem to contradict this finding, at least during the late 1990s and early 2000s, suggesting that the gap grows relatively little in standard deviation units over the latter half of elementary school. Finally, data from NAEP and NELS suggest the gaps change relatively little following eighth grade, though there is some uncertainty in these estimates, since most are based on analysis of repeated cross-sectional data (Reardon, 2007, p. 8).

Reardon (2007) does a careful analysis of changes in the Black—White test-score gap between kindergarten and fifth grade and concludes that the gap in both math and reading scores widens between kindergarten and fifth grade, and that the gap grows faster among higher-scoring students, suggesting that part of the widening gap may result from " ... black students with high skill levels in kindergarten being more likely than equally high-scoring white students to be in schools where the median skill level is far below their skills (because they are more likely to be in schools with predominantly black student populations)" (Reardon, 2007, p. 31). Thus, the increasing Black—White test-score gap might be the result of poorer schools, but schools whose quality is derived from the concentration of low-income students, in turn the result of residential segregation. Even so, the Black-White test-score gap at kindergarten entrance explains the bulk of the gap at grade five.

Carneiro et al. (2005) also argue that early environment rather than poor schooling is likely the most important reason that Blacks have lower test scores (academic skills) than Whites.

Minority deficits in cognitive and non-cognitive skills emerge early and widen. Unequal schooling, neighborhoods and peers may account for this differential growth in skills, but the main story in the data is not about growth rates but rather about the size of early deficits... .The failure of the Hispanic-white gap to widen with schooling or age casts doubt on the claim that poor schools and bad neighborhoods are the reasons for the slow growth rate in black test scores. (Carneiro et al. 21).

Explaining changes in earnings differences over time

Why has the gap in earnings between Whites and minority groups changed over time? Table 11.1 shows that full-time-employed Black males and females made large gains in relative earnings in the period 1939—79, especially in the 1940s and 1960s. The gains in the 1980s were negligible (the relative earnings of Black male college graduates fell), and Black males high school graduates made some gains in the 1990s, whereas Black female college graduates saw a decline in their earnings relative to White females. Latino males and females also made big gains in the period 1939—69, but then lost ground, particularly male high school graduates. Asian-Americans made large gains in the 1940s, 1950s, and 1960s, and college graduates continued to make gains in the 1990s and early 2000s.

The principal debate that has developed over these changes is whether they are the result of supply side forces, specifically changes in the relative investment in human capital made by the different groups, or demand side forces, specifically legal and direct employment intervention by government. Freeman (1976) maintained that the large gains in relative earnings of Blacks in the 1960s came as a result of the passage of the 1964 Civil Rights Act and subsequent federal employment legislation in 1965. Others (Card & Krueger, 1993; Donohue & Heckman, 1991; Heckman & Payner, 1989) have supported this explanation. Smith and Welch (1989), on the contrary, have argued that the single best explanation for the gains in the period 1939—79 was the relative increase in Black education, and that federal intervention had only a minor effect, primarily in raising the earnings of young Black college graduates in the early 1970s. Card and Krueger (1992b) claim that about one-fourth of the gain in Black earnings attributed to government intervention in labor markets in the 1960s and 1970s is the result of improvements in Black education in the South in the 1930s and 1940s. Juhn, Murphy, and Pierce (1991) argues that the slowdown in Black-White convergence in the 1980s was due to unmeasured skill effects, namely that the payoff to educational quality increased in the 1980s, and Blacks still received lower-quality education than Whites.

If the analysis is done decade by decade in the 50-year period 1939—89, the supply-side argument is weakened. Table 11.2 suggests that education gains by Blacks between 1939 and 1979 were correlated with a reduction in the Black-White earnings gap in those four decades. But other factors appear to have been much more important than education in that reduction. For example, Table 11.3 corrects that contribution of education differences to the income gap estimated in Table 11.2 for changes in the income distribution (specifically the income weights attached to different levels of schooling) in each decade. Wage compression in the 1940s was much more important than Black male educational gains in reducing the Black-White income gap, and was as important as education for Latinos. Although Black males' education did not increase much relative to Whites in the 1940s and racial discrimination declined only slightly, the enormous increases in incomes for all low-income earners relative to high-income

TABLE 11.3 Change in education gap adjusted for changing income weights, by decade, full-time workers, 1939–89 (percentage points of income).

Year	Latino males	Latina females	Black males	Black females
1939	29	18	27	22
1949	23	16	24	15
1949	17	12	18	11
1959	16	10	16	9
1959	15	10	15	9
1969	12	9	14	7
1969	12	9	14	7
1979	16	8	11	6
1979	16	8	11	6
1989	19	13	9	7

earners - irrespective of race - during that decade lifted Black male relative incomes more than in any decade since. In the 1940s, there was also a job shift from agriculture to manufacturing that had a power effect on Black male incomes. As a point of comparison, in the 1950s -a period of significant educational gains for minorities but no reduction in overall income inequality, much-reduced sectoral job shift, and no reductions in job discrimination — gains in relative incomes for Blacks were minimal. In the 1960s and particularly, the 1970s, Blacks made large education gains, but the major gains in income for Blacks came from the reduction in wage discrimination. In the 1980s, when the political climate on affirmative action changed, Black male and female incomes stopped rising relative to Whites' (particularly for Black male college graduates), and in the 1990s, when the climate became more favorable again, Black male relative earnings rose again. Another possible influence on Blacks' relative incomes in the 1990s may have been the relative increase in fourth- and

eighth-grade mathematics test scores in the late 1970s and 1980s, which could have been reflected in the higher relative test scores of both 25–34-year-old high school and college graduates in the 1990s and early 2000s.

From See Table 11.2 for figures based on the education gap estimated using same-year White male income weights. Figures in this table compare the education gap in 1939 with the gap in 1949 figures based on average education differences between ethnic groups in 1949 weighted by White male coefficients estimated using 1939 census data; compare the 1949 figures from Table 11.2 with 1959 figures based on average education differences in 1959 weighted by White male coefficients using 1949 census data, and so forth, for various census years. This permits comparison for each decade of the effect on income of the education gain net of changes in the distribution of income among education groups in that particular decade.

A similar analysis for Latinos and Asian-American males and females suggests that education is a more important explainer of their relative income gains than for Black and White females, although changes in sector of work (shifts from agriculture to manufacturing) are also crucial in understanding their gains in the 1940s (Latinos and Asian-Americans) and 1950s (Latinos). Both groups also profited from reduced labor-market discrimination in the 1940s and 1960s.

The recent work focusing on the relation to relative wages of pre-market skill differences between minorities and Whites has been interpreted by many as a mandate to improve the quality of education taken by Blacks and Hispanics (e.g., by Thernstrom & Thernstrom, 2003). However, both Carneiro et al. (2005) and Rothstein (2004) make convincing cases that most of the ability differences between Blacks and Whites as measured by teenage test scores of those with similar levels of schooling occur before children enter school and persist through the schooling process. This is apparently not the same pattern for Hispanics, who are able to close the ability gap as they acquire more schooling. Furthermore, almost all studies with longitudinal data show that even in the 1990s, at least for Blacks, education and test-score differences compared to Whites do not explain even part of Black–White wage differences, particularly for males.

Comparing results for Brazil and Israel

Brazil has a large Black (*preto*) and mulatto (*pardo*) population. For many years, the official ideology in Brazil was that its racial inequality was softened by the acceptance of intermarriage. In the past 10 years, however, research has identified large earnings differences between Whites and both *pretos* and *pardos* in the Brazilian labor market. The most recent of these studies uses 1996 household survey data for urban male workers and a rough proxy for the educational quality received by the individual worker (teacher–pupil ratios by state of birth and year of birth) to estimate wages of male household heads as a function of education, age, parents education, and industry worked in (Arias, Yamada, & Tejerina, 2004). The study finds that the bulk of wage differences between Whites and workers of color is explained by productivity-related worker characteristics, but unexplained wage differences remain large at higher-income levels. In the fifth quintile of income, the residual wage gap is 15% for *pretos* and 12% for *pardos,* and this increases in the top-income decile to 25% for *pretos* and 16% for *pardos.* This is reflected in lower rates of return to education for males of color than for Whites. Nevertheless, whereas *pretos* face a larger gap in education returns at the top of the income distribution, the opposite is true for *pardos.* Apparently, the common belief in Brazil that in higher socioeconomic levels, interracial marriage softens racial discrimination probably holds true.

Similar estimates have been made for Israel, where ethnic origin (European-origin vs. North African-Asian- origin immigrants) and being an Israeli Arab are potentially a source of wage discrimination (Amirs, 1983, 1988; Margalioth, 2005). The results of such estimates show that in the 1970s, the wage differential between the foreign-born males of the two ethnic groups in the Jewish population fell substantially from 25% to 16% mainly because of demographic factors such as a change in the relative age structures and period of immigration of the two groups. Unexplained differentials (wage discrimination plus quality of schooling differences) also fell from 15% to 12%. When the same estimates are made for first generation Israeli-born of North African-Asian and European extraction, the wage differential is shown to have become larger than for the foreign-born in the 1970s, rising from 26% in 1970–72 to 30% in 1980–82. This is explained mainly by an increasing age difference over the decade, with European-origin Israelis becoming increasingly older in relative terms. Nevertheless, the results also show that educational differences (larger than between the foreign born of the two ethnic groups) continued to persist even though average levels in both groups rose significantly relative to their parents. The results also show that wage discrimination fell during the decade and was relatively low (about 6% in 1980–82). Other estimates of wage differences between Israeli Arabs and Jews suggest that it is mainly the segregation of the labor market that contributes to the wage gap between the two groups. The gap is quite large: Israeli Arab employees earned about 28% less than Jewish employees. Arabs are highly overrepresented in low-paying industries such as agriculture and construction, whereas they are underrepresented in financial and business services (Margalioth, 2005). Although education differences, particularly a lower likelihood that Israeli Arabs attended university, contribute to wage differences, there is considerable evidence that an important source of wage differences is discrimination against Arabs in access to jobs on security threat and ideological grounds. Arabs also face a number of other barriers to entry, such as the requirement that potential employees have completed military service (Arabs normally do not serve in the Israeli defense forces).

See also

Human Capital; Returns to Education in Developed Countries; Returns to Education in Developing Countries; School Quality and Earnings; Education and Inequality; Desegregation, Academic Achievement and Earnings.

References

Amirs, S. (1983). *Educational structure and wage differentials of the Israeli labor force in the 1970s.* Jerusalem: Bank of Israel. Discussion Paper No. 83.07.

Amirs, S. (1988). Trends in wage differentials between Jewish males of different ethnic origin during the 1970s. *Bank of Israel Economic Review, 63,* 52—75.

Arias, O., Yamada, G., & Tejerina, L. (2004). Education, family background, and racial earnings inequality in Brazil. *International Journal of Manpower, 25*(3/4), 355—374.

Bean, F., & Tienda, M. (1988). *The hispanic population of the United States.* New York: Sage.

Becker, G. S. (1957). *The economics of discrimination.* Chicago, IL: University of Chicago Press.

Blackburn, M., & Neumark, D. (1993). Omitted-ability bias and the increase in the return to schooling. *Journal of Labour Economics, 11,* 521—544.

Bowles, S., & Gintis, H. (1975). *Schooling in capitalist America.* New York: Basic Books.

Bowles, S., Gintis, H., & Osborne, M. (2001). The determinants of earnings, a behavioral approach. *Journal of Economic Literature, 39,* 1137—1176.

Brown, M., Carnoy, M., Currie, E., et al. (2003). *Whitewashing race: The myth of a color-blind society.* Berkeley, CA: University of California Press.

Card, D., & Krueger, A. (1992a). Does school quality matter? Returns to education and the characteristics of public schools in the United States. *Journal of Political Economy, 100*(1), 1—40.

Card, D., & Krueger, A. (1992b). School quality and black/white relative earnings: A direct assessment. *Quarterly Journal of Economics, 107*(1), 151—200.

Card, D., & Krueger, A. (1993). Trends in relative Black-White earnings revisited. *American Economic Review, 83*(2), 85—91.

Carneiro, P., Heckman, J., & Masterov, D. (2005). *Labor market discrimination and racial differences in premarket factors.*

Bonn, Germany: Institute for the Study of Labor (IZA). Discussion Paper 1453.

Carnoy, M. (1994). *Faded dreams.* New York: Cambridge University Press.

Carnoy, M., Daley, H., & Hlnojosa, R. (1990). *Latinos in a changing economy. Interuniversity program for Latino research.* New York: City University of New York.

Carnoy, M., & DeAngelis, K. (1999). *Does ability influence individual earnings, and if so, by how much? School of education stanford university.* Stanford, CA: Mimeo.

Carnoy, M., Girling, R., & Rumberger, R. (1976). *Education and public sector employment.* Stanford, CA: Center for Economic Studies.

Chiswick, B. R. (1984). Differences in education attainment among racial and ethnic groups: Patterns and preliminary hypotheses. In *Paper presented at the national academy of education conference on the state of education.* Washington, DC: Mimeo.

Chiswick, B. R. (1987). Race earnings differentials. In G. Psacharopoulos (Ed.), *Economics of education: Research and studies* (pp. 232—237). Oxford: Pergamon.

Donohue, J., Ill, & Heckman, J. (1991). Continuous versus episodic change: The impact of civil rights policy on the economic status of Blacks. *Journal of Economic Literature, 29,* 1603—1643.

Farley, R. (1986). Assessing Black progress: Employment, occupations, earnings, income, poverty. *Economic Outlook United States of America, 13*(3), 14—23.

Freeman, R. (1973). Decline of labor market discrimination and economic analysis. *American Economic Review, 63*(2), 280—286.

Freeman, R. (1976). *Black elite: The new market for higher educated black Americans.* New York: McGraw-Hill.

Hanushek, E. A. (1981). *Sources of black-white earnings differentials.* Stanford, CA: Stanford University. Institute for Educational Finance and Governance.

Heckman, J., & Payner, B. (1989). Determining the impact of federal antidiscrimination policy in the economic status of blacks: A study of South Carolina. *American Economic Review, 79*(1), 138—177.

Herrnstein, R., & Murray, C. (1994). *The bell curve: Intelligence and class structure in American life.* New York: Free Press.

Jencks, C., & Phillips, M. (1998). *The black-white test score gap.* Washington, DC: The Brookings Institution.

Juhn, C., Murphy, K., & Pierce, B. (1991). Accounting for the slowdown in Black-White convergence. In M. Kosters (Ed.), *Workers and their wages: Changing patterns in the United States* (pp. 107—143). Washington, DC: American Enterprise Institute Press.

Margalioth, S. R. (2005). Labor market discrimination against Arab Israeli citizens: Can something be done? *International Law and Politics, 36,* 845—884.

Murnane, R., Willet, J., & Levy, F. (1995). The growing importance of cognitive skills in wage determination. *Review of Economics and Statistics, 77*(2), 251—266.

Myrdal, G. (1944). *American Dilemma: The Negro problem and modern democracy*. New York: Harper and Row.

Neal, D. (2004). The measured Black-White wage gap among women is too small. *Journal of Political Economy, 112,* S1–S28.

Neal, D., & Johnson, W. (1996). The role of premarket factors in Black- White wage differences. *Journal of Political Economy, 104,* 869–895.

Oaxaca, R. (1973). Male-female wage differentials in urban labor markets. *International Economic Review, 14*(3), 693–709.

Reardon, S. (2007). *Thirteen ways of looking at the Black-White test score gap*. Stanford. CA: Stanford University School of Education.

Reich, M. (1982). *Racial discrimination*. Princeton, NJ: Princeton University Press.

Rothstein, R. (2004). *Class and schools*. New York: Teachers College Press.

Smith, J., & Welch, F. (1989). Black economic progress after Myrdal. *Journal of Economic Literature, 27*(2), 519–564.

Steele, C. M. (1997). A threat in the air: How stereotypes shape intellectual identity and performance. *The American Psychologist, 52*(6), 613–629.

Thernstrom, S., & Thernstrom, A. (1997). *America in black and white: One nation, indivisible*. New York: Simon and Schuster.

Thernstrom, A., & Thernstrom, S. (2003). *No excuses: Closing the racial gap in learning*. New York: Simon and Schuster.

Welch, F. (1973). Black-White differences in returns to schooling. *American Economic Review, 63*(5), 893–907.

12

The economics of high school dropouts

Russell W. Rumberger

Gevirtz Graduate School of Education, University of California, Santa Barbara, CA, United States

Introduction

One of the major educational challenges in virtually all industrialized nations is ensuring that all students graduate from high school. Although many countries allow students to leave school prior to completing upper secondary school, a high school diploma is increasingly viewed as a minimal requirement for entry into the labor market and for further, postsecondary education. In fact, with the economy generating an increasing number of jobs that require at least some postsecondary schooling, students who earn no more than a high school diploma will likely have diminishing economic prospects.

Despite the increasing importance of graduating from high school, a large segment of the student population in many countries leave high school prior to graduation. This essay provides a brief review of the research on who drops out of high school, the economic and social consequences of dropping out, the causes of dropping out, and what can be done to improve high school graduation rates. The review relies primarily on literature in the US.

Who drops out of high school?

A number of indicators have been used by government agencies and researchers to measure the number and rate that students drop out and graduate from high school. The indicators differ with respect to: (1) the definition of dropout or graduation that is used, including the credential being measured and the time period; (2) the population being measured; and (3) the source of data.

One measure is the annual dropout rate, which measures the proportion of students who quit school each year. According Census data, 535,000 students in the US dropped out of grades 10–12 in 2014–15, or about 4.9% of the students enrolled (Snyder, de Brey, & Dillow, 2018, Table 219.57). This is no doubt an undercount because it excludes students who dropped out before grade 10. Dropout rates are higher for some demographic groups: males have higher dropout rates than females; Blacks and Hispanics have higher dropout rates than Asians and Whites; and students from low-income families have higher dropout rates than students from high income families. Annual dropout rates in the US generally declined beginning in the 1970s, reaching a low of 3.0% in 2010, then increasing more recently to reach the current rate of 4.9% in 2015 (Snyder et al., 2018, Table 219.55).

Annual dropout rates understate the likelihood that a student will drop out some time during his or her educational career. A better gauge is the proportion of dropouts in the population, which is referred to as the *status* dropout rate. Again according to Census data, in 2015 there were 2.3 million dropouts aged 16–24 in the US, representing 5.9% of the population (Snyder et al., 2018, Table 219.73). These rates too are higher for the same demographic groups mentioned above. Unlike annual dropout rate, status dropout rates have declined steadily over the last 25 years, from a high of 15.0% in 1970 to the current rate of 5.9% (Snyder et al., 2018, Table 219.75).

Yet dropout rates alone may not be sufficient to reveal the extent of the problem. Census data have been criticized because they rely on respondents' self-reported educational status, which respondents may overstate, and that may change over time because at least some dropouts return to school. Moreover, the Census considers persons who earn equivalent high school credentials by taking the General Education Development (GED) exam as completing high school even though there is extensive evidence that alternative credentials do not provide the same economic benefits as a traditional diploma (Heckman, Humphries, & Mader, 2011).

In order to provide a longitudinal perspective that captures the progress of high school students toward graduation, federal and state governments in the US are attempting to measure the proportion of entering ninth-grade students who earn a regular diploma within four years, which is known as the *ninth-grade cohort graduation rate*. Such a rate is particularly difficult to measure because it requires tracking students over several years. This is problematic, in part, because students often transfer from one educational setting to another during their high school careers. In addition, some students are retained, especially in the ninth grade, when they fail to earn enough credits to be promoted to the next grade level.

Two specific measures are currently used to estimate the ninth-grade graduation rate: the Averaged Freshman Graduation Rate (AFGR) and the Adjusted Cohort Graduation Rate (ACGR). Both of these indicators only measure graduation rates for public schools, thus ignoring the approximate 10% of high school students who graduate from private schools. The AFGR estimates the graduation rate for an entering cohort of ninth grade students by dividing the number of public high school diplomas awarded in one year with the estimated number of ninth grade students four years earlier (an average of the number of eighth graders five years earlier, the number of ninth graders four years earlier, and the number of 10th graders three years earlier). The AFGR is based on aggregated administrative data on cross-sectional counts of students reported by states to the federal government and therefore is not a true cohort rate. In contrast, the ACGR is a true cohort rate based on individual-level, longitudinal student records compiled by state education agencies and reported to the federal government. The official ACGR, as defined by the federal government in 2009, represents a four-year or "on-time" graduation rate based on the number of entering ninth grade students who earn a regular diploma within four years. This rate, therefore, does not reveal how many entering ninth grade students eventually earn a diploma. Some states do compute and report 5-year and 6-year graduation rates that typically show rates two to five percentage points high than their 4-year rates.

The national AFGR was 81.9% in 2012–13, with state rates varying from a low of 70.5.percent in Georgia to a high of 93.3% in Nebraska (Snyder et al., 2018, Table 219.40). The national AGCR was 83% in 2014–15, with state rates varying from a low of 71% in Nevada to a high of 91% in Iowa (Snyder et al., 2018, Table 219.46).

Although the on-time cohort graduation rate is perhaps the most appropriate indicator of high school completion, it suffers from a number of limitations that make it a blunt instrument for measuring high school performance and the preparation it provides for college and career success after high school. First, despite the common definition that states use to compute it, the actual requirements for a diploma vary widely among states and individual school districts. These include the number and types of courses that students must pass and whether the state requires an exit exam. Moreover, these requirements can vary over time. Some states provide alternative pathways to earn a diploma. This variation means that a high school diploma can represent vast differences in the learning and preparation it provides, ranging from a "thin" diploma that provides little preparation for future schooling and work to a "thick" diploma that provides sufficient preparation for success in college and/or a career. A recent report of nine states found that the percentage of high school graduates who earned a "college and career-ready" (CCR) diploma was substantially lower than the published ACGR (Almond, 2017). For example, the official ACGR in Nevada was 70% in 2014 while the CCR rate was 30% (Almond, 2017, p. 5, see Table 2). Moreover, traditionally disadvantaged students were less likely to earn a CCR diploma than more advantaged students. In California, for instance, the gap in the ACGR between White and Hispanic students was 11% points (88 vs. 77%) in 2014, whereas the gap in the CCR was 17% points (49 vs. 32%) (Almond, 2017, p. 15).

The Organization for Economic and Cooperative Development (OECD) computes the percentage of first-time upper secondary graduates to the population at the typical age of graduation. The average graduation rate for persons younger than 25 among OECD countries in 2016 was 81%, ranging from 57% in Mexico to 94% in Korea, with the US rate at 84% (OECD, 2018, Table B3.2).

What are the consequences?

Dropping out of school has economic and social consequences both for dropouts themselves and for the country as a whole. First, dropouts have difficulty finding jobs. Government data show that more than 37% of 16- to 24-year-olds in October 2015 who dropped out of school the previous year were unemployed (Snyder et al., 2018, Table 504.20). Among all 20- to 24-year-olds in October 2015, the unemployment rate for dropouts was 21.4%, compared to 14.5% for high school graduates and 6.0% for four-year college graduates (Snyder et al., 2018, Table 501.20). Second, even if they find a job, dropouts earn substantially less than high school graduates. In 2005, the median annual earnings of high school dropouts was almost 25% less than the income of high school graduates (Snyder et al., 2018, Table 378). Over their working lives, the Census Bureau estimates that dropouts will earn about $200,000 less than high school graduates (Day & Newburger, 2002, Fig. 3).

One reason for dropouts' poor economic outcomes is their low levels of education. Yet dropouts can return to school. Almost half of 1988 eighth-grade students who dropped out of school completed either a regular high school diploma (16%) or a GED or alternative certificate (29%) within two years of their scheduled graduation date in 1992 (Berktold, Geis, & Kaufman, 1998, Table 1). And dropouts who completed high school were more likely to enroll in postsecondary education than students who did not complete high school (42% vs. 14%) (Berktold et al., 1998, Table 15). Nonetheless, dropouts as a group are much less likely to enroll in postsecondary education than high school graduates, even though most states allow dropouts to enroll in community colleges without a high school diploma.

Dropouts experience other negative outcomes (Belfield & Levin, 2007). Dropouts have poorer health and higher rates of mortality than high school graduates; they are more likely to engage in criminal behavior and be incarcerated over their lifetimes compared to graduates. They are also more likely to require public assistance and less likely to vote. Although the observed relationship between dropping out and these economic and social outcomes does not necessarily imply a causal relationship, a growing body of research evidence has, in fact, demonstrated one. This suggests that efforts to reduce dropout rates would, in fact, reduce these negative economic and social outcomes.

The negative outcomes from dropouts generate huge social costs. Federal, state, and local governments collect fewer taxes from dropouts. The government also subsidizes the poorer health, higher criminal activity, and increased public assistance of dropouts. One recent study estimated that each new high school graduate would generate more than $200,000 in government savings, and that cutting in half the dropout rate from a single cohort of dropouts would generate more than $45 billion in savings (Belfield & Levin, 2007).

A number of economic, demographic, and educational trends could exacerbate these problems in the future. As the United States economy moves toward a higher-skilled labor force, high school dropouts will have an even harder time surviving economically. The numbers of students who are generally at greater risk of school failure—students from poor and low-income households, and racial, ethnic, and linguistic minorities—are increasing in the nation's schools. Finally, the growing push for accountability in the nation's public schools that has produced policies to end social promotion and to institute high school exit exams could increase the number of students who fail to complete high school.

Why do students drop out?

Understanding why students drop out of school is the key to addressing this major educational problem; yet identifying the causes of dropping out is extremely difficult. Like other forms of educational achievement (e.g., test scores), the causes of dropping out are influenced by an array of proximal and distal factors related to both the individual student and to the family, school, and community settings in which the student lives.

Dropouts themselves report a variety of reasons for leaving school, including school-related reasons, family-related reasons, and work-related reasons (Rotermund, 2007). The most specific reasons cited by 2002 tenth-graders who dropped out were "missed too many school days" (44%); "thought it would be easier to get a GED" (41%); "getting poor grades/failing school" (38%); "did not like school" (37%); and "could not keep up with schoolwork" (32%). But these reasons do not reveal the underlying causes of why students quit school, particularly those causes or factors in elementary or middle school that may have contributed to students' attitudes, behaviors, and school performance immediately preceding their decision to leave school. Moreover, if many factors contribute to this phenomenon over a long period of time, it is virtually impossible to demonstrate a causal connection between any single factor and the decision to quit school. Despite this difficulty, two types of factors have been identified that contribute to or increase the likelihood that students drop out of school: (1) individual factors associated with students' characteristics, attitudes, behaviors, and experiences; and (2) contextual factors associated with students' families, schools, communities, and peers.

Individual factors

A variety of individual factors are associated with dropping out (Rumberger, 2011), including several demographic factors. Generally, dropout rates are higher among males, Blacks and Hispanics, immigrants, and language minority students. Attitudes also affect dropout rates. Dropout rates are also higher among students who have low educational and occupational aspirations. Several activities and behaviors also predict dropout rates, including absenteeism, misbehavior in school, and pregnancy. Finally, poor academic achievement is a strong predictor of dropping out. Together, these factors support the idea that dropping out is influenced by both the social and academic experiences of students.

In addition to these proximal factors, a number of distal factors are associated with dropping out, such as student mobility. Both *residential* mobility (changing residences) and *school* mobility (changing schools) increase the risk of dropping out of high school (Rumberger, 2015). Student mobility may represent a less severe form of student disengagement or withdrawal from school. Another distal factor is grade retention. Although retention may have some positive impact on academic achievement in the short run, numerous studies have found that it greatly increases the likelihood that students will drop out of school. Finally, a number of long-term studies have found that lack of early academic achievement and engagement (e.g., attendance, misbehavior) in elementary and middle school predicts withdrawal from high school.

Institutional factors

While individual factors clearly contribute to students' decisions to drop out of school, individual attitudes and behaviors are shaped by the various settings or contexts in which students live—families, schools, communities, and peer groups. The importance of context in shaping behavior, including dropping out, was acknowledged in a report by the National Research Council Panel on High-Risk Youth (1993) that argued that too much emphasis has been placed on "high-risk" youth and their

families, and not enough on the high-risk settings in which they live and go to school. A number of factors within students' families, schools, and communities (and peer relationships) predict dropping out.

Families

Family background is widely recognized as the single most important contributor to success in school. Socioeconomic status, most commonly measured by *parental education* and *family income*, is a powerful predictor of school achievement and dropout behavior. Parental education influences students' aspirations and educational support; while family income allows parents to provide more resources to support their children's education, including access to better quality schools, after-school and summer school programs, and more support for learning within the home. In addition, students whose parents monitor and regulate their activities, provide emotional support, encourage independent decision-making (known as *authoritative parenting style*), and are generally more involved in their schooling are less likely to drop out of school. Additionally, students in single-parent and step-families are more likely to drop out of school than students in two-parent families.

Schools

It is widely acknowledged that schools exert powerful influences on student achievement, including dropout rates. Four types of school characteristics influence student performance: social composition of the schools, structural characteristics, school resources, and school policies and practices.

1. The social composition of schools—the characteristics of students attending the schools, particularly the socioeconomic composition of the student body—predicts dropping out even after controlling for the individual factors that influence dropping out.

2. The second characteristic has to do with the structural characteristics of schools, such as size, location, and school control (public vs. private). Dropout rates from Catholic and other private schools are lower than dropout rates from public schools, even after controlling for differences in the background characteristics of students. Yet students from private schools typically transfer to public schools instead of or before dropping out, so that student turnover rates in private schools are not statistically different than turnover rates in public schools. Smaller schools also have lower dropout rates. What is less clear is whether structural characteristics themselves account for these differences or whether they are related to differences in student characteristics and school resources often associated with the structural features of schools.

3. The third type of characteristic concerns school resources. Resources, in particular student/teacher ratios and teacher quality, appear to influence dropout rates even after controlling for a host of individual and contextual factors that might also influence dropout rates.

4. The final type has to do with school policies and practices. In particular, academic and social climate—as measured by school attendance rates, students taking advanced courses, and student perceptions of a fair discipline policy—predict school dropout rates, even after controlling for the background characteristics of students as well as the resource and structural characteristics of schools.

School factors contribute to student withdrawal in two ways. One way is indirectly, by creating conditions that influence student engagement and their *voluntary* withdrawal from school. Another way is directly, through explicit policies and conscious decisions by school personnel that cause students to *involuntarily* withdraw from school. These rules and actions may concern low grades, poor attendance, misbehavior (such as zero-tolerance policies), or being over-age and may lead to suspensions, expulsions, or forced transfers. This form of withdrawal is school-initiated and contrasts with the student-initiated form mentioned above. Some schools, for example, contribute to students' involuntary departure from school by systematically excluding and discharging "troublemakers" and other problematic students.

Community and peers

In addition to families and schools, communities and peer groups can influence students' withdrawal from school. Differences in neighborhood characteristics can help explain differences in dropout rates among communities, apart from the influence of families. Some evidence suggests that there is a threshold or tipping point on the quality of neighborhoods that results in particularly high dropout rates in the most disadvantaged neighborhoods. Poor communities may influence child and adolescent development through the lack of resources (playgrounds and parks, after-school programs) or negative peer influences. Community residents may also influence parenting practices over and above parental education and income. Students living in poor communities may also be more likely to have dropouts as friends, which increases the likelihood of dropping out of school. Another way that communities can influence dropout rates is by providing employment opportunities both during or after school. Relatively favorable employment opportunities for high school dropouts, as evidenced by low neighborhood unemployment rates, appears to increase the likelihood that students will drop out, while more favorable economic returns to graduating, as evidenced by higher salaries of high school graduates compared to dropouts, tend to lower dropout rates. Working long hours in high school can increase the likelihood of dropping out, although the impact of working in high school depends on the type of job held and on the student's gender.

What can be done?

Knowledge about why students drop out suggests several things about what can be done to design effective dropout intervention strategies (Rumberger, 2011). First, because dropping out is influenced by both individual and institutional factors, intervention strategies can focus on either or both sets of factors. That is, intervention strategies can focus on addressing the individual values, attitudes, and behaviors that are associated with dropping out without attempting to alter the characteristics of families, schools, and communities that may contribute to those individual factors. Many dropout prevention programs pursue such *programmatic strategies* by providing would-be dropouts with additional resources and supports to help them stay in school. Alternatively, intervention strategies can focus on attempting to improve the environmental contexts of potential dropouts by providing resources and supports to strengthen or restructure their families, schools, and communities. Such *systemic strategies* are often part of larger efforts to improve the educational and social outcomes of at-risk students more generally.

Second, because dropping out is associated with both academic and social problems, effective prevention strategies must focus on both arenas. That is, if dropout prevention strategies are going to be effective they must be *comprehensive* by providing resources and supports in all areas of students' lives. Because dropouts leave school for a variety of reasons, services provided them must be flexible and tailored to their individual needs.

Third, because the problematic attitudes and behaviors of students at risk of dropping out appear as early as elementary school, dropout prevention strategies can and should begin early in a child's educational career. Dropout prevention programs often target high school or middle school students who may have already experienced years of educational failure or unsolved problems. Dropout recovery programs must also attempt to overcome longstanding problems in order to get dropouts to complete school; yet such programs may be costly and ineffective. In contrast, early intervention may be the most powerful and cost-effective approach to dropout prevention.

The longstanding interest in the problem of school dropouts has spurred a great deal of effort in developing programs and strategies to improve dropout and graduation rates. They can be grouped into three basic approaches: targeted, comprehensive, and systemic.

1. Targeted Approaches. The most common approach for improving dropout and graduation rates is to develop a special program targeting students most at risk for dropping out of school. There are two targeted approaches. One is to provide supplemental services to students within an existing school program. The second is to provide an alternative school program, either within an existing school (school within a school) or in a separate facility (alternative school). Neither approach attempts to change existing institutions serving most students; instead the approaches create supplemental or alternative programs that target students who are somehow identified as being at risk of dropping out or who have already dropped out.

2. Comprehensive Approaches. A second approach to dropout prevention is through comprehensive or schoolwide reform. This approach is premised on the belief that targeted programs are insufficient to improve dropout or graduation rates either because they are not comprehensive enough or because they do not help enough students. A

school reform approach involves developing a comprehensive set of practices and programs locally or by adopting an externally developed comprehensive school reform model.

3. Systemic Approaches. Systemic approaches involve making changes to the entire educational system under the assumption that such changes can transform how all schools function in the system, what some scholars have labeled "systemic school reform." Systemic reform can occur at the federal, state, or local level of government. Although all systemic reforms may affect dropout and graduation rates by improving school performance, three specific reforms are directly connected to dropout and graduation rates. One is to raise the compulsory schooling age—the age to which students must attend school—to eighteen, as a way to force more students to remain in school.27 Another is to change high school graduation requirements, both the number and specific array of courses that students must pass to be awarded a diploma, as well as to specify whether students must pass a high school exit exam to earn a diploma. A third reform is to create alternative pathways or options for completing high school coursework and earning diplomas.

A growing number of studies have evaluated the effectiveness of these interventions. The US Department of Education established the What Works Clearinghouse (WWC) in 2002 to review scientific evidence on the effectiveness of a variety of educational interventions (US Department of Education, 2019). The WWC also convenes expert panels to recommend strategies based on the evidence published in the form of Practice Guides. An initial Practice Guide on dropout prevention was published in 2008 and a more recent one was published in 2017 (Rumberger, al., 2017). Based on the review of more than 30 dropout interventions with rigorous research

support, the expert panel identified four recommendations for reducing dropout rates and improving graduation rates in middle and high schools:

1. Monitor the progress of all students, and proactively intervene when students show early signs of attendance, behavior, or academic problems.
2. Provide intensive, individualized support to students who have fallen off track and face significant challenges to success.
3. Engage students by offering curricula and programs that connect schoolwork with college and career success and that improve students' capacity to manage challenges in and out of school.
4. For schools with many at-risk students, create small, personalized communities to facilitate monitoring and support.

While most dropout prevention programs focus on middle and high schools, research has also found interventions that focus on improving student performance in elementary school and even preschool have can significantly improve dropout and graduation rates. One such early intervention is preschool. Not only has a growing body of evidence found that high-quality preschool can improve school readiness and early school success, but long-term follow-up studies have found that preschool can also improve a wide range of adolescent and adult outcomes, including high school graduation (McCoy et al., 2017).

Research has not only found a number of interventions can reduce dropout rates and improve graduation rates, but that at least some of them yield economic benefits that exceed their costs. A recent study compared the costs and benefits of five interventions that were proven to be effective in raising high school graduation rates and found that all of them provided benefits that exceeded their costs (Belfield & Levin, 2007).

Conclusions

Successfully addressing the dropout problem in the United States will require both capacity and will. Capacity requires technical expertize to develop and implement effective dropout prevention and recovery programs, as well as more ambitious systemic school reforms. While some schools have such capacity, most require additional resources, technical expertize, and incentives to restructure existing schools. The development of such capacity will require political will; but even with the will to reform schools, it is unlikely that the United States will ever eliminate disparities in dropout rates among racial and ethnic groups without eliminating disparities in the resources of families, schools, and communities.

References

Almond, M. (2017). *Paper thin? Why all high school diplomas are not created equal.* Washington, D.C.: Alliance for Excellent Education.

Belfield, C., & Levin, H. M. (Eds.). (2007). *The price we pay: Economic and social consequences of inadequate education.* Washington, D.C.: Brookings Institution Press.

Berktold, J., Geis, S., & Kaufman, P. (1998). *Subsequent educational attainment of high school dropouts.* Washington, D.C.: U.S. Department of Education.

Day, J. C., & Newburger, E. C. (2002). *The big payoff: Educational attainment and synthetic estimates of work-life earnings.* Washington, D.C.: U.S. Census Bureau.

McCoy, D. C., Yoshikawa, H., Ziol-Guest, K. M., Duncan, G. J., Schindler, H. S., Magnuson, K., et al. (2017). Impacts of early childhood education on medium- and long-term educational outcomes. *Educational Researcher, 46*(8), 474–487. https://doi.org/10.3102/0013189X17737739.

National Research Council, Panel on High-Risk Youth. (1993). *Losing generations: Adolescents in high-risk settings.* Washington, D.C.: National Academies Press.

Organization for Economic Co-operation and Development (OECD). (2018). *Education at a glance: OECD indicators 2018.* Paris: OECD. https://doi.org/10.1787/eag-2018-en.

Rotermund, S. (2007). *Why students drop out of high school: Comparisons from three national surveys.* Santa Barbara: California Dropout Research Project, University of California, Santa Barbara. Retrieved from: http://lmri.ucsb.edu/dropouts/pubs.htm.

Rumberger, R. W. (2011). *Dropping out: Why students drop out of high school and what can be done about it.* Cambridge, MA: Harvard University Press.

Rumberger, R. W. (2015). *Student mobility: Causes, consequences, and solutions.* Boulder, CO: National Education Policy Center. Retrieved from: http://nepc.colorado.edu/files/pb_rumberger-student-mobility.pdf.

Rumberger, R., Addis, H., Allensworth, E., Balfanza, R., Duardo, D., Dynarski, M., et al. (2017). *Preventing dropout in secondary schools (NCEE 2017-4028).* Washington, DC: National Center for Education Evaluation and Regional Assistance (NCEE), Institute of Education Sciences, U.S. Department of Education. Retrieved from: https://whatworks.ed.gov.

Snyder, T. D., de Brey, C., & Dillow, S. A. (2018). *Digest of education statistics, 2016. (NCES 2007-017) U.S. Department of Education, National Center for Education Statistics.* Washington, D.C.: U.S. Government Printing Office. Retrieved from: https://nces.ed.gov/pubsearch/pubsinfo.asp?pubid=2017094.

U.S. Department of Education, Institute of Education Sciences. (2019). *What works clearinghouse.* Retrieved from: http://ies.ed.gov/ncee/wwc/.

Further reading

Alexander, K. L., Entwisle, D. R., & Kabbini, N. S. (2001). The dropout process in life course perspective: Early risk factors at home and school. *Teachers College Record, 103,* 760–882.

Bridgeland, J. M., DiIulio, J. J., Jr., & Morison, K. B. (2006). *The silent epidemic: Perspectives on high school dropouts.* Washington, D.C.: Civil Enterprises.

Depaoli, J. L., Balfanza, R., Atwell, M., & Bridgeland, J. (2018). *Grad Nation: Progress and challenge in raising high school graduation rates.* Washington, D.C.: Civic Enterprises.

Finn, J. D. (1989). Withdrawing from school. *Review of Educational Research, 59,* 117–142.

Heckman, J. J., Humphries, J. E., & Mader, N. S. (2011). The GED. In E. A. Hanshek, S. Machin, & L. Woessmann (Eds.), *Handbook of the economics of education* (Vol. 3, pp. 423–483). New York: Elsevier.

Heckman, J. J., & LaFontaine, P. A. (2010). The American high school graduation rate: Trends and levels. *The Review of Economics and Statistics, 92*(2), 244–262.

Mishel, L., & Roy, J. (2006). *Rethinking high school graduation rates and trends.* Washington, D.C.: Economic Policy Institute.

Murnane, R. J. (2013). US high school graduation rates: Patterns and explanations. *Journal of Economic Literature, 51*(2), 370–422. https://doi.org/10.1257/jel.51.2.370.

National Research Council, Committee on Increasing High School Students' Engagement and Motivation to Learn. (2004). In *Engaging schools: Fostering high school students' motivation to learn*. Washington, D.C.: The National Academies Press.

National Research Council and National Academy of Education. (2011). *High school dropout, graduation, and completion rates: Better data, better measures, better decisions*. Washington, D.C.: The National Academic Press.

Orfield, G. (Ed.). (2004). *Dropouts in America: Confronting the graduation rate crisis*. Cambridge, MA: Harvard Education Press.

Romo, H. D., & Falbo, T. (1996). *Latino high school graduation: Defying the odds*. Austin: University of Texas Press.

Rumberger, R. W., & Palardy, G. J. (2005). Test scores, dropout rates, and transfer rates as alternative indicators of high school performance. *American Educational Research Journal, 41*, 3–42.

Zaff, J. F., Donlan, A., Gunning, A., Anderson, S. E., McDermott, E., & Sedaca, M. (2017). Factors that promote high school graduation: A review of the literature. *Educational Psychology Review, 29*(3), 447–476. https://doi.org/10.1007/s10648-016-9363-5.

Relevant websites

America's Promise Alliance, *Grad Nation:* https://www.americaspromise.org/program/gradnation.

University of California, Santa Barbara, *California Dropout Research Project*: http://cdrpsb.org/.

U.S. Department of Education, Institute for Educational Sciences, What Works Clearinghouse, *Preventing Dropout in Secondary School*: https://ies.ed.gov/ncee/wwc/PracticeGuide/24.

PART III

Production, costs and financing

Education production functions

Eric A. Hanushek

Hoover Institution, Stanford University, CESifo, IZA and NBER, Stanford, CA, United States

Glossary

Educational production function A function that relates various inputs to education including those of families, peers, and schools to the maximum level of student achievement that can be obtained

Fixed effects A form of statistical analysis that removes the average effects of a factor (such as individual schools) from the analysis; in the case of teachers, the fixed effect in models of achievement growth is often interpreted as a measure of teacher quality

Value-added In the context of education production functions, the value-added of an input would be the separate contribution of learning after allowing for other inputs and the base level of knowledge of the students

Overview

Much of the analysis in the economics of education flows from a simple model of production. The common inputs are things like school resources, teacher quality, and family attributes; and the outcome is some measure of student achievement—frequently but not always student test scores. Knowledge of the production function for schools can be used to assess policy alternatives and to judge the effectiveness and efficiency of public provided services. This area of research is, however, distinguished from many because the results of analyses enter quite directly into the policy process.

The attention to education production functions is driven largely by recognition that individual skills have significant payoffs in the labor market and elsewhere. Thus, a natural question is how skills can be developed and enhanced, leading to the analysis of how schools and other educational inputs enter into skill development.

This discussion focuses largely on evidence from the US where there is a lengthy history of analysis of education production functions. The focus of this work has changed over time, moving from standard inputs and resources to the effectiveness of teachers. This analysis has been aided by the development of much more extensive data bases on school performance that come from school accountability systems. There has also been wider analysis of educational production from other countries (Woessmann, 2016).

Measuring skills and human capital

Education production functions have their roots in the more general analysis of human capital, but the two different streams of analysis have largely diverged in the past. Most human capital analysis has strong and direct linkages

The Economics of Education, Second Edition
https://doi.org/10.1016/B978-0-12-815391-8.00013-6

to labor market outcomes and the determination of earnings. Education production functions, while ostensibly closely related, have focused more on the underlying determination of skills and human capital. Until recently, the two different foci have led to quite different perspectives on both the measurement of human capital and implicitly the fundamental modeling of economic outcomes.

Historically, human capital has been considered from the labor market perspective of the individual. In its simplest form, individuals make investments that develop their skills, and this stock of skills is optimized for the labor market. In this analysis, the most frequently employed measure of individual skills, or human capital, has been school attainment, or simply years of schooling completed.

There are several justifications for relying on years of schooling to measure individual skills. First, a prime motivation for the schools is the acquisition of knowledge and skills, and this justifies the heavy governmental investment in schools of nations around the world. Second, in the early development of human capital theory, Mincer (1970, 1974) developed a simple but elegant investment model for individuals that emphasized time spent in school. This theoretical development translated into one of the most successful empirical models—the "Mincer earnings function"—that relates individual earnings to school attainment and to labor market experience. The value of school attainment as a rough measure of individual skill has subsequently been verified by a wide variety of studies of labor market outcomes (Card, 2001). Third, reliance on years of school as the human capital measure is expedient. School attainment is very commonly measured in censuses and surveys, allowing, for example, estimation of Mincer earnings functions in 139 countries (see the review in Psacharopoulos & Patrinos, 2018).

However, the difficulty with this common measure of outcomes is that it simply counts the time spent in schools without judging what

happens in schools—thus, it does not provide a complete or accurate picture of outcomes. It assumes a year of schooling produces the same amount of student achievement, or skills, over time and in every country. Importantly, it also assumes that schooling is the only input into skill development, ignoring the extensive contrary evidence discussed below. Finally, this measure of school outcomes ignores the extensive policy debates about ways to improve school quality.

A common extension in the investigation of individual human capital and labor market outcomes is the addition of cognitive skills as gauged by standardized test scores to the empirical models. Such skill measures have found their way into the literature slowly, because they have just been available for a limited number of surveys that include both achievement and labor market outcomes. Moreover, in these analyses the common interpretation of these measures is that they represent individual "ability" and thus can be added to a standard Mincer earnings function to correct for any school selection bias arising from people with higher ability continuing longer in school. Such investigations of the impact of cognitive achievement include, for example, Lazear (2003); Mulligan (1999); and Murnane, Willett, Duhaldeborde, & Tyler (2000)). In these, however, the general interpretation is still that school attainment is the measure of human capital.

A complementary line of research has considered aggregate human capital and how it affects national productivity and growth. The surge in empirical analyses of growth differences across countries begun in the early 1990s invariably included measures of school attainment to reflect the skills of the population (see Barro, 1991; Romer, 1990). In a subsequent comparison of alternative drivers of growth rate differences, Sala-i-Martin, Doppelhofer, and Miller (2004) found primary school enrollment to be among the strongest explanatory factors. Nonetheless, the estimated impacts of human capital and other inputs appeared very unstable, casting doubt on the line of empirical growth analyses (Levine & Renelt, 1992).

The parallel line of research into education production functions has concentrated on understanding the determinants of human capital. Test scores, or measures of cognitive skills more generally, have been interpreted as proxies for skills that are valued in the labor market and elsewhere and, as such, more immediate measures of human capital differences. As described below, the overall focus of this work has then been understanding how schools and other factors determine the skills of individuals.

But, this latter focus also leads to a very different interpretation of the prior labor market studies focused on school attainment. Moreover, reconsideration of the interpretation of measured cognitive skills in the prior human capital/labor market analyses helps to clarify the problems with these prior analyses and to point toward an alternative empirical approach. Specifically, these achievement measures have been interpreted as proxies for skills that are valued in the labor market, albeit the ability designation implies that these are fixed skills. An alternative interpretation is that the tested skills represent an explicit measure of human capital. If so, whether skills were determined by schools or by other inputs would in general not affect their use and interpretation in understanding variations in labor market outcomes. Thinking of skills and their measurement by test scores in this manner implies that school attainment is just one of a variety of inputs into an individual's skills.

The research considering cognitive skills as a direct measure of human capital goes a long way toward resolving some of the apparent anomalies in the prior labor market research. Using data for a representative sample of 23 countries that included test scores along with labor market information on individuals, Hanushek, Schwerdt, Wiederhold and Woessmann (2015) show that estimates of earnings functions in terms of achievement tests are readily interpreted in a human capital framework. Similarly, looking at long run growth in terms of cognitive skills helps resolve many of the difficulties with empirical growth models built on school attainment (Hanushek & Woessmann, 2008). Hanushek and Kimko (2000) demonstrate that quality differences measured by achievement have a dramatic impact on productivity and national growth rates. This is reinforced and extended in Hanushek and Woessmann (2012, 2015), who show that three-quarters of the variation in country growth rates can be explained by a simple growth model that focuses on cognitive skills. They call the aggregate test scores for countries "knowledge capital" to distinguish it from the school attainment measures that are frequently referred to as being synonymous with human capital.

These recent analyses of labor market relationships with standardized achievement test scores complete the linkage between human capital analysis from the individual labor market perspective and education production functions that seek to explain differences in test scores. This linkage provides the rationale for interpreting the results of education production estimates as indicating the longer run economic effects of schools and other inputs.

Basic production function estimates

Analysis of education production functions has a direct motivation. Because educational outcomes cannot be changed by fiat, much attention has been directed at inputs—particularly those perceived to be relevant for policy such as school resources or aspects of teachers.

Analysis of the role of school resources in determining achievement begins with the Coleman Report, the US government's monumental study on educational opportunity released in 1966 (Coleman et al., 1966). While controversial, that study's greatest contribution was directing attention to the distribution of student performance—the outputs as opposed to various school inputs such as spending per pupil or characteristics of teachers (Bowles & Levin,1968; Hanushek & Kain, 1972; Hanushek, 2016).

The underlying model that has evolved as a result of this research is very straightforward. The output of the educational process—the achievement of individual students—is directly related to inputs that both are directly controlled by policymakers (for example, the characteristics of schools, teachers, and curricula) and are not so controlled (such as families and friends and the innate endowments or learning capacities of the students). Further, while achievement may be measured at discrete points in time, the educational process is cumulative; inputs applied sometime in the past affect students' current levels of achievement.

Family background is usually characterized by such socio-demographic characteristics as parental education, income, and family size. Peer inputs, when included, are typically aggregates of student socio-demographic characteristics or achievement for a school or classroom. School inputs typically include teacher background (education level, experience, sex, race, and so forth), school organization (class sizes, facilities, administrative expenditures, and so forth), and district or community factors (for example, average expenditure levels). Except for the original Coleman Report, most empirical work has relied on data constructed for other purposes, such as a school's standard administrative records. More recent work has moved to use micro-data generated from school accountability programs. Statistical analysis (typically some form of regression analysis) is employed to infer what specifically determines achievement and what is the importance of the various inputs into student performance. Over time, attention has been increasingly directed at the statistical identification of factors that are causally related to student outcomes.

Measured school inputs

The central thrust of education production function estimation has changed over time. During the initial period—roughly 30 years starting with the Coleman Report—the analyses followed a common pattern of examining the impact on student learning of specific measures of school inputs. These studies focused on measured resources of the type typically included in school reports. The second period, following this initial estimation phase and carrying through to the present, moved to an examination of specific aspects of production, often with novel methods or data, and to concentration on teacher effects.

The state of knowledge about the impacts of basic resources is best summarized by reviewing available empirical studies from the first period. Most analyses of education production functions directed their attention at a relatively small set of resource measures, and this makes it easy to summarize the results (Hanushek, 2003). The 90 individual publications that appeared before 1995 contain 377 separate production function estimates. For classroom resources, only nine per cent of estimates for teacher education and 14% for teacher–pupil ratios yielded a positive and statistically significant relationship between these factors and student performance. Moreover, these studies were offset by another set of studies that found a similarly negative correlation between those inputs and student achievement. Twenty-nine per cent of the studies found a positive correlation between teacher experience and student performance; however, 71 percent still provided no support for increasing teacher experience (being either negative or statistically insignificant). Subsequent analysis of experience effects consistently indicates that increased experience for the first few years of teaching has a positive impact, but there is little to no additional impact past the initial teaching period (see Hanushek & Rivkin, 2012).

Studies on the direct effect of financial resources provide a similar picture, although here the analysis has been more controversial (see, for example, Hanushek,1994, 2003; Hedges, Laine, & Greenwald, 1994). These indicate that there is very weak support for the notion that simply providing higher teacher salaries or greater overall spending will lead to improved student performance. Per pupil expenditure has received the most attention, but only 27 percent of studies showed a positive and significant effect. In fact, seven per cent even suggested that adding resources would harm student achievement. It is also important to note that studies involving pupil spending have tended to be the lowest-quality studies as defined below, and thus there is substantial reason to believe that even the 27 percent figure overstates the true effect of added expenditure.

These studies make a clear case that resource usage in schools is subject to considerable inefficiency, because schools systematically pay for inputs that are not consistently related to outputs. These results of course do not indicate that money never matters or that money cannot matter. They instead point to the importance of *how* money is spent rather than *how much* is spent—a topic considered below.

Study quality

The previous discussions do not distinguish among studies on the basis of any quality differences. The available estimates can be reasonably categorized by a few objective components of quality. First, while education is cumulative, frequently only current input measures are available, which results in analytical errors and biased estimates of the effects of specific inputs. Second, schools operate within a policy environment determined almost always by higher levels of government. In the United States, state governments establish curricula, provide sources of funding, govern labor laws, determine rules for the certification and hiring of teachers, and the like. If these attributes are important—as much policy debate would suggest—they must be incorporated into any analysis of performance. The adequacy of dealing with these problems can thus be used as a simple index of study quality.

The details of these quality issues and approaches for dealing with them are discussed in detail elsewhere (Hanushek, 2003) and only summarized here. The first problem is ameliorated if one uses the "value added" versus "level" form in estimation. That is, if the achievement relationship holds across grades, it is possible to concentrate on the growth in achievement and on exactly what happens educationally between those points when outcomes are measured. This approach ameliorates problems of omitting prior inputs of schools and families, because they will be incorporated in the initial achievement levels that are measured (Hanushek, 1979). The latter problem of imprecise measurement of the policy environment can frequently be ameliorated by studying performance of schools operating within a consistent set of policies—for example, within individual states in the US. Because all schools within a state operate within the same basic policy environment, comparisons of their performance are not strongly affected by unmeasured policies (Hanushek, Rivkin, & Taylor, 1996).

If the available studies are classified by whether or not they deal with these major quality issues, the prior conclusions about research usage are unchanged (Hanushek, 2003). The best quality studies indicate no consistent relationship between resources and student outcomes. The studies finding strong resource effects, particularly for expenditure per pupil, are heavily concentrated in the group of lowest quality studies.

An additional issue, which is particularly important for policy purposes, concerns whether this analytical approach accurately assesses the causal relationship between resources and performance. If, for example, school decision-makers provide more resources to those they judge as most needy, higher resources could simply signal students known for having lower achievement. Ways of dealing with this include various regression discontinuity or panel data approaches. When done in the case of class sizes, the evidence has been mixed (Angrist & Lavy, 1999; Hoxby, 2000; Rivkin, Hanushek, & Kain, 2005).

More recent studies

The most significant innovation of recent years is the use of large administrative data bases. These data bases employ state or local records on individual student's performance and are most notable for tracking students across grades. Student performance is then related to that programs and personnel that each student is exposed to over time. These large scale data-bases, often following all students in a state over time, permit controlling for a wide range of influences on achievement through the introduction of fixed effects for schools, individuals, and time (see, for example, Rivkin et al., 2005 or Boyd, Grossman, Lankford, Loeb, & Wyckoff, 2006). These fixed effects hold constant any systematic differences that do not vary within a category (such as constant differences among the sampled schools in terms of the selection of schools by families and teachers) and obtain estimates of various inputs from their variation within each of the schools. By eliminating systematic selection and sorting of students and school personnel, they can concentrate on specific causal factors that determine individual student outcomes.

An additional aspect of the growing state data bases is that students can now be traced to subsequent outcomes—university attendance, labor market experiences, criminal behavior, and more. This type of study, while just becoming more possible, involves linking data across state and federal programs where outside-of-school

outcomes can be observed. Importantly, such studies also can validate general estimates of school and teacher effects by, for example, showing the direct linkages of estimated school factors on subsequent earnings for the students (Chetty, Friedman, & Rockoff, 2014).

There has also been continuing study of the effects of simply adding more funding on outputs. This work has in part been motivated by the introduction of production function estimates into court cases about the financing of schools (Hanushek & Lindseth, 2009). In fact, two recent studies use the imposition of court judgments against state funding rules to obtain estimates of the impact of added funding (Jackson, Johnson, & Persico, 2015; Lafortune, Rothstein, & Whitmore Schanzenbach, 2018). The estimation and interpretation of these is the subject of ongoing research.

A final alternative involves the use of random assignment experimentation rather than statistical analysis to break the influence of sample selection and other possible omitted factors. With one major US exception, this approach nonetheless has not been applied to understand the impact of schools on student performance. (Randomized trials have expanded much more rapidly in developing countries; see Duflo, Glennerster, & Kremer, 2007). The US exception is Project STAR, an experimental reduction in class sizes that was conducted in the US state of Tennessee in the mid-1980s (Word et al., 1990). To date, the use of randomized experiments has not had much impact on research or our state of knowledge about the impacts of resources. While Project STAR has entered into a number of policy debates, the interpretation of the results remains controversial because of concerns about the quality of the experiment (Krueger, 1999; Hanushek, 1999). The results of this experiment suggested a significant but small impact of lower class size but that all of the impact was concentrated in the first year of schooling (kindergarten or grade one). Smaller class sizes in later years had no additional impact on student outcomes.

Do teachers and schools matter?

Because of the Coleman Report and subsequent studies discussed above, many have argued that schools do not matter and that only families and peers affect performance. Unfortunately, these interpretations have confused measurability with true effects.

Extensive research since the Coleman Report has made it clear that teachers do indeed matter when assessed in terms of student performance instead of the more typical input measures based on characteristics of the teacher and school. The alternative approach to the examination of teacher quality concentrates on pure outcome-based measures of teacher effectiveness. The general idea is to investigate the "value-added of teacher" by looking at differences in growth rates of student achievement across teachers. A good teacher would be one who consistently obtained high learning growth from students, while a poor teacher would be one who consistently produced low learning growth. Early work relied upon very specialized samples of students (e.g., Hanushek, 1971; Murnane, 1975), but this has subsequently broadened out considerably (Hanushek & Rivkin, 2010).

The general research design is to estimate models of the growth in individual student achievement that can be attributed to various measured school and family factors and to differences in learning across the students with different teachers (see reviews in Hanushek & Rivkin, 2012; Jackson, Rockoff, & Staiger, 2014; Koedel, Mihaly, & Rockoff, 2015). The differences in student achievement growth across classrooms, which can be taken as a measure of teacher quality, appear to be consistent and very large (Hanushek & Rivkin, 2010). Hanushek (1992), for example, estimates that the variation in student outcomes from a good to a bad teacher can be as much as a full year of knowledge per academic year; in other words, while a poor teacher gets gains of 0.5 grade level equivalents during a school year, a good teacher gets gains of 1.5 grade level equivalents. Clearly, with a string of good or bad teachers, the implications for student performance could be very large.

More modern research into state administrative data bases have helped to refine the understanding of the importance of differences in teacher quality. For example, Rivkin et al. (2005) are able to provide rough bounds on the variation in teacher quality as seen within Texas (the source of their administrative database). By these studies, one standard deviation in teacher quality implies around a 0.15 standard deviation in the growth of student achievement. By this, having a series of good teachers (teachers at the 84 percentile of the quality distribution) instead of average teachers would lead to substantially different learning after just a few years. For example, 4–5 years of a good teacher could close the average achievement gap between low income and higher income students.

These estimates of magnitudes can be linked directly to studies of the economic impact of student achievement. Hanushek (2011a, 2011b) shows that a 75th percentile teacher each year generates over $400,000 in added income aggregated over a class of 30 students (compared to an average teacher). On the other hand, a 10th percentile teacher subtracts $800,000 in aggregate from a class of 30 students (again compared to an average teacher). Using a very different estimation approach that links teacher value added to the subsequent earnings of the specific students in the class, Chetty et al. (2014) confirm the order of magnitude of these teacher impacts.

These results can also be reconciled with the prior ones. These differences among teachers are simply not closely correlated with commonly measured teacher characteristics (Hanushek, 1992; Rivkin et al., 2005). Moreover, teacher credentials and teacher training do not make a consistent difference when assessed against student achievement gains (Boyd et al., 2006;

Kane, Rockoff, & Staiger, 2006). Finally, teacher quality does not appear to be closely related to salaries or to market decisions. In particular, teachers exiting for other schools or for jobs outside of teaching do not appear to be of higher quality than those who stay (Hanushek, Kain, O'Brien, & Rivkin, 2005).

The analysis of teacher value-added demonstrates the linkage between the research and policy discussions and decisions. Teacher value-added measures have been actively discussed in terms of teacher evaluations. In reviewing US state policies, the National Council on Teacher Quality (2017) finds that by 2017 39 states require teacher evaluations that include objective measures of student achievement growth, although the exact form and weight placed on these varies widely.

This linkage with policy also heightens attention to the studies, and there has been extensive analysis of the properties of value-added estimates including their stability, their accuracy, and their implications for the nature of teaching; see, for example, Braun, Chudowsky and Koenig (2010), Hanushek and Rivkin (2012), and Haertel (2013).

Benefits and costs

Throughout most consideration of the impact of school resources, attention has focused almost exclusively on whether a factor has an effect on outcomes that is statistically different from zero. Of course, any policy consideration would also consider both the magnitude of the impacts and the costs of change. For magnitude of impact, even the most refined estimates of, say, class size impacts does not give very clear guidance. The experimental effects from Project STAR indicate that average achievement from a reduction of eight students in a classroom would increase by about 0.2 standard deviations, but only in the first grade of attendance in smaller classes (kindergarten or first grade); see Word

et al. (1990); Krueger (1999). Hoxby (2000) in her regression discontinuity estimation for Connecticut schools finds no systematic effect of class size. Rivkin et al. (2005), with their fixed effects estimation, find effects half of Project STAR in grade four and declining to insignificance by grade seven.

From a policy perspective the magnitude of alternative estimates is at best small. In order to be relevant for policy, it is necessary to compare the outcomes of any change with its costs. Most educational research ignores such comparisons and neglects any consideration of costs.

It is easy to see the importance of cost considerations when put in the context of the debates over class size reduction. In economic terms the potential impacts of class size reduction are very small when contrasted with the costs of such large class size reductions, which typically involve some of the most expensive policy changes currently contemplated. The relevant alternative policy would be to compare the gains from spending on class size reduction with the potential gains from improving the quality of teachers.

Some conclusions and implications

The existing research suggests inefficiency in the provision of schooling. It does not indicate that schools do not matter. Nor does it indicate that money and resources never impact achievement. The accumulated research surrounding estimation of education production functions simply says there currently is no clear, systematic relationship between resources and student outcomes. The general conclusion from the existing work is that *how* resources are used is generally more important than *how much* is used. At the same time, more modern research into the determinants of student achievement strongly indicates that teacher quality differences are the most significant part of differences across schools.

References

Angrist, J. D., & Lavy, V. (1999). Using Maimonides' rule to estimate the effect of class size on scholastic achievement. *Quarterly Journal of Economics, 114*(2), 533–575.

Barro, R. J. (1991). Economic growth in a cross section of countries. *Quarterly Journal of Economics, 106*(2), 407–443.

Bowles, S., & Levin, H. M. (1968). The determinants of scholastic achievement–an appraisal of some recent evidence. *Journal of Human Resources, 3*(1), 3–24.

Boyd, D., Grossman, P., Lankford, H., Loeb, S., & Wyckoff, J. (2006). How changes in entry requirements alter the teacher workforce and affect student achievement. *Education Finance and Policy, 1*(2), 176–216.

Card, D. (2001). Estimating the return to schooling: Progress on some persistent econometric problems. *Econometrica, 69*(5), 1127–1160.

Chetty, R., Friedman, J. N., & Rockoff, J. (2014). Measuring the impacts of teachers II: Teacher value-added and student outcomes in adulthood. *The American Economic Review, 104*(9), 2633–2679.

Coleman, J. S., Campbell, E. Q., Hobson, C. J., McPartland, J., Mood, A. M., Weinfeld, F. D., et al. (1966). *Equality of educational opportunity*. Washington, D.C.: U.S. Government Printing Office.

Duflo, E., Glennerster, R., & Kremer, M. (2007). Using randomization in development economics research: A toolkit. In *Handbook of development economics*. North Holland.

Hanushek, E. A. (1971). Teacher characteristics and gains in student achievement: Estimation using micro data. *The American Economic Review, 60*(2), 280–288.

Hanushek, E. A. (1979). Conceptual and empirical issues in the estimation of educational production functions. *Journal of Human Resources, 14*(3), 351–388.

Hanushek, E. A. (1992). The trade-off between child quantity and quality. *Journal of Political Economy, 100*(1), 84–117.

Hanushek, E. A. (1994). Money might matter somewhere: A response to Hedges, laine, and Greenwald. *Educational Researcher, 23*(4), 5–8.

Hanushek, E. A. (1999). Some findings from an independent investigation of the Tennessee STAR experiment and from other investigations of class size effects. *Educational Evaluation and Policy Analysis, 21*(2), 143–163.

Hanushek, E. A. (2003). The failure of input-based schooling policies. *Economic Journal, 113*(485), F64–F98.

Hanushek, E. A. (2011a). The economic value of higher teacher quality. *Economics of Education Review, 30*(3), 466–479.

Hanushek, E. A. (2011b). Valuing teachers: How much is a good teacher worth? *Education Next, 11*(3).

Hanushek, E. A. (2016). What matters for achievement: Updating coleman on the influence of families and schools. *Education Next, 16*(2), 22–30.

Hanushek, E. A., Guido, S., Simon, W., & Woessmann, L. (2015). Returns to skills around the world: Evidence from PIAAC. *European Economic Review, 73*, 103–130.

Hanushek, E. A., & Kain, J. F. (1972). On the value of equality of educational opportunity as a guide to public policy. In F. Mosteller, & D. P. Moynihan (Eds.), *On equality of educational opportunity* (pp. 116–145). New York: Random House.

Hanushek, E. A., Kain, J. F., O'Brien, D. M., & Rivkin, S. G. (2005). The market for teacher quality. In *NBER working paper No. 11154*. Cambridge, MA: National Bureau of Economic Research.

Hanushek, E. A., & Kimko, D. D. (2000). Schooling, labor force quality, and the growth of nations. *The American Economic Review, 90*(5), 1184–1208.

Hanushek, E. A., & Lindseth, A. A. (2009). *Schoolhouses, courthouses, and statehouses: Solving the funding-achievement puzzle in America's public schools*. Princeton, NJ: Princeton University Press.

Hanushek, E. A., & Rivkin, S. G. (2010). Generalizations about using value-added measures of teacher quality. *The American Economic Review, 100*(2), 267–271.

Hanushek, E. A., & Rivkin, S. G. (2012). The distribution of teacher quality and implications for policy. *Annual Review of Economics, 4*, 131–157.

Hanushek, E. A., Rivkin, S. G., & Taylor, L. L. (1996). Aggregation and the estimated effects of school resources. *The Review of Economics and Statistics, 78*(4), 611–627.

Hanushek, E. A., & Woessmann, L. (2008). The role of cognitive skills in economic development. *Journal of Economic Literature, 46*(3), 607–668.

Hanushek, E. A., & Woessmann, L. (2012). Do better schools lead to more growth? Cognitive skills, economic outcomes, and causation. *Journal of Economic Growth, 17*(4), 267–321.

Hanushek, E. A., & Woessmann, L. (2015). *The knowledge capital of nations: Education and the economics of growth*. Cambridge, MA: MIT Press.

Hedges, L. V., Laine, R. D., & Greenwald, R. (1994). Does money matter? A meta-analysis of studies of the effects of differential school inputs on student outcomes. *Educational Researcher, 23*(3), 5–14.

Hoxby, C. M. (2000). The effects of class size on student achievement: New evidence from population variation. *Quarterly Journal of Economics, 115*(3), 1239–1285.

Jackson, C. K., Johnson, R. C., & Persico, C. (2015). The effects of school spending on educational and economic outcomes: Evidence from school finance reforms. *Quarterly Journal of Economics: Forthcoming*.

Jackson, C. K., Rockoff, J. E., & Staiger, D. O. (2014). Teacher effects and teacher related policies. *Annual Review of Economics, 6,* 801–825.

Kane, T. J., Rockoff, J. E., & Staiger, D. O. (2008). What does certification tell us about teacher effectiveness? Evidence from New York city. *Economics of Education Review, 27*(6), 615–631.

Koedel, C., Mihaly, K., & Rockoff, J. E. (2015). Value-added modeling: A review. *Economics of Education Review, 47,* 180–195.

Krueger, A. B. (1999). Experimental estimates of education production functions. *Quarterly Journal of Economics, 114*(2), 497–532.

Lafortune, J., Rothstein, J., & Whitmore Schanzenbach, D. (2018). School finance reform and the distribution of student achievement. *American Economic Journal: Applied Economics, 10*(2), 1–26.

Lazear, E. P. (2003). Teacher incentives. *Swedish Economic Policy Review, 10*(3), 179–214.

Levine, R., & Renelt, D. (1992). A sensitivity analysis of cross-country growth regressions. *The American Economic Review, 82*(4), 942–963.

Mincer, J. (1970). The distribution of labor incomes: A survey with special reference to the human capital approach. *Journal of Economic Literature, 8*(1), 1–26.

Mincer, J. (1974). *Schooling, experience, and earnings.* New York: NBER.

Mulligan, C. B. (1999). Galton versus the human capital approach to inheritance. *Journal of Political Economy, 107*(6, pt. 2), S184–S224.

Murnane, R. J. (1975). *Impact of school resources on the learning of inner city children.* Cambridge, MA: Ballinger.

Murnane, R. J., Willett, J. B., Duhaldeborde, Y., & Tyler, J. H. (2000). How important are the cognitive skills of teenagers in predicting subsequent earnings? *Journal of Policy Analysis and Management, 19*(4), 547–568.

National Council on Teacher Quality. (2017). *State teacher policy yearbook, 2017.* Washington: National Council on Teacher Quality.

Psacharopoulos, G., & Patrinos, H. A. (2018). Returns to investment in education: A decennial review of the global literature. *Education Economics, 26*(5), 445–458.

Rivkin, S. G., Hanushek, E. A., & Kain, J. F. (2005). Teachers, schools, and academic achievement. *Econometrica, 73*(2), 417–458.

Romer, P. (1990). Human capital and growth: Theory and evidence. *Carnegie-Rochester Conference Series On Public Policy, 32,* 251–286.

Sala-i-Martin, X., Doppelhofer, G., Ronald, I., & Miller. (2004). Determinants of long-term growth: A bayesian averaging of cassical estimates (BACE) approach. *The American Economic Review, 94*(4), 813–835.

Woessmann, L. (2016). The importance of school systems: Evidence from international differences in student achievement. *The Journal of Economic Perspectives, 30*(3), 3–32.

Word, E., Johnston, J., Pate Bain, H., DeWayne Fulton, B., Boyd Zaharies, J., Lintz, M. N., et al. (1990). *Student/teacher achievement ratio (STAR), Tennessee's K-3 class size study: Final summary report, 1985-1990.* Nashville, TN: Tennessee State Department of Education.

Further reading

Ehrenberg, R. G., Brewer, D. J., Adam, G., & Douglas Willms, J. (2001). Class size and student achievement. *Psychological Science in the Public Interest, 2*(1), 1–30.

Hanushek, E. A. (1986). The economics of schooling: Production and efficiency in public schools. *Journal of Economic Literature, 24*(3), 1141–1177.

Hanushek, E. A. (2011). The economic value of higher teacher quality. *Economics of Education Review, 30*(3), 466–479.

Hanushek, E. A., & Woessmann, L. (2015). *The knowledge capital of nations: Education and the economics of growth.* Cambridge, MA: MIT Press.

Mishel, L., & Rothstein, R. (Eds.). (2002). *The class size debate.* Washington, DC: Economic Policy Institute.

Moe, T. M. (2011). *Special interest: Teachers unions and America's public schools.* Washington, DC: Brookings Institution Press.

Peterson, P. E. (2010). *Saving schools: From Horace Mann to virtual learning.* Cambridge, MA: Belknap Press of Harvard University Press.

14

Education, knowledge capital, and economic growth

Eric A. Hanushek[a], Ludger Woessmann[b]

[a]Hoover Institution, Stanford University, CESifo, IZA, and NBER, Stanford, CA, United States;
[b]University of Munich, Ifo Institute, CESifo and IZA, Munich, Germany

Education has long been viewed as an important determinant of economic well-being. While theoretical discussions strongly emphasize the role of human capital in growth, the bulk of empirical analysis is more mixed. In large part, this mixed evidence appears to reflect measurement issues. Once corrected to allow for both quality of schools and the varied sources of skills, the skills-growth relationship becomes clear and strong.

The theoretical growth literature emphasizes at least three mechanisms through which education may affect economic growth. First, education can increase the human capital inherent in the labor force, which increases labor productivity and thus transitional growth toward a higher equilibrium level of output (as in augmented neoclassical growth theories, cf. Mankiw, Romer, & Weil, 1992). Second, education can increase the innovative capacity of the economy, and the development of new technologies, products and processes promotes growth (as in theories of endogenous growth, cf., e.g., Lucas, 1988; Romer, 1990; Aghion & Howitt, 1998). Third, education can facilitate the diffusion and transmission of knowledge needed to understand and process new information and to implement successfully new technologies devised by others, which again promotes economic growth (cf., e.g., Nelson & Phelps, 1966; Benhabib & Spiegel, 1994).

Despite these overall theoretical predictions, empirical testing has been less conclusive and open to more questions. Most people would acknowledge that a year of schooling does not produce the same cognitive skills everywhere. They would also agree that families and peers contribute to education. Health and nutrition further impact cognitive skills. Yet until recently, research on the economic impact of education—largely due to expedience—has almost uniformly ignored these aspects and has focused almost exclusively on school attainment. Recent research shows that ignoring differences in the quality of education significantly distorts the picture of how educational and economic outcomes are related.

This discussion focuses on how measures of knowledge capital—the aggregate cognitive skills of a country—reconcile the theoretical importance and the empirical evidence on the role of human capital in growth. The discussion further underscores the fundamental importance of skills for economic development.

Early studies of schooling quantity and economic growth

The majority of the empirical macroeconomic literature on economic returns to education employs measures of the quantity of schooling. The most common measure is years of schooling, averaged across the working-age population. (Woessmann (2003b) surveys issues of measuring and specifying human capital from early growth accounting to early cross-country growth regressions.) The standard method of estimating the effect of education on economic growth is to estimate cross-country growth regressions where average annual growth in gross domestic product (GDP) per capita over several decades is expressed as a function of measures of schooling and a set of other variables deemed important for economic growth.

Following the classical contributions by Barro (1991, 1997) and Mankiw et al. (1992), a vast early literature of cross-country growth regressions tended to find a significant positive association between quantitative measures of schooling and economic growth. Extensive reviews of the literature are found in Topel (1999), Temple (2001), Krueger & Lindahl (2001), and Sianesi & Van Reenen (2003). To provide an idea of the robustness of the basic association, primary schooling turns out to be the most robust influence factor (after an East Asian dummy) on growth in GDP per capita in 1960—96 in the extensive robustness analysis of 67 explanatory variables in growth regressions on a sample of 88 countries by Sala-i-Martin, Doppelhofer, & Miller (2004).

Fig. 14.1 provides a basic representation of the association between years of schooling and economic growth from 1960 to 2000. This basic relationship suggests that each year of schooling is associated with long-run growth that is 0.58% points higher, although much of the differences in growth across countries is unaccounted for.

Yet, questions developed regarding the interpretation of such relationships, and these questions persist. A substantial controversy addresses whether it is the level of years of schooling (as would be predicted by several models of endogenous growth) or the change in years of schooling (as would be predicted by basic neoclassical models) that is the more important driver of economic growth (e.g., Krueger & Lindahl, 2001)). It seems beyond the scope of current data to draw strong conclusions about the relative importance of different mechanisms for schooling quantity to affect economic growth. Even so, several recent studies suggest that education is important both as an investment in human capital and in facilitating research and development and the diffusion of technologies, with initial phases of education more important for imitation and higher education for innovation (Vandenbussche, Aghion, & Meghir, 2006).

Three more skeptical studies introduce doubts about the interpretation of the estimates. Bils & Klenow (2000) raise the issue of causality, suggesting that reverse causation running from higher economic growth to additional education may be at least as important as the causal effect of education on growth in the cross-country association. Pritchett (2001, 2006) raises questions about the plausibility of simple growth models with years of schooling and stresses that it is important for economic growth to get other things right as well, in particular the institutional framework of the economy. Third, Levine & Renelt (1992) and Levine & Zervos (1993) raise questions about the instability of empirical estimates and the sensitivity to model specification. Each issue will be discussed further below.

But most importantly, using average years of schooling as an education measure implicitly assumes that a year of schooling delivers the same

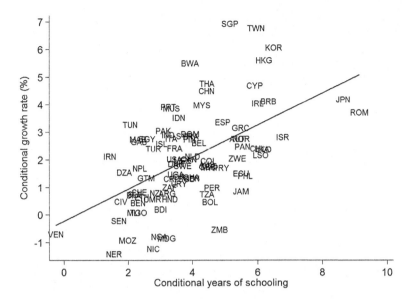

FIG. 14.1 Years of schooling and economic growth rates without considering knowledge capital. Notes: Added-variable plot of a regression of the average annual rate of growth (in percent) of real GDP per capita in 1960—2000 on average years of schooling in 1960 and initial level of real GDP per capita in 1960 (mean of unconditional variables added to each axis). *Source: Hanushek & Woessmann (2015a).*

increase in knowledge and skills regardless of the education system. This measure also assumes that formal schooling is the primary source of education and that variations in the quality of nonschool factors affecting learning have a negligible effect on education outcomes. This neglect of cross-country differences in the quality of education now appears to be the major drawback of application of school attainment as a quantitative measure of national skills.

Early evidence on the quality of education and economic growth

Quite clearly the average student in Ghana or Peru does not gain the same amount of knowledge in any year of schooling as the average student in Finland or Korea, but using measures of years of schooling in cross-country growth analysis assumes that they are equivalent. In addition, using years of schooling implicitly assumes that all skills and human capital come from formal schooling, even though extensive evidence on knowledge development and cognitive skills indicates that a variety of factors

outside of school—family, peers, and others—have a direct and powerful influence (Hanushek, 2002; Woessmann, 2003a). Ignoring these nonschool factors introduces the possibility of serious bias in the estimation of growth models based on school attainment.

Since the mid-1960s, international agencies such as the International Association for the Evaluation of Educational Achievement (IEA) and the Organization for Economic Cooperation and Development (OECD) have conducted many international tests—such as TIMSS, PISA, and their predecessors—of student performance in cognitive skills such as mathematics and science. Incorporating these measures of cognitive skills into growth analysis dramatically alters the assessment of the role of education in economic development.

Using the data from the international student achievement tests through 1991 to build a measure of educational quality, Hanushek & Kimko (2000) find a statistically and economically significant positive effect of the quality of education on economic growth in 1960—90 that is far larger than the association between the quantity of schooling and growth. Ignoring quality differences very significantly misses the true importance of education for economic growth. Their estimates suggest that one country-level standard deviation (equivalent to 47 test-score points in PISA 2000 mathematics, the same scale used in Fig. 14.2 below) higher test performance would yield about one percentage point higher annual growth.

That estimate stems from a statistical model that relates annual growth rates of real GDP per capita to the measure of educational quality, years of schooling, the initial level of income, and several other control variables (including, in different specifications, the population growth rates, political measures, openness of the economies, and the like). Adding educational quality to a base specification including only initial income and educational quantity boosts the variance in GDP per capita among the 31 countries in Hanushek and Kimko's sample that can be explained by the model from 33% to 73%. The effect of years of schooling is greatly reduced by including quality, leaving it mostly insignificant. At the same time, adding the other factors leaves the effects of cognitive skills basically unchanged.

Several studies have since found very similar results, including Barro (2001), Woessmann (2003b), Bosworth and Collins (2003), and Coulombe and Tremblay (2006); see Hanushek & Woessmann (2008) for a review. In sum, the evidence suggests that the quality of education, measured by the knowledge that students gain as depicted in tests of cognitive skills, is substantially more important for economic growth than the mere quantity of schooling.

Recent evidence on the importance of cognitive skills for economic growth

The most recent evidence, summarized in Hanushek & Woessmann (2015a), adds international student achievement tests not previously available, refines the aggregation of the various international tests, and uses the recent data on economic growth to analyze an even longer period (1960–2000).

Hanushek & Woessmann (2012a), relying on the 36 international tests from 12 testing occasions comparable between 1965 and 2003, develop a consistent metric of the aggregate cognitive skills, or knowledge capital, of nations. They adjust both the level of test performance and its variation through two data transformations. First, each of the separate international tests is benchmarked to a comparable level by calibrating the US international performance over time to the external standard of the available US longitudinal test (the National Assessment of Educational Progress, NAEP). Second, the dispersion of the tests is standardized by holding the score variance constant within a group of 13 OECD countries with relatively stable secondary school attendance rates over time. They are able to extend the sample of countries with available test-score and growth information to 50 countries. These data are also used to analyze effects of the distribution of educational quality at the bottom and at the top on economic growth, as well as interactions between educational quality and the institutional infrastructure of an economy.

The measure of knowledge capital is a simple average of the mathematics and science scores over international tests, interpreted as a proxy for the average educational performance of the whole labor force. This measure encompasses overall cognitive skills, not just those developed in schools. Thus, whether skills are developed at home, in schools, or elsewhere, they are included in the growth analyses.

After controlling for the initial level of GDP per capita and for years of schooling (Hanushek & Woessmann, 2015a), the knowledge capital measure features a highly statistically significant effect on the growth of real GDP per capita in 1960–2000 (Fig. 14.2). According to this simple specification, test scores that are larger by one standard deviation (measured at the student

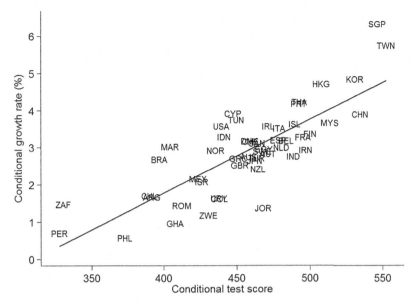

FIG. 14.2 Knowledge capital and economic growth rates across countries. Notes: Added-variable plot of a regression of the average annual rate of growth (in percent) of real GDP per capita in 1960–2000 on average test scores on international student achievement tests, average years of schooling in 1960, and initial level of real GDP per capita in 1960 (mean of unconditional variables added to each axis). *Source: Hanushek and Woessmann (2015a).*

level across all OECD countries in PISA) are associated with an average annual growth rate in GDP per capita that is two percentage points higher over the whole 40-year period.

Adding educational quality to a model that just includes initial income and years of schooling increases the share of variation in economic growth explained from 25% to 73%. As reported above, the quantity of schooling is statistically significantly related to economic growth in a specification that neglects educational quality, but the association between years of schooling and growth turns insignificant and is reduced to close to zero once the quality of education is included in the model (Fig. 14.3). Additionally, considering the variation just within each of five world regions, educational quality is significantly related to economic growth, indicating that it does not simply reflect economic differences across regions.

Recent literature on the determinants of economic growth emphasizes the importance of the institutional framework of the economy (e.g., Acemoglu, Johnson, & Robinson, 2005, 2012). The most common and powerful

measures of the institutional framework used in empirical work are the openness of the economy to international trade and the security of property rights. These two institutional variables are jointly highly significant when added to the basic growth model. But the positive effect of educational quality on economic growth is very robust to the inclusion of these controls, although its magnitude is slightly reduced by about one-third. Further, Glaeser, Porta, Lopez-de-Silanes, and Shleifer (2004) question whether the institutions themselves are an outcome of more human capital.

Other possible determinants of economic growth often discussed in the literature are fertility and geography. But when the total fertility rate and common geographical proxies, such as latitude or the fraction of the land area located within the geographic tropics, are added to the model, neither is statistically significantly associated with economic growth.

The results are remarkably similar when comparing the sample of OECD countries to the sample of non-OECD countries, with the point estimate of the effect of educational quality

FIG. 14.3 Years of schooling and economic growth rates after considering knowledge capital. Notes: Added-variable plot of a regression of the average annual rate of growth (in percent) of real GDP per capita in 1960–2000 on average years of schooling in 1960, average test scores on international student achievement tests, and initial level of real GDP per capita in 1960 (mean of unconditional variables added to each axis). *Source: Hanushek and Woessmann (2015a).*

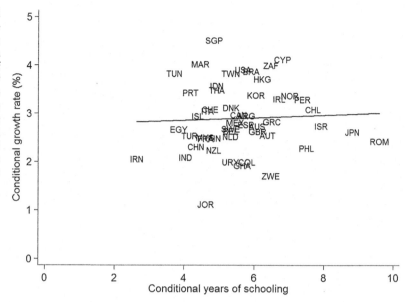

slightly larger in non-OECD countries. When the sample is separated based on whether a country was below or above the median of GDP per capita in 1960, the effect of educational quality is statistically significantly larger in low-income countries than in high-income countries (cf. Hanushek & Woessmann, 2015a). Specific analyses focusing on Latin America (Hanushek & Woessmann, 2012b) and on East Asia (Hanushek & Woessmann, 2016) confirm and extend the basic results. More recently, the importance of knowledge capital for long-run economic growth has also been shown in within-country analyses across US states (Hanushek, Ruhose, & Woessmann, 2017a, 2017b).

Causality in brief

The fundamental question is: should this tight relationship between cognitive skills and economic growth be interpreted as a causal one that can support direct policy actions? In other words, if achievement were raised, would

growth rates really be expected to go up by a commensurate amount?

The early studies that found positive effects of years of schooling on economic growth may have, indeed, been suffering from simple reverse causality, that is, improved growth was leading to more schooling rather than the reverse (Bils & Klenow, 2000). If a country gets richer, it tends to buy more of many things, including more years of schooling for its population.

There is less reason to think that higher student achievement is caused by economic growth. For one thing, scholars have found little impact of additional education spending on achievement outcomes, so it is unlikely that the relationship comes from growth-induced resources lifting student achievement (Hanushek & Woessmann, 2011a). Still, it remains difficult to develop conclusive tests of causality with the limited sample of countries included in this analysis.

Hanushek & Woessmann (2012a) present evidence on a series of tests of causality that offers some assurance that the issues most frequently cited as being potentially problematic are not affecting the results. First, the estimated relationship is little affected by including other possible determinants of economic growth. These specification tests rule out many basic problems attributable to omitted causal factors that have been noted in prior growth work.

Second, the most obvious concerns about reverse-causality issues arise because the analysis relates growth rates over the period 1960 to 2000 to test scores for roughly the same period. To address this directly, the timing of the analysis is separated by estimating the effect of scores on tests conducted only until 1984 on economic growth in the period since 1985 (and until 2009). In this analysis, available for a sample of 25 countries only, test scores strictly pre-date the growth period, making it clear that increased growth could not be causing the higher test scores of the prior period. This estimation shows a positive effect of early test scores on subsequent growth rates that is almost twice as large as that displayed above. Indeed, this fact itself may be significant, because it is consistent with the possibility that skills have become even more important for the economy in recent periods.

Third, even if reverse causality were not an issue, it does ensure that the important international differences in test scores reflect school policies and not, say, health and nutrition differences in the population or simply because of cultural differences regarding learning and testing. Nevertheless, attention can be focused just on variations in achievement that arise directly from institutional characteristics of each country's school system (exit examinations, autonomy, relative teacher salaries, and private schooling). This instrumental variable estimation of the growth relationship yields essentially the same results as previously presented, lending support both to the causal interpretation of the effect of cognitive skills and to the conclusion that schooling policies can have direct economic returns.

Fourth, a major concern is that countries with good economies also have good school systems, implying that those that grow faster because of the basic economic factors also have high achievement. In this case, achievement is simply a reflection of other important aspects of the economy and not the driving force in growth. One simple approach is to consider the implications of differences in measured skills within a single economy, thus eliminating institutional or cultural factors that may make the economies of different countries grow faster. This can readily be done for immigrants to the United States who have been educated in their home countries and who can be compared to those immigrants educated just in the United States. Since the two groups are within the single labor market of the United States, any differences in labor-market returns associated with cognitive skills cannot arise because of differences in the economy or culture of their home country. Looking at labor-market returns, immigrants from countries with higher cognitive skills tend to have higher incomes, but only if the immigrant was in fact educated in the home country. Immigrants from the same home country schooled in the United States see no economic return to home-country test scores, thus pinpointing the value of better schools. This comparative analysis rules out the possibility that test scores simply reflect cultural factors or economic institutions of the home country.

Finally, for those countries that have participated in testing at different points over the past half century, it can be observed whether or not students are getting better or worse over time. Building on this, perhaps the toughest test of causality is relating *changes* in test scores over time to *changes* in growth rates. This approach implicitly eliminates country-specific economic and cultural factors because it looks at what happens over time within each country. While considering this relationship is only possible for 12 OECD countries (because of historical testing patterns), the gains in test scores over time are very closely related to the gains in growth rates over time.

Each approach to determining causation is subject to its own uncertainty (Hanushek &

Woessmann, 2012a). Nonetheless, the combined evidence consistently points to the conclusion that differences in cognitive skills lead to significant differences in economic growth.

The interaction of educational quality with economic institutions

Economic institutions appear to interact with the effect of educational quality on economic growth. The institutional framework of a country affects the relative profitability of piracy and productive activity. If the available knowledge and skills are used in the former activity rather than the latter, the effect on economic growth may be very different, perhaps even turning negative (North, 1990).

Past work supports the possible direct effects of a country's institutions. The allocation of talent between rent-seeking and entrepreneurship matters for growth: countries with more engineering students grow faster and countries with more law students grow more slowly (Murphy, Shleifer, & Vishny, 1991). Education may not have much impact in less developed countries that lack other facilitating factors such as functioning institutions for markets and legal systems (Easterly, 2001). And due to deficiencies in the institutional environment, cognitive skills might be applied to socially unproductive activities in many developing countries (Pritchett, 2001).

Adding the interaction of educational quality and one institutional measure—openness to international trade—to the growth specification indicates not only that both have significant individual effects on economic growth but also that there is a significant positive interaction. The effect of educational quality on economic growth is indeed significantly higher in countries that have been fully open to international trade than in countries that have been fully closed. The effect of educational quality on economic growth is significantly positive, albeit

relatively low, at 0.9 per s.d. in closed economies but increases to 2.5 per s.d. in open economies. When using protection against expropriation rather than openness to trade as the measure of institutional quality, there is similarly a positive interaction term with educational quality, although it lacks statistical significance.

In sum, both the quality of the institutional environment and the quality of education seem important for economic development. Furthermore, the effect of knowledge capital on growth seems significantly larger in countries with a productive institutional framework, so that good institutional quality and good educational quality can reinforce each other. Thus, the macroeconomic effect of education depends on other complementary growth-enhancing policies and institutions. But cognitive skills have a significant positive growth effect even in countries with a poor institutional environment.

Simulating the impact of educational reform on economic growth

Development strategies invariably include education and human capital improvement as important components. These have tended until recently to focus on quantitative goals, such as achieving certain levels of educational enrollment or attainment. For example, the two Millennium Development Goals related to education that the United Nations adopted in 2000 — universal primary education and gender parity by 2015 — are solely phrased in terms of educational quantity (United Nations, 2009). Similarly, while UNESCO's Education for All initiative mentioned quality, its explicit goals mostly focused on school quantity (UNESCO, 2008).

Amidst educational progress, development strategies built just on schooling have disappointed because expansion of school attainment has not guaranteed improved economic conditions (Easterly, 2001). Thus, when the United

Nations in 2015 revisited its development goals in the Sustainable Development Goals or SDG's, the education component included explicit mention of quality, although stopping short of quantified quality targets. This is perhaps a natural acknowledgment that lower-income countries still have generally incomplete enrollment in lower secondary schools, but it still raises the possibility of overemphasis of attainment at the cost of lower quality. In general, the SDG's highlight the long standing tension between goals framed in terms of school completion (which is readily and routinely measured) and quality (which less frequently measured).

To show the value of improved quality of schooling, Hanushek & Woessmann (2015b) project the economic impacts of country changes in access and quality of schooling. Three improvements in student performance are considered. In the first, each country moves to full access to lower secondary schooling at the current quality level. In the second, all students currently in school with insufficient skills are brought up to at least to a basic skill level. In the third, both moves simultaneously occur.

Their projections rely on a simple description of how skills enter the labor market and have an impact on the economy. Improvement occurs linearly from today's schooling situation in each country to reaching the goal in 15 years. Assuming that a worker remains in the labor force for 40 years implies that the labor force is progressively made up of increasingly more skilled workers for 55 years (15 years of reform and 40 years of replacement of retiring, less-skilled workers), after which all workers are at the new improved quality level. The difference in GDP is then estimated with an improved workforce versus the existing workforce skills over 80 years, roughly the life expectancy of somebody in a developed country born today. Future gains in GDP are discounted from the present with a 3% discount rate. The resulting present value of additions to GDP is thus directly comparable to the current levels of GDP. (See Hanushek &

Woessmann (2010, 2011b, 2015b) for details of the projection methodology.)

Hanushek & Woessmann (2015b) define basic skills by a simple PISA test standard, where the OECD defines fully achieving Level 1 on the PISA test as representing the skills necessary in order to participate productively in modern economies.

Fig. 14.4 displays their projection results for four groupings of countries (according to World Bank categories): lower middle income, upper middle income, high income non-OECD, and high income OECD. Lower middle income countries include such countries as Ghana, Honduras, Indonesia, and Morocco. Examples of upper middle income are Argentina, Bulgaria, South Africa, and Turkey. The high income non-OECD includes Hong Kong, Lithuania, and several Arab oil-producing countries. Again, however, the 76 countries included in the overall projections are restricted to countries that have recently participated in PISA or TIMSS testing so that a measure of quality is available.

The first grouping of bars on the graph in Fig. 14.4 show the gains from improving quality for existing access levels to schools. The lower middle income countries on average would see gains in the average level of GDP over the next 80 years of 13%, but even high income OECD countries would on average gain three percent in GDP from bringing all students up to basic skills (PISA Level 1).

The second set of columns shows the economic impact of ensuring access of all children through lower secondary but maintaining existing quality levels. While this has essentially no impact on high income OECD countries where access is almost complete now, it has noticeable impact for the other sets of countries. For lower middle income countries, which currently average about 80% completion of lower secondary schooling, the gains would on average lift future GDP levels by 4.4%.

These two sets of projections show the tension that has existed in setting international goals for

FIG. 14.4 Projections of expanded access and improved quality of schools by level of development. *Source: Own depiction based on Hanushek and Woessmann (2015b).*

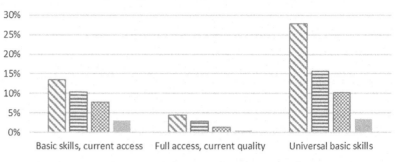

schooling. Full access clearly has value, but the value is significantly less than seen through quality improvements.

The final set of columns in Fig. 14.4 shows the result of achieving simultaneous improvements in access and quality. Lower middle income countries gain on average 28% higher GDP, and upper middle income countries gain 16% in the level of future GDP. This broader quality dimension is also relevant to upper income countries, since they today have numbers of students who do not get to basic skill levels. For example, in the US 23% of 15-year-olds do not get to Level 1 in mathematics; getting them to Level 1 implies a future GDP that would be 3.3% higher on average.

The simulations in Hanushek & Woessmann (2015b) show that the previous estimates of the effects of knowledge capital on growth have large impacts on national economies. They also suggest that directly focusing on school quality is important for economic development.

Summary

The accumulated evidence from analyses of economic outcomes is that the quality of education—measured on an outcome basis of cognitive skills—has powerful economic effects. Economic growth is strongly affected by the knowledge capital of workers.

This message is important in developed and developing countries alike. In the latter, much of the discussion of development policy today simplifies and distorts this message. It recognizes that education matters, but focuses most attention on ensuring that everybody is in school—regardless of the learning that goes on. Because of the reported findings—that knowledge rather than just time in school is what counts for economic growth—policies must pay more attention to the quality of schools.

References

Acemoglu, D., Johnson, S., & Robinson, J. A. (2005). Institutions as a fundamental cause of long-run growth. In P. Aghion, & S. N. Durlauf (Eds.), *Handbook of economic growth* (pp. 385–472). Amsterdam: North Holland.

Acemoglu, D., Johnson, S., & Robinson, J. A. (2012). The colonial origins of comparative development: An empirical investigation: Reply. *The American Economic Review, 102*(6), 3077–3110.

Aghion, P., & Howitt, P. (1998). *Endogenous growth theory.* Cambridge, MA: MIT Press.

Barro, R. J. (1991). Economic growth in a cross section of countries. *Quarterly Journal of Economics, 106*(2), 407–443.

Barro, R. J. (1997). *Determinants of economic growth: A cross-country empirical study.* Cambridge, MA: MIT Press.

Barro, R. J. (2001). Human capital and growth. *The American Economic Review, 91*(2), 12–17.

Benhabib, J., & Spiegel, M. M. (1994). The role of human capital in economic development: Evidence from aggregate cross-country data. *Journal of Monetary Economics, 34*(2), 143–174.

Bils, M., & Klenow, P. J. (2000). Does schooling cause growth? *The American Economic Review, 90*(5), 1160–1183.

Bosworth, B. P., & Collins, S. M. (2003). The empirics of growth: An update. *Brookings Papers on Economic Activity, 2*, 113–206.

Coulombe, S., & Tremblay, J.-F. (2006). Literacy and growth. *Topics in Macroeconomics, 6*(2). Article 4.

Easterly, W. (2001). *The elusive quest for growth: An economist's adventures and misadventures in the tropics.* Cambridge, MA: The MIT Press.

Glaeser, E. L., Porta, R. L., Lopez-de-Silanes, F., & Shleifer, A. (2004). Do institutions cause growth? *Journal of Economic Growth, 9*(3), 271–303.

Hanushek, E. A. (2002). Publicly provided education. In A. J. Auerbach, & M. Feldstein (Eds.), *Handbook of public economics* (Vol. 4, pp. 2045–2141). Amsterdam: North Holland.

Hanushek, E. A., & Kimko, D. D. (2000). Schooling, labor force quality, and the growth of nations. *The American Economic Review, 90*(5), 1184–1208.

Hanushek, E. A., Ruhose, J., & Woessmann, L. (2017a). Economic gains from educational reform by US States. *Journal of Human Capital, 11*(4), 447–486.

Hanushek, E. A., Ruhose, J., & Woessmann, L. (2017b). Knowledge capital and aggregate income differences: Development accounting for U.S. states. *American Economic Journal: Macroeconomics, 9*(4), 184–224.

Hanushek, E. A., & Woessmann, L. (2008). The role of cognitive skills in economic development. *Journal of Economic Literature, 46*(3), 607–668.

Hanushek, E. A., & Woessmann, L. (2010). *The high cost of low educational performance: The long-run economic impact of improving PISA outcomes.* Paris: Organisation for Economic Cooperation and Development.

Hanushek, E. A., & Woessmann, L. (2011a). The economics of international differences in educational achievement. In E. A. Hanushek, S. Machin, & L. Woessmann (Eds.), *Handbook of the economics of education* (Vol. 3, pp. 89–200). Amsterdam: North Holland.

Hanushek, E. A., & Woessmann, L. (2011b). How much do educational outcomes matter in OECD countries? *Economic Policy, 26*(67), 427–491.

Hanushek, E. A., & Woessmann, L. (2012a). Do better schools lead to more growth? Cognitive skills, economic outcomes, and causation. *Journal of Economic Growth, 17*(4), 267–321.

Hanushek, E. A., & Woessmann, L. (2012b). Schooling, educational achievement, and the Latin American growth puzzle. *Journal of Development Economics, 99*(2), 497–512.

Hanushek, E. A., & Woessmann, L. (2015a). *The knowledge capital of nations: Education and the economics of growth.* Cambridge, MA: MIT Press.

Hanushek, E. A., & Woessmann, L. (2015b). *Universal basic skills: What countries stand to gain.* Paris: Organisation for Economic Co-operation and Development.

Hanushek, E. A., & Woessmann, L. (2016). Knowledge capital, growth, and the East Asian miracle. *Science, 351*(6271), 344–345.

Krueger, A. B., & Lindahl, M. (2001). Education for growth: Why and for whom? *Journal of Economic Literature, 39*(4), 1101–1136.

Levine, R., & Renelt, D. (1992). A sensitivity analysis of cross-country growth regressions. *The American Economic Review, 82*(4), 942–963.

Levine, R., & Zervos, S. J. (1993). What we have learned about policy and growth from cross-country regressions. *The American Economic Review, 83*(2), 426–430.

Lucas, R. E., Jr. (1988). On the mechanics of economic development. *Journal of Monetary Economics, 22*(1), 3–42.

Mankiw, N. G., Romer, D., & Weil, D. (1992). A contribution to the empirics of economic growth. *Quarterly Journal of Economics, 107*(2), 407–437.

Murphy, K. M., Shleifer, A., & Vishny, R. W. (1991). The allocation of talent: Implications for growth. *Quarterly Journal of Economics, 106*(2), 503–530.

Nelson, R. R., & Phelps, E. (1966). Investment in humans, technology diffusion and economic growth. *The American Economic Review, 56*(2), 69–75.

North, D. C. (1990). *Institutions, institutional change and economic performance.* Cambridge: Cambridge University Press.

Pritchett, L. (2001). Where has all the education gone? *The World Bank Economic Review, 15*(3), 367–391.

Pritchett, L. (2006). Does learning to add up add up? The returns to schooling in aggregate data. In E. A. Hanushek, & F. Welch (Eds.), *Handbook of the economics of education* (pp. 635–695). Amsterdam: North Holland.

Romer, P. (1990). Endogenous technological change. *Journal of Political Economy, 99*(5), S71–S102. pt. II.

Sala-i-Martin, X., Doppelhofer, G., & Miller, R. I. (2004). Determinants of long-term growth: A Bayesian averaging of classical estimates (BACE) approach. *The American Economic Review, 94*(4), 813–835.

Sianesi, B., & Van Reenen, J. (2003). The returns to education: Macroeconomics. *Journal of Economic Surveys, 17*(2), 157–200.

Temple, J. (2001). Growth effects of education and social capital in the OECD countries. *OECD Economic Studies, 33*, 57–101.

Topel, R. (1999). Labor markets and economic growth. In O. Ashenfelter, & D. Card (Eds.), *Handbook of labor economics* (pp. 2943–2984). Amsterdam: Elsevier.

UNESCO. (2008). Overcoming inequality: Why governance matters. *EFA Global monitoring report 2009*. Paris: UNESCO.

United Nations. (2009). *The millennium development goals report 2009*. New York: United Nations.

Vandenbussche, J., Aghion, P., & Meghir, C. (2006). Growth, distance to frontier and composition of human capital. *Journal of Economic Growth, 11*(2), 97–127. June.

Woessmann, L. (2003a). Schooling resources, educational institutions, and student performance: The international evidence. *Oxford Bulletin of Economics & Statistics, 65*(2), 117–170.

Woessmann, L. (2003b). Specifying human capital. *Journal of Economic Surveys, 17*(3), 239–270.

Education production functions: updated evidence from developing countries

Paul Glewwe[a], Sylvie Lambert[b], Qihui Chen[c]

[a]Department of Applied Economics, University of Minnesota, St. Paul, MN, United States; [b]Paris School of Economics, Paris, France; [c]College of Economics and Management, China Agricultural University, Beijing, China

This chapter is an updated version of Glewwe and Lambert (2010). Some of the material in this article was drawn from Glewwe, Hanushek, Humpage, and Ravina (2013) and Glewwe and Muralidharan (2016).

Introduction

Economists, education researchers and other social scientists have accumulated convincing evidence that education can increase individuals' incomes by improving their productivity. Education can also generate non-pecuniary benefits, such as improved health and social integration, for individuals and for society as a whole. To the extent that much of the gap in living standards between developed and developing countries is due to wide gaps in education, efforts to raise enrollment rates and to enhance student learning could greatly improve living standards in developing countries.

This chapter addresses a central issue in education research: What education policies are most effective at raising enrollment and increasing learning in developing countries? While much research has been conducted, many estimated policy impacts may be biased, or may not apply to other countries. To provide an answer to this question, this chapter summarizes what has been learned and, equally important, what remains unclear and thus merits further research. The next section begins by providing an overview of education in developing countries in the past decades. The third section introduces the education production function, a concept used by economists for understanding how schooling generates cognitive and non-cognitive skills, and several other relevant relationships. The fourth section reviews estimation issues. The fifth section summarizes research on enrollment and learning in developing countries. The last section concludes and points out a number of directions for future research.

Education in developing countries

Despite dramatic increases in school enrollment in most developing countries, they still lag behind developed countries. One widely available indicator is the *gross enrollment rate*, the number of children enrolled in education at a particular level, regardless of age, divided by the population in the age group associated with that level. In 1960, primary school gross enrollment rates were 65% in low-income countries, 83% in middle-income countries, and over 100% in high-income countries (Table 15.1). By 2016, primary gross enrollment rates reached or exceeded 100% in low- and middle-income countries, and in all regions (except that Sub-Saharan Africa, at 97%, was slightly below 100%). Secondary gross enrollment rates have increased even more dramatically since 1960 (Table 15.2). Yet except for OECD countries and other European countries and Central Asian countries, there is still room for improvement in secondary enrollment around the world, especially in Sub-Saharan Africa.

Note that gross enrollment rates above 100% do *not* imply that all children are enrolled. Grade repetition can cause gross rates to exceed 100% even when some children never enroll. Another measure of education progress that avoids such ambiguity is *net enrollment rates*, the number of children enrolled in education at a particular schooling level *of the age associated with that level*, divided by all children of that age. Net enrollment rates cannot exceed 100%; they remove the upward bias in gross rates caused by enrollment of "overage" children (due to repetition or delayed enrollment). Table 15.1 shows that primary net enrollment rates are much lower than gross rates. The net enrollment rate in Sub-Saharan Africa is particularly low, only 78% in 2016. Sub-Saharan Africa's educational outcomes are low even compared to low-income non-African countries; its primary and secondary net rates are well below those of South

TABLE 15.1 Primary enrollment rates.

Area	Gross enrollment rate				Net enrollment rate	
	1960	1980	2000	2016	2000	2016
World	80	97	99	104		91
Country group						
Low-income	65	66	74	101	55	80
Middle-income	83	99	101	105	87	93
High-income	109	101	101	102	96	97
Region						
Sub-Saharan Africa	40	77	82	97	61	78
Middle East/North Africa	59	86	96	104	84	94
Latin America	91	115	118	109	96	95
South Asia	41	78	91	113	79	94
East Asia and Pacific Islands	87	109	107	103	95	96
Europe and Central Asia	103	103	103	102	96	97
Organization for Economic Cooperation and Development (OECD)	109	102	102	102	98	97

Sources: UNESCO Institute for Statistics (uis.unesco.org): https://data.worldbank.org/indicator/SE.PRM.ENRR.FE, https://data.-worldbank.org/indicator/SE.PRM.ENRR.MA.(accessed on October 15,2018).

TABLE 15.2 Secondary school enrollment rates (percent of students of secondary school age).

Area	Gross enrollment rate				Net enrollment rate	
	1960	1980	2000	2016	2000	2016
World	29	49	60	76	55	66
Country group						
Low-income	14	19	23	40	19	32
Middle-income	21	44	57	78	54	67
High-income	63	86	99	107	87	93
Region						
Sub-Saharan Africa	5	19	26	43	21	34
Middle East/ North Africa	13	42	68	80	61	70
Latin America	14	72	85	95	66	76
South Asia	10	27	43	71	39	60
East Asia and Pacific	20	46	62	88	65	79
Europe and Central Asia	55	87	95	106	84	91
OECD	65	81	95	105	83	90

Sources: UNESCO Institute for Statistics (uis.unesco.org): https://data.worldbank.org/indicator/SE.SEC.ENRR.FE, https://data.worldbank.org/indicator/SE.SEC.ENRR.MA.(accessed on October 15,2018).

Asia, which is as poor as Sub-Saharan Africa. Note also that these averages hide some gender disparities; girls still have lower enrollment rates in the Middle East and in Africa (Table 15.3).

Turning to learning outcomes, in 2016, the adult literacy rate in developing countries reached 84%, but was only 61% in "least developed" countries.[1] Illiteracy arises because many adults never attend school and/or because attending school may not develop literacy. Sub-Saharan Africa exemplifies the latter. It is estimated that 88% of all children and adolescents in that region will not be able to read proficiently by the time they are of age to complete primary and lower secondary education, among whom 54% are in school (UNESCO Institute for Statistics, 2017).

Problems in attaining literacy likely reflect low school *quality* in many developing countries; children learn much less per year of schooling than their counterparts in developed countries. This may reflect the rapid expansion of education in developing countries in recent decades (see Tables 15.1 and 15.2), which strained financial and human resources. Comparisons of education quality across countries require internationally comparable data on academic performance. Two sources of such data are the Trends International Mathematics and Science Study (TIMSS) and Progress in International Reading Literacy Study (PIRLS), administered by the International Association for the Evaluation of Educational Achievement.

The first four columns of Table 15.4 show the TIMSS mathematics test scores in 1999 for grade 7 and 8 students and in 2015 for grade 4 and 8 students. The scores for the four developed countries (France, Japan, the UK and the US) range between 488 and 593. A few developing economies score above 500 (Kazakhstan, Malaysia, South Korea and Taiwan). Yet most developing countries score much lower. A similar pattern holds for reading scores (columns 5 and 6 in Table 15.4), which are available only for grade 4. On a more optimistic note, the lowest performing developing country on mathematics in 1999, South Africa, had made dramatic improvements (from 275 to 372) by 2015.[2]

[1] Source: World Bank World Development Indicators. Available at: https://databank.worldbank.org/data/reports.aspx?source=2&series=SE.ADT.LITR.ZS&country=LIC (accessed April 10, 2019). "Least developed" are those classified as low-income countries by the World Bank.

[2] For more on the South African case, see van der Berg and Gustafsson (2019).

TABLE 15.3   Gender disparities in gross primary and secondary enrollment rates.

	A. Gender disparities in gross primary school enrollment			
	2005		2016	
	Male	Female	Male	Female
World average	105	100	104	105
Country group				
Low income	99	85	104	98
Middle income	106	102	104	106
High income	101	100	102	102
Region				
Sub-Saharan Africa	99	87	100	95
Middle East & North Africa	104	97	106	102
Latin America & Caribbean	118	114	110	108
South Asia	106	101	108	118
East Asia & Pacific	105	104	103	102
Europe & Central Asia	102	101	103	102
OECD members	102	101	102	102

	B. Gender disparities in gross secondary school enrollment			
	2005		2016	
	Male	Female	Male	Female
World average	66	62	77	76
Country group				
Low income	33	24	44	36
Middle income	64	61	78	78
High income	101	101	108	107
Region				
Sub-Saharan Africa	36	28	46	40
Middle East & North Africa	74	70	82	77
Latin America & Caribbean	83	90	92	97
South Asia	54	45	71	71
East Asia & Pacific	68	67	87	88
Europe & Central Asia	96	94	106	105
OECD members	98	98	105	106

Notes: Countries with populations of less than 1 million are excluded.

Sources: *UNESCO Institute for Statistics (uis.unesco.org); https://data.worldbank.org/indicator/SE.PRM.ENRR.FE, https://data.worldbank.org/indicator/SE.PRM.ENRR.MA, https://data.worldbank.org/indicator/SE.SEC.ENRR.MA, https://data.worldbank.org/indicator/SE.SEC.ENRR.FE. (accessed on October 15, 2018).*

TABLE 15.4 Mean mathematics and reading achievement, TIMSS and PIRLS studies.

Country	Mathematics (TIMSS) 1999		Mathematics (TIMSS) 2015		Reading (PIRLS) 2001	Reading (PIRLS) 2016
	Grade 7	Grade 8	Grade 4	Grade 8	Grade 4	Grade 4
France	—	—	488	—	525	511
Japan	—	579	593	586	—	—
U.K. (England)	—	—	546	518	553	559
U.S.	—	502	539	518	542	549
Argentina					420	480
Azerbaijan						472
Bahrain			451	454		446
Belize					327	
Botswana			—	391		
Chile	—	392	459	427	—	494
Colombia	—	—			422	
Egypt			—	392		330
Georgia			463	453		488
Indonesia	—	403	397	—	—	
Iran	—	422	431	436	414	428
Jordan	—	428	388	386	—	
Kazakhstan			544	528		536
South Korea	—	587	608	606	—	—
Kuwait	—	—	353	392	396	393
Macao SAR						546
Lebanon			—	442		
Malaysia	—	519	—	465	—	—
Morocco	337	—	377	384	350	358
Oman			425	403		418
Philippines	345	—	535	—	—	—
Qatar			439	437		442
Saudi Arabia			383	368		430
South Africa	—	275	376	372	—	320
Thailand	—	467	—	431	—	—
Tunisia	—	448			—	—

(Continued)

III. Production, costs and financing

TABLE 15.4   Mean mathematics and reading achievement, TIMSS and PIRLS studies.—cont'd

Country	Mathematics (TIMSS) 1999		Mathematics (TIMSS) 2015		Reading (PIRLS) 2001	Reading (PIRLS) 2016
	Grade 7	Grade 8	Grade 4	Grade 8	Grade 4	Grade 4
Turkey	—	429	483	458	449	—
Trinidad and Tobago						479
United Arab Emirates			452	465		452

Source: Mullis et al. (2000); Mullis, Martin, Gonzalez, and Kennedy (2003); Mullis, Martin, Foy, and Hooper (2016, 2017).

These assessments imply that raising learning in developing countries requires not just increased enrollment but also more learning per year enrolled. Policy interventions that increase enrollment and/or learning can be classified into those that increase the demand for education and those that improve the supply of education services. The following subsections review both types. Table 15.5 summarizes the findings. The discussion is limited to policy impacts on enrollment and learning; see Damon and Glewwe (2009), Glewwe and Muralidharan (2016), Damon, Glewwe, Sun, and Wisniewski (2019) for comparisons of the costs and benefits of specific policies.

The education production function

Formal education increases individuals' well-being primarily through their acquisition of skills, both cognitive (e.g. literacy and numeracy) and non-cognitive (e.g. social and organizational skills). Thus an understanding of the process by which formal education produces those skills is crucial for crafting effective education policies. Economists characterize this process as *education production*.

Economists have studied factories, farms and other productive organizations for more than two centuries. They have gradually developed a comprehensive yet flexible framework for thinking about production processes. At first glance, depicting education as a production process may seem strange, but upon further reflection this approach is useful because it provides a comprehensive framework for thinking about how cognitive and non-cognitive skills were generated through formal education. Most importantly, this framework provides crucial guidance on how to use education data to estimate the impact of education policies (and other causal factors) on students' acquisition of skills.

The process by which both cognitive and non-cognitive skills are learned is determined by many different factors. Production functions simply depict this process as a mathematical relationship between inputs and skills acquired. This relationship can be very flexible, allowing for almost any learning process. In this sense, an education production function always exists, although the fact that it exists does not guarantee that one can estimate it.

Everything that determines learning, henceforth referred to as "factors" or "inputs" in the production process, can be divided into school, child and household variables. A simple yet flexible skills production function is:

$$A = a(S, \mathbf{Q}, \mathbf{C}, \mathbf{H}, \mathbf{I}) \tag{15.1}$$

where A is skills learned ("achievement"), S is years of schooling, $\mathbf{Q}$ is the set of all school and teacher characteristics ("quality") that affect learning, $\mathbf{C}$ is all child characteristics (including "ability") and $\mathbf{H}$ is all household characteristics that affect learning, and $\mathbf{I}$ is educational "inputs" that households

TABLE 15.5 Summary of empirical results.

Demand-side policies	Studies	Countries	Impact on enrollment/ time in school	Impact on learning
Unconditional transfers (including pensions)	Carvalho (2000)	Brazil	Yes	Not estimated
	Baird et al. (2011)	Malawi	Yes	No
	Benhassine et al. (2015)	Morocco	Yes	No
	Edmonds (2006)	South Africa	Yes	Not estimated
Conditional cash transfers	de Janvry et al. (2012)	Brazil	Yes	Not estimated
	Glewwe and Kassouf (2012)	Brazil	Yes	Not estimated
	Barrera-Osorio and Filmer (2016)	Cambodia	Yes	No
	Mo et al. (2013)	China	Yes	No
	Attanasio et al. (2010)	Colombia	Yes	Not estimated
	Baez and Camacho (2011)	Colombia	Yes	No/negative
	Barrera-Osorio et al. (2016)	Colombia	Yes	Not estimated
	Galiani and McEwan (2013)	Honduras	Yes	Not estimated
	Baird et al. (2011)	Malawi	Yes	Yes
	Baird et al. (2016a)	Malawi	Yes	Yes
	Schultz (2004)	Mexico	Yes	Not estimated
	Behrman et al. (2009)	Mexico	Yes	Not estimated
	Behrman et al. (2011)	Mexico	Yes	Not estimated
	Gitter and Barham (2008)	Nicaragua	Yes	Not estimated
	Barham et al. (2013)	Nicaragua	Yes	Yes
	Chaudhury and Parajuli (2010)	Pakistan	Yes	Not estimated
Merit-based scholarships	Blimpo (2014)	Benin	Not estimated	Yes
	Li et al. (2014)	China	Not estimated	Yes

(Continued)

TABLE 15.5   Summary of empirical results.—cont'd

Demand-side policies	Studies	Countries	Impact on enrollment/ time in school	Impact on learning
	Kremer et al. (2009)	Kenya	Yes	Yes
	Friedman et al. (2016)	Kenya	Yes	Yes
Reduction/abolition of school fees	Filmer and Schady (2014)	Cambodia	Yes	No
	Yi et al. (2014)	China	Yes	Not estimated
	School Fees Abolition Initiative (2006)	Kenya	Yes	Not estimated
	Borkum (2012)	South Africa	No	Not estimated
Vouchers	Angrist et al. (2002)	Colombia	Yes	Yes
	Angrist et al. (2006)	Colombia	Yes	Yes
	Muralidharan and Sundararaman (2015)	India	No estimated	Yes
	Hsieh and Urquiola (2006)	Chile	No	No
	Lara et al. (2011)	Chile	Not estimated	No
Matching funds	Ambler et al. (2015)	El Salvador	Yes	Not estimated
In-kind transfers	Hidalgo et al. (2013)	Ecuador	Yes	Negative
	Kremer et al. (2003)	Kenya	Yes	Not estimated
Information-based intervention	Loyalka et al. (2013)	China	Negative impact	No
	Wang et al. (2014)	China	Yes	Not estimated
	Jensen (2010)	Dominican Republic	Yes	Not estimated
Other: child learning/ mother literacy	Banerji et al. (2013)	India	No	Yes
Other: adult literacy	Handa (2002)	Mozambique	No	Not estimated
Other: female sanitary products	Oster and Thornton (2011)	Nepal	No	Not estimated
Other: funds to purchase bicycles	Muralidharan and Prakash (2017)	India	Yes	Not estimated
Supply-side policies				
School construction	Burde and Linden (2013)	Afghanistan	Yes	Yes

TABLE 15.5 Summary of empirical results.—cont'd

Demand-side policies	Studies	Countries	Impact on enrollment/ time in school	Impact on learning
	Kazianga et al. (2013)	Burkina Faso	Yes	Yes
	Duflo (2001)	Indonesia	Yes	Not estimated
	Handa (2002)	Mozambique	Yes	Not estimated
	Alderman et al. (2003)	Pakistan	Yes	Not estimated
Longer school days	Bellei (2009)	Chile	Not estimated	Yes
	Orkin (2013)	Ethiopia	Not estimated	Yes
Class size	Urquiola (2006)	Bolivia	Not estimated	Yes
	Urquiola and Verhoogen (2009)	Chile	Not estimated	Yes
	Duflo et al. (2015)	Kenya	Not estimated	No
Teacher attendance	Duflo et al. (2012)	India	Not estimated	Yes
	Muralidharan and Sundararaman (2010)	India	Not estimated	No
Contract teachers	Muralidharan and Sundararaman (2013)	India	Not estimated	Yes
	Duflo et al. (2015)	Kenya	Not estimated	Yes
Teachers incentives	Contreras and Rau (2012)	Chile	Not estimated	Yes
	Muralidharan and Sundararaman (2011)	India	Not estimated	Yes
	Muralidharan (2012)	India	Not estimated	Yes
	Glewwe, Ilias, et al. (2010) and Glewwe, Lambert, et al. (2010)	Kenya	No	No
Remedial education	Banerjee et al. (2007)	India	Not estimated	Yes
	Banerjee et al. (2010)	India	Not estimated	Yes
	Lakshminarayana et al. (2013)	India	Not estimated	Yes
	Banerjee et al. (2016)	India	Not estimated	Yes
Material inputs (textbooks etc.)	Tan et al. (1999)	The Philippines	Yes	Yes
	Abeberese et al. (2014)	The Philippines	Not estimate	Yes
	Borkum et al. (2012)	India	No	No
	Chin (2005)	India	Yes	Not estimated

(Continued)

TABLE 15.5 Summary of empirical results.—cont'd

Demand-side policies	Studies	Countries	Impact on enrollment/time in school	Impact on learning
	Glewwe et al. (2009)	Kenya	No	No
	Glewwe et al. (2004)	Kenya	Not estimated	No
Technology-enhanced instruction	Lai et al. (2013)	China	Not estimated	Yes
	Lai et al. (2015)	China	Not estimated	Yes
	Yang et al. (2013)	China	Not estimated	Yes
	Mo et al. (2015)	China	Not estimated	Yes
	Barrera-Osorio and Linden (2009)	Colombia	Not estimated	No
	Banerjee et al. (2007)	India	Not estimated	Yes
	Beuermann et al. (2015)	Peru	Not estimated	Yes
	Cristia et al. (2014)	Peru	No	Not estimated
	Malamud and Pop-Eleches (2011)	Romania	Not estimate	Negative
School meals	Adrogue and Orlicki (2013)	Argentina	No	Yes
	Kazianga et al. (2012)	Burkina Faso	Yes	Yes
	McEwan (2013)	Chile	No	No
	Tan et al. (1999)	the Philippines	No	Yes
	Alderman et al. (2012)	Uganda	No	No
Health: deworming	Miguel and Kremer (2004)	Kenya	Yes	No
	Baird et al. (2016b)	Kenya	Yes	Not estimated
	Ozier (2014)	Kenya	Not estimated	Yes
Health: iron supplementation tablets	Luo et al. (2012)	China	Not estimated	Yes
	Sylvia et al. (2013)	China	Not estimated	Yes
Health: health insurance	Chen and Jin (2012)	China	No	Not estimated
Health: eyeglasses	Glewwe et al. (2016)	China	Not estimated	Yes

contribute, such as children's daily attendance and purchases of textbooks and other school supplies. While years of schooling (S) and educational inputs (I) can be grouped with child or household variables, Eq. (15.1) separates them from **C** and **H** because they are almost always under parents' control.

Eq. (15.1) shows how each variable affects learning *holding other variables constant*. This qualification is important. Consider an improvement in one school quality variable, call it Q_j, such as a reduction in class size. Eq. (15.1) shows how changing Q_j affects learning *for given values of the other variables*. But changing Q_j (or any school quality variable) could change household behavior, that is change S or one or more I variables. For example, parents may keep children in school longer (increase S) or reduce educational inputs (reduce **I** variables) in response to improved school quality. Thus the "full" impact of changing Q_j on skills (A) is *not* entirely captured by the impact of that variable as depicted in Eq. (15.1).

To obtain the "full" impact of changing school quality, one must know how changes both in the **Q** variables and in other variables affect S and **I** in Eq. (15.1). These relationships can be expressed as:

$$S = f(\mathbf{Q}, \mathbf{C}, \mathbf{H}, \mathbf{P}) \qquad (15.2)$$

$$\mathbf{I} = g(\mathbf{Q}, \mathbf{C}, \mathbf{H}, \mathbf{P}) \qquad (15.3)$$

where **P** denotes the prices relevant for these household decisions, such as tuition, prices of school supplies, and even child wages (the "price" of children's time spent in school).

Inserting (15.2) and (15.3) into (15.1) gives another expression for skills acquired (A):

$$A = h(\mathbf{Q}, \mathbf{C}, \mathbf{H}, \mathbf{P}) \qquad (15.4)$$

which economists call a "reduced form" relationship, the right-hand side of which involves only exogenously determined variables (but not endogenous "choice" variables, S and I). It shows the *full* causal impact of school quality variables (and other variables) on learning. Eq. (15.4) is not a production function because it depends on households' preferences (which guide households' decisions) and because it includes prices, which, in theory, should not have direct impacts on learning. While the production function in (15.1) shows the "direct" impacts of all

variables that influence learning, when analyzing policy impacts one must estimate the "full" impact depicted in (15.4), which includes not only direct impacts captured in (15.1) but also *indirect* impacts that work by changing variables that are under households' control.

Which equation, (15.1) or (15.4), should education policymakers focus on estimating? In fact, estimates of both (15.1) and (15.4) are useful for policymakers. Eq. (15.4) is useful because it shows actual changes in A after the **Q** and **P** variables change, and government policies primarily affect these two sets of variables. Yet the impacts of **Q** on A in Eq. (15.1) are also important because they better capture overall welfare effects. Intuitively, if increases in Q_j induce parents to reduce educational inputs (**I**), household welfare increases because savings from these reduced purchases can be spent on other goods. Eq. (15.4) captures the drop in A from reducing **I**, but not the increased household welfare from purchasing other goods. In contrast, the structural impact measured in (15.1) ignores both effects. Since they have opposing impacts on household welfare, they largely cancel each other out. Thus overall welfare effects are better approximated by changes in A measured in (15.1); see Glewwe, Kremer, Moulin, and Zitzewitz (2004) for details.

Of course, some government policies cannot be described as changes in school quality (**Q**) or schooling prices (**P**). Examples are policies that decentralize decision-making processes or change teachers' contracts. Such policies affect schooling outcomes by changing what happens in classrooms, or changing prices for education goods and services. Glewwe and Kremer (2006) explain that one can depict **Q** and **P** as determined by (functions of) education policies, and perhaps by community characteristics as well. Ultimately, both skills (A) and years of schooling

(S) are determined by child and household characteristics, education policies, and community characteristics. Knowledge of these "ultimate" relationships can directly link education policies to education outcomes S and A.

Estimation of education production functions

While knowledge of skills production functions and other education relationships is crucial for effective education policies, these relationships are very difficult to estimate. This section explains the methods used, potential problems, and possible solutions.

Consider estimating the production function in Eq. (15.1). (These estimation issues also apply to other education relationships, such as the determinants of years of schooling, Eq. (15.2).) This can be estimated using linear regression methods. The linearity assumption is not restrictive if one adds squared and interaction terms to the variables in Eq. (15.1). A simple linear specification of Eq. (15.1) is:

$$A = \beta_0 + \beta_1 S + \beta_{Q1} Q_1 + \beta_{Q2} Q_2 + \ldots + \beta_{C1} C_1$$
$$+ \beta_{C2} C_2 + \ldots (14.1)$$
$$+ \beta_{H1} H_1 + \beta_{H2} H_2 + \ldots + \beta_{I1} I_1 + \beta_{I2} I_2 + \ldots + u_A$$

where each variable in **Q**, **C**, **H** and **I** is shown explicitly. An "error term", u_A, is added, for several reasons. First, data never exist for all variables in **Q**, **C**, **H**, and **I**, so u_A accounts for all variables in Eq. (15.1) that are not in the data. Second, u_A indicates that Eq. (15.1') is only a linear approximation of Eq. (15.1). Third, observed test scores (A) may measure actual skills with error, so u_A includes the difference between the observed A and the "true" A. Finally, the right-hand side variables in Eq. Eq. (15.1') may also contain measurement errors, so differ- ences between their true and measured values are also in u_A.

While u_A may seem unimportant because it is unobserved, the causal impacts of the *observed* variables in Eq. (15.1') on learning, which are the β coefficients, can be consistently estimated by ordinary least squares (OLS) *only if u_A is uncorrelated with ALL the observed "explanatory" variables*. Unfortunately, u_A is very likely to be correlated with those variables. The following paragraphs offer four reasons.

Omitted variable bias. The explanatory variables in Eq. (15.1') could be correlated with u_A because of omitted variables: no dataset contains all the variables in each set of explanatory variables (**Q**, **C**, **H**, and **I**), and many unobserved variables (which end up in u_A) may well be correlated with some observed variables. Difficult to observe variables include: teachers' motivation (a **Q** variable), school principals' management skills (**Q**), children's ability (**C**) and motivation (**C**), and parents' willingness (**H**) and capacity (**H**) to help, and the time they spend helping their children with schoolwork (**I**). OLS estimates of the β's in Eq. (15.1') may be biased because these variables, if unobserved, are probably correlated with some observed variables in Eq. (15.1'). For example, "high quality" schools are usually better in many dimensions, both observed and unobserved. This produces positive correlation between u_A and observed school and teacher quality variables, leading to overestimation of the impacts of those variables. Similarly, parental tastes for children's education are rarely observed and probably positively correlated with parental education, causing overestimation of the latter's impact. Omitted variable bias can also induce underestimation of observed variables' impacts. For example, high school quality may lead parents to reduce time spent helping their children, generating negative correlation between school quality and u_A (assuming some parental efforts are unobserved, which is likely, and thus are in u_A).[3] Omitted variable bias affects the estimated β terms not only for observed variables correlated with u_A but also for those uncorrelated with u_A.

Selection and attrition bias. Sometimes changes in school and teacher characteristics (**Q**) affect which children attend school. Improved school or teacher quality should increase enrollment, but newly enrolled students may differ from "original" students in unobserved ways. New students' parents may care more about education and take (unobserved) actions to help their children beyond enrolling them in better schools. Alternatively, improved schools could attract students who would otherwise drop out (students with lower academic ability or less parental support). The former effect overestimates impacts of school quality variables on learning; the latter leads to underestimation. Bias due to changes in enrollment is called selection bias. A related phenomenon is attrition bias: current students are less likely to drop out if school quality improves. If weaker students would otherwise have left, the β's on many school quality variables would be underestimated (due to their negative correlation with u_A).

Endogenous program placement bias. School quality could also be correlated with u_A if governments improve schools with unobserved education problems (Pitt, Rosenzweig, & Gibbons, 1993). Governments may also raise school quality in areas with good education outcomes, if those areas have political influence (World Bank, 2001). The former causes underestimation of school quality variables' impacts on learning, while the latter causes overestimation.

Measurement error bias. Anyone who has seen household or school survey data collected in developing countries understands that even the best data contain many errors. Data on school characteristics (including tuition fees) may be inaccurate or out of date. Child, household and school input variables are prone to errors. Because measurement error is the difference between the true and observed values of a variable, it causes u_A to be correlated with the observed variable. Random measurement error typically causes underestimation of true impacts, while nonrandom errors could cause underestimation or overestimation.

Whatever the cause, the key point is: anything that induces correlation between u_A and the observed variables in Eq. (15.1') will lead to biased estimates.

The above estimation problems are difficult to solve. When estimating the impacts of policy variables (**P** or **Q**) on learning, all difficulties arise because students facing different policy variables probably differ in unobserved ways. One approach to address omitted variable, measurement error, and endogenous program placement biases is instrumental variables, which uses other variables (that must be uncorrelated with u_A) to predict the variable(s) correlated with u_A. Unfortunately, it is difficult to find plausible instruments. Glewwe and Kremer (2006) provide further discussion. Another approach uses panel data to estimate the impact of changes (over time) in observed variables on changes in test scores; if the unobserved variables correlated with observed variables do not change, they are "differenced out" of the equation (their change over time is zero). But many unobserved variables could change, and such "differencing" may exacerbate measurement error bias.

The ideal solution to these estimation problems is randomized trials: randomly divide the population into two groups, one is "treated" but not the other. Random assignment of policy "treatment" ensures that unobserved characteristics do not

---

[3] When unobserved variables correlated with u_A are endogenous in the sense that households choose them, researchers sometimes call the resulting bias *endogeneity bias*.

differ across groups statistically, so they are uncorrelated with the policy treatment of interest. Comparison of outcomes for these groups provides unbiased estimates of the impact of that policy. Unfortunately, this approach might be costly or infeasible for other reasons (including ethical reasons).[4] Yet many recent studies have used this approach, raising one's confidence in their results. Other methods, especially those exploiting policy experiments (e.g. difference-in-differences) and quasi-experiments (e.g. regression discontinuity design), can also provide credible evidence. To ensure that the evidence we summarize is of high quality, the next section focuses only on studies that adopted randomized trials, difference-in-differences or regression discontinuity methods.

Evidence of policy impacts from developing countries

This section reviews the evidence from developing countries on the impacts of various education policies (both demand-side and supply-side interventions) on school enrollment and learning. For detailed reviews, see Glewwe and Kremer (2006), Glewwe and Miguel (2008), Glewwe et al. (2013), and Glewwe and Muralidharan (2016).

Demand-side interventions

Policies that raise demand for education increase learning mainly by increasing time in school.[5] This can be done by increasing available household income (an **H** variable) and/or reducing education costs (**P** variables). (Raising school quality **Q** can also increase demand, but for convenience we treat school provision as a

supply-side intervention; see the next subsection.) Existing policy options to raise demand for education include unconditional and conditional cash transfers, school fee reductions (including non-merit-based scholarships and vouchers), merit-based scholarships, information-based interventions and other more indirect household-based interventions.

(1) Unconditional cash transfers

Income transfers directly raise parental income (an **H** variable). *Unconditional* cash transfers (UCT) may increase households' education spending (which increases **I**), presumably by relaxing households' budget constraints and the resulting income effect. A number of recent studies, based on pension reforms, found significant (unconditional) income effects on enrollment, but not on learning. Examining Brazil's new pension scheme, Carvalho (2000) found that a benefit increase of R$100 (about half the minimum wage) raised girls' enrollment by 4.5 percentage points, although its impact on boys' enrollment was much smaller. Edmonds (2006) showed that, in South Africa, receiving a generous pension (about 125% of black households' median income) increased enrollment among children living with pensioners. For example, male pension eligibility increased rural boys' school attendance by 18 percentage points. More recently, Baird, McIntosh, and Ozler (2011), evaluating a UCT program in Malawi, found that for girls who were already in school when the program began, the number of terms that they were enrolled over the next two years increased from 4.79 to 5.02 (a statistically significant impact), but they found no significant impact on these girls' test scores. Benhassine, Devoto, Duflo, Dupas, and Pouliquen (2015) examined a program in Morocco that provided monthly

---

[4] Deaton (2010) raises several objections to randomized trials, but does not focus on randomized trials for research on education. See Imbens (2010) for responses to Deaton's arguments.

[5] For a detailed theoretical discussion, see Glewwe and Jacoby (2004).

payments of $8 to $13 to primary school students' parents, with higher amounts for upper grades.[6] They found that the program increased children's enrollment rate by 7.4 percentage points (average over boys and girls), but had no effect on their test scores. Overall, these findings suggest that while higher household income does increase enrollment, it has little effect on learning.

(2) Conditional cash transfers

To ensure that income transfers increase enrollment, one could condition them on education choices, which helps to simultaneously alleviate poor households' resource constraints and provide an incentive to invest in their children's education. *Conditional* cash transfer (CCT) programs provide transfers to households only if their children are enrolled in, and regularly attending, school.[7]

The earliest and best known CCT program is Mexico's PROGRESA (later called *Opportunidades*) program, which was implemented in 1997. PROGRESA provided monthly payments ($7 to $25, depending on child gender and grade) to the mothers of students in grades 3—9 whose daily attendance rate was 85% or higher in the previous month. Exploiting the randomized treatment assignment of PROGRESA, Schultz (2004) estimated that 3 years after the program, years of schooling of rural children aged 6—16 in 1999 increased by 0.66 years. Focusing on a slightly younger cohort (aged 6—14 in 2003) in both urban and rural areas, Behrman, Parker, and Todd (2009) found that 5.5 years after the program, PROGRESA raised grades completed by 0.25 for boys and 0.32 for girls, although its short-run impacts (1.5 years post

implementation) are small and statistically insignificant. A later study (Behrman, Parker, & Todd, 2011) focused on rural children aged 15—21 in 2003, who were old enough to have completed their schooling (thus the impact on grades completed for this cohort is likely the full impact of the program). The authors found that the program raised grades completed by 0.7 grades for younger girls (aged 15—18 in 2003) and by nearly 1 grade for boys of that age; its impacts for older children (aged 19—21 in 2003) were smaller, especially for girls, likely because they had fewer years of program exposure.

Brazil's *Bolsa Familia* program (originally called *Bolsa Escola*), is likely the largest CCT program in the world. Conditional on an 85% attendance rate, poor parents of children aged 6—15 received about $8 per month per child for up to three children. Since the program was not implemented as a randomized trial, its impacts have been evaluated using other methods. Using a difference-in-differences approach, de Janvry, Finan, and Sadoulet (2012) found that the program reduced children's dropout rate by 9.6 percentage points. Glewwe and Kassouf (2012), also using a difference-in-differences strategy, found that the program increased enrollment by about 3 percentage points and reduced the dropout rate by 3 percentage points.[8]

Colombia also has a national CCT program, *Familias en Acción*, which provided monthly cash grants to parents of primary ($7 per month) and secondary ($14 per month) school students, conditional on a monthly attendance rate of 80%. Similar to Brazil's *Bolsa Familia*, this program was not implemented as a randomized trial; thus

---

[6] The payments were "labeled" as assistance for education costs, but there was no formal requirement for children's enrollment or regular school attendance for their parents to receive the payments (thus this is a UCT program).

[7] For a detailed description and comprehensive assessment of CCT programs, see Fiszbein et al. (2009).

[8] The likely cause of the difference in these two studies' estimated reductions in the dropout rates is that de Janvry et al. examined only four states in the poor Northeast region of Brazil, while Glewwe and Kassouf used nationwide data; the impact of the program is likely to be larger among less wealthy populations.

evaluations of its impacts have used other methods. Using a difference-in-differences method, Attanasio et al. (2010) found small but statistically significant increases in enrollment for children aged 8–13 (1.4 and 2.8 percentage points, respectively, for urban and rural children), as well as larger, statistically significant impacts for children aged 14–17 (4.7 and 6.6 percentage points for urban and rural children, respectively). Using matching and regression discontinuity methods, Baez and Camacho (2011) found that the program increased the probability of completing secondary school by 4–8 percentage points. The program's impact on math test scores was statistically insignificant; somewhat surprisingly, its impact on Spanish scores was negative (−0.5 standard deviations, SDs) and marginally significant, which may be due to the fact that weaker students whose parents did not receive cash transfers had dropped out and were not tested.

The impacts of another CCT program in Colombia, studied by Barrera-Osorio, Bertrand, Linden, and Perez-Calle (2011), are also informative. The program was implemented as a randomized trial with three different versions. The first was a standard CCT program providing $15 per month to students' families conditional on a daily attendance rate of 80% or higher in the previous month; the other two versions both included a "forced savings" component, depositing part of the payments into a bank account that was made available on a future date, when the decision on enrollment in the next school year (the second version) or in tertiary

education (the third version) needed to be made.[9] While all three versions led to statistically significant increases in the daily attendance rate (by 3–5.6 percentage points) among secondary school students, their impacts on enrollment differed. The first version, with no "forced savings", had no significant effect on enrollment; in contrast, the other two versions both increased the enrollment rate significantly by about 4 percentage points. These findings suggest that CCT programs can be made more effective by changing their design, for example, by providing "commitment devices" that can lead to greater educational investments, especially for households that have difficulties committing to long-term investments in education.

Many other developing countries have also implemented CCT programs. Most of these were implemented as randomized trials, which greatly facilitates evaluation of their impacts on schooling outcomes. Most of these programs were found to be effective at increasing both enrollment and learning. Implemented as a randomized trial in the early 2000s, Honduras' CCT program targeted children aged 6–12 in grades 1–4, whose mothers received monthly payments of about $6, conditional on daily attendance of 85% or higher. This program increased these children's enrollment by 8.3 percentage points (Galiani & McEwan, 2013). Nicaragua's CCT program also targeted children in grades 1–4, providing annual payments (on average $302 per year) to their households. Gitter and Barham's (2008) experimental evaluation found

---

[9] More specifically, the second version imposed the same conditionality as the first but reduced the payments to $10 per month and put $5 per month into a bank account that was made available around the time when students were about to enroll in the next year of schooling. To provide an incentive to enroll in tertiary education, the third version provided payments of $10 per month for regular attendance but put $5 per month into a fund that was made available six years later, at the time of graduation from secondary school, conditional on the student's enrolling in tertiary education. If the student did not enroll in tertiary education he or she had to wait another year to receive the money.

that before the control group was allowed to participate in 2003, the program increased the current enrollment of children aged 7–13 by 16.6 percentage points. Examining this program's longer-run effect on boys,[10] Barham, Macours, and Maluccio (2013) found that the program increased the number of grades attained by 0.50. Moreover, 10 years post implementation, test scores were significantly higher (by 0.20 SDs for home language and 0.12 SDs for math)[11] for boys with longer program exposure (5 years instead of 2 years). Malawi's CCT program provided monthly transfers of $4 to $10 to parents of girls aged 13–22. Baird et al. (2011) found that for girls who were already enrolled in school when the program started, this program raised the number of terms enrolled over the next 2 years by 0.54 and the daily attendance rate over the 2 years by 8.0 percentage points. Two years of program exposure also raised their English and math test scores, both by 0.12 SDs. Further focusing on girls who were not in school when the program began, many of whom returned to school due to the program, Baird, Chirwa, de Hoop, and Ozler (2016a) found a much larger impact on terms enrolled over the 2-year period, an increase of 2.35. The 2-year program exposure also increased these girls' English and math scores by, respectively, 0.13 SDs and 0.16 SDs.

Relatively few studies have been conducted to rigorously evaluate CCT programs in Asian countries. The existing few studies have found significant impacts of CCT programs on enrollment, but not on test scores. Mo et al. (2013) examined a randomized trial in rural China, which offered about $70 to grade 7 students' households conditional on an attendance rate of 80% or higher over one semester. This program

reduced these students' dropout rate by 8%, but had a small and statistically insignificant impact on their test scores. Chaudhury and Parajuli (2010) evaluated a CCT program in Pakistan that targeted girls in grades 6–8; these girls' families received about $3 per month conditional on a monthly attendance rate of 80% or higher. Estimates based on difference-in-differences and regression-discontinuity methods indicated that this program increased girls' enrollment by 8.7%. Finally, Barrera-Osorio and Filmer (2016) implemented a randomized trial in Cambodia, which had two versions. The first provided a "poverty scholarship" of $10 to poor households, twice per year, conditional on enrollment and maintaining passing grades. The second was a merit-based scholarship targeting students in grades 4–6 conditional on their performance in grade 3; it provided $10, also twice per year, to scholarship recipients who stayed enrolled, attended regularly, and maintained passing grades, up to the end of grade 6. Both versions significantly raised enrollment and attendance – the probability of reaching grade 6 increased by 19 and 14 percentage points, respectively, for the poverty and merit scholarship recipients. However, only the latter had a positive impact on test scores, raising recipients' math test scores by 0.17 SDs and memory test scores by 0.15 SDs.

(3) Merit-based scholarships

Another kind of conditionality provides cash payments based on students' academic performance, usually in the form of *merit-based scholarships*. As demonstrated by the Barrera-Osorio and Filmer study discussed above, conditioning on student performance may be more effective than conditioning on enrollment and attendance, presumably because the former links incentive

---

[10] Girls were not included in the study since their enrollment rates at ages 9–12 were quite high. Note also that this study had no pure control group; instead one set of randomly selected communities had the program for 5 years (2000–05) while the other set had the program for only 2 years (2003–05).

[11] SD refers to the standard deviation of the overall distribution of test scores.

more tightly to students' learning. Recent studies suggest that merit-based scholarships can be quite effective at increasing both enrollment and learning, although different incentive designs may yield different outcomes.

Kremer, Miguel, and Thornton (2009) experimentally evaluated a scholarship program in rural Kenya that targeted grade 6 girls; those girls who scored in the top 15% on end-of-year exams would be given, for each of the next 2 years (grades 7 and 8), a scholarship of $6.40 to cover school fees. Their parents would also be given a payment of $12.80. The program significantly increased these girls' daily attendance by 3.2 percentage points and their scores on a grade 6 year-end exam by 0.27 SDs. A follow-up study, conducted by Friedman, Kremer, Miguel, and Thornton (2016), examined the educational outcomes of the same girls 4–5 years after the program started (about 2 years after the program had ended). Significant positive impacts were found on enrollment in secondary school (8.6 perentage points higher) and enrollment in any school (7.9 percentage points higher); test scores were also significantly higher (by 0.20 SDs).

A number of scholarship programs have tried different incentive schemes, creating opportunities for understanding how incentives should be provided. A program in Benin, studied by Blimpo (2014), randomly assigned 100 secondary schools to a control group or to one of three types of scholarships with different incentives: an individual-incentive design, a group-incentive design and a tournament.[12] All three types of incentives had statistically significant (and similar)

impacts, increasing grade 10 test scores by 0.24–0.28 SDs. A scholarship program in China, evaluated by Li, Han, Zhang, and Rozelle (2014), was based on a tournament with two different versions, which yielded quite different results. In the first version (individual incentive), groups of 10 low-performing students would compete for prizes with each other in terms of improvement in test scores over time. In the second version (peer incentive), each of the 10 low-performing students, while competing with each other for prizes identical to those in the first version, was paired with a high-performing student; the latter received a reward as an encouragement to assist the low-performing student paired up with him or her. While the individual-incentive intervention had no statistically significant impact, the peer-incentive intervention increased weaker students' test scores by 0.27 SDs, suggesting that in some cases student incentives on their own may be ineffective unless accompanied by pedagogical support.

(4) School fee reductions

While CCT programs appear to increase demand by raising incomes (an **H** variable), they also reduce the price of education (**P**). Indeed, the price becomes negative because parents are paid for enrolling their children. Policies that directly reduce education prices have similar effects. Several African countries, including Ethiopia, Ghana, Kenya, Malawi, Mozambique, Tanzania and Uganda, have abolished school fees (School Fees Abolition Initiative, 2006). Indeed, in the past two to three decades many

---

[12] More specifically, these three schemes were: scholarships based on individual-level performance with respect to a set goal, with no limit on the number of scholarships offered; scholarships based on average performance for (randomly assigned) teams of four students, again with respect to a set goal with no limit on the number of scholarships; and a "tournament" in which 84 teams of four students each (randomly assigned) from 28 schools competed for a large prize that was given only to the three top performing teams. For the first two types, the payments were $10 per person ($40 for a team of four) for a relatively low level of performance, and $40 per person ($160 for a team of four) for a high level of performance. For the third type, the prizes were much larger, at $640 for each of the top three teams.

developing countries, especially in Sub-Saharan African, have eliminated primary school fees.

School fees elimination and non-merit-based scholarships. A number of recent studies have examined the impact of school fee reductions in developing countries, but their findings are mixed. Borkum (2012), using a regression-discontinuity approach, examined the impact of school fees elimination in South African primary and secondary schools that served poor populations. Unlike the above-mentioned results for CCT programs, little effect of school fees elimination was found on enrollment at either the primary or the secondary level. Using a randomized trial, Yi et al. (2014), evaluated a non-merit-based scholarship program that promised to pay for upper secondary school for poor students in grades 7 and 9 in two Chinese provinces (Shaanxi and Hebei), conditional on admission to upper secondary school. For ninth graders, the intervention increased the continuation rate into upper secondary school by 7.9 percentage points, but had no statistically significant impact for seventh graders. Using a regression-discontinuity method, Filmer and Schady (2014) estimated impacts of a Cambodian program that provided scholarships to low-income students in grades 7–9 who were deemed at risk of dropping out, conditional on their staying in school and not repeating a grade. They found that five years after the scholarships were offered, the average number of grades completed increased by 0.6, but the impact on test scores was small and statistically insignificant.

Vouchers. Several countries have implemented *vouchers*, which provide poor households funds to enroll their children in private schools. Again,

existing findings are mixed. Angrist, Bettinger, Bloom, King, and Kremer (2002) evaluated Colombia's *Programa de Ampliacíon de Cobertura de la Educacíon Secundaria* (PACES), which awarded vouchers to over 125,000 poor urban students from 1992 to 1997. In most communities, demand for vouchers exceeded supply, so eligibility was determined by lottery. Exploiting this "natural experiment", Angrist et al. found that three years after receiving the voucher, voucher winners scored higher on math and reading tests (by 0.16 SDs), completed more years of education, and had lower rates of grade repetition. A follow-up study, Angrist, Bettinger, and Kremer (2006), found that seven years after receiving the voucher, voucher winners had significantly higher high-school graduation rates (5.6 percentage points) and scored 0.2 SDs higher on college entrance exams.[13]

In contrast, two studies in Chile found insignificant effects of using vouchers to attend private schools on learning. Using a difference-in-differences approach, Lara, Mizala, and Repetto (2011) found a very small impact (0.02 SDs) of being awarded vouchers on the test scores of grade 10 students, all of whom were in public primary schools but some used vouchers to move into private secondary schools. Also using a difference-in-differences approach, Hsieh and Urquiola (2006) examined the impact of using vouchers to enroll in a private school on the test scores of fourth and eighth graders. No statistically significant effects were found on these students' math and language (Spanish) test scores.

More recently, Muralidharan and Sundararaman (2015) experimentally evaluated the impact

---

[13] While both studies suggest that the PACES voucher program was highly effective, the estimated effect may not include only the differential "productivity" of private schools because the PACES program allowed vouchers to be topped up by parents (to attend a better school than they could have afforded without a voucher), and required students to maintain minimum academic standards to continue receiving the voucher. Thus while the results point to the effectiveness of the PACES program, the estimates reflect a combination of private school productivity, additional education spending, and student incentives.

of a school-choice voucher program in the Indian state of Andhra Pradesh. They found no difference between the test scores of lottery winners and losers on the two main subjects of native language and math at the end of year 2 and year 4 of the program. But they found positive effects of winning the voucher on other tests after four years of the program: English (0.12 SDs), science and social studies (0.08 SDs), and language (Hindi) (0.55 SDs).

Matching funds for educational opportunities. There are other ways to reduce the direct costs of attending schools. A program in El Salvador matched remittances sent by Salvadoran migrants in the United States to students of their choosing if those remittances are committed to educational purposes. Using a randomized trial, Ambler, Aycinena, and Yang (2015) found that when the match amount is three times the amount of remittance, the program significantly increased enrollment in a private school (by 10.9 percentage points). However, the overall increase in enrollment of 3.1 percentage points was statistically insignificant.

In-kind transfers. Finally, in-kind transfers, such as providing uniforms, which also reduces the direct costs of attending school, may also increase enrollment. Existing findings are mixed, however. Based on a randomized trial in Kenya, Kremer, Moulin, and Namunyu (2003) estimated that free uniforms increased pupils' participation by 15 percentage points. In contrast, Hidalgo, Onofa, Oosterbeek, and Ponce (2013), evaluating a randomized trial that provided free school uniforms to poor primary school students in urban Ecuador, found a surprising 2 percentage point reduction in daily attendance. Unfortunately, their data do not allow them to determine why providing uniforms had this unexpected effect.

(5) Information-based interventions

Motivated by the finding that poor children in developing countries often assume low rates of return to schooling, several recent interventions have provided information to students and their parents about the benefits of education and how to take advantage of educational opportunities. Existing findings are inconclusive. Jensen (2010) implemented a randomized trial that provided information on returns to schooling to poor grade 8 boys in the Dominican Republic. He found that boys who received the information were 4.1% more likely to be in school one year after receiving the information, and, four years after the intervention had completed, on average, 0.2 more years of schooling. In contrast, for a similar but more intensive intervention in China, Loyalka et al. (2013) found little effect of providing information. The intervention, also implemented as a randomized trial, provided a 45-mininute information session on earnings associated with different levels of schooling to grade 7 students in poor rural areas of Hebei and Shaanxi provinces. No significant effects on the dropout rate or test scores were found. Another information-based intervention examined by the same authors provided four 45-min career counseling sessions to students. Again, this program had no statistically significant impact on students' test scores and, somewhat surprisingly, had a significantly negative impact on time in school.[14] Wang et al. (2014) evaluated another information-based program in China, a randomized school counseling intervention targeting seventh and eighth graders who were preparing to take upper secondary school entrance exams, with a goal to reduce their anxiety. This program reduced the dropout rate by

---

[14] The authors speculate that this may reflect that students learned that upper secondary and postsecondary entrance requirements were more difficult than they previously thought.

about 2% in the first half of the school year, but had no effect at the end of the school year.

(6) Other household-based interventions

Several other types of interventions have been implemented to directly affect households (rather than in schools) to improve schooling outcomes, often by raising households' demand for schooling indirectly. One such intervention provided information to mothers on how to develop their child's learning. Banerji, Berry, and Shotland (2013) evaluated the impacts of such an intervention, a mother literacy intervention, and the combination of both interventions, in India. Neither of the interventions, nor their combination, had an impact on children's enrollment or daily attendance. Yet they did improve learning. The lessons on child learning induced a small but statistically significant increase (0.04 SDs) in the test scores (average over literacy and mathematics) of children in grades 1–4; a somewhat higher impact (0.06 SDs) on test scores was found for children of women who took both classes. Using a difference-in-differences approach, Handa (2002) examined the impact of an adult literacy program in Mozambique on children's enrollment rate, but found no significant effect.

Another type of household-based intervention provides female sanitary products to school-age girls, since the unavailability of such products is often claimed to inhibit female school participation after puberty. Oster and Thornton (2011) experimentally evaluated the impact of such an intervention in Nepal, but found no effect of the intervention on girls' daily attendance.[15] A more successful intervention was implemented in India, which offered families funds to purchase bicycles for their (secondary school age) daughters to ride to school. Using a difference-in-differences strategy, Muralidharan and Prakash (2017) found

that this program increased secondary school enrollment by 5.2 percentage points. For girls who lived more than three kilometers from the nearest secondary school, the impact was about 9 percentage points. These are very large impacts given that the initial enrollment rate for these girls was only 17.2%.

In summary, recent evidence from many countries indicates that higher household incomes and especially lower schooling costs greatly increase school enrollment, but this does not necessarily improve children's learning outcomes. Incentives, especially those tied directly to students' learning outcomes are generally effective at improving both enrollment and learning outcomes. The results for information-based and other types of household-based interventions remain mixed.

Supply-side policies

Many education policies operate not through increasing education demand but instead by improving the supply. Most supply-side policies take one of following forms: 1) increasing the *quantity* of schooling services offered, which involves building more schools and/or raising the capacity of existing schools; 2) raising the *quality* of schooling services, which involves providing more learning materials, providing technology-enhanced learning and "teaching at the right level", etc.; 3) providing other inputs such as nutrition and medical services that may enhance students' learning.

(1) Interventions that raise the quantity of school services

School construction. The most "obvious" supply-side policy that increases the quantity of school services is *building new schools* to reduce households' distance to the nearest

---

[15] This may reflect that only 1% of girls stated that the lack of sanitary products was a binding constraint to school participation.

school, as long distance to school discourages enrollment (Filmer, 2004). Some regard distance as particularly harmful to girls' schooling (Bommier & Lambert, 2000; Foster & Rosenzweig, 2004). Recent research suggests that building more schools significantly raises both the enrollment rate and students' test scores. Using a difference-in-differences method to examine a large school construction program in Indonesia in the 1970s, Duflo (2001) found that an additional school built per 1000 school-age children increased years of education by 0.19 years. Handa (2002), also using a difference-in-differences method, found that the construction of new primary schools in Mozambique increased children's probability of enrollment by 0.3 percentage points for each new school built within an "administrative post" area.[16] Alderman, Kim, and Orazem (2003) experimentally evaluated an intervention in Pakistan, which provided funding to construct new (or support existing) private primary schools for girls. They found that the program increased the enrollment rate by 25 and 15 percentage points, respectively, for girls in urban and rural areas. More recently, Burde and Linden (2013), examining a randomized trial in Afghanistan, found that the opening of primary schools in rural villages that previously had no schools increased enrollment rates of primary-school-age girls and boys by, respectively, 51.5 and 34.6 percentage points; it also raised girls' and boys' test scores by, respectively, 0.66 and 0.41 SDs. Finally, Kazianga, Levy, Linden, and Sloan (2013) evaluated the impact of providing "girl-friendly" schools – schools with amenities particularly attractive to girls, such as sources of clean water and separate latrines for boys and girls – in rural Burkina Faso. They found that opening these schools increased the enrollment rate of all children by 18.5 percentage points; it also increased test scores by 0.41 SDs for children in villages that previously had no primary schools.

Longer school days. The second most obvious policy to increase the quantity of school services is to increase the time that children spend in school. There are only two studies of this policy, one in Chile (Bellei, 2009) and another in Ethiopia (Orkin, 2013), both of which were based on difference-in-differences estimation. Both support the common-sense notion that longer school days increase student learning.

Hiring more teachers. Another "quantity" policy is hiring more teachers to increase existing schools' capacity. Existing evidence suggests that smaller classes lead to improved learning in general. Exploiting a policy in Bolivia that schools with pupil-teacher ratios above 30 can apply to the authorities for another teacher, Urquiola (2006) found that schools that obtained another teacher have significantly higher language test scores (but not math scores). Adopting a similar approach, Urquiola and Verhoogen (2009) found that, in Chilean private schools, increased class size significantly reduced both math and language test scores for children in grades K-8.[17] More recently, Duflo, Dupas, and Kremer (2015) examined an intervention in Kenya that randomly assigned some schools an extra contract teacher, and then randomly divided students within these schools into classes taught by the current, civil-service teacher and those taught by the newly-assigned contract teacher. By comparing the classes taught by the current civil-service teacher to those taught by same type of teacher in the control schools, which had much higher pupil-teacher ratios, the authors found that the reduction in class size (due to the newly-assigned contract teacher) increased test scores (by 0.09 SDs), but the increases were not statistically significant.

[16] Administrative post areas are relatively large areas with on average about 20 primary schools.

[17] About half of students in Chile are enrolled in private schools.

Increasing teacher attendance. Raising teachers' attendance, which is low in many developing countries, may be another way to increase the "quantity" of school services. Duflo, Hanna, and Ryan (2012) experimentally evaluated an intervention in informal schools in India that paid teachers salaries as a function of the number of days of teacher attendance, using cameras with time-date stamps to record their attendance. This program reduced teacher absence by half (from 42% to 21%) and significantly increased student test scores (by 0.17 SDs). In contrast, another randomized intervention in India, evaluated by Muralidharan and Sundararaman (2010), provided only low-stakes (no consequences) monitoring and feedback; it had no impact on either teacher attendance or test scores. These results suggest that while "low-stakes" monitoring may not be very effective at reducing teacher absence, providing teachers with "high-stakes" incentives to reduce absence can be effective.

(2) Interventions that raise the quality of education services

Provision of material inputs. One way to improve education *quality* is to provide additional material inputs to students, yet available findings have been mixed. Two randomized trials in Kenya, one providing textbooks (Glewwe, Kremer, & Moulin, 2009) and another supplying flipcharts (Glewwe et al. 2004), were found to be ineffective at improving learning: neither textbooks nor flipcharts raised students' test scores, except that textbooks raised learning among the best students.[18] Another randomized trial, conducted by Borkum, He, and Linden (2012), provided school libraries (both in-school libraries and traveling libraries) to primary schools in India. No effect of either library was

found on students' daily attendance (which was quite high, around 90%). Nor did they increase learning – "in school" libraries had no effect, and traveling libraries had an unexpected negative effect, on students' language scores. In contrast, two interventions examined by Tan, Lane, and Lassibille (1999), which provided "multilevel learning materials" to primary school students in the Philippines, were found to be effective. The first intervention provided only these materials; the second combined them with "parent-teacher partnerships". The "materials only" intervention significantly reduced the probability of dropping out, and significantly raised scores on two of three tests (Filipino, math and English); the "materials + parent-teacher partnerships" intervention had no significant impact on dropping out but significantly increased scores on all three tests.

The Tan et al. study shows that, when combined with other interventions, provision of additional educational materials may be more effective at enhancing learning. Chin (2005) used a difference-in-difference approach to evaluate a program in India that provided both additional educational materials and extra teachers to very small primary schools. This program significantly raised students' primary school completion rates (by 1–2 percentage points), although one cannot determine how much of this effect is due to the extra teachers and how much is due to the additional educational materials. Abeberese, Kumler, and Linden (2014) experimentally evaluated the impacts of a reading program in the Philippines that provided age-appropriate reading materials to students and trained teachers to incorporate reading into their teaching. After only four months, the reading scores of program school students were 0.13 SDs higher, although this

---

[18] Another study that examined the impact of textbooks, the Sabarwal, Evans, and Marshak (2014) study of Sierra Leone, found no impact. But this resulted from the fact that few of the textbooks reached the students due to school administrators' misunderstanding of the policy.

impact declined over time; no effect was found on math scores.

Technology-enhanced instruction. Another way to improve education quality is to combine instruction with modern information technology. The most common examples of this are computer-assisted learning (CAL) programs. There is only one study of the impact of technology-enhanced instruction on students' time in school, that of Cristia, Czerwonko, and Garofalo (2014) in Peru. It found no significant effect of the program on either repetition or dropout rates. In contrast, there is much more evidence on the impact of technology-enhanced instruction on student learning, yet existing findings yield widely varying magnitudes of impact, ranging from positive impacts to no impact or even negative impacts. These differences in estimated impacts underscore the importance of context, and perhaps more importantly the importance of program design in creating effective technology-aided instruction interventions.

Studies that found significant positive impacts of CAL include one conducted in India (Banerjee, Cole, Duflo, & Linden, 2007) and four in China (Lai et al. 2013, 2015; Mo et al. 2015; Yang et al. 2013). The program in India provided 2 h per week of computer-based math instruction. It had a very large positive effect (0.48 SDs) on students' math scores at the end of year 2 of the program, although the gains were not long-lasting. Lai et al. (2015) evaluated a CAL program in schools for migrant children in Beijing, China, which provided two 40-min sessions of remedial math instruction per week to grade 3 students; after one year their math test scores were 0.14 SDs higher than those of children in the control group. Lai et al. (2013) examined a similar program in China's remote Qinghai province, which focused on improving Chinese language skills; significant increases in

both Chinese (0.20 SDs) and math (0.22 SDs) scores were found after one year. Yang et al. (2013) studied a CAL program in three Chinese provinces and found modest (0.12 SDs) but significantly positive effects on test scores. Finally, Mo et al. (2015) examined a CAL program that provided remedial math instruction to boarding school students in rural areas of Shaanxi province; they found that it significantly increased math scores for both third graders (0.25 SDs) and fifth graders (0.26 SDs).

Three studies found no impact or even negative impacts. Barrera-Osorio and Linden (2009) studied a school-level program that provided computers and teacher training to randomly selected schools in Colombia; they found no impact of the program on Spanish or math test scores.[19] Beuermann, Cristia, Cruz-Aguayo, Cueto, and Malamud (2015) used a large-scale randomized trial to evaluate the *One Laptop per Child* program in Peru. They found that while the program increased the ratio of computers to students from 0.12 to 1.18 in treatment schools, there was no impact on either school enrollment or (math and language) test scores. Finally, Malamud and Pop-Eleches (2011) used a regression-discontinuity method to estimate the impact of providing vouchers for purchasing computers to the families of middle-school students in Romania. They found that students who received the voucher had significantly lower grade-point average; a possible explanation is that these students spent more time playing computer games and less time reading or doing homework.

Teacher incentives. Teachers' effort is a key determinant of education quality, so a natural policy option is to provide teachers incentives to exert more effort. A common policy is to link teachers compensation to their students' performance. The evidence thus far suggests that

---

[19] The authors argue that the lack of impact resulted from poor implementation, with teachers failing to incorporate the new technology effectively in their teaching.

teacher incentives are often quite effective. Muralidharan and Sundararaman (2011) present experimental evidence on impacts of a program in Andhra Pradesh (India) that provided bonus payments (the mean bonus was 3% of annual pay) to teachers based on the average improvement of their students' scores on independently administered tests. After two years, students in incentive schools outperformed those in control schools by 0.27 and 0.17 SDs in math and language tests, respectively. Students in incentive schools also performed better on subjects that had no incentives, suggesting positive spillovers from improved performance on math and language onto untested subjects (science and social studies). Muralidharan (2012) presents evidence from a long-term follow up in the same setting that extended teacher performance pay by five years to a subset of the original schools. He found that students who completed all five years in primary school under one of the two incentive schemes – an individual-teacher incentive and a group-teacher incentive – performed significantly better than those in control schools, by 0.54 SDs and 0.35 SDs, respectively, on math and language tests.[20] Glewwe, Ilias, et al. (2010) and Glewwe, Lambert, et al. (2010) evaluated a randomized trial in Kenya that provided school-level group incentives using prizes for high-achieving schools. Based on a tournament design, the prizes were awarded to the best schools (those with the highest average student test scores) and the most-improved schools (those with the highest average improvements). The program increased teachers' test preparation efforts but not in activities that would increase long-term learning (such as reduced teacher absence). Students in treatment schools performed better on high-stakes tests but not on

low-stakes tests; and these gains dissipated after the program ended. Finally, Contreras and Rau (2012) used a difference-in-difference procedure to evaluate Chile's National System of School Performance Assessment program, which provided teachers bonus payments based on students' test scores and was gradually rolled out to all public schools. This program led to a large (0.29 SDs) significant increase in students' math scores.

Contract teachers. A different way to motivate teachers to exert effort is to make employment contracts subject to periodic renewal, and not renew contracts for underperforming teachers. In recent years many developing countries have started to employ new teachers (who are often not professionally trained) on short-term renewable contracts in response to challenges such as a lack of qualified teachers for rapidly expanding school systems, the high cost of teachers, and the reluctance of qualified teachers to serve in rural areas where the education system is expanding the most. The growing use of "contract teachers" in public schools is a major change in the provision of primary education in developing countries since the 1990s. Contract teachers comprise a third of public-school teachers across twelve countries in Africa (Bourdon, Frölich, & Michaelowa, 2010). Their share among public-school teachers in India grew from 6% in 2003 to 30% in 2010 (Muralidharan, Das, Holla, & Mohpal, 2017). However, the use of contract teachers is contentious. Proponents consider them to be an efficient way to expand education access to millions of first-generation learners, and argue that contract teachers face strong incentives relative to tenured civil-service teachers, to exert effort. Opponents worry that using underqualified and untrained teachers may not

---

[20] The original program featured two different (randomized) bonus payment interventions: the first based bonuses on the average performance of groups of teachers, while the second based bonuses on each teacher's individual performance. While both sets of incentive schools experienced significantly positive impacts, students in individual-incentive schools scored higher than those in group-incentive schools.

improve learning outcomes, and that using contract teachers reduces the prestige of the teaching profession, and reduces the motivation of other teachers (Kumar, Priyam, & Saxena, 2005).

While studies on the impact of contract teachers are sparse, available evidence suggests that their use raises students' test scores. The Kenyan program examined by Duflo et al. (2015), discussed above, provided a randomly selected set of schools with an extra contract teacher; students within these schools were then randomly assigned to the contract teacher and to the current civil-service teacher. As mentioned above, simply reducing class sizes had a positive by statistically insignificant impact on test scores. But students in reduced-size classes taught by a contract teacher scored significantly higher (0.29 SDs, averaged across subjects) than those in control schools. Also, holding class size constant, students taught by contract teachers significantly outscored those taught by civil-service teachers even though contract teachers had much lower salaries. Muralidharan and Sundararaman (2013) evaluated a program that provided an extra contract teacher to randomly chosen government-run rural primary schools in Indian (Andhra Pradesh). After two years, students in schools with an extra contract teacher performed significantly better than those in comparison schools, by 0.16 SDs and 0.15 SDs in math and language tests, respectively. Contract teachers were also significantly less likely to be absent from school than civil-service teachers (16% vs. 27%). These findings suggest that contract teachers are at least as effective at improving student learning as civil-service teachers.

Remedial education. Given the large variation in children's initial preparation upon school entry, and differential progress in school, another way to improve learning outcomes is to teach children "at the right level", especially for those who have fallen behind. Available evidence from India suggests that remedial education can greatly improve learning. Banerjee et al. (2007) evaluated a randomized trial implemented in two Indian

cities that targeted grade 3—4 students in public schools who had not achieved basic reading and arithmetic competencies. These children were removed from their regular classrooms for 2 h per day to receive remedial instruction that was tailored to their current learning level, delivered by an informal, locally hired teacher. Although this program had no statistically significant impact on daily attendance, it significantly increased learning – students' test scores (average of math and English) increased by 0.14 SDs after one year of the program and by 0.28 SDs after two years. Banerjee, Banerji, Duflo, Gelnnerster, and Khemani (2010) examined several other interventions designed to improve community participation in education in India. Of all the interventions examined, only remedial instruction was effective at increasing learning. That instruction was delivered by youth volunteers hired from the village, who received one week of training and then conducted after-school reading camps for 2—3 months. While only 13.2% of students actually attended the camps, the increases in learning were substantial – among children who could read nothing at the baseline, exposure to the program increased the fraction of those able to read letters by 7.9 percentage points. Subsequently, Lakshminarayana et al. (2013) examined a program that recruited community volunteers to provide remedial education to rural children in India. Remedial instruction, tailored to students' needs and learning levels, was provided for 2 h per day in their school after normal school hours. The program's impact was quite large: two years after the program, students' test scores in program villages were 0.74 SDs higher than those in the comparison group. Finally, Banerjee et al. (2016) evaluated different methods of implementing remedial instruction in public schools on a large scale. Their findings support the hypothesis that "teaching children at the right level" can significantly increase learning. In particular, implementing this approach in dedicated learning camps held outside of normal school hours, using learning-appropriate remedial materials, was effective at raising test scores. However, programs that attempted to incorporate this pedagogy into the regular school day had no impact. This suggests that while the remedial pedagogy can be successful, it was difficult to get teachers to implement it during normal school hours, and that successfully scaling up remedial pedagogy within an existing school system can be challenging because teachers tend to focus on completing the syllabus prescribed in standard textbooks.

(3) Other complementary inputs

Given the extensive evidence that well-nourished children have better educational outcomes in developing countries (Glewwe & Miguel, 2008), interventions that improve children's nutrition and health should improve their schooling outcomes.

School meals. The most common nutrition intervention is the provision of school meals. Existing evidence suggests that school meals usually do not increase students' time in school, but they do increase learning, at least in some cases. Among five studies conducted in five different countries, namely, Argentina (Adrogue & Orlicki, 2013), Burkina Faso (Kazianga, de Walque, & Alderman, 2012), Chile (McEwan, 2013), the Philippines (Tan et al., 1999), and Uganda (Alderman, Gilligan, & Lehrer, 2012), only the one in Burkina Faso found a significantly positive impact of school feeding on enrollment of children aged 6—15 (Kazianga et al. 2012); take-home rations provided by the same program also had a significant and positive impact (4.8 percentage points) on enrollment. Only the Ugandan study by Alderman et al. (2012) measured the impact of school meals on daily attendance, yet it found no statistically significant effect. In contrast, these studies generally found that school meal programs increased student learning. More specifically, in Argentina, Adrogue and Orlicki

(2013) found a large impact (0.17 SDs) of school feeding on third graders' language test scores, although its impact on math scores is small and statistically insignificant. The study by Kazianga et al. (2012) in Burkina Faso found that the school meal program increased math scores by 0.10 SDs; take-home rations provided by this program had a similar impact (0.08 SDs). In the Philippines, Tan et al. (1999) found significantly positive impacts of school feeding on first graders' math (0.25 SDs) and Filipino (0.16 SDs) test scores.

Medical services. A natural extension of providing food to improve students' educational outcomes is the provision of basic medical services. Four such interventions have been rigorously evaluated: deworming medicine, iron supplementation tablets, health insurance, and eyeglasses.

Many school-age children in developing countries have various types of worm infections (e.g. roundworm, hookworm, whipworm, and schistosomiasis), which can lead to anemia and other problems that may reduce children's attentiveness in school. Miguel and Kremer (2004) conducted a randomized trial in rural Kenya that provided deworming medicine to primary school students. This intervention reduced students' absence rate by 7—8 percentage points, but had no impact on test scores. A follow-up study (Baird, Hicks, Kremer, & Miguel, 2016b) found that 10 years after the program, women who were eligible for the program as school girls were 25% more likely to have attended secondary school, and men who were eligible were more likely to have completed primary school. In another follow-up study, Ozier (2014) estimated this program's spillover effects onto younger siblings of the treated children, who were less than a year old when the program started. He found that, 10 years after the program, these children's test score gains were quite large, equivalent to 0.5—0.8 years of schooling.

Evidence of other types of medical services interventions comes from China. Chen and Jin (2012), using a difference-in-differences estimation procedure (combined with propensity score matching), examined impacts of a health insurance program in China, but found no impact on enrollment of children aged 6–16. Two experimental studies in China, Luo et al. (2012) and Sylvia et al. (2013), provide evidence that the provision of iron supplements improved student learning, at least under some circumstances. Lastly, Glewwe, Park, and Zhao (2016) examined a randomized intervention in rural areas of China's Gansu province, which provided eyeglasses to nearsighted students in grades 3–5. They found that the intervention significantly increased test scores (average across Chinese, math and science) by at least 0.16 SDs for targeted students.

Finally, other supply-side interventions have attempted to increase student enrollment and learning, such as school-based management (e.g. decentralizing more management authority to schools and local communities) and large-scale provision of resources (e.g. provision of entire packages of school inputs or of large amounts of money for schools to buy educational inputs). However, for such interventions it remains unclear which specific inputs, policies, or activities are the ones that increase enrollment and learning. Thus, we do not summarize these interventions in this chapter. For detailed surveys of these interventions, see Glewwe et al. (2013) and Glewwe and Muralidharan (2016).

Conclusions and suggestions for future research

Developing countries have made great strides to ensure that all children complete primary school and most enroll in secondary school. Researchers have demonstrated that several policies can raise enrollment (see Table 15.5). Yet school enrollment does not ensure that students learn fundamental cognitive (and non-cognitive) skills. While hundreds of policies have been advocated to increase learning, relatively few have been rigorously evaluated, and even fewer appear to be effective. Randomized evaluations of proposals to increase learning deserve the highest priority for future research.

In our opinion, six specific phenomena require further study. First, grade repetition is high in many countries (on average, 13% in Sub-Saharan African and 12% in Latin America; see Glewwe & Kremer, 2006). Repetition is an inefficient policy for helping students who fall behind. The real issue is: How should schools accommodate students with very different backgrounds and abilities? Some advocate "tracking" (grouping students by academic performance). Others argue that tracking is inherently unequal. In any case, the impact of repetition on education outcomes and alternatives to that policy merit further research.

Second, to pass entrance exams to secondary or post-secondary education, many public school students in developing countries attend private tutoring classes (see Dang, 2007; and Jayachandran, 2014). Tutors are often teachers from the students' own school, which may tempt teachers to reduce effort during the school day to generate demand for tutoring services. One policy that may avoid this is to forbid teachers from tutoring their own students. More research is needed on both possible problems and effective remedies.

A third issue is how to provide teachers with sufficient and effective incentives to exert more effort. A common policy is to link teachers' compensation to their students' performance, yet there are several different ways to design such incentives. For example, evidence from developed countries suggests that awards framed in the form of "loss" (i.e. awards that may be taken back if students failed to improve) are more effective those framed as "gains" (Levitt, List, Neckermann, & Sadoff, 2016). A different way to motivate teachers to exert effort is to make employment contracts subject to periodic renewal, and not renew contracts for under-performing teachers. Yet the exact forms of these contracts, as well as their effectiveness, remain to be examined.

A fourth is the timing of education services: hours per school day, days per year, and vacation times. In some countries, schools operate during periods of high demand for agricultural labor, which may greatly raise the opportunity cost of school attendance. Another issue related to timing is the timing of school entry. Delayed school entry is prevalent in developing countries, but how it affects children's cognitive development in developing countries remains unclear.

Fifth, little is known about peer effects in developing countries.[21] Peer effects may magnify the impacts of many policy interventions. For example, a primary school intervention that increases students' learning may increase learning among children those students are grouped with in secondary school.

A final question concerns language. In most Sub-Saharan African countries, and in some Asian and Latin American countries, children who enroll in primary school face a language (such as English, French or Spanish) that they do not know. Teaching in local languages, at least during the first years, facilitates initial learning but may inhibit mastering the "academic" language used in higher education. Thus teaching in local languages deserves further study.

References

Abeberese, A. B., Kumler, T. J., & Linden, L. L. (2014). Improving reading skills by encouraging children to read in school: A randomized evaluation of the Sa Aklat Sisikat reading program in the Philippines. *Journal of Human Resources, 49*(3), 611−633.

Adrogue, C., & Orlicki, M. E. (2013). Do in-school feeding programs have an impact on academic performance? The case of public schools in Argentina. *Education Policy Analysis Archives, 21*(50), 1−23.

Alderman, H., Gilligan, D. O., & Lehrer, K. (2012). The impact of food for education programs on school participation in northern Uganda. *Economic Development and Cultural Change, 61*(1), 187−218.

Alderman, H., Kim, J., & Orazem, P. F. (2003). Design, evaluation, and sustainability of private schools for the poor: The Pakistan urban and rural fellowship school experiment. *Economics of Education Review, 22,* 265−274.

Ambler, K., Aycinena, D., & Yang, D. (2015). Channeling remittances to education: A field experiment among migrants from El Salvador. *American Economic Journal: Applied Economics, 7*(2), 1−27.

Angrist, J., Bettinger, E., Bloom, E., King, E., & Kremer, M. (2002). Vouchers for private schooling in Colombia: Evidence from a randomized natural experiment. *The American Economic Review, 92*(5), 1535−1558.

Angrist, J., Bettinger, E., & Kremer, M. (2006). Long-term educational consequences of secondary school vouchers: Evidence from. *Administrative Records in Colombia" Amer*ican Economic Review, 96(3), 847−862.

Attanasio, O., Fitzsimons, E., Gomez, A., Gutierrez, M. I., Meghir, C., & Mesnard, A. (2010). Children's schooling and work in the presence of a conditional cash transfer program in rural Colombia. *Economic Development and Cultural Change, 58*(2), 181−210.

Baez, J. E., & Camacho, A. (2011). *Assessing the long-term effects of conditional cash transfers on human capital: Evidence from Colombia.* Washington, DC: World Bank. World Bank Policy Research ` No. 5681.

Baird, S. J., Chirwa, E., de Hoop, J., & Ozler, B. (2016a). Girl power: Cash transfers and adolescent welfare. Evidence from a cluster-randomized experiment in Malawi. In S. Edwards, S. Johnson, & D. N. Weil (Eds.), *African successes, volume II: Human capital* (pp. 139−164). Chicago: University of Chicago Press.

Baird, S., Hicks, J. H., Kremer, M., & Miguel, E. (2016b). Worms at work: Long-run impacts of a child health

---

[21] Duflo, Dupas, and Kremer (2011) provide an early attempt to experimentally estimate peer effects in developing countries.

investment. *Quarterly Journal of Economics, 131*(4), 1637−1680.

Baird, S., McIntosh, C., & Ozler, B. (2011). Cash or condition? Evidence from a cash transfer experiment. *Quarterly Journal of Economics, 26*(4), 1709−1753.

Banerjee, A. V., Banerji, R., Berry, J., Duflo, E., Kannan, H., Mukherji, S., et al. (2016). *Mainstreaming an effective intervention: Evidence from randomized evaluations of "teaching at the right level" in India.* NBER Working Papers No. 22746.

Banerjee, A., Banerji, R., Duflo, E., Gelnnerster, R., & Khemani, S. (2010). Pitfalls of participatory programs: Evidence from a randomized evaluation in education in India. *American Economic Journal: Economic Policy, 2*(1), 1−30.

Banerjee, A. V., Cole, S. A., Duflo, E., & Linden, L. L. (2007). Remedying education: Evidence from two randomized experiments in India. *Quarterly Journal of Economics, 122*(3), 1235−1264.

Banerji, R., Berry, J., & Shotland, M. (2013). *The impact of mother literacy and participation programs on child learning: Evidence from a randomized evaluation in India.* Cambridge, MA: Abdul Latif Jameel Poverty Action Lab (J-PAL).

Barham, T., Macours, K., & Maluccio, J. A. (2013). *More schooling and more learning?: Effects of a three-year conditional cash transfer program in Nicaragua after 10 years.* Inter-American Development Bank.

Barrera-Osorio, F., Bertrand, M., Linden, L., & Perez-Calle, F. (2011). Improving the design of conditional transfer programs: Evidence from a randomized education experiment in Colombia. *American Economic Journal: Applied Economics, 3*, 167−195.

Barrera-Osorio, F., & Filmer, D. (2016). Incentivizing schooling for learning: Evidence on the impact of alternative targeting approaches. *Journal of Human Resources, 51*(2), 461−499.

Barrera-Osorio, F., & Linden, L. (2009). In *The use and misuse of computers in education: Evidence from a randomized experiment in Colombia. World bank policy research working paper #4836, impact evaluation series No. 29.*

Behrman, J. R., Parker, S. W., & Todd, P. E. (2009). Schooling impacts of conditional cash transfers on young children: Evidence from Mexico. *Economic Development and Cultural Change, 57*(3), 439−477.

Behrman, J. R., Parker, S. W., & Todd, P. E. (2011). Do conditional cash transfers for schooling generate lasting benefits? A five-year follow-up of PROGRESA/opportunidades. *Journal of Human Resources, 46*(1), 93−122.

Bellei, C. (2009). Does lengthening the school day increase students' academic achievement? Results from a natural experiment in Chile. *Economics of Education Review, 28*, 629−640.

Benhassine, N., Devoto, F., Duflo, E., Dupas, P., & Pouliquen, V. (2015). Turning a shove into a nudge? A "labeled cash transfer" for education. *American Economic Journal: Economic Policy, 7*(3), 86−125.

van der Berg, S., & Gustafsson, M. (2019). Educational outcomes in post-apartheid South Africa: Signs of progress despite great inequality. In N. Spaull, & J. Jansen (Eds.), *South African schooling: The enigma of inequality.* Springer.

Beuermann, D., Cristia, J., Cruz-Aguayo, Y., Cueto, S., & Malamud, O. (2015). Home computers and child outcomes: Short-term impacts from a randomized experiment in Peru. *American Economic Journal: Applied Economics, 7*(2), 53−80.

Blimpo, M. P. (2014). Team incentives for education in developing countries: A randomized field experiment in Benin. *American Economic Journal: Applied Economics, 6*(4), 90−109.

Bommier, A., & Lambert, S. (2000). Education demand and age at school enrollment in Tanzania. *Journal of Human Resources, 35*(1), 177−203.

Borkum, E. (2012). Can eliminating school fees in poor districts boost enrollment? Evidence from South Africa. *Economic Development and Cultural Change, 60*(2), 359−398.

Borkum, E., He, F., & Linden, L. (2012). *School libraries and language skills in Indian primary schools: A randomized evaluation of the Akshara library program.* Working Paper, Abdul Latif Jameel Poverty Action Lab, MIT.

Bourdon, J., Frölich, M., & Michaelowa, K. (2010). Teacher shortages, teacher contracts and their impact on education in Africa. *Journal of the Royal Statistical Society: Series A, 173*, 93−116.

Burde, D., & Linden, L. L. (2013). Bringing education to Afghan girls: A randomized controlled trial of village-based schools. *American Economic Journal: Applied Economics, 5*(3), 27−40.

Carvalho, I. E. (2000). *Income effects on child labor and school enrollment in Brazil* (Ph.D. thesis). Cambridge, MA: Massachusetts Institute of Technology, Department of Economics.

Chaudhury, N., & Parajuli, D. (2010). Conditional cash transfers and female schooling: The impact of the female school stipend programme on public school enrolments in Punjab, Pakistan. *Applied Economics, 42*(28), 3565−3583.

Chen, Y., & Jin, G. Z. (2012). Does health insurance coverage lead to better health and educational outcomes? Evidence from rural China. *Journal of Health Economics, 31*(1), 1−14.

Chin, A. (2005). Can redistributing teachers across schools raise educational attainment: Evidence from operation blackboard in India. *Journal of Development Economics, 78*(2), 384−405.

Contreras, D., & Rau, T. (2012). Tournament incentives for teachers: Evidence from a scaled-up intervention in Chile. *Economic Development and Cultural Change, 61*(1), 219–246.

Cristia, J., Czerwonko, A., & Garofalo, P. (2014). Does technology in schools affect repetition, dropout and enrollment? Evidence from Peru. *Journal of Applied Economics, 17,* 89–112.

Damon, A., & Paul, G. (2009). Three proposals to improve education in Latin American and the Caribbean: Estimates of the costs and benefits of each strategy. In B. Lomborg (Ed.), *Latin American development priorities.* New York, NY: Cambridge University Press.

Damon, A., Paul, G., Sun, B., & Wisniewski, S. (2019). *What education policies and programs affect learning and time in school in developing countries?* Review of education (in press).

Dang, H.-A. (2007). The determinants and impact of private tutoring classes in Vietnam. *Economics of Education Review, 26*(6), 683–698.

Deaton, A. (2010). Instruments, randomization, and learning about development. *Journal of Economic Literature, 48*(2), 424–455.

Duflo, E. (2001). Schooling and labor market consequences of school construction in Indonesia: Evidence from an unusual policy experiment. *The American Economic Review, 91*(4), 795–813.

Duflo, E., Dupas, P., & Kremer, M. (2011). Peer effects, teacher incentives, and the impact of tracking: Evidence from a randomized evaluation in Kenya. *The American Economic Review, 101,* 1739–1774.

Duflo, E., Dupas, P., & Kremer, M. (2015). School governance, teacher incentives, and pupil-teacher ratios: Experimental evidence from Kenyan primary schools. *Journal of Public Economics, 123,* 92–110.

Duflo, E., Hanna, R., & Ryan, S. P. (2012). Incentives work: Getting teachers to come to school. *American Economics Review, 102*(4), 1241–1278.

Edmonds, E. (2006). Child labor and schooling responses to anticipated income in South Africa. *Journal of Development Economics, 81*(2), 386–414.

Filmer, D. (2004). *If you build it, will they come? School availability and school enrollment in 21 poor countries.* The World Bank. Policy Research Working Paper Series No. 3340.

Filmer, D., & Schady, N. (2014). The medium-term effects of scholarships in a low-income country. *Journal of Human Resources, 49*(3), 663–694.

Fiszbein, A., Schady, N., et al. (2009). *Conditional cash transfers: Reducing Present and future poverty.* Washington, DC: The World Bank.

Foster, A., & Rosenzweig, M. (2004). Technological change and the distribution of schooling: Evidence from green-revolution India. *Journal of Development Economics, 74*(1), 87–111.

Friedman, W., Kremer, M., Miguel, E., & Thornton, R. (2016). Education as liberation? *Economia, 83,* 1–30.

Galiani, S., & McEwan, P. J. (2013). The heterogeneous impact of conditional cash transfers. *Journal of Public Economics, 103,* 85–96.

Gitter, S., & Barham, B. (2008). Women and targeted cash transfers in Nicaragua. *The World Bank Economic Review, 22*(2), 271–290.

Glewwe, P., & Muralidharan, K. (2016). Improving education outcomes in developing countries: Evidence, knowledge gaps, and policy implications. In S. Machin, L. Woessmann, & E. A. Hanushek E.A. (Eds.), *Handbook of the Economics of Education.* North Holland.

Glewwe, P., Hanushek, E., Humpage, S., & Ravina, R. (2013). School resources and educational outcomes in developing countries. In P. Glewwe (Ed.), *Education policy in developing countries.* Chicago: University of Chicago Press.

Glewwe, P., Ilias, N., & Kremer, M. (2010). Teacher incentives. *American Economic Journal: Applied Economics, 2*(3), 205–227.

Glewwe, P., & Jacoby, H. (2004). Economic growth and the demand for education: Is there a wealth effect? *Journal of Development Economics, 74*(1), 33–51.

Glewwe, P., & Kassouf, A. L. (2012). The impact of the Bolsa Escola/Familia conditional cash transfer program on enrollment, dropout rates and grade promotion in Brazil. *Journal of Development Economics, 97*(2), 505–517.

Glewwe, P., & Kremer, M. (2006). Schools, teachers, and education outcomes in developing countries. In E. Hanushek, & F. Welch (Eds.), *Handbook of the economics of education.* North Holland.

Glewwe, P., Kremer, M., & Moulin, S. (2009). Many children left behind? Textbooks and test scores in Kenya. *American Economic Journal: Applied Economics, 1*(1), 112–135.

Glewwe, P., Kremer, M., Moulin, S., & Zitzewitz, E. (2004). Retrospective vs. Prospective analyses of school inputs: The case of flip charts in Kenya. *Journal of Development Economics, 74,* 251–268.

Glewwe, P., & Lambert, S. (2010). Education production functions: Evidence from developing countries. In D. J. Brewer, P. J. McEwan, E. Baker, B. McGaw, & P. Peterson (Eds.) (3rd ed.)*The international encyclopedia of educationEconomics of education.* Elsevier.

Glewwe, P., & Miguel, E. (2008). The impact of child health and nutrition on education in less developed countries. In T. P. Schultz, & J. Strauss (Eds.), *Handbook of development economics* (Vol. 4). North Holland.

Glewwe, P., Park, A., & Zhao, M. (2016). A better vision for development: Eyeglasses and academic performance in rural primary schools in China. *Journal of Development Economics, 122,* 170–182.

Handa, S. (2002). Raising primary school enrolment in developing countries: The relative importance of supply and demand. *Journal of Development Economics, 69*, 103−128.

Hidalgo, D., Onofa, M., Oosterbeek, H., & Ponce, J. (2013). Can provision of free school uniforms harm attendance? Evidence from Ecuador. *Journal of Development Economics, 103*, 43−51.

Hsieh, C.-T., & Urquiola, M. (2006). The effects of generalized school choice on achievement and stratification: Evidence from Chile's school voucher program. *Journal of Public Economics, 90*, 1477−1503.

de Janvry, A., Finan, F., & Sadoulet, E. (2012). Local electoral incentives and decentralized program performance. *The Review of Economics and Statistics, 94*(3), 67γ2−685.

Imbens, G. W. (2010). Better LATE than nothing: Some comments on Deaton (2009) and Heckman and Urzua (2009). *Journal of Economic Literature, 48*(2), 399−423.

Jayachandran, S. (2014). Incentives to teach badly: After-school tutoring in developing countries. *Journal of Development Economics, 108*, 190−205.

Jensen, R. (2010). The (perceived) returns to education and the demand for schooling. *Quarterly Journal of Economics, 25*(2), 515−548.

Kazianga, H., de Walque, D., & Alderman, H. (2012). Educational and child labour impacts of two food-for-education schemes: Evidence from a randomized trial in rural Burkina Faso. *Journal of African Economy, 21*(5), 723−760.

Kazianga, H., Levy, D., Linden, L. L., & Sloan, M. (2013). The effects of "girl-friendly" schools: Evidence from the BRIGHT school construction program in Burkina Faso. *American Economic Journal: Applied Economics, 5*(3), 41−62.

Kremer, M., Miguel, E., & Thornton, R. (2009). Incentives to learn. *The Review of Economics and Statistics, 91*(3), 437−456.

Kremer, M., Moulin, S., & Namunyu, R. (2003). *Decentralization: A cautionary tale*. Mimeo, Harvard University.

Kumar, K., Priyam, M., & Saxena, S. (2005). The trouble with para-teachers. *Frontline, 18*.

Lai, F., Luo, R., Zhang, L., Huang, X., & Rozelle, S. (2015). Does computer-assisted learning improve learning outcomes? Evidence from a randomized experiment in migrant schools in Beijing. *Economics of Education Review, 47*, 34−48.

Lai, F., Zhang, L., Qu, Q., Hu, X., Shi, X., Boswell, M., et al. (2013). *Does computer-assisted learning improve learning outcomes? Evidence from a randomized experiment in public schools in rural minority areas in Qinghai*. China: Rural Education Action Program Working Paper.

Lakshminarayana, R., Eble, A., Bhakta, P., Frost, C., Boone, P., Elbourne, D., et al. (2013). The support to rural India's public education system (STRIPES) trial: A cluster randomised controlled trial of supplementary teaching, learning material and material support. *PLoS One, 8*(7), e65775.

Lara, B., Mizala, A., & Repetto, A. (2011). The effectiveness of private voucher education: Evidence from structural school switches. *Education Evaluation and Policy Analysis, 33*(2), 119−137.

Levitt, S., List, J., Neckermann, S., & Sadoff, S. (2016). The behavioralist goes to school: Leveraging behavioral economics to improve educational performance. *American Economic Journal: Economic Policy, 8*(4), 183−219.

Li, T., Han, L., Zhang, L., & Rozelle, S. (2014). Encouraging classroom peer interactions: Evidence from Chinese migrant schools. *Journal of Public Economics, 111*, 29−45.

Loyalka, P., Liu, C., Song, Y., Yi, H., Huang, X., Wei, J., et al. (2013). Can information and counseling help students from poor rural areas go to high school? Evidence from China. *Journal of Comparative Economics, 41*, 1012−1025.

Luo, R., Shi, Y., Zhang, L., Liu, C., Rozelle, S., Sharbono, B., et al. (2012). Nutrition and educational performance in rural China's elementary schools: Results of a randomized control trial in Shaanxi province. *Economic Development and Cultural Change, 60*(4), 735−772.

Malamud, O., & Pop-Eleches, C. (2011). Home computer use and the development of human capital. *Quarterly Journal of Economics, 126*, 987−1027.

McEwan, P. (2013). The impact of Chile's school feeding program on education outcomes. *Economics of Education Review, 32*, 122−139.

Miguel, T., & Kremer, M. (2004). Worms: Identifying impacts on education and health in the presence of treatment externalities. *Econometrica, 72*(1), 159−217.

Mo, D., Zhang, L., Wang, J., Huang, W., Shi, Y., Boswell, M., et al. (2015). The persistence of gains in learning from computer assisted learning (CAL): Evidence from a randomized experiment in rural schools in Shaanxi province in China. *Journal of Computer Assisted Learning, 31*(2), 562−581.

Mo, D., Zhang, L., Yi, H., Luo, R., Rozelle, S., & Brinton, C. (2013). School dropouts and conditional cash transfers: Evidence from a randomised controlled trial in rural China's junior high schools. *Journal of Development Studies, 49*(2), 190−207.

Mullis, I. V. S., Martin, M. O., Foy, P., & Hooper, M. (2016). *TIMSS 2015 international results in mathematics*. MA: Boston College: Chestnut Hill.

Mullis, I. V. S., Martin, M. O., Foy, P., & Hooper, M. (2017). *PIRLS 2016 international results in reading*. Chestnut Hill, MA: Boston College.

Mullis, I. V. S., Martin, M. O., Gonzalez, E. J., Gregory, K. D., Garden, R. A., O'Connor, K. M., et al. (2000). *TIMSS 1999 international mathematics report: Findings from IEA's repeat* of the Third International Mathematics and Science Study at the eighth grade. Chestnut Hill, MA: Boston College.

Mullis, I. V. S., Martin, M. O., Gonzalez, E. J., & Kennedy, A. M. (2003). *PIRLS 2001 international report: IEA's study of reading literacy achievement in primary schools in 35 countries.* Chestnut Hill, MA: Boston College.

Muralidharan, K. (2012). *Long-term effects of teacher performance pay: Experimental evidence from India.* JPAL Working Paper.

Muralidharan, K., Das, J., Holla, A., & Mohpal, A. (2017). The fiscal costs of weak governance: Evidence from teacher absence in India. *Journal of Public Economics, 145,* 116–135.

Muralidharan, K., & Prakash, N. (2017). Cycling to school: Increasing secondary school enrollment for girls in India. *American Economic Journal: Applied Economics, 9*(3), 321–350.

Muralidharan, K., & Sundararaman, V. (2010). The impact of diagnostic feedback to teachers on student learning: Experimental evidence from India. *Economic Journal, 120*(546), F187–F203.

Muralidharan, K., & Sundararaman, V. (2011). Teacher performance pay: Experimental evidence from India. *Journal of Political Economy, 119*(1), 39–77.

Muralidharan, K., & Sundararaman, V. (2013). *Contract teachers: Experimental evidence from India.* JPAL Working Paper.

Muralidharan, K., & Sundararaman, V. (2015). The aggregate effect of school choice: Evidence from a two-stage experiment in India. *Quarterly Journal of Economics, 130*(3), 1011–1066.

Orkin, K. (2013). *The effect of lengthening the school day on Children's achievement in Ethiopia.* Young Lives Working Paper No.119.

Oster, E., & Thornton, R. (2011). Menstruation, sanitary products, and school attendance: Evidence from a randomized evaluation. *American Economic Journal: Applied Economics, 3*(1), 91–100.

Ozier, O. (2014). *Exploiting externalities to estimate the long-term effects of early childhood deworming.* World Bank Policy Research Working Paper 7052. World Bank.

Pitt, M. M., Rosenzweig, M. R., & Gibbons, D. M. (1993). The determinants and consequences of the placement of government programs in Indonesia. *The World Bank Economic Review, 7*(3), 319–348.

Sabarwal, S., Evans, D. K., & Marshak, A. (2014). *The permanent input hypothesis: The case of textbooks and (no) student

learning in Sierra Leone.* Policy Research working paper, no. WPS 7021. Washington, DC: World Bank Group.

School Fees Abolition Initiative. (2006). *Building on what we know and defining sustained support.* UNICEF and the World Bank. www.ungei.org/infobycountry/files/HighlightsSFAIWorkshopNairobiApril2006.pdf.

Schultz, T. P. (2004). School subsidies for the poor: Evaluating the Mexican PROGRESA poverty program. *Journal of Development Economics, 74*(1), 199–250.

Sylvia, S., Luo, R., Zhang, L., Shi, Y., Medina, A., & Rozelle, S. (2013). Do you get what you pay for with school-based health programs? Evidence from a child nutrition experiment in rural China. *Economics of Education Review, 37,* 1–12.

Tan, J.-P., Lane, J., & Lassibille, G. (1999). Student outcomes in Philippine elementary schools: An evaluation of four experiments. *The World Bank Economic Review, 13*(3), 493–508.

UNESCO Institute for Statistics. (2017). *More than one-half of children and adolescents are not learning worldwide.* UIS Fact Sheet No. 46 http://uis.unesco.org/sites/default/files/documents/fs46-more-than-half-children-not-learning-en-2017.pdf.

Urquiola, M. (2006). Identifying class size effects in developing countries: Evidence from rural Bolivia. *The Review of Economics and Statistics, 88*(1), 171–177.

Urquiola, M., & Verhoogen, E. (2009). Class-size caps, sorting, and the regression discontinuity design. *The American Economic Review, 99*(1), 179–215.

Wang, H., Chu, J., Loyalka, P., Tao, X., Shi, Y., Qu, Q., et al. (2014). *Can school counseling reduce school dropout in developing countries?.* REAP Working Paper #275.

World Bank. (2001). *World development report 2000/2001.* Washington, DC: Attacking Poverty.

Yang, Y., Zhang, L., Zeng, J., Pang, X., Lai, F., & Rozelle, S. (2013). Computers and the academic performance of elementary school-aged girls in China's poor communities. *Computer Education, 60,* 335–346.

Yi, H., Song, Y., Liu, C., Huang, X., Zhang, L., Bai, Y., et al. (2014). Giving kids a head start: The impact and mechanisms of early commitment of financial aid on poor students in rural China. *Journal of Development Economics, 113,* 1–15.

Schooling inputs and behavioral responses by families

Birgitta Rabe

Institute for Social and Economic Research, University of Essex, Colchester, Essex, United Kingdom

Introduction

Governments around the world are investing a substantial proportion of national resources into educating children in schools. On average OECD countries spent 3.5% of GDP on primary, secondary and post-secondary (non-tertiary) education in 2015 (OECD, 2018). To what extent students benefit from these investment is a central question in education and for public policy. There is remarkable disagreement in the schooling quality literature over how much schooling inputs matter in producing cognitive skills in children. In an influential early investigation of the relationship between school inputs and child achievements Coleman et al. (1966) found only small effects of school resources on student outcomes, and this result has been both confirmed and challenged over the years (e.g. Hanushek, 2003; Jackson, Johnson, & Persico, 2016; Krueger, 2003; Lafortune, Rothstein, & Whitmore Schanzenbach, 2018). While the more recent literature generally does find positive resource impacts, in particular if these ae concentrated on disadvantaged schools or students (Gibbons & McNally, 2013), these impacts

are often small. There are several possible reasons for this, one of which is that there may be behavioral responses that may amplify or reduce the impact of educational quality and which are often not separately identified in empirical work. For example, parents might plausibly react to changes in school resources by adjusting effort and engagement in the educational process, as highlighted in an early paper by Becker and Tomes (1976). To the extent that parents' changes in behavior are compensatory — parents lower their own inputs at home as school resources increase — this will mask the impacts of resource differences.

There is a small but growing literature that looks at how parents respond to children's schooling opportunities, highlighting that public inputs can encourage or crowd out parental inputs such as help with homework, engaging with the child in activities that enhance learning, investing money into learning resources or paying for tutors to help with school subjects (Rabe, 2019). If public inputs encourage parental involvement this would amplify the overall impact on children, while if they crowd out parents' efforts the impact of public investments would be mitigated. Whether school investments displace parental efforts can potentially depend on many factors, for example the type of input, whether the change in input provided is large or small, anticipated or not, and the ability and constraints of the parents.

When evaluating the causal effects of educational policies, behavioral responses by parents and other agents will need to be taken into account. There is little value in devoting public funds to activities or goods which crowd out parental effort and investments. However, policy makers need detailed insight into the nature of these responses and how they vary across public investments and parents if they want to learn which school inputs to prioritize and how best to target them to children to maximize their impact on school performance. Knowledge of this could strengthen the relationship between spending and children's test score outcomes.

This article describes and discusses the emerging research looking explicitly at the interactions between school inputs and parental behavioral responses.

Conceptual framework: education production and input interactions

To illustrate the relationship between public and parental investments into children we use the framework set out in Todd and Wolpin (2003) who focus on behavioral responses by parents to changes in school investments. They adopt an education production function approach that likens the process of a child's skill development to the production process of a firm. Cognitive achievements are produced in a cumulative process that depends on the history of family and school inputs as well as inherited endowments. There are three periods, period $t = 0$ is the pre-school period, and $t = 1$ and $t = 2$ correspond to the first and second year in school. F_t represents family inputs into skill production in period t and μ stands for a child's innate

ability. A_t is the child's achievement at the beginning of period t and at the time of school entry depends only on family inputs and innate ability:

$$A_1 = g_0(F_0, \mu),$$

where g_t is a period-specific production function. Family inputs are determined by the family's wealth, W, and the child's innate ability in period 0 ($F_0 = \theta_0(\mu, W)$). Families decide the level of school inputs $\overline{S_1}$ they wish their child to receive by choosing where to live and which school to send their child to. However, while parents choose the school, the school will determine the level of inputs S_1 applied to each child within the school. This may vary across children in a school by ability, for example. At the start of the second year of school, achievement is assumed to depend on the history of family and school inputs in period $t = 1$ as well as on the child's innate ability:

$$A_2 = g_1(S_1, F_1, F_0, \mu).$$

The family inputs in period $t = 1$ are determined by the following decision rule:

$$F_1 = \theta\left(A_1, \mu, W, S_1 - \overline{S_1}\right)$$

That is, families choose their inputs based on the child's achievement at the beginning of the school year, his/her endowments, the family's wealth and the difference between the actual and the targeted level of school inputs received during the year, $S_1 - \overline{S_1}$. Family input decisions are made after the school has chosen its inputs. In this setup, the effect on achievement of exogenously changing a school input in the first period while holding all other inputs constant are given by:

$$\frac{dA_2}{d\left(S_1 - \overline{S_1}\right)} = \frac{\partial g_1}{\partial S_1}.$$

This is the *ceteris-paribus* effect which is determined by the period-specific production technology, g_1, and is often referred to as production function parameter because it depends on the properties of the production function.

However, the total effect of a change in the school input while *not* holding all other inputs constant will have to consider the indirect effects, that is, the behavioral responses by parents. This policy effect is given by:

$$\frac{dA_2}{d\left(S_1 - \overline{S_1}\right)} = \frac{\partial g_1}{\partial S_1} + \frac{\partial g_1}{\partial F_1}\frac{\partial F_1}{\partial \left(S_1 - \overline{S_1}\right)}.$$

This makes clear that the contribution of parents to how achievement changes with school inputs in the second year of schooling depends on how reactive they are to differences in school inputs and how effective their inputs are in the education production technology. The policy effect is of interest because it informs on the total impact of public investments on children's achievement. However, the policy effect can vary between populations in different settings and can therefore not be extrapolated from one situation to the other. Moreover, without knowing the family input decision rule, $\partial F_1 / \partial \left(S_1 - \overline{S_1}\right)$, the production function parameters cannot be derived from a policy effect observed, say, in an experiment.

The average policy effect can be smaller or larger than the *ceteris-paribus* effect. Let's assume that parental inputs have a positive effect on achievement, i.e. $\partial g_1 / \partial F_1 > 0$. If parents reduce their inputs as school resources increase, $\left(\partial F_1 / \partial \left(S_1 - \overline{S_1}\right) < 0\right)$, the average policy effect will be smaller than the production function parameter. For example, if parents see that children receive more individual attention in school because class sizes decrease, they may decide to spend less time helping their children with homework. In this case school and family inputs are *substitutes* in education production and public investments crowd out private investments into children. On the other hand, if parents increase their inputs when they see school resources increase, $\left(\partial F_1 / \partial \left(S_1 - \overline{S_1}\right) > 0\right)$, the policy effect will be larger than the *ceteris-paribus* effect. In this case school and family inputs are *complements* in education production and the impact of school investments is amplified by parental responses. An example of this would be if the increased attention students receive in smaller classes leads to more challenging homework that encourages more parental involvement.

Therefore, if we want to understand how school inputs determine cognitive achievement outcomes, we will be interested both in the production function parameter and the (context-specific) behavioral responses by parents, and in particular whether parental inputs are substitutes or complements in education production.

Extensions

Todd and Wolpin's (2003) model can easily be adapted to include further agents and inputs. For example, it may be that apart from parents we want to consider children who choose how much effort to exert in period $t = 1$ based on the inputs that schools and parents provide (Greaves, Hussain, Rabe, & Rasul, 2019; Pop-Eleches & Urquiola, 2013). Here achievement would be determined by inputs from schools, parents and children, $A_2 = g_1(S_1, F_1, F_0, C_1, \mu)$, and the total policy effect would be given by:

$$\frac{dA_2}{d\left(S_1 - \overline{S_1}\right)} = \frac{\partial g_1}{\partial S_1} + \frac{\partial g_1}{\partial F_1}\frac{\partial F_1}{\partial \left(S_1 - \overline{S_1}\right)}$$
$$+ \frac{\partial g_1}{\partial C_1}\left[\frac{\partial C_1}{\partial S_1} + \frac{\partial C_1}{\partial F_1}\right]$$

Further, it might be possible that teachers are agents who react to changes in school inputs by reducing or increasing their own effort. For example, they may devote less time and effort into math instruction once the school makes video clips available through an online math platform. More generally, we might want to consider more than one type of school input, S_1^x and S_1^y. While in a randomized experiment it may be possible to vary one input while holding the other constant, in the case of an extensive and sustained policy, increasing or decreasing S_1^x would mean that the school system has a chance to adjust the quantity S_1^y (Pop-Eleches & Urquiola, 2013). Finally, it may be useful to distinguish different types of families, as their responses may differ. For example, school investments are often found to have different effects for children from high versus low income families, with children from low socioeconomic status (SES) families benefitting more from education interventions. This may be because their parents are less likely to adjust their own inputs in response to school investments.

Methodological approaches to estimation

There are two main reasons why there are only a small number of empirical studies of interactions between schools' and parents' inputs in the production of educational outcomes to date. One reason this area of research is relatively under-developed is that data comprehensively measuring both school and parental inputs are hard to come by. Much of the literature evaluating the effects of school inputs on children's test score outcomes is based on administrative school data which usually includes detailed measures of school inputs and child outcomes but few measures of family background, let alone of parental investments. In contrast, the child development literature which focuses on the impact of parent's investments tends to use survey data which typically includes a rich set of family-level inputs and background characteristics but limited information on school inputs. Therefore, research on input interactions has mostly relied on linking administrative and survey data sets at the level

of the child or school, or on supplementing administrative data by primary data collection from parents (e.g. Das et al., 2013; Greaves et al., 2019; Pop-Eleches & Urquiola, 2013).

Secondly, the main methodological challenge in establishing a causal relationship between school and parental inputs is that researchers require a setting where school inputs vary for reasons that are unrelated to the unobserved characteristics of families. For example, there may be factors motivating families to send their children to schools that deliver an intense curriculum, and at the same time to be very involved in their children's school work. In this situation it is impossible to know whether an observed correlation between school and parental inputs is caused by a parental response to the level of school resources received or related to these unobserved factors. Therefore, to determine a causal relationship researchers usually look at the outcomes of experiments or of 'quasi-experiments' where school inputs vary randomly, but these do not often occur in practice.

One approach taken in a number of papers has been to use maximum class size rules (Bønnesronning, 2004; Datar & Mason, 2008; Fredriksson, Öckert, & Oosterbeek, 2016). Several countries have a strict legal upper limit on the number of students that can be taught together in one class, and classes are split in two once student numbers exceed a maximum. This leads to variation in the number of pupils taught by one teacher that are unrelated to characteristics of students and their parents and allows researchers to assess how parents respond to student-teacher ratios.

Another approach has been to use school admission lotteries (Cullen, Jacob, & Levitt, 2006) or test score thresholds that channel children with very similar scores into higher and lower quality schools, allowing comparisons of investments between families whose children just made it into the better school with those that missed it by a small margin and who are assumed to be very similar in both observed and unobserved characteristics (Pop-Eleches & Urquiola, 2013). Das et al. (2013) use variation in school funds induced by a randomly assigned school grant program to investigate parental responses.

Finally, a recent contribution by Greaves et al. (2019) uses a set-up where school resources are not changing, but instead parents' beliefs about the quality of the school is impacted by information release from government school inspections. Outcomes from school inspections are made public to parents and reveal information about their child's school that parents cannot generally observe. To the extent that the news deviates from parents' beliefs about the school — quality is better or worse than anticipated — we expect parents to respond to the news.

Empirical findings

For a number of years the focus of research on parental responses to school quality has been on so-called extensive margin choices, i.e. parents choosing a school for their children, sometimes alongside a residential move, in search for improved schooling (Burgess, Greaves, Vignoles, & Wilson, 2015; Gibbons, Machin, & Silva, 2013). This literature looks at the level of school resources that parents target for their children, corresponding to $\overline{S}_1$ in Todd and Wolpin's (2003) framework described above. It examines the factors that determine school choices, often in the context of school accountability policies which involve publishing school quality information (Figlio & Loeb, 2011; Hastings & Weinstein, 2008). A part of this literature has looked at how school quality is capitalized into house prices, with significant house price premia documented for residential areas which give access to good schools (Black, 1999; Black & Machin, 2011; Fack & Grenet, 2010; Figlio & Lucas, 2004; Hussain, 2017). However, as Todd and Wolpin (2003) point out, a family may choose a school

at a given time in a given location, but there may be a difference between the school-level inputs parents chose and those received by their child within the school. If moving school is not an option in the short-term, parents can make intensive margin choices, i.e. adjust the amount of resources they expend on the child, conditional on school choice. Given high transaction costs when changing school, intensive margin responses to school quality are the relevant margin of adjustment for many families in practice.

Among the papers studying family intensive-margin responses to schooling inputs a majority finds that school and parental inputs are substitutes, i.e. that parents reduce their own efforts as schooling improves. Evidence from randomly assigned school grants in India worth around $3 per student and mainly spent on notebooks, writing materials, workbooks and stationery shows that for each additional $1 of funding parents reduce their own spending on similar inputs by $0.76 (Das et al., 2013). However, this only happens if parents anticipate increases in school spending, and not if these grants come as a surprise. Similarly, based on evidence for Zambia, the authors show that unpredictable funding sources have larger test score impacts than predictable grants, suggesting that households may offset own spending if they know that school resources are increasing.

Two papers come to similar results in the high-income context of the US by looking at parental time inputs and school spending. Both find that as per pupil school expenditure goes up, parents reduce their own effort with their children. The first paper captures parental effort by using measures of how often parents discuss various school issues with their child and engage in activities with the school (Houtenville & Conway, 2008). The authors find a negative association between per-student expenditure on instructional salaries and parental effort, although the effort reduction is small in magnitude. The second paper proxies parental involvement by using maternal labor force participation

(Liu, Mroz, & van der Klaauw, 2010). The authors model parents' choice of schools and involvement with their children and consider that choosing where to live and how much to work will also depend on employment opportunities and wages. In policy simulations based on their structural model estimates the authors find that maternal employment rates increase — and therefore maternal time inputs into the child decrease — in response to 25% school funding increases. As before, the adjustment by mothers is small (employment rates increase by 0.5% points or 0.75% from the mean) but there is a negative net impact on test scores.

Consistent with this, evidence from variation in class size triggered by maximum class size rules in Sweden shows that parents decrease their help with homework as classes get smaller (Fredriksson et al., 2016). Interestingly, these results are found for higher income parents but not those with lower incomes. Higher income parents are 43% less likely to help their children with homework if class size drops by 5 students. Class size does not affect the amount of homework set by teachers, so high-income parents are less likely to help for a given amount of homework, while low income parents do not respond. Fredriksson et al. (2016) also examine whether parents switch schools in reaction to larger classes. They find that both high and low income parents have a substantially increased probability of switching to schools with smaller class sizes in these circumstances. Although differences are not statistically significant, point estimates are larger for low income families, perhaps because transaction costs are lower for this group which lives in rental housing more often than high income families. Taken together the study suggests that families respond differentially depending on their abilities and costs.

All of these papers finding evidence of substitutability of family and school inputs in the education production function look at how parents react to changes in particular inputs from schools. A few further studies take a broader

approach to schooling inputs by using measures of school quality. The first proxies school quality by peer ability. It is set in Romania where children are sorted into schools and tracks of different quality based on their achievement scores (Pop-Eleches & Urquiola, 2013). Parents whose children just made it into a higher quality school reduce their help with homework, compared to parents of children who just failed to get into the better school. There is a 3–4% point decrease in the proportion of parents helping with homework often, but these effects reduce over time. Cullen et al. (2006) look at randomized lotteries that determine high school admission into Chicago Public Schools. School quality is measured in terms of achievement levels and gains, graduation rates and poverty rates among the student body. Similarly to Pop-Eleches and Urquiola (2013) parents of students who win access to schools that are better are less likely to help with homework.

A further study uses ratings from a nationwide school inspections regime in England to capture quality referring to factors such as leadership, quality of teaching, students' personal development and academic outcomes (Greaves et al., 2019). Parents are not able to observe all of these dimensions of school quality so that inspection ratings provide news to parents that shift inputs into their children. Parents reduce their help with homework when they learn that their children's school is better than anticipated. Parents who receive good news about the quality of their child's school are 14% points less likely to increase and 24% points more likely to decrease help with homework than parents who receive bad news are.

While the majority of studies come to the conclusion that parental and school inputs are substitutes, there are some papers that show the opposite, i.e. that parents increase their investments when schools do. For example, evidence based on the US Head Start program which provided pre-school education and care for low income families and was randomly assigned to applicants increased parental involvement along a number of dimensions (Gelber & Isen, 2013). However, in this case specific steps were taken to improve parental involvement so it does not generalize to other policies which do not. Another example is a paper that looks at class size increases in Norway (Bonesrønning, 2004). In contrast to evidence for Sweden (Fredriksson et al., 2016), larger classes here led to reductions in measures of parental effort. A related paper surveys parents in England to find out how they perceive the returns to public and private investments and the extent to which they are exchangeable. Based on elicited parental beliefs this paper finds that parents' spending on children will go up if school quality improves (Attanasio, Boneva, & Rauh, 2018). There are also a few studies that find no reactions from parents to changes in school inputs, at least for some types of inputs or parents (Datar & Mason, 2008; Fredriksson et al., 2016).

Factors driving heterogeneous results

Todd and Wolpin (2003) emphasize in their framework on input interactions that behavioral responses to public policies are likely to be setting specific. Therefore it comes as no great surprise that the empirical evidence accumulated to date has results that are sometimes at odds with each other.

One way to reconcile conflicting evidence is to look more closely at the *types of inputs* from parents and schools considered in the research. Not all inputs may be substitutable to the same extent. For example, the school grant program in India provided pens, workbooks and stationary (Das et al., 2013) which are easily substituted so that if more pens are provided by schools we expect parents to buy fewer. There are also diminishing returns from providing more learning materials which suggest substitution is likely to happen in this case. Other inputs, such as teacher attention for example (proxied by

class size), is perhaps not as easily substituted for at home. Some types of school inputs on the other hand might naturally inspire parents to do more, for example if schools invest into improving feedback and communication with parents this might enable them to input more, and better, into their children.

Information is likely to play an important role in this. School inputs that are not easily observed by parents are less likely to provoke a response than those that are seen by everyone. The study for England using school quality inspections shows that information release in the context of school accountability systems can provoke significant responses by parents (Greaves et al., 2019). Likewise, the study comparing anticipated and unanticipated school grants in India and Zambia shows that parents only react to resource changes if they are aware they are happening (Das et al., 2013). Therefore responses to changes in school inputs can evolve over time as parents learn about them and may only emerge after a policy has been taken to scale and sustained over a period of time. (Pop-Eleches & Urquiola, 2013). The ability to observe subtle changes in resources such as per student expenditure may differ between low and high socio-economic status families, as suggested by evidence from Malawi where parents' knowledge about their children's academic performance was worse among the poor (Dizon-Ross, 2019).

Fredriksson et al. (2016) highlight that parents are likely to be differentially able or motivated to adjust their investment behavior in response to variation in school inputs and to face different costs in doing so, stressing the need to distinguish between *types of families*. The study on class size in Sweden showed that while higher income parents step up their help with homework or change schools as class size increases, less educated parents if anything tend to switch schools. A similar result comes from the study of school inspections in England (Greaves et al., 2019). Here heterogeneity analysis shows that it is high and not low educated parents who react to news about the quality of their children's school. This suggests that behavioral responses to changes in schooling inputs will depend on the population affected by such changes, and on their ability, access to information, financial means and preferences.

Multiple inputs and agents

There are considerable limitations and gaps in our knowledge of input interactions which are linked to the available data. Based on survey data, several papers aggregate responses to questions on parent-child interactions into a measure of parental involvement, but they often lack measures of parents' other inputs such as monetary investments into their children. Few studies are able to look simultaneously at different dimensions of parental inputs, and these tend to indicate that conclusions derived from focusing on only one input type may miss that there are further, and possibly opposite direction, adjustments of inputs in other domains. For example, evidence for kindergartens in the US suggests that parents react to increases in group sizes by reducing parent-child interactions - consistent with the evidence from Norway but not Sweden (Bonesrønning, 2004; Fredriksson et al., 2016) - but at the same time increase parent-financed activities such as paid lessons and clubs (Datar & Mason, 2008). Similarly, the study of school quality inspections in England finds that parents spend fewer hours helping their children with homework when the children's school is of higher quality than expected and they also spend less time talking to their children about important matters, indicating that both parent-child interactions are substitutes to beliefs over school quality (Greaves et al., 2019). The study of randomized high school admissions in Chicago demonstrates that parents of students who win the lottery and enter higher quality schools subsequently help

less with homework but are at the same time more likely to discuss school-related issues (Cullen et al., 2006). In other words, parents may react to changes in school inputs by adjusting multiple margins of behavior and these adjustments may go in the same or opposite directions. If empirical studies are unable to observe the whole range of behaviors they may draw incomplete conclusions.

Adding to this, it will be important to take into account that apart from parents, other agents may adjust to changes in schooling quality too. We have shown above how the framework by Todd and Wolpin (2003) can be extended to consider responses by children, for example. Children's own time investments have a significant role for educational achievement, with growing importance in adolescence (Caetano, Kinsler, & Teng, 2019; Del Boca et al., 2017). Greaves et al. (2019) can observe a range of parent and child outcomes in their survey data and find that while parents substitute school inputs for own inputs, children's time inputs move in the opposite direction: when a family receives good news about school quality, the child is more likely to increase time spent on homework, partly compensating for the loss of parental inputs. Pop-Eleches and Urquiola (2013) find that students who make it into better schools more often have negative interactions with peers, while Cullen et al. (2006) find that they experience improvements in disciplinary incidents. A study for Britain finds that by exerting more effort, parents induce their child to also exert more effort, and vice versa (De Fraja, Oliviera, & Zanchi, 2010).

Teachers and schools are further agents who may react to changes in the resources available to them. Fredriksson et al. (2016) show that changes in class size do not affect the amount of homework set by teachers, and similarly Greaves et al. (2019) show that there are no within-year school responses to information release about school quality along a large number of dimensions related to teaching practices.

On the other hand, in the context of Kenya Duflo, Dupas, and Kremer (2015) find that individual teachers exert less effort once more teachers are hired in their school and class sizes get smaller, and this undoes the positive impact of reduced class size. Moreover, teachers tend to sort into higher quality schools, exacerbating the differences between them (Pop-Eleches & Urquiola, 2013).

Test score impacts

Ultimately we are interested in how parental and school inputs combine to produce children's educational outcomes. Therefore it is important to understand the extent to which any parental responses drive a wedge between the effect of public policy and children's schooling outcomes, and several papers on input interactions look at impacts on test scores. However, as discussed above, empirical evidence on the test score impacts of changes in school inputs usually captures the sum of the *ceteris paribus* production function parameter and the behavioral responses by families without being able to disentangle the two. Interesting suggestive evidence comes from studies that find a parental response only from one of two groups, allowing them to compare the achievement of children in absence and presence of parental adjustments. One such study is that on school grants in India where parents did not respond to the unanticipated grants in the first year but did reduce their own spending on learning materials in the second year once they had learned about the existence of the grants (Das et al., 2013). Here there was a sizable test score impact of school spending in the first year which was zero in the second year, indicating that crowding out of parental investments had wiped out the benefits of public spending. However, we cannot rule out that the impact of the grant would have been zero in the second year even if parents had continued to spend.

Another study is the one on class size increases in Sweden which prompted higher educated parents to help their children more with homework, but not lower educated parents, and both types of parents to move school (Fredriksson et al., 2016). This study, like much of the previous class size literature, finds a negative effect of larger classes on children of lower educated parents only, and we might infer that this is because of the differential parental response. On the other hand the authors also show that lower income children find it harder to follow the teacher than higher income children once class sizes increase, so what we are observing may be a heterogeneous treatment effect. Taken at face value, both studies suggest that we should expect parental behavior to have sizable effects on children's outcomes.

Further evidence on test score impacts of behavioral responses by families comes from the study based on school inspections in England (Greaves et al., 2019). In contrast to other papers there is release of information on school quality but no change to school quality or inputs, and checks indicate that schools do not react to information release in the short-term. Assuming that there is no adjustment by schools, the observed test score impacts would be from behavioral responses by families and not from school quality. Test scores significantly reduce, by 9% of a standard deviation, for families that receive good news about school quality earlier in their exam year, compared to those who receive it later in the same year. Because parents reduce their time investment in response to good news while children increase theirs, the negative overall effect suggests that parental inputs are either more productive than childrens' or they adjust more upon receiving the news.

Conclusions

Theory has long highlighted that family and school-based inputs can be substitutes or complements in producing children's human capital. If public inputs encourage parental involvement this would amplify the overall impact on children, while if they crowd out parents' efforts the impact of public investments would be mitigated. To understand how school inputs determine cognitive achievement outcomes, we need information on both the production function parameter and the (context-specific) behavioral responses by parents. Policy makers need detailed insight into the nature of these responses and how they vary across public investments and parents if they want to learn which school inputs to prioritize and how best to target them to children to maximize their impact on test scores.

The empirical evidence on input interactions is still scarce. Overall, existing studies indicate that there can be significant and sizable responses by parents to changes in school quality. The majority of studies finds that schooling and parental inputs are substitutes: parents reduce their own investments when they see school inputs increase, and this is likely to drive a wedge between policy intentions and outcomes and reduce the test score impacts of schooling investments. However, the evidence is not entirely conclusive and, as emphasized by Todd and Wolpin (2003), responses are setting specific. Therefore it is important to understand the precise features of school policies that affect how families respond. Where data allows, evidence should take into account multiple margins of adjustments by multiple agents and across different socio-economic groups. It has become clear that we might expect different responses by socio-economic background to occur because of differences in parents' ability, access to information, financial means and preferences. This implies that the distributional impact of school policies may be affected by program features that are relevant for behavioral responses. Families can respond to changes in school inputs only if they are aware of them, indicating the importance for policy makers to carefully consider the provision of information, how it is framed and who it targets.

References

Attanasio, O., Boneva, T., & Rauh, C. (2018). *Parental beliefs about returns to different types of investments in school children*. HCEO Working Paper 2018-032.

Becker, G. S., & Tomes, N. (1976). Child endowments and the quantity and quality of children. *Journal of Political Economy, 84*(4), S143–S162.

Black, S. (1999). Do better schools matter? Parental valuation of elementary education. *Quarterly Journal of Economics, 114*(2), 578–599.

Black, S., & Machin, S. (2011). Housing valuations of school performance. In E. A. Hanushek, S. Machin, & L. Woessmann (Eds.), *Handbook of the economics of education* (Vol. 3).

Bonesrønning, H. (2004). The determinants of parental effort in education production: Do parents respond to changes in class size? *Economics of Education Review, 23*(1), 1–9.

Burgess, S., Greaves, E., Vignoles, A., & Wilson, D. (2015). What parents want: School preferences and school choice. *Economic Journal*, 1262–1289.

Caetano, G., Kinsler, J., & Teng, H. (2019). Towards causal estimates of children's time allocation on skill development. *Journal of Applied Econometrics, 34*(4), 588–605.

Coleman, J., Campbell, E., Hobson, C., McPartland, J., Mood, A., Weinfeld, F., et al. (1966). *Equality of educational opportunity*. Washington, D.C.: U. S. Government Printing Office.

Cullen, J. B., Jacob, B. A., & Levitt, S. (2006). The effect of school choice on participants: Evidence from randomized lotteries. *Econometrica, 74*(5), 1191–1230.

Das, J., Dercon, S., Habyarimana, J., Krishnan, P., Muralidharan, K., & Sundararaman, V. (2013). When can school inputs improve test scores? *American Economic Journal: Applied Economics, 5*(2), 29–57.

Datar, A., & Mason, B. (2008). Do reductions in class size 'crowd out' parental investment in education? *Economics of Education Review, 27*(6), 712–723.

De Fraja, G., Oliviera, T., & Zanchi, L. (2010). Must try harder: Evaluating the role of effort in educational attainment. *The Review of Economics and Statistics, 92*(3), 577–597.

Del Boca, D., Monfardini, C., & Nicoletti, C. (2017). Parental and child time investments and the cognitive development of adolescents. *Journal of Labor Economics, 35*, 565–608.

Dizon-Ross, R. (2019). Parents' beliefs about their children's academic ability: Implications for educational investments. *American Economic Review, 108*(8), 2728–2765.

Duflo, E., Dupas, P., & Kremer, M. (2015). School governance, teacher incentives, and pupil–teacher ratios: Experimental evidence from Kenyan primary schools. *Journal of Public Economics, 123*, 92–110.

Fack, G., & Grenet, J. (2010). When do better schools raise housing prices? Evidence from paris public and private schools. *Journal of Public Economics, 94*, 59–77.

Figlio, D. N., & Loeb, S. (2011). School accountability. In *Handbook of the economics of education* (Vol. 3, pp. 383–421). Elsevier.

Figlio, D. N., & Lucas, M. E. (2004). What's in a grade? School report cards and the housing market. *American Economic Review, 94*, 591–604.

Fredriksson, P., Öckert, B., & Oosterbeek, H. (2016). Parental responses to public investments in children. Evidence from a maximum class size rule. *Journal of Human Resources, 51*(4), 832–868.

Gelber, A., & Isen, A. (2013). Children's schooling and parents' behavior: Evidence from the Head start impact study. *Journal of Public Economics, 101*, 25–38.

Gibbons, S., Machin, S., & Silva, O. (2013). Valuing school quality using boundary discontinuities. *Journal of Urban Economics, 75*, 15–28.

Gibbons, S., & McNally, S. (2013). *The effects of resources across school phases: A summary of recent evidence.* CEP Discussion Paper No 1226.

Greaves, E., Hussain, I., Rabe, B., & Rasul, I. (2019). *Parental responses to information about school quality: Evidence from linked survey and administrative data.* Working Papers of the Institute for Social and Economic Research no. 2019-03.

Hanushek, E. A. (2003). The failure of input-based schooling policies. *Economic Journal, 113*, F64–F98.

Hastings, J., & Weinstein, J. M. (2008). Information, school choice, and academic achievement: Evidence from two experiments. *Quarterly Journal of Economics, 123*(4), 1373–1414.

Houtenville, A. J., & Conway, K. S. (2008). Parental effort, school resources, and student achievement. *Journal of Human Resources, 43*(2), 437–453.

Hussain, I. (2017). *Do consumers respond to short-term innovations in school productivity?, evidence from the housing market and parents' school choices.* University of Sussex mimeo.

Jackson, C. K., Johnson, R. C., & Persico, C. (2016). The effects of school spending on educational and economic outcomes: Evidence from school finance reforms. *The Quarterly Journal of Economics, 131*(1), 157–218.

Krueger, A. B. (2003). Economic considerations and class size. *Economic Journal, 113*, F34–F63.

Lafortune, J., Rothstein, J., & Whitmore Schanzenbach, D. (2018). School finance reform and the distribution of student achievement. *American Economic Journal: Applied Economics, 10*(2), 1–26.

Liu, H., Mroz, T. A., & van der Klaauw, W. (2010). Maternal employment, migration, and child development. *Journal of Econometrics, 156*, 212–228.

OECD. (2018). *Education at a glance 2018: OECD indicators.* Paris: OECD Publishing. https://doi.org/10.1787/eag-2018-en.

Pop-Eleches, C., & Urquiola, M. (2013). Going to a better school: Effects and behavioural responses. *American Economic Review, 103*(4), 1289–1324.

Rabe, B. (2019). Do school inputs crowd out parental investments into children? *IZA World of Labor, 460*.

Todd, P. E., & Wolpin, K. I. (2003). On the specification and estimation of the production function for cognitive achievement. *Economic Journal, 113*(485), F3–F33.

The economics of early childhood interventions

M. Nores

NIEER, Rutgers University, New Brunswick, NJ, United States

The last decades have been ones of particular attention to early childhood development policies and programs globally. Most recently, the early years have been integrated into the Sustainable Development Goals (Britto et al., 2017), as well as the G20 2018 communiqué (point 14). These trends have been increasingly driven by developments in neuroscience and its implications for education, health, and in economic, particularly the research on human capital formation. An understanding of early opportunities, as well as the consequences of early adversity, have increased the importance of early interventions for later educational, social, and economic outcomes. The labor-market pressures on women also come into play in some contexts and countries.

Early childhood education has developed at a slower pace than primary education did 60 or so years ago, but has increased continuously since the 1970s. Global pre-primary gross enrollment ratios are currently 49%. Enrolments in pre-primary education reach over 130 million children and are 33% in sub-Saharan Africa, 28% in the Middle East and North Africa, 78% in East Asia and the Pacific, around 74% in Europe and Central Asia (95% in

the European Union), 73% in Latin America and the Caribbean, and 69% in North America (World Bank, 2018). Coverage has increased significantly in the last four decades and remains extremely low in the developing world. Most provision is based in the public sector, though child care continues to be provided mostly by private institutions, with the private sector accounting for 42% of pre-primary services. Public funding predominates, yet remains low, with only an average 0.07% GNP spent on pre-primary education (Valerio & Garcia, 2013). Donor aid from bilateral and multilateral agencies has increased over the last decades, yet only amounts to 2% of basic education aid (Putcha, Upadhahyay, Neuman, Cjhoi, & Lombardi, 2016). Ultimately, with 250 million children not reaching their developmental potential, the cost of inaction has been estimated to average a loss of about a quarter of an average adult income per year per person, a significant loss to countries (Daelmans et al., 2017).

The economic rationale

Why do governments provide early childhood education and child care? Why is early

The Economics of Education, Second Edition
https://doi.org/10.1016/B978-0-12-815391-8.00017-3

childhood education increasing in developing and first world country policy and aid agendas? From an economic perspective, there are three fundamental rationales for early childhood education and child care interventions (and education interventions in general): (1) market failures, (2) equity and redistribution, and (3) human capital formation (Gruber, 2007; Heckman & Raut, 2016; Barnett & Nores, 2015). All of these perspectives support viewing early childhood programs as public goods worth investing in by governments and not dependent solely on individual family choices or constraints.

Market failures

Market failures in education include (1) positive externalities (Barnett & Nores, 2015), and (2) credit market failures (Gruber, 2007). Externalities are benefits accrued to society (social benefits) when an individual chooses to consume a good or service, beyond those accrued to the individual (private benefits). Some private benefits, in particular earnings, are commonly known as private returns to education and may also be accrued, but other examples include our own health (or happiness).

On the other hand, social benefits are benefits that increase social welfare. Examples of social benefits are increased productivity of the labor force (contributing to economic growth and development), less welfare use of individuals with higher earnings, reduced crime, increased tax collection, and increased female productivity (by shifting women to the labor market). There are also a series of intangible social benefits that are harder to measure and relate to having a more educated society and less inequity (active participation and the quality of the democratic process).

Families do not account for externalities when deciding about education (they are not willing to pay for them and these are not included in the price of schooling); therefore, they consume less than what is socially desirable (the social

optimum). For example, a family knows that by investing in education his/her child will benefit through increased productivity and therefore earn higher wages as an adult. Therefore, they would be willing to pay for education to the extent that the cost of educating their child is as least equal to or less than the extra benefits the child will accrue in the future. However, society also benefits from this investment and families are not taking these benefits into account, therefore underinvesting in education. In addition, they may have imperfect information about what the benefits may be, which would also lead to underinvestment.

Credit market failures relate to the inability of families to borrow to finance education (especially early childhood or basic education). This type of market failure can be addressed through loans to finance education but these are absent in early childhood (unlike for higher education). Governments have chosen to provide early childhood services directly (e.g., preschool, home-visitation) or fund other providers (e.g., vouchers and subsidized daycare, grants for home-visitation interventions), but they do not to provide low-interest loans the way they do for higher education.

Equity and redistribution

The consumption of education, like the consumption of most goods, is dependent on the financial ability to pay for the service (i.e., the capacity of families to pay for education and the indirect costs of education, e.g., school uniforms, books, remedial classes, transportation, and parent association fees). Since higher family income renders higher spending capacities, inequalities in income have the potential to translate into inequalities in educational attainment (and in the quality of education), and consequently, into differences in lifelong earning streams. Without government intervention, education has the potential to reproduce income inequalities. Through equality in access and educational opportunities, governments in democratic and nondemocratic societies have seen education as a way of redistributing income across generations. Public support for education based on distributional concerns is based on a belief that a children's access to education (and lifelong chances) should not be based on their parent's financial capital.

Similarly, whether or not most parents might be altruistic and prioritize expenditure on their children's education, the distributional argument also covers children whose parents might prioritize their consumption over their own children's consumption (what is known as egotistic utility functions). Public provision of education and child care, as an alternative to money for child care or loans, ensures that all children are provided the same opportunities regardless of their parents' preferences.

Human capital formation

The focus on looking at early childhood within studies of human capital formation has more recently emerged in economics. Based on what is known in neurobiology about sensitive periods in development, and high brain plasticity of the early years, the field of economics is currently interested in disentangling what interventions and at which points in a children's life cycle determine higher latter productivity, and the long-results in health, crime and other areas observed in experimental studies in early childhood (Heckman & Raut, 2016). Analyses of human capital formation along the life cycle have shown that gaps in skill formation arise early on and that cannot be reduced later in life through schooling or training. Therefore, early processes and the impacts of early investments has emerged as a plausible means to offset the detrimental effects of poverty. When, where, and how these interventions are effective is being addressed by this research and aspects of quality have been highlighted (Barnett, 2011). Suggested pathways for effects include

snowballing effects of early success on motivation and effort, effects executive function and meta-cognitive abilities, reduction of the effects on brain development from excessive stress and inadequate nutrition, and family responses to children's early performance (Barnett & Nores, 2015).

Types of early childhood interventions

In the presence of market failures and a concern with redistribution, governments have three alternatives for intervention: regulation, funding, and provision. Although the motivations for government intervention described require a combination of regulation and funding, provision of early childhood education and child-care alternatives has prevailed in many countries. Provision does not equate quality, and this is a central issue of concerns as it relates to the goals of reducing disparities and in terms of human capital formation (Barnett, 2011).

Across countries, provision of early childhood education and care differ significantly. They support different aspects of childhood, from children's growth, development, and learning (childhood education programs and preschool programs) to health, nutrition, hygiene, and cognitive, social, physical, and emotional development. They take place in formal, informal, and nonformal settings, in arrangements ranging from center-based, to formal preschool education, to parent/community-based arrangements or home-visiting. Stronger integrated and aligned cross-sectoral programming (in health, nutrition, education and social protection) promote children's development comprehensively and across their life-cycle (Richter et al., 2017). Early childhood education has gained strength as a cost-effective way of reducing disparities in educational outcomes and increasing schools' effectiveness. Because early environments (and disadvantages) define later outcomes, early childhood education allows increasing educational attainment of the individual (productivity), as well as reducing social inefficiencies in the provision of education later on (reducing grade repetition, and the need for remedial or dropout prevention programs) (Carneiro & Heckman, 2003; Heckman & Masterov, 2007). Studies on cost effectiveness (measuring the cost of providing high-quality preschool education vs. the benefits produced by it in the form of higher productivity of the labor force, reduced welfare, reduced crime, and higher tax collection, have strengthened the argument for early childhood interventions.

In the international arena, as part of the sustainable development goals of ensuring inclusive and equitable quality education and promoting lifelong learning opportunities for all by 2030, early childhood is included as a target. Specifically, it addresses ensuring that all children have access to quality early childhood development, care and pre-primary education so as to be ready for primary education. The overall argument on early childhood has moved from providing it as a basic human right to providing it because it is an effective way of reducing disparities and increasing individual productivity (the human capital argument). Because it leads to higher educational attainment, it increases individual welfare and reduces the probability of poverty in adulthood (the equity argument), while in parallel increasing efficiencies in the education system, reducing social costs, and increasing social welfare (the externality argument).

Evidence in the US, and internationally, has shown that high-quality early childhood interventions have direct effects on cognitive and noncognitive development (Barnett, 2011; Barnett & Nores, 2015; Camilli, 2010; Engle et al., 2011; Heckman & Masterov, 2007; Nores & Barnett, 2010). Meaningful lasting effects across different child developmental dimensions have been present in several small controlled interventions, including random assignments,

focused on disadvantaged populations. Among these are the Carolina Abecedarian Full-Day School Program, the Early Training Project, the Elmira Prenatal/Early Infancy Project, the Infant Health and Development Program, the integrated responsive stimulation and nutrition interventions in the Lady Health Worker program in Pakistan, the Jamaican Study, the Mauritius Preschool Study, the Milwaukee New Hope Project, the Perry Preschool Project, and the Turkish Early Enrichment Project.

These studies are particularly valuable because randomization increases internal validity, namely, inferring causality between the program and the observed cognitive and noncognitive outcomes. On the other hand, as long as interventions remain small, external validity, or the degree to which conclusions can be generalized, remains small; that is, it is not clear whether the size of the results would remain the same when interventions are extended to a large-scale (i.e., national) level. This makes larger-scale interventions (such as those of Head Start program in the US, the Chicago Child–Parent Centers, the Michigan School Readiness Program, the South Carolina Pre-K, the New York Pre-K, the Effective Provision of Pre-School Education Project of the University of London, and the studies of preschool expansion in Argentina and Uruguay, among others) substantiating the benefits of early childhood education and the persistence of long-term effects, of fundamental importance (Barnett, 2011; Heckman & Masterov, 2007; Melhuish; 2008).

Among the programs mentioned, the Perry Preschool Program is among the most-studied early childhood interventions, following a sample of 128 low-income children through age 40 (Barnett, 2011; Schweinhart, 2005). Children were randomly assigned to treatment and control groups (58 experiment and 65 control), and the treatment group received half-day (2.5 h per day) high-quality preschooling (teachers had a BA) and weekly home visits for 2 years. The Abecedarian program consisted of a study following 111 children until the age of 21. Randomization was done at birth (54 experiment and 51 control) with the treatment group receiving center-based child care with an emphasis on language development, 8 h a day through the age of 5 (Ramey, 2018). Similarly, the Chicago Child–Parent Center consisted on matching treatment individuals with similar children (of the same age, which would also be eligible for the program and of similar education and economic family background) rather than on random assignment of individuals. The program provided health and social services, free meals, and center-based half-day preschooling for 3-and 4-year-olds during the school year (Reynolds et al., 2011).

The different types of benefits resulting from these interventions, as well as those from international studies, are summarized below. These are differentiated as cognitive (school progress and performance outcomes), noncognitive (social, behavioral, and labor-market outcomes), and indirect benefits to society.

Cognitive and academic outcomes

In the short and medium term, early childhood interventions, particularly those that focus on the developmental and cognitive aspects of childhood (Nores & Barnett, 2010), may impact children's cognitive development, school progress, and educational attainment. These three types of indicators have been used as the basis for evaluating success of most early childhood educational interventions.

Indicators such as achievement tests and intelligence quotients (IQs), usually measure cognitive development. Several studies evidence positive effects of high-quality center-based care on children's cognitive growth. That is, children come into these programs extremely disadvantaged, and end they up performing better than similar peers who did not have access to the program. While in some cases IQ outcomes

have been large, they have been short termed, sustained until school entry, and converging through the first years of schooling except for the Abecedarian and Milwaukee programs. Not all types of interventions have impacts on cognitive development. Quality matters in early childhood; well-designed, intensive programs that focus on quality interactions and include involvement with children and families show the strongest results. Moreover, children from impoverished homes have benefitted more generally across these studies (Engle et al., 2011). The evidence from developing countries substantiates these findings (Boocock, 1995; Engle et al., 2011; Schady, 2006).

Early childhood programs have also shown that they can have important medium- and long-term effects on achievement; reducing grade repetition, reducing placement in remedial or special education, and increasing educational attainment. From random assignment studies, there is evidence of positive and lasting impacts of early child education on achievement (e.g., Milwaukee, Florida, Abecedarian, and Perry) (Barnett, 2011; Blau & Currie, 2005). Among the international research, there is evidence of increased achievement from various programs and evaluations, i.e., a carefully designed study in Sweden (Boocock, 1995), a large program to construct preschool facilities in Argentina, a nutritional and early stimulation program in Jamaica (Schady, 2006), the Colombian Hogares Comunitarios program (Attanasio et al., 2014), the Cali Study (Boocock, 1995) on dosage, and the Pakistan Study (Yousafsai et al., 2014), integrating nutritional and child-care components.

Increased school readiness, achievement, and social development set the stage for improvements in school progress and educational attainment. It reduces the chances that a child will repeat grades, need remedial education, be a special-needs child, or drop out of school. The evidence shows reduced grade retention, and the estimates for dropout reduction across the Abecedarian, Chicago, and Perry studies are quite similar (around 20—30%). There is also evidence of reduced special education rates and in the number of years of special education necessary when it is still required (e.g., Abecedarian, Perry, Chicago, and Early Training Project). Center-based experiences in Argentina, Burma, Cambodia, Chile, Colombia, Ethiopia, and Mexico evidence improvements in enrollment, age of entry, retention, and performance (Britto et al., 2017; Engle et al., 2011; Schady, 2006).

Since children that have experienced early programming enter school more prepared and progress through it more smoothly, they are also more likely to succeed in attaining a secondary education degree. In developing countries, transitioning into secondary education is an area of concern. Few studies in the US and none in the international arena have followed children through high school and beyond. Abecedarian, Perry, Chicago, and the Florida studies, as well as evaluations on Head Start, have indicated effects on secondary school graduation rates of participants (Barnett & Nores, 2015; Blau and Currie, 2005).

Noncognitive outcomes

Focusing on cognitive development indicators ignores the full array of social and economic noncognitive responses motivated by schools, families, and institutions. Short-term evidence on scores does not measure relevant nutritional, social, emotional, and overall developmental dimensions. Some examples of developmental outcomes due to early childhood interventions are: improvements in the health and nutritional indicators of the child, effects on socialization (aggression and behavior indicators), which in the long term relate to delinquency and crime outcomes, and effects on motivation, self-discipline, and attentiveness that relate to long-term educational attainment.

While some interventions might not successfully affect IQs, they may still provide benefits by affecting social and emotional skills, leading to increased educational success, reduced criminal activity, integration of disadvantaged population into mainstream society, etc. (Carneiro & Heckman, 2003). This human capital approach has addressed path dependency of circumstances and behaviors resulting from early education. Growing attention is being given to how early cognitive development defines later attainments, life behaviors, opportunities, and experiences (Heckman & Masterov, 2007). When preschool programs deter children from transgressions, they may dissuade them from crime later on. A similar argument goes for health-related behavior. While many programs are critically evaluated on cognitive development indicators, medium- and long-run behavioral changes have economics implications.

In the developing world, in the context of high child mortality rates, stunting, and serious child illnesses and hunger, health and nutrition take on added importance for child development (Barnett, 2011; Engle et al., 2007). Health, nutritional, and developmental improvements have been evidenced across interventions in developing countries (e.g., Chile, Colombia, Egypt, Guinea, Jamaica, Kenya, Mexico, Mauritius, Pakistan, and Vietnam; Britto et al., 2017; Engle et al., 2011; Nores & Barnett, 2010; Raine, Kjetil, Liu, Venables, & Mednick, 2003) and the US (Elmira Pre-natal/Early Infancy Project), with improvements varying from improvements in iodine and iron deficiencies, to improvements in height/weight measures. The Abecedarian program showed strong results on the long-term health of its participants (Campbell et al., 2014).

Substantial lifetime (long-term) effects are mediated through higher educational attainment. The effects of educational attainment on earnings are well established and long lasting. Higher educational attainment reflects cognitive advantages and enhanced noncognitive attributes, for example, self-discipline or diligence. Overall, higher attainment is associated with higher economic well-being over the long term, in particular, higher earnings and employment status. The Perry Preschool Program followed children up to age 40, observing their earnings well into adulthood. Program participants showed considerable higher earnings than the control group (Nores, Belfield, Barnett, & Schweinhart, 2005). While increased earnings are a private benefit, these directly translate into higher amounts of tax payments (income taxes, through increased annual earnings, and sales taxes through increased consumption) (Heckman, Pinto, & Savelyev, 2013).

Reduced crime is another indication of social and emotional effects of early childhood. The Perry Preschool Project evidenced substantial lower rates of criminal activity for the treatment group. The Chicago Child— Parent Center (and an expansion program later on) showed reduced delinquency and crime. Evaluations of the Florida and Colorado Head Start (for females only), the Panel Study of Income Dynamics (PSID), the Head Start study (comparing Head Start to non-Head Start participants between the ages of 18 and 31) and the Mauritius Preschool Study, support the findings from the Perry and Chicago random studies. Many of the benefits from reduced crime can be summarized into victims (some, such as pain, being intangible), policing, criminal justice system, and incarceration costs. Private benefits from reduced crime may vary from increased quality of life, to intergenerational benefits (discussed below), and a series of intangible benefits (such as freedom).

As individuals attain higher levels of education, subsequent increased earnings, and evidence reduced criminal behavior, the aggregation of such behavioral and economic changes is expected to reduce welfare use. The Perry Preschool Program indicates lower welfare reliance of the treatment group (the PSID Head Start evaluation also looked at welfare but found no difference across groups).

Other indicators of social and behavioral changes relate to improvements in the quality of life, health-related behavioral changes, and teenage pregnancy. Teenage pregnancy effects might be the consequences of postponing childbirth through increased educational attainment or through behavioral changes. For youth and adults, the Abecedarian and Perry studies provided indication of health-related behavior in terms of drug usage and tobacco. These two programs also generated increases in the age when the participants had their first child (Schweinhart et al., 2005; Blau and Currie, 2005).

Indirect effects: female labor supply

Besides benefits realized through the child's increased educational attainment and lifetime behavioral responses, early childhood interventions impact a child's family by freeing up women's time. As an increasing number of mothers enter the labor market, especially with global trends in urbanization and industrialization, the question arises on how to take care of their children. Even though child protection and the enhancement of child development and school readiness has been at the center of government interventions, increased female labor participation has increased awareness on the issues of early child care and education, as well as other policies such as parental leave, that support early child development.

Early childhood interventions offer opportunities for maternal participation in the labor market and increased school participation of older siblings (usually females) freed from child-care responsibilities. Child care and labor-market choices are competing uses of the time of the mother and child-care prices affect labor-market choices, in particular, for married women who evidence a higher elasticity (option to decide depending on the price) in their labor supply with respect to child-care prices than single women who have no choice but to work, depend on welfare, or a relative. Mothers in non-wage jobs (e.g., agricultural work in their household) tend to overlap work and family responsibilities.

Evidence from the expansion of child-care policies and subsidies in the US and developing countries show a substantial relation between women's decision to work, in particular for single and low-earning mothers, and child-care prices (e.g., see Gelbach (2002) and Bainbridge, Meyers, and Waldfogel (2003) for the US, Berlinski and Galiani (2007) for Argentina, and Lokshin, Glinskaya, and Garcia (2000) for Kenya). This decision to work is accompanied with increases in household earnings and reductions in welfare dependency. However, some studies do not find positive effects, which emphasizes the need to understand context and when expansion of programs increase access or just subsidize existing programs (Ruhm, 2011).

Economic returns

Returns for the three programs described in detail above (Perry, Abecedarian and Chicago Child Parent Cetners) have been estimated to be between $2.5 to $16 per dollar invested (Barnett & Masse, 2007; Temple & Reynolds, 2007). While these types of estimates are still the exception, rather than the norm, various studies have estimated effects on earnings (Engle et al., 2011; Daelmans et al., 2017; Richter et al., 2017) which accounted for less than half of the benefits in the US studies. Ultimately, the level of returns will depend on the quality of the programs and policies and the degree to which these fit the needs of the population and context (Barnett & Nores, 2015).

Conclusions

The economic rationale for early childhood interventions is similar to that of providing primary and secondary education. Early childhood interventions are argued based on the existence of externalities, family credit constraints, and equity. However, research on human capital formation and the early years has also indicated that there are meaningful implications for investments in early childhood, that also have consequences on children's formal education trajectory and beyond. Expected benefits from high-quality early childhood interventions vary from short-term impacts on cognitive measures such as IQ, to higher achievement, school progress, reduced repetition, reduced special education placement, higher educational attainment, higher earnings, more taxes paid, reduced crime, reduced welfare reliance, reduced teenage pregnancy, and improved health-related behaviors and health outcomes. Moreover, early childhood interventions also free mothers (and in some contexts, older female siblings) for labor-market opportunities, increasing female productivity.

Because many of the externalities of early childhood education have been quantified, it has gained support as a policy alternative to interventions later on. Early childhood education has gained strength as a cost-effective way of reducing disparities in educational outcomes and increasing schools' effectiveness. In parallel, while developed and developing contexts vary in terms of impact and needs (e.g., nutrition), the equity argument has gained strength as an outcome of early childhood provision over time. Early childhood interventions increase educational progress and attainment, increasing individual welfare and reducing the probability of disadvantages in adulthood. The literature on human capital formation has emphasized connections among all of the above, heavily informed by developments in the fields of neuroscience and genomics.

See also

Cost—Benefit Analysis and Cost—Effectiveness Analysis; Education Production Functions: Concepts.

References

Attanasio, O. P., Fernández, C., Fitzsimons, E. O., et al. (2014). Using the infrastructure of a conditional cash transfer program to deliver a scalable integrated early child development program in Colombia: Cluster randomized controlled trial. *BMJ, 349*, g5785.

Bainbridge, J., Meyers, M. K., & Waldfogel, J. (2003). Child care policy reform and the employment of single mothers. *Social Science Quarterly, 84*(4), 771–791.

Barnett, W. S. (2011). Effectiveness of early educational intervention. *Science, 333*, 975–978.

Barnett, W. S., & Masse, L. N. (2007). Comparative benefit–cost analysis of the Abecedarian program and its policy implications. *Economics of Education Review, 26*(1), 113–125.

Barnett, W. S., & Nores, M. (2015). Investment and productivity argument for ECCE. In *Investing against Evidence* (p. 73).

Berlinski, S., & Galiani, S. (2007). The effect of a large expansion of pre-primary school facilities on preschool attendance and maternal employment. *Labour Economics, 14*(3), 665–680.

Boocock, S. S. (1995). Early childhood programs in other nations: Goals and outcomes. *Future of Children, 5*(3), 94–114.

Britto, P. R., Lye, S. J., Proulx, K., et al. (2017). Nurturing care: Promoting early childhood development. *Lancet, 389*, 91–102.

Camilli, G., Vargas, S., Ryan, S., & Barnett, W. S. (2010). Meta-analysis of the effects of early education interventions on cognitive and social development. *Teachers College Record, 112*(3), 579–620.

Campbell, F., Conti, G., Heckman, J. J., et al. (2014). Early childhood investments substantially boost adult health. *Science, 343*(6178), 1478–1485.

Carneiro, P., & Heckman, J. (2003). *Human capital policy.* NBER Working Paper No. W9495. Cambridge: National Bureau of Economic Research.

Daelmans, B., Darmstadt, G. L., Lombardi, J., et al. (2017). Early childhood development: The foundation of sustainable development. *The Lancet, 389*(10064), 9–11.

Engle, P. L., Black, M. M., Behrman, J. R., De Mello, M. C., Gertler, P. J., Kapiriri, L.,... & International Child Development Steering Group. (2007). Strategies to avoid the loss of developmental potential in more than 200 million children in the developing world. *The Lancet, 369*(9557), 229–242.

Engle, P. L., Fernald, L. C., Alderman, H., et al. (2011). Strategies for reducing inequalities and improving developmental outcomes for young children in low-income and middle-income countries. *The Lancet, 378*(9799), 1339–1353.

Gelbach, J. B. (2002). Public schooling for young children and maternal labor supply. *American Economic Review, 92*(1), 307–322.

Gruber, J. (2007). *Public finance and public policy* (2nd ed.). New York: Worth Publishers.

Heckman, J. J., & Masterov, D. V. (2007). The productivity argument for investing in young children. *Applied Economic Perspectives and Policy, 29*(3), 446–493.

Heckman, J., Pinto, R., & Savelyev, P. (2013). Understanding the mechanisms through which an influential early childhood program boosted adult outcomes. *American Economic Review, 103*(6), 2052–2086.

Heckman, J. J., & Raut, L. K. (2016). Intergenerational long-term effects of preschool-structural estimates from a discrete dynamic programming model. *Journal of Econometrics, 191*(1), 164–175.

Lokshin, M. M., Glinskaya, E., & Garcia, M. (2000). *The effect of early childhood development programs on women's labor force participation and older children's schooling in Kenya.* World Bank Policy Research Working Paper No. 2376. Washington, DC: World Bank.

Melhuish, E. C., Phan, M. B., Sylva, K., et al. (2008). Effects of the home learning environment and preschool center experience upon literacy and numeracy development in early primary school. *Journal of Social Issues, 64*(1), 95–114.

Nores, M., & Barnett, W. S. (2010). Benefits of early childhood interventions across the world: (under) investing in the very young. *Economics of Education Review, 29*, 271–282.

Nores, M., Belfield, C. R., Barnett, W. S., & Schweinhart, L. (2005). Updating the economic impacts of the high/scope Perry preschool program. *Educational Evaluation and Policy Analysis, 27*(3), 245.

Putcha, V., Upadhahyay, A., Neuman, M., Cjhoi, M., & Lombardi, J. (2016). *Financing early childhood development: An analyses of international and domestic sources in low-and middle- income countries.* Washington, D.C.: Results for Development.

Raine, A., Kjetil, M., Liu, J., Venables, P., & Mednick, S. A. (2003). Effects of environmental enrichment at ages 3–5 years on schizotypal personality and antisocial behavior at ages 17 and 23 years. *American Journal of Psychiatry, 160*(9), 1627–1635.

Ramey, C. T. (2018). The Abecedarian approach to social, educational, and health disparities. *Clinical Child and Family Psychology Review, 21*(4), 527–544.

Reynolds, A. J., Temple, J. A., White, B. A. B., et al. (2011). Age 26 costbenefit analysis of the child-parent center early education program. *Child Development, 82*(1), 379–404.

Richter, L. M., Daelmans, B., Lombardi, J., et al. (2017). Investing in the foundation of sustainable development: Pathways to scale up for early childhood development. *The Lancet, 389*(10064), 103–118.

Ruhm, C. J. (2011). Policies to assist parents with young children. *Future of Children, 21*, 37–68.

Schady, N. R. (2006). Early childhood development in Latin America and the Caribbean. *Economia, 6*(2), 185–225.

Schweinhart, L. J., Montie, J., Xiang, Z., et al. (2005). *Lifetime effects: The high/scope Perry preschool study through age 40.* Ypsilanti, MI: High/Scope Press.

Temple, J. A., & Reynolds, A. J. (2007). Benefits and costs of investments in preschool education: Evidence from the Child–Parent Centers and related programs. *Economics of Education Review, 26*(1), 126–144.

The World Bank. (2018). *The World Bank open data.* Washington, D.C.: The World Bank Group.

Valerio, A., & Garcia, M. (2013). Effective financing. In P. Rebello Britto, P. Engle, & C. Super (Eds.), *Handbook of early childhood development research and its impact on global policy.* New York: Oxford University Press.

Yousafzai, A. K., Rasheed, M. A., Rizvi, A., et al. (2014). Effect of integrated responsive stimulation and nutrition interventions in the lady health worker programme in Pakistan on child development, growth, and health outcomes: A cluster-randomised factorial effectiveness trial. *The Lancet, 384*(9950), 1282–1293.

Further reading

Campbell, F. A., Ramey, C. T., Pungello, E., Sparling, J., & Miller-Johnson, S. (2002). Early childhood education: Young adult outcomes from the Abecedarian project. *Applied Developmental Science, 6*(1), 42–57.

Connelly, R., & Kimmel, J. (2003). The effect of child care costs on the employment and welfare recipiency of single mothers. *Southern Economic Journal, 69*(3), 498–520.

Conti, G., Heckman, J. J., & Pinto, R. (2016). The effects of two influential early childhood interventions on health and healthy behaviour. *The Economic Journal, 126*(596), F28–F65.

Kimmel, J. (2006). Child care, female employment and economic growth. *Community Development: Journal of the Community Development Society, 37*(2), 71–85.

Lokshin, M. (2004). Household childcare choices and women's work behavior in Russia. *Journal of Human Resources, 39*(4), 1094–1115.

McLeod, G. F., Horwood, L. J., Boden, J. M., & Fergusson, D. M. (2018). Early childhood education and later educational attainment and socioeconomic well-being outcomes to age 30. *New Zealand Journal of Educational Studies*, 1–17.

Rao, N., Sun, J., Chen, E. E., & Ip, P. (2017). Effectiveness of early childhood interventions in promoting cognitive development in developing countries: A systematic review and meta-analysis. *Hong Kong Journal of Paediatrics, 22*, 14–25.

Shonkoff, J. P., Radner, J. M., & Foote, N. (2017). Expanding the evidence base to drive more productive early childhood investment. *The Lancet, 389*(10064), 14–16.

Relevant websites

http://www.fpg.unc.edu. Frank Porter Graham Child Development Institute.

http://www.highscope.org. High Scope Educational Research Foundation.

http://www.nber.org. National Bureau of Economic Research.

http://nieer.org. National Institute for Early Education Research.

http://secc.rti.org. The National Institute of Child Health and Human Development Study of Early Childhood and Youth Development.

http://www.unicef.org. United Nations Children's Fund.

https://data.worldbank.org/.

https://en.unesco.org/themes/early-childhood-care-and-education. United Nations Education, Scientific and Cultural Organization (UNESCO). (UNESCO provides the leading source on the Education for All (EFA) Global Monitoring actions, including the in early childhood interventions as means for increasing primary and secondary educational attainment and equity.

https://sustainabledevelopment.un.org/sdg4.

Parental socioeconomic status, child health, and human capital

J. Currie[a], *J. Goodman*[b]

[a]Columbia University, New York, NY, United States; [b]Harvard University, Cambridge, MA, United States

Glossary

Fetal origins hypothesis A biological theory suggesting that the environment an individual Is exposed to as a fetus can have long-term effects on his or her health
Grossman health model A theoretical model describing how an individual's health refates to his or her previous health and choices of medical inputs, such as medical care, food, and housing
Sibling fixed effects A regression analysis technique that compares siblings to each other in order to remove the statistical bias due to family background.

Introduction

Investments in education pay off in the form of higher future earnings, and differences in educational attainments explain a significant fraction of the adult variation in wages, incomes, and other outcomes. But what determines a child's educational success? Most studies point to family background as the primary factor. But why does background matter? While many aspects are no doubt important, research increasingly implicates health as a potentially major factor. The importance of health for education and earnings suggests that if family background affects child health, then poor child health may in turn affect education and future economic status.

What evidence exists about the effect of parental socioeconomic status (SES) on child health? What evidence exists about the effect of child health on future outcomes, such as education? A great deal of evidence shows that low SES in childhood is related to poorer future adult health (Smith, Hart, Blane, & Hole, 1998). The specific question at the heart of this article is whether low parental SES affects future outcomes through its effects on child health. In most of the studies cited, SES is defined by parental income or poverty status, although some measure SES through residential neighborhood or parental schooling attainment. The article focuses primarily on children from developed countries because it is more obvious why the common and severe health problems of children in many developing countries might impede human capital development.

The Economics of Education, Second Edition
https://doi.org/10.1016/B978-0-12-815391-8.00018-5

Does parental socioeconomic status affect child health?

External benefits of parental SES

Parental SES may impact both parents' own health and the health of their children. Schooling attainment, in particular, has a stronger correlation with a parent's own good health than does income or other measures of SES (Grossman, 2007). The association between education and parents' own health is only partially explained by better health knowledge and may be better explained by the fact that more highly educated parents tend to exhibit better health behaviors. Even after controlling for income, parents with more schooling smoke less, drink less alcohol, exercise more, and work less often in dangerous occupations. They also adhere more carefully to prescribed medical therapies and are more likely to use newer medical technologies to address health problems. These tendencies may be caused by education, or they may indicate that people who plan for the future better tend both to pursue more schooling and to behave in healthier ways.

This article focuses, however, not on the internal benefits of parental SES (i.e., for parents' own health) but on the external benefits of parental SES for children's health. Through what channels might these benefits flow? In the health model presented by Grossman (2000), a health production function Qj describes how a child's current health depends on health inputs such as medical care, food, and housing, as well as previous health levels Qj-i, *Qj-2*, etc. This is similar to an education production function that models how a child's test score depends on inputs such as teachers and textbooks as well as previous test scores. Grossman's health model yields several insights into how parental SES might affect child health. First, and perhaps most obviously, budget constraints bind more in poorer families, preventing them from buying more or better material health inputs such as better-quality medical care and food, as well as safer housing and neighborhoods.

Second, SES affects what parents choose to do with the health inputs they can afford, as parents of lower SES may have different past experiences with the healthcare system, or different health preferences, or different health beliefs (e.g., whether it is normal for a child to wheeze).

Parental education may play a particularly important role in this regard. Maternal schooling is strongly correlated with neonatal mortality rates and children's overall health, which may indicate the importance of health knowledge but is more likely explained by the association between schooling and various health behaviors (Grossman, 2007). More highly educated mothers smoke less, drink less, take more vitamins, and receive more prenatal medical care. In other words, they treat health inputs that impact their children, like cigarettes and alcohol, differently than do less-educated mothers. Once these inputs are controlled for, maternal schooling has little additional association with child health, suggesting that parental education may affect child health largely through the use of such health inputs.

Finally, children of lower SES families are likely to have lower health status at birth. This is not necessarily due to a worse genetic endowment but may stem from differing environmental triggers that activate certain genes (Rutter, 2006). Thus, a low SES child may have poor health at birth because of the circumstances surrounding gestation and birth, rather than because of worse genetic endowments. All of the above may be mechanisms through which SES affects child health.

Evidence

Correlation

Differences in the health of high and low SES children are apparent at birth. Data from Britain and California show that low SES children are more likely to have low birth weight than high SES children. Maternal reports of overall child health from the US, Britain, and Canada all show that the health gap between high and low SES children continues through early childhood and beyond (Currie, Shields, & Wheatley Price, 2007). The health gaps are smaller in Britain and Canada than in the US, perhaps due to universal health insurance coverage, but are still present.

Variations in the incidence of health insults (such as hospitalizations or new diagnoses of chronic conditions) may be of particular importance in explaining the gap in health status between rich and poor. Evidence from the US, Britain, and Canada suggests that poor children are more likely to receive health insults and suffer from chronic conditions than rich children (Currie & Lin, 2007). More than twice as many poor children than nonpoor children are reported by their mothers to be in less than very good health, a gap that increases as children age. Further, 32.4% of poor children suffer from a chronic condition, compared to 26.5% of nonpoor children, a gap that would likely be even larger if differences in diagnosis probabilities were accounted for. Such chronic conditions also limit poor children more than nonpoor children. The percentage of poor children report being limited by their chronic conditions is 11.4% as compared to 7.0% of non-poor children. The fraction of children with a limitation due to a chronic condition rises with age, and rises more sharply for poor children than for others. By their teenage years, poor children have almost double the probability of being limited by their chronic condition: 14.1% compared to 7.8% of nonpoor children.

Theoretical models suggest that persistent poverty is likely to have worse effects on health than transitory poverty. Although more research is needed, evidence from several studies suggests that persistent poverty affects child mental health, particularly aggressive behavior, more than current poverty (Strohschein, 2005).

Causation

The fact that children of low SES parents are less healthy on average than other children does not necessarily imply that low SES causes poor child health. A third factor such as poor parental health may, for example, cause both poverty and poor child health. Alternatively, poor child health may cause low SES by reducing parental earnings. Identifying causal effects matters very much because interventions to improve parental SES will not necessarily improve child health if parental SES does not directly affect child health. Unfortunately, relatively little literature attempts to identify causal impacts of parental SES on child health in a developed country context, perhaps because of the difficulty of finding interventions that affect parental SES but that do not also directly affect children's health. Research in this area uses one of two approaches. The first approach is to ask whether the correlation between SES and child health remains once other variables are controlled for. The second is to examine the effect of natural experiments that randomly change some parents' SES relative to a control group.

Mother's education, one measure of SES, seems to have a positive impact on child health. In the US, the great expansion of higher education in the 1960s and 1970s raised women's education levels, which in turn improved infant health as measured by birth weight and gestational age (Currie & Moretti, 2003). The effect may have occurred through increased rates of marriage and prenatal care, as well as through substantial reductions in smoking.

Income itself, as a measure of SES, seems to have relatively little effect on child health. Welfare-to-work experiments, for example, have had little impact on child health, either positive or negative. Income may, however, matter more in a developing country context. For example, black South African girls increased their height-for-age when their grandmothers started receiving old-age pensions, suggesting increased investment in nutrition (Duflo, 2000). Finally, the state of the economy may impact child health. Dutch citizens born during recessions have higher mortality rates at all ages compared to those born just prior to the recession, though the precise pathway for this effect is unclear (Van den Berg, Lindeboom, & Portrait, 2006).

Studies of American and British families find that the apparent effect of income on child mental health is considerably lessened once other factors, such as parenting skills and physical home environment, are controlled for (Berger, Paxson, & Waldfogel, 2006). Estimates from the American study suggest that even cash subsidies to bring every family up to the poverty line would not eliminate the observed gaps in child outcomes.

Neighborhoods are often said to be an important pathway for SES to affect outcomes. Some evidence on this point comes from a US social experiment that randomly assisted some public housing residents to move to low-poverty neighborhoods. This moving-to-opportunities experiment improved the mental health of girls through reductions in generalized anxiety disorders and psychological distress (Orr et al., 2003). Curiously, there was no such positive effect for boys.

Some recent research has attempted to control for unobserved family background characteristics by examining children born to the same mother (i.e., estimating models with sibling fixed effects). Some studies of American mothers suggest that on average, maternal income during pregnancy does not affect the probability of having a child with low birth weight, but that it does matter if the mother herself had a low birth weight. Evidence from California birth records suggests that, even among women with the same mother, being born in a poor area increased the probability of being low birth weight and of later delivering a baby with low birth weight (Currie & Moretti, 2007). One final piece of evidence that maternal SES affects infant health comes from examination of the health improvements black women experienced as a result of the US Civil Rights movement. Infants of black women who themselves had healthier infancies as a result of the Civil Rights movement (which improved hospital access for blacks in southern states) show large gains in birth weight relative to the infants of black women born just a few years earlier (Almond et al., 2019).

In summary, it is difficult to prove that the strong and exceedingly robust correlation between parental SES and child health is a causal relationship. The literature attempting to do so is underdeveloped. There is, however, evidence that maternal SES early in the child's life matters, and that child mental health may be particularly susceptible to the effects of early deprivation.

Does child health affect future outcomes?

Possible channels

Poor child health may impact adult labor supply and productivity through two channels. First, it may damage adult health. Cohorts that suffer high death rates in childhood may also show high death rates in adulthood, in part because of the direct effects of childhood health conditions on future morbidity. In rich countries, cohorts that suffer a higher disease burden in childhood have higher adult death rates, though in poor countries the relation is reversed because only relatively healthy people survive to adulthood (Bozzoli, Deaton, & Quintana-Domeque, 2007). In the US, adults' reports about their overall childhood health are highly correlated with current adult outcomes, a pattern that continues to hold even once family background is controlled for by comparing siblings to each other. Thus, adult siblings who had better health in childhood have 24% higher incomes, higher wealth, more weeks worked per year, and a higher growth rate of income (Smith, 2007).

Comparing siblings to each other reduces the apparent effect of childhood health on future education, suggesting that childhood health may affect future income through mechanisms other than educational attainment. Sickly children may, for example, be less able to work hard as adults.

Second, poor child health may impair children's educational attainment and thus skill acquisition. Among older children, school absences may be a mechanism for health to affect education, although overall absenteeism is quite small for both poor and nonpoor children. It is more likely that poor health impacts skill acquisition by impairing children's ability to learn while they are in school. Conditions such as anemia and lead poisoning have this effect, though today they are relatively rare in developed countries. Conditions such as tooth decay and ear infections are much more common and might therefore have a greater overall impact. Mental health conditions may be a particularly important mechanism because they are common and have worse effects on schooling attainment than most physical chronic conditions.

Evidence

In developing countries, children in poor health tend to have lower educational attainments, but surprisingly little examination of this relationship has occurred in developed countries. Data on older Americans show that the apparent effect of a retrospective measure of childhood SES on future health, education, and income shrinks when child health measures are included (Luo & Walte, 2005). This result implies that child health may explain some of the impact of low childhood SES on future outcomes.

The primary deficiency of this literature is that correlations between child health and future outcomes, including those mentioned above, may be due to other characteristics of households that are associated both with poor child health and worse outcomes. Until the last decade, most studies claiming a causal connection between child health and future educational attainment suffered from methodological weaknesses, but in the past decade an outpouring of research on this topic has paid careful attention to the causal question. The remainder of this section examines specific child health problems that may work through the two channels described above, starting with conditions *in utero* and low birth weight, for which there is much causal evidence, and continuing with nutrition, mental health, asthma, acute conditions, and environmental toxins, for which there are fewer causal studies.

Conditions **in utero**

Increasing numbers of studies have focused on the hypothesis that fetal conditions are related to adult risk of disease, an idea that has become known as the fetal origins or the Barker hypothesis (Barker, 1998; Gluckman & Hanson, 2005). This literature strongly suggests that conditions *in utero* affect not only birth weight but features such as basic metabolism, which in turn affect future health outcomes. Fetuses starved *in utero* may develop more efficient metabolisms that raise the risk of future obesity, heart disease, and diabetes. As adult health is strongly linked to adult economic well-being, this suggests a relationship between health *in utero* and future outcomes.

The most compelling tests of the hypothesis look for sharp exogenous shocks in fetal health caused by conditions outside the mother's control. Dutch adults who were *in utero* during the 1944–45 famine caused by Nazi occupation were more likely to suffer various health impairments including nervous disorders, heart disease, and antisocial personality disorders. Swedes who were *in utero* when the 1986 Chernobyl disaster exposed their mothers to low-dose fallout were less likely to qualify for high school and had lower grades (Almond, Edlund, & Palme, 2007). Americans who were *in utero* during the 1918 influenza epidemic were much less likely to graduate from high school, had lower wages, were more likely to be poor and receiving transfer payments, and as adults suffered more from schizophrenia, diabetes, and stroke (Almond, 2006). In general, health shocks in early life due to wars, famines, and other crizes can have large, lasting effects on health.

Cognitive functioning can also be directly affected by conditions *in utero* and in infancy. For example, maternal alcohol consumption can lead to permanent brain damage, as can trauma during the birth itself. Extreme deprivation in early childhood, such as that experienced by some Romanian orphans in state-run nurseries, demonstrably impairs cognitive functioning (O'Connor, Rutter, & the English and Romanian Adoptees Study Team, 2000). Severe health insults *in utero* or in early childhood clearly can cause permanent cognitive impairments, but questions remain about how sensitive these sensitive periods are and whether damage due to less-extreme deprivation is noteworthy or widespread.

Birth weight

More direct evidence is provided by recent literature linking low birth weight to negative future outcomes. In the US, low-birth-weight babies have a much higher infant mortality rate than their heavier counterparts (Conley et al., 2003). They also have lower average scores on a variety of tests of intellectual and social development. British children with low birth weight have lower test scores, educational attainments, wages, and probabilities of being employed as adults, even conditional on many measures of family background (Case, Fertig, & Paxson, 2005).

Many of the studies exploring the effect of birth weight on future outcomes compare siblings or twins in an attempt to control for unobserved family characteristics that might otherwise bias the results. Some small-sample studies that do this in an American context

conclude that siblings with lower birth weight tend to attain less education. More recently, several studies have employed individual-level national vital statistics (birth certificate) data in Canada, Norway, and Scotland to examine this question. All of these studies show a link between low birth weight and lower educational attainment, and some show a negative effect on height and intelligence, even among siblings or twins (Black, Devereux, & Salvanes, 2007). Similar findings occur in the US, where a number of studies confirm that siblings (or twins) with lower birth weight attain less education than their higher birth-weight counterparts (Currie & Moretti, 2007). Data from the US also suggests that lower birth weight is associated with a higher probability of living in a poor area, a lower probability of being married, lower earnings, worse health, and worse cognitive abilities.

Nutrition

Nutrition may play a significant role in the child's cognitive development. Randomized trials in developing countries such as Guatemala, for example, indicate that poor nutrition can harm cognition (Maluccio et al., 2006). It is less obvious that nutritional supplementation should have a large effect on the cognitive achievement of children in richer countries. Several US studies have, however, found positive effects of prenatal participation in the special supplemental nutrition program for women, infants, and children (WIC), which provides coupons that can be redeemed for specific foods to women, infants, and children who are deemed to be nutritionally at risk (Kowaleski-Jones & Duncan, 2002). Children of mothers participating in WIC had better outcomes on cognitive tests even when compared to a control group of higher income, better-educated women also receiving prenatal care in clinic settings. Children born while their mothers participated in WIC show better temperament, although not better motor or social skills, than their siblings born while their mothers were not participating. These studies underline the importance of the prenatal period.

Further evidence on the importance of nutrition comes from the fact that height is a good measure of a population's average health. Interestingly, the well-established relationship between adult height and earnings disappears when early childhood cognitive test scores are controlled for (Case & Paxson, 2006). Since much of the variation in adult height is due to childhood nutrition, this suggests that poor childhood nutrition likely affects both cognitive performance and adult height, leading to the observed correlation between height and earnings.

Mental health

The prevalence and importance of child mental health problems have been increasingly recognized. Approximately one in five children and adolescents in the US exhibit some impairment from a mental or behavioral disorder, 11% have significant functional impairments, and 5% suffer extreme functional impairment. Moreover, mental health problems are one of the leading causes of days lost in the workplace because they strike many people of working age. Retrospective questions asked to US adults suggest that those with early-onset psychiatric problems were less likely to have graduated from high school or attended college. Children's mental health problems are usually grouped into four categories: anxiety, depression, hyperactivity, and conduct disorders (aggressive or antisocial behavior). The evidence to date suggests that these last two externalizing problems have the greatest impact on outcomes.

Children with behavioral problems in Britain and New Zealand have poorer schooling, earnings, and employment outcomes as young adults than their counterparts without such problems. Hyperactivity and conduct disorders seem to cause these negative outcomes, while anxiety and depression have little effect. US data also suggest that children with behavior problems

at young ages are less likely to graduate from high school or to attend college, even after conditioning on maternal characteristics (McLeod & Kaiser, 2004). American children with attention-deficit hyperactivity disorder (ADHD) complete less schooling and are more likely to have continuing mental health problems than a group of control children consisting either of children from the same school or nonpsychiatric patients in the same medical center (Mannuzza & Klein, 2000).

Beyond adding available controls to regression models, many of these studies do not address the possibility that the negative outcomes might be caused by other factors related to a diagnosis of mental health problems, such as poverty or the presence of other learning disabilities. Recent studies address these challenges by comparing siblings, thus eliminating any family background characteristics as a source of bias (Currie & Stabile, 2006). In both the US and Canada, siblings with high scores on an ADHD screener had lower math and reading scores and higher probabilities of being in special education or having repeated a grade than their siblings with low scores on the ADHD screener. ADHD appears to have larger effects on academic outcomes than childhood depression, conduct disorders, or other mental problems, and the effects of ADHD are large relative to those of physical chronic conditions.

Asthma

Poor children are more likely to suffer from and be limited by asthma, the most prevalent childhood chronic condition, than are nonpoor children. Though siblings with controlled asthma show no difference in achievement scores than siblings without asthma, several studies indicate that asthmatic children are more likely than similar but nonasthmatic children to have behavior problems, even when the asthma is well controlled (Calam et al., 2003). Asthmatic children are absent more frequently from school, have higher incidence of learning disabilities, and repeat grades more often. They also have lower scores on a test of school readiness skills and their parents were three times more likely to report that they needed extra help with learning, particularly if children reported that their asthma caused activity limitations. These studies suffer from the deficiency that the apparent connection between asthma and outcomes could reflect omitted third factors because asthma is more prevalent among poor and minority children. The fact that several of the studies do, however, use very homogeneous groups of children and still find behavioral differences suggests that uncontrolled asthma probably does have a causal effect on behavior.

Acute illnesses

Poor children are more likely to suffer from acute illnesses such as tooth decay and ear infections than their richer peers. Ear infections affect most young children at one time or another and are the most common reason children visit a doctor. Roughly 5% of 2−4-year-old children have hearing loss because of middle-ear effusion lasting 3 months or longer. Hearing loss can delay language development, but little research has been done to determine how important these effects might be in explaining disparities in cognitive or academic outcomes.

Environmental toxins

One final category of health problems that may explain disparities in outcomes between poor and nonpoor children is exposure to environmental toxins. The most obvious of these toxins is lead, as lead poisoning has been shown to significantly decrease I (X, and majority of affected children are from low-income families). Lead may also worsen children's mental health, making them more prone to antisocial behavior. Adoption of public health measures such as banning lead in paint and gasoline have, however, caused the number of US children with

unsafe lead levels to decline from 13.5 million in 1988 to less than half a million in 2000. Relatively little research examines the health effects of exposure to other environmental toxins at the level now generally occurring in the population. Data on possible human health effects generally come from either animal studies, or disastrous releases. Residents of areas near hazardous waste sites are more likely to be poor and have lower levels of education than people in the remainder of the country and therefore their children's health outcomes are likely to differ even in the absence of negative health effects from exposure. Some studies try to control for observable confounding factors, but unobservable characteristics of people who live near hazardous waste sites may tend to cause bad outcomes.

One approach that avoids this omitted variable problem uses variation in pollution levels stemming from implementation of the 1970 and 1977 Clean Air acts, which caused exogenous changes in air-pollution levels across counties. Countries that experienced larger air-pollution reduction also experienced decreased rates of infant mortality (Chay & Greenstone, 2003). The Clean Air acts also reduced prenatal exposure to lead, which in turn decreased infant mortality and the proportion of low-birth-weight babies (Reyes, 2005). Other papers account for omitted characteristics such as ground-water pollution and SES by examining changes in pollution over time within single zip-code areas. These studies reveal that reducing pollutants such as carbon monoxide lowers infant mortality rates, as well as hospitalization rates for childhood asthma (Currie & Neidell, 2005). These studies show that pollution can have causal effects on child health, but there has been little investigation of whether these effects have long-term consequences for children's outcomes. The National Children's Study attempts to remedy this by examining the effects of environmental exposures on 100,000 children from birth to age 21 years.

Can health account for gaps in Children's educational outcomes?

In order for a given health problem to lead to a disparity in educational outcomes, the health problem must either be more prevalent among the poor or have a larger negative effect on the poor, and must also be associated with lower educational attainments. Few of the specific health problems mentioned above fit both these criteria. Mental health problems are much more prevalent among the poor and have large negative effects, but are still too rare to explain observed human capital disparities. Similarly, the long-term effects of low birth weight are statistically significant but relatively small. The same is true for many of the other specific conditions, while for some of the other large categories, such as injuries and exposure to environmental toxins, too little evidence currently exists to determine the likely long-term effects or the extent of the disparity in exposures. One exception to this generalization is the fetal injuries mentioned above, which have very large effects on future outcomes. Children of US mothers infected during the flu epidemic were 15% less likely to graduate from high school, and Swedish children exposed to low-level radiation after Chernobyl were 5.6% less likely to qualify for high school. These results raise the provocative idea that one of the best ways to safeguard children's health and educational attainments may be to start with their pregnant (or prepregnant) mothers.

To summarize, this article surveys literature focusing on two questions: Do parental circumstances affect child health at early ages? Does child health matter for future educational attainments? The answer to both questions appears to be yes. It is too early to tell how important these feedbacks between health and more conventional measures of human capital may be. We know too little about the cumulative and interactive effects of health insults. The available evidence suggests that fetal health may be particularly important. We need to understand more about the reasons why poor children suffer a higher incidence of negative health events, even *in utero*, so that we can do more to prevent them. Much of the literature reviewed here is extremely recent, suggesting that this topic will continue to be a fruitful area of research.

See also

Education and health; Education production functions: concepts; Education production functions: evidence from developed countries; Education production functions: evidence from developing countries; Human capital; The external benefits of education.

References

Almond, D. (2006). Is the 1918 influenza pandemic over? Long-term effects of *in utero* influenza exposure in the post-1940 U.S. Population. *Journal of Political Economy, 114*, 672–712.

Almond, D., Chay, K., & Greenstone, M. (2019). Civil rights, the war on poverty, and black-white convergence in Infant mortality in Mississippi. *The American Economic Review* (forthcoming).

Almond, D., Edlund, L., & Palme, M. (2007). *Chernobyl's subclinical legacy: Prenatal exposure to radioactive fallout and school outcomes in Sweden*. NBER Working Paper 13347.

Barker, D. J. P. (1998). *Mothers, babies and health in later life* (2nd ed.). Edinburgh: Churchill Livingston.

Berger, L., Paxson, C., & Waldfogel, J. (2006). *Income and child development*. Working Paper.

Black, S. E., Devereux, P. J., & Salvanes, K. G. (2007). From the cradle to the labor market? The effect of birth weight on adult outcomes. *Quarterly Journal of Economics, 122*, 409–439.

Bozzoli, C., Deaton, A., & Quintana-Domeque, C. (2007). *Child mortality, income and adult height*. NBER Working Paper 12966.

Calam, R., Gregg, L., Simpson, B. M., et al. (2003). Childhood asthma, behaviour problems and family functioning. *The Journal of Allergy and Clinical Immunology, 122*, 499–504.

Case, A., Fertig, A., & Paxson, C. (2005). The lasting Impact of childhood health and circumstance. *Journal of Health Economics, 24*, 365–389.

Case, A., & Paxson, C. (2006). *Stature and status: Height, ability, and labor market outcomes*. NBER Working Paper 12466.

Chay, K. Y., & Greenstone, M. (2003). *Air quality, infant mortality, and the Clean Air Act of 1970*. NBER Working Paper 10053.

Coniey, D., Strully, K., & Bennett, K. (2003). *The starting gate: Birth weight and life chances*. Berkeley, CA: University of California Press.

Currie, J., & Lin, W. (2007). Chipping away at health: More on the relationship between income and child health. *Health Affairs, 26*, 331–344.

Currie, J., & Moretti, E. (2003). Mother's education and the Intergenerational transmission of human capital: Evidence from college openings. *Quarterly Journal of Economics, 118*, 1495–1532.

Currie, J., & Moretti, E. (2007). Biology as destiny? Short and long-run determinants of intergenerational transmission of birth weight. *Journal of Labor Economics, 25*, 231–264.

Currie, J., & Neidell, M. (2005). Air pollution and Infant health: What can we learn from California's recent experience? *Quarterly Journal of Economics, 120*, 1003–1030.

Currie, A., Shields, M. A., & Wheatley Price, S. (2007). The child health/family income gradient: Evidence from England. *Journal of Health Economics, 26*, 213–232.

Currie, J., & Stabile, M. (2006). Child mental health and human capital accumulation: The case of ADHD. *Journal of Health Economics, 25*, 1094–1118.

Duflo, E. (2000). Child health and household resources in South Africa: Evidence from the old age pension program. *The American Economic Review, 90*, 393–398.

Gluckman, P., & Hanson, M. (2005). *The fetal matrix: Evolution, development, and disease*. New York: Cambridge University Press.

Grossman, M. (2000). The human capital model. In A. Culver, & J. P. Newhouse (Eds.), *The handbook of health economics* (pp. 347–408). Amsterdam: North Holland.

Grossman, M. (2007). Education and nonmarket outcomes. In E. Hanushek, & F. Welch (Eds.), *Handbook of the economics of education* (pp. 577–633). Amsterdam: North-Holland.

Kowaleski-Jones, L., & Duncan, G. J. (2002). Effects of participation in the WIC food assistance program on children's health and development: Evidence from NLSY children. *American Journal of Public Health, 92*, 799–804.

Luo, Y., & Walte, L. J. (2005). The impact of childhood and adult SES on physical, mental and cognitive well-being in later life. *Journal of Gerontology, 60B*, S93–S101.

Malucclo, J., Hoddinott, J., Behrman, J., et al. (2006). *The impact of nutrition during early childhood on education among Guatemalan adults*. University of Pennsylvania. Population Studies Center Working Paper 06-04.

Mannuzza, S., & Klein, R. G. (2000). Long-term prognosis in attention- deficit/hyperactivity disorder. *Child and Adolesecent Psychiatric Clinics of North America, 9*, 711–726.

McLeod, J., & Kaiser, K. (2004). Childhood emotional and behavioral problems in educational attainment. *American Sociological Review, 69*, 636–658.

O'Connor, T. G., Rutter, M., & the English and Romanian Adoptees Study Team. (2000). Attachment disorder behavior following early severe deprivation: Extension and longitudinal follow-up. *Journal of the American Academy of Child & Adolescent Psychiatry, 39*, 703–712.

Orr, L., Feins, J., Jacob, R., et al. (2003). *Moving to opportunity: Interim impacts evaluation*. Washington, DC: U.S. Department of Housing and Urban Development.

Reyes, J. W. (2005). *The impact of prenatal lead exposure on infant health* (Working Paper).

Rutter, M. (2006). *Genes and behavior: Nature-nurture interplay explained*. Oxford: Blackwell.

Smith, J. P. (2007). The impact of SES on health over the lifecourse. *Journal of Human Resources, 52*, 739–764.

Smith, G. D., Hart, C., Blane, D., & Hole, D. (1998). Adverse socioeconomic conditions in childhood and cause specific adult mortality: Prospective observational study. *British Medical Journal, 316*, 1631–1635.

Strohschein, L. A. (2005). Household income histories and child mental health trajectories. *Journal of Health and Social Behavior, 46*, 359–375.

Van den Berg, G., Lindeboom, M., & Portrait, F. (2006). Economic conditions early in life and Individual mortality. *The American Economic Review, 96*(1), 290–302.

Further reading

Costello, J. E., Compton, S. N., Keeler, G., & Angold, A. (2003). Relationships between poverty and psychopathology: A natural experiment. *Journal of the American Medical Association, 290*, 2023–2028.

Currie, J. (2009). Healthy, wealthy, and wise: Socioeconomic status, poor health in childhood, and human capital development. *Journal of Economic Literature, 47*, 87–122.

Heckman, J. J. (2007). The technology and neuroscience of capacity formation. *Proceedings of the National Academy of Sciences, 104*, 13250–13255.

Relevant websites

http://www.cdc.gov. Centers for Disease Control and Prevention (CDC).

http://papers.nber.org. National Bureau of Economic Research.

http://www.nationalchildrensstudy.gov. National Children's Study.

http://www.who.int. World Health Organization.

Monetary and non-monetary incentives for educational attainment: design and effectiveness

H. Schildberg-Hörisch[a], V. Wagner[b]

[a]University of Düsseldorf, Düsseldorf, Germany; [b]University of Mainz, Mainz, Germany

Introduction

The use of extrinsic incentives to steer individual behavior is at the heart of economics. The "basic law of behavior" is that higher incentives will lead to higher levels of effort provision (Gneezy, Meier, & Rey-Biel, 2011). Education is one area in which regular provision of effort is key in order to realize large returns (Oreopoulos, 2007). The returns to education do not only encompass higher levels of human capital and higher wages (Angrist & Krueger, 1991), but also various positive externalities of education such as reduced crime (Lochner & Moretti, 2004) and teenage pregnancy (Black, Devereux, & Salvanes, 2008), better health (Lleras-Muney, 2005), higher political involvement (Milligan, Moretti, & Oreopoulos, 2004), and higher levels of productivity and growth of GDP per capita for a country as a whole (Hanushek & Wößmann, 2012).

However, students often invest too little in their own education and drop out of school too early, given that, according to the standard framework of the education production function, investments in education should reflect the discounted returns to schooling net of costs (Sadoff, 2014). Many of the tasks students perform in school (e.g., homework assignments) yield benefits only in the far future. Thus, time-inconsistent preferences (Bettinger & Slonim, 2007), or neglect of positive externalities may induce students to make sub-optimal investment decisions in education. Extrinsic incentives for educational inputs or outputs can possibly tackle these sub-optimal investment decisions by offering immediate rewards to students. If students lack sufficient motivation, strongly discount the future, or have inaccurate

The Economics of Education, Second Edition
https://doi.org/10.1016/B978-0-12-815391-8.00019-7

information on the returns to education, immediate rewards can increase students' performance in education (Fryer, 2011).[1]

In principle, extrinsic incentives can be of monetary or non-monetary nature. The effects of monetary-incentives for students, parents, and teachers on educational attainment have been studied widely. However, the use of monetary incentives may be difficult to scale up because they are potentially expensive and educators and parents may be skeptical about "cash for grades". Non-monetary incentives have the potential to mitigate these problems while being cost-effective in increasing educational attainment. A growing body of academic research therefore evaluates the effectiveness of non-monetary incentives, in particular among younger children who might be more responsive to non-monetary incentives than older children (Levitt, List, Neckermann, & Sadoff, 2016a). Moreover, enhancing the motivation of young children to invest in their education by providing extrinsic incentives early on is considered especially effective due to self-productivity and dynamic complementarity of skills in the process of skill formation over time (Cunha & Heckman, 2007).

This chapter reviews the literature on providing extrinsic, monetary and non-monetary incentives to increase educational attainment. Thereby, we focus on the design and implementation of extrinsic incentives in the field. We cover financial incentives only in brief, focusing on the role of cash size and recipient (students, parents, or teachers). We then discuss different types of non-monetary incentives, review which types of incentives are preferred by students if they are free to choose, and report evidence on the effectiveness of non-monetary incentives to raise educational achievement, mainly in primary and secondary education. The literature on financial incentives and educational nudges (such as feedback, deadlines and goal setting) which are closely related to non-monetary incentives is reviewed in greater depth in chapters 41 and 2 of this handbook, respectively.

Monetary incentives

For economists, extrinsic financial incentives are a "natural way" to motivate individuals. Different types of financial incentives have been tested so far, e.g., cash for grades, end of year prizes, cash for attendance and enrollment, tuition fee wavers, and teacher merit pay. Gneezy et al. (2011) summarize the empirical evidence on the effectiveness of financial incentives from large-scale field experiments as follows: (i) financial incentives work well in increasing attendance and enrollment, (ii) financial incentives have mixed results regarding effort provision and achievements, and (iii) financial incentives seem to work for some students, but not for others.

Since our focus lies on the *design* of extrinsic incentive schemes, we proceed by discussing whether and how the effectiveness of monetary incentives relates to variations in cash size or recipient of monetary incentives.

Sensitivity to cash size

Standard economic theory predicts that higher cash incentives lead to greater effort and

---

[1] Fryer (2011) also argues though that extrinsic incentives have little impact on performance if students lack resources or knowledge to convert effort into achievement or if the production function has important complementarities out of their control. Moreover, extrinsic incentives may have negative effects on education outcomes in case they undermine intrinsic motivation.

higher educational outcomes.[2] Leuven, Ooster-beek, and Klaauw (2010), De Paola, Scoppa, and Nisticô (2012), and Barrow and Rouse (2018) test this prediction among university students by varying the amount of money that students can earn. Leuven et al. (2010) and De Paola et al. (2012) offer incentives of similar magnitude. In Leuven et al. (2010), students earn €681 in the high incentive treatment and €227 in the low incentive treatment if they collect all possible credit points for the first year within one year. De Paola et al. (2012) use a rank-based incentive scheme in which only the 30 best-performing students (about 19–20% of students in the treatment groups) receive either €250 or €700. Although the two studies use different incentive schemes (for absolute vs. relative performance, respectively), both find a positive effect of financial incentives on the performance of high-ability students only and, on average, no significant difference between the high and low incentive treatments. Barrow and Rouse (2018) analyze the effects of varying the cash size of The California Scholarship Program. Students receive incentives ranging from $500 to $1000 per semester, (i) either for meeting the end-of-semester performance benchmark (a final average grade of "C" or better in at least 6 credits) only during fall semesters or (ii) half of the incentive is paid for enrolling for six or more credits and half for meeting the performance benchmark during spring semesters. Based on survey data, Barrow and Rouse (2018) find an overall positive effect of financial incentives on students' time spent on educational activities, their quality of effort, and engagement with their studies (measured by learning strategies, academic self-efficacy, and motivation). However, larger cash incentives

do not generate larger increases in time spent on academic activities and effort than smaller incentive payments. In a developing country context, Baird, Mcintosh, and Özler (2011) experimentally investigate both the sensitivity to cash size and the role of the recipient (Malawian parents or adolescent daughters). Enumeration areas are either randomized to one of the treatment conditions and receive cash transfers or to the control group receiving no transfers. Moreover, in the treatment conditions, recipients either receive unconditional or conditional cash transfers, i.e. for 80% or above school attendance per month. Cash transfers to parents vary between $4, $6, $8, and $10 and cash transfers to girls (15–16 years) are $1, $2, $3, $4, or $5 per month. Overall, conditional cash transfers outperform unconditional ones in terms of schooling outcomes (enrollment, attendance given enrollment, and achievement tests). Increasing transfer amounts has no effect on educational outcomes if they are conditional or paid to girls. Only increasing unconditional cash transfers to parents increases enrollment rates of girls, but seems to decrease their performance in test scores. Using a sample that is largely comprised of low income, minority students, Levitt et al. (2016a) find that second to tenth graders in the US obtain significantly better test scores in low stakes tests if they receive a cash reward of $20 for a performance increase compared to their previous test result, but not for a reward of $10.

Overall, larger cash rewards for educational inputs or performance do not seem to produce different results than smaller cash rewards among university students. The findings of Levitt et al. (2016a) suggest that younger and/or more disadvantaged students might be more

---

[2] If students (or parents) maximize utility by balancing marginal benefits from obtaining better educational outcomes and marginal costs from exerting effort, monetary incentives on educational inputs (such as effort provision) or educational outcomes increase their marginal benefits and thus their provision.

responsive to varying cash size for performance increases. However, more research on the sensitivity to cash size among students of different age groups and backgrounds is needed for more reliable conclusions. A further open question refers to how the context under consideration affects a possible lower limit for financial incentives to become effective.

Who should be rewarded?

Students' motivation is a key input for educational attainment and can be influenced by parents, teachers, and peers. When designing financial incentive schemes in education, it is thus critical to know who should be rewarded to raise educational outcomes most (cost-) effectively. Parental inputs such as their attitude toward or involvement at school are important determinants of children's cognitive and non-cognitive skills (Avvisati, Gurgand, Guyon, & Maurin, 2014; Bergman, 2017; Bergman & Chan, 2017; Cunha, Lichand, Madeira, & Bettinger, 2017) and getting parents involved in school seems promising to modify students' behavior. Financial incentives to parents that are conditional on children's educational outcomes provide information to parents and might be effective because they reduce or eliminate information frictions between parents and children. In contrast, unconditional financial incentives contain no informational value for parents. Bursztyn and Coffman (2012), for example, show that parents prefer conditional cash transfer programs over unconditional

transfers, suggesting that parents desire to reduce information asymmetries between them and their children and seek for methods to help them control their children.

The majority of studies vary the recipient of monetary incentives within the household and find little evidence for a differential impact of offering financial incentives to parents as opposed to their children. Berry (2015) reward either Indian parents or their children with 100 rupees conditional on children's performance increase in a reading test, Baird et al. (2011) provide conditional or unconditional cash transfers to parents or their daughters in Malawi, and de Walque and Valente (2018) investigate the impact of equally sized financial incentives for high attendance rates to either children or their parents in Mozambique. Levitt, List, and Sadoff (2016b) reward either parents or children in Chicago high schools with $50 or participation in a lottery with a 10% probability of winning $500 if children meet monthly, minimum achievement standards for attendance, behavior, grades and test scores. These studies find no evidence that the recipient of the reward impacts educational outcomes, i.e. treatment effects do not differ significantly between treatments that incentivize students and parents.[3]

Behrman, Parker, Todd, and Wolpin (2015) vary whether students or their teachers are eligible to receive financial rewards and additionally investigate an aligned incentive treatment, in which students, teachers, and school administrators simultaneously receive financial rewards contingent on students' performance in an end-of-year mathematics test. The authors

---

[3] The treatment effects per se are typically positive. Berry (2015) does not have a randomized control group, but comparing his experimental results to a quasi-experimental control group suggests that incentives substantially improve test scores. Baird et al. (2011) find that both conditional and unconditional cash transfers tend to increase school enrollment, while tests scores increase for conditional transfers only. In de Walque and Valente (2018), incentives to both children and parents are effective in increasing attendance rates, with a 38%, but not significantly larger effect for incentivizing children than parents. Levitt et al. (2016b) find positive and significant treatment effects which are modest in size.

find no effect on students' performance if only teachers receive incentives. However, incentivizing only students yields positive and significant effects on math performance and aligning incentives produces even larger effects. Fryer, Devi, and Holden (2017) test aligned, simultaneous incentives to students, parents, and teachers only. Students and their parents receive $2 each for each math assignment mastered (answering at least four out of five questions correctly) by the students, parents are additionally paid $20 for each parent-teacher review session they attend, and teachers receive $6 for each academic conference held with a parent plus possibly high performance bonuses for students' achievements on standardized tests. While Fryer et al. (2017) find large and significant positive treatment effects on incentivized achievements in math, achievements in reading, which are not incentivized, decrease significantly. In contrast, List, Livingston, and Neckermann (2018) find no significant effects of aligning incentives of students, parents, and teachers. They pay either students and their parents $45 each or students, parents, and teachers $30 each if a student meets predefined standards (improvement of test scores, maintaining course grades, and avoidance of unexcused absences and suspensions). In three further treatments, List et al. (2018) test three individual incentive schemes in which they either pay students, parents, or teachers $90. Their findings in the individual treatments are in line with the aforementioned literature (Baird et al., 2011; Berry, 2015; Levitt et al., 2016b)—treatment effects are positive, large and significant (0.30–0.37 standard deviations) and sign and significance of the treatment effects do not change regardless of who receives the reward.

Overall, the recipient of financial incentives (students, parents, or teachers) does not seem to make a difference for their effectiveness. The so far limited research on aligning student, parent, and teacher incentives shows promising results in terms of increasing students'

educational achievements even further, but the existing evidence is not completely equivocal.

Non-monetary incentives

Whether non-monetary incentives can affect students' educational attainment as well has recently received increasing attention in the economics of education literature. When providing non-monetary incentives to students, researchers first have to identify and choose appropriate non-monetary incentives before they can assess their impact on educational attainment. So far, little is known about students' valuation of different types of non-monetary incentives. We therefore first propose a categorization of non-monetary incentives which is based on Wagner and Riener (2015). We then review studies reporting students' incentive choice and summarize the literature examining the effectiveness of non-monetary incentives on students' educational attainment.

Types of non-monetary incentives

Non-monetary incentives for students can be broadly categorized into (providing) tangible non-monetary incentives on the one hand and granting rights and privileges on the other hand. *Tangible non-monetary incentives* comprise trophies, certificates, candies, or toys, for example. Non-monetary incentives in the category *granting rights and privileges* are mostly non-tangible (although they might be given in the form of a voucher) and grant students privileges such as getting out of one homework assignment or having the privilege to go off campus during the school day. Incentives such as bonus points for the next exam also fall into this category, as they can be interpreted as a privilege to start the exam with a lead compared to others.

Wagner and Riener (2015) propose to further subdivide the above mentioned two main categories: (i) "mastery goal incentives", (ii) "social recognition incentives", and (iii) "curiosity incentives" are classified as tangible non-monetary incentives, (iv) "work avoidance incentives", and (v) "consumption rights" as granting rights and privileges.[4] We further add the sub-category "toys and candies" to the tangible non-monetary incentives as many studies use these kind of rewards. Table 19.1 gives an overview about the two main categories, their sub-categories and examples of experimental studies.

Mastery goal incentives support the joy of learning and the motivation to expand knowledge in one subject. Hence, this category mainly consists of incentives which constitute educational inputs such as books and science kits. *Social recognition incentives* acknowledge students' achievements either in private or in public. *Curiosity incentives* could be any type of non-monetary incentives but, importantly, students do not know ex ante what exactly the incentive is. As indicated by their name, *toys and candies incentives* are incentives students can play with or eat. *Work avoidance incentives* compensate students for their past educational investments in the future, e.g., by giving them extra points in the next exam or reducing the work load of their homework. *Consumption rights* give students the right to do something which is usually forbidden in school (e.g., using the cell phone during class) or determined by the teacher (e.g., choose games in the physical educational lesson).

Selection of non-monetary incentives

So far, most studies have offered predetermined non-monetary rewards to students without reporting students' perceived valuation of the reward or on which grounds they have chosen the incentive. However, knowing students' perceived valuation is crucial for designing effective incentive schemes.

Moreover, if the valuation of various non-monetary incentives differs between students, e.g., by gender or ability, incentive schemes should be tailored to the target audience.

To our knowledge, only Wagner and Riener (2015) report the results of a survey in which they ex ante elicit students' preferences for different non-monetary incentives. Wagner and Riener (2015) survey 241 high school students attending fifth and sixth grades in Germany in the run-up of a field experiment and ask students to name their most preferred incentive among a list of 17 non-monetary incentives. Based on students' answers in this survey, the authors select four non-monetary incentives among which students can choose in the main experiment.

Fig. 19.1 presents the survey results. Overall, students prefer work-avoidance incentives and private social recognition incentives over mastery incentives and public social recognition incentives. The modal choice of students is *bonus points* for the next exam, followed by *homework-voucher* and *surprise*. In their main experiment, Wagner and Riener (2015) use homework-vouchers[5] and surprise incentives but not bonus points because teachers were not allowed to use them. However, other studies test bonus points and assessment weighting (e.g., the average of one or several graded problem sets or homeworks counts toward the final class grade) among university students (Bigoni, Fort, Nardotto, & Reggiani, 2015; Chevalier, Dolton, & Lührmann, 2018; De Paola, Gioia, & Scoppa, 2015; Emerson & Mencken, 2011; Grove & Wasserman, 2006) and find positive effects on students' motivation. Granting the right to use a cell phone for 5 min during class is another highly ranked incentive (rank 5 out of 17). Since cell phones are not allowed in the classroom in

---

[4] These categories are mainly motivated by the concept of Goal Theory, a widely used concept in pedagogical research (see Ames, 1992).

[5] On request, Levitt et al. (2016a) report that they also tested a *homework pass* in one school district.

TABLE 19.1 Categorization of non-monetary incentives for students used in experimental studies.

	Tangible non-monetary incentives				Granting rights and privileges	
	Mastery goal	Social recognition	Curiosity	Toys and candies	Work avoidance	Consumption rights
	Book (Voucher): Guryan et al. (2016); Chevalier et al. (2018)	Letter to Parents: Wagner and Riener (2015)	Surprise Wagner and Riener (2015)	Pizza-Party: Levitt et al. (2016a)	Homework- Voucher: Levitt et al. (2016a); Wagner and Riener (2015)	Right to Obtain a Driving License: Barua and Vidal-Fernandez (2014)
	Science Kits: Guryan et al. (2016)	Trophy/Medal: Levitt et al. (2016a); Wagner and Riener (2015)		(Refillable) Pencil: Jalava et al. (2015); Visaria et al. (2016)	Bonus Points: Chevalier et al. (2018); Bigoni et al. (2015); De Paola et al. (2015); Emerson and Mencken (2011); Grove and Wasserman (2006); Baumert and Demmrich (2001)	Off Campus: Lichtman-Sadot (2016)
	Drawing/Art/Crafts Sets: Berry (2015); Guryan et al. (2016); Martorell et al. (2016)	Certificate: Jalava et al. (2015); Springer et al. (2015); Robinson et al. (2018)		Various Toys: Berry (2015); Guryan et al. (2016); Martorell et al. (2016)		Extra Curricular Sports: Vidal-Fernández (2011)
	Access to Exercise Solutions: Chevalier et al. (2018)			Credits for cell phone: Fryer (2016)		High-value Event: Burgess et al. (2016)
	School materials (school uniforms, bags etc.): de Walque and Valente (2018)					

Note: This table presents categories of non-monetary incentives used in experimental studies. The difference between *toys and candies* and *consumption rights* is that in the latter category students are only granted the right to consume something, whereas in the first category students also receive toys or candies.

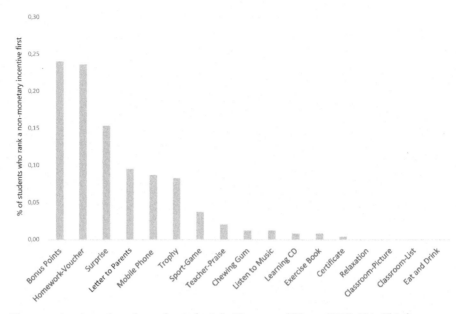

FIG. 19.1 **Non-monetary incentives chosen by students in Wagner and Riener (2015).** *Note:* This figure presents the share of students who rank a non-monetary incentive first out of 17 in the survey of Wagner and Riener (2015). The authors distinguish between five categories of non-monetary incentives, with the following specific incentives that are described in detail below: (i) mastery goal incentives exercise book and learning CD: (ii) social recognition incentives teacher-praise, classroom-picture, letter to parents, trophy, and certificate: (iii) curiosity incentive getting a small surprise reward: (iv) work avoidance incentive bonus points and homework-voucher: (v) consumption rights incentives chewing gum, listen to music, eat and drink, mobile phone, relaxation, and sport-game. *Exercise Book:* receiving a booklet with mathematical exercises. *Teacher-Praise:* being praised in front of the class. *Letter to the parents-,* teacher sends a letter to the parents that praises the pupil's performance. *Surprise-,* getting a small surprise reward. *Homework-voucher:* no homework in math: voucher can be used once until the end of semester. *Chewing Gum:* being allowed to eat a chewing gum in one lesson. *Learning CD:* receiving a CD with mathematical games. *Classroom-Picture:* picture of the pupil who could improve his/her test score is hung up in the classroom. *Trophy:* getting a small medal. *Relaxation:* relaxing 5 min of one lesson. *Listen to Music:* being allowed to listen to music for 5 min. *Classroom-List,:* list of all who could improve their test score is hung up in the classroom. *Certificate:* receiving a certificate stating that a test score has improved. *Bonus points:* receiving extra points for the next written exam. *Eat and Drink:* being allowed to eat and drink during class. *Mobile Phone:* being allowed to play 5 min with the mobile phone in one lesson. *Sport-Game:* determining one game in the sports class.

most German schools, Wagner and Riener (2015) could not test this incentive, but Fryer (2016) does. He rewards students with credits to talk if they read books outside of school and finds no effect on effort or test scores. Notably, students evaluate a *letter to parents* which is praising the students' performance as valuable (rank 4 out of 17). Students' rather frequent choice of the letter to parents could indicate that students want to sent a positive signal and might want their parents to get involved in their education.

This result is especially interesting as recent research shows that getting parents involved in the education of their children is an important input for students' academic careers (Avvisati et al., 2014; Bergman, 2017; Bergman & Chan, 2017; Cunha et al., 2017).

Rewards of the category *(public) social recognition*—incentives that make students' academic achievements salient to their peers in the classroom, e.g. *classroom-picture* and *classroom-list*—are almost never chosen in the survey.

Testing a public recognition award, Bursztyn and Jensen (2015) find that performance declines if a leaderboard is installed and sign-up rates for an online SAT preparatory course are lower if students' decisions are made public. Another unpopular reward is a certificate which is awarded privately, although Jalava, Joensen, and Pellas (2015) find that girls respond strongly to being rewarded with a certificate. It would be interesting to explore in future research whether these stated preferences differ by culture or institutional setting.

Several further studies give students the opportunity to choose a reward out of a predetermined set of rewards during the experiment (Berry, 2015; Burgess, Metcalfe, & Sadoff, 2016; de Walque & Valente, 2018; Guryan, Kim, & Park, 2016),[6] but do not conduct or report results of a pre-survey. Only Guryan et al. (2016) and Wagner and Riener (2015) provide detailed information on students' incentive choices. In Guryan et al. (2016), students receive points for reading books which can be exchanged for various toys (e.g., a razor scooter, an interactive robot toy, a watercolor paint, and easel set), or combinations of prizes. 25% of students who receive points do not claim a prize and students claiming a prize are significantly more likely to choose non-book prizes than book prizes (*mastery goal incentive*), at a ratio of approximately 5 to 1. This is in line with the survey results of Wagner and Riener (2015) that mastery goal incentives seem to be unpopular among students. Wagner and Riener (2015) discuss students' incentive choice among their four predetermined incentives (receiving a medal, a homework-voucher, a letter to parents, or a surprise for grade improvements) in depth.

Overall, the surprise reward proves to be very popular and is the modal choice of students— approximately one-third of students opt for it. The letter to parents (27%), the homework-voucher (21%) and the medal (20%) seem to be similarly popular. With respect to school type— schools preparing for the academic track or vocational training—and gender, the authors do not find notable differences in students' incentive choice, except that boys are slightly more likely to choose the medal, while girls more often go for the surprise. Furthermore, the authors distinguish students by ability based on their past midterm grade in math. The surprise incentive is popular for all ability levels, but low ability students choose the letter to parents significantly more often than high ability students. Only 8% of high ability students chose the letter to parents, 32% the medal, and 26% the homework-voucher. In contrast, 42% of low ability students chose the letter to parents, 10% the medal, and 16% the homework-voucher.

These results indicate a heterogeneous valuation of non-monetary incentives by students' ability and that the target audience (peers or parents) of the signaling value of non-monetary incentives might play a crucial role for their effectiveness (as indicated by Bursztyn & Jensen, 2015).

Effectiveness of non-monetary incentives

Non-monetary incentives for students

Non-monetary incentives for students have been studied to a larger extent than non-monetary incentives for parents or teachers.

---

[6] In Berry (2015), students could choose between a cricket set, a doll, a car, or a drawing set or they received (in another treatment arm) a voucher redeemable for a toy in a shop. Girls in the study of de Walque and Valente (2018) get vouchers to buy school uniforms, shoes, school bags, or smaller school materials, de Walque and Valente (2018) report that their incentive selection is based on information gathered during focus group discussions but do not present detailed results of these discussions. In Burgess et al. (2016), students do not choose from a predefined set—but choose the event for a school trip, jointly with the school administration.

Table 19.2 gives an overview of the relevant literature and highlights differences in the design of incentive schemes with respect to subjects' age, stakes of the test, incentives offered, whether incentives were predetermined, and whether they were offered for educational inputs or outputs.

All studies on tangible non-monetary incentives, such as toys, books, trophies, or certificates, have in common that they provide non-monetary incentives in a low stakes testing environment, i.e. for tests that do not count for the final course grade. Non-monetary incentives are either provided for educational inputs or outputs and in most studies students cannot choose their incentive. Moreover, tangible non-monetary incentives have been offered predominantly to rather young children (below grade 8). One reason might be that schools are more comfortable rewarding younger students with non-monetary incentives and are therefore more likely to participate in those studies. Furthermore, younger children might be less familiar with cash, might receive higher utility from non-monetary incentives, and might be more likely to overestimate the value of non-financial rewards (Levitt et al., 2016a). Levitt et al. (2016a) compare the effectiveness of a trophy—either framed as a loss or a gain—among elementary school students to middle and secondary school students and find that younger students respond stronger to non-monetary incentives only if they are framed as a loss.

Overall, the effects of tangible non-monetary incentives are mixed: They have either no effect or positively affect students' motivation and performance. These mixed results are prevalent independently of whether incentives reward investments into educational inputs or outputs. Positive results are mostly found for a subsample of students under investigation and results differ in for whom the rewards are motivating. For example, Springer, Rosenquist, and Swain (2015) find that girls, in particular, respond to non-monetary incentives, while

Levitt et al. (2016a) find suggestive evidence that boys are more responsive than girls. These heterogeneous findings by gender could be explained by the different non-monetary incentives in place. Girls might be more motivated by a certificate (Springer et al., 2015) than by a trophy (Levitt et al., 2016a). Using non-monetary incentives provided for educational outputs (improvements in literacy), Berry (2015) finds positive effects for low-performing students, while Guryan et al. (2016) incentivize educational inputs (reading books) and tend to find somewhat stronger positive results for already motivated students. Clearly, further research is needed to investigate why the results of these studies differ. Other design features of non-monetary incentives which might be fruitful areas for future research are the timing of non-monetary incentive payments and the effects of repeated incentive payments. We are aware of only one study showing that delayed as opposed to immediate incentive payments are ineffective (Levitt et al., 2016a) and, to our knowledge, no study has investigated the effectiveness of repeated non-monetary incentive payments.

Extrinsic incentives in education are often criticized on the basis that they crowd out the intrinsic motivation of students permanently leading to lower educational attainment once the incentives are removed. Fryer (2016) examines whether non-monetary incentives crowd out motivation in the ACT college entrance exam four years after students have been incentivized for reading books outside of school—students could earn cell phone minutes which could be used outside of school. Martorell, Miller, Santibanez, and Augustine (2016) investigate whether "goody bags" for attendance in a summer-school program have an impact on attendance rates and standardized test scores during the regular school year following the summer program. Levitt et al. (2016a) explore whether a trophy for performance in a low stakes test is detrimental for performance in a test of the same subject months later and Visaria,

TABLE 19.2 Summary of research on non-monetary incentives for students.

Author	Grade/Age	Stakes	Type of incentive	Country	Predetermined	What is incentivized?	Overall assessment
Type of incentive: tangible							
Berry (2015)	Grades 1-3	Low	Toy (cricket set, doll, car, drawing set) or toy voucher	Developing	No	Output - test score	Positive (for low-performing students): attendance & test score
Chevalier et al. (2018)	19.5 years	Low	Book voucher, exercise solutions	Developed	Yes	Input - quiz participation (exercise solution) Output - quiz performance (book voucher)	No effect: quiz participation & final class examination grade
de Walque and Valente (2018)	Grades 6-7	Low	Vouchers for school uniforms, shoes, school bag, smaller materials (pens, notebooks, etc ...)	Developing	No	Input - school attendance	Positive: attendance & test score
Fryer (2016)	Grades 6-7	Low	Credits to talk and text for cellular phone	Developed	Yes	Input - reading books outside of school	No effect: student effort, attendance suspensions & test score
Guryan et al. (2016)	Grades 4-5	Low	Captain Underpants books, art sets, board games, sports equipment, t-shirts, hats, magazine subscriptions, science kits	Developed	No	Input - reading books during summer	Positive: number of books read; no effect: reading comprehension test score
Jalava et al. (2015)	Grade 6	Low	Certificate, refillable pencil	Developed	Yes	Output - test score	No effect: test score
Levitt et al. (2016a)	Grades 2-10	Low	Trophy	Developed	Yes	Output - test score	Positive (for younger children): test score
Martorell et al. (2016)	Grades 1-5	Low	"Goody bags": toys, crafts projects, stuffed animals	Developed	Yes	Input - attendance in summer program	No effect: suspensions & test score

Continued

TABLE 19.2 Summary of research on non-monetary incentives for students.—cont'd

Author	Grade/Age	Stakes	Type of incentive	Country	Predetermined	What is incentivized?	Overall assessment
Robinson et al. (2018)	Grades 6-12	Low	Certificate for attendance	Developed	Yes	Input - attendance in school	No effect (prospective reward) or negative effect (retrospective reward): attendance
Springer et al. (2015)	Grades 5-8	Low	Certificate of recognition	Developed	Yes	Input - attendance in supplemental educational services	Positive (especially for females): attendance
Visaria et al. (2016)	Grade 3	Low	Two pencils and a brightly colored eraser shaped like an animal	Developing	Yes	Input - attendance in school	(i) Short term: positive on attendance, no effect on test scores: (ii) Long term: no effect (high baseline attendance) or negative effect (low baseline attendance) on attendance & test score
Wagner and Riener (2015)	Grades 5-6	Low	Medal, parent-letter, homework-voucher, surprise	Developed	No	Output - test score	No effect: test score
Type of incentive: Granting rights/privileges							
Barua and Vidal-Fernandez (2014)	15–18 years	High	Having the right to obtain a driving license only if certain minimum academic requirements are met	Developed	Yes	Input - attendance/enrollment in school & Output - passing courses	Positive (for blacks and males): High school graduation, years of education, hours of homework, fewer hours watching TV, fewer working hours as student
Baumert and Demmrich (2001)	Grade 9	High	Test grade counts toward final course grade	Developed	Yes	Output - test score	No effect: test score
Bigoni et al. (2015)	21 years	High	Extra points for course grade	Developed	Yes	Output - test score	–

Study	Age/Grade	Stakes	Incentive	Developed	Outcome	Effect
Burgess et al. (2016)	Grade 11	Low	Chance to qualify for a high-value event	No	Input - attendance, conduct, homework, and classwork	No effect: test score, positive (students predicted to have above median treatment effects): classwork & homework
Chevalier et al. (2018)	19.5 years	High	Assessment weighting	Yes	Output - quiz score	Positive: quiz participation & final class examination grade
De Paola et al. (2015)	20.5 years	High	Bonus points for final exam	Yes	Output - test score	–
Emerson and Mencken (2011)	19–20 years	High	Students' homework counts 12–18% toward final course grade	Yes	Output - performance on homework	Positive: test score
Lichtman-Sadot (2016)	Grades 9-11	High	Granting high school students privileges to go off campus during the school day	Yes	Input - student behavior (absences, probation) Output - students' GPA, test scores	Positive: test score & high school dropout rate
Vidal-Fernández (2011)	14 years	High	Participation in high school extra curricular sports	Yes	Output - passing courses	Positive (boys): high school graduation
Grove and Wasserman (2006)	19 years	High	Assessment weighting	Yes	Output - performance on problem sets	Positive (for freshmen): test score

Note: This table summarizes research on non-monetary incentives for students. We define an incentive as high stakes if the incentivized action has a direct impact on a student's final course grade or GPA and low stakes otherwise. In column "Predetermined", we indicate whether students could choose their incentive out of a given set of incentives ("no") or whether the incentive was predetermined by the researcher ("yes"). The last column "Overall assessment" summarizes the impact of non-monetary incentives compared to a control group. Such an assessment is not possible for Bigoni et al. (2015) and De Paola et al. (2015) because these studies do not have a control group in which students receive no incentive. As Bigoni et al. (2015), for instance, compare a tournament, piece rate and cooperative treatment. In all three treatments, students can earn bonus points for the next exam. As Levitt et al. (2016a) reported upon our request, they also use a "Homework Pass" that pupils can use to get out of one homework assignment and a "Pizza Party" for which researchers brought pizza to school for qualifying pupils.

Dehejia, Chao, and Mukhopadhyay (2016) test the long-term effects of non-monetary incentives (two pencils and an eraser) for attendance in nonformal schools in India. Fryer (2016), Levitt et al. (2016a), and Martorell et al. (2016) find no evidence that tangible non-monetary incentives crowd out intrinsic motivation: there is no or no clear impact on performance or attendance rates after the incentives have been removed. In Visaria et al. (2016), non-monetary incentives increase attendance rates while in place, but have heterogeneous long-run effects for students with high and low baseline attendance. Students with low baseline attendance decrease their attendance rate after the removal of the incentive and their performance in a test three months later is lower than if there had been no incentive at all. In contrast, students with high baseline attendance are not affected by the removal of the reward in the long-term.

In contrast to tangible non-monetary incentives, studies using granting rights and privileges as incentives have mainly relied on older students (14–21 years old). Most studies in this category incentivize students' behavior (e.g., test performance, attendance) with bonus points for the next exam or the course grade (Baumert & Demmrich, 2001; Bigoni et al., 2015; Chevalier et al., 2018; De Paola et al., 2015; Emerson & Mencken, 2011; Grove & Wasserman, 2006). We classify these incentives as high stakes since they directly influence students' final course grade or GPA. Besides bonus points, incentives in this category grant rights to students if certain academic performance and/or behavior requirements are fulfilled such as having the right to obtain a driver's license (Barua & Vidal-Fernandez, 2014), qualifying for a high-value event (Burgess et al., 2016), going off campus during the school day (Lichtman-Sadot, 2016), or participating in high school extra curricular sports (Vidal-Fernández, 2011).

Overall, granting rights incentives have positive effects on educational attainment. Barua and Vidal-Fernandez (2014) find that a "No Pass No Drive" law at the state level increases males' additional years of education by 0.064 years and their likelihood to graduate from high school by 1.5%, while the effects are not significant for girls. Lichtman-Sadot (2016) report a 0.1 standard deviation increase in test scores if a conditional open campus policy is in place compared to an unconditional policy. Vidal-Fernández (2011) finds a 2% points increase in the likelihood of graduation if student athletes are required to pass one additional course in order to be allowed to participate in school sports. Bonus points or assessment weighting are also effective to motivate students. Grove and Wasserman (2006) document an increase in students' exam performance by one-third to two-thirds of a letter grade if graded problem sets comprise 15% of the final grade, Chevalier et al. (2018) estimate the return to a 10% assessment weighting to be around 0.27 of a standard deviation in the final in-term examination grade, and Emerson and Mencken (2011) find that if homework counts toward the final course grade, students improve course-specific achievement measures, but do not perform better on standardized tests. Only Baumert and Demmrich (2001) do not find positive effects for students in grade 9 if a test counts toward the final course grade. One reason could be an age effect because students in their sample are much younger than students in the other studies using bonus points or assessment weighting (grade 9 vs. university students). Interestingly, the survey findings of Wagner and Riener (2015) indicate that bonus points are perceived as attractive by even younger children (grades 5 and 6) as well. Thus, it would be promising to test bonus points for the next exam among younger children as they are easy and costless to implement and potentially reduce the stress level of students while sitting for an exam.

To summarize, tangible non-monetary incentives have been mostly given to younger children with mixed results: they have been found to either increase or not to change students' motivation and performance. Nonmonetary incentives in the form of granting rights have been analyzed predominantly among (older) high school students, while bonus points and assessment weighting have been analyzed predominantly among university-students. Both types of incentives have typically produced positive results.

Non-monetary incentives for parents and teachers

The effects of non-monetary incentives for parents on students' educational attainment have been rarely. We are aware of only one study testing a social recognition reward.[7] Mayer, Kalil, Oreopoulos, and Gallegos (2018) equip parents of children who attend a subsidized preschool with an electronic tablet and a preloaded application with children's books. Parents are asked to read to their children and are incentivized to increase the time using the digital library by a "social recognition reward". Parents receive a private congratulatory message and a cartoon bear does a celebratory dance if parents meet their self-set goal. Further, all treated parents receive a message about who reads the most to their child.[8] Thus, this incentive can be categorized as a combination of a private and public (but anonymous) social recognition reward. At the same time, Mayer et al. (2018) also implement a *soft commitment device*—parents set a goal how much time to read to their children—and receive *reminders* to work toward their reading goal every weekday. These behavioral tools are simultaneously implemented with the recognition rewards and jointly increase the time parents spend reading to their children by one standard deviation compared to parents receiving "placebo" information only. Unfortunately, the experimental design does not allow to disentangle the effect of the social recognition incentive from the soft commitment device and the reminders.

Evidence on the effectiveness of non-monetary incentives for teachers is extremely scarce, despite the fact that in many institutional settings teachers are legally not allowed to accept financial incentives paid by third parties such that only non-monetary incentives could be applied. Studies on non-monetary teacher incentives exclusively report results of teacher surveys on the popularity of various incentives or propose potentially effective nonmonetary incentives, but do not empirically test their effectiveness. Two categories of non-monetary incentives that might be popular among teachers are *work avoidance* and *social recognition* incentives. For example, Jacobson and Kennedy (1992) report on deferred salary leave plans in Canada, this is, teachers are allowed to defer a portion of their salary each year to self-fund a leave of absence. In Kobakhidze (2010), teachers' proposals for non-monetary incentives include *mastery goal incentives* to teachers such as free textbooks, free or discounted professional development literature and training, free classroom materials, financing of extracurriculum activities (e.g., excursions), and classroom technologies (e.g., computers and projectors) as well as *social recognition* incentives such as "best teacher" or "teacher of the year" awards, greetings on special occasions (e.g., Teacher's Day), moral support

---

[7] There is a growing body of literature which does not use non-monetary incentives as per our definition but uses behaviorally informed interventions to get parents involved in their children's education. In particular, sending parents text messages with information about their children's performance and behavior in school seems to be a cost-effective and easy to implement way to enhance educational outcomes (Bergman, 2017; Bergman & Chan, 2017; Berlinski, Busso, Dinkelman, & Martinez, 2017; Cunha et al., 2017; Rogers & Feller, 2018).

[8] Each tablet had a unique number and parents received the message " ... *the parent with [tablet number! did the most reading with their child! Congratulations to that parent!"*

from school principals, oral praise and encouragement from the school administration, changes in societal attitudes toward teachers, raising the prestige of teachers, and organizing special events for teachers. Vaillant and Rossel (2012) discuss teachers' status and their public recognition as an important source of teacher motivation and present initiatives in Latin America that seek to raise the status and prestige of the teaching profession. These initiatives award innovative projects, outstanding teachers or classroom activities in a public ceremony which is covered by the most important media of the country and often combined with monetary incentives such as prizes. Vegas and Umansky (2005) and Chapman, Snyder, and Burchfield (1993) are two further studies that propose social recognition incentives to motivate teachers.

Despite many ideas on their design, there is a striking lack of knowledge concerning the effectiveness of non-monetary incentives for parents and teachers in raising students' educational attainment. In principle, we consider them an equally promising tool as non-monetary incentives for students and see a strong demand for future research.

Discussion and conclusion

In this chapter, we have focused on the design and effectiveness of monetary and non-monetary incentive schemes in education. Regarding monetary incentives, we report results on two design features which have received rather little attention to date: the sensitivity to cash size and the recipient of the reward. While increasing the cash size of the reward does not seem to impact educational outcomes of university students, there is evidence that younger and/or more disadvantaged students seem to respond stronger to higher monetary-incentives (Levitt et al., 2016a). Moreover, monetary incentives work equally well for students, parents, and teachers; this is, the recipient of a financial reward of a given size does not make a difference for its effect on students' educational outcomes. Aligning incentives by providing simultaneous monetary incentives to students, parents, and teachers tends to increase their effect sizes beyond those of individual incentives.

During recent years, non-monetary incentives to motivate students have received increasing attention due to their potential cost-effectiveness and higher acceptance among teachers and parents. With respect to nonmonetary incentives, we synthesize the existing literature by the type of incentive and shed light on students' valuation and selection of rewards. We propose to broadly differentiate between two categories of non-monetary incentives: (i) tangible incentives and (ii) granting rights and privileges. So far, tangible non-monetary incentives have been mainly applied in low stakes testing environments among younger students and have produced either no or positive impacts on educational outcomes. In contrast, incentives of the category granting rights and privileges have largely been tested among older students in high stakes environments. These types of incentives, among them bonus points for the next exam and assessment weighting, have been found to be effective in raising students' performance.

An integral part of non-monetary incentives to effectively raise educational attainment or modify students' behavior in class is their ability to induce value for their recipient, typically the students. The aforementioned studies provide first insights in identifying students' valuation for different types of non-monetary incentives. Future research on non-monetary incentives in education should expand this knowledge by reporting on which grounds researchers have chosen certain incentives, by offering students a choice among various incentives to learn which incentives students value most, and by documenting that more highly valued incentives are more effective. The ultimate aim should be to equip teachers with a broad set—a "toolbox"—of effective incentives tailored to the respective target group, taking into account students' age, gender, ability, intrinsic motivation, and family background, for example. As Levitt et al. (2016a) acknowledge, we also need a better understanding whether the same incentives offered on a regular basis maintain their motivational power and thus can be used to promote sustained effort provision, habit formation, learning, and educational attainment in the long run.

With the knowledge of a "toolbox" of effective incentives, teachers could possibly alternate the incentive scheme which might be more effective than using always the same incentive if rewards are paid repeatedly.

In the attempt to identify new and effective non-monetary incentives, "Induced Value Theory" (Smith, 1976) can give guidance in choosing incentives which are worth testing in the field. According to "Induced Value Theory", the experimenter achieves control over agents' characteristics if the incentive ("reward medium") satisfies three conditions (Friedman & Sunder, 1994): monotonicity, salience, and dominance. That is, incentives should be chosen such that (i) individuals prefer more of the reward medium to less, and do not become satiated (*monotonicity*), (ii) the reward depends on individuals' actions as defined by the institutional rules that the individual understands (*salience*), and (iii) changes in individuals' utility from the experiment come predominantly from the reward medium and other influences are negligible (*dominance*).[9]

While dominance is hard to fulfill in educational settings, researchers should seek for non-monetary incentives that satisfy salience and monotonicity. In particular, dominance may not be met if students are intrinsically motivated to perform well, effectively pressurized by their parents, and/or aware of the high returns to education. Additionally, students likely care about the rewards earned by their peers and experimental procedures cannot always be designed to make it impossible for students to learn about others' rewards. Moreover, dominance could be violated by experimenter demand effects that can potentially arise if researchers are present in the classroom to explain the experimental procedures.[10] In contrast, salience is usually fulfilled as the conditions to receive the reward can be clearly communicated: i.e., the receipt of incentives typically depends on measures of educational performance or educational inputs that are straightforward to understand for students. For many types of non-monetary incentives, it is less clear whether monotonicity is met or not, e.g., whether students become satiated after receiving the second or third trophy, certificate, or letter to the parents. Bonus points for the next exam clearly fulfill salience and monotonicity and the predominantly positive results of this incentive on students' performance indicate that they induce value to students. Another incentive for younger students which could satisfy salience and monotonicity, but has not yet been tested in studies that aim at raising educational attainment are golden toy coins.

[9] Friedman and Sunder (1994) give the following intuition for the three features: " ... the experimenter can freely choose any relationship between intrinsically worthless objects and the reward medium. As long as he can explain the relationship clearly to the subjects (salience) and subjects are motivated by the reward medium (monotonicity) and no other influences (dominance), then the experimenter can control subjects' characteristics to implement the chosen relationship in the laboratory."

[10] There is a trade-off between running the experiment by the researcher in order to maintain high levels of control over the experiment and delegating the administration of the experiment to teachers to maintain the natural class environment. An additional reason for delegating the experimental implementation to teachers is to decrease the role of experimenter demand effects in order to aim at satisfying the dominance condition.

Two recent papers provide evidence that golden toy coins induce value to elementary school children (Hermes et al., 2019; Schunk, Berger, Hermes, Winkel, & Fehr, 2017).

Acknowledgments

We thank Laura Breitkopf and Daniel Kamhofer for helpful comments on an earlier version of this chapter.

References

Ames, C. (1992). Classrooms: Goals, structures, and student motivation. *Journal of Educational Psychology, 84*(3), 261–271.

Angrist, J., & Krueger, A. (1991). Does compulsory school attendance affect schooling and earnings? *Quarterly Journal of Economics, 106*(4), 979–1014.

Avvisati, F., Gurgand, M., Guyon, N., & Maurin, E. (2014). Getting parents involved: A field experiment in deprived schools. *The Review of Economic Studies, 81*(1), 57–83.

Baird, S., Mcintosh, C., & Özler, B. (2011). Cash or condition? Evidence from a cash transfer experiment. *Quarterly Journal of Economics, 126*(4), 1709–1753.

Barrow, L., & Rouse, C. (2018). Financial incentives and educational investment: The impact of performance-based scholarships on student time use. *Education Finance and Policy, 13*(4), 419–448.

Barua, R., & Vidal-Fernandez, M. (2014). No Pass No drive: Education and allocation of time. *Journal of Human Capital, 8*(4), 399–431.

Baumert, J., & Demmrich, A. (2001). Test motivation in the assessment of student skills: The effects of incentives on motivation and performance. *European Journal of Psychology of Education, 16*(3), 441–462.

Behrman, J., Parker, S., Todd, P., & Wolpin, K. (2015). Aligning learning incentives of students and teachers: Results from a social experiment in Mexican high schools. *Journal of Political Economy, 123*(2), 325–364.

Bergman, P. (2017). *Parent-child information frictions and human capital investment: Evidence from a field experiment* (Unpublished manuscript).

Bergman, P., & Chan, E. (2017). *Leveraging parents: The impact of high-frequency information on student achievement* (Unpublished manuscript).

Berlinski, S., Busso, M., Dinkelman, T., & Martinez, C. (2017). *Reducing parent-school information gaps and improving education outcomes: Evidence from high frequency text messaging in Chile* (Unpublished Manuscript).

Berry, J. (2015). Child control in education decisions: An evaluation of targeted incentives to learn in India. *Journal of Human Resources, 50*(4), 1051–1080.

Bettinger, E., & Slonim, R. (2007). Patience among children. *Journal of Public Economics, 91*(l-2), 343–363.

Bigoni, M., Fort, M., Nardotto, M., & Reggiani, T. (2015). Cooperation or competition? A field experiment on non-monetary learning incentives. *The B.E. Journal of Economic Analysis & Policy, 15*(4), 1753–1792.

Black, S., Devereux, P., & Salvanes, K. (2008). Staying in the classroom and out of the maternity ward? The effect of compulsory schooling laws on teenage births. *The Economic Journal, 118*(530), 1025–1054.

Burgess, S., Metcalfe, R., & Sadoff, S. (2016). *Understanding the Response to financial and non-financial incentives in education: Field experimental evidence using high-stakes assessments*. Technical report, IZA Discussion Paper No. 10284.

Bursztyn, L., & Coffman, L. (2012). The schooling decision: Family preferences, intergenerational conflict, and moral hazard in the Brazilian Favelas. *Journal of Political Economy, 120*(3), 359–397.

Bursztyn, L., & Jensen, R. (2015). How does peer pressure affect educational investments? *Quarterly Journal of Economics, 130*(3), 1329–1367.

Chapman, D., Snyder, C., & Burchfield, S. (1993). Teacher incentives in the third world. *Teaching and Teacher Education, 9*(3), 301–316.

Chevalier, A., Dolton, P., & Lührmann, M. (2018). "Making it count": Incentives, student effort and performance. *Journal of the Royal Statistical Society: Series A, 181*, 323–349.

Cunha, F., & Heckman, J. (2007). The technology of skill formation. *The American Economic Review, 97*(2), 31–47.

Cunha, N., Lichand, G., Madeira, R., & Bettinger, E. (2017). *What is it about communicating with parents?* (Unpublished manuscript).

De Paola, M., Gioia, F., & Scoppa, V. (2015). Are females scared of competing with males? Results from a field experiment. *Economics of Education Review, 48*, 117–128.

De Paola, M., Scoppa, V., & Nisticô, R. (2012). Monetary incentives and student achievement in a depressed labor market: Results from a randomized experiment. *Journal of Human Capital, 6*(1), 56–85.

Emerson, T., & Mencken, K. (2011). Homework: To require or not? Online graded homework and student achievement. *Perspectives on Economic Education Research, 7*(1), 20–42.

Friedman, D., & Sunder, S. (1994). *Experimental methods: A primer for economists*. Cambridge University Press.

Fryer, R. (2011). Financial incentives and student achievement: Evidence from randomized trials. *Quarterly Journal of Economics, 126*(4), 1755–1798.

Fryer, R. (2016). Information, non-financial incentives, and student achievement: Evidence from a text messaging experiment. *Journal of Public Economics, 144*, 109–121.

Fryer, R., Devi, T., & Holden, R. (2017). *Vertical versus horizontal incentives in education: Evidence from randomized trials.* Technical report, National Bureau of Economic Research Working Paper 17752.

Gneezy, U., Meier, S., & Rey-Biel, P. (2011). When and why incentives (Don't) work to modify behavior. *The Journal of Economic Perspectives, 25*(4), 191–209.

Grove, W., & Wasserman, T. (2006). Incentives and student learning: A natural experiment with economics problem sets. *The American Economic Review, 96*(2), 447–452.

Guryan, J., Kim, J., & Park, K. (2016). Motivation and incentives in education: evidence from a summer reading experiment. *Economics of Education Review, 55*, 1–20.

Hanushek, E., & Wößmann, L. (2012). Do better schools lead to more growth? Cognitive skills, economic outcomes, and causation. *Journal of Economic Growth, 17*(4), 267–321.

Hermes, H., Hett, F., Mechtel, M., Schmidt, F., Schunk, D., & Wagner, V. (2019). Do children cooperate conditionally? Adapting the strategy method for first-graders. *Journal of Economic Behavior & Organization.* https://doi.org/10.1016/j.jebo.2018.12.032.

Jacobson, S., & Kennedy, S. (1992). Deferred salary leaves in education: a canadian alternative to reductions in the teaching work force. *Educational Evaluation and Policy Analysis, 14*(1), 83–87.

Jalava, N., Joensen, J., & Pellas, E. (2015). Grades and rank: impacts of non-financial incentives on test performance. *Journal of Economic Behavior & Organization, 115*, 161–196.

Kobakhidze, M. (2010). Teacher incentives and the future of merit-based pay in Georgia. *European Education, 42*(3), 68–89.

Leuven, E., Oosterbeek, H., & Klaauw, B. (2010). The effect of financial rewards on students' achievement: evidence from a randomized experiment. *Journal of the European Economic Association, 8*(6), 1243–1265.

Levitt, S., List, J., Neckermann, S., & Sadoff, S. (2016a). The behavioralist goes to school: leveraging behavioral economics to improve educational performance. *American Economic Journal: Economic Policy, 8*(4), 183–219.

Levitt, S., List, J., & Sadoff, S. (2016b). *The effect of performance-based incentives on educational achievement: Evidence from a randomized experiment.* Technical report, National Bureau of Economic Research Working Paper 22107.

Lichtman-Sadot, S. (2016). Improving academic performance through conditional benefits: open/closed campus policies in high school and student outcomes. *Economics of Education Review, 54*, 95–112.

List, J., Livingston, J., & Neckermann, S. (2018). Do financial incentives crowd out intrinsic motivation to perform on standardized tests? *Economics of Education Review, 66*, 125–136.

Lleras-Muney, A. (2005). The relationship between education and adult mortality in the United States. *The Review of Economic Studies, 72*(1), 189–221.

Lochner, L., & Moretti, E. (2004). The effect of education on crime: Evidence from prison inmates, arrests, and self-reports. *The American Economic Review, 94*(1), 155–189.

Martorell, P., Miller, T., Santibanez, L., & Augustine, C. (2016). Can incentives for parents and students change educational inputs? Experimental evidence from summer school. *Economics of Education Review, 50*, 113–126.

Mayer, S., Kalil, A., Oreopoulos, P., & Gallegos, S. (2018). Using behavioral insights to increase parental engagement: The parents and children together intervention. *Journal of Human Resources.* https://doi.org/10.3368/jhr.54.4.0617.8835R.

Milligan, K., Moretti, E., & Oreopoulos, P. (2004). Does education improve citizenship? Evidence from the United States and the United Kingdom. *Journal of Public Economics, 88*(9–10), 1667–1695.

Oreopoulos, P. (2007). Do dropouts drop out too soon? Wealth, health and happiness from compulsory schooling. *Journal of Public Economics, 91*(11), 2213–2229.

Robinson, C., Gallus, J., Lee, M., & Rogers, T. (2018). *The demotivating effect (and unintended message) of retrospective awards.* Faculty Reseach Working Paper Series RWP18-020. Harvard Kennedy School.

Rogers, T., & Feller, A. (2018). Reducing student absences at scale by targeting parents' misbeliefs. *Nature Human Behavior, 2*, 335–342.

Sadoff, S. (2014). The role of experimentation in education policy. *Oxford Review of Economic Policy, 30*(4), 597–620.

Schunk, D., Berger, E., Hermes, H., Winkel, K., & Fehr, E. (2017). *The KIDS-WIN-study: Design of a working memory training intervention in primary schools* (Unpublished manuscript).

Smith, V. (1976). Experimental economics: Induced value theory. *The American Economic Review, 66*(2), 274–279.

Springer, M., Rosenquist, B., & Swain, W. (2015). Monetary and nonmonetary student incentives for tutoring services: A randomized controlled trial. *Journal of Research on Educational Effectiveness, 8*(4), 453–474.

Vaillant, D., & Rossel, C. (2012). The recognition of effective teaching in Latin America: Awards to excellence. *Teacher Development, 16*(1), 89–110.

Vegas, E., & Umansky, I. (2005). *Improving teaching and learning through effective incentives: What can we learn from education reforms in Latin America?* Washington D.C.: World Bank.

Vidal-Fernández, M. (2011). The effect of minimum academic requirements to participate in sports on high school graduation. *The B.E. Journal of Economic Analysis & Policy, 11*(1).

Visaria, S., Dehejia, R., Chao, M., & Mukhopadhyay, A. (2016). Unintended consequences of rewards for student attendance: Results from a field experiment in indian classrooms. *Economics of Education Review, 54*, 173–184.

Wagner, V., & Riener, G. (2015). *Peers or parents? On non-monetary incentives in schools*. Technical report, DICE Discussion Paper 203.

de Walque, D., & Valente, C. (2018). *Incentivizing school attendance in the presence of parent-child information frictions*. Technical report, IZA Discussion Paper No. 11637.

Further reading

Allan, B. M., & Fryer, R. G. (2011). *The power and pitfalls of education incentives* (Policy Paper, Hamilton Project).

Angrist, J. D., Lang, D., & Oreopoulos, P. (2009). Incentives and services for college achievement: Evidence from a randomized trial. *American Economic Journal: Applied Economics, 1*(1), 1–29.

Angrist, J. D., & Lavy, L. (2009). The effects of high stakes high school achievement awards: Evidence from a randomized trial. *The American Economic Review, 99*(4), 1384–1414.

Angrist, J. D., Oreopoulos, P., & Williams, T. (2014). When opportunity knocks, who answers? New evidence on college achievement awards. *Journal of Human Resources, 49*(3), 572–610.

Bettinger, E. P. (2012). Paying to learn: the effect of financial incentives on elementary school test scores. *The Review of Economics and Statistics, 94*(3), 686–698.

Bettinger, E. P., Long, B. T., Oreopoulos, P., & Sanbonmatsu, L. (2012). The role of application assistance and information in college decisions: Results from the H&R Block Fafsa Experiment. *Quarterly Journal of Economics, 127*(3), 1205–1242.

Bishop, J. (2006). Drinking from the fountain of knowledge: Student incentive to study and learn - externalities, information problems and peer pressure. In E. A. Hanushek, & F. Welch (Eds.), *Handbook of the economics of education* (Vol. 2, pp. 909–944). Amsterdam: North Holland.

Damgaard, M. T., & Nielsen, H. S. (2018). Nudging in Education. *Economics of Education Review, 64*, 313–342.

Duflo, E., Dupas, P., & Kremer, M. (2015). School governance, teacher incentives, and pupil - teacher ratios: experimental evidence from Kenyan Primary Schools. *Journal of Public Economics, 123*, 92–110.

Fryer, R. G. (2013). Teacher incentives and student achievement: Evidence from New York City Public Schools. *Journal of Labor Economics, 31*(2), 373–427.

Fryer, R. G., Levitt, S. D., List, J., & Sadoff, S. (2012). *Enhancing the efficacy of teacher incentives through loss aversion: A field experiment*. Working Paper 18237. National Bureau of Economic Research.

Glewwe, P., Ilias, N., & Kremer, M. (2010). Teacher Incentives. *American Economic Journal: Applied Economics, 2*(3), 205–227.

Koch, A., Nafziger, J., & Nielsen, H. S. (2015). Behavioral Economics of Education. *Journal of Economic Behavior & Organization, 115*, 3–17.

Lavecchia, A. M., Liu, H., & Oreopoulos, P. (2015). Behavioral Economics of Education: Progress and Possibilities. In E. A. Hanushek, S. Machin, & L. Woessmann (Eds.), *Handbook of the economics of education* (Vol. 5, pp. 1–74). Amsterdam: North Holland.

Lavy, V. (2002). Evaluating the effect of teachers' group performance incentives on pupil achievement. *Journal of Political Economy, 110*(6), 1286–1317.

Neal, D. (2011). The design of performance pay in education. In E. A. Hanushek, S. Machin, & L. Woessmann (Eds.), *Handbook of the economics of education* (Vol. 4, pp. 495–550). Amsterdam: North Holland.

Oswald, Y., & Backes-Gellner, U. (2014). Learning for a bonus: How financial incentives interact with preferences. *Journal of Public Economics, 118*, 52–61.

Woessmann, L. (2011). Cross-country evidence on teacher performance pay. *Economics of Education Review, 30*(3), 404–418.

Educational mismatch in developing countries: A review of the existing evidence

H. Battu, K.A. Bender

University of Aberdeen, Aberdeen, Scotland

Introduction

Over the last thirty to forty years, many low and middle-income countries have invested heavily in their educational systems and have made tremendous strides with respect to the quantity of education with significant improvements in enrolments across primary, secondary and tertiary levels plus improvements in literacy rates (Glewwe & Muralidharan, 2016). Gross enrollment rates in low income countries have risen from around 46% in 1970 to around 100% in 2016. The equivalent rises at the secondary level are from 13 to 40% (UNESCO Institute for Statistics) with gross enrolments at the tertiary level rising from 12% in 1999 to 26% in 2013 (UNESCO Institute for Statistics).

Nevertheless, there has been some cynicism and disappointment surrounding the investment in human capital in developing countries. This is reflected in the titles of two seminal contributions from 2001, namely by Lant Pritchet ("Where Has all the Education Gone?) and William Easterly ("Educated for What"). Pritchet

(2001) identifies three issues: the poor institutional environment, the lack of labor demand to absorb the increased supply and the poor quality of education whereby increased years of schooling are not translated into increased human capital. Indeed, a number of studies have documented the poor quality of education especially at the school level, with low levels of educational learning, grade repetition, high drop-out rates, a lack of textbooks, low level of teacher's engagement and high absenteeism (Kremer, Brannen, & Glennerster, 2013; Murnane & Ganimian, 2014; World Bank, 2018). Easterly (2001; p. 84) takes a more macroeconomic approach and does not see increased education as resulting in increased GDP growth with the damning conclusion that, "Education is another magic formula that failed us on the quest for growth".

Here we focus on the capacity of labor markets in poor countries to absorb the increased supply of educated labor. The concern for many of these countries is with weak labor markets combined with low levels of job generation.

The Economics of Education, Second Edition
https://doi.org/10.1016/B978-0-12-815391-8.00020-3

In all of this, one has to recognise that labor markets of the developing world are quite distinct relative to those in the industrialised, developed countries. There is an absence of unemployment insurance, and so few individuals in developing countries can afford to be openly unemployed, the informal sector alongside self-employment and micro-firms are important sources of employment, there are low rates of employment amongst the working age population and there is relatively weak state regulation.

Underutilisation and underemployment of workers, then, is more important than unemployment and can take a variety of forms. This could mean working at fewer hours than desired or accepting jobs whose skills and educational requirements are below those attained. Where individuals have more education (skills) than required, this is referred to as overeducation (overskilling). These types of mismatch capture both the quantity and quality of jobs and as such represent a useful measure of underutilisation.[1]

Whilst in the developed countries there is a huge literature examining the mismatch between a worker's education and skills and that required in the workplace (Mehta, Felipe, Quising, & Camingue, 2011), there is little attention paid here to developing countries. Indeed, the various reviews by Hartog (2000), Leuven and Oosterbeek (2011), McGuinness (2006), Sloane (2003) make little or no mention of matching in low or middle-income labor markets. This stems principally from a lack of data in these countries on the education or skills required to perform or obtain a job (Mehta et al., 2011). Nevertheless, voices have long been raised about the capacity of labor markets in developing countries to absorb an increased supply of highly educated,

highly skilled labor. Mark Blaug in his classic study from 1973 wrote about education and employment in developing countries and the incapacity of the industrial sector to mop up the rising supply of educated labor. In particular, he identified graduates in India as accepting lower paid jobs that were incompatible with their educational qualifications.[2] More recently there has been an upsurge in interest reflected in three reports examining mismatch in developing countries (Handel, Valerio, & Sanchez Puerta, 2016; Kupets, 2015b; McGuinness, Redmond, & Bergin, 2017).

Given that labor markets in developed and developing economies are quite different, it is reasonable to ask whether the findings from the general mismatch and overeducation literature for high income countries also hold for low and middle-income countries? What are the outstanding gaps in our knowledge with respect to low and middle countries? Inevitably, we have to bear in mind two things when approaching these broad questions. First, there is considerable heterogeneity within and across developing countries. Mismatch in China is perhaps a very different beast to that of mismatch in Senegal and mismatch in urban China may be quite different from that in rural China. Second, whilst there are only a small number of published papers and reports looking at low and middle-income countries, it is still unrealistic to try to cover all countries. Instead we will be more focused and concentrate on a set of middle-income countries (the so-called, 'BRIC' countries of Brazil, Russia, India and China) and a representation of low-income countries.

In particular, we address what the literature has to say about the following sets of questions.

---

[1] More broadly others have looked at skill shortages and skill gaps.

[2] Education and skills mismatch especially amongst graduates may also be an important driver of protest, conflict and unrest in society (see Habibi & El-Hamidi, 2016 for Egypt) and may also be associated with increased migration and a brain drain.

First, is mismatch higher in less developed countries? Is this reflected in higher overeducation or higher undereducation? Does it matter whether we look at low or middle-income countries? Indeed, is undereducation more of a cause for concern in low-as opposed to middle income countries? Second, what are the causes of mismatch in developing countries and how do the specific characteristics of developing country labor markets impact upon match quality? In particular, what role does labor market segmentation and informality play? Is overeducation higher in the informal sector and to what extent are highly educated workers pushed into the informal sector? What is the relationship between educational quality and mismatch? Does better quality education (i.e. better skills) improve educational match quality? More fundamentally, why would there be overeducation in many of these countries when the level of educational attainment is still relatively low? Third, what are the consequences of mismatch in these countries in terms of wages, productivity, job satisfaction and also economic growth? Are the types of regularities that we see in the developed country context also evident within the developed countries? Finally, what can be done to reduce mismatch in developing countries and are there lessons (if any) to be learnt from the developed countries?

The paper has the following structure. Section Introduction offers an overview of the measurement issues in the matching literature and offers a brief summary of the main findings. Section Measurement issues focuses on the incidence of mismatch, Section The degree of mismatch on the determinants of mismatch, Section

Explanations for mismatch on the consequences and the penultimate section focuses on policy and also.

Measurement issues

Recent research has focused on several different ways of thinking about educational and skills mismatch, often driven by the data that are available. McGuinness, Pouliakas, and Redmond (2018) offer a deeper discussion of these issues particularly the advantages and disadvantages of each method, but here we give a brief overview of how the literature measures educational and skills mismatch.

In order to measure over- and undereducation, the key component is to what to compare a worker's education. There are three common ways to calculate this comparator. Some papers use an 'objective' measure by calculating the average, median or modal level of education of the occupation in which the worker is employed and then compares worker education levels with this average, median or mode (the so-called 'realized matches').[3] An alternative to this data driven methodology to determine the comparator group is to use an independent evaluation method (such as the SOC in the UK or DOT or O*NET in the US) that evaluates the skills and education necessary for a job. However, since this has to be done by external and independent evaluators, this information is not typically available to researchers. A final method relies on workers themselves to identify subjectively whether they have the education to do their job or not, particularly upon entry.

---

[3] Generally, the more detailed the occupation, the better the estimate for the average level of education in the occupation. However, unless the dataset is large, the ability to go to very disaggregated occupations is limited by data. In addition, because of the (sometimes large) variation in education in the occupations, there can be sizable variation around the average educational levels, typically leading researchers to look at deviations of at least one standard deviation above or below the mean in order to determine under- or overeducation, respectively.

While determining over- or undereducation has a longer history and broader coverage in the mismatch literature, there is a growing recognition that comparing the actual skills of workers and the required skills of jobs might be a better way of defining mismatch. Some research combines both education and skill mismatches to create a more 'genuine' (Chevalier, 2003; Mavromaras, Sloane, & Wei, 2012) measure of mismatch. However, the same requirement is needed to calculate skills mismatch as with educational mismatch — namely the comparator level of skills. This is made more difficult since skills can be changed after accumulating formal education. While it is possible to use skills dictionaries as mentioned above (CEDEFOP, 2015), most academic articles investigating skills mismatch use subjective data from workers.

These measures of mismatch are often referred to as measures of 'vertical' mismatch since they attempt to measure the amount or incidence of being over- or undereducated or over- or underskilled. Other measures of mismatch, however, focus not on the quantity of education or skills but whether there is a match in the field of study and the job. Such mismatches are called 'horizontal' in the sense that such workers may have the same level of education or skills, but in an area that is not a match for the job (Somers et al. forthcoming). As with vertical mismatch, this can be measured subjectively through worker self-assessment of whether his or her field of study matches the one required for the job, but there are objective measures as well by determining an average or modal field in an occupation or using a 'correspondence table' (Béduwé & Giret, 2011) that externally assigns a discipline to an occupation.[4]

General findings

As stated earlier the large majority of research on any of the kinds of mismatch described above has been done on developed countries. As seen in the review by McGuinness et al. (2018), there is a large variation in the rates of mismatch across countries, but also between different ways of measuring mismatch. However, in their Table 2 (Table 4) the average rate of overeducation (overskilling) across all countries showed that over 20% of workers were overeducated (over 25% were overskilled) for each of the three measures of vertical mismatch. Their Table 3 (Table 5) indicated a range of average rates of undereducation from 10 to 26% depending on the measure (just over 13% for underskilling). Finally, the rate of horizontal mismatch is just over 25% for the studies in Mavromaras, McGuinness, O'Leary, Sloane, and Wei (2013, Table 5) which is comparable to the rates found in Somers et al. (forthcoming).

These two survey articles also find consistent correlations with labor market outcomes such as wages and job satisfaction. Generally matched workers enjoy the highest earnings, although there can be a positive return to being overeducated (first found by Duncan & Hoffman, 1981). Estimates in McGuinness et al. (2018), indicate an average penalty of almost 14% for overeducation and nearly 8% for overskilling, which are relatively robust to controlling for individual heterogeneity (Mavromaras et al. 2013). Although results are not universally consistent, many papers also find a negative relationship between mismatch and job satisfaction.

[4] These measures examine mismatch from the worker's side, but there could be mismatches from the employer's side as well. Skills gaps and skills shortages (McGuinness & Ortiz, 2016; Weaver & Osterman, 2017) impact the ability for firms to find the skills they need.

The degree of mismatch

There has though been a recent upsurge in interest in examining mismatch in developing countries. The fact that educational attainment remains relatively low in developing countries means that overeducation may be seen as a somewhat contradictory phenomenon for these economies. One may argue that overeducation is more prevalent in labor markets where the average educational level of the workers is higher (i.e. developed countries). For developing countries, there seems to be two simultaneous phenomena: relatively low educational attainment resulting in undereducation married to overeducation amongst those who have decent education. Undereducation then may be a bigger issue in the poorest developing labor markets.

Rates of overeducation and undereducation

Brazil

Since the 1990s higher education in Brazil has expanded significantly and largely because of an expansion in private education. More generally, average years of schooling have increased significantly from 2004 to 2013 with the proportion of those aged 25–34 years old having higher education rising from around 8%–15% (da Silva Marioni, 2018). The general consensus seems to be that demand has not kept pace with supply. However, there has been relatively little research into mismatch in South American, generally, and Brazil, in particular. Leuven and Oosterbeek (2011) estimate that the percentage of overeducated workers in Latin America is on average 24% (with 21% undereducated). An early paper is Diaz and Machado (2008) who use 2000 Census data in Brazil and job evaluations of

required education to estimate a rate of overeducation of between 14 and 19% depending on the region, while the rate of undereducation was between 49 and 58%. Reis (2017), on the other hand, uses survey data for six large metropolitan areas in 2012 to estimate the incidence of over- and undereducation at 26 and 29%, respectively. Finally, da Silva Marioni (2018) using a job analysis measure find similar estimates to Reis (2017) with 25% overeducated and 26% undereducated.

Russia (and post-communist transition economies)

There is real paucity of research examining educational or skill mismatch in Russia. Kupets (2015a) in a comparison of a number of countries reports (Figure 3) that Russia at over 35% had the highest incidence of self-assessed overeducation compared to a number of EU and OECD countries, with undereducation in Russia standing at around 10%. There was some variation, however, using different types of realised matches with a modal-based comparator generating much smaller levels of overeducation. Shevchuk, Strebkov, and Davis (2015) examine free-lance IT workers in Russia using a question about educational match quality and find a very high level of mismatch of 57% for men and 64% for women, though this may be due to the specialised sample.

While there is little research specifically on Russia, there is a growing literature looking at Post-communist countries. Robert (2014) uses data on recent graduates from Hungary, Lithuania, Poland and Slovenia and uses both vertical and horizontal measures of mismatch to find rates of horizontal mismatch lower than rates of vertical mismatch except for in Poland in 2008/9. Hungary had the highest rate of vertical mismatch at 38.7%, while it was about a quarter of the workforce for Slovenia and Lithuania and 10.7% in Poland. Horizontal mismatch, on the other hand, was found to be much lower in Slovenia at 11.7%, and around 20% for the other three countries.[5] Kiersztyn (2013), using data for Poland, finds an increasing incidence of overeducation from 7.5% in 1988 to over 20% in 2003, where 10.7% are persistently overeducated. Kupets (2015a) examines subjective measures of over- and undereducation in urban areas of Armenia, Georgia, Macedonia and Ukraine and finds rates of overeducation of around 30% in Armenia, Georgia and Ukraine, but only 20% in Macedonia, while the rates of undereducation in each country are less than 10%. Using different data and a statistical based methodology, Kupets (2016) examines over- and undereducation in Ukraine from 2004 to 2013 to find that overeducation has remained relatively constant at around 20%, while the rate of undereducation has been falling from almost 20% to just under 10%. Myrsíkova (2016) looks at a number of ways to calculate mismatch in the Czech labor market, finding rates of overeducation of 6–7% using job evaluations, 14–19% for realised matches and subjective rates of overeducation of 25%. For the incidence of undereducation for these three methodologies, the rates are 22–26%, 12–17% and 15%, respectively.

India

As with Russia, there are not many papers examining mismatch in the Indian context. On the demand side, the performance of the Indian economy post the reforms of 1991 has been patchy with the shares of industrial and service sector output as a percentage of GDP increasing but with the informal sector still having significant shares of employment. On the supply side, illiteracy rates have fallen, the share of secondary educated workers has risen and the share of high

skilled workers has increased (Mukherjee & Paul, 2012). India also has a high and rising non-employment rate among the educated young (aged 18–29 years) alongside labor and skill shortages for industry (Banerjee & Chiplunkar, 2018).

Mukherjee and Paul (2012) focus on educational mismatch in Indian using an objective measure. They find overeducation rates of between 13 and 19% depending on occupation and find differences across religion and caste. Unni (2015) looks at the difference between worker education and the proportion of university graduates by occupation. For older cohorts who did not have much access to higher education, the rate of mismatch was around 20% (Table 2, for 'Low' and 'Non-graduate' occupations) while it was 24% for the younger cohort. Sharma and Sharma (2017) calculate over and undereducation by looking at average education in an occupation to find (Table III) a rate of overeducation of 19.2% and undereducation of 23.5%, though when there is overeducation it is 2.2 years on average when the difference in undereducation is only 1.6 years. Younger workers, males, urban workers, part time workers and those in larger firms are more likely to be overeducated.

China

China is interesting because of its huge expansion in educational attainment. Bai (2006) documents the increase in enrollment in higher education in China after 1999 going from an enrollment rate of 9.8%–19% in 2004. Yang (2018) reports that the enrollment rate continued to increase to over 26% by the late 2000s with over 14 million undergraduates enrolled and 1.7 million postgraduates enrolled in 2012. Unlike many other low- and middle-income countries, it has also had impressive rates of

---

[5] The average rates of mismatch were not reported in Robert (2014), but in personal communication with the authors.

economic growth. We would then expect a greater capacity to absorb the increased supply of educated labor. Has this turned out to be the case? Bai (2006) and Yang (2018) suggest that because of substantially higher unemployment rates among graduate's post reform, the increased capacity due to growth has not kept pace with the production of new graduates. More generally there are concerns about the quality of education provided (see Molnar & Koen, 2015).

Yue and Yang (2005) estimate the incidence of graduate overeducation to be around 20% where this rises with education and graduate undereducation at just over 17%. This is based on the self-report method using survey data funded by the Ministry of Education of China collected from 45 universities in China in 2003. Yang and Mayston (2012) report very similar estimates for the same time period and using the same data. The next two studies use the uses waves of the China Health and Nutrition Survey (CHNS) and construct a realised match measure using the mean and mode level of education. Ren and Miller (2012a) use seven waves of the CHNS and find a slightly higher incidence of overeducation at 27% with the percentage of correctly matched worker standing at 46%. These estimates are, though, for rural China with males having higher overeducation (37.5%) than females (24.9%). Yin (2016) use all eight waves of the CHNS and find that 18% of workers are overeducated and 20% are undereducated (using the mean level of education). The gender disparity in overeducation here is very small. Their mode measure gives an overeducation rate which is higher at 26% which is nevertheless dominated by undereducation at 30%. Male overeducation here is two percentage points higher than for females. A more recent study by Wu and Wang (2018), uses the World Bank's Skills Toward Employability and Productivity (STEP) dataset for 2012 and finds a higher incidence of overeducation at 34% with undereducation below 10%. Note that the STEP survey measure of mismatch is subjective and the survey itself was conducted in only one urban area in China namely Kunmin city, which is the capital of Yunnan Province.

Wu (2008) argues that in the state sector, monopolised industries and developed areas, the incidence of overeducation is higher than in enterprises, competitive industries and less developed areas. Market reforms and greater competition should then reduce overeducation.

Yang and Mayston (2012) also investigate the incidence of overeducation, which they claim stems from the hierarchical nature of the Chinese labor market. According to their results, PhD graduates are reported to have the highest rate of overeducation (42%), followed by those with a master level qualification (36%). College Diploma graduates are estimated to have the lowest incidence of overeducation (13%). In terms of subjects, Yang and Mayston (2012) point out that agriculture graduates have the highest incidence of overeducation (28%) and somewhat surprisingly Art graduates have the lowest overeducation rate in China (17%).

Much less is known about skills mismatch in China. One exception is Molnar et al. (2015) which uses subjective evaluations from workers regarding skills mismatch, finding that 31% of university graduates and 38% of vocational students report being mismatched due to skills. In particular, technical skills such as programming are highlighted as being the ones that have the biggest gaps between proficiency and demand by employers. In a variant on skills mismatch, Zhu (2014) examines subjective evaluations of how well matched a worker's educational discipline matches the one of the job. They emphasise how Chinese higher education differs from other countries, with a greater focus on providing general skills with a four-year degree structure. 27% of male graduates are mismatched compared to 30% for females. Graduates from 211 Universities (the top 100 top research universities in China) have lower mismatch as do graduates in medicine and workers in the information industry.

Mismatch for workers in the financial service industry is very high at 38.4%, and this is the highest of all industries.

Finally, there is one paper on mismatch for female graduates in Taiwan in the early 2000s by Tao and Hung (2014). They look at a combination of horizontal and vertical mismatch combining measures of over and undereducation with subjective measures of whether a worker's education is related to her job. No overall rate is given, but there is a lot of variation in mismatch for graduates that depends upon the ranking of the university, with better matches for graduates of higher ranked universities.

Low-income countries

There are also a handful of studies looking at mismatch in lower income countries. El-Hamidi (2009) estimates rates of over and undereducation in Egypt using the realised match method and compares 1998 to 2006 to find the male overeducation rate in the private sector to be actually falling from 43 to 11% while for women it fell from 29 to 17%. The rates of undereducation have gone in the opposite direction increasing for men from 8 to 31% and growing slightly for women from 16 to 18% (Table 2). The authors offer little in the way of explanation for these dramatic changes but do point to changes in the makeup of the Egyptian labor market and significant changes in the educational qualification of workers. David and Nordman (2017) examine mismatch among remainers and return migrants in Egypt and Tunisia using the realised match approach. The overall overeducation rate in Egypt is confirmed to be low at 11.4% with returnees having a rate of 10.7%. In Tunisia the overeducation is a little higher at 12.2%. Undereducation in both countries is higher at 16% for Egypt and 22% for Tunisia.

There are three studies that examine mismatch across a range of low and middle-income countries. Handel et al. (2016, Table 5.2) examine multiple forms of mismatch across 12 low- and middle-income countries. The mean overeducation rate across the countries is 34% but for the lowest income countries (e.g. Lao PDR, Ghana, Kenya, Vietnam and Sri Lanka), they estimate quite high rates of overeducation of 41, 40, 25, 70 and 46% respectively, while the rates of undereducation are 14, 13, 40, 4, and 10%, respectively. Kupets (2017) uses the ILO's School to Work Transition Survey (SWTS) for 34 low- and middle-income countries. Their sample only looks at the young (aged 15 to 29), and they present estimates using both subjective and objective measures. By contrast to Handel et al. (2016), under-qualification also tends to be much more widespread in Sub-Saharan Africa, Southern Asia and in low-income countries (where levels of informal employment are highest). Over-qualification tends to be more widespread in regions with lower levels of informal employment; this is true for Northern Africa, the Arab States, Europe and Central and Western Asia, as well as in middle-income countries (Table 2). Most countries facing an over-qualification mismatch 'have experienced rapid growth in enrollment to tertiary education and overall educational attainment of population' (Kupets, 2017, p. 13). McGuinness et al. (2018) using Labor Force Surveys (LFS) from 20 low- and middle- and high income countries calculate mismatch using the realised match approach. They find that on average, over-education is a larger issue in those countries compared to high-income countries. The greater mismatch the authors argue stems from the higher degrees of informality in these economies.

Herrera and Merceron (2013) examine under-education and mismatch and focus on sub-Saharan countries, including Benin, Burkina Faso, Cote d'Ivoire, Mali, Niger, Senegal, Tonga, and cities in Cameroon and the capital of Madagascar. An average rate of overeducation of 20% is found with undereducation ranging between 15 and 25% depending on the measure used (Herrera & Merceron, 2013, Table 2.1). These averages also hide wide disparities in both rates across countries, particularly in undereducation, which was nearly 50% in both Burkina Faso, Mali and Niger.

Chort (2017) offers a slightly different framework for examining mismatch. She looks at migrant workers from Senegal in four countries — two developed economies (France and Italy) and two developing economies (Mauritania and Cote d'Ivorie). She finds that the rate of mismatch to be greater in the developed economies although the rate of horizontal mismatch is similar. Vertical mismatch (overeducation) is found to be much higher in the developed economies (12.7 compared to 2.2%). Chort argues that these differences occur because of the imperfect transferability of skills across countries, though strong networks of immigrants as seen by the Senegalese in Mauritania and Cote d'Ivoire have a strong mitigating effect on overeducation rates. These results are consistent with Visintin, Tijdens, and van Klaveren (2015) who use data across 86 countries, finding that rates of overeducation are generally greater for migrants, but that these rates are dependent upon where the country of origin and the country of migration.

Moving to East Asia, there have been several studies examining Malaysia. Zakariya (2014, Table 4) looks at a 2007 sample of Malaysian workers finding that in Manufacturing and Business Support industries the rate of overeducation is 18.5 and 12.6% respectively and the rate of undereducation is substantially higher at 32.9 and 22.6%, respectively, with little difference by gender. In a later study (Zakariya, 2017, Table 2)[6] with a subjective mismatch measure for Malaysia, it is found that 24% are moderately mismatched while less 9% are severely mismatched — again with little difference by gender.

Explanations for mismatch

Introduction

A whole host of factors have been identified as generating mismatch including frictions (imperfect information or information asymmetry whereby the "right" workers/firms cannot find one another), business cycle effects (the unemployed may more readily compromise and take any job), life cycle effects (the young), work and family preferences (females, mothers with young children) where some choose to work in jobs for which they are overeducated since they offer compensating non-pecuniary advantages, discrimination (socio-economic status, ethnic minorities, immigrants). Other additional factors include failures in terms of education (education level, low achievement, "wrong" field of study, poor skills) and failures in terms of the job market (low employment rates, low investment, informality, low-quality jobs, low-skill equilibrium, self-employment) (Handel et al. 2016). Each of these factors is associated with varying degree of seriousness. Frictions and preferences would point to mismatch being transient whereas informality points the blame toward the demand side with low job creation which implies mismatch as being of a more longer-term nature.

Underlying these explanations are a variety of theories, many of which are motivated by and embedded in an understanding of labor markets in developed economies. One of the earliest (Thurow, 1975) relies on institutional theories of the labor force to suggest that internal labor markets make firms base pay on observable characteristics of workers and jobs rather than being determined by the quality of the match of worker and job. A later set of theories (Freeman, 1976) suggested that educational

---

[6] The paper also offers interesting results on the increased prevalence of on-the-job search by the severely mismatched, *ceteris paribus*, though the paper does not look at any other labor market outcomes such as wages.

mismatch was caused by the subsidisation of higher education, leading to an oversupply of highly educated workers. This clearly has a resonance in some of the low- and middle-income countries.

Another early theory of mismatch stems from search and information problems (Spence, 1973; Tsang, Rumberger, & Levin, 1991; Tsang & Levin, 1985). Since observing of productivity is costly and takes time (Habermalz, 2006), employers use education as a means of job-screening in labor markets with imperfect information. Similarly, workers use additional education as a signal to potential employers. Of course, these informational gaps may be more acute in low and middle-income countries perhaps generating higher overeducation. More specifically, with asymmetric information, workers have an incentive to invest in additional education so that the overeducated may be more likely to be hired causing overeducation to dominate undereducation. Mismatch can also be persistent over years, particularly if it is expensive for the worker to search for a new job with a better match or for the firm to search for a new worker. Mismatch, therefore, does not necessarily mean the same thing throughout the career (Battu, Belfield, & Sloane, 1999 for the UK and Bender & Heywood, 2009, 2016 for the US) where mismatch early in the career is mostly a function of frequent job changes due, in part, to the informational challenges mentioned previously. Mismatch later in the career, however, could be explained by rapidly changing human capital requirements, particularly where there is substantial job specific human capital or due to persistence effects from a bad match early in a career (Summerfield & Theodossiou, 2017).

Informality

At the heart of labor markets in low and middle-income countries is dualism and informality. Whilst there is considerable debate in the literature about measurement and definitions (Levy, 2008), the informal economy 'refers to all economic activities by workers and economic units that are — in law or in practice — not covered or insufficiently covered by formal arrangements' (ILO, 2015). A basic definition of informal employment then includes those not receiving social security benefits via employment (ILO, 2002). More broadly informal labor markets are seen as having a relative ease of entry, low labor productivity, labor regulations that are non-existent or unenforceable, missing social benefits and tax evasion. Jobs also tend to be heterogenous and precarious from selling lottery tickets, shoe shining to garbage recycling. The informal sector is also often associated with sprawl and urban slums, environmental damage and pollution and also employment in sweatshops (see Levy, 2008 and Meghir et al., 2015). Informal workers also tend to be younger, have fewer skills, and earn less than their counterparts in the formal sector (Maloney, 1999; Thomas, 1992).[7]

The consensus also seems to be that the informal sector is larger in Sub-Saharan Africa than in other parts of the developing world and accounts for around 60—80% of total non-agricultural employment. The informal sectors in the South and Southeast Asia are also

---

[7] There is also an increasing recognition that a simple dichotomy between informal and formal does not capture well labor markets in developing countries. Indeed, Fields (2007: 29) suggests four labor market states in low income countries, where "[workers] might be employed (be it in wage employment or self-employment) in … the formal sector, the free entry part of the urban informal sector, the upper tier of the urban informal sector, and rural agriculture [and they] might also be unemployed".

considered equally large but in Latin America and North Africa they seem to be smaller with estimates of between 30 and 60% of non-agricultural employment (ILO, 2002; Maloney & Núñez, 2004). In addition, nearly three-quarters of informal sector workers are self-employed and the share of the informal sector in output is much lower than the share in employment.

The informal sector is also seen as a depository for those who cannot access and obtain formal sector jobs. In the Harris and Todaro (1970) model, jobs are rationed in the formal sector due to labor market rigidities. As a result some workers are forced to accept informal sector jobs. Informal jobs then belong to a residual sector made up of workers queuing for a formal job.[8] A highly skilled worker who is unable to obtain a high-skill job in the formal sector, since formal sector jobs may be rationed, may accept a low-skill job in the informal sector for which she is overeducated. Those stuck in the informal sector, even if they are just as productive (or educated) as those in the formal sector, may then be less well rewarded. On the other hand, the informal sector employment may be seen as attractive to workers because their level of human capital does not match the requirements for performing formal jobs. Undereducation may then be the result and would be consistent with the relatively high rates of under-education seen in developing economies described above.

The evidence on the relationship between informality and overeducation is limited. Handel et al. (2016) examines overeducation across 12 low and middle-income countries using data from the STEP survey covering largely urban households. Overeducation is measured using a subjective measure comparing individuals' actual education with that required or necessary for their current job. They find an average overeducation rate of 36% and this dominates undereducation which stands at a lowly 12%. Informality seems to be driven by a lack of employment options with 40% of respondents indicating that they would be willing to take informal jobs with the main reason being that they had no other employment choices (Handel, 2017). Handel et al. (2016) also find that employment in the formal (public) sector is strongly associated with better matches but employment in the informal, formal private sectors and self-employment are associated with greater over-education. In addition, informality is negatively associated with undereducation; the higher is informality the lower is undereducation.

There are two Columbian micro studies testing the relationship between informality and overeducation. Herrera-Idárraga, López-Bazo, and Motellón (2012), using a statistical measure of mismatch (with the mean level of education across occupations), find that 15% of Columbian urban workers are overeducated. This is higher for formal workers (17%) relative to those employed in informal workers (11%). They hypothesise that in the presence of a large informal sector, educated workers who cannot find high skilled formal sector jobs accept an unskilled informal job for which they are overeducated. Upon controlling for the endogeneity of employment into formal and informal sector jobs, they find that while male informal sector workers are more likely to be overeducated, this is not evident for females. Overeducation

---

[8] There is a considerable literature that sees a more fluid setup with labor markets being more competitive (fully or weakly) with fewer or no barriers to mobility (see Heckman & Pagés, 2004; Maloney, 1999). Indeed, there may be significant job mobility across sectors and this could be in either direction (Maloney, 1999), workers may report being better off or no worse off by taking jobs in the informal sector (Meghir et al. 2015; Pratap & Quintin, 2006) and informal workers may have greater job satisfaction than formal workers with respect to job flexibility.

they argue may be caused in part by the desire of male workers to obtain a formal, protected job. Herrera-Idárraga, López-Bazo, and Motellón (2015) build on their earlier study and gauge whether the wage gap between the formal and informal sectors is related to the degree of mismatch across the two sectors. Does lower pay in the informal sector reflect the greater degree of overeducation there? They use the standard Duncan and Hoffman (1981) ORU wage specification controlling for endogeneity into employment. In line with the existing literature they find that the returns to overeducation are lower than the return to a required year of education and this is evident for both formal and informal sectors. Well matched workers in the formal sector earn around double what their equivalent earn in the informal sector and they also have higher returns than informal workers who are overeducated. The return to a year of overeducation is also found to higher in the formal sector than in the informal sector.

Quality of education

By quality of education, we refer to the variability of educational institutions and the educational system, which may be reflected in a lower quality and inappropriateness of accumulated skills. Al-Samarrai and Bennell (2007), focusing on Sub-Saharan Africa, argue that critical thinking and problem-solving skills are lacking for post-secondary education school leavers in many countries without strong educational systems. Chapman and Chien (2014) find that in 2011—12, only 16% and 14% of university instructors held doctoral degrees in China and in Vietnam, respectively. In addition, the countries may be producing graduates but they may be of the wrong type. For example, in China there are perhaps sufficient graduates in finance and management but not enough in the high technology sector and also in nursing (Ra, Chin, & Liu, 2015).

The relationship between various aspects of education quality and mismatch is not well investigated or understood. Handel et al. (2016) capture quality via literacy test scores for eight of the 12 STEP countries and ask whether having higher-level skills (i.e. higher performance on literacy tasks) aids workers in getting higher-level jobs given their education attainment and also whether the overeducated come from the lower end of the ability distribution (measured via test scores). Those with better ability (better reading test scores) would then obtain better jobs than their formal education alone would allow, resulting in greater undereducation as traditionally measured. On the other hand, those with lower ability would struggle and end up in lower level jobs given their (higher) education and have higher probability of being overeducated. Their empirical findings are inconclusive and indicate that test scores play no role with respect to undereducation but those with greater ability do have a lower probability of being overeducated, albeit the effects are small relative to other factors such as informality, years of tertiary education and field of study. In addition, they argue that tertiary educated overeducated workers are not drawn exclusively from the lowest achievers.

University quality and its impact on mismatch are not that well explored in the literature. Obviously there are a range of potential measures of quality here including grades of the students upon commencement of their education, the official rank or reputation of the institution, public versus private institutions, the resources expended on education, the skills and training of instructors and official research and teaching quality evaluations. We would expect that having a degree from a high-quality university significantly reduces the probability of being overeducated. One interesting possibility is that low-ability individuals use education to signal an ability trait that they do not hold and enter into low quality universities in order to send a distorted signal of their productivity

(Ordine & Rose, 2009). Ordine and Rose (2009) present some supporting empirical estimates showing that the extent of overeducation depends on education quality. Using a sample of Italian graduates and after controlling for pre-college ability, academic fields, households' and jobs' characteristics, they find that having a degree from research-oriented universities significantly reduces the probability of being overeducated. Boccanfuso et al. (2015) examine the effects of an education reform in Senegal which endeavored to increase the quality of higher education and using a difference-in-difference approach find that this boosted employment and the probability of obtaining a better job implying a reduction in mismatch.

Again, there is limited evidence on the effects of university quality on mismatch in low- or middle-income countries. Most of the research here focuses on primary and secondary schools and on the effects on poor quality education on general achievement and labor market outcomes (Behrman, Ross, & Sabot, 2008; Hanushek, 2009; Hanushek, Lavy, & Hitomi, 2008). Nevertheless, Yamada, Lavado, and Martinez (2015) using Peruvian data find that education quality (i.e. lower quality universities) is a key determinant of the probability of being overeducated. Li, Morgan, and Ding (2008) for China also place significant emphasis on the quality of Chinese higher education and argue that graduates from institutions with a good reputation have a greater probabilities of obtaining employment but also a higher salary upon employment.

What about the role of type of education and whether the accumulated education is general, specific and more vocational? In the developed country literature, overeducation tends to lower for those who studied health related, engineering, technical or science degrees and higher for those in arts and humanities (Dolton & Vignoles, 2000; Robst, 2007). The argument here is that these provide students with occupation-specific skills which reduces the likelihood that graduates search for jobs out with their own field

(Wolbers, 2003). Nevertheless, more recent analysis points to a greater fragility amongst science and engineering graduates, with greater technological change associated with rapidly changing skill requirements reducing any immunity to mismatch (Bender & Heywood, 2011). The evidence in the low- and middle-income countries is scant but generally in line what we see elsewhere. A study by Zhu (2014) focusing on China presents some interesting findings. Using a subjective measure of mismatch (whether their job is unrelated to their major), graduates in medicine have the lowest mismatch at less than 7% whereas graduates in history and philosophy have mismatch rates of 50%. In terms of industry, they find that workers in the information industry are least likely to be mismatched and workers in the financial service industry of rates of over 38% (the highest among all industries in the study).

Other factors

Aside from examining the effects of informality, Handel et al. (2016) also find that strong predictors of overeducation include educational level and years of tertiary education plus public versus private sector employment. As such these findings are line with the developed economies literature. The role of the informal economy is again found to be important with both informal self-employed and employed workers more likely to be overeducated.

Chua and Chun (2016) use the STEP survey to examine what drives mismatch in six Asian countries focusing on urban areas. Their research is one of the few that examines the impact of search frictions on mismatch. Search frictions are defined as capturing credit constraints and high search costs. The argument is that these perhaps push low-income workers to compromise and take jobs which involve mismatch. Using self-reported data on difficulty in finding vacancies, in navigating the job application process and certifying educational qualifications as proxies for increased frictions as well as the quality of match, their empirical analysis is supportive since such constraints for those with lower socioeconomic status pushes them to enter less desirable informal sector jobs rather than accept unemployment. Those who remain unemployed in developing countries are perhaps those who can afford to keep searching for a job that is better matched.

Mukherjee and Paul (2012) take a more unique tack by examining the relationship between educational mismatch and cultural and religious identity in India. Though there is some research in high income countries examining mismatch across ethnicity and migrant status, the literature in the low and middle countries is sparse. Their argument is that particular community groups are more likely to be discriminated against and their networks are perhaps a relative hindrance, so there may be an incentive to obtain additional education as a means of compensation. They find support this in that being Muslim and being from a lower caste is associated with higher probability of being overeducated.[9]

Consequences of mismatch

The overeducated typically have lower earnings and productivity, lower job satisfaction and greater job mobility although it not evident that the latter necessarily improves match quality. Here we ask whether these general findings hold for low- and middle-income countries.

Brazil

Again-there is little research on the earnings penalties in South America or Brazil. Leuven

and Oosterbeek (2011) find that the wage penalty is important: while the wage returns per year of education for an individual properly educated for the job that he/she has is 7.5%, for overeducated workers the wage returns of the "surplus" years is only 4.1%, a penalty of over 3%. Reis (2017) finds a penalty of around 6% for the overeducated (compared to those having the required education) and a penalty of over 26% for the undereducated, though he estimates that controlling for fixed effects reduces that penalty significantly to about 1% and 3% for the over- and undereducated respectively. Diaz and Machado (2008) find an overeducation penalty of about 4% and an undereducation penalty of about 26% - with men and women having very similar penalties. Reis and Machado (2016) find that those with a close match of training and required training have an earnings advantage of over 10% compared to those whose training is not at all related to their graduate job. This falls to a 2% advantage for those who have a partial match, showing that any mismatch is detrimental to earnings. A very recent contribution by da Silva Marioni (2018) uses panel data for Brazil and controls for individual heterogeneity. The key findings are that overeducated individuals earn significantly less and undereducated individuals earn significantly more than those who hold a well-matched job. Incorporating individual fixed effects reduces the loss to overeducation to less than 4% and the gains from undereducation to just over 4%.

Russia and post-communist countries

Only a subset of the papers above estimate penalties for mismatch in Russia or post-communist countries. Lamo and Messina (2010) in their study on Estonia estimate an

---

[9] Using an objective measure of overeducation, they find rates of overeducation of between 13 and 19% with the highest rates being for blue collar and traditional jobs mainly in the informal sector. On the other hand, undereducation is found to be higher for sales, managerial and administrative workers.

overeducation penalty of between 24 and 27% for women, but a somewhat smaller penalty of 18—24% for men. On the other hand, Mysikova (2016) finds an overeducation penalty of 4—8% while the undereducation penalty was 9—17% in Czechoslovakia. Finally, in an admittedly quite selected sample of free-lance IT professionals in Russia, Shevchuk et al. (2015) found a 23% penalty for subjectively identifying as mismatched for men, while the penalty was 19% for women, though it is considerably higher at nearly 40% for women with childminding responsibilities.

India

Only Sharma and Sharma (2017) examine earnings penalties from mismatch in India. They find (Table VIII) that there is between a 9—11% penalty for overeducation (with the higher penalty found when endogeneity is controlled for) and between a 14—18% penalty for undereducation.

China

Ren and Miller (2012b) find that the return to overeducation for both males and females is around 7.1% percent and this is only slightly lower than the 5.83% return for females. Interestingly, for males, this is higher than the return to required years of education (5.3%), but for females, the return is lower than the return for required education (13.6%). Wu and Wang (2018) estimate that for those with tertiary degrees, there is at least a 20% penalty for overeducation in OLS models (Table 5) although treatment effects from endogeneity corrected results push this to over 30% penalty (Table 7). Yang and Mayston (2012) also report a negative effect of mismatch on earnings. Yin (2016), on the other hand finds that the wage penalty for overeducation declines (or even disappears) when controlling for unobserved heterogeneity.

Zhu (2014) finds that while OLS estimates of the effect of field of discipline mismatch is around -6%, this declines dramatically when using a nonparametric estimation method to -1.3%. Tao and Hung (2014, Table 3) in their study of Taiwanese women find a strong relationship with better matches generating higher returns with the best matched having a 14% premium over those who are overeducated and not in a job in a related field to their education. Undereducation also generates a premium of about 13% compared to that same overeducated group.

Low-income countries

For Egypt, El-Hamidi (2009, Table 5), interestingly, has found results counter to most of the literature with a positive premium paid to the overeducated and sometimes the undereducated, compared to the adequately educated. For Sub-Saharan Africa, Herrera and Merceron (2013, Table 2.3) estimate a wage premium for the undereducated of around 18% and a wage penalty of about 9% for the overeducated with some variation by gender — with men having a higher undereducation premium and a larger overeducation penalty, though they show that the overeducated do have an advantage in job security (op. cit. Table 2.5). Zakariya (2014, Table 5) shows that in Malaysia the penalty for overeducation is around 10% while there is between an 8—11% premium for undereducation with slightly larger effects in Manufacturing than in Business Services (Table 7).

Handel's (2017) analysis of STEP data found that 'over-education is associated with a large wage penalty in ten of twelve' STEP countries; the average pay penalty among self-employed workers in the STEP sample was 23%. Kupets' (2017) analysis of the ILO's school-to-work transition surveys found that over qualification is associated with lower wages, job dissatisfaction and an increased willingness to change jobs.

The literature on developed economies show that wages of overeducated workers are higher than wages for well-matched workers doing the same job, but returns to the years of schooling beyond the required level are lower (albeit still positive). The overeducated also earn less than those who have the same level of education but have a job that matches their education. Undereducated workers earn less than the well-matched employees in the same job, but more than workers with the same educational level and a job that matches their education (Groeneveld and Hartog, 2004; Hartog, 2000; Rubb, 2003).

According to McGuiness and co-authors, the penalty in low and middle income countries from overeducation is higher than that found in developed countries. (McGuinness et al., 2017, p. 24). This is line with the idea that those who cannot obtain a match in the formal sector end up compromising in the informal sector and thereby are underutilised and receive pay penalty.

Overeducation, job satisfaction and economic growth

The effect of overeducation on economic growth is not well researched. There is an old literature that focuses on the effects of overeducation in particular industries or firms. Overeducated individuals are found to be less satisfied with their job than adequately educated workers with a similar educational background (Allen & van der Velden, 2001; Hartog, 2000). The overeducated may be likely to engage in job-search (Wald, 2005) and behave in a disruptive manner in the workplace (Tsang and Levin (1985). Again the evidence from outside the developed countries is quite limited. Kupets' (2017) analysis of the ILO's school-to-work transition surveys for low- and middle-income countries, found that overeducation is associated with job dissatisfaction and an increased willingness to change jobs. Yin (2015) in an interesting study using Chinese data finds that the overeducated tend to

have higher job satisfaction than those who are well matched and those who are undereducated. This holds with respect to general job satisfaction but also with respect to satisfaction with workload, working conditions, and relationships with colleagues. Taking a job which is not commensurate with one's education may offer compensating benefits, though this seems to be an exception rather than the rule in this literature.

The potential effects on job satisfaction as well the impacts via informality, quality of education, insufficient graduates in technology and science all could mean that increased investment in education is not necessarily reflected in increased economic growth. Whilst there is a huge literature examining the effects of human capital on growth, the effects of overeducation on economic growth is not well studied. There is a recent study by Sam (2018) that examines the impact of graduate overeducation on economic growth across thirty-eight developing countries. A job analysis measure is employed and unobserved heterogeneity between countries and the endogeneity of overeducation is accounted for. He finds that a higher rate of overeducated graduates reduces GDP growth per capita especially over the medium-term (five years) and when the endogeneity of overeducation is accounted for.

Policy, conclusions and reflection

The evidence on mismatch in developing countries is small, is scattered across countries and is subject to a series of measurement problems due to a lack of the right kinds of data. Care then needs to be taken in interpreting any findings. For example, higher overeducation may reflect the lower quality of education in the poorer economies where indviduals years of education may be inflated due to repeat years etc. Nevertheless, we find that there are a number of patterns found in the small, but growing literature. First, most developing countries experience relatively high rates of overeducation/overskilling, though there is wide variation in the rates. Rates of undereducation/underskilling are generally lower than for more developed countries, though, again, there is wide variability. Second, there are differences across genders in the rates of mismatch, though whether these stem from differences in educational or job opportunities is an underdeveloped research area. Third, wage penalties seem to be in line with the extant literature on mismatch. Finally, the reasons for mismatch are very different in developing countries, compared to developed countries. Lack of established strongly institutionalised education systems and labor market informality are much more important factors for the countries reviewed here than in the literature in more economically developed countries.

Overeducation clearly means different things in different country contexts so that offering policy prescriptions, whilst possible, is really geared toward the general. On top of this, most policy focuses on educational attainment, skills shortages and skills gaps and says little or nothing about overeducation or overskilling. This is evident for both developing and developing countries and this despite the significant amount of research especially in developed countries on mismatch. This literature seems to have made little real impact on policy. In a developing country context and given the nascent research in this area this, is even more evident.

One obvious policy is that developing countries should focus on improving the quality of their education system and institutions from the primary to the tertiary level so that students will graduate with the actual skills that correspond to their educational level. There is also merit in strengthening the links between the higher education sector and the labor market by increasing the vocational content of programmes. Governments could also reduce the information gaps between employers and workers through improved systems of job matching and reducing search costs for both workers and firms. Improving rates of educational attainment at both basic and intermediate levels would also be sensible interventions. More fundamentally, there needs to be greater attention to the demand side boosting labor demand via continued growth of per capita GDP (Sharma & Sharma, 2017) and improving the rates of formal employment. Whilst fears about jobless growth are perhaps overplayed there is definitely a need to boost growth to absorb the increased supply of educated labor. High rates of self-employment plus high degrees of informality suggest that good jobs that utilise existing workforce skills are in short supply. Weak investment, unattractive business conditions and low levels of overall economic activity play a role. Boosting local consumption may not be enough as local consumption is hindered by low local wages. These do not require high skills. Instead a greater attention to openness and exports would a key way to boost the demand for higher skills. This is easier to say than deliver given the current atmosphere surrounding protectionism within the developed countries. Weak job creation, whilst central, may be endogenous and reflect the poor skills base. Furthermore, reducing informal employment is simply not feasible so that policy needs to focus on the quality of employment in the informal sector.

References

Al-Samarrai, S., & Bennell, P. (2007). Where has all the education gone in sub-saharan Africa? Employment and other outcomes among secondary school and university leavers. *Journal of Development Studies, 43*, 1270–1300. https://doi.org/10.1080/00220380701526592.

Allen, J., & van der Velden, R. (2001). Education mismatches versus skill mismatches. *Oxford Economic Papers, 53*, 434–452. https://doi.org/10.1093/oep/53.3.434.

Bai, L. (2006). "Graduate unemployment: Dilemmas and challenges in China's move to mass higher education. *The China Quarterly, 185*, 128–144. https://doi.org/10.1017/S0305741006000087.

Banerjee, A., & Chiplunkar, G. (2018). *How important are matching frictions in the labour market? Experimental &*

non-experimental evidence from a large Indian firm. PEDL Research Paper.

Battu, H., Belfield, C. R., & Sloane, P. J. (1999). Over eduation among graduates: A cohort view. *Education Economics, 7*, 21–38. https://doi.org/10.1080/09645299900000002.

Béduwé, C., & Giret, J.-F. (2011). Mismatch of vocational graduates: What penalty on French labour market? *Journal of Vocational Behavior, 78*, 68–79. https://doi.org/10.1016/j.jvb.2010.09.003.

Behrman, J. R., Ross, D., & Sabot, R. (2008). Improving quality versus increasing the quantity of schooling: Estimates of rates of return from rural Pakistan. *Journal of Development Economics, 85*(1–2), 94–104.

Bender, K. A., & Heywood, J. S. (2009). Educational mismatch among Ph.D.s: Determinants and consequences. In R. B. Freeman, & D. F. Goroff (Eds.), *Science and engineering Careers in the United States: An Analysis of Markets and employment* (pp. 229–255). Chicago, IL: University of Chicago Press and National Bureau of Economic Research.

Bender, K. A., & Heywood, J. S. (2011). Educational mismatch and the careers of scientists. *Education Economics, 19*, 253–274. https://doi.org/10.1080/09645292.2011.577555.

Bender, K. A., & Heywood, J. S. (2016). Educational mismatch and retirement. *Education Economics, 25*, 347–365. https://doi.org/10.1080/09645292.2016.1234586.

CEDEFOP. (2015). *Skills, qualifications and jobs in the EU: The making of a perfect match?: Evidence from cedefop's european skills and jobs survey.* Cedefop Reference Series 103. Luxembourg: Publications Office of the European Union.

Chapman, D., & Chien, C.-L. (2014). *Higher education in Asia: Expanding out, expanding up. "* Montreal: UNESCO Institute for Statistics.

Chevalier, A. (2003). Measuring over-education. *Economica, 70*, 509–531. https://doi.org/10.1111/ecca.2003.70.issue-279.

Chort, I. (2017). Migrant network and immigrants' occupational mismatch. *Journal of Development Studies, 53*, 1806–1821. https://doi.org/10.1080/00220388.2016.1219344.

Chua, K., & Chun, N. (2016). *"In search of a better match: Qualification mismatches in developing Asia."* Asian Development Bank. Economics Working Paper No. 476.

David, A., & Nordman, C. J. (2017). Education mismatch and return migration in Egypt and Tunisia. *Espace Populations Sociétés, 2017*(1). https://doi.org/10.4000/eps.7110.

Diaz, M. D. M., & Machado, L. (2008). Overeducation e Undereducation no Brasil: Incidencia e Retornos. (Overeducation and Undereducation in Brazil: Incidence and Returns. With English summary. *Estudos Economicos, 38*, 431–460. https://doi.org/10.1590/S0101-41612008000300001.

Dolton, P., & Vignoles, A. (2000). The incidence and effects of overeducation in the U.K. Graduate labour market. *Economics of Education Review, 19*, 179–198. https://doi.org/10.1016/S0272-7757(97)00036-8.

Duncan, G. J., & Hoffman, S. D. (1981). The incidence and wage effects of overeducation. *Economics of Education Review, 1*, 75–86. https://doi.org/10.1016/0272-7757(81)90028-5.

Easterly, W. (2001). *The elusive quest for growth: Economists' adventures and misadventures in the tropics.* Cambridge, MA: MIT Press.

El-Hamidi, F. (2009). *"Education—Occupation mismatch and the effect on wages of Egyptian workers".* ERF Working Paper, March, No. 474 (Cairo).

Freeman, R. B. (1976). *The overeducated American.* New York: Academic Press.

Glewwe, P., & Muralidharan, K. (2016). Improving school education outcomes in developing countries: Evidence, knowledge gaps, and policy implications. In E. Hanushek, S. Machin, & L. Woessmann (Eds.), *Handbook of the economics of education* (Vol. 5). North Holland/Elsevier.

Groeneveld, S., & Hartog, J. (2004). Overeducation, wages and promotions within the firm. *Labour Economics, 11*, 701–714.

Habermalz, S. (2006). More detail on the pattern of returns to educational signals. *Southern Economic Journal, 73*, 125–135.

Habibi, N., & El-Hamidi, F. (2016). *Why are Egyptian youth burning their university diplomas? The overeducation crisis in Egypt.* Crown Centre for Middle Eastern Studies. Middle East Brief, No. 102.

Handel, M. (2017). *"Predictors and consequences of mismatch in developing countries: results from the World Bank STEP survey."* Geneva: ILO.

Handel, M. J., Valerio, A., & Sanchez Puerta, M. L. (2016). *Accounting for mismatch in low- and middle-income countries: Measurement, magnitudes, and explanations.* Washington DC: World Bank Group.

Hanushek, E. A. (2009). School policy: Implications of recent research for human capital investments in South Asia and other developing countries. *Education Economics, 17*, 291–313. https://doi.org/10.1080/09645290903142585.

Hanushek, E. A., Lavy, V., & Hitomi, K. (2008). Do students care about school quality? Determinants of dropout behavior in developing countries. *Journal of Human Capital, 2*, 68–105. https://doi.org/10.1086/529446.

Harris, J. R., & Todaro, M. P. (1970). Migration, unemployment and development: A two-sector analysis. *American Economic Review, 60*, 126–142.

Hartog, J. (2000). Over-education and earnings: Where are we, where should we go? *Economics of Education Review,*

19, 131–147. https://doi.org/10.1016/S0272-7757(99)00050-3.

Heckman, J., & Pagés, C. (2004). *Law and employment: Lessons from Latin America and the caribbean*. University of Chicago Press for the National Bureau of Economic Research.

Herrera-Idárraga, P., López-Bazo, E., & Motellón, E. (2012). *Informality and overeducation in the labor market of a developing country*. XREAP Working Papers 20/2012. Barcelona: Xarxa de Referència en Economia Aplicada.

Herrera-Idárraga, P., López-Bazo, E., & Motellón, E. (2015). Double penalty in returns to education: Informality and educational mismatch in the Colombian labour market. *Journal of Development Studies, 51*, 1683–1701. https://doi.org/10.1080/00220388.2015.1041516.

Herrera, J., & Merceron, S. (2013). Underemployment and job mismatch in sub-saharan Africa. In *Urban labor Markets in sub-saharan Africa, a copublication of the agence Francaise de developpement and the World Bank. Africa development forum* (pp. 83–107). Washington, D.C.: World Bank.

International Labour Office. (2015). *The transition from the informal to the formal economy*. Report V(1).International Labour Conference, 104th Session, 2015. Geneva: ILO.

International Labour Organization. (2002). *Men and women in the informal economy*. Geneva: International Labour Office.

Kiersztyn, A. (2013). Stuck in a mismatch? The persistence of overeducation during twenty years of the postcommunist transition in Poland. *Economics of Education Review, 32*, 78–91. https://doi.org/10.1016/j.econedurev.2012.09.009.

Kremer, M., Brannen, C., & Glennerster, R. (2013). The challenge of education and learning in the developing world. *Science, 340*, 297–300. https://doi.org/10.1126/science.1235350.

Kupets, O. (2015a). *Education in transition and job mismatch: Evidence from the skills survey in non-EU transition economies*. Kier Discussion Paper Series, Kyoto Institute of Economic Research.

Kupets, O. (2015b). Skill mismatch and overeducation in transition economies. *IZA World of Labor, 224*. https://doi.org/10.15185/izawol.224.

Kupets, O. (2016). Education-job mismatch in Ukraine: Too many people with tertiary education or too many jobs for low-skilled? *Journal of Comparative Economics, 44*, 125–147. https://doi.org/10.1016/j.jce.2015.10.005.

Kupets, O. (2017). *Educational mismatch among young workers in low- and middle-income countries: Evidence from 34 school to work transitions surveys in 2012–2015*. Geneva: ILO.

Lamo, A., & Messina, J. (2010). Formal education, mismatch and wages after transition: Assessing the impact of unobserved heterogeneity using matching estimators. *Economics of Education Review, 29*, 1086–1099. https://doi.org/10.1016/j.econedurev.2010.06.002.

Leuven, E., & Oosterbeek, H. (2011). Overeducation and mismatch in the labor market.. In E. A. Hanushek, S. Machin, & L. Woessmann (Eds.), *Handbook of the economics of education* (Vol. 4, pp. 283–326) Amsterdam: Elsevier Science.

Levy, S. (2008). *Good intentions, bad outcomes*. Washington, D.C: Brookings Institution Press.

Li, F., Morgan, W., & Ding, X. (2008). The expansion of higher education, employment and over-education in China. *International Journal of Educational Development, 28*, 687–697. https://doi.org/10.1016/j.ijedudev.2007.10.002.

Maloney, W. F. (1999). Does informality imply segmentation in urban labor markets? Evidence from sectoral transitions in Mexico. *World Bank Economic Review, 13*, 275–302. https://doi.org/10.1093/wber/13.2.275.

Maloney, W. F., & Núñez, J. (2004). Measuring the impact of minimum wages: Evidence from Latin America. In J. J. Heckman, & C. Pagés (Eds.), *Law and employment: Lessons from Latin America and the Caribbean* (pp. 109–130). Chicago, IL: University of Chicago Press.

Mavromaras, K., McGuinness, S., O'Leary, N., Sloane, P., & Wei, Z. (2013). Job mismatches and labour market outcomes: Panel evidence on university graduates. *Economic Record, 89*, 382–395. https://doi.org/10.1111/1475-4932.12054.

Mavromaras, K., Sloane, P., & Wei, Z. (2012). The role of education pathways in the relationship between job mismatch, wages and job satisfaction: A panel estimation approach. *Education Economics, 203*, 303–321. https://doi.org/10.1080/09645292.2012.672556.

McGuinness, S. (2006). Overeducation in the labour market. *Journal of Economic Surveys, 20*, 387–418. https://doi.org/10.1111/joes.2006.20.issue-3.

McGuinness, S., & Ortiz, L. (2016). Skill gaps in the workplace: Measurement, determinants and impacts. *Industrial Relations Journal, 47*, 253–278. https://doi.org/10.1111/irj.12136.

McGuinness, S., Pouliakas, K., & Redmond, P. (2018). Skills mismatch: Concepts, measurements and policy approaches. *Journal of Economic Surveys, 32*, 985–1015. https://doi.org/10.1111/joes.12254.

McGuinness, S., Redmond, P., & Bergin, A. (2017). *Educational mismatch in low and middle income countries*. Geneva: ILO.

Meghir, C., Narita, R., & Robin, J.-M. (2015). Wages and Informality in Developing Countries. *American Economic Review, 105*(4), 1509–1546. https://doi.org/10.1257/aer.20121110.

Mehta, A., Felipe, J., Quising, P., & Camingue, S. (2011). Overeducation in developing economies: How can we test for it, and what does it mean? *Economics of Education Review, 30*, 1334–1347. https://doi.org/10.1016/j.econedurev.2011.06.004.

Molnar, M., & Koen, V. (2015). *Providing the right skills to all in China: From "made in China" to "created in China.* OECD Working paper 1219.

Mukherjee, A., & Paul, S. (2012). Community identity and skill mismatch: A study on Indian labour market. In *The annual conference on economic growth and development, New Delhi.*

Murnane, R. J., & Ganimian, A. J. (2014). *Improving educational outcomes in developing countries: Lessons from rigorous evaluations.* Working Paper 20284. Cambridge, MA: National Bureau of Economic Research.

Ordine, P., & Rose, G. (2009). Overeducation and instructional quality: A theoretical model and some facts. *Journal of Human Capital, 3*, 73–105. https://doi.org/10.1086/599836.

Pratap, S., & Quintin, E. (2006). Are labor markets segmented in developing countries? A semiparametric approach. *European Economic Review, 50*, 1817–1841. https://doi.org/10.1016/j.euroecorev.2005.06.004 1700.

Pritchet, L. (2001). Where has all the education gone? *The World Bank Economic Review, 15*, 367–391. https://doi.org/10.1093/wber/15.3.367.

Ra, S., Chin, B., & Liu, A. (2015). *Challenges and opportunities for skills development in Asia: Changing supply, demand, and mismatches.* Manila: Asian Development Bank.

Reis, M. C. (2017). Educational mismatch and labor earnings in Brazil. *International Journal of Manpower, 38*(2), 180–197. https://doi.org/10.1108/IJM-02-2016-0030.

Reis, M. C., & Machado, D. C. (2016). "Uma Analise dos Rendimentos do Trabalho entre Individuos com Ensino Superior no Brasil. (An Analysis of the Labor Earnings among Workers with Tertiary Education in Brazil. With English summary.)" Economia Aplicada/Brazilian. *Journal of Applied Economics, 20*, 415–437.

Ren, W., & Miller, P. W. (2012a). Changes over time in the return to education in urban China: Conventional and ORU estimates. *China Economic Review, 23*, 154–169. https://doi.org/10.1016/j.chieco.2011.08.008.

Ren, W., & Miller, P. W. (2012b). Gender differentials in the payoff to schooling in rural China. *The Journal of Development Studies, 48*, 133–150. https://doi.org/10.1080/00220388.2011.561326.

Robert, P. (2014). Job mismatch in early career of graduates under post-communism. *International Journal of Manpower, 35*, 500–518. https://doi.org/10.1108/IJM-05-2013-0113.

Robst, J. (2007). Education and job match: The relatedness of college major and work. *Economics of Education Review, 26*, 397–407. https://doi.org/10.1016/j.econedurev.2006.08.003.

Rubb, S. (2003). Overeducation in the labor market: A comment and Re-analysis of a meta-analysis. *Economics of Education Review, 22*, 621–629. https://doi.org/10.1016/S0272-7757(02)00077-8.

Sam, V. (2018). *Overeducation among graduates in developing countries: What impact on economic growth?.* MPRA Paper No 87674. University of Munich.

Sharma, S., & Sharma, P. (2017). Educational mismatch and its impact on earnings: Evidence from Indian labour market. *International Journal of Social Economics, 44*, 1778–1795. https://doi.org/10.1108/IJSE-05-2016-0134.

Shevchuk, A., Strebkov, D., & Davis, S. N. (2015). Educational mismatch, gender, and satisfaction in self-employment: The case of Russian-language internet freelancers. *Research in Social Stratification and Mobility, 40*, 16–28. https://doi.org/10.1016/j.rssm.2015.02.004.

da Silva Marioni. (2018). *Overeducation in the labour market: Evidence from Brazil.* RES Conference.

Sloane, P. J. (2003). Much ado about nothing? What does the overeducation literature really tell us?". In F. Buchel, A. de Grip, & A. Mertens (Eds.), *Overeducation in Europe: Current Issues in Theory and policy* (pp. 11–48). Cheltenham: Edward Elgar.

Somers, M. A., Cabus, S. J., Groot, W., & Maassen van den Brink, H. (2018). Horizontal mismatch between employment and field of education: Evidence from a systematic literature review. *Journal of Economic Surveys.* https://doi.org/10.1111/joes.12271.

Spence, M. (1973). Job market signalling. *Quarterly Journal of Economics, 87*, 355–374.

Summerfield, F., & Theodossiou, I. (2017). The effects of macroeconomic conditions at graduation on overeducation. *Economic Inquiry, 55*, 1370–1387. https://doi.org/10.1111/ecin.12446.

Tao, H.-L., & Hung, C.-Y. (2014). Vertical and horizontal educational mismatches of female graduates in taiwan. *Asian Economic Journal, 28*, 181–199. https://doi.org/10.1111/asej.12032.

Thomas, J. (1992). *Informal economic activity, London school of economics handbooks in economics.* London: London School of Economics.

Thurow, L. C. (1975). *Generating inequality: Mechanisms of distribution in the U.S. Economy.* New York: Basic Books, Inc.

Tsang, M. C., & Levin, H. M. (1985). The economics of overeducation. *Economics of Education Review, 4*, 93–104. https://doi.org/10.1016/0272-7757(85)90051-2.

Tsang, M. C., Rumberger, R. W., & Levin, H. M. (1991). The impact of surplus schooling on worker productivity. *Industrial Relations: A Journal of Economy and Society, 30*, 209–228. https://doi.org/10.1111/j.1468-232X.1991.tb00786.x.

Unni, J. (2015). Skill gaps and employability: Higher education in India. *Journal of Development Policy and Practice, 1*, 18–34. https://doi.org/10.1177/0000000315612310.

Visintin, S., Tijdens, K., & van Klaveren, M. (2015). Skill mismatch among migrant workers: Evidence from a large multi-country dataset. *IZA Journal of Migration, 4*, 1–34. https://doi.org/10.1186/s40176-015-0040-0.

Wald, S. (2005). The impact of overqualication on job search. *International Journal of Manpower, 26*, 140–156. https://doi.org/10.1108/01437720510597649.

Weaver, A., & Osterman, P. (2017). Skill demands and mismatch in U.S. Manufacturing. *Industrial and Labor Relations Review, 70*, 275–307. https://doi.org/10.1177/0019793916660067.

Wolbers, M. H. J. (2003). Job mismatches and their labour-market effects among school-leavers in Europe. *European Sociological Review, 19*, 249–266. https://doi.org/10.1093/esr/19.3.249.

World Bank. (2018). *World development report 2018: Learning to realize education's promise.*

Wu, W. (2008). The impact of overeducation on earnings in China. *Frontiers of Education in China, 3*, 123–136. https://doi.org/10.1007/s11516-008-0008-4.

Wu, N., & Wang, Q. (2018). Wage penalty of overeducation: New micro-evidence from China. *China Economic Review, 50*, 206–217. https://doi.org/10.1016/j.chieco.2018.04.006.

Yamada, G., Lavado, P., & Martinez, J. J. (2015). *An unfulfilled promise? Higher education quality and professional underemployment in Peru.* IZA Discussion Paper, 9591. Bonn: IZA.

Yang, L. (2018). Higher education expansion and post-college unemployment: Understanding the roles of fields of study in China. *International Journal of Educational Development, 62*, 62–74. https://doi.org/10.1016/j.ijedudev.2018.02.009.

Yang, J., & Mayston, D. (2012). Impact of overeducation on wages in China. *Chinese Economy, 45*(2), 65–89. https://doi.org/10.2753/CES1097-1475450204.

Yin, L. (2015). *Educational mismatch, skill mismatch and job satisfaction.* University of Sheffield, Mimeo.

Yin, L. (2016). *Overeducation in the Chinese labour market.* Ph.D. thesis. University of Sheffield.

Yue, C., & Yang, J. (2005). Overeducation or undereducation: Some evidence form Chinese graduates. In *Proceedings of the Chinese economics association 2005 conference paper.*

Zakariya, Z. (2014). Wage effect of over-education and mismatch in Malaysia: A random effect approach. *Jurnal Ekonomi Malaysia, 48*, 3–17.

Zakariya, Z. (2017). Job mismatch and on-the-job search behavior among university graduates in Malaysia. *Asian Economic Journal, 31*, 355–379. https://doi.org/10.1111/asej.12135.

Zhu, R. (2014). The impact of major-job mismatch on college graduates' early career earnings: Evidence from China. *Education Economics, 22*, 511–528. https://doi.org/10.1080/09645292.2012.659009.

Peer effects in education: recent empirical evidence

Alfredo R. Paloyo

University of Wollongong, RWI - Leibniz-Institut fur Wirtschaftsforschung, Forschungsinstitut zur Zukunft der Arbeit (IZA), ARC Center of Excellence for Children and Families over the Life Course (ARC LCC), Global Labor Organization (GLO), Wollongong, NSW, Australia

Introduction

Research on peer effects in education has a rich history in economics.[1] Generally, peer effects may arise whenever economic agents interact within a group or a network,[2] but we are particularly interested in the education context because the existence of peer effects therein creates another lever for policymakers to adjust when attempting to improve academic outcomes. If externalities arise from group characteristics or behavior—that is, if peer effects exist—then group composition itself becomes a potential policy instrument.

Consider a typical education production function (Hanushek, 1979), where an outcome could be, say, final marks. We may posit that the outcome is determined by educational inputs, such as innate cognitive and noncognitive skills, nutritional status, teacher ability, school resources, and the quality of the home environment. Evidence of peer effects would suggest that we ought to include classroom, school, and neighborhood compositions as additional inputs in the production function as well. To the extent that parents and school principals, for example, are able to adjust the composition of these various reference groups, researchers who deliberately or inadvertently ignore peer effects are painting an incomplete picture of what determines final marks.

The existence of peer effects has important practical implications in the education space. For instance, in a number of countries, students

---

[1] The Equality of Education Opportunity Study—otherwize known as the Coleman Report (Coleman, Campbell-HobsonMcPartland, WoodWeinfeld, & York, 1966)—is arguably among the earliest to provide some structure to the idea that peers matter. It is widely cited and likely induced many researchers and policymakers to invest resources into studying this field.

[2] Thus, a more inclusive term would be "social-interaction effects" instead of merely "peer effects", but I use these terms interchangeably when there is no risk of confusion or dilution of meaning.

The Economics of Education, Second Edition
https://doi.org/10.1016/B978-0-12-815391-8.00021-5

are segregated into different schools on the basis of ability (a practice known as tracking, streaming, or phasing). A notable example is Germany, where most children are segregated into three separate school tracks.[3] In many schools worldwide, classes are grouped according to ability to minimize the difference between the weakest and strongest students in one classroom. This is a consequence of the belief that teaching is more effective if students comprising the class are relatively more homogeneous.[4] In both cases—whether one is contemplating school tracking or ability grouping—peer composition is directly manipulated.[5] This naturally raises the question of whether the resulting mix of students is optimal or if one can rearrange students to improve outcomes we typically care about.[6]

In this chapter, I survey the recent empirical evidence on peer effects in education. I take off from the earlier panoptic surveys of Vigdor and Ludwig (2010), Epple and Romano (2011), Sacerdote (2011), and—from a social-networks perspective—Jackson (2011), so empirical contributions which are already discussed in these earlier surveys are not extensively covered

here. Although the articles I review are limited to the economics literature, I acknowledge that allied social scientists have made and continue to make substantial contributions to the evidence base as well.[7] The survey is limited only for tractability and focus.

Earlier evidence discussed in the surveys mentioned above uncovered rather mixed results.[8] At the university level, peer effects are somewhat modest if not nonexistent for academic performance even if the social impacts (such as on binge drinking) are stronger. Impacts at earlier schooling stages (primary and secondary) are less definitive, with about half of the studies finding no impact and the rest showing that there is either a modest or even strong impact on test scores. As pointed out by Vigdor and Ludwig (2010) and emphasized more recently by Angrist (2014), estimates from studies with exogenous (i.e., experimental) variation in peer quality are typically less in magnitude than non-experimental estimates.

Recent empirical evidence presented here does not mitigate the ambiguity in previous results. However, there is a clear path to move

---

[3] In increasing levels of ability, most students are put on any of the following tracks: *Hauptschule, Realschule,* and *Gymnasium.* There are other school types, too, such as the *Gesamtschule,* or the *Stadtteilschule* in Hamburg and the *Sekundarschule* in Berlin, with the latter two being created after the formal abolition of the *Realschulen* in the two states following reforms in their respective school systems.

[4] One can argue that school tracking or ability-based sorting within schools may exacerbate existing inequalities. A small difference in achievement between two students early in their life courses may be amplified after sorting due to the varied experiences between separate but homogeneous groups. See, e.g., Gorard and Siddiqui (2018), who note that stratification and the resulting "clustering of relative advantage is potentially dangerous for society."

[5] Other policies that alter student composition—whether directly or indirectly—include, among others, racial desegregation, the operation of single-sex or coeducational schools, and the use of private-school vouchers. As one can surmise, peer effects cast a wide net in terms of policy relevance.

[6] Two studies discussed below—Carrell, Sacerdote and West (2013) and Booij, Leuven and Oosterbeek (2017)— do precisely that: the authors assigned students into peer groups that were designed to maximize their performance.

[7] Sociologists—typically from a social-networks perspective—have also intensively studied the issue, perhaps even earlier than economists. As examples, see Lerman (1967), Barnes (1969), and Booth and Babchuk (1969). Statisticians have naturally applied their techniques to this area as well. As Graham [2015, p. 482] notes, "The analysis of networks has always been a multidisciplinary endeavor. Economists are relative latecomers to this project."

[8] See, in particular, Table 4.2 in Sacerdote (2011) and Table 1 in Sacerdote (2014). The range of estimates is quite wide.

forward, especially as new datasets are created which explicitly map social networks, including those within classrooms, schools, and neighborhoods. Advances in estimation strategies, especially from network economics, are bringing new insights into the literature. Future work on this topic could clarify contexts in which one may expect peer effects to manifest, how large these spillovers are, which factors amplify or mitigate the impacts, and whether nonlinearities and heterogeneities can be exploited for optimal network design, all while accounting for endogenous margins of adjustment available to the various relevant economic agents.

Recent empirical evidence

The economics literature on peer effects in education is extremely active, reflecting the importance that researchers and policymakers attach to the issue. Since 2012 to the present, over three dozen papers were published on the topic of peer effects in education in economics journals alone, with the majority making an empirical contribution.[9] The student samples range from primary schools to universities, covering a variety of outcomes such as test scores in different subjects, college enrollment, and longer-term characteristics (e.g., occupational choice and earnings). Countries range from the US, Germany, Brazil, and China, among others. The identification of peer effects rests on a diverse set of estimation strategies, including regression-discontinuity designs, instrumental variables, fixed effects, and random assignment.[10]

The estimation strategy is relevant because network formation is endogenous (Jackson, 2005; Sacerdote, 2014).[11] This presents problems in the identification of peer effects. For example, "homophily"—a feature of networks where individuals who are similar in some or another dimension are grouped together (McPherson, Smith-Lovin, & Cook, 2001)—may result in the overestimation of the peer effect. If we observe a particular student with high-ability classmates to be peforming well academically, to what extent can we attribute this outcome to her peers rather than to some unobserved characteristic that she and her classmates share, such as teacher quality? In the absence of explicit random assignment, the answer comes with great difficulty and necessarily with some untestable but maintained assumption.

Deliberate random assignment

A number of recent papers capitalized on explicit random assignment. Three studies generated exogenous variations in peer quality via direct, experimental manipulation. In Carrell, Sacerdote and West (2013), the authors randomly assigned half of the freshmen at the US Air Force Academy (USAFA) to peer groups that were designed to benefit the low-ability students. Oosterbeek and van Ewijk (2014) and Booij, Leuven and Oosterbeek (2017) deliberately varied peer characteristics of Economics and Business undergraduate students at the University of Amsterdam.

Carrell, Sacerdote and West (2013) used insights from Bhattacharya (2009), who

[9] A Google Scholar search of "peer effects in education" actually turns up 793 results as of 26 March 2019. An equivalent search on EconLit returns 496 results.

[10] Details of these various strategies are beyond the scope of this survey, but the interested reader can get acquainted with them with reference to Imbens and Wooldridge (2009).

[11] Cicala, Fryer and Spenkuch (2018) couches this process in a Roy (1951)-type self-selection model where individuals select their peers based on comparative advantage. See also Graham (2016) and Graham (2017) from a networks perspective.

demonstrated that the optimal peer assignment can be solved through mathematical programming. The first stage of the experiment involved generating pre-treatment data by randomly assigning USAFA students into different peer groups (squadrons). Estimates of nonlinear peer effects were then obtained, and these informed the constrained optimization problem, which was to find the mix of students across and within squadrons that would maximize the achievement of the lowest-ability incoming freshmen students.

Contrary to expectations, Carrell, Sacerdote and West (2013) found that the students whose outcomes they intended to improve performed significantly worse. In particular, assigning the lowest-ability students into a squadron that would have presumably maximized their performance instead reduced their GPA by - 0.061.[12] Middle-ability students actually peformed better by 0.082. The authors attributed this negative result among lowest-ability students to behavioral adjustments: the target population, it turned out, selected low-ability study partners and low-ability friends.[13] Homophily strikes again.

Booij, Leuven and Oosterbeek (2017) deployed an experiment in the Netherlands that is similar to Carrell, Sacerdote and West (2013). The more recent study is superior in having a broader support in peer quality—that is, it has a wider distribution of peer ability by experimental design. That said, despite a significant difference in contexts (USAFA vs. University of Amsterdam), Booij, Leuven and Oosterbeek (2017) obtained qualitatively similar results. In particular, low-ability students performed worse than expectations following experimental

variation that was designed ex *ante* to maximize their performance. Like Carrell, Sacerdote and West (2013) in the US, the authors of the Dutch study attribute the effects to endogenous behavioral changes that the experiment induced.

Oosterbeek and van Ewijk (2014) looked at the impact of the share of females in the classroom on the achievements of males and females on dropout rates, absenteeism, and subject-specific performance. The authors conclude that the sex composition of the peer group only marginally influences the outcome variables within the subgroup of males. Interestingly, males end up doing worse in math-intensive subjects when there are more females—who, in the sample, perform better at math than males—in the group.

Two recent studies used the well-known Project STAR (Student-Teacher Achievement Ratio) experiment in Tennessee, US, which was originally designed as an experiment on the impact of class size on student achievement (Word, Johnston, Bain, Fulton, Zaharias, Achilles, Lintz, Folger and Breda, 1990). Since class assignment was randomized, peer composition is exogenous to the outcome of interest. Sojourner (2013) used lagged peer academic achievement (measured in kindergarten) and found that it has a sizable positive impact on own achievement at the end of first grade. Bietenbeck, forthcoming estimated the impact of exposure to grade repeaters on longer-term outcomes. He found that having at least one retained classmate reduced performance in math at the end of kindergarten (this effect dissipates), improved noncognitive skills, and increased the likelihoods of graduating from high school and taking a college entrance exam.

[12] The grade point average (GPA) in the US goes from 0 to 4, with 4 being the best grade. The negative overall estimate is shown to be driven by males, with an estimated effect of -0.094 while the corresponding estimate for female students was not statistically significant (although positive).

[13] These behavioral responses that magnify or mitigate the impact are called "equilibrium effects" by Pop- Eleches and Urquiola (2013).

In the School of Business and Economics of Maastricht University in the Netherlands, the assignment of students and teachers to classes is essentially randomized. Feld and Zölitz (2017) used this fact to demonstrate that, on average, students benefit from the presence of better peers. Instead of teachers or students adjusting their behavior, the authors' analysis of course evaluations suggest that peer effects in this case seem to come from better class interaction. The evidence is suggestive, not definitive, since the course-evaluation survey is voluntary and self-completed. The authors showed that high-achieving students are more likely to complete the survey.

Many studies in the peer effects literature are concerned with either school-level or classroom-level peer effects. What makes Hong and Lee (2017) extremely rare is that the authors estimated peer effects within subclassroom groups. For identification, the authors leveraged the "fixed-seat system" in Sogang University in Korea, where students are given seat assignments that they follow throughout the semester. They showed that students are especially affected by their seatmates, but classmates that are farther away become less relevant.[14] This implies that evidence of peer effects using the whole set of class- or schoolmates may be understating the true peer effect because of a peculiar type of measurement error where irrelevant peers are included—a point previously made by Ammermueller and Pischke (2009) and Angrist (2014), among others, in the peer-effects literature, but also by Jackson (2014) in the networks literature.

Finally, Angrist et al. (2016) exploited the fact that oversubscribed charter schools[15] in Massachusetts allocate places via a lottery. Using data from Boston, the authors estimated the impact of going to charter schools on a number of scholastic outcomes. They showed that students from charter schools improved performance in the state's school exit exam and the likelihood of qualifying for a state-sponsored scholarship. Charter-school attendance also improved SAT scores and other measures related to the Advanced Placement exams; it also shifted students from two-to four-year institutions, which is presumably a better outcome.

Charter schools have superior characteristics relative to other public schools in Boston (e.g., the student-teacher ratio is lower), and the pool of applicants for charter schools is also academically better (Angrist, Cohodes, Dynarski, Pathak and Walters, 2016). Students from charter schools, for instance, score better in the English and Math components of the Massachusetts Comprehensive Assessment System. Since a number of factors are better in charter schools apart from peer quality, it is impossible to conclude from this study that peer effects are what drives the estimated positive impacts. However, one can view the evidence as suggesting that better peers—in conjunction with other school inputs—may improve certain academic outcomes that we ought to care about.

Regression-discontinuity design

When deliberate random assignment is not available, researchers have used quasi-experimental exogenous variations generated by discontinuities. In two studies (Pop-Eleches & Urquiola, 2013; Vardardottir, 2013), the authors identified peer effects from the

---

[14] The First Law of Geography is that "everything is related to everything else, but near things are more related than distant things" (Tobler, 1970, p. 236).

[15] Charter schools, as contemplated in the US, are autonomous public schools in the sense that they operate independently of the typical state school system. They receive public funds, but operate under a contract or "charter" with some other agency.

discontinuity in the probability of being assigned to high-ability groups in secondary school based on some measure of ability crossing a threshold level. Billings, Deming and Rockoff (2014) used students in the same neighborhood but lived on opposite sides of a school boundary after it was redrawn, which resulted in an increase in race-based school segregation, and thus a change in the race composition of schoolmates. Finally, Dustmann, Puhani and Schönberg (2017) used a discontinuity in the school-starting age based on the date of birth.[16] The idea is that older students in a cohort peform better relative to younger cohort members, and this increases the likelihood of the former to enter higher-ability secondary schools.

Pop-Eleches and Urquiola (2013) estimated the impact of going to a better secondary school using administrative data covering the entirety of Romania. In their case, they use peer ability as a proxy for the quality of the school. The discontinuity in the probability of going to a better school arises because a student's ability to choose which secondary school to go to depends on whether a composite score based on her primary school GPA and her performance in a national test crosses a known threshold. The authors' outcome variable of interest is the student's performance in a baccalaureate exam.[17] Being in a school with better peers raises performance in this high-stakes exam by 0.02 to 0.10 standard deviation.

As in Carrell, Sacerdote and West (2013), Pop-Eleches and Urquiola (2013) also investigated the behavioral responses or equilibrium effects that were generated after having been assigned to a particular school or peer group. In this case, they showed that better teachers were also assigned to the higher-achieving students, parental effort declined, and students who scored just above the cutoff had worse self-perceptions relative to their peers. The latter two effects concerning parents and students, however, dissipated over time.[18]

Using data from post-compulsory schooling in Iceland, Vardardottir (2013) showed that being assigned to a high-ability class improves academic achievement as measured by end-of-first-year grade and Spring Session exam results, which increased by 0.47 and 0.32 standard deviation, respectively. The discontinuity exploited here involves a cutoff based on academic performance in the 10th grade. Students who score better than the cutoff are assigned into high-ability classes in this particular commercial college (upper secondary or senior high school) while the rest are distributed to constitute the remaining sections.

In Fall 2002, the district of Charlotte-Mecklenburg Schools (CMS) in the US was ordered by the North Carolina State Supreme Court to stop race-based busing that was originally intended to desegrate schools. In response, CMS switched to a school-choice plan that was based

---

[16] This approach—essentially using the date of birth as an instrument for some endogenous variable—is well-known in the economics literature. See, e.g., Angrist and Krueger (1991) and McEwan and Shapiro (2008).

[17] Students must pass the exam to enter university, and the grade is used as part of the admissions criteria (Pop-Eleches & Urquiola, 2013).

[18] In a structural model estimated using data from the Early Childhood Longitudinal Study, Fu and Mehta (2015) showed that ignoring behavioral effort adjustments would lead to an overestimation of the peer effects. Using data from the Progress in International Reading Literacy Study (PIRLS) and the National Educational Panel Study (NEPS), Kiss (2017) showed that parents send their children to extra remedial classes to compensate for being assigned into a high-ability class where a teacher would tend to grade tougher. Students also adjust their effort: Mehta, Stinebrickner and Stinebrickner (2019), using data from the Berea Panel Study, showed that increased achievement associated with better peers occurs because college study time increases.

on residential choice. To implement this switch, school boundaries were redrawn, and families were assigned to neighboring schools. This resulted in an increase in school segregation (Billings, Deming, & Rockoff, 2014, p. 443): "the proportion of students attending a middle or high school with a high concentration of black students (over 65%) jumped from 12% to 21%, while the proportion attending a relatively integrated school—35 - 65% black—fell from 53% to 40%."

Redrawing school boundaries resulted in situations where students who lived in the same neighborhood but on either side of the boundary could go to vastly different schools, especially in terms of the schools' racial composition. To the extent that these boundaries are exogenous to outcomes, however, Billings, Deming and Rockoff (2014) can use this geographic discontinuity to estimate the impact of being assigned to a less integrated school, which is, of course, what they did. Being assigned to a school with more minority students reduced performance in high school exams for both white and minority students. In addition, the rates of high school graduation and attendance in a four-year college declined for whites. The authors concluded that ending race-based busing in CMS widened racial inequality.

As mentioned in Footnote 3 (p. 2), Germany tracks students into three school types after Age 10, with the *Gymnasium* preparing students for higher education. This track enlists students who have superior academic performance earlier in their schooling. Hence, average peer quality is higher in *Gymnasien*. Dustmann, Puhani and Schönberg (2017) estimated the effects of attending this type of school on long-term labor-market outcomes, such as wages, employment, and being in a white-collar occupation.

The identification of the effect comes from a discontinuity in school-starting age and the assumption that one's date of birth has no direct impact on future labor-market outcomes. Being born on or after July 1 implies being older in a school cohort relative to those born earlier in the year because these children must wait longer to start school, which typically results in better academic performance. Dustmann, Puhani and Schönberg (2017) showed that date of birth is a strong predictor of which track a student is eventually assigned to, and they exploited this relationship to demonstrate that attending a *Gymnasium* does not lead to better labor-market outcomes in the long run.[19]

Instrumental variable

Bramoullé, Djebbari and Fortin (2009) showed that it is possible to identify peer effects in the presence of endogenous peer outcomes and behavior via an instrumental-variable (IV) approach which exploits a particular network structure. The average peer characteristics of one's peers may serve as an instrument for one's average peer characteristics as long as one has not interacted with the peers of one's peers.[20] This insight was used by de Giorgi, Pellizzari and Redaelli (2010)—who described this social-network structure as "partially overlapping groups"—to analyze the impact of peer characteristics on course or major choice in Bocconi University in Italy.

[19] Similar to the Angrist et al. (2016) study on Boston charter schools discussed in Section 2.1, many factors that are different between *Gymansien* and the other two school types (*Hauptschulen* and *Realschulen*). To the extent that the econometrician is unable to control for these other characteristics, it would be difficult to disentagle the effect of better peers from the effects of these unobserved confounders.

[20] The formulation in Bramoullé, Djebbari and Fortin (2009, p. 44) is not less taxing to read: "the characteristics of the friends' friends of a student who are not his friends may serve as instruments for the actions of his own friends."

More recently, Mendolia, Paloyo and Walker (2018) used this "peers-of-peers" IV strategy to estimate the impact of peer quality on high-stakes test scores and the probability of attending university in England.[21] The sample consisted of students in secondary schools drawn from the Longitudinal Study of Young People in England (Next Steps) which were successfully matched with the National Pupil Database (NPD). For concreteness, say we consider a specific student, Student 1. The authors calculated her average peer characteristics, but the coefficient associated with this variable in a least-squares regression will not represent the true impact of these characteristics due to the aforementioned endogeneity issue. As an instrument, average peers-of-peers characteristics measured in primary school where Student 1 did not go to is used, with the additional restriction that these peers of peers did not go to the same secondary school as Student 1.[22] The authors demonstrated that peer quality has a small, positive impact on test scores.

Mendolia, Paloyo and Walker (2018) only observed a subset of classmates for each individual, which implied that the average peer characteristics and behavior were measured with some error. As suggested by Ammermueller and Pischke (2009), this problem can be addressed with the use of an instrumental variable, as in the classical solution to the errors-in-variables model.[23] Using the well-known Program for International Student Assessment (PISA) dataset matched with the NPD for England, Micklewright, Schnepf and Silva (2012) demonstrated that this type of measurement error would result in the attenuation of the coefficient estimate if left unaddressed.

Fixed effect

Even if sorting is generally endogenous, many economists have argued that the distribution of peers can be characterized as exogeneous at lower levels of aggregation in certain contexts. Suppose, for instance, that Student 1 chooses a school. She and her parents may have chosen this school for a number of unobserved reasons that made other students choose the same school. Her cohort may consist of ten sections or classes that stay together for the duration of the academic year. In which section she ends up may be entirely random (say, the school administrator uses a program to randomize the distribution of the cohort over the ten sections). Within a school, therefore, exposure to a particular peer group—here, construed as the section— is random; thus, average peer quality is exogenous.[24] Econometrically, this involves including a school fixed effect in the regression model, but this can be varied and extended to account for school-by-grade, track-by-school, university-by-course fixed effects, and so on.

This identification strategy—either used exclusively or in conjunction with another approach— is applied in many recent studies. Ficano (2012) and Foster (2012) used course fixed effects in a small liberal arts college (presumably in the US) and in two members of the Australian Technology Network (University Technology

---

[21] Patacchini, Rainone and Zenou (2017) also used this approach to resolve the endogeneity arising out of "correlated effects" (Manski, 1993), where group-specific unobservable factors affect both the individual and her peers. This paper is discussed in Section 2.4 in the context of a network fixed-effects approach.

[22] This last restriction—one of the main contributions of Mendolia, Paloyo and Walker (2018)—is important because including peers of peers that go to the same secondary school would violate the necessary exclusion restriction for the instrument to be valid. See the well-known "reflection problem" attributed to Manski (1993).

[23] For a recent take on the use of instrumental variables in this context, see von Hinke, Leckie and Nicoletti (2019).

[24] In this case, we set aside the reflection problem for simplicity of exposition.

Sydney and University of South Australia), respectively. Carrell, Hoekstra and Kuka (2018) and Vardardottir (2015) introduced school-by-grade and track-by-school fixed effects, respectively. The former used students from Alachua County in Florida while the latter examined the Swiss subsample of PISA.

Tonello (2016) exploited cohort-to-cohort random variation in peer characteristics in Italian junior high schools. In this literature, Hoxby (2000) is perhaps the most well-known application of this approach. Gibbons and Telhaj (2016) used the change in peers as students transitioned from primary to secondary school in England, which is the same school transition exploited in Lavy, Silva and Weinhardt (2012). Rao (2019) used a natural experiment in schools in Delhi, India, where a policy change increased the proportion of poor students in elite private schools. The introduction was staggered, so Rao leveraged the variation over time and across schools to pin down the peer effect using a difference-in-differences strategy.[25] All these authors augmented their respective identification strategies with fixed effects to account for non-random sorting.

Ficano (2012), Foster (2012), Vardardottir (2015), Tonello (2016), Carrell, Hoekstra and Kuka (2018), Dills (2018), and Rao (2019) looked at the impact of peer characteristics on measures of achievement while Gibbons and Telhaj (2016) estimated the impact of peer outcomes on one's own outcomes. In particular, Foster (2012), Tonello (2016), Dills (2018) used the share of international students, students from non-English-speaking backgrounds, non-native

students, or minority-student status as a regressor of interest; Ficano (2012) used the sex ratio, Vardardottir (2015) and Rao (2019) used socioeconomic status; and Carrell, Hoekstra and Kuka (2018) used exposure to children from families linked to domestic violence. As a measure of peer quality, Gibbons and Telhaj (2016) use prior achievement before transitioning to secondary school.

The majority of papers in the peer-effects literature posits that class- or schoolmates constitute the relevant peer or reference group. Hong and Lee (2017) in Section 2.1 and Lu and Anderson (2015) earlier used the microenvironment of being seatmates in class. Patacchini, Rainone and Zenou (2017) locates itself in the networks literature, where relationships between individuals ("nodes") are made more explicit and exact. The National Longitudinal Study of Adolescent to Adult Health (Add Health) allowed Patacchini, Rainone and Zenou to examine the impact of self-nominated friends—that is, people with whom a student actually interacts, not simply those with whom she shares a subject, school, or neighborhood.[26] While this approach avoids the measurement-error problem that Angrist (2014) and Jackson (2014) recently illustrated, network formation nonetheless remains an endogenous process where unobserved characteristics shared by nodes in the same network may render naïve estimators of peer effects biased. To address this issue, a network fixed effect should be included to account for non-random sorting into schools, universities, or tracks (Bramoullé, Djebbari, & Fortin, 2009).

[25] He can also exploit exogenous variation within classrooms since some schools assign group work and study partners alphabetically.

[26] Since the network structure is explicit in the dataset, one can imagine applying spatial econometric techniques to analyze this issue. Hsieh and Lin (2017) did this to estimate heterogeneities in the impact of the sex and race composition of nominated friends in Add Health. Spatial econometrics is beyond the scope of this review, but Lin (2010) and Hsieh and Lin (2017) are examples of where this technique has been applied.

Variance restriction

The average outcome for students in a classroom can be construed as being generated by the teacher and the student effects. Thus, heterogeneity in these outcomes across classrooms may be the result of classroom-level heterogeneity generated by differences in teacher ability or non-random sorting into different classrooms by students. If some of these factors are unobserved to the econometrician, then the observed variation in average outcomes across classrooms is likely to exhibit "excess variance" or differences that cannot be explained by observed characteristics (Graham, 2008).

In the peer-effects literature, it is typically acknowledged that this excess variance is partly explained by the "endogenous effect" generated by social interactions within the peer group.[27] In linear models without exogenous variation in peer quality, however, it is impossible to disentangle the two effects—that is, the endogenous effect cannot be separately identified from the "exogenous effect" of group characteristics (Manski, 1993). This identification problem is extremely difficult to solve. As a result, many researchers have instead estimated a combined "social-interaction effect" (Sacerdote, 2011).[28]

Graham (2008) showed that one can recover the endogenous effect in linear models by imposing conditional-variance restrictions.[29] His application used data from the class-size reduction experiment, Project STAR, in Tennessee, US (Word et al. 1990). The variance in mean outcomes across classes of small sizes is larger than the corresponding variance across classes of large sizes. The reason is that sub-class groupings in large classes would offset each other's effects on the class average. Since classroom assignment was randomized in Project STAR, within-class variance can be instrumented by class size.

Recently, Jahanshahi (2017) used this approach to estimate the social multiplier and the impact of the sex ratio in class using Project STAR data and, separately, data from primary and secondary schools in Italy. The author demonstrated that failing to account for the endogenous effect could inflate the estimate of the exogenous effect. He concluded that the sex composition of one's peers in school is less important than the behavior or achievement of one's classmates.

Nonlinearity and heterogeneity

Although average peer effects are interesting *per se*, welfare-enhancing opportunities—in a Pareto sense—exist only if peer effects are heterogeneous or nonlinear (Hoxby & Weingarth, 2005; Sacerdote, 2014; Vigdor & Ludwig, 2010). If peer effects were linear, then moving a student from one classroom to the other will have a symmetric impact. To illustrate, suppose Student 1 in a high-ability Class 1 is a pupil with high ability who generates a positive peer effect which

---

[27] The effect is also known as the "social multiplier" because behavioral characteristics of one's peers influence oneself, but one also influences her peers (Angrist, 2014).

[28] Although from a policy perspective, one should care about distinguishing the endogenous effect from the exogeneous effect because of their different policy implications.

[29] In some cases, nonlinearity allows identification when a linear model would otherwise not (Brock & Durlauf, 2001, 2007).

benefits her classmates.[30] Moving her to a different class with lower-ability students will reduce the average academic performance in Class 1 as she brings her positive peer effect to her new classroom. In contrast, reconsider what would happen if there were nonlinear peer effects. Suppose, for example, the nonlinearity takes the following form with respect to the ability distribution: high-ability students are not affected by the behavior of their peers, but low-ability students are improved by having high-ability classmates. Transferring our high-ability Student 1 to a new class with some low-ability pupils will not change the mean outcome of her original class but will improve the mean outcome of her new classmates.[31]

Many previous studies (some discussed above) considered the existence of nonlinear and heterogeneous peer effects. I will not rehash all of them here; instead, I select a few to illustrate the variety of these identified effects. Feld and Zölitz (2017) showed that the sex ratio does not significantly make a difference in outcomes. This is in contrast to Jahanshahi (2017), who noted that increasing the proportion of females in class is detrimental. The former looked at students at Maastricht University while the latter used earlier school data from US (kindergarten) and Italy (primary and secondary schools). Conditioning on one's sex, Hong and Lee (2017) showed that peer effects exists for males, but not for females in Sogang University. This is qualitatively the same result obtained by Ficano (2012) from a private liberal arts college in the US.

Fruehwirth (2013) examined heterogeneity in effects by race and ability using data from public elementary schools in North Carolina, US Similar to Billings, Deming and Rockoff (2014)

in Section 2.2, Fruehwirth (2013) looked at the percentage of minorities in the classroom but, in addition, she also tested whether the magnitude of endogenous peer effects vary by race. For a Hispanic student, for example, will she be more affected by the average achievement of other Hispanics in the classroom or will she respond more to the average achievement of the whole class? The answer will have equity and efficiency implications, especially since minorities—for a variety of reasons unrelated to underlying ability—are typically associated with poorer academic outcomes. Fruehwirth showed that peer effects are indeed stronger among students of the same race. Using Add Health data, Hsieh and Lin (2017) showed that intra-race spillover effects are stronger for whites relative to non-whites.

The strength of the within-race endogenous effect identified in Fruehwirth (2013), however, diminishes as one moves to higher percentiles of the ability distribution. In other words, low-ability students are affected more than high-ability students by increases in mean peer achievement. The increased responsiveness of low-ability students is also found in English secondary schools by Mendolia, Paloyo and Walker (2018), who showed that increasing the proportion of low-ability peers has a significantly worse impact on low-ability students. In Tennessee kindergartens, however, Sojourner (2013) did not find nonlinearities across the ability distribution.

In higher education, low-achieving Maastricht University students are harmed by the presence of high-achieving peers (Feld & Zölitz, 2017). In nearby University of Amsterdam, the results from an experiment are more nuanced

---

[30] Where I went to high school, these "sections" (classes within a "batch" or cohort of students) are called the "pilot classes". Teachers taught specific subjects, and they taught it in different sections, but the class or section composition stayed constant throughout the academic year. The teachers moved around different classrooms while the students remained in the same one throughout the day (except for out-of-classroom activities).

[31] Benabou (1996) notes that, beyond the mean, the dispersion is also important.

(Booij, Leuven and Oosterbeek 2017). Low-ability students benefit from high-ability students if the group is more heterogeneous, unless it is dominated by low-ability students. High-ability students seem to be impervious to peer effects, no matter the configuration. This is slightly different from Sogang University students in Korea, where Hong and Lee (2017) found that peer effects are indeed nonlinear across the ability distribution, but that both low- and high-achieving students are responsive to these effects. Dills (2018) demonstrated that low-ability (racial) minority students with more non-white classmates perform worse academically in a selective, private, Catholic liberal arts college in the US.

Conclusion

Peer effects are alluring. It gives rise to the possibility of designing and implementing policies that supposedly maximize a specific objective function, such as academic performance, with a rearrangement of group members. From the perspective of a school principal, for instance, imagine the temptation of being able to increase average school performance simply by moving students across different classrooms. As a parent, one can insist on putting a child in a setting where she can realize her full potential or avoid putting her in a potentially detrimental environment. This policy lever is probably cheaper than providing free uniforms and textbooks, building new infrastructure and increasing capital investment, or hiring better teachers.

Indeed, one may argue that the major focus should be on primary and secondary schooling. If peer effects matter, then the largest impacts could occur at this stage of the life course. In virtually all cases, self-selection is limited, screening is minimal, and attendance is compulsory. Even if individual effects are small, it could aggregate to a large total impact given the volume of students. Effects could also accumulate over time (García, Heckman, Leaf, & Prados, 2016), so optimally mixing students at earlier stages could pay off over the life course.[32]

However, despite the rich history of the peer-effects literature, it is clear that even the recent evidence is ambiguous. Part of the reason, of course, is that peer-effects are extremely context-specific. What may work in kindergarten may not necessarily apply in higher education, especially across different levels of national development. This is obvious, though no less important. A more nuanced takeaway—earlier pointed out by Sacerdote (2014, p. 269)—is that "we do not yet know enough about the nature of peer effects to engage in social engineering of peer groups to affect students' outcomes in a desired direction." We are just now uncovering behavioral adjustment mechanisms that amplify or dampen the peer effects that we estimate: parents adjust (Fu & Mehta, 2015; Kiss, 2017) and students adjust (Mehta, Stinebrickner and Stinebrickner 2019), for example. It is not inconceivable that school principals, teachers, and education policymakers also adjust, yet we have not yet been able to provide extensive evidence on where and how large these margins of adjustment occur.

From an estimation perspective, it is clear that the merging of the peer-effects literature and the networks literature is inevitable. The use of class, school, or neighborhood groups as a proxy for actual peers was clearly a second-best outcome in a world when network data did not exist and when networks-based statistical estimators and their properties were unknown. Even if the data and estimators existed, computational power then did not allow such estimation. These days, more studies collect explicit social connections (e.g., Add Health), and social-media

---

[32] I thank Amnon Levy for raising this point.

networks (e.g., Facebook, Twitter, and LinkedIn) are undoubtedly exploiting their in-house data to estimate spillover effects.

Jackson (2014) highlighted the importance of understanding the micro- and macro-level characteristics of networks. The micro-level involves how nodes are interconnected within a network, and the macro-level would pertain to the structure of the network itself (e.g., the existence of clustering and homophily). The language is expressed in discrete math and graph (network) theory (Graham, 2015). Recent papers are more explicit in their acknowledgment of the social-network structure, and these are providing new insights. For instance, van Leeuwen, Offerman and Schram (2019) noted the importance of a key player or "superstar" in realizing efficiency gains for the entire network. Landini et al. (2016) showed that there is a bias associated with self-nominated networks because respondents may misreport with whom they interact. Jain and Langer (2019) demonstrated that the size and degree of closeness within a network are important: there is a tradeoff between increasing the network size, which increases the available information, and the cost of processing the information transmitted within the network.

The lesson from Carrell, Sacerdote and West (2013) and Booij, Leuven and Oosterbeek (2017) is clear: even if we think we know what we are doing, endogenous adjustments within peer groups can put a spanner in the works. In both studies, the peer-group compositions that were implemented to maximize the academic performance of a specific target group made them worse. Of course, this is not to say that we ought to stop experimenting. On the contrary, we should encourage more experimentation to have a deeper understanding of how these causal mechanisms come about. What I would caution against, however, are large-scale policy experiments of this type, where the potential harm is significant. That said, new datasets and estimation strategies—with computational power increasing to accommodate them—would allow more researchers to make further advances on the nature of peer effects.

References

Ammermueller, A., & Pischke, J.-S. (2009). Peer effects in European primary schools: Evidence from the progress in international reading literacy study. *Journal of Labor Economics, 27*(3), 315–348.

Angrist, J. D. (2014). The perils of peer effects. *Labour Economics, 30*(C), 98–108.

Angrist, J. D., Cohodes, S. R., Dynarski, S. M., Pathak, P. A., & Walters, C. R. (2016). Stand and deliver: Effects of boston's charter high schools on college preparation, entry, and choice. *Journal of Labor Economics, 34*(2), 275–318.

Angrist, J. D., & Krueger, A. B. (1991). Does compulsory school attendance affect schooling and earnings? *Quarterly Journal of Economics, 106*(4), 979–1014.

Barnes, J. A. (1969). Graph theory and social networks: A technical comment on connectedness and connectivity. *Sociology, 3*(2), 215–232.

Benabou, R. (1996). Equity and efficiency in human capital investment: The local connection. *Review of Economic Studies, 63*(2), 237–264.

Bhattacharya, D. (2009). Inferring optimal peer assignment from experimental data. *Journal of the American Statistical Association, 104*(486), 486–500.

Bietenbeck. (2019). The long-term impacts of low-achieving childhood peers: Evidence from project STAR. *Journal of the European Economic Association.* forthcoming.

Billings, S. B., Deming, D. J., & Rockoff, J. (2014). School segregation, educational attainment, and crime: Evidence from the end of busing in charlotte-mecklenburg. *Quarterly Journal of Economics, 129*(1), 435–476.

Booij, A. S., Leuven, E., & Oosterbeek, H. (2017). Ability peer effects in university: Evidence from a randomized experiment. *Review of Economic Studies, 84*(2), 547–578.

Booth, A., & Babchuk, N. (1969). Personal influence networks and voluntary association affiliation. *Sociological Inquiry, 39*(2), 179–188.

Bramoullé, Y., Djebbari, H., & Fortin, B. (2009). Identification of peer effects through social networks. *Journal of Econometrics, 150*(1), 41–55.

Brock, W. A., & Durlauf, S. N. (2001). Discrete choice with social interactions. *Review of Economic Studies, 68*(2), 235–260.

Brock, W. A., & Durlauf, S. N. (2007). Identification of binary choice models with social interactions. *Journal of Econometrics, 140*(1), 52–75.

Carrell, S. E., Hoekstra, M., & Kuka, E. (2018). The long-run effects of disruptive peers. *American Economic Review, 108*(11), 3377–3415.

Carrell, S. E., Sacerdote, B. I., & West, J. E. (2013). From natural variation to optimal policy? The importance of endogenous peer group formation. *Econometrica, 81*(3), 855–882.

Cicala, S., Fryer, R. G., & Spenkuch, J. L. (2018). Self-selection and comparative advantage in social interactions. *Journal of the European Economic Association, 16*(4), 983–1020.

Coleman, J. S., Campbell, E. Q., Hobson, C. J., McPartland, J., Wood, A. M., Weinfeld, F. D., et al. (1966). *Equality of education opportunity*. Summary Report. US Department of Health, Education, and Welfare.

Dills, A. K. (2018). Classroom diversity and academic outcomes. *Economic Inquiry, 56*(1), 304–316.

Dustmann, C., Puhani, P. A., & Schönberg, U. (2017). The long-term effects of early track choice. *Economic Journal, 127*(603), 1348–1380.

Epple, D., & Romano, R. E. (2011). Peer effects in education: A survey of the theory and evidence. In J. Benhabib, A. Bisin, & M. O. Jackson (Eds.), *Handbook of social economics* (Vol. 1B, pp. 1053–1163). Elsevier B.V.

Feld, J., & Zölitz, U. (2017). Understanding peer effects: On the nature, estimation, and channels of peer effects. *Journal of Labor Economics, 35*(2), 387–428.

Ficano, C. C. (2012). Peer effects in college academic outcomes — gender matters! *Economics of Education Review, 31*, 1102–1115.

Foster, G. (2012). The impact of international students on measured learning and standards in Australian higher education. *Economics of Education Review, 31*, 587–600.

Fruehwirth, J. C. (2013). Identifying peer achievement spillovers: Implications for desegregation and the achievement gap. *Quantitative Economics, 4*(1), 85–124.

Fu, C., & Mehta, N. (2015). Ability tracking, school and parental effort: A structural model and estimation. *Journal of Labor Economics, 36*(4), 923–979.

García, J. L., Heckman, J. J., Leaf, D. E., & Prados, M. J. (2016). *Quantifying the life-cycle benefits of an influential early childhood program*. Human Capital and Economic Opportunity Working Group Working Paper No. 2016-35.

Gibbons, S., & Telhaj, S. (2016). Peer effects: Evidence from secondary school transition in England. *Oxford Bulletin of Economics and Statistics, 78*(4), 548–575.

de Giorgi, G., Pellizzari, M., & Redaelli, S. (2010). Identification of social interactions through partially overlapping peer groups. *American Economic Journal: Applied Economics, 2*(2), 241–275.

Gorard, S., & Siddiqui, N. (2018). Grammar schools in England: A new analysis of social segregation and academic outcomes. *British Journal of Sociology of Education, 39*(7), 909–924.

Graham, B. S. (2008). Identifying social interactions through conditional variance restrictions. *Econometrica, 76*(3), 643–660.

Graham, B. S. (2015). Methods of identification in social networks. *Annual Review of Economics, 7*(1), 465–485.

Graham, B. S. (2016). *Homophily and transitivity in dynamic network formation*. CEMMAP Working Paper No. 16/16.

Graham, B. S. (2017). An econometric model of network formation with degree heterogeneity. *Econometrica, 85*(4), 1033–1063.

Hanushek, E. A. (1979). Conceptual and empirical issues in the estimation of educational production functions. *Journal of Human Resources, 14*(3), 351–388.

Hong, S. C., & Lee, J. (2017). Who is sitting next to you? Peer effects inside the classroom. *Quantitative Economics, 8*(1), 239–275.

Hoxby, C. M. (2000). *Peer effects in the classroom: Learning from gender and race variation*. NBER Working Paper No. 7867.

Hoxby, C. M., & Weingarth, G. (2005). *Taking race out of the equation: School reassignment and the structure of peer effects*.

Hsieh, C.-S., & Lin, X. (2017). Gender and racial peer effects with endogenous network formation. *Regional Science and Urban Economics, 67*, 135–147.

Imbens, G. W., & Wooldridge, J. M. (2009). Recent developments in the econometrics of program evaluation. *Journal of Economic Literature, 47*(1), 5–86.

Jackson, M. O. (2005). A survey of models of network formation: Stability and efficiency. In G. Demange, & M. Wooders (Eds.), *Group formation in economics: Networks, clubs, and coalitions* (pp. 11–57). Cambridge University Press.

Jackson, M. O. (2011). An overview of social networks and economic applications. In J. Benhabib, A. Bisin, & M. O. Jackson (Eds.), *Handbook of social economics* (Vol. 1A, pp. 511–585). Elsevier B.V.

Jackson, M. O. (2014). Networks in the understanding of economic behaviors. *Journal of Economic Perspectives, 28*(1), 3–22.

Jahanshahi, B. (2017). Separating gender composition effects from peer effects in education. *Education Economics, 25*(1), 112–126.

Jain, T., & Langer, N. (2019). Does whom you know matter? Unraveling the influence of peers' network attributes on academic performance. *Economic Inquiry, 57*(1), 141–161.

Kiss, D. (2017). How do ability peer effects operate? Evidence on one transmission channel. *Education Economics, 26*(3), 253–265.

Landini, F., Montinari, N., Pin, P., & Piovesan, M. (2016). Friendship network in the classroom: Parents bias on peer effects. *Journal of Economic Behavior and Organization, 129*, 56–73.

Lavy, V., Silva, O., & Weinhardt, F. (2012). The good, the bad, and the average: Evidence on ability peer effects in schools. *Journal of Labor Economics, 30*(2), 367–414.

van Leeuwen, B., Offerman, T., & Schram, A. (2019). Competition for status creates superstars: An experiment on public good provision and network formation. *Journal of the European Economic Association.* forthcoming.

Lerman, P. (1967). Gangs, networks, and subcultural delinquency. *American Journal of Sociology, 73*(1), 63–72.

Lin, X. (2010). Identifying peer effects in student academic achievement by spatial autoregressive models with group unobservables. *Journal of Labor Economics, 28*(4), 825–860.

Lu, F., & Anderson, M. L. (2015). Peer effects in microenvironments: The benefits of homogeneous classroom groups. *Journal of Labor Economics, 33*(1), 91–122.

Manski, C. F. (1993). Identification of endogenous social effects: The reflection problem. *Journal of Econometrics, 60*(3), 531–542.

McEwan, P. J., & Shapiro, J. S. (2008). The benefits of delayed primary school enrollment: Discontinuity estimates using exact birth dates. *Journal of Human Resources, 43*(1), 1–29.

McPherson, M., Smith-Lovin, L., & Cook, J. M. (2001). Birds of a feather: Homophily in social networks. *Annual Review of Sociology, 27*, 415–444.

Mehta, N., Stinebrickner, R., & Todd, S. (2019). Time-use and academic peer effects in college. *Economic Inquiry, 57*(1), 162–171.

Mendolia, S., Paloyo, A. R., & Walker, I. (2018). Heterogeneous effects of high school peers on educational outcomes. *Oxford Economic Papers, 70*(3), 613–634.

Micklewright, J., Schnepf, S. V., & Silva, P. N. (2012). Peer effects and measurement error: The impact of sampling variation in school survey data (evidence from PISA). *Economics of Education Review, 31*, 1136–1142.

Oosterbeek, H., & van Ewijk, R. (2014). Gender peer effects in university: Evidence from a randomized experiment. *Economics of Education Review, 38*, 51–63.

Patacchini, E., Rainone, E., & Zenou, Y. (2017). Heterogeneous peer effects in education. *Journal of Economic Behavior and Organization, 134*, 190–227.

Pop-Eleches, C., & Urquiola, M. (2013). Going to a better school: Effects and behavioral responses. *American Economic Review, 103*(4), 1289–1324.

Rao, G. (2019). Familiarity does not breed contempt: Generosity, discrimination, and diversity in Delhi schools. *American Economic Review, 109*(3), 774–809.

Roy, A. D. (1951). Some thoughts on the distribution of earnings. *Oxford Economic Papers, 3*(2), 135–146.

Sacerdote, B. (2011). Peer effects in education: How might they work, how big are they and how much do we know thus far?. In E. A. Hanushek, S. Machin, & L. Wößmann (Eds.), *Handbook of the economics of education* (Vol. 3, pp. 249–277) Elsevier B.V.

Sacerdote, B. (2014). Experimental and quasi-experimental analysis of peer effects: Two Steps forward? *Annual Review of Economics, 6*(1), 253–272.

Sojourner, A. (2013). Identification of peer effects with missing peer data: Evidence from project STAR. *Economic Journal, 123*(569), 574–605.

Tobler, W. (1970). A computer movie simulating urban growth in the Detroit region. *Economic Geography, 46*, 234–240.

Tonello, M. (2016). Peer effects of non-native students on natives' educational outcomes: Mechanisms and evidence. *Empirical Economics, 51*(1), 383–414.

Vardardottir, A. (2013). Peer effects and academic achievement: A regression discontinuity approach. *Economics of Education Review, 36*, 108–121.

Vardardottir, A. (2015). The impact of classroom peers in a streaming system. *Economics of Education Review, 49*, 110–128.

Vigdor, J., & Ludwig, J. (2010). Neighborhoods and peers in the production of schooling. In D. J. Brewer, & P. J. McEwan (Eds.), *Economics of education* (pp. 163–169). Elsevier B.V.

von Hinke, S., Leckie, G., & Nicoletti, C. (2019). The use of instrumental variables in peer effects models. *Oxford Bulletin of Economics and Statistics, 81*(5), 1179–1191.

Word, E., Johnston, J., Bain, H. P., Fulton, B. D., Zaharias, J. B., Achilles, C. M., et al. (1990). *The state of Tennessee's student/teacher achievement ratio (STAR) project.* Technical Report 1985–1990. Tennessee State Department of Education.

The role of teacher quality in education production

Bjarne Strøm[a], Torberg Falch[b]

[a]Department of Economics, Norwegian University of Science and Technology, Norway; [b]Department of Teacher Education, Norwegian University of Science and Technology, Norway

Introduction

Most people find it obvious that the quality of teachers matter for students' outcomes. Credible measurement of the quantitative importance of teachers is challenging, and in particular what characterizes strong and weak teachers. The last years have witnessed an explosion of studies of teacher quality, especially from the US, as a result of increased availability of longitudinal administrative data matching students, teachers and schools.

This chapter summarizes recent attempts to measure the effect of teacher quality on student outcomes within an education production framework. We consider to what extent different research strategies are able to provide credible evidence on teacher quality. Estimated teacher effects on student achievement may reflect that some teachers are better at teaching to the test rather than generating true knowledge. Thus, we also discuss to what extent teacher quality measures based on student achievement translate into education and labor market outcomes after students have left school, which illustrates

the potential economic value of increased teacher quality. We discuss to what extent teacher quality is related to individual teacher characteristics and teacher labor market conditions. The chapter also discusses the potential usefulness of value added based teacher quality measures in teacher evaluation systems and pay policies.

Estimating teacher quality

Our point of departure is the education production function as formulated recently in Koedel, Mihaly, and Rockoff (2015), but building heavily on the novel insights provided by Ben-Porath (1967) and Hanushek (1979).

$$y_{it} = f(X_i(t),\ S_i(t), T_i(t), \alpha_{i0}, \varepsilon_{it}) \qquad 22.1$$

y_{it} is an outcome measure for student i at time (grade) t. The outcome is assumed to be generated by the history of inputs relevant for the student where, $X_i(t)$ represents the history of individual and family inputs for student i up to time t. $S_i(t)$ similarly represents all school inputs, such as resource use and class size, while $T_i(t)$ represents teacher quality. α_{i0} is student i's initial ability, while ε_{it} is a stochastic idiosyncratic term.

A main question in the literature of teacher quality is how to specify and estimate the production function in order to obtain unbiased estimates of the relationship between student outcomes and teacher quality. In other words, the question is to what extent similar students exposed to different teachers, all else equal, end up having different outcomes. Ideally, one would like to perform an experiment where teachers are randomly allocated across students, while the researcher observes the achievement of students after being exposed to the teacher. However, for obvious reasons, such an experiment is hard to conduct in practice, so studies of the relationship between student outcomes and teacher quality needs to be based on non-experimental data.

We consider two approaches obtaining credible estimates of teacher quality in non-experimental settings. The first approach (the value added approach) requires data for outcome variables (typically test scores or exam results) available for the same student at different points in time. The second approach (the between subject approach) is relevant in cases where test scores are available at a single point in time on several subjects taught by different teachers.

The value added approach

Following Koedel et al. (2015), a tractable and estimable version of the general formulation of the education production function in (1) is the following linear value added model

$$y_{isj,t} = \beta_0 + \beta_1 y_{i,t-1} + \beta_2 X_{is,t} + \beta_4 T_{isj,t} + \varepsilon_{it}$$

$$22.2$$

$y_{isj,t}$ is the achievement of student i exposed to teacher j in school s at time (grade) t. Here, $X_{is,t}$, $S_{is,t}$ and $T_{isj,t}$ represents levels of the

individual, family and school inputs and the quality of teacher j experienced by individual i in school s at time (grade) t. This value added model assumes that the inclusion of a lag, $y_{i,t-1}$ in the achievement variable captures all cumulative (dynamic) features of the educational production process. This is consistent with a restriction that the effects of all inputs evolve in a common geometrically declining pattern.

On the other hand, this is a very data demanding strategy as it requires longitudinal data linking individual students to individual teachers within schools and across grades. This type of data has typically become available in some US states. But in many countries, linked student-teacher data are not available or unreliable and hence assessments of teacher quality must still be based on other approaches.

By exploiting the fact that a student has been exposed to different teachers throughout his/her school career, total teacher effects can be identified, holding observed and unobserved school, and to some extent also family and individual variables, constant. One strength of this approach is the possibility to quantify the potential gains from increasing teacher quality due to both observed and unobserved characteristics of the teacher.

In the value added framework, the approach is to use indicator variables for each teacher the students have been exposed to during the period under investigation. This removes sorting of students across schools and districts as a source of bias. Moreover, if students are followed and tested at different grades and exposed to different teachers over time, the inclusion of fixed student effects also effectively removes potential bias from omitted time-invariant individual and family characteristics, such as innate ability. An early study using this approach was Hanushek (1971), using test scores at the end of third grade and controlling for second grade test scores and a range of control variables. Recent studies, most prominently Chetty et al. (2014a,b) have further developed and refined the value added approach by exploiting data over cohorts and grades in schools in New York City, and the literature expands rapidly. Recent reviews of the literature can be found in Jackson, Rockoff, and Staiger (2014) and Koedel et al. (2015).

A crucial first question is to what extent these value-added based estimates represents unbiased estimates of the true teacher quality. Or put differently: Do the value added estimates adequately account for the effect teachers have on student's knowledge or do they to some extent reflect unobserved student characteristics or school or teacher behavior not related to true knowledge generation?

A first challenge is that the value added approach may not account sufficiently for endogenous assignment of teachers to classes within schools, as suggested by Rothstein (2010) and followed up in Rothstein (2017),.[1] Kane and Staiger (2008) and Kane, McCaffrey, Miller, and Staiger (2013) validates the value added approach by exploiting random assignment of students to teachers in field experiments. They find that the estimated teacher effects based on historical non-experimental data and the value added approach are unbiased predictors of student achievement under random assignment. Although Chetty et al. (2014 a) find that less advantaged students tend to be assigned to teachers with lower value added,

they find that controlling for test scores in previous grades and a small set of other student characteristics is sufficient to account for the bias due to this sorting. They reach this conclusion using two approaches. Their first approach is to estimate bias based on the degree of selection on observable characteristics excluded from the value added model. Their second approach is to exploit changes in teacher assignments across adjacent grades due to teacher turnover in order to assess the bias due to unobservables. Using this quasi-experimental approach, they find that the entry (exit) of a high value added teacher in a cohort induces a higher (lower) than average end-of-year test score for this cohort. They conclude that the degree of bias in the value added measures due to endogenous assignment of teachers within schools is low. Bacher-Hicks, Kane, and Staiger (2014) replicates their analysis using data from Los Angeles. They confirm the Chetty et al. (2014) conclusion that value added estimates are fairly unbiased estimates of teacher effects.[2]

However, whether assignment of teachers across classes within school after conditioning on past performance and a small set of controls can be viewed as fairly random or systematically related to student characteristics is still a controversial issue. The problem is likely to vary across schools, school districts and countries, see also Dieterle, Guarino, Reckase, and

---

[1] An important element in Rothstein's critique of the value added approach is the use of a "placebo" or falcification test. The argument goes like this: If teacher value added represents an ubiased measure of teacher quality, teacher value added in later grades should not be able to predict value added in earlier grades. However, he finds that this is not the case using data from North Carolina schools. Chetty, Friedman, and Rockoff (2017) argue theoretically that the "placebo" test used by Rothstein (2017) is not a valid approach. Put simply, their argument is that prior test scores cannot be used to conduct placebo test because value added measures are themselves estimated from prior test scores and gives a mechanical relationship between prior and current value added measures. See also Goldhaber and Chaplin (2015) for discussion and evidence on the relevance of the Rothstein test.

[2] Bacher-Hicks et al. (2014) also study to what extent teacher effectiveness vary with student characteristics and find that teacher value added forecast the causal impact on student achievement independently of whether teachers move across schools that differ substantially in terms of student composition. However, they also find that disadvantaged students by race and parental background are disproportionally matched with low value added teachers. This contribute to widening achievement gaps between groups and may have adverse distributional effects.

Wooldridge (2014) for a recent study of the assignment of students to teachers within schools.

A second challenge for the value added approach is whether estimated teacher quality only captures short term effects, for example some sort of "teaching to the test"-effects. Is estimated teacher quality able to predict student performance in the education and labor markets in the future? To investigate this issue, Chetty, Friedman, and Rockoff (2014b) compare outcomes at later points in life between students assigned to high and low value added teachers. They find that students of higher value added teachers have both higher earnings and are more likely to attend college than students of lower value added teachers.

What do the value added studies tell us about the numerical contribution of teacher quality to student outcomes? According to the review article by Koedel et al. (2015), the variation in teacher quality is substantial and much of the variation occurs within schools. Hanushek and Rivkin (2012) use several representative estimates of the labor market returns to cognitive test scores as well as a number of estimates of total teacher effects from value added studies to assess the importance of teachers on earnings. They estimate that the economic value of a teacher who is one standard deviation above the mean is $420 000 for a class of 20 students. Chetty et al. (2014b) suggest that a hypothetical replacement of an average teacher with one in the top 5% will increase students' lifetime income by around $1.4 million per classroom taught. These are large gains compared to possible costs connected with such a replacement of teachers. They illustrate that policies that are able to increase teacher quality have a large potential to increase labor productivity.

The between subject approach

A between subject approach has been proposed when the data includes information on several test scores at the same point in time, but from classes with different teachers for the same student. This format allows the researcher to account for student and school fixed effects. Removing the student fixed effect by measuring all variables as deviations from subject specific means (denoted by a bar over the variable), effectively also absorbing all school level effects. Equations of the following format are estimated

$$ y_{ij} - \overline{y_j} = \beta\left(T_{ij} - \overline{T_j}\right) + \left(\varepsilon_{ij} - \overline{\varepsilon_j}\right) \qquad 22.3 $$

where j denote subject. Clotfelter, Ladd, and Vigdor (2010) notice that while the concern in value added models is that students' assignment to classrooms (teachers) can be correlated with time varying unobserved determinants of student achievement, the concern in the between subject approach is that assignment of students to classrooms (teachers) is correlated with unobserved student characteristics that differs across subjects.[3]

Formally, the identification assumption in the between subject approach is that the within student by subject error term, ε_{ij}, is uncorrelated with teacher characteristics T_{ij}. Thus, researchers using this strategy need to argue that this assumption is valid in their specific context. For instance, Clotfelter et al. (2010) try to assess the credibility of the assumption in their analysis of teacher effects in US high schools by measuring to what extent students is assigned to different classes by subject based on their relative ability across subjects. They conclude that the matching of students to classes (teachers) is to a large extent based on general ability and not relative ability across subjects. However, this conclusion is of course limited to their

---

[3] Another difference between the value added and between subject approach is that the latter does not account for the cumulative feature of the learning process as current achievement is only related to current teacher characteristics.

sample and specific institutional context and need not apply in other settings.[4] Another challenge with the between subject approach is that other variables important for student achievement such as peer groups is also likely to vary across subjects. Although control variables meant to account for across subject differences in peer groups can sometimes be included, teacher effects may to some extent reflect unobserved peer characteristics.

What explains teacher quality variation?

While a lot of research effort in the last 10–15 years has been directed toward the estimation of teacher quality based on the value added approach and the reliability of these quality measures, an increasing amount of studies also investigate the relationship between teacher quality and individual teacher characteristics and teacher labor market conditions.

There are two approaches to investigating factors related to teacher quality. The two-step approach relates estimated overall teacher quality, T, to teacher characteristics, C, in the following way

$$T_i = \alpha C_i + \varepsilon_i$$

The alternative approach, which is more commonly used, is to estimate the effect of teacher characteristics directly by including teacher characteristics in the education production function 21.2 and 21.3 instead of indicator variables for teachers. One challenge to this approach is potential endogenous sorting of teachers and students across schools and classrooms within schools.[5] The possibility that teacher wages and teacher characteristics are jointly determined in the teacher labor market is a further source of endogeneity. Studies using this approach typically include school fixed effects in the model in order to control for time-invariant school or district level variables, in addition to control variables to account for relevant within school or within school district variation. Examples of studies in this tradition are Loeb and Page (2000), Harris and Sass (2011) and Britton and Propper (2016).

Individual teacher characteristics

Teacher experience

According to the review of the earlier research in Palayo and Rees (2010), teacher productivity in terms of student achievement gains improves in the first few years of the career but stops improving thereafter. Using data from different states and school districts in the US, Papay and Kraft (2015), Wiswall (2013) and Harris and Sass (2011) indicate that earlier findings were partly a result of restrictive model assumptions, failure to take account of endogenous teacher attrition, and dynamic matching of better students to teachers with higher productivity as teachers gain experience. They find that improvement in teacher quality continues far longer into the

---

[4] Gronqvist and Vlachos (2016) use cross section data on students' achievement in Swedish compulsory schools to estimate teacher effects and argue that since formal tracking is forbidden in Sweden, the between-subjects strategy is well suited there. Their evidence also suggest that the matching of teachers and students is unrelated to variables characterizing teachers' cognitive ability, while they cannot completely rule out the possibility of systematic relationship between matching and teachers non-cognitive ability. Slater, Davies, and Burgess (2012) use the between subject approach to obtain measures of variation in teacher effectiveness in England using matched data for students, schools and teachers from 33 schools. They also include prior subject specific student performance.

[5] Hanushek, Kane, and Rivkin (2004), Clotfelter, Ladd, and Vigdor (2006) and Dieterle et al. (2014) contain US evidence on teacher-student matching across school districts, schools and within schools. Falch and Strøm (2005) and Bonesranning et al. (2005) provide evidence on teacher sorting across schools and school districts in Norway.

career than the earlier results indicate. On-the-job training throughout much of the career seems to improve teacher quality.

Teacher skills, formal training and education

Earlier research reviewed in Palayo and Rees (2010) emphasize that teacher test scores and attending selective educational institutions positively affect student performance in the US, while formal teacher credentials in terms of advanced degrees and certification does not. Recent studies have extended this research by looking at a broader set of teacher skills, exploring data from other countries, and using more credible estimation strategies.

Rockoff, Jacob, Kane, and Staiger (2011) conduct a survey of new math teachers in New York City in order to measure the association between a set of observable teacher characteristics and teacher quality using the two-step approach. While relying on a small sample, their investigation indicates that a much broader set of observational credentials than those traditionally used when recruiting teachers are positively associated with student achievement gains.

Harris and Sass (2011) studies the relationship between teacher education and training using the value added format and exploits variation over time within teachers in these variables to assess the contribution to student achievement using data from Florida public schools while conditioning on teacher, school and student fixed effects. While their general results support earlier research findings that formal teacher training and graduate coursework did not affect student outcomes, some heterogeneity exist across subjects and grade levels. Moreover, it is an open question to what extent the results applies outside the Florida school system and in

other institutional contexts. A recent paper by Bastian (2019) using data from North Carolina gives a more comprehensive and nuanced picture of the effectiveness of teachers with graduate degrees.

Clotfelter et al. (2010) use the between subject approach for high schools in North Carolina. They find that subject specific teacher credentials (licensure and certification) in math and English language increase student achievement. According to their results, the achievement gain of having a teacher with strong teacher credentials compared to a teacher with weak teacher credentials is 0.23 standard deviations. Moreover, they judge that the teacher credentials account for more than one-fifth of the overall distribution of teacher quality in their sample. While they also find that teacher test scores are predictive of student test scores, the effect of licensure and certification variables are more important than teacher test scores. However, it is also in this case a question of the external validity to other contexts. Slater et al. (2012) find for English schools that teacher credentials are not associated with their measures of total teacher quality based on the between subject approach.

Gronqvist and Vlachos (2016) use matched student-teacher register data from upper secondary schools in Sweden and the between subject approach to study the effect of teacher cognitive and noncognitive skills.[6] Their conclusion is that teacher skills have negligible effects on average student achievement, but that the average effect hides important heterogeneities. First, cognitive and non-cognitive teacher skills seems to be complementary, i.e., students having a teacher with high cognitive skills and high social interaction skills increase student achievement, while having a teacher with low social interaction skills

---

[6] Teacher skills are measured by three measures: From military drafts they have measures of cognitive skills and social interaction skills for Swedish men. In addition, for all teachers GPA from upper secondary school which may be associated with both cognitive and noncognitive skills are available. All teacher skill measures are obtained before teachers started tertiary education.

and high cognitive skills decrease achievement. Second, while increased cognitive skills seems to increase the achievement gap between high and low-achieving students, increased social interaction skills decrease the gap.

A recent paper by Hanushek, Piopiunik, and Widerhold (2019) investigates the relationship between student achievement and teacher cognitive skills across 31 countries using a between subject approach and test scores in math and reading from the PISA surveys. To measure country differences in teacher skills, they exploit information from adult test scores in numeracy and literacy from the PIAAC survey. They show that relative teacher skills vary substantially across countries. The results suggest that student achievement is strongly associated with teacher cognitive skills. The results imply that one standard deviation increase in teacher skills increases student achievement with 0.1−0.15 standard deviations. One limitation with the study is that teacher relative skills across subjects are only measured at the country level. Although they show that results are robust to the inclusion of a range of observable country specific variables and placebo tests, the results might to some extent reflect unobserved country differences in subject specific skills rather than teacher skills.

Teacher labor market variables

If teacher wages were determined in a well-informed competitive market, teacher quality and teacher wages would be jointly determined. High-quality teachers would have higher wage than low-quality teachers. Moreover, exogenous negative shifts in teacher supply, for instance due to improved outside options, would increase teacher wages to equilibrate the market.

However, actual teacher labor markets are very far from this stylized free market model as emphasized in Lankford and Wyckoff (2010). Instead, teacher wages are to a large extent determined within rigid wage scales, often within collectively bargained contracts with teacher trade unions. Since teacher quality is important for student performance, understanding how structural changes in the teacher labor market affect teacher quality is important in order to design policies to retain and recruit effective individuals in the teaching profession. This section reviews some recent empirical evidence of the effects of teacher wages, wage setting systems, and other labor market characteristics on teacher quality.

Teacher wages and teacher wage systems

While earlier research from the US, as reviewed in Hanushek and Rivkin (2006), suggests that teacher quality is not systematically associated with teacher wages, recent evidence from other countries and other institutional contexts paints a more nuanced picture. While several recent studies find that teacher wages and wages in alternative jobs have causal effects on teacher supply, Britton and Propper (2016) takes this line of research a step further by assessing the effect of relative teacher wages on student outcomes in English schools.[7] They exploit the fact that the centralized and regulated pay system in English schools implies large regional variation in the pay gap between teacher jobs and alternative jobs in the private sector. Such a gap may affect the recruitment of teachers to the school as well as the productivity of current teachers as suggested by efficiency wage theories. They find that a ten percent negative shock to the wage gap implies a 2% loss in

---

[7] Falch (2011) find that an exogenous pay increase in hard to staff schools in Northern Norway increase supply of teachers to these schools. Leigh (2012) find that increased teacher pay boosts the average aptitude of students entering teacher education courses.

average school performance on key exams taken at the end of compulsory education.

A recent paper by Willén (2018) provides a more direct study of the effect of different pay setting systems. He exploit that the pay determination system of teachers in Sweden changed dramatically in 1996 from a uniform national pay schedule to a system with pay determined at the individual level. Exploiting pre-reform variation in regional non-teacher pay, he finds a long run elasticity of teacher pay with respect to pre-reform non-teacher pay of 0.2. The reform implied an increase in entry wages and a flattening of the age-wage relationship. However, he finds no effect on this change on teacher composition, nor on student performance.

Hanushek et al. (2019) study whether their estimated effects of cognitive teacher skills on student performance across countries is associated with cross country differences in factors related to teacher pay. Their results suggest that observed cognitive teacher skill differences across countries are positively associated with differences in women's access to high skilled non-teacher occupations and to salary premiums for teachers.[8]

Teacher unions

In most countries, teacher unions affect teacher wage setting and, in addition, the operation of schools through, e.g., recruitment and layoff policies. While there is agreement that teacher unions are important actors in the teacher labor market, the theoretical effects of unions on teacher productivity is ambiguous due to the conflicting effects of pure rent-seeking activities and the potential efficiency gain through collective voice. Credible empirical evidence on the actual effect of teacher unions on student outcomes is limited. Earlier studies look at the effects of teacher collective bargaining on relatively short-run measures of student outcomes. Hoxby (1996) finds that unionization increases high school dropout, while Lovenheim (2009) finds no effect. A recent paper by Lovenheim and Willén (2019) estimates the effects of teacher collective bargaining laws on long run student outcomes as labor market performance. Their identification strategy exploits the staggered introduction of duty-to-bargain laws across cohorts within states. They find that exposure to collective bargaining laws reduces future labor market success in terms of earnings and labor market participation, especially among black and Hispanic men. The effects are not evident for women. Moreover, they also find that collective bargaining laws are associated with lower non-cognitive skills among young men.

A recent paper by Baron (2018) reaches quite different conclusions. He exploits that the state of Wisconsin limited teacher bargaining power in 2011 by imposing legal restrictions on unions funding and bargaining ability in order to reduce the state budget deficit in the aftermath of the Great Recession. To identify effects on student outcomes he exploits variation in the timing of the decrease in teacher bargaining power due to variation in the expiration dates of existing union contracts across school districts in the state. He finds that the reduction in teacher union power reduced student achievement, in particular among students in the lower part of the achievement distribution. He argues that the reduction in achievement was due to a reduction in teacher salaries combined with an increase in teacher turnover. His results may

---

[8] This is consistent with the evidence in Bacolod (2007) indicating a marked decline in the quality of young women going into teaching between 1960 and 1990 in the US as measured by standardized test scores and undergraduate institution selectivity together with an increase in the non-teacher alternatives available for females. Dolton and Marcenaro-Gutierrez (2011) also conclude that teacher pay differences contributes significantly to explain differences in cross-country student performance.

indicate that the effect of changes in teacher union power on student outcomes is not symmetric. Further analysis is needed to conclude whether this conclusion extends to student outcomes in the longer run.

As a result of the reform in Wisconsin, some school districts replaced the old seniority-pay system with a flexible-pay system. Biasi (2018) finds that high-quality teachers, measured using a value-added approach, moves away from school districts with a seniority-pay system to districts with a flexible-pay system, increasing average teacher quality in the latter school districts. To gauge the general effects of such moves she performs a simulation exercise based on a structural model of the teacher labor market. The simulations show that the implementation of individual salary models in all school district generates smaller improvement in teacher quality entirely connected to the exit of low quality teachers.

Teacher mobility

Since the evidence clearly shows that teacher quality is important for student outcomes, knowledge about the link between teacher mobility and teacher quality is crucial in order to understand the determination of overall teacher quality as well as quality distribution across schools. Teachers' decisions about job changes is a choice among different job alternatives that maximizes individual utility. This choice will depend on relative wages, as well as nonpecuniary job conditions and teacher characteristics. Previous studies have shown that teachers are more likely to quit schools with large shares of minority and disadvantaged students.[9]

However, an important and difficult issue is to gain empirical knowledge of the change in overall teacher quality and the quality distribution across schools and students as teachers

exit the public school sector or move across schools. Feng and Sass (2017) tries to answer this question using matched school, teacher and student data from North Carolina and Florida. Using the two-step approach, they estimate the effect of both own quality as well as the quality of their peers on the teachers' decisions to move to another school within or across school districts or leave the public school sector. They do not find strong relationships between teacher quality and intra or interdistrict teacher mobility. Regarding exit from the public school sector, they find that both the most effective teachers and the least effective teachers are most likely to exit while teachers in the middle of the quality distribution are most likely to stay. Moreover, the quality of ones' peer teachers are important for the mobility decision. Top quality teachers are more likely to stay if surrounded by high quality peers and teachers tend to move to schools where the average teacher quality is roughly similar to their own. The broad conclusion is that teacher mobility tend to exacerbate quality differences across schools.

Use of teacher quality measures in pay and evaluation systems

The evidence suggest that teacher quality are only weakly related to specific teacher characteristics traditionally included in pay schedules (formal education, experience and teacher credentials). Thus, it would be tempting to replace traditional pay schedules with individual pay setting based on teacher quality measures obtained from value added models. There is also some evidence that performance pay systems contribute positively to student outcomes (Lavy (2009)), although the literature does not provide definitive evidence in support of performance pay.

---

[9] See Hanushek et al. (2004) for evidence from the US and Falch and Strøm (2005) for evidence from Norway.

First, practical problems arise when trying to implement value added based evaluation systems. Evaluation systems must have legitimacy inside the institution, i.e., among the teachers. Research have demonstrated the importance of teachers, but even unbiased value added estimates are measured with error. For example, the precision depends on the number of students assigned to the teacher. Ignoring measurement error may imply that two teachers with the same true quality will be treated differently just because they have different number of students. How to handle measurement error and other practical implementation problems is not trivial in this context as emphasized by Ballou and Springer (2015). Implementation issues are also discussed in Staiger and Kane (2014).

Second, when value added based teacher quality estimates become high stake, the incentives for teachers to teach to the test, manipulate assignment of students to teachers and outright cheat or manipulate tests becomes apparent. Earlier research has shown that test based school accountability systems are vulnerable to manipulation or cheating by the actors involved, see Figlio and Winicki (2005) and Jacob (2005) for evidence and examples. Arguably, such behavior will be exaggerated when implemented at the individual teacher level, although Lavy (2009) finds that introduction of a teacher performance pay system in Israel did not lead to teacher manipulation of test scores.

Third, the quality of a single teacher is likely to depend on the quality of his/her peers as shown in Jackson and Bruegmann (2009). Based on the value added approach, they show that a single teachers' students has larger achievement gains in math and reading if the teacher have effective colleagues. This makes it difficult to isolate the single teacher's contribution to student achievement and is rather an argument for group based performance pay systems, although such systems face serious problems with free-riding. Goodman and Turner (2013) present evidence that a group based bonus program to teachers in New York City schools had no effects on student achievement in general, although small positive effects on math achievement were detected when the program contained small groups of teachers.

A related problem with regard to individual teacher pay systems based on teacher performance is that large pay differences themselves may reduce effort and productivity as suggested by the fair-wage mechanism in efficiency wage models introduced by Akerlof and Yellen (1990). Recent experimental evidence indicates that pay differences which are not regarded as fair may reduce effort, see Cohn, Fehr, and Goette (2015) and Breza, Kaur, and Shamdasani (2018)[10].

Summary and the way forward

There are large differences in teacher quality. This is demonstrated in a large number of studies, using impressive data-sets and sophisticated empirical methods. The value-added approach is most common, but the between-subject approach is a fruitful alternative because it relies on different assumptions on the underlying education production function and is less demanding with regard to data.

One important question is how this insight can be used in policy. In a recruitment situation, estimates of teacher quality will typically be unobservable and the principal must rely on other types of information. However, teacher quality seems only weakly related to observable teacher characteristics. There is firm evidence that teacher quality is positively associated with the experience of the teacher, the cognitive skill of the teacher and some teacher credentials.

---

[10] Ashraf and Bandiera (2018) contains a broader discussion of the role of social incentives in organizations.

However, the findings in this literature seems to depend on the specific context of the data.

One might think that estimated teacher quality can be used in an incentive pay system. However, the design of pay and teacher evaluation systems based on estimated teacher quality face important practical implementation problems and a risk of behavior that is gaming the system. Careful empirical research taking implementation and institutional details into account is needed to conclude whether such systems will enhance teacher productivity and student long run outcomes.

A fruitful future avenue of research is to explore what we may denote the teacher "production function", which can be loosely described as

$$T_j = f(C_j, M_j, \varepsilon_j)$$

where T is teacher quality, C is teacher characteristics, M is teaching methods and ε is the error term. Some experimental studies identify effective teaching methods. Such findings have the potential to increase teacher quality along the whole distribution of teacher quality. Arguably, the potential is largest at the low end of teacher quality distribution, because high-quality teachers presumably use effective teaching methods already. An early study on teaching methods is Machin and McNally (2008). They find that the introduction of a "literacy hour" in English schools increased student achievement. Another more recent example is Jerrim and Vignoles (2016) who study the effect of introducing Singaporean inspired 'mastery' approach to teaching mathematics into schools in England. They find a small positive effect of the change in teaching method. A third example is Machin, McNally, and Viarengo (2018) studying the effect of an intervention that changes how teachers teach young children to read represented by the staggered introduction of "synthetic phonics" in English primary schools. They provide evidence that the intervention had a positive causal effect on young childrens' literacy and especially among children with disadvantaged background and non-native speaking English background.

References

Akerlof, G. A., & Yellen, J. L. (1990). The fair wage-effort hypothesis and unemployment. *Quarterly Journal of Economics, 105,* 255–283.

Ashraf, N., & Bandiera, O. (2018). Social incentives in organizations. *Annual Review of Economics, 10,* 439–463.

Bacher-Hicks, A., Kane, T. J., & Staiger, D. O. (2014). *Validating teacher effect estimates using changes in teacher assignments in Los Angeles.* NBER Working Paper No. 20657.

Bacolod, M. P. (2007). Do alternative opportunities matter? The role of female labor markets in the decline of teacher quality. *Review of Economics and Statistics, 89,* 737–751.

Ballou, D., & Springer, M. G. (2015). Using student test scores to measure teacher performance: Some problems in the design and implementation of evaluation systems. *Educational Researcher, 44,* 77–86.

Baron, E. J. (2018). The effect of teachers' unions on student achievement: Evidence from Wisconsin's act 10. *Economics of Education Review, 67,* 40–57.

Bastian, K. C. (2019). A degree above? The value-added estimates and evaluation ratings of teachers with a graduate degree. *Education Finance and Policy, 14,* 652–678.

Ben-Porath, Y. (1967). The production of human capital and the life-cycle of earnings. *Journal of Political Economy, 75,* 352–365.

Biasi, B. (2018). *The labor market for teachers under different pay schemes.* NBER Working Paper 24813.

Bonesrønning, H., Falch, T., & Strøm, B. (2005). Teacher sorting, teacher quality, and student composition. *European Economic Review, 49,* 457–483.

Breza, E., Kaur, S., & Shamdasani, Y. (2018). The morale effects of pay inequality. *Quarterly Journal of Economics, 133,* 611–663.

Britton, J., & Propper, C. (2016). Teacher pay and school productivity. *Journal of Public Economics, 133,* 75–89.

Chetty, R., Friedman, J. N., & Rockoff, J. N. (2014a). Measuring the impacts of teachers I: Evaluating bias in teacher value-added estimates. *American Economic Review, 104,* 2593–2632.

Chetty, R., Friedman, J. N., & Rockoff, J. N. (2014b). Measuring the impacts of teachers II: Teacher value added and student outcomes in adulthood. *American Economic Review, 104,* 2633–2679.

Chetty, R., Friedman, J. N., & Rockoff, J. N. (2017). Measuring the impacts of teachers: Reply. *American Economic Review, 107,* 1685–1717.

Clotfelter, C. T., Ladd, H. F., & Vigdor, J. L. (2006). Teacher-student matching and the assessment of teacher effectiveness. *Journal of Human Resources, 41*, 778−820.

Clotfelter, C. T., Ladd, H. F., & Vigdor, J. L. (2010). Teacher credentials and student achievement in high school: A cross subject analysis with student fixed effects. *Journal of Human Resources, 45*, 655−681.

Cohn, A., Fehr, E., & Goette, L. (2015). Fair wages and effort provision: Combining evidence from a choice experiment and a field experiment. *Management Science, 61*, 1777−1794.

Dieterle, S. G., Guarino, C. M., Reckase, M. M., & Wooldridge, J. M. (2014). How do principals assign students to teachers? Finding evidence in administrative data and the implications for value-added. *Journal of Policy Analysis and Management, 34*, 32−58.

Dolton, P., & Marcenaro-Gutierrez, O. D. (2011). If you pay peanuts do you get monkeys? A cross-country analysis of teacher pay and performance. *Economic Policy, 26*, 5−55.

Falch, T. (2011). Teacher mobility responses to wage changes: Evidence from a quasi- natural experiment. *American Economic Review, 101*, 460−465.

Falch, T., & Strøm, B. (2005). Teacher turnover and non-pecuniary factors. *Economics of Education Review, 24*, 611−631.

Feng, L., & Sass, T. R. (2017). Teacher quality and teacher mobility. *Education Finance and Policy, 12*, 396−418.

Figlio, D., & Winicki, J. (2005). Food for thought? The effects of school accountability plans on school nutrition. *Journal of Public Economics, 89*, 381−394.

Goldhaber, D., & Chaplin, D. D. (2015). Assessing the "Rothstein falsification test": Does it really show teacher value-added models are biased? *Journal of Research on Educational Effectiveness, 8*, 8−34.

Goodman, S. F., & Turner, L. J. (2013). The design of teacher incentive pay and educational outcomes: Evidence from the New York city bonus program. *Journal of Labor Economics, 31*, 409−420.

Gronqvist, E., & Vlachos, J. (2016). One size fits all ? The effects of teachers' cognitive and social abilities on student achievement. *Labour Economics, 42*, 138−150.

Hanushek, E. A. (1971). Teacher characteristics and gains in student achievement: Estimation using micro data. *American Economic Review, 61*, 280−288.

Hanushek, E. A. (1979). Conceptual and empirical issues in the estimation of educational production functions. *Journal of Human Resources, 14*, 351−388.

Hanushek, E. A., Kane, J. F., & Rivkin, S. G. (2004). Why public schools lose teachers. *Journal of Human Resources, 39*, 326−354.

Hanushek, E. A., Piopiunik, M., & Widerhold, S. (2019). The value of smarter teachers: International evidence on teacher skills and student performance. *Journal of Human Resources, 54*, 857−899.

Hanushek, E. A., & Rivkin, S. G. (2006). Teacher quality. In E. A. Hanushek, & F. Welch (Eds.), *Handbook of the Economics of Education* (volume 2, pp. 1051−1078). North Holland: Elsevier.

Hanushek, E. A., & Rivkin, S. G. (2012). The distribution of teacher quality and implications for policy. *Annual Review of Economics, 4*, 131−157.

Harris, D. N., & Sass, T. R. (2011). Teacher training, teacher quality and student achievement. *Journal of Public Economics, 95*, 798−812.

Hoxby, C. M. (1996). How teachers' unions affect education production. *Quarterly Journal of Economics, 111*, 671−718.

Jackson, C. K., & Bruegmann, E. (2009). Teaching students and teaching each other: The importance of peer learning for teachers. *American Economic Journal: Applied Economics, 1*, 85−108.

Jackson, C. K., Rockoff, J. E., & Staiger, D. A. (2014). Teacher effects and teacher-related policies. *Annual Review of Economics, 6*, 801−825.

Jacob, B. (2005). Testing, accountability, and incentives: The impact of high-stakes testing in Chicago public schools. *Journal of Public Economics, 89*, 761−796.

Jerrim, J., & Vignoles, A. (2016). The link between East Asian 'mastery' teaching methods and English children's mathematics skills. *Economics of Education Review, 50*, 29−44.

Kane, J., McCaffrey, D. F., Miller, T., & Staiger, D. O. (2013). *Have we identified effective teachers? Validating measures of effective teaching using random assignment.* Seattle, WA: Bill & Melinda Gates Foundation.

Kane, T. J., & Staiger, D. O. (2008). *Estimating teacher impacts on student achievement: An experimental evaluation.* NBER Working Paper No.14607.

Koedel, C., Mihaly, K., & Rockoff, J. E. (2015). Value-added modeling: A review. *Economics of Education Review, 47*, 180−195.

Lankford, H., & Wyckoff, J. (2010). Teacher labor markets: An overview. In D. J. Brewer, & P. J. McEwan (Eds.), *Economics of education*. Elsevier. Academic Press.

Lavy. (2009). Performance pay and teachers' effort, productivity, and grading ethics. *American Economic Review, 99*, 1979−201.

Leigh, A. (2012). Teacher pay and teacher aptitude. *Economics of Education Review, 31*, 41−53.

Loeb, S., & Page, M. E. (2000). Examining the link between teacher wages and student outcomes: The importance of alternative labor market opportunities and non-pecuniary variation. *Review of Economics and Statistics, 82*, 393−408.

Lovenheim, M. F. (2009). The effect of teachers' unions on education production: Evidence from union election certifications in three midwestern states. *Journal of Labor Economics, 27*, 525−587.

Loevenheim, M. F., & Willén, A. (2019). The long-run effects of teacher collective bargaining. *American Economic Journal: Economic Policy, 11,* 292–324.

Machin, S., & McNally, S. (2008). The literacy hour. *Journal of Public Economics, 92,* 1441–1462.

Machin, S., McNally, S., & Viarengo, M. (2018). Changing how literacy is taught: Evidence on synthetic phonics. *American Economic Journal: Economic Policy, 10,* 217–241.

Papay, J. P., & Kraft, M. A. (2015). Productivity returns to experience in the teacher labor market. Methodological challenges and new evidence on long-term career improvement. *Journal of Public Economics, 130,* 105–119.

Rockoff, J. E., Jacob, B. A., Kane, T. J., & Staiger, D. O. (2011). Can we recognize an effective teacher when we recruit one? *Education Finance and Policy, 6,* 43–74.

Rothstein, J. (2010). Teacher quality in educational production: Tracking, decay, and student achievement. *Quarterly Journal of Economics, 125,* 175–214.

Rothstein, J. (2017). Measuring the impacts of teachers: Comment. *American Economic Review, 107,* 1656–1684.

Slater, H., Davies, N. M., & Burgess, S. (2012). Do teachers matter? Measuring the variation in teacher effectiveness in England. *OxfordBulletin of Economics and Statistics, 74,* 629–645.

Staiger, D. O., & Kane, T. J. (2014). The relationship between annual student achievement gains and a teacher's career value added. In T. J. Kane, K. A. Kerr, & R. C. Pianta (Eds.), *Designing teacher evaluation systems: New guidance from the measures of effective teaching project.* San Fransisco, CA: John Wiley & Sons Inc.

Willén, A. (2018). *From a fixed national pay scale to individual wage bargaining: The labor market effects of wage decentralization.* Working Paper.

Wiswall, M. (2013). The dynamics of teacher quality. *Journal of Public Economics, 100,* 61–78.

The economics of class size

D.W. Schanzenbach

University of Chicago, Chicago, IL, United States

Introduction

Class-size reduction is a politically popular but relatively expensive education reform. Understanding the causal relationship between class size and student achievement is critical for determining whether class-size reduction can be recommended as a policy to improve student outcomes. We begin with a review of the theory of why class size might matter, followed by a discussion of the empirical strategies for identifying the causal impact of class size on student achievement. Next, the empirical literature on class-size reduction is reviewed, focusing on studies using experimental and quasi-experimental techniques because these rely on the most credible strategies for identifying the true causal relationship between class size and student achievement.

Why class size might matter

For most readers, class size and academic outcomes are probably intuitively linked. Nonetheless, it may be helpful to formalize the idea somewhat. Lazear (2001) puts forth a useful theory of educational production. In it, reducing class size decreases the amount of time that the classroom is disrupted, increasing time devoted to productive tasks. A simple summary of the model is as follows: a child is behaving in class at a given moment with probability p, and misbehaving with probability $(1 - p)$. In the model, misbehavior is broadly defined, ranging from talking or fighting, to behaviors such as asking questions that slow down the class or monopolizing the teacher's time. When there are n children in the classroom, p^n is the probability that the entire class is behaving and learning is taking place (assuming that p is independent across children). Assuming a constant disruption rate, having fewer students in the class means that learning is taking place in a larger fraction of time.

In the model, the impact of reducing class size depends not only on the size of the class, but also on the behavior of the students in it. As a result, the Lazear theory predicts that class-size effects should be larger for classes with more poorly behaved students. For example, on average p may decrease with age, so the impact of class-size reduction might be smaller for high school students than elementary school students. The impact of class-size reduction — all else equal — is predicted to be larger for groups with lower propensities to behave.

Empirical approaches to studying the impact of class size

Economists typically model the relationship between student achievement and class size for student/in school j as

$$Y_{ij} = aS_{ij} + bF_{ij} + \varepsilon_{ij} \qquad [1]$$

where Y represents a measure of student achievement. S contains information on school-level inputs that impact achievement, such as class size, F contains family inputs, such as parental education, and e is an error term. Both S and F measure inputs over the child's entire lifetime, and may contain inputs that are not observable to the econometrician. A negative co-efficient on class size would suggest that student achievement declines as class size increases.

The problem with estimating Eq. (1) (and similar versions of it) is that class size may be endogenous such that $E(\varepsilon|S, F) \neq 0$. For example, if students are assigned to small classes or better teachers in a compensatory manner — perhaps, because of low baseline test scores, or low levels of family inputs — but that information is not available to the researcher, the estimated impact of school resources will be biased. The most obvious such example is remedial or special-education courses, which tend to be small in size. Similarly, bias will result if parents who are more involved in their children's education are more likely to push for a smaller class or better teachers, and parental involvement is not measured in the dataset.

Due to these confounding factors, researchers have relied on strategies that use (plausibly) exogenous variation in class size in order to identify the causal impact of class size on student achievement. In other words, to identify the effect of class size, the variation in class size must come from factors that are more or less out of the control of decision makers such as parents and educators. The easiest example of this is where students are randomly assigned to classes of different size. The benefit of using a randomized experiment is that the treatment assignment is unrelated to any omitted characteristics. Such a design allows researchers to isolate the impact of the policy they are trying to test, without confounding factors such as parental pressure or compensating assignments. Thus, an experimental study typically offers more compelling evidence than a nonexperimental study, which simply observes the relationship between Y and S in the real world.

With a well-designed experimental assignment, a straightforward comparison of means by class type will provide an unbiased estimate of the impact of class size on achievement. In the case of (an idealized version of) a class-size experiment in which students are randomized within schools, the equation to be estimated might be as follows:

$$Y_{ics} = \beta_0 + \beta_1 \, SMALL_{cs} + X_{ics}\gamma + \alpha_s, + v_{ics} \qquad [2]$$

where $SMALL$ is an indicator variable for randomly assigned small-class treatment, and c indexes class c in school s. X is a vector of student-level characteristics. When treatments are randomized, student-level covariates are not related to class assignment and their inclusion should not change the estimated effect on class size, but should just contribute to the overall explanatory power of the model. A school-level fixed effect, α, is included, so that identification of small-class effects are identified off of within-school comparisons. Finally, the error term v contains class-level and individual-level components, reflecting random differences in teacher and student quality.

Nonexperimental research

There have been volumes of research looking at the relationship between class size and student performance in nonexperimental settings. These are well summarized in a pair of influential meta-analyses by Hanushek (1986, 1997). In them, he argues that the lion's share of the economics of education literature finds no consistent relationship between class size and student performance. In the 277 estimates from 59 published studies included in the 1997 paper, only 15% showed a positive, statistically significant impact of class size on student outcomes. A reanalysis by Krueger (2003) raised questions about the validity of the meta-analysis, and argued that the literature largely supports a positive impact of reduced class size. Interested readers are encouraged to refer to Hanushek (2003) for an overview of the debate.

The usefulness of the Hanushek meta-analyses is limited by the underlying quality of the studies included in them. Most - but certainly not all - of the underlying studies relied only on observational variation and did not have a research design that would allow the estimation of the causal impact of class size on student achievement. This is problematic for several reasons. For one, within-school variation in class size (in the absence of a true experiment) is seldom random. If, for example, there is compensatory assignment to smaller classes, then the coefficient on class size will not only pick up the true effect of being in a smaller class but also any correlated omitted variables such as special-education status or poor prior achievement as discussed above (see also Boozer & Rouse, 2001). In addition, if there are only small differences in class size within school - for example, one classroom with 22 students and the other with 23 students — then one would need a large amount of data to precisely estimate the effect of such a small difference in class size. In general, it is inappropriate to base public policy on research that does not have a compelling identification strategy. As a result, much more weight should be placed on the experimental and quasi-experimental evidence outlined below.

Experimental research

The most influential studies of class-size reduction are based on data from Project STAR, a large-scale randomized trial in the US state of Tennessee to test the impact of reducing class sizes in grades K-3. Mosteller (1995) described Project Steps to Achieving Resilience (STAR) as "one of the most important educational investigations ever carried out and illustrates the kind and magnitude of research needed in the field of education to strengthen schools." In the experiment, students were randomly assigned within school to one of three treatment types: a small-size class (target of 13—17 students), a regular-size class (target of 22—25 students), or a regular-size class with a full-time teacher's aide. Importantly, teachers were also randomly assigned to class types. The experiment took place in 79 public schools across a variety of geographic locations (inner-city, suburban, and rural; predominantly low income, and middle class) for a single cohort of students in kindergarten through third grade in the years 1985—89. An eventual 11 600 students and 1330 teachers took part in the experiment. It is worth noting that the experiment made some students better off than they would have been, but of course did not otherwise increase class sizes beyond their normal range in the state at the time. Thus, no students were made worse off by being assigned to abnormally large classes.

In the ideal implementation of this experiment, students were to remain with the same randomly assigned class type from kindergarten through the end of third grade. In practice, though, there were several major sources of deviation from this model. Students who entered a participating school while the cohort was in first, second, or third grades were added to the experiment and randomly assigned to a class type. There were a substantial number of new entrants — 45% of eventual participants entered after kindergarten. A relatively large fraction of students also exited Project STAR schools (45% of overall participants), due to school moves, grade retention, or grade skipping, which also caused deviations from the original plan (see Krueger (1999) and Hanushek (1999) for further discussion). Fortunately, many of these exiting students are recaptured in the follow-up analysis described below, which includes all students in Tennessee in grades 4–8, and a nationwide match of college-entrance-exam takers when the cohort is around 12th grade. In addition, in response to parental concerns about fairness to students, all students in regular and regular-aide classes were re-randomized across the two treatment groups in first grade. This deviation is less problematic for evaluation of the program, because it involved new randomization. In general, studies have found no difference in performance between regular and regular-aide classes, so these two groups are sometimes combined as the control group.

Finally, a smaller number of students (about 10% of participants) were moved from one class type to another in a nonrandom manner. It has been reported that most of these moves were due to student misbehavior, and were not typically the result of parental requests for moves to small classes (Krueger, 1999). Of all transitions, 25% were into small (more desirable) classes. This weakness of the experiment can be addressed through use of an intent-to-treat setup — that is, to use the variation caused by initial randomly assigned class type instead of the actual (possibly nonrandom) class type attended.

In practice, the nonrandom transitions and new entrants described above complicate the approach somewhat. Due to nonrandom transitions after initial assignment, it would be inappropriate to use current-year class type; instead, initial class-type assignment (the intent-to-treat measure) is typically used in studies using Project STAR data. That is, all impacts are measured with regard to the class that students were assigned to, and not the class

that they actually attended. The intent-to-treat measure used in this case likely understates the impact of small classes by up to 15% (Krueger, 1999). Nonetheless, the conservative intent-to-treat measure based on random assignment is typically considered preferable to models which measure the impact of actual class type attended in cases in which there is nonrandom movement between classes. A simple example may help illustrate this: if a child were moved from a regular class to a small class because his parents insisted on the move, it is also reasonable to assume that the parents are especially active in other aspects of the student's education. For example, they may monitor homework closely or provide other education-enhancing opportunities. Researchers cannot control for these characteristics because they do not have perfect measures of the home environment. In the ideal case in which class type is randomly assigned, these home-environment measures are uncorrelated with class type and their impacts are absorbed in the error term in Eq. (2). When the effect of actual (nonrandom) class attended is measured instead, some of the impacts of the active home environment also may be picked up because actual attendance may be correlated with this home-environment component of the error term. Using the experimentally induced variation in this case means that not all students actually attend their assigned class type, and some students' test scores will count toward the regular-size class they were assigned to, even though they actually attended small classes. This approach circumvents the causation problem, but provides an understatement of the true impact. Krueger (1999) provides a more detailed discussion of this matter.

As described above, new entrants into the program were randomly assigned to class types. So, even though new entrants in first, second, and third grades on average are more disadvantaged than the kindergarten entrants, randomization allows us to compare new entrants in each grade to other new entrants in the same school across class types. In practice, then, the school-level fixed effect in Eq. (3) is replaced with a fixed effect that combines school with a student's grade of entry (K, 1, 2, or 3) to the experiment, as this is the pool within which random assignment was determined (K representing kindergarten). In general, work on Project STAR has employed the following approach:

$$Y_{igs} = \beta_{0g} + \beta_{1g} SMALL_{is} + \beta_{2g} AIDE_{is}$$
$$+ \beta_{3g} X_{is} + \alpha_{sw} + \varepsilon_{igs} \qquad [3]$$

Here g indexes the grade of the outcome measure. Both the SMALL and AIDE variables are measured as initial assignment, and not actual class attendance. The fixed effect varies by the randomization pool — school interacted with entry wave w. The coefficient on the control for classes with a teacher aide is sometimes omitted, as there appears to be no difference in outcomes between regular and regular-aide classes. As a result, the coefficient of interest measuring the small-class effect is similar whether or not aide classes are separately controlled. For precision, other student-level covariates such as gender, race, and free-lunch status are included in the vector X of control variables, but because of random assignment, including these controls does not change the magnitude of the small-class effect. The dependent variable is an outcome such as the mean math and reading score on the Stanford Achievement Test (SAT)

for each grade, or whether a student took a college entrance exam.

Checks for randomization

Due to the experimental design, impacts of reduced class size are straightforward to measure as the within-school (and entry wave) difference between class types, provided the randomization was done correctly. A compelling check of randomization is to examine a pretest to ensure that there are no measurable differences in the dependent variable between class types before the program begins. Unfortunately, no baseline test measure was collected in Project STAR. Another way to investigate whether randomization was done properly is to compare student characteristics that are related to student achievement but cannot be manipulated in response to treatment, such as student race, gender, and age. If there are no systematic differences in observable characteristics across class types, this provides support that the randomization was done properly. A similar check should be done on observable teacher characteristics.

Table 23.1 presents estimates of differences in mutable characteristics across initial treatment assignment. This is similar to tables presented in Krueger (1999) and Krueger and Whitmore

TABLE 23.1 Testing whether covariates appear randomly assigned.[a]

	(1)	(2)	(3)	(4)
Panel A: Student characteristics	Female = 1	White = 1	Free lunch = 1	Age in 1985 (in years)
	0.000	-0.002	-0.014	-0.012
	(0.012)	(0.006)	(0.011)	(0.011)
Panel B: Teacher characteristics	Female = 1	White = 1	Master's degree or higher = 1	Total experience (in years)
	-0.001	-0.001	-0.051	-0.155
	(0.006)	(0.018)	(0.027)	(0.470)

[a] Each entry represents a separate regression. Only coefficients on initial assignment to small class are reported. Standard errors, in parentheses, are clustered by randomization pool. Other covariates include randomization-pool fixed effects.

(2001). The estimating equation is similar to Eq. (3) above, with student or teacher characteristic on the left-hand side and indicators for small-class assignment and school-by-entry-wave fixed effects. Standard errors are clustered at the school level. Each table entry represents a separate regression, and only the coefficient and standard error on small-class assignment are reported. Since none of the coefficients are large or statistically significant, this is evidence that the randomization was done correctly, at least with regard to observable characteristics. The single exception is that the teacher having a master's degree or higher is marginally significant ($p = 0.06$). This means that teachers with more education were slightly less likely to be assigned to small classes. The results below are virtually unchanged if direct controls for teacher characteristics are included. Now that the randomization is validated, it is straightforward to turn to results of the experiment.

Achievement results

Table 23.2 reports the impact of initial assignment to a small class on student test scores in grades K–3. Eq. (3) is estimated, and each table entry reflects a separate regression. Test scores are normalized into z-scores based on the regular and regular-aide population. Average math and reading scores are reported in most cases, though if a student was missing a test score for one test but not both, the score for the non-missing test is used. The coefficient on the indicator variable for small class can be interpreted as the standard-deviation impact of the treatment. As many researchers have found (Krueger, 1999; Krueger & Whitmore, 2001; Word et al., 1990), the table indicates that overall, students benefit about 0.15 standard deviations from assignment to a small class. When the results are disaggregated by race, it appears that black students benefited more from being assigned to a small class than the overall population, suggesting that reducing class size might be an effective strategy to reduce the black–white achievement gap. Krueger and Whitmore (2002) find that this result is largely driven by a larger treatment effect for all students regardless of race in predominantly black schools, suggesting that benefits from additional resources are higher in such schools. Benefits are also larger for students from low socioeconomic status families, measured by whether they receive free or reduced-price lunch.

TABLE 23.2 Small-class effects on test scores during the experiment.[a]

	(1)	(2)	(3)	(4)
Panel A: Overall	Kindergarten	Grade 1	Grade 2	Grade 3
	0.187	0.189	0.141	0.152
	(0.039)	(0.035)	(0.034)	(0.030)
Panel B: Black students only	Kindergarten	Grade 1	Grade 2	Grade 3
	0.214	0.249	0.207	0.242
	(0.074)	(0.063)	(0.054)	(0.060)
Panel C: Free-lunch students only	Kindergarten	Grade 1	Grade 2	Grade 3
	0.188	0.195	0.174	0.174
	(0.046)	(0.042)	(0.041)	(0.039)

[a] *Each entry represents a separate regression. Only coefficients on initial assignment to small class are reported. Standard errors are in parentheses, clustered by randomization pool. Other covariates include randomization-pool fixed effects and student demographic characteristics.*

In fourth grade, the class-size reduction experiment concluded and all students were returned to regular-sized classes. At the same time, the assessment test was changed from the SAT to the Comprehensive Test of Basic Skills (CTBS). Both tests are multiple-choice standardized tests that measure reading and math achievement, and are taken by students at the end of the school year. The CTBS results are scaled in the same manner as the SAT, in terms of standard deviation units. One important difference in the data is that all students in public schools statewide who had ever participated in Project STAR are included in the follow-up study, even if they had been retained a grade. It is estimated that 20% of students had been retained a grade by eighth grade, but this did not vary with initial class assignment. As a result, some students took the fourth-grade test in 1990, while others took it in later years or even took it more than once. In the analysis reported here, all scores from grade $g-$ no matter what year a student was in that grade - are compared. In the event of multiple attempts at grade $\_g's$ test, the first available score is used. As in Table 23.2, all estimates are conditional on school-by-entry wave fixed effects and only the coefficient on small class is reported.

Results for grades 4–8 are reported in Table 23.3. Overall, there is a persistent positive impact of small-class assignment that is statistically significant (or borderline significant) through eighth grade, as has been found in previous studies (e.g., Krueger & Whitmore, 2001). The magnitude of the gain is one-third to one-half the size that was observed while the students were in the experimental classes. When the results are disaggregated, though, the impact appears to remain stronger with black and free-lunch students than with more advantaged students. There is also some evidence that nonacademic outcomes such as the rates of criminal behavior and teen pregnancy are improved (Krueger & Whitmore, 2002).

Another potential measure of student achievement is whether these students take the SAT or the American College Test (ACT) college-entrance exam, which can be used as an early proxy for college attendance. In order to measure this, Project STAR student data were matched to the national databases of college-entry test records, as described in Krueger and Whitmore (2001, 2002). To examine whether

TABLE 23.3 Small-class effects on long-term test scores.[a]

	Grade 4 (z-score) (1)	Grade 5 (z-score) (2)	Grade 6 (z-score) (3)	Grade 7 (z-score) (4)	Grade 8 (z-score) (5)	Took college entrance test (1 = yes) (6)
Panel A: Overall	0.035	0.048	0.060	0.040	0.036	0.024
	(0.025)	(0.024)	(0.025)	(0.025)	(0.025)	(0.010)
Panel B: Black	0.078	0.080	0.105	0.066	0.063	0.050
Students only	(0.048)	(0.043)	(0.045)	(0.042)	(0.046)	(0.018)
Panel C: Free-lunch	0.029	0.058	0.080	0.067	0.064	0.031
Students only	(0.036)	(0.031)	(0.034)	(0.031)	(0.034)	(0.014)

[a] Each entry represents a separate regression. Only coefficients on initial assignment to small class are reported. Standard errors are in parentheses, clustered by randomization pool. Other covariates include randomization pool-fixed effects and student demographic characteristics.

assignment to a small class influences the college-entrance exam test-taking rate, a binary variable indicating that a college-entrance exam was taken is the dependent variable in Eq. (3). The impact of small-class assignment on college test taking is included as the final column in Table 23.3. Overall, test-taking rates increase by about 2% points. Black students were 5% points more likely to take the SAT or ACT if they were assigned to a small rather than regular-size class. On average, 38% of black students assigned to small classes took at least one of the college-entrance exams, compared with 33% in regular classes. Such a striking difference in test-taking rates between the small and regular class students could occur by chance less than one in 10 000 tries. Krueger and Whitmore (2002) interpret the magnitude of these effects by reference to the resulting reduction in the black–white test-taking gap. In regular classes, the black–white gap in taking a college entrance exam was 12.9% points, compared to 5.1% points for students in small classes. Thus, assigning all students to a small class is estimated to reduce the black–white gap in the test-taking rate by an impressive 60%. After controlling for increased selection into the test among small-class students, the impact on test scores for blacks is 0.15 standard deviations – about the same as the test-score impact in third grade.

Additional caveats

An important limitation to the experiment was nonrandom movement across class-type assignment, as well as sample attrition during the treatment phase. As discussed briefly above (and at much greater length in the referenced works, especially Krueger, 1999), nonrandom movement can be addressed through using initial class-type assignment and not the actual (nonrandom) class-type attended. The attrition problem is significantly addressed through the

statewide and nationwide matches used for the follow-up analyses.

Another concern often raised about the results of randomized experiments generally is that the measured effect may be driven by Hawthorne effects and might not be generalized to nonexperimental settings. That is, people participating in the experiment might act differently than they normally do because they know they are being studied. Although one cannot directly test for Hawthorne effects, Krueger (1999) attempts to shed light on the issue by investigating differences in achievement using the variation across only regular-sized classes, as there is little reason to think that Hawthorne effects would cause some classes in the treatment group to behave differently relative to other treatment-group classes. Class size in regular-sized classes ranged from 16 to 30 students, but the bulk of the distribution was between 20 and 26 students. Whether or not school effects are controlled for, students in a regular class with slightly fewer members out-scored larger regular classes. The estimated magnitude of a one-student reduction in class size was consistent with the magnitude of the experimental results (which estimates the impact of a seven-student reduction).

Finally, another concern is whether the findings of this experiment may be generalized to other settings. Along many measures, Tennessee in the mid-1980s looks reasonably similar to other places that might be interested in implementing a class-size reduction policy, so it would be reasonable to expect similar effects as those in the experiment. On the other hand, the Tennessee sample has lower levels of education inputs than the United States overall at the time, as measured by spending per student and education level of teachers. If adding resources has a greater impact when the baseline levels are already low, this might mean that schools with higher levels of spending could experience a smaller impact of class-size reduction. In addition, in order to be eligible for the experiment, schools were required to have a large enough enrolment to support three classrooms per grade. As a result, Project STAR schools were about 30% larger than average schools in Tennessee or across the United States. If larger schools are somehow differently effective with additional resources, then the findings in Project STAR may not be generalizable to smaller school settings (see Schanzenbach (2007) for further discussion of these points).

Quasi-experimental research

As true randomized experiments are rare, researchers must also look for quasi-experimental approaches that allow isolation of the causal impact of class-size reduction. One of the strengths of quasi-experimental approaches is that the participants are unaware that they are being studied, so Hawthone effects are unlikely.

The most famous quasi-experimental approach to studying class-size reduction comes from Angrist and Lavy's (1999) use of a strict maximum class-size rule in Israel and a regression discontinuity (RD) approach. In Israel, maximum class size is dictated by Maimonides' rule, which specifies that no more than 40 students shall be in one class. As a result, if the school's total enrolment in a grade is 40 students or fewer, there will only be one classroom with a class size equal to the total enrolment. If the enrolment increases from 40 to 41 students, though, a second class must be added, and the average class size declines precipitously from 40 students to 20.5 students. Similarly, if enrolment increases from 80 to 81 students, a school must move from two to three classes and the average class size falls from 40 students to 27 students.

Using the local variation around the enrolment sizes that are multiples of 40 students, Angrist and Lavy isolate the causal impact of class-size reduction. They find strong improvements overall in both math and reading scores, of a magnitude that is consistent with Project STAR's experimental results. Like in Project STAR, they also find larger improvements among disadvantaged students.

Urquiola (2006) uses a similar RD approach in Bolivia and finds that a one standard-deviation reduction in class size (about eight students in his data) improves test-score performance by 0.2–0.3 standard deviations. Browning and Heinesen (2007) also find similar results on data from Denmark, even though average class size is much smaller in their study (20 pupils per classroom, compared to 31 students in Angrist and Lavy's Israeli data). Urquiola and Verhoogen (2009) provide a cautionary tale about possible endogenous responses of schools to class-size caps, and show that in Chilean data, these endogenous responses of schools lead to violations of the assumptions of the RD design. In addition, caveats about the external validity of these studies are required as was the case with Project STAR.

Another quasi-experimental approach comes from Hoxby's (2000) study of class size in the US state of Connecticut. In the study, Hoxby isolates the variation in enrolment that comes from random fluctuations in cohort sizes across adjacent years. That is, taking away any preexisting trends in enrolment that might signify that a school district is waning or booming, the effect of class size is identified by variation in cohort size that reflects a temporary random shock in population size that may have been caused by an unusually small (or large) birth rate in a given year. Using this approach, Hoxby finds no positive effect of reduced class size, but has the statistical precision to rule out an effect as large as about one-fifth the size found in Project STAR. The discrepancy between these results and those of other well-identified experimental and quasi-experimental studies remains a puzzle.

Policy-induced variation

Another potentially promising approach to studying the effects of class-size reduction comes from sharp changes in policies regarding class size. The most famous recent example comes from the US state of California, where in 1996 a law was passed to give strong monetary incentives to schools to reduce class size in grades K–3 to 20 or fewer students. Unfortunately, from a research-design perspective, the take-up of the policy was nearly universal within a short period of time, so there was very little variation to exploit and evaluate its impact. In addition, test scores are only available starting in grade 4, so any evaluation of the policy was forced to use later test scores (instead of scores during the year that the reduced class size was experienced) as the outcome measure. Not surprisingly, the best evaluation of the policy found inconclusive results (Bohrnstedt & Stecher, 2002). It is unfortunate that this policy intervention, costing more than $1 billion per year, did not yield useful information about the impact of class-size reduction on student outcomes.

Discussion

The bulk of the research using credible identification of the impacts of class-size reduction suggests that reducing class size will significantly improve test scores. In addition, the benefits appear to be larger for disadvantaged groups such as African American students and children from families with low socioeconomic status. The long-term follow-up of the Project STAR class-size experiment finds that the gains appear to persist even after students are returned to regular-sized classes. The prior research has been less able to credibly isolate potential nonlinear effects of class size, which is an important consideration for policymakers considering a potential class-size reduction.

An important question that policymakers must ask prior to embarking on class-size reduction is whether the projected benefits outweigh the costs. A cost-benefit study of Project STAR found that the overall benefits outweighed the

costs (Krueger & Whitmore, 2001). The answer in other cases will depend on the school's situation. What is the current level of educational inputs? Are there many disadvantaged students? Do we want to put extra weight on questions of equity - for example, the potential for small classes to reduce the black-white achievement gap? Is there a ready supply of qualified individuals available to meet the increased demand for classroom teachers? And, of course, what is the next best use of the available funds?

See also

Empirical Research Methods in the Economics of Education; Education Production Functions: Concepts; Education Production Functions: Evidence from Developed Countries; Education Production Functions; Evidence from Developing Countries.

References

Angrist, J. D., & Lavy, V. (1999). Using Maimonides' rule to estimate the effect of class size on scholastic achievement. *Quarterly Journal of Economics, 114*(2), 533–575.

Bohrnstedt, G. W., & Stecher, B. M. (2002). *What we have learned about class size reduction in California.* CSR Research Consortium Capstone Report.

Boozer, M., & Rouse, C. (2001). Intraschool variation in class size: Patterns and implications. *Journal of Urban Economics, 50*(1), 163–189.

Browning, M., & Heinesen, E. (2007). Class size, teacher hours and educational attainment. *Scandinavian Journal of Economics, 109*(2), 415–438.

Hanushek, E. A. (1986). The economics of schooling: Production and efficiency in public schools. *Journal of Economic Literature, 24,* 1141–1177.

Hanushek, E. A. (1997). Assessing the effects of school resources on student performance: An update. *Educational Evaluation and Policy Analysis, 19*(2), 141–164.

Hanushek, E. A. (1999). Some findings from an independent investigation of the Tennessee STAR experiment and from other investigations of class size effects. *Educational Evaluation and Policy Analysis, 21,* 154–164.

Hanushek, E. A. (2003). The failure of inputs-based schooling policies. *The Economic Journal, 113*(485), F64–F98.

Hoxby, C. M. (2000). The effects of class size on student achievement: New evidence from population variation. *Quarterly Journal of Economics, 115*(4), 1239–1285.

Krueger, A. B. (1999). Experimental estimates of education production functions. *Quarterly Journal of Economics, 114*(2), 497–532.

Krueger, A. B., & Whitmore, D. M. (2001). The effect of attending a small class in the early grades on college-test taking and middle school test results: Evidence from project STAR. *Economic Journal, 111,* 1–28.

Krueger, A. B., & Whitmore, D. (2002). Would smaller classes help close the black-white achievement gap? In J. E. Chubb, & T. Loveless (Eds.), *Bridging the achievement gap* (pp. 11–46). Washington, DC: Brookings Institution Press.

Kureger, A. B. (2003). Economic considerations and class size. *The Economic Journal, 113*(485), F34–F63.

Lazear, E. P. (2001). Educational production. *Quarterly Journal of Economics, 116,* 777–803.

Mosteller, F. (1995). The Tennessee study of class size in the early school grades. *Future of Children, 5*(2), 113–127.

Schanzenbach, D. W. (2007). What have researchers learned from project STAR? *Brookings Papers on Education Policy, 2007,* 205–228.

Urquiola, M. (2006). Identifying class size effects in developing countries: Evidence from rural Bolivia. *Review of Economics and Statistics, 88*(1), 171–177.

Urquiola, M., & Verhoogen, E. (2009). Class-size caps, sorting, and the regression-discontinuity design. *American Economic Review, 99*(1), 179–215.

Word, E., Johnston, J., Bain, H. P., et al. (1990). *Student/teacher achievement ratio (STAR): Tennessee's K-3 class size study.* Final Summary Report 1985–1990. Nashville, TN: Tennessee State Department of Education.

Further reading

Achilles, C. M., Nye, B. A., Zaharias, J. B., & DeWayne Fulton, B. (1993). *The lasting benefits study (LBS) in grades 4 and 5 (1990-1991).* A legacy from Tennessee's four-year (K-3) class-size study (1985-1989), project STAR. Research Paper, HEROS. Ehrenberg, R. G., Brewer, D. J., Gamoran, A., & Wiilms, J. D. (2001). Does class size matter? Scientific American 285(5), 78–86.

School finance: an overview

Jennifer King Rice[a], David Monk[b], Jijun Zhang[a,c]

[a]University of Maryland, College Park, MD, United States; [b]The Pennsylvania State University, State College, PA, United States; [c]American Institutes for Research, Washington, DC, United States

Introduction

School finance is a broad and evolving field encompassing three resource-related functions — revenue generation, resource allocation, and resource utilization — all aimed at providing educational opportunities and producing educational outcomes. All of these activities occur in a broader context of educational goals and societal values that shape how finance systems are structured and executed. In this chapter, we provide an overview of school finance, emphasizing the enduring challenges and highlighting new ways of thinking about them. We begin by exploring contextual factors that influence school finance decisions; this includes a discussion of the goals and purposes of public education and the broader societal values that frame public finance. The next section describes traditional and contemporary mechanisms for raising revenue to support education systems, and examines the role of different levels of government in supporting public education. The section that follows discusses how resources are allocated across education systems, and emphasizes the evolution of equity and efficiency considerations

in our allocation decisions. We conclude with a set of critical resource utilization issues that are at the center of current school finance policy deliberations.

Throughout the chapter, our goal is to provide a sense of how this field has evolved, and we emphasize longstanding challenges and new ways of thinking about enduring issues. With the goal of offering an overview of the field, we prioritize breadth over depth and refer readers to other sources for additional information on the complexities and nuances of the topics covered. In addition, many of the ideas touched on in this chapter are given more in-depth attention elsewhere in this volume. Our focus here is on K-12 public education systems in the US Issues related to financing higher education, non-public education, and education in international contexts are addressed in other chapters in the *Encyclopedia*.

School finance in context

The goals and purposes of public education are to meet both individual and societal demands for schooling. In general, purposes of education are to produce individuals who can contribute to the economic, political, civic, social, and cultural institutions in our society. As such, we expect high school graduates to have acquired a wide range of competencies, skills, and personal qualities. These ideas are consistent with those of early proponents of public education including Horace Mann and Thomas Jefferson. Further, they reflect the work of international efforts to identify the array of "key competencies that contribute to a successful life and a well-functioning society" (Rychen & Salganik, 2003).

While many of the benefits of formal education are enjoyed by individuals in the form of better employment opportunities, higher wages, better health, expanded options for leisure time, and a better life for themselves and their children, it is the social benefits of education that justify a publicly-financed system of schools. These social or collective benefits include all of the benefits enjoyed by individuals in the society, plus additional benefits that are uniquely collective in nature (Cohn & Geske, 2004). For instance, from a societal perspective, investments in public education pay returns in the form of national economic productivity and growth, good citizenship and a working democracy, a more peaceful society, and lower costs associated with prisons and social services. Analysts typically classify educational benefits into a four-cell matrix, as shown in Table 24.1.

Calculating the returns on investments in education has been the focus of research, and estimates depend on a number of contextual factors including the developmental status of the nation, and the level and type of education (Psacharapolous, 2006). Taken together, studies show that education is a good investment for individuals and for society, with a rate of return typically exceeding 10% (Becker, 1993, chap. 2, pp. 15–25; Card & Krueger, 1996; Montenegro & Patrinos, 2014). Estimating the "full" returns to education has long been a challenge due to the difficulties of quantifying many of the non-market benefits, though some progress has been made capturing the value of benefits like lower crime rates, better child education, household health resulting from investments in education, and the civic returns to education (Barnett & Masse, 2007; Baum & Payea, 2013; Dee, 2004; Haveman & Wolfe, 1984)

The estimated benefits of education, particularly education at the elementary level that gives rise to basic literacy skills, make a compelling case for a public investment in education. Each year, hundreds of billions dollars in federal, state, and local revenues are dedicated to public K-12 education (National Center for Education Statistics, 2018).[1] Over the past 50 years, 4–5% of the Gross Domestic Product has been invested in elementary and secondary education in the US (NCES, 2018). Decisions about how best to raise and allocate these resources are influenced by three broad and sometimes competing goals: efficiency, equity, and liberty (Garms, Guthrie, & Pierce, 1978).[2] The goal of efficiency holds that resources should be used to pursue the best set of outcomes in ways that minimize the use of resources. The goal of equity emphasizes the

---

[1] In 2015–16, expenditures for elementary and secondary education in the U.S. totaled $707 billion. K-12 education spending as a percentage of gross domestic product increased from 4.1 in 1995–96 to 4.5 in 2009–10, but has declined since then to 3.9% in 2015–16 (NCES, 2018).

[2] While the ideas presented here are relatively straightforward, each of these goals is multi-faceted and complex. For instance, our definition of efficiency deals with production efficiency, but efficiency in exchange is also an important consideration (See Monk, 1990). Likewise, the concept of equity has been defined in numerous ways (see, for example, Wise, 1972). Finally, how to apply the goal of liberty in the provision of public education is wrought with complexities, particularly with respect to early childhood education.

TABLE 24.1   Classification of the benefits of education.

Benefit type	Private	Social
Market	Employability	Higher productivity
	Higher earnings	Higher net tax revenue
	Labor market flexibility	Less reliance on government financial support
	Greater mobility	
Nonmarket	Greater consumer efficiency	Lower crime rates
	Better household health	Less spread of infectious diseases
		Desired family size
		Better social cohesion
	Non-wage remuneration (fringe benefits and working conditions)	Civic participation (voter participation, volunteerism, charity; service in public agencies)
	Future opportunities for children	Technological change

Source: Adapted from Wolfe and Zuvekas (1997), and Psacharopoulos (2006).

fairness in the distribution of a good, service, or burden. The goal of liberty holds that revenue generation and resource allocation should be conducted in a way that properly balances individual in contrast to collective interests. While each of these goals is important in its own right, they are often in tension with one another requiring policymakers to strike a reasonable balance among them as they consider options for raising, distributing, and utilizing resources to realize the goals of public education.

Raising revenue: multiple and evolving roles

Historically, school finance in the US was largely a local function.[3] Families and communities raised resources to provide local schools so that children would learn the knowledge, skills, and values needed to be competent and productive adult members of the community. As the broader civic, social, and economic benefits of public education became more apparent, state laws requiring children to attend school were adopted. Compulsory education laws, first enacted in the mid-1600s, obligated states to establish school systems to finance and administer public education. By the mid 1800s, systems of universal, tax-support education involving multiple levels of government spread throughout the country. Most often these systems were organized around school districts that were responsible for raising revenue, typically through the use of the local property tax, and providing educational services for students. This local system of education finance coupled with the uneven distribution of wealth across districts, however, resulted in large disparities across communities in education spending, services, and outcomes. Despite the efficiencies expected to result from this decentralized system of school finance (i.e., the potential for local systems to better meet the preferences of their constituencies), the inherent inequities associated

[3] For a history of education finance, see Guthrie et al. 2007.

with such a heavy reliance on the local property tax for revenue generation led to court cases challenging the legality of state systems of school finance.[4] One outcome of these court cases was a gradual shift to more state involvement in revenue generation for public education. Over the period from 1919 to 2014, the state share of revenue for public education increased from 16.5 to 46%, while the local share decreased from 83 to 45% (NCES, 2018). This dramatic shift over time in the share of revenue provided by states and districts reflects a normative shift in school finance from the traditional emphasis on liberty to a greater emphasis on equity that could only be ensured through an increase in state involvement.

Since education is fundamentally a state responsibility, the federal role has always been relatively modest. The federal government share peaked at 12.7% in 2009−10 and has faded to 8.7% of total government revenues for K-12 public education in 2013−14 (NCES, 2018). In general, federal funding for education has been motivated by three key concerns: ensuring opportunity for all students, countering underinvestment that might result in national labor shortages, and realizing scale economies through a national research and development efforts (Guthrie, Springer, Rolle, & Houck, 2007). Federal expenditures to promote equity include programs like Head Start that provides early educational opportunities for disadvantaged students, the Elementary and Secondary Education Act that supports education for low-income students, and Public Law 94−142 that funds education for handicapped students. Federal policies to promote efficiency include vocational education initiatives, the National Assessment of Educational Progress and policy efforts to monitor the effectiveness of schools, and data collection and research efforts to guide decision making. Finally, the federal government has

recently promoted the goal of liberty through policies that expand school choice.

In addition to local, state, and federal revenue sources, many schools benefit from funding and resources from non-government sources. Since states have varied in their reporting requirements, information about the types, amounts, and distributions of non-governmental resources is limited. Much of the evidence is based on specific states and school districts (Addonizio, 1999; Schwartz, Armor, & Fruchter, 2002; Zimmer, Krop, Kaganoff, Ross, & Brewer, 2001). Since 2006, the federal government has required districts to report private contributions, and analyses have shown that private contributions to public schools can be substantial, giving rise to related questions about the implications these resources have for funding disparities across schools and districts (Mcintyre, 2016; Vara-Orta, 2017).

The different levels of government tend to rely on different types of revenue raising instruments, and these instruments have been studied in terms of their effects on equity and efficiency. As noted above, local districts tend to rely most heavily on the property tax, states have typically used a combination of sales and income taxes, and the federal government relies primarily on income taxes. Evaluations of these taxes tend to focus on five criteria: tax base, yield, equity, economic effects, and administrative and compliance costs (Odden & Picus, 2013). The most desirable taxes have a broad base and a low rate, a stable yield, minimal economic effects, and low administrative costs. Education finance systems typically incorporate a combination of taxes across levels of the education system, balancing the strengths and weakness of each instrument. Further, as will be discussed in the next section, intergovernmental grants are often used by federal and state agencies to encourage

---

[4] For a detailed review of school finance litigation, see Minorini & Sugarman, 1999.

local districts to shoulder their share of the tax burden for public education.

In addition to the more traditional taxes used to raise funds for education, lotteries have been considered by many states legislatures as a potential revenue source for public education. Lotteries provide fungible revenues (Erekson, DeShano, Platt & Ziegert, 2002) that are often earmarked for public education (Novarro, 2005). Lotteries are popular alternatives in the face of constrained resources, and earmarking lottery profits for K–12 education tends to increase spending (Evans & Zhang, 2007). However, revenue from lotteries tends to be unstable and regressive, qualities that make this strategy less attractive – on both practical and normative grounds – as a sustainable and fair means to generate revenue for public education (Campbell, 2003; McAuliffe, 2006).

Distributing resources: multiple and competing goals

As described above, states assumed a more active role in school finance following court cases that challenged the equity of heavy reliance on the local property tax to fund education. This section describes the dominant approaches used by states to allocate education funds, reviews school finance litigation challenging the equity and adequacy of school finance systems, and explores issues related to the efficient use of educational resources.

Mechanisms for distributing revenue across school districts

Several state equalization formulas have become common tools to distribute funds in more equitable ways than would occur by relying on the local property tax (Odden & Picus, 2013). Four approaches have dominated the landscape. Flat grants have been used to ensure that all schools are funded to provide a basic education for students. These programs provide all schools a grant, typically based on enrollment. However, by treating all schools the same, flat grants fail to recognize (a) the varying fiscal capacity of different districts that gives rise to inequities in the first place, and (b) the differential needs and costs across schools.

Foundation programs were introduced in the early 1900s in direct response to the shortcomings of flat grants. The foundation program is rooted in the philosophy that states have an obligation to provide a minimum level of education. The state sets a foundation, the per-pupil expenditure needed to provide a minimum quality education, and requires a minimum tax rate to ensure local effort as a condition for state aid. States typically fund the difference between the per-pupil expenditure that districts are able to generate at the minimum tax rate and the state-established per-pupil foundation expenditure. In this way, states distribute funds inverse to local wealth with the goal of helping all school districts to provide a minimum foundation of education services. Districts are free to tax themselves above the minimum required rate to supplement this foundation level of spending, but the revenues generated beyond the foundation are a function of local wealth alone. So long as the foundation level and the minimum tax rates are set at relatively low levels, inequities stemming from differences in the fiscal capacity of school districts remain a problem.

Guaranteed tax base (GTB) programs were introduced in the 1970s in response to school finance litigation based on unequal local fiscal capacity arguments. A GTB program guarantees, through the allocation of state aid, that each school district in a state can function as if it had an equal tax base. Essentially, the state establishes the tax base that will be "guaranteed" for all school districts and provides aid such that any district with an actual tax base less than the GTB will generate revenue as if they had the GTB. This "wealth equalization" program grants school districts the liberty to determine their own tax rate, and equalizes fiscal capacity up to the level of the GTB. State aid is awarded inversely to local wealth, thereby improving equity without limiting liberty. However, to the degree that the GTB is high and low-wealth districts tax themselves at a high rate, the cost to the state can be excessive.

The fourth formula that states have used to allocate funds to support education is a combination foundation and GTB program. This combination approach can offset the problems of each of the formulas; the foundation program requires that districts provide at least a basic level of education, and the GTB ensures equity if districts choose to spend beyond the foundation level.

Beyond these four basic formulas, states have employed a variety of strategies to promote greater equity. For instance, state-determined-spending programs prescribe the per pupil expenditure across districts in the state. This per pupil expenditure may be funded by the state or some combination of state and local revenues. States have also placed revenue limits on local school districts to restrict the difference in spending across jurisdictions. While these sorts of programs are intended to promote greater equity, they can have serious implications for liberty through limits on local control.

Regardless of the state formula used to distribute general education funds to districts, additional adjustments are commonly made to account for student needs and geographic cost differences across school districts. Adjustments for special-needs students tend to take the form of categorical grants or weights that recognize the higher-than-average costs associated with educating low-income, limited-English proficient, and special education students. States typically provide this additional funding through grants or weighted student adjustments, but

some research indicates that states tend to underestimate the influence of poverty, special education. and limited English proficiency status on cost (Baker & Duncombe, 2004). Determining student eligibility and the magnitude of the weights to be assigned to various "types" of students is a process that varies across states and involves a number of assumptions about the costs of providing education services to students with special needs.[5]

A second type of adjustment recognizes differences in what a dollar can purchase across different jurisdictions. There is broad consensus that the cost of educational inputs varies geographically due to differences in local labor markets, housing prices, transportation and energy costs, and so forth. While measuring cost differentials can be difficult due to the multiple factors and data requirements, some useful tools have been developed and most focus on teacher costs given that salaries and benefits account for about 80% of current expenditures in elementary and secondary schools (NCES, 2018). For example, the Geographic Cost of Education Index (GCEI) developed by Chambers (1997) adjusts teacher salary to account for differences in worker and workplace characteristics. Likewise, Taylor and Fowler (2006) developed the Comparable Wage Index (CWI) to adjust for differences in the cost of education that are beyond the control of school districts. The CWI is constructed on salary differentials of non-educators and reflects the systematic, regional labor cost variation due to differences in both the cost of living and local community characteristics (such as crime rate).[6]

Challenges to state funding systems

While the distribution formulas and weighting mechanisms that states use to allocate

---

[5] For additional discussion, see Chambers, Parrish, and Harr (2002), Duncombe and Yinger (2005), Moore, Strang, Schwartz, and Braddock (1988), Schwartz, Steifel, and Amor (2005).

[6] For updates on the NCES Comparable Wage Index, go to http://bush.tamu.edu/research/faculty/Taylor_CWI/.

resources across school districts are intended to promote greater equity in education finance than would be realized through exclusive reliance on the local property tax, the equity and adequacy of state funding systems have been challenged in the courts. But defining what, specifically, constitutes a fair funding system has been an evolving process, one driven largely by the courts. And, in most cases, remedies to promote greater equity have required greater state investment in public education, which has shifted control away from local decision makers to state policy makers — revealing a tension between liberty (local control) and equity (resulting from greater state involvement).

School finance litigation has been categorized into three "waves" (Guthrie et al., 2007; Baker, Green, & Richards, 2008). During the first wave, which spanned the 1960s through 1973, plaintiffs challenged school finance systems through the federal Constitution's equal protection clause. This wave ended with *Rodriguez v San Antonio* in which the court ruled that school funding based on the local property tax was justified through its rational relationship with local control. The second wave, from 1973 through 1989, was characterized by challenges based on state education clauses and state equal protection clauses. These cases hinged on whether courts viewed (a) education as a fundamental right and (b) local wealth as a suspect classification; if not, the existing system was often upheld in the name of local control. The third wave, from 1989 to the present, includes cases based on claims that school finance formulas prevent poor school districts form providing an adequate educational services and opportunities, as defined by state education clauses and standards, to all students. An adequate education is one that provides resources sufficient to ensure that all students, regardless of background or residential district, have the opportunity to realize a clearly defined set of goals (Baker & Green, 2009, 2014).

Given the simultaneous emphasis on inputs and outcomes, the goal of adequacy inextricably links goals of equity and efficiency. The tie that binds adequacy to equity is the principle that a state's educational resources should be fairly allocated across all student groups in all state locales. The tie that binds adequacy to excellence is the principle that all students can and should be expected to achieve an absolute level of academic proficiency (Allgood & Rice, 2003).

Several methodologies have been developed to determine an adequate expenditure level, including the professional-judgment approach (Chambers & Parrish, 1994, pp. 45—74; Gutherie & Rothstein, 1999), the successful schools approach (Augenblick, 1997), and the cost function approach (Reschovsky & Imazeki, 2003). Taken together adequacy studies suggest, almost without exception, that additional resources are needed to provide all students the opportunity to realize specified educational outcomes.[7] The *Campaign for Fiscal Equity v. The State of New York* offers an illustration of how courts have used the concept of adequacy to identify a comprehensive and essential array of resources. In this lawsuit, plaintiffs successfully argued that the state's school finance system underfunded New York City public schools and, in so doing, denied its students their constitutional right. The case created a new constitutional standard for a "sound basic education," which NY State Supreme Court Justice DeGrasse, writing

---

[7] In most cases, these studies call for substantial increases in state funding. For example, an adequacy cost study in Pennsylvania estimated the need for an additional $4.38 billion in state spending. Likewise, studies estimated additional costs of adequacy at $3.45 billion in Washington, $1.3 billion in Nevada, and $6—8 billion in New York State. Information retrieved on July 20, 2015 from http://www.schoolfunding.info/policy/CostingOut/factsheetslist.php3.

for the majority, defined as the "foundational skills that students need to become productive citizens capable of civic engagement and sustaining competitive employment." To ensure a sound basic education, the court held that the state must provide at least the following resources: (1) sufficient numbers of qualified teachers, principals, and other personnel; (2) appropriate class sizes; (3) adequate and accessible school buildings; (4) sufficient and up-to-date books, technology, and learning materials; (5) suitable curricula, including an expanded platform of programs to help at-risk students by giving them "more time on task"; (6) adequate resources for students with extraordinary needs; and (7) a safe orderly environment (*CFE v. State*, 295 A.D. 2d at 9–10). Research suggests that litigation, and the public and judicial pressure resulting from litigation, has improved equity, typically as a result of "leveling up," or increasing overall state funding such that the additional funds are allocated to lower-wealth districts (Evans, Murray, & Schwab, 1999; Thompson & Crampton, 2002).

Utilization of resources: current policy issues for school finance

Education expenditures are of interest to the extent that they are used to purchase resources that translate into meaningful learning opportunities for students, and, ultimately, desired outcomes like economic productivity, social responsibility, and civic participation (Rice, 2015). In this section, we describe several current policy issues that have implications for education finance systems.

Teacher compensation

A first set of policy issues relates to teachers and teacher compensation. Teacher compensation consumes more that half of K-12 public education operating expenditures. This

substantial investment in teachers is justified on the grounds that teachers are the most important school resource provided to students (e.g., Ferguson, 1998; Rivkin et al., 2005; Sanders & Rivers, 1996). Nonetheless, concern about the supply and quality of teachers, particularly in geographic and subject shortage areas, has induced policymakers and researchers to consider how compensation can be used to attract and retain quality teachers into the profession and to the schools that need them the most. Research has also found that money, along with other factors such as working conditions, student characteristics, and school leadership, influences teachers' decisions about where to work, whether to remain in the profession, and what kinds of ongoing professional development to pursue (Rice, Roellke, Sparks, & Kolbe, 2009; Springer, Swain, & Rodriguez, 2016). Further, evidence suggests that annual incentive payments, or bonuses, may be an effective tool for retaining teachers in subject-shortage areas and disadvantaged schools (Clotfelter et al., 2005). Research has found that large financial payments coupled with threats of dismissal may precipitate improvements in teacher performance (Dee & Wyckoff, 2015), but that the success of incentive systems may hinge on factors related to their design and implementation (Rice & Malen, 2017).

Despite some experimentation with alternative compensations systems, most school districts have relied on single salary schedules that pay teachers based on objective criteria like education units, university degrees, and years of teaching experience. For the most part, these salary schedules do not account for the difficulty of the teaching assignment, the productivity of the teacher, or the competitiveness of the surrounding labor market (Goldhaber & Player, 2005). While an array of historical, social, and political factors explain the traditional reliance on salary schedules, some districts have begun to experiment with alternative compensation structures that may help increase teacher supply and performance (Podgursky & Springer, 2007). For example, districts have used a variety of economic incentives – e.g., signing bonuses, tuition remission for university credits, and housing assistance – to attract teachers to geographic and subject shortage areas. Clearly, more research is needed to understand how to structure teacher compensation in ways that advance the overarching goals of public education.

Expanding the scope of educational services

Another current policy issue that has implications for resource utilization in school finance relates to expanding the scope of educational services. Initiatives like investing in early childhood education and linking education with other social services are typically advanced as efforts to improve the education opportunities for students from economically disadvantaged families. Research suggests that these kinds of initiatives may also have important implications for efficiency.

While policies aimed at narrowing the achievement gap typically target school-age children, research shows that a substantial gap exists at the outset of formal schooling (Lee & Burkham, 2002; Stipek & Ryan, 1997). Proponents of early education programs recognize that investments in the young have relatively high returns (Carneiro & Heckman, 2003). Cost-benefit analyses of preschool programs for disadvantaged children have shown that the long-term effects of early education are associated with monetary benefits that exceed the costs of the programs. High-quality resource-intensive programs have returns that range from $2.50 to $10 for every dollar invested. These monetary returns come in the form of lower education costs, higher earnings, lower crime rates, and lower welfare rates (Barnett & Lamy, 2013; Barnett & Masse, 2007; Belfield, Nores, Barnett, & Schweinhart, 2006; Reynolds, Temple, Robertson, & Mann, 2002).

Less resource-intensive, large-scale Head Start program also have been found to have benefits that outweigh the costs (Ludwig & Phillips, 2007; Oppenheim & MacGregor, 2002). While the price tag associated with these programs may be high, the investment may be wise on both equity and efficiency grounds.

The conventional bounds of public education finance are also challenged by proposals to expand the role of schools. The idea is that efforts to narrow the achievement gap must recognize the wide range of social and economic factors – including health care quality, nutrition, housing quality and stability, parental occupation and aspirations – that affect student achievement (Rothstein, 2004). Proposals to address these multiple influences may involve greater collaboration between schools and other social service fields, or they might require providing a broader set of services (e.g., health and dental care) to low-income students within the school setting. Either approach has implications for fiscal policy and the potential to advance goals of efficiency, equity and liberty.

References

Addonizio, M. F. (1999). New revenues for public schools: Alternatives to broad-based taxes. In W. J. Fowler, Jr. (Ed.), *Selected papers in school finance, 1997*. Washington, D.C.: Department of Education, National Center for Education Statistics.

Allgood, W., & Rice, J. K. (2003). The adequacy of urban education: Focusing on teacher quality. In C. F. Roellke, & J. K. Rice (Eds.), *Fiscal policy issues in urban education* (pp. 155–180). Greenwich, CT: Information Age Publishing, Inc.

Augenblick, J. (1997). *Recommendations for a base figure and pupil-weighted adjustments to the base figure for use in a new school finance system in Ohio*. Columbus: Ohio Department of Education.

Baker, B., & Duncombe, W. D. (2004). Balancing districts needs and student needs: The role of economies of scale adjustments and pupil need weights in school finance formulas. *Journal of Education Finance, 29*(3), 195–222.

Baker, B., & Green, P. C. (2009). Conceptions, measurement and application of educational adequacy standards. In

D. N. Plank (Ed.), *AERA handbook on education policy*. New York: Routledge.

Baker, B., & Green, P. (2014). Conceptions of equity and adequacy in school finance. In H. Ladd, & E. Fiske (Eds.), *Handbook of research in education finance and policy* (pp. 203–221). New York, NY: Lawrence Erlbaum Associates, Inc.

Baker, B., Green, P., & Richards, C. E. (2008). *Financing education systems*. Upper Saddle River, NJ: Pearson.

Barnett, W. S., & Lamy, C. E. (2013). Achievement gaps start early: Preschool can help. In P. L. Carter, & K. G. Welner (Eds.), *Closing the opportunity gap: What America must due to give every child a chance* (pp. 98–110). New York, NY: Oxford University Press.

Barnett, W. S., & Masse, L. N. (2007). Comparative benefit-cost analysis of the Abecedarian program and its policy implications. *Economics of Education Review, 26*, 113–125.

Baum, S., & Payea, K. (2013). *Education pays 2013: The benefits of higher education for individuals and society. Trends in Higher Education Series*. The College Board Retrieved 10/29/2018, from https://trends.collegeboard.org/sites/default/files/education-pays-2013-full-report.pdf.

Becker, G. S. (1993). *Human capital: A theoretical and empirical analysis with special reference to education* (3rd ed.). Chicago: University of Chicago Press.

Belfield, C. R., Nores, M., Barnett, S., & Schweinhart, L. (2006). The high/scope perry preschool program: Cost-benefit analysis using data from the age-40 follow-up. *Journal of Human Resources, 41*(1), 162–190.

Campell, N.,D. (2003). Do lottery funds increase educational expenditure? Evidence from Georgia's lottery for education. *Journal of Education Finance, 28*(3), 383–401.

Card, D., & Krueger, A. B. (1996). Labor market effects of school quality: Theory and evidence. In G. Burtless (Ed.), *Does money matter: The effect of school resources on student achievement and adult success* (pp. 97–140). Washington, D.C.: Brookings.

Carneiro, P., & Heckman, J. J. (2003). Human capital policy. In J. J. Heckman, & A. B. Krueger (Eds.), *Inequality in America: What role for human capital policies?* Cambridge, MA: MIT Press.

Chambers, J. (1997). *Geographic variations in public school costs*. Washington, DC: U.S. Department of Education, National Center for Education Statistics.

Chambers, J., & Parrish, T. (1994). State-level education finance. *Advances in educational productivity*. Greenwich, CT: JAI Press.

Chambers, J., Parrish, T., & Harr. (2002). *What are we spending on special education services in the United States, 1999–2000*. Palo-Alto, CA: Center for Special Education Finance, Special Education Expenditure Project.

Clotfelter, C., Glennie, E., Ladd, H., & Vigdor, J. (2005). In *Teacher bonuses and teacher retention in low performing schools: Evidence from North Carolina's $1,800 teacher bonus program. Maxwell policy research symposium, Syracuse University*.

Cohn, E., & Geske, T. G. (2004). *The economics of education* (3rd ed.). Mason, Ohio: South-Western Publishing, Thomson Learning.

Dee, T. S. (2004). Are there civic returns to education? *Journal of Public Economics, v88*(9–10), 1697–1720.

Dee, T. S., & Wyckoff, J. (2015). Incentives, selection, and teacher performance: Evidence from IMPACT. *Journal of Policy Analysis and Management, 34*(2), 267–297.

Duncombe, W. D., & Yinger, J. M. (2005). How much more does a disadvantaged student cost? *Economics of Education Review, 24*(5), 513–532.

Erekson, O. H., Deshano, K. M., Platt, G., & Andrea, Z. (2002). Fungibility of lottery revenues and support of public education. *Journal of Education Finance, 28*(2), 310–312.

Evans, W. N., Murray, S. E., & Schwab, R. M. (1999). The impact of court-mandated school reform. In J. Ladd, R. Chalk, & J. Hansen (Eds.), *Equity and adequacy in education finance: Issues and perspectives*. Washington DC: National Research Council.

Evans, W. N., & Zhang, P. (2007). The impact of earmarked lottery revenue on k–12 educational expenditures. *Education Finance and Policy, 2*(1), 40–73.

Ferguson, R. F. (1998). Can schools narrow the black-white test score gap? In C. Jencks, & M. Phillips (Eds.), *The black-white test score gap* (pp. 318–374). Washington, D.C.: Brookings.

Garms, W. I., Guthrie, J. W., & Pierce, L. C. (1978). *School finance: The economics and politics of public education*. Englewood Cliffs, NJ: Prentice-Hall.

Goldhaber, D., & Player, D. (2005). What different benchmarks suggest about how financially attractive it is to teach in public schools. *Journal of Education Finance, 30*(3), 211–231.

Gutherie, J., & Rothstein, R. (1999). Enabling adequacy to achieve reality: Translating adequacy into school finance arrangements. In H. F. Ladd, R. Chalk, & J. Hansen (Eds.), *Equity and adequacy in education finance: Issues and perspectives* (pp. 209–259). Washington, DC: National Academy Press.

Guthrie, J. W., Springer, M. G., Rolle, R. A., & Houck, R. A. (2007). *Modern education finance and policy*. Boston, MA: Pearson Education.

Haveman, R., & Wolfe, B. (1984). Schooling and economic well-being: The role of non-market effects. *Journal of Human Resources, 19*(3), 377–407.

Lee, V., & Burkham, D. (2002). *Inequality at the starting gate: Social background differences in achievement as children begin school*. Washington, DC: Education Policy Institute.

Ludwig, J., & Phillips, D. A. (2007). *The benefits and costs of Head Start*. Ann Arbor, MI: The National Poverty Center.

McAuliffe, E. W. (2006). The state-sponsored lottery: A failure of policy and ethics. *Public Integrity, 8*(4), 367–379.

Mcintyre, E. (2016). *Should private funding be allowed in public schools?* Educationdive. https://www.educationdive.com/news/should-private-funding-be-allowed-in-public-schools/419978/.

Minorini, P. A., & Sugarman, S. (1999). Educational adequacy and the courts: The promise and problems of moving to a new paradigm. In H. F. Ladd, R. Chalk, & J. Hansen (Eds.), *Equity and adequacy in education finance: Issues and perspectives*. Washington, D.C.: National Academy Press.

Monk, D. H. (1990). *Educational finance: An economic approach*. New York: McGraw-Hill.

Montenegro, C. E., & Patrinos, H. A. (2014). *Comparable estimates of returns to schooling around the world*. Policy Research Working Paper 7020. Washington, DC: World Bank Group.

National Center for Education Statistics. (2018). *Digest of education statistics: 2016*. Washington, D.C.: US Department of Education.

Novarro, N. K. (2005). Earmarked lottery profits: A good bet for education finance? *Journal of Education Finance, 31*(1), 23–44.

Odden, A. R., & Picus, L. O. (2013). *School finance: A policy perspective* (5th ed.). New York, NY: McGraw-Hill.

Oppenheim, J., & MacGregor, T. (2002). *The economics of education: Public benefits of high-quality preschool education for low-income children*. Building Communities for Change. (ERIC Document Reproduction Service No. ED480538) Retrieved July 16, 2007, from ERIC database.

Parrish, T., & Esra, P. (2006). *The special education expenditure project (SEEP): Synthesis of findings and policy implications*. InForum.

Picus, L.O., & Odden, A.R..

Podgursky, M., & Springer, M. G. (2007). Teacher performance pay: A review. *Journal of Policy Analysis and Management, 26*(4), 909–949.

Psacharopoulos, G. (2006). The value of investment in education: Theory, evidence, and policy. *Journal of Education Finance, 32*(2), 113–136.

Reschovsky, A., & Imazeki, J. (2003). Let no child be left behind: Determining the cost of improved student performance. *Public Finance Review, 31*(3), 263–290.

Reynolds, A. J., Temple, J. A., Robertson, D. L., & Mann, E. A. (2002). Age 21 cost-benefit analysis of the title I Chicago child-parent centers. *Educational Evaluation and Policy Analysis, 24*(4), 267–303.

Rice, J. K. (2015). *Investing in equal opportunity: What would it take to build the balance wheel?* Denver, CO: National Education Policy Center.

Rice, J. K., & Malen, B. (2017). *Performance-based pay for educators*. New York, NY: Teachers College Press.

Rice, J. K., Roellke, C. F., Sparks, D., & Kolbe, T. (2009). Piecing together the teacher policy landscape: A policy-problem typology. *Teachers College Record, 111*(2), 511–546.

Rivkin, S., Hanushek, E. A., & Kain, J. F. (2005). Teachers, schools and academic achievement. *Econometrica, 73*(2), 417–458.

Rothstein, R. (2004). *Class and schools: Using social, economical and educational reform to close the black-white achievement gap. Washington, DC: Economic Policy Institute*. New York: Teachers College, Columbia University.

Rychen, D. S., & Salganik, L. (2003). *Key competencies for a successful life and a well-functioning society*. Toronto: Hogrefe & Huber.

Sanders, W. L., & Rivers, J. C. (1996). *Research progress report: Cumulative and residual effects of teachers on future student academic achievement*. University of Tennessee Value-Added Research and Assessment Center.

Schwartz, A. E., Amor, H. B. H., & Fruchter, N. (2002). Private money/public schools: Early evidence on private and non-traditional support for New York city public schools. In C. F. Roellke, & J. K. Rice (Eds.), *Fiscal policy issues in urban education* (pp. 231–253). Greenwich, CT: Information Age Publishing, Inc.

Schwartz, A. E., Steifel, L., & Amor, H. B. (2005). Measuring school performance using cost functions. In L. Stiefel, R. Rubenstein, A. E. Schwartz, & a. J. Zabel (Eds.), *Measuring school performance and efficiency: Implications for practice and research—2005 yearbook of the American education finance association* (pp. 67–92). New York: Eye on Education.

Springer, M. G., Swain, W. A., & Rodriguez, L. A. (2016). Effective teacher retention bonuses: Evidence from Tennessee. *Educational Evaluation and Policy Analysis, 38*(2), 199–221.

Stipek, D. J., & Ryan, R. H. (1997). Economically disadvantaged preschoolers: Ready to learn but further to go. *Developmental Psychology, 33*, 711–723.

Taylor, L. L., & Fowler, W. J., Jr. (2006). *A comparable wage Approach to geographic cost adjustment (NCES 2006-321). U.S. Department of education*. Washington, DC: National Center for Education Statistics.

Thompson, D.,C., & Crampton, F. E. (2002). The impact of school finance litigation: A long view. *Journal of Education Finance, 27*(3), 783–816.

Vara-Orta, F. (2017). Can private funds deepen disparities? *Education Week, 36*(28), 1, 10, 14.

Wise, A. E. (1972). *Rich schools, poor schools: The promise of equal educational opportunity.* Chicago, IL: University of Chicago Press.

Wolfe, B., & Zuvekas, S. (1997). Non-market effects of education. *International Journal of Educational Research, 27*(6), 491–502.

Zimmer, R., Krop, C., Kaganoff, T., Ross, K. E., & Brewer, D. (2001). *Private giving to public schools and districts in Los Angeles County.* Santa Monica, CA: Rand Education.

The economics of tuition and fees in American higher education

R.G. Ehrenberg

Cornell University, Ithaca, NY, United States

Glossary

Tuition discount rate Percentage of undergraduate tuition revenue that goes back to undergraduate students in the form of institutional grant aid.

Net tuition Tuition paid by students minus the average amount of institutional and other grant aid they receive.

Introduction

Tuition and fee policies in higher education vary widely across countries and, in some countries, widely across academic institutions within the country. This article focuses on one country, the United States. Readers interested in policies in other nations can consult the website of the Center for International Higher Education at Boston College, which provides a comprehensive listing of international higher education journals and has numerous working papers dealing with the subject.

The American higher education system is a highly decentralized one. There are over 4200 degree-granting institutions in the United States. While the majority of institutions are private, not for profits, about two-thirds of all undergraduate students enrolled in four-year colleges attend public institutions; this share rises to about four-fifths when one takes into account the students enrolled in 2-year colleges, which are predominately public institutions. A small but growing share of students are enrolled in private for-profit degree-granting institutions.

For a number of years, the College Board has been collecting data on tuition and fees and publishing it in annual volume *Trends in College Pricing*. In 2007−08, the average tuition and fees at 2-year public institutions, 4-year publics, and 4-year privates were US$2361, US$6185, and US$23 712, respectively (College Board, 2007). The figures for public institutions are for students who reside in the same state as the institution is located; students from out of the state and foreign countries are charged higher levels of tuition at the publics. The average public 4-year out-of-state tuition and fees was US$16640 during that period.

These averages mask considerable variation in the tuition and fees that students pay to attend both public and private institutions. For example, in 2007−08 about 19% of the students attending private 4-year institutions faced tuition and fees that were over US$33 000, while almost 18% faced tuition and fees that were less than US$15 000. Similarly, while 45% of the in-state and out-of-state students attending public 4-year institutions faced tuition and fee levels that were less than US$6000, 13% faced tuition and fee levels that were more than US$12 000.

It is important to stress that an institution's tuition and fee level does not reflect the full cost that the institution incurs in educating undergraduate students. Gordon Winston from Williams College has very carefully documented that no undergraduate student at a public or private nonprofit college or university (including those who receive no financial aid) pays the full cost of his or her education because of subsidies that are provided to them (Winston, 1999). In private higher education, these subsidies come from the income that the endowments of the university provide, from annual-giving streams to the institutions provided by alumni, foundations, corporations, and other donors, and from the value of the services of the buildings on campus that were constructed using funds from external donors. In public higher education, these subsidies come from all of the previous sources, as well as from current state appropriations and previous state appropriations for buildings and capital equipment. For future reference, it is important to note that Winston has also documented that the subsidies students receive are largest in absolute value at the nation's most selective (in terms of admission standards) and wealthiest private colleges and universities.

An institution's tuition and fee level also overstates the costs that many students incur to attend the institution because of financial aid provided to students by the federal government, state governments, the institutions themselves, and private donors. At the federal level, aid currently takes the form of grant aid for students from lower and lower-middle income families, subsidized loans for students from lower and middle income families, and tax credits. A number of states have grant-aid programs for students who reside in their state and attend colleges within the state. Sometimes, these grant programs are restricted to students attending public colleges in the state. Depending upon the state, these grant programs may be either need-based or merit-based; an example of the latter is the Georgia HOPE scholarship program. HOPE provides grant aid to Georgia students who attain a B average in high school and attend either a public or private academic institution in the state. Continuation of the aid after a student's first year of college is contingent on the student's maintaining a B average in college. A number of states also have special scholarship programs or loan-forgiveness programs for students who are employed in the state after graduation in relatively low-paying occupations that are deemed to be of critical importance to the state.

Researchers and policymakers have long worried whether academic institutions will try to capture some of the grant aid that governments provide to help students afford college by raising their tuition levels. To date, the empirical evidence on whether this has occurred is ambiguous (Long, 2004).

Institutions also provide grant aid to students. Grant aid may be based upon financial need (as at the nation's most selective private colleges and universities) or it may be based upon merit. Merit is broadly defined here to include efforts by institutions to attract students with strong academic or strong athletic backgrounds. For a number of years, the National Association of College and University Business Officers (NACUBO) conducted an annual tuition-discounting survey to estimate how undergraduate grant aid provided by an institution compared to the tuition revenue that the institution was receiving; recently, this survey has been taken over by the College Board. These surveys suggest that the typical private American college or university has a discount rate in the range of 33%, in the sense that it returns roughly this share of the tuition revenue that it receives back to undergraduate students in the form of grant aid (Baum & Lapovsky, 2006). Of course, at the richest private institutions, much of these grant funds come from endowment income. Increasingly, public colleges and universities also provide grant aid to students; in recent years, the average tuition discount rate at public 4-year institutions was in the range of 15% of tuition revenues.

Tuition keeps rising in private higher education

In 1967, William Bowen published an important book that examined what had happened to tuition and fee levels at a set of selective private colleges and universities in the United States during the first two-thirds of the twentieth century (Bowen, 1967). He found that, on average, the institutions increased their tuition and fee levels by 2—3% more than the rate of inflation (as measured by the increase in the consumer price index (CPI)) each year. He attributed this partially to the growth of new knowledge and graduate programs, which added costs to the academic institutions. But first and foremost, he attributed this to the fact that higher education institutions were not sharing in the productivity gains that were occurring in the rest of the economy.

To understand Bowen's argument, consider a very simple model in which tuition is the only source of revenue for an academic institution and faculty salaries are the only cost for the university. Suppose also that the institution believes that a high-quality undergraduate education is dependent upon maintaining a fixed student/faculty ratio. In such a world, faculty members' productivity does not increase over time; each year they educate the same number of students. However, in the rest of the economy, productivity is increasing because of investments in new capital equipment and changes in technology

and since real wages (wages adjusted for inflation) depend upon productivity growth, they too are increasing.

In such a world, the administrators at the academic institutions face a dilemma. If they restrict tuition increases to the rate of inflation, salaries of faculty would remain constant (in inflation-adjusted terms) and would fall behind the earnings of people in other professional occupations. This would make it difficult to retain existing faculty members and to attract new people into graduate study and then faculty positions in academia. Inevitably then, the quality of higher education would decline. Alternatively, the administrators could bite the bullet, raise tuition by more than inflation, and try to keep the salaries of faculty members competitive with salaries in the rest of the economy. The pattern of tuition increases during the first two-thirds of the twentieth century suggests that they chose the second option.

As documented in *Tuition Rising* (Ehrenberg, 2000), throughout this period of time, tuition and fees at selective private higher education in the United States did not increase as a share of median family income, because median family income also increased more rapidly than inflation because of the growth in labor productivity and the growth in the number of two-income-earner families in the United States. However, the decade of the 1980s was one of virtually no real income growth in the United States, yet tuition kept increasing throughout this decade at rates greater than the rate of inflation. As a result, while tuition and fees at the typical selective private college and university in the United States was in the range of 30% of median family income in 1975, today it is over 50% of median family income. While the growth in financial aid has caused net tuition to rise by a smaller amount, it too is still much higher today as a share of median family income than it was 30 years ago.

In *Tuition Rising* there has been a detailed description of the forces that have allowed the selective private colleges and universities to keep increasing their tuition and fees at rates that substantially exceed the rate of increase in the CPI. A few of the more important ones have been highlighted in this article.

First, the selective private colleges and universities have but one objective; they want to be the very best that they can in every dimension of their activities. They want to have the best instructional and research facilities, attract the best students and faculty, provide the highest quality education and support services, and the like. To do all these things takes money. While they try to diversify their revenue streams (by attracting more annual giving to support current operations, to build the endowment and to finance new construction, and by trying to commercialize their faculty members' research findings), in the absence of any market forces that limit tuition increases, increasing tuition is an easy way to generate increased revenues. After all, the institutions can always price discriminate (and they do); they can use a share of the increased revenue that they generate from a tuition increase to provide more grant aid to students who otherwise would not be able to afford to attend the institution to ensure that the tuition increase does not restrict access.

Each year, the number of students who apply to attend these institutions keeps getting larger, while the number of positions in their first-year students has increased only slightly. These institutions have focused primarily on maintaining or increasing their quality rather than increasing their size (although several are now marginally doing so) and despite their increased tuition and fees, students increasingly flock to them. This has occurred in large part because, as the distribution of earnings becomes more disperse in the United States, students and their parents instinctively understand that where one goes to college may matter as much as whether one goes to college. In what has become an increasingly winner-take-all society, there is increased pressure on students and their families, in the words

of my colleague Robert Frank "to buy the best" (Frank & Cook, 1995). And empirically, with one exception, all empirical research on the topic suggests that students who attend selective private colleges and universities in the United States, which Winston's research indicates, provide the greatest subsidy to their students, are making a rational economic choice; they receive benefits in the form of higher post-college earnings and increased probability of being admitted to high-quality professional and graduate programs than would otherwise be the case. Put simply, as long as long lines of students keep knocking on the doors of these selective private institutions clamoring to gain admission to them, there are no market forces to hold the rate of increase in tuition down at these institutions.

Of course, these institutions could try to be socially responsible, improve the efficiency of their operations, and get better by substitution rather than by increasing expenditures. Often they do try to do this, especially in the nonacademic sphere of their operations. However, there are a number of forces that prevent them from doing this in the academic sphere of their operations. One is the system of shared governance that prevails within them that gives faculty members an extraordinary amount of influence over academic decisions. Faculty members are crucial to the reputation of these institutions because they are the creators of new knowledge and the ones who educate undergraduate and graduate students. Administrators strive to keep the faculty happy because the labor market for faculty at these top institutions is very competitive and top faculty are mobile; often, this requires the administrators to make greater expenditures than they otherwise would prefer to do.

Another factor is the important role that alumni and other external constituents play. Alumni are vital to these institutions because they help recruit new students, provide internship opportunities and summer employment opportunities for existing students, provide job opportunities for graduates, and provide financial support in the form of donations for current operations, endowment, and new buildings. However, alumni often have very strong preferences for specific programs (often ones that they were involved with when they were students) and any attempt to cut back the scale of, or eliminate a program, may lead to a threat to withhold contributions or other sources of support for the institution if the action is undertaken. This makes it difficult for administrators to cut any program that an external constituent really cares about.

A third factor is the role that the annual *US News & World Report (USNWR)* rankings, which in many respects is now the gold standard in rankings, now plays in American higher education. Empirical research shows that when an institution improves in the rankings, other factors held constant, it attracts more applicants, can be more selective and admit a smaller fraction of these applicants, a greater fraction of the students it admits will enroll at the institution, these enrolled students will have higher test scores, and the institution will be able to spend less on grant aid to attract the students (Monks & Ehrenberg, 1999). Conversely, when an institution falls in the rankings, just the reverse occurs. Administrators passionately care about these outcomes and while administrators often claim that they pay no attention to the *USNWR* rankings and that the rankings do not influence anything that goes on at the university, such statements are simply false.

The formula that *USNWR* uses to compute its rankings gives positive weight to the educational expenditures per student that an academic institution makes. Hence, any academic institution that unilaterally reduced its expenditures per student, or even the rate of growth of its expenditures per student relative to its competitors' rate of growth, would find that it would fall in the rankings. Hence, the *USNWR* ranking methodology does not reward academic institutions for holding their costs down; it puts pressure on the institutions to spend more.

Of course, to say that the selective private colleges and universities continue to have long lines of applicants clamoring to gain admission is not to say that most private colleges in the United States face this situation. In fact, many private colleges and universities admit large fractions, if not virtually all, of the individuals that apply to them. Yet, these other private colleges and universities, for the most part, have increased their tuitions at roughly the same rates over time as the most selective privates.

They have been able to do this in part because of the belief that in the higher-education market, posted price (tuition and fees) is taken by many to be an indicator of quality; if an institution lets its tuition fall relative to its competitors, it runs the risk of being perceived as an inferior institution. In part, they have been able to do this because students and their families do not seem to respond in a symmetric fashion to tuition increases and grant aid increases; Christopher Avery and Caroline Hoxby have found that in awarding accepted students a merit-based grant has a larger effect on their enrollment probabilities than reducing tuition by an equal amount (Avery & Hoxby, 2004).

Not surprisingly, tuition discount rates tend to be higher at smaller less-selective private liberal art colleges than they do at the more-selective private liberal art colleges and the private research universities. The more selective an institution is, the less it needs to use grant aid to try to attract students to it.

Tuition keeps rising at public institutions

During the last 30 years, rates of tuition and fee increase at 4-year public higher education institutions in the United States have been equal to or greater than the rates of tuition increases at the 4-year privates. However, while tuition increases at the privates have always been associated with increases in expenditures per student, tuition increases at the publics have often been associated with decreases in expenditures per student. This occurs because in addition to the factors described above that influence tuition growth in private higher education, tuition growth in public higher education is influenced by changes in the state appropriations that public higher education institutions receive. As described in *The Perfect Storm* (Ehrenberg, 2006), tight budgets faced by the states during the period due to several recessions, limitations on the willingness of the public to increase state tax rates, competing demands on state budgets from elementary and secondary education, Medicaid, and the criminal justice system, and large increases in college-age populations, have limited the ability of states to increase their support for their higher education institutions. On a real per-student basis, state appropriations per student today are only slightly greater than they were at the start of the period. As a result, tuition has risen and state appropriations have fallen as a share of public college and university budgets in the United States.

Although tuition has risen at roughly the same rate (in recent years roughly 3% more than the rate of increase in the CPI) at public and private higher education institutions in the United States, because state appropriations have failed to grow at a similar rate, expenditures per student have fallen in public higher education relative to that in private higher education. As a result, faculty salaries in public higher education have fallen relative to faculty salaries in private higher education, which makes it more difficult for the public institutions to attract and retain high-quality faculty. Student-faculty ratios have also risen in public higher education relative to those in private higher education. Great concern has been expressed that these changes are causing a decline in the relative quality of public higher education in the United States.

To try to reduce these financial pressures, public higher education institutions are pursuing a number of strategies. Public colleges and universities have always charged higher tuition and fee levels to students enrolling in their institutions who are not residents of the state in which the institution is located. Many public institutions have substantially increased the dollar gap between what in-state and out-of-state students are charged and, when possible, have sought to increase the share of their students they enroll from out-of-state as a way of generating additional revenues.

A number of them have moved toward charging differential tuition and fee rates for undergraduate students depending upon the program in which the student is enrolled. Historically, colleges and universities charged the same rate for all students; the notion being that students should be able to choose what to study based upon their intellectual interest, not based on costs. However, financial pressures have led public institutions to begin to charge higher tuition and fees for high-cost majors (due to small class sizes or the need for expensive equipment) and/or for majors that promise to lead to jobs with high economic returns. The intellectual justification for such strategies was articulated long ago by Stephen Hoenack and William Weiler (Hoenack & Weiler, 1975).

Graduate and professional program tuition and fees

The discussion above all deals with undergraduate education. American colleges and universities also enroll graduate students in professional degree programs in law (JD), medicine (MD), business and management (MBA), and a host of other fields. They also enroll students in research masters (MA or MS) and Ph.D. programs. Tuition and fees for professional degree programs are often market determined and are often higher than the tuition charged to undergraduate students at the same institution. The higher tuition levels are justified by the high earnings that entry into these professional fields promises to potential students. Students bear the cost of tuition and fees in most professional degree programs, although increasingly professional programs award both need- and merit-based aid to attract a diverse student body and to improve its academic profile.

In 2007–08, annual tuition and fees at many top private law, graduate business, and medical schools were in the US$40 000-US$45 000 range. With tuition levels this high, many students have extremely large loan burdens upon graduation. To encourage law students to enter low-paying public service law careers, many of the selective private law schools have funded their own programs that provide for loan forgiveness if graduates are employed in public service positions for a specified number of years. A recent study by Erica Field looked at an interesting quasi-experiment that the NYU law school conducted (Field, 2006). Applicants who expressed interest in entering public law careers were offered either a loan-forgiveness program or free tuition, with the understanding that the tuition would have to be paid back if they did not enter public interest law careers upon graduation. The two options were developed to have identical present value to participants. Field's striking finding was that providing tuition remission upfront was much more effective in inducing students to enter public interest law careers.

Tuition levels for students enrolled in most Ph.D. programs are much more similar to undergraduate tuition levels. However, at the best private and public universities, very few students actually pay tuition on their own. Doctoral programs must provide financial support to doctoral students to induce them to enroll in their programs because the economic return upon graduating from a Ph.D. program in many fields is relatively low. This support often comes in the form of a multi-year guarantee, with the support being either a fellowship (no work expectation), a teaching assistantship, or a research assistantship; students often have a variety of these forms of support during the time as doctoral students. Tuition remission and increasingly the provision of health insurance are part of these packages.

Concluding remarks

Looking to the future, the most pressing issue relating to tuition and fees at American colleges and university is whether undergraduate tuition and fees can continue to increase in the years ahead at rates that exceed the rate of inflation. America no longer leads the world in the fraction of its recent cohorts of young people who attain college degrees. The major growth in its populations is coming from groups that traditionally have been under-represented in higher education, who are least able to afford higher education. Congressional debate over the rate of increase in college tuitions has intensified and recent legislation winding its way through Congress, if enacted, would begin to publicize those institutions whose tuition increases are above average. A decade from now, an article in the next edition of this encyclopedia on tuition might look very different.

References

Avery, C., & Hoxby, C. (2004). Do and should financial aid affect students' college choices? In C. Hoxby (Ed.), *College choice* (pp. 239–299). Chicago, IL: University of Chicago Press.

Baum, S., & Lapovsky, L. (2006). *Tuition discounting: Not just a private college practice.* New York: The College Board.

Bowen, W. G. (1967). *The economics of the major private research universities.* Berkeley, CA: Carnegie Commission on Higher Education.

College Board. (2007). *Trends in college pricing 2007.* New York: The College Board.

Ehrenberg, R. G. (2000). *Tuition rising: Why college costs so much.* Cambridge, MA: Harvard University Press.

Ehrenberg, R. G. (2006). The perfect storm and the privatization of public higher education. *Change, 38,* 47–53.

Field, E. (2006). *Educational debt burdens and career choice: Evidence from a financial aid experiment at NYU Law School.*

National Bureau of Economic Research Working. Paper No. 12282.

Frank, R. H., & Cook, P. J. (1995). *The winner-take-all society*. New York: Free Press.

Hoenack, S. A., & Weiler, W. C. (1975). Cost-related tuition policies and university enrollments. *Journal of Human Resources, 10*, 332–360.

Long, B. T. (2004). How do financial aid policies affect colleges? The Georgia HOPE scholarship. *Journal of Human Resources, 39*, 1045–1066.

Monks, J., & Ehrenberg, R. G. (1999). U.S news and world reports college rankings: Why do they matter? *Change, 31*, 42–57.

Winston, G. C. (1999). Subsidies, hierarchies and peers: The awkward economics of higher education. *Journal of Economic Perspectives, 13*, 13–36.

Further reading

Brewer, D. J., Eide, E. R., & Ehrenberg, R. G. (1999). Does it pay to attend an elite private college? Cross-cohort evidence on the effects of college type and earnings. *Journal of Human Resources, 34*, 104–123.

Dale, S. B., & Krueger, A. B. (2002). Estimating the payoff to attending a more selective college: An application of selection on observables and unobservables. *Quarterly Journal of Economics, 117*, 1491–1527.

Ehrenberg, R. G. (Ed.). (2004). *Governing academia*. Ithaca, NY: Cornell University Press.

Ehrenberg, R. G. (Ed.). (2007). *What's happening to public higher education?*. Baltimore, MD: Johns Hopkins University Press.

Eide, E. R., Brewer, D. J., & Ehrenberg, R. G. (1998). Does it pay to attend an elite private college? Evidence on the effects of undergraduate college quality on graduate school attendance. *Economics of Education Review, 17*, 371–376.

Groen, J. A., & White, M. J. (2004). In-state versus out-of-state students: The divergence of interest between public universities and state governments. *Journal of Public Economics, 88*, 1793–1814.

Long, B. T. (2004). How do financial aid policies affect colleges? The institutional impact of the Georgia HOPE scholarship. *Journal of Human Resources, 39*, 1045–1066.

Rizzo, M. J., & Ehrenberg, R. G. (2004). Resident and nonresident tuition and enrollment at flagship state universities. In C. Hoxby (Ed.), *College choice* (pp. 303–349). Chicago, IL: University of Chicago Press.

Singell, L. D., & Stone, J. A. (2007). For whom the pell tolls: The response of university tuition to federal grants-in-aid. *Economics of Education Review, 26*, 285–295.

Relevant websites

http://www.bc.edu. Higher Education at Boston College. A leading source for information on international higher education.

http://www.ilr.cornell.edu. Research Institute. A large number of conference and working papers dealing with the economics of higher education are available on this site.

http://www.grapevlne.ilsu.edu. Study of Education Policy at Illinois State University. An annual compilation of state tax appropriations for higher education institutions in the United States.

http://www.sheeo.org. (SHEEO). The reader can download its annual "Survey of State Tuition, Fees and Financial Assistance Policies for Public Colleges and Universities.

http://www.collegeboard.com. The reader can download the most recent edition of the college board's publications trends in college pricing and trends in student aid from this site.

http://webcaspar.nsf.gov. Institutional data base that provides annual data on tuition and fees (and many other variables) for all higher education institutions in the United States.

PART IV

Teacher labour markets

Teacher labor markets: An overview

Jessalynn James[1], James Wyckoff[2]

[1]Annenberg Institute, Brown University, Providence, RI, United States; [2]Curry School of Education, University of Virginia, Charlottesville, VA, United States

Introduction

The market for K-12 teachers is important, both for its sheer size and because teachers can have outsized impacts on the life outcomes of the students they teach. Elementary and secondary teachers are estimated to account for more than 1 of every 12 workers with a bachelor's degree.[1]

More impressive is the impact that teachers can have on student outcomes. By many measures students are not realizing their learning potential; this is especially true among nonwhite, low-income students. For example, the most recent results from the National Assessment of Educational Progress (NAEP) find that— depending on grade and subject—only 20 to 30% of students from large public cities are proficient.[2] The production of student outcomes like these are determined by a variety of factors in and out of school (Duncan & Murnane, 2011). However, rigorous empirical research has now documented the many ways that teachers influence their students' short-term

achievement outcomes (Aaronson, Barrow, & Sander, 2007; Chetty, Friedman, & Rockoff, 2014a, 2014b; Kane & Staiger, 2008; Rivkin, Hanushek, & Kain, 2005; Rockoff, 2004), socio-emotional outcomes (Gregory et al., 2014; Jackson, 2012; Ruzek, Domina, Conley, Duncan, and Karabenick, 2015), and later life outcomes like teen pregnancy rates, college attendance, earnings, and retirement savings (Chetty, Friedman, & Rockoff, 2014b). Research also documents that differences in effectiveness among teachers substantially alter these proximal and later life outcomes. For example, having one teacher with value-added scores one standard deviation above the average may increase a student's undiscounted lifetime earnings by $39,000 (Chetty et al., 2014b). As a result, the focus on teachers has substantially increased.

The challenge of developing a more-effective teacher workforce of this magnitude is daunting, yet the stakes of not doing so are high. What determines the teacher quality a particular student receives? The allocation of teacher quality can be

---

[1] U.S Census Bureau Educational Attainment in the United States 2016 Detailed Tables (https://www.census.gov/data/tables/2016/demo/industry-occupation/acs-2016.html).

[2] NAEP proficiency rates are available at https://www.nationsreportcard.gov/.

The Economics of Education, Second Edition
https://doi.org/10.1016/B978-0-12-815391-8.00026-4

viewed as a function of demand, supply, and market-specific institutional constraints.

$$T^d = g(A*, w, r, C, X) \qquad 26.1$$

$$T^s = h(w, C, Y, Z) \qquad 26.2$$

Demand for teacher quality, T^d, is a function of the desired outcomes for students (A*), teacher wages (w), prices of other inputs (r), the exogenous attributes of students (C), and restrictions placed on employers regarding the hiring of teachers (X), e.g., regulations and a single salary schedule. Teacher supply, T^s, is also a function of the wage (w), the characteristics of students (C), other working conditions (Y), and requirements associated with eligibility to teach (Z), e.g., certification requirements.

In response to an increased policy focus on the importance of teachers, and a variety of policy initiatives intended to improve the overall quality and distribution of teachers, the research literature on teacher labor market policies has grown dramatically. Much of this work addresses three related research questions:

- What policies facilitate the recruitment of effective teachers?
- What policies are most effective for differentially retaining effective teachers?
- What policies are most effective for developing an effective teaching workforce?

The effectiveness of policies is built on a causal understanding of the effect of an intervention on the desired outcome and depends on a number of more nuanced issues. For example, how does one define and measure teacher quality? What is the supply elasticity of teacher quality to changes in wages and working conditions? How does teacher turnover affect the production function of student learning? And many others.

The research literature on teacher labor markets is well established and several recent articles provide useful insights (Dee & Goldhaber, 2017; Goldhaber, 2015; Hanushek & Rivkin, 2006; Ladd, 2007; Murnane & Steele, 2007). The articles

following this overview provide excellent summaries of specific features of teacher labor markets. Our intent in this chapter is to provide a conceptual and empirical framework within which to situate more-specific research questions. We begin by describing some features of teacher labor markets that importantly influence teacher labor market policies and research intended to improve student outcomes.

Constrained teacher labor markets

Markets are inevitably influenced by the context in which they operate. Three features of the labor market for teachers in the US importantly influence the ability to build an effective teaching workforce:

- Teachers' preferences for where they teach,
- The economic and racial segregation of families, coupled with the common use of neighborhood catchment areas for schools,
- Compensation typically driven by a rigid salary structure, and
- The difficulty of differentiating quality.

Each of these features influences teacher labor markets and the nature of the policies intended to improve teacher effectiveness and student outcomes. Each can be altered, but each reflects the preferences of influential stakeholders that have persisted over decades. These attributes also complicate research on policy effects. We briefly discuss each of these features in turn.

First, teachers typically prefer to teach in schools with smaller percentages of poor, non-white and low-performing students (Boyd, Lankford, Loeb, & Wyckoff, 2005; Clotfelter, Ladd, & Vigdor, 2005; 2011; Jackson, 2009; Kalogrides, Loeb, & Bèteille, 2012; Lankford, Loeb, & Wyckoff, 2002; Sass, Hannaway, Xu, Figlio, & Feng, 2012). In addition, many teachers prefer to teach closer to where they grew up (Boyd et al., 2005; Reininger, 2012) and in schools similar to those they attended (Ronfeldt, 2012).

These preferences, when coupled with other aspects of teacher labor markets, have important implications for recruiting and retaining an effective teaching workforce.

The economic and racial segregation of students likewise has implications for teacher labor markets. Perhaps most importantly, there is ample evidence that socio-economic status, race, and a host of correlates (e.g., healthcare, stable housing, and family supports) are the prime determinants of achievement and other student outcomes (Brooks-Gunn & Duncan, 1997; Crowder & South, 2011; Reardon & Bischoff, 2011; Wodke, Harding, & Elwert, 2011). Concentrating these disadvantages in neighborhoods coincident with school and district boundaries creates heterogeneous schools and districts which increase the challenges of student learning (Card & Payne, 2002), financing education (Hyman, 2017; USCCR, 2018), and the recruitment and retention of teachers as described above (Jackson, Johnson, & Persico, 2016).

Employers in many labor markets would react to such supply reductions by increasing wages to elicit sufficient numbers of effective teachers. The US market for public school teachers, however, consistently compensates teachers according to a school-district-determined single salary schedule—a matrix that fixes a teacher's salary based solely on the years of experience teaching in that school district and his or her educational attainment. All teachers in the district are subject to the same schedule regardless of the attributes of their school or their productivity. Teachers' experience and education, however, have been shown to be only loosely tied to teacher effectiveness for improving student outcomes (Aaronson et al., 2007; Clotfelter, Ladd, & Vigdor, 2006; 2007; Wayne & Youngs, 2003). To the extent that other working conditions differ across schools within a district, as described above, the single salary schedule results in some schools and subjects having chronic staffing problems and low-performing students being disproportionately taught by less-qualified teachers.

This outcome is easily depicted in a simple teacher labor market diagram (Fig. 26.1). Assume that, based on constant enrollments and norms about class size, the demand for high-

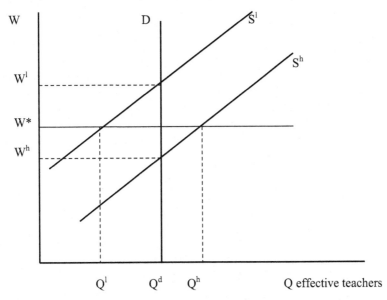

FIG. 26.1   The demand and supply of effective teachers.

quality teachers is perfectly inelastic at Q^d. Due to accountability or other external forces, assume the demand for high-quality teachers is the same for schools within a district regardless of their student composition; schools with disproportionately low-achieving students have the same demand for teacher quality as schools with mostly high-achieving students. Also assume that schools prefer to hire high-quality teachers but will hire low-quality teachers if insufficient numbers of high-quality teachers are available at the prevailing wage. Finally, assume that at any given wage high-quality teachers prefer to work with higher-rather than lower-achieving students. S^l and S^h in Fig. 26.1 represent the supply of high-quality teachers in schools having lower- and higher-scoring students, respectively. If teacher salaries could freely adjust to take into account this difference in supply, schools with low-achieving students could attract sufficient numbers of high-quality teachers by paying the salary W^l, which is higher than the salary W^h needed to attract sufficient numbers of high-quality teachers in schools with high-achieving students. Note that teachers view the schools as being equally attractive even though salaries differ between the schools.[3] Such an outcome is precluded by the single salary schedule. The typical case is depicted by a district-wide wage W^*, where there is excess supply of high-quality teachers in schools with high-achieving students $(Q^h - Q^d)$ and a shortage of high-quality teachers in schools with low-achieving students $(Q^d - Q^l)$. The shortage of high-quality teachers is especially apparent in schools with low-achieving students in subject areas such as math, science or special education, where teacher supply is generally more limited.

Many of the important issues in teacher labor markets reflect issues of teacher quality. For example, when policymakers talk of teacher shortages, they usually mean shortages of teachers who meet some threshold of effectiveness. The importance of teachers to improving student outcomes reflects the ability of more-effective teachers to differentially improve student achievement relative to their less-effective peers. However, explicating what is meant by an effective teacher has been empirically challenging. One straightforward, but controversial, approach has been the use of standardized student achievement tests to create estimates of teacher value-added. Despite its appeal as an outcome-focused metric with good internal (Chetty et al., 2014a) and predictive validity (Chetty et al., 2014b), annual value-added measures often have meaningful measurement error (Koedel, Mihaly, & Rockoff, 2015), focus solely on achievement—just one of many student outcomes schools aspire to produce—, lack transparency, and can only be estimated for teachers in grades and subjects with standardized tests—typically about 20% of all teachers. Depending on its use, these limitations may constrain the utility of value-added and are the reason that other measures of teacher effectiveness are generally more prominent in practice. In response to federal policy initiatives (e.g., Race to the Top, Teacher Incentive Fund) many states and districts revised their teacher evaluation systems to include more rigorous teacher observation protocols and other measures to capture other domains of teacher performance and to provide quality measures for all teachers. While initially promising, concerns have been raised about whether the implementation of these

---

[3] $W^l - W^h$ is the compensating wage differential that results in high-quality teachers being indifferent between teaching in the two school types. A compensating differential for teaching low-achieving students also could be made with combinations of other endogenous school variables, such as better leadership or better facilities, rather than salaries. In fact, adjusting other working conditions may be a more cost-efficient means to induce sufficient supply of high-quality teachers to schools with low-achieving students.

systems effectively differentiates teacher quality (Kraft & Gilmour, 2017).

In addition to each of the features of teacher labor markets described above, researchers confront empirical challenges in identifying the effects of policies intended to improve teacher quality.

Methodological challenges

Due to improvements in data systems and methodological advancements over the past decade, the quantity and quality of evidence about teacher labor markets have improved considerably. Research on teacher labor markets addresses a range of theoretical and empirical questions. While many empirical questions explore the causal effects of interventions often intended to improve student outcomes by increasing the quality of teaching, other questions are purely descriptive, attempting to understand mechanisms or patterns that inform causal questions (Loeb et al., 2017). A substantial increase in randomized control trials, the increasing sophistication of quasi-experimental methods, and more readily available panel data have all contributed. Despite these advances, research on teacher labor markets must frequently confront two important methodological challenges: 1) the non-random sorting of teachers to some interventions and to the students they teach; and 2) the identification of a credible counterfactual. Each of these has the potential to mislead policymakers if researchers are not careful in describing the strength of causality associated with their research designs.

The most difficult methodological challenge remains the identification of causal effects. Isolating causal effects relies on having a counterfactual that credibly controls for all other factors that could influence the outcome, while varying the treatment (Angrist, 2004; Barrow & Rouse, 2005). As discussed earlier, the study of teacher labor markets is complicated by the numerous ways in which teachers and students sort themselves to schools. Students can be endogenously sorted to schools through defacto segregation resulting from residential location decisions and from school choice opportunities that concentrate low-achieving students in some schools. Teachers can be endogenously sorted to schools based on their preferences for attributes of schools, including the characteristics of students, such as student achievement, and geographic proximity to their homes. Such sorting can make it difficult to isolate the effects of teachers from other school-based factors. For example, if treatment and control teachers are differentially sorted to students of varying abilities, interventions attempting to identify the causal effects of the treatment on student outcomes may be biased.

In many situations, randomized control trials (RCTs) have the potential to address the challenge of confounders, producing unbiased treatment effects, and are increasingly employed in education research broadly and on issues related to teacher labor markets. RCTs are viewed as the 'gold standard' for identifying the effects of a treatment. However, RCTs may not be appropriate in some situations for practical or ethical reasons. For example, it would be difficult to randomly assign teachers to particular preparation programs, to better understand the development effects of those programs. However, it is easy to envision random assignment to some of the courses or experiences teacher preparation students might have in a preparation program.

Teacher recruitment, teacher retention, and teacher development each are influenced by some factors that are rarely directly measured; in the absence of random assignment, omitted variables may bias measured attributes. For example, teacher surveys indicate that retention decisions turn on the quality of school leadership and the work environment, importantly influenced by the principal. Quality of leadership and school culture are rarely observed and when they are, it is for small samples with limited external validity. In the absence of controlling for such measures, estimates may misattribute their effects to correlates, such as attributes of the students.

In addition, there are several other criteria besides bias by which to evaluate research designs. For example, precision and cost might argue against RCTs (Deaton & Cartwright, 2018). Below are a few prominent examples RCTs used in teacher labor market research:

- Pathways to teacher preparation: Glazerman, Meyer, and Decker (2006), Constantine, Player, Silva, Hallgren, Grider, and Deke (2009).
- Pay for performance: Fryer (2013), Goodman and Turner (2013).
- Transfer incentives: Glazerman, Protik, Teh, Bruch, and Max (2013).
- Professional development: Wayne, Yoon, Zhu, Cronen, and Garet (2008).

Identifying cause is challenging in any policy area, and that challenge is heightened given the endogeneity prevalent in teacher labor markets described above. While well-executed RCTs with a clearly defined treatment are the ideal approach, they remain relatively rare. Quasi-experimental methods, such as regression discontinuity designs, have also become popular. Observational data on teachers collected over time—permitting panel data estimation—remain the most commonly employed approach for understanding teacher labor markets. This approach may control for a variety of competing explanations, which increases confidence that the intervention led to the outcome, but does so imperfectly. Estimates from such designs must be treated with care to avoid misleading policymakers.

Regardless, the evidence to date has provided meaningful information about three core facets of teacher labor markets: recruitment, retention, and teacher development. In the following sections, we discuss each of these aspects of teacher labor markets in turn.

Recruiting effective teachers

Recruiting an effective teaching workforce epitomizes several of the issues confronting policy and research on teacher labor markets, including an understanding of the scope of labor markets, an ability to discern differences in teacher quality, and a more nuanced understanding of the features of teaching that attracts potentially effective teachers.

First, the market for teachers is local, and as we describe above, meaningful differences can exist between schools within the same districts. While some factors may influence most of these markets, in general the demand and supply of teachers is local. For example, as women gained greater access to other occupations in the 1960s and 1970s, the supply of teachers decreased, resulting in less-qualified teachers and upward pressure on salaries across most schools (Bacalod, 2007; Corcoran, Evans, and Schwab, 2004).

Much has been made of widespread teacher shortages in the US. These reports are often based on limited information that cites declining numbers by policymakers (Daniel, 2016; Milliard, 2015; Rebora, 2016), by the popular press (Betancourt, 2018; Rich, 2015; Strauss, 2015), and by researchers (Sutcher, Darling-Hammond, & Carver-Thomas, 2016). Many of these reports, however, lack nuance in their analysis of the nature and extent of teacher shortages. For example, these shortages tend to be concentrated in specific, hard-to-staff subjects (e.g., STEM and special education) and high-need schools (Dee & Goldhaber, 2017). An understanding of the nature of where teachers are most needed is imperative for designing policies that facilitate the recruitment of high-quality teachers.

There are multiple criteria that a school leader might use to recruit effective teachers. To do so successfully, however, administrators must select criteria that will help them identify which educators will be effective in the classroom.

Often the data available to school leaders will include such information as the teachers' training and preparation route (e.g., through an accredited college or university teacher preparation program, or through an alternative route such as Teach for America) and their performance in that program, or the teachers' prior experience, though school administrators may collect additional information about teachers during the job application process.

Unfortunately, however, much of the information meant to signal teachers' preparedness is poorly predictive of teachers' actual performance in the classroom. While principals can be good assessors of teachers' quality once the teachers are already in the classroom (Jacob & Lefgren, 2008), they are not always likely to have access to information that is predictive of teachers' quality in advance of hiring. Educational background, graduate coursework, and degree attainment, for example, are largely unassociated with teacher quality (Aaronson et al., 2007; Clotfelter, Ladd, & Vigdor, 2007, 2006 and; Wayne & Youngs, 2003). The selectivity of the college a teacher has attended, as measured by Barron's ratings, is likewise a poor predictor of teacher quality (Aaronson et al., 2007; Kane, Rockoff, & Staiger, 2008), as is whether the teacher is certified (Aaronson et al., 2007; Clotfelter et al., 2007, 2006; Constantine et al., 2009; Darling-Hammond, Chung, and Frelow, 2002; Goldhaber, 2007).

Non-traditional measures, such as those that are intended to identify skills, knowledge, or personality traits with a proven association with effective teaching may be more useful for selecting teachers from an applicant pool. Measures of teachers' pedagogical content knowledge (Hill, Rowan, & Ball, 2005; Rockoff, Jacob, Kane, & Staiger, 2011)—that is, their knowledge not only of the content, but also knowledge of how to explain concepts to students, accurately use representations, provide examples, and interpret student work—and measures of teachers' personality traits and belief systems (Dobbie,

2011; Rockoff et al., 2011), such as extraversion, conscientiousness, perseverance, and personal efficacy are both predictive of teachers' success on the classroom.

Multiple measures combined, however, can be more informative of teachers' future performance. There is evidence of school districts, such as the District of Columbia Public Schools' (DCPS; Jacob, Rockoff, Taylor, Lindy, & Rosen, 2016), New York City Public Schools (Rockoff et al., 2011), and Spokane Public Schools (Goldhaber, Grout, & Huntington-Klein, 2017), as well as alternative preparation programs such as Teach for America (TFA; Dobbie, 2011) collecting application data across multiple measures that are together predictive of effective teaching. Yet, while scores on these measures can be used to select a higher-quality teaching force (e.g., Goldhaber et al., 2017), school administrators do not always take full advantage of these data for hiring. For example, teachers' composite application scores in DCPS are predictive of their classroom performance, but not of their probability of being hired by the district (Jacob et al., 2016).

Regardless of the measures used to select from teaching applicants, school administrators will have difficulty composing a highly-effective teaching staff if they are unable to persuade these highly-skilled teachers to apply to—and accept positions at—their schools. One mechanism by which districts might recruit high-caliber teachers is through compensation. While some districts have attempted to use compensation as a lever for *retaining* their most-effective teachers (e.g., Dee & Wyckoff, 2015; Fullbeck, 2014; Glazerman et al., 2013), few studies have explicitly examined the role that greater compensation might play in altering the composition of teachers who might *apply* for and accept certain teaching positions in the first place. Simulations of incentive-based evaluation on entry into the teacher labor market (Rothstein, 2015) suggest that performance-based contracts can alter the performance distribution of the teaching workforce by enticing higher-ability teachers while dis-incentivizing the entry or retention of lower-ability teachers. These effects, however, may be extremely small, given that those who are new to teaching generally have little confirmation of their performance ability from which to assess their probability of earning incentives.

Evidence of incentive effects in practice largely comes from two studies of programs designed to induce educators to teach in traditionally hard-to-staff schools. The first such evidence comes from California, which briefly offered a $20,000 fellowship the state's most-competitive students in accredited post-baccalaureate teacher licensure programs in return for teaching in low-performing schools. Steele, Murnane, and Willett (2010) found that these novice teachers were significantly more likely to begin their teaching careers in low-performing schools than they would have in the absence of the Fellowship program. The second key source of evidence on the use of incentives for recruitment comes from a large-scale initiative that offered high-performing teachers $10,000 per year for up to two years to transfer to low-performing schools (Glazerman et al., 2013). The Talent Transfer Initiative (TTI) led to 88% of vacancies being filled by incentivized teachers, though the share of teachers offered the incentive who chose to transfer to lower-performing schools was low (5%) and retention in these schools returned to the status quo once the two-year incentive period ended.

These two initiatives targeted teachers at different points in their careers; the California fellowship was directed toward teacher candidates who were not already working in schools, while the TTI was focused on existing teachers who had at least two years of experience. Notably, both programs successfully encouraged teachers to enter the profession, and specifically to enter low-performing schools, which are on average more difficult to staff (Boyd, Lankford, Loeb, & Wyckoff, 2013; Clotfelter et al., 2006; Loeb, Kalogrides, & Béteille, 2012). Both

programs had similarly high costs; however, the benefits from student achievement gains may make the return on investment higher than that of other education interventions, such as class size reduction (Glazerman et al., 2013).

The timing of hiring is also important for school administrators' ability to recruit effective teachers, and structural barriers that lead to late hiring may explain inefficiencies in teacher recruitment and hiring. When districts hire later in the summer, they risk losing applicants to other positions that are quicker to make offers—and the more appealing candidates are typically hired earlier in the application cycle (Levin & Quinn, 2003). Reasons driving these hiring delays include: a lack of—or insufficient-length—notification requirements for teachers leaving their positions; transfer requirements from the teachers' unions that prevent districts from making new hires until existing teachers looking to transfer positions have been placed; and budget shortfalls or delays that lead to financial uncertainty about which positions can be filled (Levin & Quinn, 2003). Each of these mechanisms can lead to unfilled teaching positions at the start of the school year, or positions that have been filled with less-desirable teachers. Delays in hiring ultimately lead to lower student achievement, as students are taught by less effective teachers than might have otherwise been in their classrooms, and barriers to timely hiring tend to be more acute in urban districts, where there are higher shares of underserved students (Engel, Cannata, & Curran, 2018; Levin, Mulhern, & Schunck, 2005; Papay & Kraft, 2016). Importantly, early hires tend to be better fits with their hiring schools, in terms of both needs and culture, given that principals are more concerned later in the hiring season with finding *someone* to fill a position than with making their ideal hire (Rutledge, Harris, Thompson, & Ingle, 2008). In turn, teachers who are better matched with their hiring schools are on average more productive and less likely to later transfer to another school (Jackson, 2013).

An additional tool that school leaders may use to recruit effective teachers is to expand their pool of teaching applicants by hiring from multiple pipelines. For example, teachers have historically been hired predominantly from traditional teacher preparation programs within colleges and universities. However, districts have recently loosened teacher training and certification requirements to hire Teach for America (TFA) participants, Teaching Fellows, or graduates of other non-traditional teacher preparation programs. Several studies have found that the more-selective pipelines (e.g., TFA and the New York City Teaching Fellows) produce teachers who are on average at least as effective in math as their traditionally-prepared peers, though with mixed effects in reading (Boyd et al., 2012; Constantine et al., 2009; Glazerman, Mayer, & Decker, 2006; Kane et al., 2008).

Retaining effective teachers

Recruitment alone is insufficient for creating and maintaining a high-quality teaching force; the most effective teachers should ideally be retained after they have been hired, and at higher rates than their less-effective peers. In general, attrition can be harmful for student outcomes; student achievement in math and ELA is lower in schools with higher rates of teacher turnover, and these effects are more pronounced in schools with higher shares of minority and low-achieving students (Ronfeldt, Loeb, & Wyckoff, 2013). Importantly, students whose teachers do not attrit also experience negative effects from turnover, suggesting that high rates of attrition may lead not just to compositional effects but also might disrupt teaching and learning in a school more broadly (Ronfeldt et al., 2013).

There are a number of factors that might affect teachers' retention decisions, including their school's culture, their principal's leadership, professional development, the quality of relationships among their colleagues, academic expectations, and school safety (Johnson, Kraft, & Papay, 2012; Kraft, Marinell, & Yee, 2016). Across studies that have examined factors associated with teachers' attrition decisions, leadership consistently emerges as a key motivator. While school leaders have limited influence over some workplace conditions, there are others that are directly within their control—specifically, their relationships with and the supports and feedback they give to their teachers. Few highly-effective teachers, however, report receiving the sorts of communication from their leaders (e.g., positive feedback, public recognition from their school, or encouragement to return for another year) that is associated with increased retention (TNTP, 2012). Meanwhile, less effective teachers are offered recognition in the form of leadership roles at the same rates as their highly-effective peers, and are rarely counseled out by their school leaders, given poor evaluation ratings, or assigned less-desirable opportunities (TNTP, 2012).

In addition to workplace conditions, some of the tools used to recruit highly effective teachers may also support the differential retention of effective teachers by targeting teachers on either end of the performance distribution; these approaches can be designed to induce attrition in low-performing teachers or to encourage the retention of high-performing teachers. For example, incentive programs have shown some success at increasing retention for targeted teachers. The Talent Transfer Initiative is one such program, having had effects not simply on selection into the profession, but also teachers' retention. 93% of TTI teachers were retained during the payout period, relative to 70% of their control peers; however, the difference in retention after payouts ceased was no longer significant (Glazerman et al., 2013). In another example, Fullbeck (2014) found that Denver Public School district's Pro-Comp program, which awards additional financial compensation for teaching in high-poverty schools, in combination with performance- and credential-based criteria, is associated with significantly improved teacher retention, though these retention effects are substantially smaller for high-poverty schools where retention concerns are most acute. North Carolina had similar success with a briefly-implemented program that awarded bonuses to teachers of high-need subjects who taught in low-income and low-performing schools, though this program was open to all appropriately-credentialed teachers, regardless of their effectiveness; in this case, turnover was reduced by 12%, with a larger effect on more-experienced teachers (Clotfelter, Glennie, Ladd, & Vigdor, 2008). Given that teachers' effectiveness generally improves with experience (Boyd, Lankford, Loeb, Rockoff, & Wyckoff, 2008; Harris & Sass, 2011; Papay & Kraft, 2015; Rockoff, 2004), the program may have inadvertently led to higher retention among more-effective teachers.

Among other incentive programs that have contributed to differential retention of highly-effective teachers is Chicago's Teacher Advancement Program, which awarded bonuses according to value-added and classroom observation scores as well as to teachers who took on leadership and mentorship roles within their schools. This program was also associated with improved school-level retention (Glazerman & Seifullah, 2012). In Tennessee, teachers in low-performing schools who earned performance bonuses were more likely to be retained than their peers who scored just below the threshold of bonus eligibility, but this effect was concentrated only among teachers in tested grades and subjects (Springer, Swain, & Rodriguez, 2016).

In general, incentive policies are targeted at differentially retaining highly effective teachers, or retaining all teachers in general. However, school administrators may instead—or in addition—choose to improve the composition of teaching quality within their schools by encouraging attrition among their lower-performing teachers. Arguably the highest-profile example of this approach is used by the Washington, DC public schools (DCPS), where teachers who fail to perform above a certain threshold or make adequate performance gains over time on the DCPS teacher evaluation program, IMPACT, are immediately dismissed. The share of teachers who directly lose their jobs as a result of their performance rating is quite low; only about 3% of teachers are dismissed each year due to their IMPACT ratings. However, there are also indirect effects on low-performing teachers' retention within DCPS. Specifically, being near the score threshold for ratings associated with separation consequences leads to an increase in *voluntary* attrition of more than 50% (Dee & Wyckoff, 2015), indicating that the program successfully induces the voluntary departure of its weaker teachers. While teacher turnover can be undesirable if the effectiveness of new teachers is lower than that of the teachers they are replacing, the differential retention of low performing teachers in DCPs means that those who leave are on average replaced with teachers who are better at driving student achievement (Adnot, Dee, Katz, & Wyckoff, 2017).

A more commonly-available policy option for school leaders is simply to dismiss or deny tenure to teachers who are in the probationary period of employment (e.g., Jacob, 2011; Drake, Goldrink, Grissom, et al., 2016). This option, however, is often limited only to teachers who are at the start of their careers; it is less feasible to dismiss experienced, but low-performing teachers. In most school districts, tenure policies can make it difficult to implement programs like IMPACT or to formally dismiss teachers beyond their first years in the classroom, so school leaders may instead choose less stringent options to encourage the voluntary departure of their lowest-performing teachers. Strategies could include putting less-effective teachers on professional improvement plans, the stigma of which can induce the targeted teachers to resign (Cohen-Vogel, 2011; Drake et al., 2016; Weisberg, Sexton, Mulhern, and Keeling, 2009), or simply being candid about poor performance and counseling less effective teachers out of the profession (TNTP, 2012).

This is not to say that all low-performing teachers should inherently be dismissed or that all high-performing teachers are performing at their highest potential. Given that teachers make considerable gains in their first three to five years in the classroom, some relatively low-performing first-year teachers may make sufficient improvements to merit their retention. Principals, as the de facto instructional leaders within their schools, can facilitate and encourage teachers' professional development, such that they improve not just the composition of teachers within their schools, but also the quality of those who they have hired and retained.

Developing an effective teacher workforce

Evidence suggests that teacher evaluation is a powerful tool for teachers' development. The act of lesson observation and evaluation can have significant effects on teachers' behaviors and practices—particularly when the evaluation system incorporates feedback to its teachers about how to improve their practice in meaningful ways. This can be true even in low-stakes settings. A recent evaluation program used by the Cincinnati Public Schools (CPS) provides evidence of such effects. In CPS, teachers were evaluated throughout the academic year by their school administrators and peer evaluators; evaluations were based on a combination of classroom observations and a review of classroom artifacts. Taylor and Tyler (2012) found that evaluated teachers' students scored significantly higher on standardized math assessments in the year following their evaluations, with larger gains for lower-performing teachers. Importantly, these performance effects persisted and even grew in the years following the evaluation. These findings suggest that teachers can be responsive to the feedback they receive in their evaluations in ways that meaningfully affect student outcomes, and teachers can retain the improved teaching practices that they have adopted in response to

these evaluations. In another low-stakes evaluation setting, Steinberg and Sartain (2015) leveraged the randomized implementation of a pilot program in the Chicago Public Schools, the Excellence in Teaching Project (ETP), which consisted of a three-part evaluation process: principal training on the program, classroom observations, and a principal-teacher conference in which teachers received feedback on their performance. Pilot schools demonstrated meaningful improvements in the first year of the program, and sustained effects the following year, relative to non-participating schools.

Performance effects from evaluation programs have also been demonstrated in higher-stakes settings where the act of evaluation is combined with powerful sanctions (i.e., threat of dismissal) or financial rewards according to a teacher's performance level. For example, in their analysis of DCPS's IMPACT program, Dee and Wyckoff (2015) also examined the effect of strong incentive contrasts at consequential performance thresholds on retained teachers' performance. They found positive performance effects for high-performing teachers facing potentially large financial rewards, as well as for low-performing teachers who faced potential dismissal but remained teaching in DCPS. Among those who returned teaching the next year, teachers who scored at consequential thresholds improved by approximately 25% of a standard deviation of IMPACT points. Adnot (2016) built on these findings to explore the effects of these sharp incentive thresholds on teachers' practice, as measured their scores on a classroom evaluation rubric. She found that teachers at the threshold associated with involuntary dismissal made large gains on their instructional practice by the following year.

School leaders' strategies for improving the composition and development of their teaching force can also compound, given that the presence of highly-skilled peer teachers can lead to spillover effects for their colleagues. Jackson and Bruegmann (2009) find, for example, that teachers can learn good teaching from their peers. These spillover effects are strongest for the lowest-performing and least-experienced teachers within a school, and not only persist but also accumulate over time. Loeb et al. (2012) likewise find that teachers in more-effective schools make larger gains to their own effectiveness.

Looking forward

The measurement and distribution of effective teachers remains one of the most challenging problems confronting policymakers. The last decade has substantially improved the evidence base to address this issue, providing useful methodological and substantive insights. Yet, there remains much to learn, conceptually and methodologically that would inform policy to improve teacher effectiveness in low-performing schools, including:

- For decades, the research literature has documented the misdistribution of teacher *qualifications*; more experienced, better educated teachers are more likely to teach in schools with higher concentrations of poor and nonwhite students. However, these qualifications appear to be only loosely linked to teacher *effectiveness*. When researchers attempt to isolate exogenous variation to identify the distribution of effectiveness as measured by value-added they are confronted with a puzzle. There is good reason to believe that less effective teachers are sorted to schools with higher concentrations of poor and nonwhite students, as a result of the preferences of both teachers and hiring officials. Research also documents that classrooms with higher concentrations of poor students are likely to have smaller mean achievement gains attributable to out of school factors which should be controlled when assessing teacher effectiveness. By controlling for these factors researchers may well inappropriately bias upwards teacher effectiveness in schools with large concentrations of poor students, assuming such sorting exists. Efforts to isolate variation free of such sorting has been unconvincing to date.

- Researchers have made good progress identifying policies that can improve teacher retention but improving retention in high-poverty schools remains a challenge. In general, there is good evidence that factors such as school leadership, school supports, and school culture can be influential. How can policymakers attract and retain effective leaders to these schools? Research also documents the importance of compensation. What mix of working conditions and compensation in budget-constrained school districts is most effective?

- Improving the skills of teachers in high-poverty schools remains the most likely path to improving teacher effectiveness in these schools. The research evidence on how best to do so at scale is quite limited. Some promising evidence comes from the teacher evaluation literature, but we need to learn much more. Substantial research documents that teachers markedly advance in their ability to improve student achievement over the first 5—7 years of their careers. What do these teachers learn while on the job? Could it be frontloaded into teacher preparation programs or first-year professional development? Doing so would have a disproportionate effect on the schools with concentrations of poor students where these less experienced teachers are more likely to teach.

References

Aaronson, D., Barrow, L., & Sander, W. (2007). Teachers and student achievement in the Chicago public schools. *Journal of Labor Economics, 25*(1), 95—135.

Adnot, M. (2016). *Effects of incentives and feedback on instructional practice: Evidence from the District of Columbia Public Schools' IMPACT teacher evaluation system*. Doctoral Dissertation. University of Virginia.

Adnot, M., Dee, T., Katz, V., & Wyckoff, J. (2017). Teacher turnover, teacher quality, and student achievement in DCPS. *Educational Evaluation and Policy Analysis, 39*(1), 54–76.

Angrist, J. (2004). Treatment effect heterogeneity in theory and practice. *The Economic Journal, 114*(494), C52–C83.

Bacalod, M. P. (2007). Do alternative opportunities matter? The role of female labor markets in the decline of teacher quality. *The Review of Economics and Statistics, 89*(4), 737–751.

Barrow, L., & Rouse, C. E. (2005). *Causality, causality, causality: The view of education inputs and outputs from economics (WP 2005–15)*. Chicago, IL: Federal Reserve Bank of Chicago.

Betancourt, S. (September 6, 2018). *Teacher shortages worsening in majority of US states, study reveals*. The Guardian. Retrieved from https://www.theguardian.com/us-news/2018/sep/06/teacher-shortages-guardian-survey-schools.

Boyd, D., Grossman, P., Hammerness, K., Lankford, H., Loeb, S., Ronfeldt, M., et al. (2012). Recruiting effective math teachers: Evidence from New York city. *American Educational Research Journal, 49*(6), 1008–1047.

Boyd, D., Lankford, H., Loeb, S., Rockoff, J., & Wyckoff, J. (2008). The narrowing gap in New York city teacher qualifications and its implications for student achievement in high-poverty schools. *Journal of Policy Analysis and Management, 27*(4), 793–818.

Boyd, D., Lankford, H., Loeb, S., & Wyckoff, J. (2005). Explaining the short careers of high-achieving teachers in schools with low-performing students. *American Economic Review, 95*(2), 166–171.

Boyd, D., Lankford, H., Loeb, S., & Wyckoff, J. (2013). Analyzing the determinants of the matching of public school teachers to jobs: Disentangling the preferences of teachers and employers. *Journal of Labor Economics, 31*(1), 83–117.

Brooks-Gunn, J., & Duncan, G. J. (1997). The effects of poverty on children. *The Future of Children, 7*(2), 55–71.

Card, D., & Payne, A. A. (2002). School finance reform, the distribution of school spending, and the distribution of student test scores. *Journal of Public Economics, 83*(1), 49–82.

Chetty, R., Friedman, J. N., & Rockoff, J. E. (2014a). Measuring the impacts of teachers 1: Evaluating bias in teacher value-added estimates. *American Economic Review, 104*(9), 2593–2632.

Chetty, R., Friedman, J. N., & Rockoff, J. E. (2014b). Measuring the impacts of teachers II: Teacher value-added and student outcomes in adulthood. *American Economic Review, 104*(9), 2633–2679.

Clotfelter, C., Glennie, E., Ladd, H., & Vigdor, J. (2008). Would higher salaries keep teachers in high-poverty schools? Evidence from a policy intervention in North Carolina. *Journal of Public Economics, 92*(5–6), 1352–1370.

Clotfelter, C., Ladd, H. F., & Vigdor, J. L. (2005). Who teaches whom? Race and the distribution of novice teachers. *Economics of Education Review, 24*(4), 377–392.

Clotfelter, C., Ladd, H. F., & Vigdor, J. L. (2006). Teacher-student matching and the assessment of teacher effectiveness. *Journal of Human Resources, 41*(4), 778–820.

Clotfelter, C., Ladd, H. F., & Vigdor, J. L. (2007). Teacher credentials and student achievement: Longitudinal analysis with student fixed effects. *Economics of Education Review, 26*(6), 673–682.

Clotfelter, C., Ladd, H. F., & Vigdor, J. L. (2011). Teacher mobility, school segregation, and pay-based policies to level the playing field. *Education Finance and Policy, 6*(3), 399–438.

Cohen-Vogel, L. (2011). "Staffing to the test": Are today's school personnel practices evidence based? *Educational Evaluation and Policy Analysis, 33*(4), 483–505.

Constantine, J., Player, D., Silva, T., Hallgren, K., Grider, M., Deke, J., et al. (2009). *An evaluation of teachers trained through different routes to certification, Final report (No. NCEE 2009-4043)*. Washington, DC: National Center for Education Evaluation and Regional Assistance, Institute of Education Sciences, U.S. Department of Education.

Corcoran, S. P., Evans, W. N., & Schwab, R. M. (2004). Changing labor-market opportunities for women and the quality of teachers, 1957–2000. *American Economic Review, 94*(2), 230–235.

Crowder, K., & South, S. J. (2011). Spatial and temporal dimensions of neighborhood effects on high school graduation. *Social Science Research, 40*(1), 87–106.

Daniel, A. (October 17, 2015). *Williams: Texas must expand teacher pool*. The Texas Tribune. Retrieved from http://www.texastribune.org/2015/10/17/michael-williams-reflects-his-time-texas-education/.

Darling Hammond, L., Chung, R., & Frelow, F. (2002). Variation in teacher preparation: How well do different pathways prepare teachers to teach? *Journal of Teacher Education, 53*(4), 286–302.

Deaton, A., & Cartwright, N. (2018). Understanding and misunderstanding randomized control trials. *Social Science and Medicine, 210*, 2–21.

Dee, T. S., & Goldhaber, D. (2017). *Understanding and addressing teacher shortages*. Washington, DC: The Hamilton Project, The Brookings Institution.

Dee, T. S., & Wyckoff, J. (2015). Incentives, selection, and teacher performance: Evidence from IMPACT. *Journal of Policy Analysis and Management, 34*(2), 267–297.

Dobbie, W. (2011). *Teacher characteristics and student achievement: Evidence from Teach for America.* Unpublished manuscript.

Drake, T. A., Goldring, E., Grissom, J. A., Cannata, M. A., Neumerski, C., Rubin, M., et al. (2016). Development or dismissal? Exploring principals' use of teacher effectiveness data. In J. A. Grissom, & P. Youngs (Eds.), *Improving teacher evaluation systems: Making the most of multiple measures* (pp. 169–183). New York, NY: Teachers College Press.

Duncan, G. J., & Murnane, R. J. (Eds.). (2011). *Whither opportunity? Rising inequality, schools, and children's life chances.* New York, NY: Russell Sage Foundation.

Engel, M., Cannata, M., & Curran, F. C. (2018). Principal influence in teacher hiring: Documenting decentralization over time. *Journal of Educational Administration, 56*(3), 277–296.

Fryer, R. (2013). Teacher incentives and student achievement: Evidence from New York city public schools. *Journal of Labor Economics, 31*(2), 373–427.

Fullbeck, E. S. (2014). Teacher mobility and financial incentives: A descriptive analysis of Denver's ProComp. *Educational Evaluation and Policy Analysis, 36*(1), 67–82.

Glazerman, S., Mayer, D., & Decker, P. (2006). Alternative routes to teaching: The impacts of Teach for America on student achievement and other outcomes. *Journal of Policy Analysis and Management, 25*(1), 75–96.

Glazerman, S., Protik, A., Teh, B., Bruch, J., & Max, J. (2013). *Transfer incentives for high-performing teachers: Final results from a multi-site experiment (NCEE 2014-4003).* Washington, DC: National center for Education Evaluation and Regional Assistance, Institute of Education Sciences, U.S. Department of Education.

Glazerman, S., & Seifullah, A. (2012). *An evaluation of the Chicago teacher advancement program (TAP) after four years: Final report.* Princeton, NJ: Mathematica Policy Research, Inc.

Goldhaber, D. (2015). Exploring the potential of value-added measures to affect the quality of the teacher workforce. *Educational Researcher, 44*(2), 87–95.

Goldhaber, D., Grout, C., & Huntington-Klein, N. (2017). Screen twice, cut once: Assessing the predictive validity of applicant selection tools. *Education Finance and Policy, 12*(2), 197–223.

Goodman, S. F., & Turner, L. J. (2013). The design of teacher incentive pay and educational outcomes: Evidence from the New York city bonus program. *Journal of Labor Economics, 31*(2), 409–420.

Gregory, A., Allen, J. P., Mikami, A. Y., Hafen, C. A., & Pianta, R. C. (2014). Effects of a professional development program on behavioral engagement of students in middle and high school. *Psychology in the Schools, 51*(2), 143–163.

Hanushek, E. A., & Rivkin, S. G. (2006). Teacher quality. In E. Hanushek, & F. Welch (Eds.), *Handbook of the economics of education* (Vol. 2, pp. 1052–1080). Amsterdam: Elsevier.

Harris, D. N., & Sass, T. R. (2011). Teacher training, teacher quality and student achievement. *Journal of Public Economics, 95*(7–8), 798–812.

Hill, H. C., Rowan, B., & Ball, D. L. (2005). Effects of teachers' mathematical knowledge for teaching on student achievement. *American Educational Research Journal, 42*(2), 371–406.

Hyman, J. (2017). Does money matter in the long run? Effects of school spending on educational attainment. *American Economic Journal: Economic Policy, 9*(4), 256–280.

Jackson, C. K. (2009). Student demographics, teacher sorting, and teacher quality: Evidence from the end of school desegregation. *Journal of Labor Economics, 27*(2), 213–256.

Jackson, C. K. (2012). *Non-cognitive ability, test scores, and teacher quality: Evidence from 9th grade teachers in North Carolina.* NBER Working Paper No. 18624. Cambridge, MA: National Bureau of Economic Research.

Jackson, C. K. (2013). Match quality, productivity, and worker mobility: Direct evidence from teachers. *Review of Economics and Statistics, 95*(4), 1096–1116.

Jackson, C. K., & Bruegmann, E. (2009). Teaching students and teaching each other: The importance of peer learning for teachers. *American Economic Journal, 1*(4), 85–108.

Jackson, C. K., Johnson, R. C., & Persico, C. (2016). The effects of school spending on educational and economic outcomes: Evidence from school finance reforms. *The Quarterly Journal of Economics, 131*(1), 157–218.

Jacob, B. A. (2011). Do principals fire the worst teachers? *Educational Evaluation and Policy Analysis, 33*(4), 403–434.

Jacob, B. A., & Lefgren, L. (2008). Can principals identify effective teachers? Evidence on subjective performance evaluation in education. *Journal of Labor Economics, 26*(1), 101–136.

Jacob, B. A., Rockoff, J. A., Taylor, E. S., Lindy, B., & Rosen, R. (2016). *Teacher applicant hiring and teacher performance: Evidence from DC public schools.* NBER Working Paper No. 22054. Cambridge, MA: National Bureau of Economic Research.

Johnson, S. M., Kraft, M. A., & Papay, J. P. (2012). How context matters in high-need schools: The effects of teachers' working conditions on their professional satisfaction and their students' achievement. *Teachers College Record, 114*(10), 1–39.

Kalogrides, D., Loeb, S., & Bèteille, T. (2012). Systematic sorting: Teacher characteristics and class assignments. *Sociology of Education, 86*(2), 103–123.

Kane, T. J., Rockoff, J. E., & Staiger, D. O. (2008). What does certification tell us about teacher effectiveness? Evidence from New York city. *Economics of Education Review, 27,* 615–631.

Kane, T. J., & Staiger, D. O. (2008). *Estimating teacher impacts on student achievement: An experimental evaluation.* NBER Working Paper No. 14607. Cambridge, MA: National Bureau of Economic Research.

Koedel, C., Mihaly, K., & Rockoff, J. (2015). Value-added modeling: A review. *Economics of Education Research, 47*, 180–195.

Kraft, M. A., & Gilmour, A. (2017). Revisiting the widget effect: Teacher evaluation reform and the distribution of teacher effectiveness. *Educational Researcher, 46*(5), 234–249.

Kraft, M. A., Marinell, W. H., & Yee, D. S. (2016). School organizational contexts, teacher turnover, and student achievement: Evidence from panel data. *American Educational Research Journal, 53*(5), 1411–1449.

Ladd, H. (2007). Teacher labor markets in developed countries. *Future of Children, 17*(1), 201–217.

Lankford, H., Loeb, S., & Wyckoff, J. (2002). Teacher sorting and the plight of urban schools: A descriptive analysis. *Educational Evaluation and Policy Analysis, 24*(1), 37–62.

Levin, J., Mulhern, J., & Schunck, J. (2005). *Unintended consequences: The case for reforming the staffing rules in urban teachers' union contracts.* New York, NY: The New Teacher Project.

Levin, J., & Quinn, M. (2003). *Missed opportunities: How we keep high-quality teachers out of urban classrooms.* New York, NY: The New Teacher Project.

Loeb, S., Dynarski, S., McFarland, D., Morris, P., Reardon, S., & Reber, S. (2017). *Descriptive analysis in education: A guide for researchers. (NCEE 2017–4023).* Washington, DC: U.S. Department of Education, Institute of Education Sciences, National Center for Education Evaluation and Regional Assistance.

Loeb, S., Kalogrides, D., & Béteille, T. (2012). Effective schools: Teacher hiring, assignment, development, and retention. *Education Finance and Policy, 7*(3), 269–304.

Milliard, T. (2015). Schools in 'crisis': Nevada short nearly 1,000 teachers. *Reno Gazette-Journal.* p. A9, Retrieved from http://www.rgj.com/story/news/education/2015/10/08/schools-crisis-nevada-short-nearly-1000-teachers/73618992/.

Murnane, R., & Steele, J. (2007). What is the problem? The challenge of providing effective teachers for all children. *Future of Children, 17*(1), 15–44.

Papay, J. P., & Kraft, M. A. (2015). Productivity returns to experience in the teacher labor market: Methodological challenges and new evidence on long-term career improvement. *Journal of Public Economics, 130*, 105–119.

Papay, J. P., & Kraft, M. A. (2016). The productivity costs of inefficient hiring practices: Evidence from late teacher hiring. *Journal of Policy Analysis and Management, 35*(4), 791–817.

Reardon, S. F., & Bischoff, K. (2011). Income inequality and income segregation. *American Journal of Sociology, 116*(4), 1092–1153.

Rebora, A. (2016). Faced with deep teacher shortages, Clark County, Nev., district looks for answers. *Education Week, 35*(19), s2.

Reininger, M. (2012). Hometown disadvantage? It depends on where you're from: Teachers' location preferences and the implications for staffing schools. *Educational Evaluation and Policy Analysis, 34*(2), 127–145.

Rich, M. (August 9, 2015). *Teacher shortages spur a nationwide hiring scramble (credentials optional)* (p. A1). New York Times.

Rivkin, S. G., Hanushek, E. A., & Kain, J. F. (2005). Teachers, schools, and academic achievement. *Econometrica, 73*(2), 417–458.

Rockoff, J. E. (2004). The impact of individual teachers on student achievement: Evidence from panel data. *American Economic Review, 94*(2), 247–252.

Rockoff, J. E., Jacob, B. A., Kane, T. J., & Staiger, D. O. (2011). Can you recognize an effective teacher when you recruit one? *Education Finance and Policy, 6*(1), 43–74.

Ronfeldt, M. (2012). Where should student teachers learn to teach? Effects of field placement school characteristics on teacher retention and effectiveness. *Educational Evaluation and Policy Analysis, 34*(1), 3–26.

Ronfeldt, M., Loeb, S., & Wyckoff, J. (2013). How teacher turnover harms student achievement. *American Educational Research Journal, 50*(1), 4–36.

Rothstein, J. (2015). Teacher quality policy when supply matters. *American Economic Review, 105*(1), 100–130.

Rutledge, S. A., Harris, D. N., Thompson, C. T., & Ingle, W. K. (2008). Certify, blink, hire: An examination of the process and tools of teacher screening and selection. *Leadership and Policy in Schools, 7*(3), 237–263.

Ruzek, E. A., Domina, T., Conley, A. M., Duncan, G. J., & Karabenick, S. A. (2015). Using value-added models to measure teacher effects on students' motivation and achievement. *The Journal of Early Adolescence, 35*(5–6), 852–882.

Sass, T. R., Hannaway, J., Xu, Z., Figlio, D. N., & Feng, L. (2012). Value added of teachers in high-poverty schools and lower poverty schools. *Journal of Urban Economics, 72*(2), 104–122.

Springer, M. G., Swain, W. A., & Rodriguez, L. A. (2016). Effective teacher retention bonuses: Evidence from Tennessee. *Educational Evaluation and Policy Analysis, 38*(2), 199–221.

Steele, J. L., Murnane, R. J., & Willett, J. B. (2010). Do financial incentives help low-performing schools attract and keep academically talented teachers? Evidence from California. *Journal of Policy Analysis and Management, 29*(3), 451–478.

Steinberg, M. P., & Sartain, L. (2015). Does teacher evaluation improve school performance? Experimental evidence from Chicago's excellence in teaching project. *Education Finance and Policy, 10*(4), 535–572.

Strauss, V. (August 24, 2015). *The real reasons behind the U.S. teacher shortage*. The Washington Post. Retrieved from https://www.washingtonpost.com/news/answer-sheet/wp/2015/08/24/the-real-reasons-behind-the-u-s-teacher-shortage/?utm_term=.4e0b6d48a817.

Sutcher, L., Darling-Hammond, L., & Carver-Thomas, D. (2016). *A coming crisis in teaching? Teacher supply, demand, and shortages in the U.S.* Palo Alto, CA: The Learning Policy Institute.

Taylor, E. S., & Tyler, J. H. (2012). The effect of evaluation on teacher performance. *American Economic Review, 102*(7), 3628–3651.

TNTP. (2012). *The irreplaceables: Understanding the real retention crisis in America's urban schools*. New York, NY: TNTP.

U.S. Commission on Civil Rights [USCCR]. (2018). *Public education funding inequity in an era of increasing concentration of poverty and resegregation. Briefing Report*. Washington, DC: USCCR.

Wayne, A. J., Yoon, K. S., Zhu, P., Cronen, S., & Garet, M. S. (2008). Experimenting with teacher professional development: Motives and methods. *Educational Researcher, 37*(8), 469–479.

Wayne, A. J., & Youngs, P. (2003). Teacher characteristics and student achievement gains: A review. *Review of Educational Research, 73*(1), 89–122.

Weisberg, D., Sexton, S., Mulhern, J., Keeling, D., Schunck, J., Palcisco, A., et al. (2009). *The widget effect: Our national failure to acknowledge and act on differences in teacher effectiveness*. New York, NY: New Teacher Project.

Wodke, G. T., Harding, D. J., & Elwert, F. (2011). Neighborhood effects in temporal perspective: The impact of long-term exposure to concentrated disadvantage on high school graduation. *American Sociological Review, 76*(5), 713–736.

Teachers in developing countries

Paul Glewwe[a], Rongjia Shen[a], Bixuan Sun[a], Suzanne Wisniewski[b]

[a]Department of Applied Economics, University of Minnesota, St. Paul, MN, United States; [b]University of
St. Thomas, Saint Paul, MN, United States

Introduction to review of literature on teachers in developing countries

This chapter reviews rigorous high-quality evaluations of teaching and teacher interventions in developing countries.[1] Teachers can have large impacts on student learning in both developed and developing countries (see Azam & Kingdon, 2015, and the references therein). This review focuses on three main questions: (1) What teaching, teacher and pedagogical policies increase students' time spent in school, as measured by student enrollment, attendance, dropout rates and completed years of schooling? (2) What teaching, teacher and pedagogical policies and programs increase student learning as measured by test scores? and (3) What policies lead to improved teacher outcomes, such as teachers' time in school, attitudes, and pedagogical practices?

To answer these questions, our review of high-quality evaluations of education interventions builds upon Damon, Glewwe, Wisniewski,

and Sun (2019), extending their analysis to 2017 but limiting the scope to policies that focus on teachers in developing countries. We divide these policies into three types: teaching inputs, pedagogy, and school governance. Interventions that focus on teaching inputs (e.g. computers, extra teachers) can improve teacher quality and thereby make classroom activities more effective. We focus on inputs that directly affect teachers' ability to teach, including teacher training. School inputs that target teaching quality can have an impact on a student's time in school, but more likely affect student learning. Pedagogical interventions, such as new curriculum and tracking of students, can directly increase teacher quality when accompanied by teaching training. These interventions mostly focus on improving students' performance once they enroll in school, but continued enrollment and attendance may depend on school and teacher quality because parents take the quality of pedagogy into account when deciding whether to continue to enroll their child in

---

[1] In this chapter, developing countries include both emerging and developing countries as defined by the International Monetary Fund (2014). The complete list of developing countries used in the literature search is in the Appendix.

The Economics of Education, Second Edition
https://doi.org/10.1016/B978-0-12-815391-8.00027-6

school. School governance interventions, such as teacher performance pay, contract teachers and teacher monitoring, can increase teacher effort and improve instructional quality through well-designed incentives. We also build upon Damon et al. (2019) by extending our analysis to examine high-quality evaluations that focus on teacher outcomes, such as teachers' time in school and improvements in teachers' attitudes and pedagogical practices, as these teacher outcomes are likely to improve student outcomes.

Methods for literature selection and categorization

A key challenge when assessing the impacts of different types of teacher and teaching policies and programs on student and teacher outcomes is identification of causal impacts. This chapter presents evidence from 52 high-quality studies, 34 of which are based on randomized controlled trials, published between 1990 and 2017.[2] Six steps were used to select studies that have credible estimates of the impacts of teacher and teaching programs and policies on student and teacher educational outcomes:

1. Included papers from Damon et al. (2019) that focus on teaching in developing countries. Dropped working papers that were not published within five years after they appeared as a working paper.
2. Searched all past volumes of the *Handbook of the Economics of Education* for papers that focus on teacher outcomes but were beyond the scope of the studies covered by Damon et al. (2019).

3. Searched the EconLit and ERIC databases for recent working papers and papers published from 2015 through 2017.[3]
4. Reviewed abstracts to eliminate duplicates and papers that do not estimate the impacts of teacher and teaching programs or policies for developing countries.
5. Reviewed full papers, and eliminated papers based on lack of relevance or lack of quantitative analysis.
6. Excluded papers that are not "high quality" (RCT, RDD, DD).[4]

For studies with multiple estimates of program impacts, only those that are most representative of the sampled population are included in the analysis of each paper. Also, for studies that evaluate the impacts of interventions on test scores, the estimated impacts were converted to standard deviations of test scores.

Analysis of teacher interventions that increase time in school

Impacts of teacher inputs on time in school

Providing sufficient teaching or teacher inputs may increase students' time in school because providing more of these inputs, such as more teachers and more pedagogical materials, can make schools more attractive to students (and their parents). Three papers evaluated such impacts of programs providing teaching inputs (including teachers) in developing countries. Of these papers, only Battaglia, Marianna and Lebedinski (2015), who evaluated

---

[2] All cited papers with publication dates after 2017 are revised or final versions of working papers circulated in 2017 or earlier. Working papers not published within five years after they first appeared are excluded under the assumption that such delays may reflect serious methodological problems.

[3] Econlit is the most comprehensive database for the economic literature, and ERIC has the most extensive coverage of the education literature.

[4] Randomized Controlled Trials (RCTs), Regression Discontinuity Design (RDD), Difference-in-Differences (DD).

the Roma Teaching Assistant Program (RTAP), found significant impacts on students' time in school. To improve the school performance of the Roma minority in Serbia, RTAP provided an extra teacher assistant to each treatment school. After one year, student absences in participating schools fell by 17 h per year, and boys' absences fell by 26 h per year. However, this program did not affect the dropout rate.

There are two other papers on input interventions. Chin (2005) studied a program which provided extra teachers and additional educational materials (including blackboards) to one-teacher primary schools in India. She found significantly positive impacts on students' primary school completion rates (1−2% points), but since the program combined provision of both extra teachers and educational materials, the impact from extra teachers alone cannot be estimated. Lastly, Tan, Lane, and Lassibille (1999) evaluated two teacher centered interventions in the Philippines. One provided multi-level teaching materials that were designed to pace teachers' teaching according to their students' abilities, and a week-long training for teachers on using those materials. This intervention decreased students' probability of dropping out by 43%. However, a second intervention that provided school feeding with parent-teacher partnerships, which was designed to persuade parents to participate in their children's education, had no significant impact on dropping out.

Impacts of pedagogy interventions on time in school

Four papers focus on changing pedagogical practices. These practices can influence not only student learning but also time in school because high-quality pedagogy can make schooling more attractive to students.

Wang et al. (2016) conducted an RCT to examine the impact of a social−emotional learning (SEL) program for seventh and eighth grade students in rural high schools in Shaanxi province, China. The interventions included: (1) designating teachers of noncore courses to serve as (part-time) SEL teachers; (2) providing these teachers 32 fully-scripted, 45-min sessions of emotional adjustment curriculum; and (3) providing these teachers a five-day professional training. The authors found that this program decreased dropping out by 1.6% points at midline (8 months), but this impact faded away by endline (15 months). The program had greater impacts on dropping out among students in the top 20% of the age distribution. They concluded that the program successfully helped students cope with anxiety, with greater impacts for at-risk students.

Three studies that considered the impact of pedagogical interventions on time in school indicators found no significant impacts. Banerjee, Banerji, Duflo, Gelnnerster, and Khemani (2010) measured the impact of combining tutoring with a community information campaign in India on students' daily attendance, and Cristia, Czerwonko, and Garofalo (2014) evaluated the impact of providing computer software, hardware and relevant teacher training to grade 7 students in urban public secondary schools in Peru. Neither intervention affected enrollment, attendance or dropout rates significantly. Loyalka, Popova, Li, Liu, and Shi (2017) implemented an RCT to evaluate a high-profile professional development program in Henan Province, China. The program provided a 15-day training course focused on improving teacher math knowledge, pedagogy, ethics, personal growth, and classroom management strategies, plus supplemental online material, a communication platform, and post-training follow-up. There were several varieties of interventions, but none of them affected student dropping out.

Impacts of teacher-related governance interventions on time in school

Teacher governance constitutes schools' organization and operation, especially how schools manage teachers and improve teacher quality through hiring policy, monitoring and compensation. Several papers have examined teacher governance interventions. Unfortunately, none of these interventions affected students' time in school.

Two studies examined monitoring of teachers in India. Duflo, Hanna, and Ryan (2012) studied an intervention that assigned students to take pictures of their teacher and other students at the beginning and end of the day, and rewarded teachers according to their attendance. Banerjee et al. (2010) evaluated a community-level information campaign that encouraged local monitoring of schools, including teacher and student attendance. Both studies found no impact on student attendance.

Teachers' salaries in developing countries are rarely linked to their performance. This provides no incentive to teachers to improve their performance. In contrast, pay-for-performance schemes may increase teachers' performance. Three studies have explored such schemes in developing countries.

Glewwe, Ilias, and Kremer (2010) evaluated of a teacher incentive program in Kenya that gave teachers prizes, using a tournament design based on (school-average) performance of all students in grades 4–8. There was no impact on student absence. The authors speculate that the school-average nature of the incentive (across 12 teachers, on average) caused free riding and thus weakened the incentives to individual teachers. Barrera-Osorio and Raju (2017) present results from an RCT of a teacher performance pay program in Punjab, Pakistan, for public primary schools with very low student exam scores. The program provided bonuses to teachers and principals in these schools. The bonuses were determined by a composite score based on annual change of school enrollment, change in the school's mean score and the exam participation rate. To increase enrollment, the program encouraged out-of-school children to enroll by encouraging treatment school teachers to conduct enrollment drives when the school year started. The authors found little program impact; the only positive effect was on Grade 1 enrollment in the program's third year. Finally, Pugatch and Schroeder (2018) used regression discontinuity methods to estimate the impact of the Hardship Allowance program, which provided a 30–40% salary increase to primary school teachers in remote locations (≥ 3 km from a main highway) in Gambia. The program did not effect enrollment.

Analysis of teacher interventions that improve learning outcomes

Impacts of teacher inputs on learning

Interventions that provide additional teacher or teaching inputs can increase classrooms resources, and thereby may make teachers more effective and help students learn more.

Computer-assisted learning

Eleven studies examine the impact of computer-assisted instruction on student learning. Most of the estimated impacts are positive and statistically significant, but a few have statistically insignificant or significantly negative results. This heterogeneity in results underscores the importance of program design, as well as combining high technology inputs with teacher training and instruction.

Eight high-quality studies report significant and positive impacts on student learning from information and communication (ICT) interventions. One is from India, six are from China, and one from Costa Rica.

In India, Banerjee, Cole, Duflo, and Linden (2007) found that a two-year program providing computer-based mathematics instruction for 2 h per week increased test scores by 0.48 standard deviations of the distribution of test scores (henceforth denoted by σ). Unfortunately, this gain faded to 0.10σ one year after the program ended. The authors also found that this intervention was less cost effective than a remedial instruction program.

In China, Lai, Luo, Zhang, Huang, and Scott (2015) used an RCT to evaluate the impact after one year of an ICT program in schools in Beijing for migrants' children. The program provided 80 min of computer-assisted remedial math instruction per week for Grade 3 students. The authors found that math scores increased by 0.14σ. Also in China, Lai et al. (2013) evaluated an ICT program, similar to the one in Beijing, that focused on Chinese language in Qinghai province. After one year, the authors found significantly positive increases in both Chinese (0.20σ) and mathematics (0.22σ).

Mo et al. (2013) studied the impact of a "One Laptop per Child" program on 300 migrant third graders in Beijing, where computers had computer games consistent with the schools' curriculum. They found significantly positive impacts on math, language and computer skills tests. Mo et al. (2014a) evaluated remedial mathematics software for rural boarding school students in Shaanxi Province. They found large and statistically significant increases in math scores of Grade 3 (0.25σ) and Grade 5 (0.26σ) students. Mo et al. (2014b) evaluated a similar intervention, but included both boarding students and students living at home. One year later, the average increase in Grade 3 and 5 math scores was significantly positive (0.16σ). Finally, Yang et al. (2013) evaluated an ICT program in three Chinese provinces; they found modest (0.12σ) but statistically significant increases in test scores.

Alvarez-Marinelli et al. (2016) evaluated two computer-assisted language learning (CALL) programs in Costa Rica using an RCT. Treatment A provided computer-assisted English Language learning software, tests, assessment tools, and teacher training. Treatment B provided a research-based language acquisition CALL curriculum designed for non-English speakers to learn English. The average time-on-task for treatment A was 67 min per week, while time-on-task for treatment B was 127 min per week. When

Treatments A and B are combined into a single CALL intervention, the authors found no significant impact after controlling for initial difference in pre-intervention test scores. They suggest that this could reflect that the intervention was too short to rule out an initial unbalance of oral English proficiency between the intervention and control groups. However, Treatment A generated a significantly positive effect compared to Treatment B and the control group. The authors also estimated that Treatment A increased scores on Picture Vocabulary and Understanding Direction tests by 0.32σ and 0.40σ, respectively.

In contrast, two studies on Latin America found no impacts of ICT programs. Barrera-Osorio and Linden (2009) studied an intervention that gave computers and teacher training to randomly selected Colombian schools. They found no impact of the program on either math or Spanish skills, and suggest that the reason was poor implementation, and more specifically that teachers did not use this new technology effectively. Beuermann, Cristia, Cueto, Malamud, and Cruz-Aguayo (2015) obtained similar results for Peru. They conducted a large-scale RCT of the "One Laptop per Child" program. The program increased the computer-to-student ratio from 0.12 to 1.18 in program schools, but had no impact on either math or language scores. These results are striking given the program's coverage and expense; it gave each student a laptop computer and allowed students to take them home, which provided much more time to use them than any other ICT intervention to date.

Finally, one study found negative impacts of ICT interventions. In Romania, Malamud and Pop-Eleches (2011) studied a program that provided vouchers to purchase computers to the parents of middle-school students. They estimate that receiving such vouchers significantly reduced students' academic performance. They believe that the result stems from the fact that students reported increases in the time spent playing games and less time spent reading and doing homework.

Pupil-teacher ratio

Five high-quality studies have examined the impact of having more teachers, measured by pupil-teacher ratios, on student learning. In Bolivia, Urquiola (2006) used the fact that schools in Bolivia with pupil-teacher ratios above 30 can (and do) apply for another teacher. He found that schools which obtained an additional teacher, reducing the pupil-teacher ratio, have significantly higher scores on language exams, but not consistently for mathematics exams. He also points out that class size reductions may have nonlinear effects; effects are larger for substantial class size reductions from high initial levels, but smaller when the class size reduction is from a lower level. Because of potential of non-linearities, these results should be interpreted cautiously. In Chile, Urquiola and Verhoogen (2009) estimated the impact of class size caps of 45 students on students' test scores. They found that class size reductions led to significantly higher math and language test scores. Battaglia and Lebedinski (2015) used difference-in-differences methods to evaluate Serbia's Roma Teaching Assistant Program, implemented among Grade 1–4 Roma minority students. The program placed one Roma teaching assistant in participating schools. There was no significant impact on Serbian and math test scores in the full sample, but interacting a variable indicating schools with fewer than 43 Roma students, the effect on both test scores became significantly positive; these effects are driven by female students.

In contrast, two other studies found statistically insignificant effects. Duflo, Dupas, and Kremer (2015) implemented an RCT in Kenya that randomly assigned contract teachers to some schools, and students in those schools were randomly assigned to classes that were taught either by a current teacher (a civil-service teacher) or by a newly hired contract teacher. Comparing classes of different sizes taught by civil-service teachers, they found that reducing class size from about 80 to about 40 increased test scores

by about 0.09σ, but this estimate was statistically insignificant. Anderson, Gong, Hong, and Zhang (2016) used regression discontinuity to estimate the impact of students selected into elite high schools on subsequent college entrance exam scores in China. The authors also estimated the effect of student/teacher ratio on college entry exam scores, and did not find statistically significant impacts for either attending elite schools or higher student/teacher ratio.

Literacy programs with teacher training

Literacy programs with teacher training provide teachers more resources and skills to deliver better learning outcomes. Two high-quality studies found significantly positive impacts on test scores.

Jukes et al. (2017) conducted an RCT to evaluate the HALI literacy program for Grade 1 students in Kenya. The evaluation randomly allocated 101 primary schools to one of four groups: (1) malaria intervention alone; (2) literacy intervention alone; (3) both interventions combined; and (4) neither intervention. The literacy intervention provided teachers sequential, semi-scripted lesson plans, gave training workshops, sent weekly motivational text messages with instructional tips, and provided $0.50 per week of mobile phone credit to encourage teachers to use them. Nine months after program implementation, the authors found significantly positive impacts of the literacy (teacher training) intervention on spelling, Swahili letter sounds and Swahili word reading, but no effect on English letter knowledge. These results persisted to 24 months post-program implementation. The program did not affect non-literacy outcomes (reasoning, numeracy and sustained attention). Finally, the estimated effect on numeracy at 24 months was negative; this may reflect teachers teaching literacy at the expense of numeracy. The program cost was US$32,940, or US$531 per teacher and US$8.57 per child. The main limitations of the study are: (1) the evaluation was conducted by the same people who designed the program;

(2) there are four primary outcomes and ten secondary outcomes increasing the likelihood of Type I error, particularly for effects of borderline significance.

Fuje and Tandon (2015) used an RCT to evaluate the Rural Education and Development (READ) project, implemented in primary schools in rural Mongolia. The program provided high-quality children's books and in-service teacher training. The authors use propensity score matching to compare the treated students to students in a control group who received the treatment only after the experiment. Overall, the program increased the total test score by 0.35σ. The authors also provide disaggregated effects for vocabulary (Peabody), mathematics, listening, reading and writing. The effects on these subjects are significantly positive except for listening. Subpopulation analyses show that the program helps students: 1. Who did not have access to extra-lesson sessions; 2. Whose parents are educated; and 3. Who are girls. The average costs (in 2008 US$) of a single book and a set of shelves were $2.1 and $71.5. The training cost was $ 3.14 per day per teacher.

Longer school days

Lengthening school days provides teachers with more instructional time, which should increase student learning. Two high-quality studies estimate the impacts of longer schools days, one of which evaluated a program with longer school hours coupled with teacher training. Both found significantly positive impacts on test scores.

Cruz, Loureiro, and Sa (2017) used difference-in-differences with year and school fixed effects to evaluate Rio de Janeiro's "Single-Shift Schools" program in Brazil that extends the school day to a 7-h daily shift from 7:30 a.m. to 2:30 p.m. The analysis is at the school level, not the student level. Overall, the authors find that the program had positive effects in "certified" schools,[5] but not in regular schools, suggesting that extending the school day should be combined with structured organization of what is done in the additional hours. Specifically, the certified elementary schools experienced significantly positive impact of 0.26σ on the IDEB index, which is the national Education Development Index based on the student performance in national standardized tests and student pass rates. The certified middle schools had a significantly positive impact of 0.81σ on the IDEB index. The authors conclude that, for the single shift program, having 7 h for the students does not seem to increase student performance without organizing what is done in these 7 h, such as teachers with 40 h of dedication to the school, teacher training, and curriculum.

Orkin (2013) used difference-in-differences to evaluate the effect of lengthening the school day on primary school students in Ethiopia. The treated schools provided five-and-a-quarter hours of instruction per day. The control group schools provided 4 h of instruction per day. Overall, lengthening the school day did not affect reading scores, but increased writing and numeracy scores. Also, the program had larger effects on girls than on boys, for non-stunted children than for stunted children, for urban children than for rural children, and for children from families with above-median wealth. However, the author thinks that the results for reading should be treated with caution; they may reflect pre-treatment differences between treated and control schools.

Unique interventions

As mentioned in Impacts of teacher inputs on time in school section, Tan et al. (1999) examined

---

[5] Schools were certified "when they included aspects such as all teaching staff dedicated 40 h of their weekly working hours to a single school" (Cruz et al., 2017).

several teacher-centered interventions in the Philippines. One program combined school feeding with parent-teacher partnerships, and another combined multi-level learning materials with parent-teacher partnerships. Both interventions significantly increased student learning, however it is not possible to separate the individual contributions of each element of these interventions.

Chay, McEwan, and Urquiola (2005) use regression discontinuity to examine Chile's P-900 school program, which had four components: (1) School infrastructure improvements, such as building repairs (implemented in 1990 and 1991); (2) Provision of instructional materials, such as textbooks, classroom libraries, cassette recorders and copy machines (in 1990 and 1991); (3) Weekly training programs for teachers, focusing on language and mathematics (in 1992); and (4) After-school workshops for third and fourth grade students who lagged behind (in 1992). The authors found no significant program effect one year into program implementation at the end of 1990, but found significantly positive effects on the 1992 mathematics and language scores three years into program implementation. They offered possible explanations on the lack of effect in 1990: (1) One year of exposure was insufficient to affect achievement; (2) The 1990 program differed from the 1992 program; (3) Scores increased by a small amount each year, but did not become significant until 1992.

Impacts of pedagogy interventions on learning

Teaching at the right level, remedial education, tutoring

Remedial programs target students who are lagging behind by "teaching at the right level", that is teaching in a way that accounts for students' current skill levels. In theory, such interventions should help students who are falling behind, reducing the heterogeneity of students' skills in a given classroom. Several high-quality studies have found that remedial programs greatly increase student learning, even when taught by individuals with little or no formal training and who are paid only a fraction of the regular civil-service teachers' salaries.

Three papers on India have estimated the impact on student learning of programs that "teach at the right level". Banerjee et al. (2007) used an RCT to evaluate a program operated by Pratham, an Indian non-profit organization. This program focused on the weakest public school students in Mumbai and Vadodara. It provided schools locally hired informal teachers, known as *Balsakhi* ("child friend"). These students were taken out of their regular classrooms for 2 h per day for remedial instruction from the *Balsakhi*. After one year of the program, students' average math and English test scores increased by 0.14σ, and after two years their scores increased by 0.28σ. These gains occurred primarily among the weaker students who received the remedial instruction, rather than the non-participating students who could have benefited from a smaller class size for 2 h per day. The authors conclude that the students who received remedial instruction benefitted from being taught at a level that better matched their actual skills, rather than the level in the official curriculum.

Banerjee et al. (2010) evaluated several interventions for increasing community participation in education. Only one of these interventions increased student learning, a 2–3 month remedial instruction program taught by locally hired youths. The youths had only one week of training before implementing after-school reading camps. The authors found substantial increases in learning, even though only 13% of the students participated in the camps. Most children in this sample were completely illiterate before the program. This program increased the proportion of students who could read letters by 7.9% points. For the children who could not read *and* participated in the camp, the proportion able to read letters increased sharply, from zero to 60%.

In another paper, Banerjee et al. (2016) evaluated four different ways to scale up Pratham's approach to teaching at the right level (TaRL) in India between 2008 and 2014. In Bihar, they evaluated a summer camp implemented by trained government teachers and village volunteers; it increased language and mathematics scores by $0.07-0.09\sigma$. In a second intervention, in Bihar and Uttarakhand, Pratham's method was introduced into government schools with three different treatment arms. For both states, neither providing Pratham materials alone nor providing materials plus teacher training was successful; government teachers continued using traditional methods. The third arm, which added trained volunteers, was successful (language and math scores increased by 0.1σ) only in Bihar, where the volunteers worked outside the schools. In Uttarakhand, the volunteers worked in classrooms as teacher assistants, and continued using traditional methods. In a more recent study (2012−13) in Haryana (a state with good teaching resources), the intervention first trained government officials in Pratham's method, who subsequently trained teachers, provided materials and dedicated 1 h per day to Pratham's reading program. Language test scores increased by 0.15σ. Finally, in Uttar Pradesh (a state with low teaching resources), Pratham staff and village volunteers ran 40 day camps during school, which increased language and mathematics test scores by $0.61-0.70\sigma$.

Banerjee et al. (2016) note that the two key ingredients to Pratham's system are: (1) grouping children by initial learning level; and (2) focusing on skills appropriate to that level. In India, this TaRL program works when implemented: (1) by volunteers outside the classroom; (2) by trained teachers supported by government monitors and taught during a dedicated class hour; and (3) by volunteer camps within schools.

Two studies on remedial tutoring were conducted outside of India. Jayachandran (2014) studied the impact of offering after-school for-profit tutoring by the school's teachers on academic pass rates for Nepal's grade 10 school-leaving exam. This tutoring reduced the school-level pass rate (across three subjects) by 11% points for students in government schools. Jayachandran hypothesizes that teachers reduced the time and/or quality of teaching during school hours to increase the demand for their for-profit tutoring. Since the estimate includes those who were not tutored, the effect was negative when all students are combined.

In Peru, Saavedra, Nashlund-Hadley and Alfonso (2017) estimated the impact of remedial science tutoring by trained public-sector primary school teachers on grade 3 science, mathematics and reading scores. Tutoring had a positive impact on science, but no spillovers onto mathematics or reading. The positive impact of remedial science tutoring was strong (students scored 0.12σ higher) given that compliance was low; treated students attended, on average, only 4.5 of 16 tutoring sessions.

Tracking

Tracking students into classrooms based on learning levels reduces the variation in students' skills within a classroom, making it easier for teachers to match their lessons to their students' skills. However, students tracked to "lower" level classrooms may experience negative peer effects and reduced self-esteem. Further, tracking may be ineffective if the data used for tracking are noisy.

Duflo, Dupas, and Kremer (2011), using an RCT in Kenya, found that tracking pupils according to their skills significantly increased student learning (0.18σ). These positive impacts benefitted students in all quartiles of the initial test score distribution: lower-achieving students improved their basic skills while higher-achieving students developed more advanced skills. This suggests that teachers altered their teaching to match their students' skills. Importantly, the study found no adverse peer effects.

Cummins (2017) reassesses Duflo et al. (2011), arguing that their study does not show that tracking increases the test scores of all students if teacher effort is low and incentives are misaligned. Cummins notes that a significantly positive impact of tracking depended on whether a standard civil-servant teacher or a contract teacher (who faces strong incentives to teach well in the hope of obtaining a civil-servant position) taught the class. Tracking with a contract teacher increased low-ability students' test scores by 0.24σ, but had no effect with a civil-servant teacher.

Teacher training with materials/curriculum

Four evaluations focused on literacy curriculum and materials. In the Philippines, Abeberese, Kumler, and Linden (2014) evaluated a program that provided reading materials and trained teachers to use those materials. After four months, students' reading scores in the treatment schools were 0.13σ higher than students' scores in the control group, although after seven months this impact was only 0.06σ. In contrast, the program had no effect on mathematics scores. Lucas et al. (2014) evaluated a new literacy curriculum for Kenyan and Ugandan primary schools, which was accompanied by training for teachers, principals and school management committees. They found that the new curriculum increased literacy test scores by 0.02σ in Kenya and 0.20σ in Uganda. They suggest that the differential effect may reflect Kenyan students' higher baseline scores and better access to learning materials, which reduced the scope for improvement. In contrast, Ugandan students had much lower scores and access to learning materials before the intervention, and so had more room for growth. In Congo (DRC), Aber et al. (2017) conducted an RCT to evaluate the impact of "Learning to Read in a Healing Classroom" (LRHC) on the reading and math skills of conflict-affected students in grades 2−4. Teachers were trained on, and provided, a reading curriculum infused with social and

emotional learning principles intended to improve student well-being and security. Teachers formed learning circles to exchange information, collaborate, problem solve and support one another, and received continued training, peer coaching, and support from master teacher trainers. The program had marginally significant (10% level) impacts on reading and geometry test scores, but no impact on addition/subtraction. The authors suggest that a literacy-focused teacher training program may, in general, better improve literacy, yet social-emotional learning programs in conflict-affected countries may improve both student well-being and math and reading outcomes.

Loyalka et al. (2017) evaluated the impact of a national teacher professional development program in China on lower secondary (grades 7−9) mathematics test scores and the student dropout rate (discussed in Section Impacts of pedagogy interventions on time in school). Their RCT evaluated three separate treatments. The first was a 15-day teacher training program focused on improving teachers' math knowledge, pedagogy, ethics, personal growth and classroom management. Teachers also received access to an online platform with additional professional development materials. The second treatment combined the teacher training program with post-training follow-up that provided text messages or phone calls with supplementary information and reports on how much teachers were using an online platform. The third treatment included the first two treatments plus post-training evaluation of the teachers. The results were disappointing; none of these treatments affected these students' mathematics scores. The authors argue that, despite high teacher participation, the nationally-designed teaching materials were neither relevant nor accessible to teachers. In particular, the training materials were extremely theoretical with little application to actual teaching, and the teachers were not taught how to apply the theoretical material. Also, in some cases new technologies (e.g.

multi-media graphing) were presented in the training, but were not available for the teachers to use.

Impacts of teacher-related governance interventions on learning

Some argue that even when teachers use appropriate pedagogy and have adequate inputs, learning requires good governance: a well-organized and well-managed education system. The following paragraphs consider governance interventions that focus on teaching or teachers' impacts.

Teacher performance pay

Teacher performance pay, evaluated over eight studies, has had mixed success at increasing student learning, as viewed across five studies. An RTC study conducted in Andhra Pradesh, India, found that giving teachers additional payments for increasing their students' test scores raised student learning. Muralidharan and Sundararaman (2011) found that, two years after the program started, the students in the teacher incentive schools had math and language test scores that were 0.27σ and 0.17σ higher than those of control school students, respectively.

In Chili, Contreras and Rau (2012) evaluated a program that provided bonus payments to public school teachers based on their students' test scores. This program significantly increased students' mathematics test scores by 0.29σ. In contrast, the impact on language scores was smaller and insignificant.

Glewwe et al. (2010) evaluated a group-level teacher incentive program in Kenya that provided prizes for schools with the highest performing students or the most-improved students. They found that students in the teacher-incentive schools scored higher on high-stakes tests (those that determined the prizes) but not on low-stakes tests (for which high scores did not entail prizes). They also found that these gains faded quickly after the program ended. They conclude that teacher incentives may not produce long-term learning.

Barrera-Osorio and Raju (2017) conducted an RCT for a teacher performance-pay program in Pakistan among grade 5 students in 600 primary schools. The program's three arms offered performance pay to either the head teacher alone, all teachers, or the head teacher receiving twice the bonus to teachers. The bonus was a function of the change in school enrollment, participation in the test and the change in test scores. While the program did increase exam participation, it had no impact on test scores or enrollment (see Section Impacts of teacher-related governance interventions on time in school). The authors believe the program provided an incentive to increase exam participation, but not test scores. They also note that using administrative data to measure changes in exam scores can limit teacher effort when the previous year's scores were high, making a higher score difficult in the subsequent year.

Loyalka, Sylvia, Liu, Chu, and Shi (2016) conducted RCTs for three teacher performance-pay schemes in rural China. For grade 6 students, they find that a "pay-for-percentile" incentive increased students' mathematics scores by 0.15σ, while teacher pay-for-performance schemes that pay teachers according to "levels" (average scores) or gains had no impact. They also found that the reward amounts did not matter. Finally, they found that the pay-for-percentile scheme resulted in teachers covering more material, and more advanced material.

Three studies examine the impact of unconditional teacher pay. De Ree, Jaitze, Muralidharan, Pradhan, and Rogers (2018) evaluated an unconditional doubling of teacher salaries in Indonesia. The program's original intent was to tie the salary increase to a process that rewarded teachers for higher knowledge and pedagogical skills, and provided training where needed. In reality, it doubled teacher salaries with almost no requirements. After three years, this doubling of teacher salaries did not affect mathematics, science, Indonesian and English test scores in either primary or secondary schools. The teacher outcome results were also largely insignificant (see Section Governance interventions). Kusumawardhani (2017) evaluated the same program, and also found no impacts on student test scores and teacher performance. Pugatch and Schroeder (2018) used a geographic discontinuity design to evaluate Gambia's hardship allowance, which provides a 30–40% salary premium to primary school teachers in remote locations. Teachers earned this allowance if they lived more than three kilometers from a main highway. The program had no effects on grade 3 and 5 English and math test scores, nor on grade 1–6 enrollment (see Section Impacts of teacher-related governance interventions on time in school). The program did increase the quantity and quality of teachers in those schools (see Section Governance interventions); however, the authors found no association between qualified teachers and student outcomes.

Contract teachers

There are only two high-quality studies on contract teachers. In the Kenya, Duflo et al. (2015) conducted an RCT for a program that provided schools an extra first grade contract teacher, reducing class sizes from about 80 to about 40. The authors studied two distinct interventions: 1. A class size reduction for classes taught by regular civil-service teachers; and 2. Being taught in a "small" class of about 40 students by a contract teacher (relative to a "small" class with a regular civil-service teacher). The class size reduction impact was discussed above. Regarding the impact of contract teachers, the authors find that, holding class size constant, students taught by contract teachers learned significantly more than those taught by civil-service teachers.

Muralidharan and Sundararaman (2013) studied a program that provided additional contract teachers to rural primary schools in Andhra Pradesh, India. After two years, the students whose schools received contract teachers had significantly higher test scores than the students in comparison schools (0.16σ for mathematics and 0.14σ for language). Unfortunately, the combination of a lower pupil-teacher ratio with adding a contract teacher prevents one from disentangling the effects of these two interventions. They did, however, find that absenteeism among contract teachers (16%) was significantly lower than among civil-service teachers (27%), and suggest that the main effect is primarily from the contract teachers rather than the pupil-teacher ratio reduction.

A related intervention is centralized deployment of teachers. Han, Liu, and An (2017) studied the impact of centralized teacher deployment on students, age 9–12, in rural China. Rural schools typically lack qualified teachers, and a proposed solution is mandatory assignment via centralized deployment. Combining difference-in-difference modeling with matching, they found that the average increase in students' math scores in the centralized townships was 0.3σ lower than in the comparison townships. There was no impact on Chinese test scores. These results, combined with the finding of lower work hours in centralized townships (see Section Governance interventions) suggest that centrally deployed teachers can undermine school quality.

Teacher monitoring and diagnostic feedback provided to teachers

Three studies examine a possible solution to teacher absenteeism: monitoring. Duflo et al. (2012) implemented an RCT that used cameras to monitor teacher attendance in small informal schools in Rajasthan, India. The cameras automatically recorded the time and date of each photograph, and thus could verify teacher attendance. The program not only monitored teachers but also provided them additional payments based on their monthly attendance (low attendance yielded no additional payments). The authors estimated that this program reduced teacher absence by half and increased student test scores by 0.17σ. They suggest that these impacts were due not to monitoring alone, but required the monetary incentives linked to teacher attendance. In contrast, Muralidharan and Sundararaman (2010) found no impact of a program in India that only monitored teacher absenteeism, without penalties or rewards based on attendance; this intervention affected neither teacher attendance nor student learning.[6] Combined, these results indicate that monitoring is effective only if it includes positive consequences for teacher attendance (or negative consequences for teacher absence).

De Hoyos, Ganimian, and Holland (2017) evaluated the impact of diagnostic feedback and capacity building on grade 3 and 5 reading and math scores and teacher outcomes in Argentina. The diagnostic feedback treatment provided schools with reports of grade 3 and 5 math and reading (in Spanish) test scores. In a second treatment, schools also received capacity building: five professional development workshops and two school visits. The impact of diagnostic feedback alone increased students' math and reading test scores by 0.29−0.38σ. However, the diagnostic feedback plus capacity building intervention had smaller impacts, and only for grade 5 scores. The authors contend that these treatment schools had had lower baseline achievement, low take-up of treatment and little impact from the capacity building.

Multi-dimensional teacher interventions

Bassi, Meghir, and Reynoso (2016) evaluate the impact of a nation-wide program in Chile to increase student learning in mathematics, reading and science from pre-K through grade 4 in low-performing public and subsidized private schools. The program provided teachers a package of pedagogical materials and tools, as well as promotion of class planning and class observation, and staff meetings to discuss students' progress. After one year, the program increased grade 4 students' reading test scores by 0.13σ, but not math or science. It had no impact on any scores after two years. The authors speculate that the program was not implemented as rigorously in the second year, suggesting that these programs are difficult to maintain momentum over time.

Bruns, Costa, and Cunha (2017) evaluated a program that provided secondary schools in Brazil with classroom observation feedback and expert coaching. Teachers received feedback from classroom observers on time use and student engagement. Self-help materials were provided to the principal pedagogical coordinator and to teachers, and the pedagogical coordinator received expert coaching. The program provided no direct training, rather teachers were supported by the school's pedagogical coordinator (who received coaching). Regarding impact, grade 10 students performed 0.5−0.8σ higher on math and Portuguese tests and 0.6σ higher on grade 12 Portuguese tests. The authors also found that teachers changed their allocation of classroom time (see Section Governance interventions).

Analysis of interventions that improve teacher outcomes

Teacher outcomes, including teachers' time in school, attitudes, and pedagogical practices, are often assessed when studying educational programs' impacts on student outcomes. Changes

---

[6] Muralidharan and Sundararaman (2010) has no estimates of the impact of monitoring on teacher attendance, and thus is not discussed in Analysis of interventions that improve teacher outcomes section. The claim of no impact on attendance is from lack of differences in absence across treatment and control schools.

in teacher outcomes may explain, at least in part, changes in student outcomes.

School input interventions

Only one study estimated the impact of school inputs on teacher outcomes. Yamada, Lavado, and Montenegro (2016) studied the impact on two teaching methods of the "One Laptop per Child" provision of low-cost laptops to primary schools in impoverished areas of Peru. Method A stressed students' cooperation and teachers' supervision (student-centered method), while Method B used a traditional lecture approach (teacher-centered method). To measure these two types of teaching methods, the authors measured whether: (1) students worked in groups; (2) students requested help from classmates during class; (3) students provided support to their classmates; (4) students engaged in cooperative work in class; (5) teachers conducted group work. The results show that providing laptops reduced teachers' use of student-centered pedagogical practices (Method A) by 6–13% points.

Pedagogy interventions

Some pedagogy interventions change students' performance through changing teachers' attitudes and pedagogical practices. It is informative to analyze how pedagogy interventions affect teacher outcomes to understand the success or failure of these interventions. Only one study examined pedagogy interventions, but it found very little effect on teacher outcomes.

In China, Loyalka et al. (2017) evaluated the professional development component of the National Teacher Training Program and its two post-training interventions − post-training follow-up and post-training evaluation − on several teacher outcomes. This program had no impact on students' time in school and test performance. To investigate why this program

failed, the authors estimated the impact of the program on student-reported teaching behaviors and teacher knowledge, attitudes, and beliefs. The interventions affected almost none of the teaching behaviors and teacher knowledge, attitudes, and beliefs. Since the program and its two post-training interventions focused on improving teacher math knowledge, pedagogy, ethics, personal growth, and classroom management, the negligible impact on teachers' outcomes suggest that the program failed not because teacher behaviors do not affect student performance, but because the program did not change those behaviors.

Governance interventions

Almost all high-quality studies of teacher governance interventions show impacts on teacher outcomes.

Teacher performance pay

Five of the studies that examined in the impact of teacher performance pay and unconditional teacher pay on test scores also looked at teacher outcomes. In Andhra Pradesh, India Muralidharan and Sundararaman (2011) tested for differences in teacher outcomes between the control and treatment groups, but did not measure the intensity of teacher efforts. They found no impact on teacher absence nor on observed indicators of classroom activities. However, indicators of teacher behavior from teacher interviews were statistically significant. The authors suggest that changes in teacher behavior may have been missed by classroom observations, and that teachers improved students' performance not by increasing their attendance but by increasing effort when present.

The group-level teacher incentive program in Kenya evaluated by Glewwe et al. (2010) measured teacher outcomes mostly by classroom visits or student surveys. The authors provide difference-in-difference estimates of program impacts on teacher attendance and measures of pedagogy. All estimates were statistically insignificant. However, test preparation sessions provided by treatment school teachers were 7.4% points higher than those of control school teachers. The authors conclude that teachers' efforts focused on increasing scores on the formula used to reward teachers, not on general learning.

In rural China, Loyalka et al. (2016) evaluated three teacher performance-pay schemes. They used curricular coverage to measure teaching competence, and estimated that pay-for-percentile increased curricular coverage by 2.7% points, while incentives based on levels and gains had no impact on curricular coverage. Moreover, pay-for-percentile incentives increased both the coverage and intensity of instruction, and teachers covered more difficult curricula. These results are consistent with the finding that the "pay-for-percentage" incentive also worked to increase test scores.

Two studies on unconditional increases in teacher pay show some impacts on teacher outcomes. In Indonesia, De Ree et al. (2017, 2018) evaluated the impact of unconditionally doubling teachers' base pay. Although the intervention improved teachers' satisfaction with their income and reduced their holding of outside jobs, this program had virtually no impact on student learning or self –reported teacher absence. The authors note that teachers' financial situation, job satisfaction, and ability to focus on teaching (due to less need for outside jobs) all improved. In The Gambia, Pugatch and Schroeder (2018) used regression discontinuity design to check the efficiency of the Hardship Allowance program, which provided an unconditional 30–40% salary premium to primary school teachers in remote locations in Gambia. They found that the program increased the number of qualified teachers and lowered the pupil-teacher ratio. They also found that the relationship between teacher qualifications and student test scores was statistically insignificant,

and conclude that improved teacher qualifications does not necessarily increase student learning.

Contract teachers

Duflo et al. (2015) estimated the impact of providing a contract teacher on teacher effort, measured during unannounced spot checks, and pedagogical behavior, measured by teacher surveys. Both civil-servant and contract teachers reported having more time to provide individual attention to children, including slow learners, and provide feedback on individual work. However, civil-service teachers work less after adding more contract teachers, who may be given some civil-service teacher responsibilities. The authors find that school-based management training for school committee members (and interested parents) to monitor the program appeared to reduce teacher attendance but increased the likelihood that teachers were in class teaching if present.

Muralidharan and Sundararaman (2013) evaluated an Extra Contract Teacher program in India. Schools hired new contract teachers, paying them 1/5 the salary of civil-service teachers. The authors compared contract and civil-service teachers' absence and level of teaching activities, and found that contract teachers had lower absence rates (-12.2% points) and higher rates of teaching activity (7.3% points). They noted that the additional contract teachers fully compensated for the reduction in civil-service teachers' effort.

Han et al. (2017) evaluated a related intervention: centralized deployment of teachers in rural China from 2000 to 2004. Using difference-in-differences methods, the authors found that centralized deployment decreased weekly teaching and grading hours and decreased weekly hours spent on preparation and out-of-class tutoring. They also compared these outcomes with contract teachers, who were not affected by the centralized deployment, and found similar results. The authors note that reduced working hours, combined with lower student test scores, suggest that civil-service teachers reduced their effort without improving teaching efficiency.

Teacher monitoring and diagnostic feedback

Designing effective monitoring mechanisms is important for reducing teacher absenteeism in developing countries. Two studies in India evaluated the impacts of teacher monitoring on teacher outcomes. Duflo et al. (2012) studied a performance-incentive program targeting teachers in non-formal education centers. They found that the program reduced teacher absence rates by 21% points, with similar results for both low- and high-quality teachers. However, the authors find no significant impact of this program on measures of teacher performance (percent of children sitting in the classroom),[7] teachers interacting with students, or blackboard utilization.

Pandey, Goyal and Sundararaman (2009) studied the impact of community meetings that provided villagers information on the roles and responsibilities of the school oversight committee, and benefits that students were entitled to receive. Using difference-in differences methods, they found increases in teachers' engagement in teaching (9% points) in Madhya Pradesh, increases in teachers' attendance (7% points) in Uttar Pradesh, and no impact on either in Karnataka, where teacher attendance and engagement in teaching were much higher at baseline. The authors mentioned that the differential impact across states may reflect differences in the extent to which teachers are governed by the school's oversight committee; for example, in Madhya Pradesh school committees verify teacher attendance but in Karnataka there is no such verification.

Lastly, recall that De Hoyos et al. (2017) evaluated the impact of diagnostic feedback and/or capacity building primary school students' test scores. The treatment of diagnostic feedback alone may have increased students' scores because, as the authors show, it significantly increased teacher activity and improved student-teacher interactions. As with the test score results, there were no impacts when diagnostic feedback and capacity building were combined.

Multi-dimensional teacher interventions

The final study is by Bruns et al. (2017), who evaluated an intervention in Brazil that combined performance feedback on teacher practice, provision of self-help materials, and coaching of the school pedagogical coordinator regarding classroom observation and teacher feedback. The program increased the share of class time devoted to instructional activities by 5.2% points, decreased classroom management by 2.8% points, and decreased off-task activities by 2.5% points. The authors also found that coordinators helped teachers at the low end of the skill distribution to improve their practice.

Conclusion

The abundance of high-quality evaluations of teaching and teacher interventions in developing countries provides much information on the effectiveness of programs designed to increase student time in school and student learning, and improve teacher outcomes.

Regarding time in school, there are relatively few (12) studies on the impact of teacher-related inputs, pedagogy or teacher-related school governance. Unfortunately, there is little evidence of impact, except for adding extra teachers or teaching assistants.

There is much more research on the impacts of teacher related-inputs, pedagogy or teacher-related school governance on student learning.

---

[7] The authors admit that this is a crude measures of teacher performance.

The most widely studied teacher-related input is different forms of information and communication technology (11 studies), such as laptops and computer-assisted learning. The majority of studies find significantly positive impacts on test scores. However, three studies show no or negative impacts, revealing that high-technology inputs may not succeed without effective teaching training or appropriate software. There is some evidence on other teacher inputs, including pupil-teacher ratio reductions, literacy programs (with teacher training), longer school days and multi-dimensional intervention. Of these, two studies on literacy programs with teacher training found improved learning outcomes, but the other interventions were less effective. Regarding the pupil-teacher ratio, the reductions evaluated may have been too small. For longer school days, the additional time may have been poorly structured. Thus, input interventions must ensure that inputs are well-targeted and appropriate to the local context.

Eleven studies have considered the impact of teaching pedagogy, in India, Nepal, Peru, the Philippines, Kenya, Uganda, Congo (DRC) and China. They range from teaching at the right level, to student tracking into classrooms based on performance, to teacher training programs. Many of these interventions increased student learning. Teaching at the right level program is most effective when it is carefully implemented. For example, effective programs provide atypical teachers (volunteers or locally trained informal teachers) or regular (civil service) teachers in the classroom who are under government monitoring, who dedicate a class hour to tutoring. Extensive teacher training programs are most effective when the training and curriculum are relevant to the local teaching context and level of student learning.

Teacher-related governance interventions can improve learning outcomes, but the 16 studies from India, Chile, Kenya, Pakistan, China, Argentina, and Brazil reveal that getting the incentives right matters. The eight studies on pay-for-performance or unconditional pay increases reveal that more research is needed on payment schemes' structures (e.g. pay-for-percentile, size of pay increase, short vs. Long term, unconditional vs. Conditional) to understand the different impacts on student learning. While research remains limited, two promising interventions are use of contract teachers and monitoring teachers combined with incentives. Both of provide incentives to teachers to increase student learning goals, while civil-servant teachers currently are less accountable.

Finally, we examined papers on teacher outcomes, which may clarify pathways through which teaching and teacher interventions may improve school or student learning outcomes. We found only 14 studies that examined the impact of teacher interventions on teacher outcomes, such as time in school, attitudes, and pedagogical practices. Only two studies considered the impact of teacher related inputs pedagogy (professional development programs in China and Chile) on teacher outcomes. Neither program in China or Chile altered teaching behaviors and knowledge, attitudes, beliefs, or teacher-student interactions, and subsequently did not affect student learning.

Yet some teacher-related governance interventions had positive impacts on teacher outcomes, including performance pay, contract teachers and monitoring with diagnostic feedback. As with impacts of teacher governance on student learning, incentives seem to matter. For example, in China a "pay-for-percentile" teacher incentive scheme seemed to increase teaching intensity and curriculum coverage, as well as test scores.

References

*55 total studies: 34 *RCT, 18 high quality (RDD-DD design) and 3 cited in the introduction.*

* Abeberese, A. B., Kumler, T. J., & Linden, L. L. (2014). Improving reading skills by encouraging children to

read in school: A randomized evaluation of the Sa Aklat Sisikat reading program in the Philippines. *Journal of Human Resources, 49*(3), 611–633.

* Aber, J. L., Torrente, C., Starkey, L., Johnston, B., Seidman, E., Halpin, P., et al. (2017). Impacts after one year of "Healing Classroom" on children's reading and math skills in DRC: Results from a cluster randomized trial. *Journal of Research on Educational Effectiveness, 10*(3), 507–529.

Alvarez-Marinelli, H., Blanco, M., Lara-Alecio, R., Irby, B. J., Tong, F., Stanley, K., et al. (2016). Computer assisted English Language learning in Costa Rican elementary schools: An experimental study. *Computer Assisted Language Learning, 29*(1), 103–126.

Anderson, K., Gong, X., Hong, K., & Zhang, X. (2016). Do selective high schools improve student achievement? Effects of exam schools in China. *China Economic Review, 40*, 121–134.

Azam, M., & Kingdon, G. G. (2015). Assessing teacher quality in India. *Journal of Development Economics, 117*, 74–83.

* Banerjee, A., Banerji, R., Duflo, E., Gelnnerster, R., & Khemani, S. (2010). Pitfalls of participatory programs: Evidence from a randomized evaluation in education in India. *American Economic Journal: Economic Policy, 2*(1), 1–30.

* Banerjee, A., Banerji, R., Berry, J., Duflo, E., Kannan, H., Mukherji, S., et al. (2016). *Mainstreaming an effective intervention: Evidence from randomized evaluations of "teaching at the right level" in India (No. w22746)*. National Bureau of Economic Research.

* Banerjee, A., Cole, S., Duflo, E., & Linden, L. (2007). Remedying Education: Evidence from two randomized experiments in India. *Quarterly Journal of Economics August*, 1235–1264.

* Barrera-Osorio, & Linden, L. (2009). *The use and misuse of computers in education: Evidence from a randomized experiment in Colombia*. World Bank Policy Research Working Paper #4836. Impact Evaluation Series No. 29.

* Barrera-Osorio, F., & Raju, D. (2017). Teacher performance pay: Experimental evidence from Pakistan. *Journal of Public Economics, 148*, 75–91.

* Bassi, M., Meghir, C., & Reynoso, A. (2016). *Education quality and teaching practices.*. National Bureau of Economic Research Working Paper No. 22710.

Battaglia, M., & Lebedinski, L. (2015). Equal access to education: An evaluation of the Roma teaching assistant program in Serbia. *World Development, 76*, 62–81.

* Beuermann, D., Cristia, J., Cueto, S., Malamud, O., & Cruz-Aguayo, Y. (2015). One laptop per child at home: Short-term impacts from a randomized experiment in Peru. *American Economic Journal: Applied Economics, 7*(2), 53–80.

* Bruns, B., Costa, L., & Cunha, N. (2017). Through the looking glass: Can classroom observation and coaching improve teacher performance in Brazil?. *Economics of Education Review, 64*, 214–250.

Chay, K. Y., McEwan, P. J., & Urquiola, M. (2005). The central role of noise in evaluating interventions that use test scores to rank schools. *The American Economic Review, 95*(4), 1237–1258.

Chin, A. (2005). Can redistributing teachers across schools raise educational attainment? Evidence from operation blackboard in India. *Journal of Development Economics, 78*(2), 384–405.

Contreras, D., & Rau, T. (2012). Tournament incentives for teachers: Evidence from a scaled-up intervention in Chile. *Economic Development and Cultural Change, 61*(1), 219–246.

* Cummins, J. R. (2017). Heterogeneous treatment effects in the low track: Revisiting the Kenyan primary school experiment. *Economics of Education Review, 56*, 40–51.

Cristia, J., Czerwonko, A., & Garofalo, P. (2014). Does technology in schools affect repetition, dropout and enrollment? Evidence from Peru. *Journal of Applied Economics, 17*, 89–112.

Cruz, T., Loureiro, A., & Sa, E. (2017). *Full-time teachers, students, and curriculum: The single-shift model in Rio de Janeiro*. The World Bank.

Damon, A., Glewwe, P., Wisniewski, S., & Sun, B. (2019). What education policies and programmes affect learning and time in school in developing countries? A review of evaluations from 1990 to 2014. *Review of Education, 7*(2), 295–387.

* De Ree, Jaitze, J., Muralidharan, K., Pradhan, M. P., & Rogers, H. F. (2018). Double for nothing? Experimental evidence on an unconditional teacher salary increase in Indonesia (English). *Quarterly Journal of Economics, 133*(2), 993–1039.

* De Hoyos, R., Ganimian, A. J., & Holland, P. A. (2017). *Teaching with the test: Experimental evidence on diagnostic feedback and capacity building for public schools in Argentina*. World Bank Working Paper No. WPS8261.

* Duflo, E., Dupas, P., & Kremer, M. (2011). Peer effects, teacher incentives, and the impact of tracking: Evidence from a randomized evaluation in Kenya. *The American Economic Review, 101*, 1739–1774.

* Duflo, E., Dupas, P., & Kremer, M. (2015). School governance, teacher incentives, and pupil-teacher ratios: Experimental evidence from Kenyan primary schools. *Journal of Public Economics, 123*, 92–110.

* Duflo, E., Hanna, R., & Ryan, S. P. (2012). Incentives work: Getting teachers to come to school. *American Economic Review, 102*(4), 1241–1278.

Fuje, H., & Tandon, P. (2015). *When do in-service teacher training and books improve student achievement? Experimental evidence from Mongolia*. The World Bank.

* Glewwe, P., Ilias, N., & Kremer, M. (2010). Teacher incentives. *American Economic Journal: Applied Economics*, 205−227.

Han, L., Liu, M., & An, X. (2017). Centralized deployment and teacher incentives: Evidence from reforms in rural China. *Economic Development and Cultural Change, 65*(2), 297−337.

International Monetary Fund. (2014). *World economic outlook (statistical Appendix). Washington, DC.* https://www.imf.org/external/pubs/ft/weo/2014/01/pdf/statapp.pdf.

Jayachandran, S. (2014). Incentives to teach badly: After-school tutoring in developing countries. *Journal of Development Economics, 108*, 190−205.

Jukes, M. C., Turner, E. L., Dubeck, M. M., Halliday, K. E., Inyega, H. N., Wolf, S., & et al. (2017). Improving literacy instruction in Kenya through teacher professional development and text messages support: A cluster randomized trial. *Journal of Research on Educational Effectiveness, 10*(3), 449−481.

Kusumawardhani, P. N. (2017). Does teacher certification program lead to better quality teachers? Evidence from Indonesia. *Education Economics, 25*(6), 590−618.

* Lai, F., Luo, R., Zhang, L., Huang, X., & Scott, R. (2015). Does computer-assisted learning improve learning outcomes? Evidence from a randomized experiment in migrant schools in Beijing. *Economics of Education Review, 47*, 34−48 [1].

* Lai, F., Zhang, L., Qu, Q., Hu, X., Shi, Y., Boswell, M., et al. (2013). *Does computer-assisted learning improve learning outcomes? Evidence from a randomized experiment in public schools in rural minority areas in Qinghai, China.* Rural Education Action Program Working Paper.

* Loyalka, P., Popova, A., Li, G., Liu, C., & Shi, H. (2017). *Unpacking teacher professional development.* Rural Education Action Program (REAP) Working Paper No. 314.

* Loyalka, P., Sylvia, S., Liu, C., Chu, J., & Shi, Y. (2016). *Pay by design: Teacher performance pay design and the distribution of student achievement..* Rural Education Action Program (REAP) Working Paper No. 306.

* Lucas, A., & Mbiti, I. (2014). Effects of school quality and student achievement: Discontinuity * evidence from Kenya. *American Economic Journal: Applied Economics, 6*(3), 234−263.

Malamud, O., & Pop-Eleches, C. (2011). Home computer use and the development of human capital. *The Quarterly Journal of Economics, 126*, 987−1027.

* Mo, D., Swinnen, J., Zhang, L., Yi, H., Qu, Q., Boswell, M., et al. (2013). Can one-to-one computing narrow the digital divide and the educational gap in China? The case of Beijing migrant schools. *World Development, 46*, 14−29.

* Mo, D., Zhang, L., Wang, J., Huang, W., Shi, Y., Boswell, M., et al. (2014). *The persistence of gains in learning from computer assisted learning (CAL): Evidence from a randomized experiment in rural schools in Shaanxi Province in China.* REAP Working Paper 268.

* Mo, D., Zhang, L., Lui, R., Qu, Q., Huang, W., Wang, J., & Rozelle, S. (2014). Integrating computer-assisted learning into a regular curriculum: Evidence from a randomized experiment in rural schools in Shaanxi. *Journal of Development Effectiveness, 6*(3).

* Karthik, M., & Sundararaman, V. (2010). The impact of diagnostic feedback to teachers on student learning: Experimental evidence from India.. *The Economic Journal, 120*(546), F187−F203.

* Muralidharan, K., & Venkatesh, S. (2011). Teacher performance pay: Experimental evidence from India. *Journal of Political Economy, 119*(1), 39−77.

* Muralidharan, K., & Venkatesh, S. (2013). *Contract teachers: Experimental evidence from India.* JPAL Working Paper. Available at http://www.povertyactionlab.org/evaluation/extra-contract-teachers-andhra-pradesh-india.

Orkin, K. (2013). *The effect of lengthening the school day on children's achievement in Ethiopia.* No. Working Paper 119. Young Live.

* Pandey, P., Goyal, S., & Venkatesh, S. (2009). Community participation in public schools: Impact of information campaigns in three Indian states. *Education Economics, 17*(3), 355−375.

Pugatch, T., & Schroeder, E. (2018). Teacher pay and student performance: Evidence from the Gambian hardship allowance. *Journal of Development Effectiveness, 10*(2), 249−276.

* Saavedra, J., Näslund-Hadley, E., & Alfonso, M. (2017). *Targeted remedial education: Experimental evidence from Peru (No. w23050).* National Bureau of Economic Research.

* Tan, J.-P., Lane, J., & Lassibille, G. (1999). Student outcomes in philippine elementary schools: An evaluation of four experiments. *World Bank Economic Review, 13*(3), 493−508.

Urquiola, M. (2006). Identifying class size effects in developing countries: Evidence from rural Bolivia. *Review of Economics and Statistics, 88*(1), 171−177.

Urquiola, M., & Verhoogen, E. (2009). Class-size caps, sorting, and the regression discontinuity design. *American Economic Review, 99*(1), 179−215.

* Yamada, G., Lavado, P., & Montenegro, G. (2016). *The effect of one laptop per child on teachers' pedagogical practices and students' use of time at home.* IZA Working Paper.

* Yang, Y., Zhang, L., Zeng, J., Pang, X., Lai, F., & Scott, R. (2013). Computers and the academic performance of elementary school-aged girls in China's poor communities. *Computers & Education, 60*(2013), 335−346.

* Wang, H., Chu, J., Loyalka, P., Xin, T., Shi., Y., Qu, Q., et al. (2016). Can social−emotional learning reduce school dropout in developing countries?. *Journal of Policy Analysis and Management, 35*(4), 818−847.

Teacher supply

Peter Dolton

Department of Economics, University of Sussex, Brighton, UK

The supply of high quality school teachers must be one of the main education policy priorities of any government since the education of the next generation is their responsibility. Any education system needs to recruit and retain the high-quality teachers and understand the role of pay and other incentives intended both to attract people to the profession and to retain them.

Every country needs a relatively large number of teachers, as on average, in OECD countries 2.6% of the total labor force are teachers. In most countries, this means the education sector is the largest employer of university graduates. Accordingly, teachers pay is the largest component of a country's educational expenditure taking up over 60% of the educational budget in most countries.

In any consideration of the quality of teachers we must be aware of the forces of supply and demand and the decisions governments choose to make about desirable pupil teacher ratios, teacher working hours, the length and quality of teacher training, teacher pay and incentives and the other non-pecuniary conditions in teaching which must be affected by government educational spending priorities.

Many countries have experienced recurrent cricrises NOT crizeszes in the recruitment and retention of teacher. Indeed, in many countries there is a more or less continuous shortage of teachers, notably in secondary schools and in the most technical subjects. The shortage tends to be particularly acute in subjects like mathematics and science and in specific geographical areas, where the 'opportunity wage' for 'would be' teachers is much higher.

The labor market position of teachers and specifically their pay has been shown to be clearly related to the educational outcomes for pupils (see Dolton and Marcenaro Gutierrez (2011,2013); Dolton et al. (2018). The consequences of teacher supply problem are also inequitably felt across different socioeconomic groups in any society. It is also clear that there are many other factors which are crucial in the supply of graduates entering the profession like the occupational status which is accorded to teachers. (See Dolton and Marcenaro, 2013; Dolton et al., 2018). These factors are hugely important in the quality of graduates who enter teaching and this has well-documented consequences for pupil performance.

The labor market for teachers

The labor market for teachers can be thought of within a traditional supply and demand

The Economics of Education, Second Edition
https://doi.org/10.1016/B978-0-12-815391-8.00028-8

framework, with the additional complication that the government is virtually the sole hirer of labor. The demand for teachers can determined by the number of children in the country of school age, and the government's desired pupil-teacher ratio (PTR). For a given such ratio, the demand for teaschers is therefore a constant, denoted by Q^* in Fig. 28.1. Under the reasonable assumption that the supply of teachers is a positive function of average teacher earnings, an upward-sloping labor supply schedule can be drawn as S. In a perfectly competitive market, a teacher wage of W^* would therefore clear this labor market. However, the teachers' labor market is of course not competitive, and the government, in its role as (almost) exclusive purchaser of teaching labor, has other considerations, prime among which is the level of expenditure on teachers' salaries in total. For a given level of such expenditure, an inverse relationship can be plotted between teachers' earnings and the number of teachers hired, labeled E_1 in Fig. 28.1; if the government wants to raise the salaries of teachers, it can afford to hire fewer of them, given a fixed budget. The number of

teachers hired is therefore Q_g at average earnings of W^g, and the excess demand for teachers is $Q^* - Q_g$. This can only be eradicated by a relaxing of the budget constraint leading to higher earnings, or other factors changing to make teaching more attractive, so that more potential teachers supply their labor at any given wage.

Of course, the above analysis is simplistic in that it treats all teachers as being the same. In reality, within the same country, there may be teacher shortages in particular geographical locations or regions or in particular subjects, with an over-supply elsewhere. In addition, the PTR is typically been different in primary and secondary schools and hence the real market position is very different for teachers in the different sectors. We can amend Fig. 28.1 to allow for such possibilities by creating a simple distinction of different kinds of teachers. A simple analysis would suggest that the possibility of differential wages by subject, in different regions or between primary and secondary sectors could be adopted to solve the problems of short supply in particular areas. Whether this solution

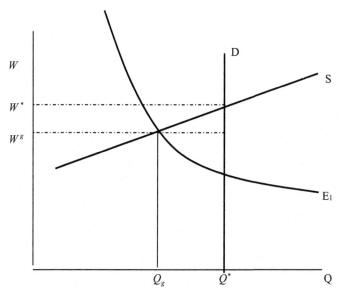

FIG. 28.1 The labor market for teachers.

is actually viable, given the demands of teachers' unions, is another question.

Fig. 28.2 shows the teacher demand and supply elements that may be used to determine if the teacher labor market is in shortage or in surplus. Demand is dependent on the number of pupils in the country and on the Government's desired PTR. The higher the number of pupils enrolled in

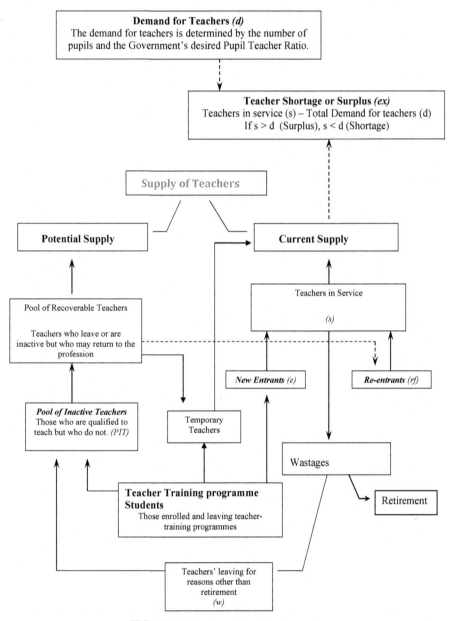

FIG. 28.2 Teacher demand and supply.

IV. Teacher labour markets

schools, or the lower is the PTR target set by the Government, then the higher will be the demand for teachers.

The supply of teachers as outlined in Fig. 28.2 can be divided into two: the current supply of teachers and the potential supply. The current supply of teachers, consists of those who are currently in service in the teaching workforce. These teachers in service *(s)* and would contain those who are continuing teachers, the new entrants *(e)* and the re-entrants *(rf)*. The new entrants are those who are first timers teaching in public schools while re-entrants are those with previous teaching experience in public schools, who left and are now returning to teaching. The number of students enrolled in the Initial Teacher Training (ITT) courses sustains the flow of new entrants as they can enter into teaching upon completion of their training. A shortage *(ex)* occurs when the demand for teachers is not matched by supply and a surplus occurs when the current supply of teachers exceeds the demand of teachers.

To complete the teacher supply and demand model, the outflow of teachers needs to be considered as well. Wastage makes up the outflow of teachers from the current supply.

This group of leavers can be divided into those who leave at retirement age and those who leave for reasons other than retirement (i.e. those below the age of 60—65). This includes those leaving to pursue a different career and those seeking a career break for family or other reasons. When teachers (and those who are qualified to teach) leave the profession, they become inactive and enter the stock of potential teachers in the Pool of Inactive Teachers *(PIT)*. In addition to the leavers below retirement age, the PIT also contains the ITT graduates who do not enter into teaching. A second component in the potential supply of teachers is the Pool of Recoverable Teachers *(PRT)*. The teachers in the PRT are those who leave the profession but can be enticed to return to teaching and are therefore the main source of potential supply.

The demand for teachers

The first key element in the demand for teachers is the demographic pattern of pupil numbers which will fluctuate all the time with changing fertility patterns. In many OECD countries, projected numbers of pupils will be falling over the next 5—10 years.

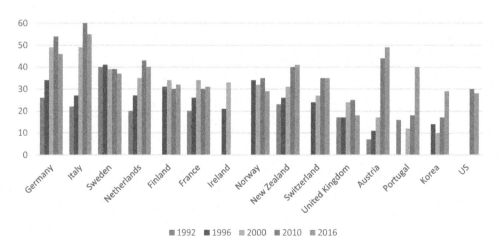

FIG. 28.3   Percentage of teacher aged 50 years and over in lower secondary school by country over time. *Source: OECD.Stat (https://stats.oecd.org/).*

The second demographic trend affecting the demand for new teachers relates to the age distribution of the stock of existing teachers. Fig. 28.3 shows that in many OECD countries the teacher stock is aging as an increasing proportion of teachers in the years from 1992 to 2016 are over 50. This will lead to an increase in the demand for new teachers to replace those retiring over the next 10—15 years.

A third factor in the demand for teachers is the size of class the government chooses for its pupils. This varies remarkably across countries as Fig. 28.4 shows that Pupil/Teacher ratios in primary schools are over 25 to 1 and lower than 20 to in some countries. This will not only condition the demand for teachers but the quality of the teaching which is imparted to the children as larger classes may mitigate against individual pupil attention. In many OECD countries Pupil/Teacher ratios have been falling. In

the USA, average class size in 2016 has fallen to 21in Primary schools and 26 in Lower Secondary schools. This represents a growth in teacher supply over the last 35 years in the USA Of course what these aggregate figures hide are the increasing need for specialist teachers of subject like ICT.

A fourth factor in demand is the governments choice of the length of the working day for teachers and how many teaching days there are in a year. Most countries make their elementary teachers teach between 650 and 800 hours in the year but some teach a lot more — including some that teach around 1000 hours a year like the USA Fig. 28.5 illustrates the variability of teacher hours in a year across countries and these differences must be reflected in the quality and intensity of the effort required of teachers in their job and hence the relative attractiveness of the job compared to alternatives.

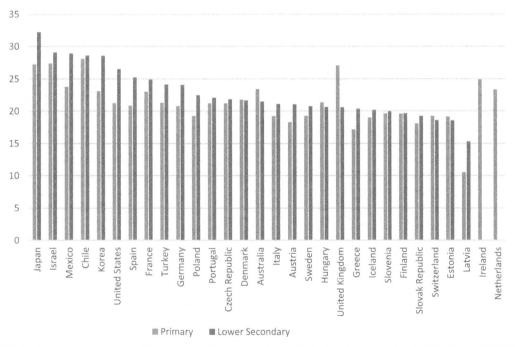

■ Primary ■ Lower Secondary

FIG. 28.4 Average class size in public educational institutions by level of education by country in 2016. *Source: OECD / UIS / Eurostat (2018). (https://doi.org/10.1787/eag-2018-36-en).*

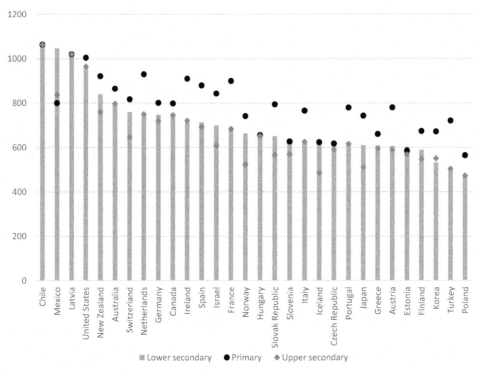

FIG. 28.5 Number of teaching hours per year, by level of education 2017. Net contact time in hours per year in public institutions. *Source: Education at a Glance (2018) Chart D4.1. (https://doi.org/10.1787/eag-2018-en).*

Several other features may complicate the demand for teachers in different countries. First, if the financial administration of education is performed at a local level resourcing decisions will depend on local and school specific factors. Secondly, the determination of desired pupil-teacher ratios and teacher recruitment may be influenced by educational criteria at the state or local level. Thirdly, the most governments control the nature of length of teacher training — this can and has been changed in times of crisis. Finally, different countries have different conventions about the extent to which school subjects, like Mathematics may be taught by non-specialists. Fig. 28.6 clearly shows that in many countries over 20% of Principals report that instruction is hindered by a lack of Mathematics and Science teachers. Clearly, allowing non-specialists to teach such shortage subjects

will solve the short run problem of having a teacher in front of a class — but at what cost to the quality of teaching? Ultimately the demand for teachers will depend on the political will that creates the policy on educational expenditure balanced with the importance on spending on health, welfare, defense and other priorities.

The supply of teachers

The supply of teachers can be regarded as all those currently in teaching, plus those currently not teaching, but who are qualified to teach, and would consider teaching if the conditions were right. An additional central component is the retention of the present stock of teachers. The supply issues at stake are therefore ones of recruitment and retention, as well as inducing

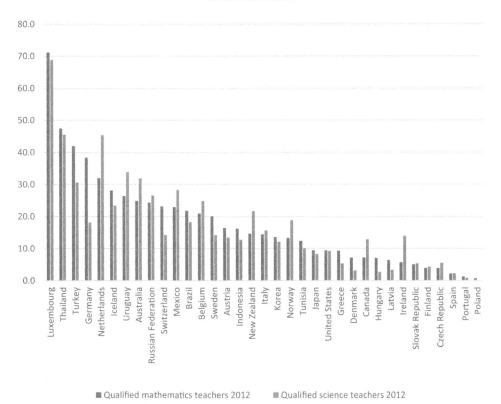

FIG. 28.6 Percentage of principals reporting that the school's capacity to provide instruction is hindered a lot by a lack of qualified mathematics or science teachers, 2012. *Source: Effective teacher policies: Insights from PISA, 2018, Figure 4.2 (https://doi.org/10.1787/9789264301603-en).*

the return of qualified individuals who have left the profession. There are many factors that are likely to influence the supply of teachers, such as the relative earnings on offer in teaching and other careers, other labor market opportunities, and varying relative non-pecuniary conditions of work. To a certain extent, some of these factors can be controlled by the government or federal authorities since it can determine how many places are provided on courses at universities to train teachers. In many countries teacher training courses are not always filled, and attendance varies by subject. The measurement of teacher supply and most specifically the changes in teacher supply from year to year is problematic. Various studies have tried to measure teacher

supply by changes in the pool of inactive teachers or the pool of recoverable teachers; changes in the stock of those teachers actually in service; the number of new entrants or the numbers leaving teaching or teacher training programmes.

It is evident that the flow of newly qualified teachers does not necessarily indicate the level of overall supply. Focusing on those currently working as a teacher ignores individuals who are available for (and possibly seeking) work in teaching, but who are not currently employed as a teacher. Supply can be calculated as consisting of those entering the profession and those remaining in teaching from the previous year.

But the difficulty is not just recruiting teachers but keeping them in the classroom. Some trainees drop out and others decide not to become teachers. Recently in some countries, kine the UK, there has also been an unprecedented rise in newly qualified teachers leaving the profession within the first 5 years. This wastage and turnover not only adds to the costs of providing teacher training but also has negative effects on child performance. The evidence is that higher teacher turnover is associated with lower educational pupil outcomes (Dolton & Newson, 2003). This is of particular concern since we know that teacher turnover is highest in the most deprived areas.

Policies to increase the retention of trainees and new teachers have been on the forefront of the political agenda on education. The most prominent measures are repayment of student loans for up to ten years and a hardship allowance for students in shortage subjects committing to become teachers, bursaries for undertaking and completing teacher training and cash 'golden hellos' of for new teachers in shortage subjects.

It is hard to find direct evidence of the interrelation between teacher supply and shortage and the quality of teachers. How do schools react when faced with a teacher shortage? In the usual course of events we would expect a school to advertise and hire a fully qualified teacher. If teachers are in short supply the school may resort to hiring a teacher with less than a full qualification; expanding the size of the classes; add hours to other teacher's courses, appoint or use more teaching auxiliary staff, or cancel the planned course. Even in the latest OECD publications there is virtually no clear evidence on how schools currently cope.

What individuals can earn as teachers, relative to what they could earn in alternative occupations (the opportunity wage), is one of the key determinants of the decision to become a teacher. In particular, the lower are relative wages (or wage growth) in teaching, the less likely is a graduate to choose that career. Relative earnings affect both initial career choices, as well as

choices made later in an individual's career. Dolton (1990) also found that there is considerable inertia to remain in teaching, and suggested that this effect may be partially due to the different individuals' subjective evaluation of the relative pecuniary and non-pecuniary rewards to teaching. It is also likely that non-pecuniary factors such as workload, job stress, physical surroundings and related factors also play an important role in the decision to enter teaching or to leave if these working conditions change.

While relative pay affects the decision to become a teacher, it also affects the decision to remain a teacher. Analyzing the decision to leave teaching, Dolton and Van der Klaauw (1995) show that the higher the relative earnings of teachers, the less likely they are to leave teaching. Work using US data suggests that raising teacher pay could improve the quality of the stock of teachers. But attracting more able students to teaching is not the only difficulty for policy-makers. Since individuals with higher ability generally command higher wages, high ability teachers are at a higher risk of leaving the profession than less talented teachers. To negate the lure of improved outside opportunities on 'able' teacher retention, some countries have introduced fast track programmes with the aim of recruiting and retaining the most able graduates by shortening pay scales and providing them with additional training, support and supervision.

Another important aspect of teacher supply is that teaching is a career that is relatively popular with female graduates. In nearly all OECD countries the majority of teachers are women particularly in primary education, where women consist of 80% or over of the teacher labor force. A crucial aspect of the distinction between male and female occupational choice is that often women are simultaneously making decisions about starting a family and hence deciding whether to participate in the labor market. This is particularly true in teaching since a teaching career has complementarities with family formation and in particular, the ease with which one can return to teaching after a career interruption. Hence for women the choice of teaching as a career is intimately related to the decision to participate in the labor market (Dolton & Makepeace, 1993).

Labor market conditions at the time the occupational choice is made are also important. The most recent evidence from Dolton & Chung (2003) look at time series data in the UK and finds that aggregate labor market conditions, particularly unemployment levels, are important determinants of teacher supply. Notably, they find that the supply of graduates to teaching is counter-cyclical with most graduates' perception of teaching (and willingness to enter the profession) improving when teacher pay is high compared to alternative occupations and when graduate unemployment is high.

Teacher quality is extremely difficult to observe. That is to say — it is very difficult accurately measure, the amount of effort exerted or output produced by any individual teacher. This is important because teacher effectiveness is an important determinant of pupil attainment. It is unclear whether teachers with better qualifications are necessarily better teachers. There is some evidence in the UK (see Chevalier, Dolton, & McIntosh, 2007) that teachers are being drawn from a lower part of the educational achievement or ability distribution than they were in the past.

What we seek to do is recruit the individuals with the most appropriate personalities to be good teachers. To some extent this does not necessarily mean the most able individuals — but often those with the capacities to be good teachers. What makes a good teacher is not something which can be easily measured. Naturally governments and state agencies should try to maximize the effective use of the tax-payers money spent on education — this means that there should be appropriate attempts to monitor spending on teachers. The problem with this is

that we do not fully understand: how to measure teacher quality, how teacher quality affects pupil performance, how to measure effective teacher input or effort. Under these circumstances it is tempting for governments to try to introduce various incentive mechanisms and even performance related pay for teachers. The current state of knowledge is overviewed in Dolton, McIntosh, and Chevalier (2003). Although the popularity of this measure appears to be waning (see Dolton and Marcenaro-Gutierrez, 2013; Dolton et al. 2018).

Teachers' pay

The most important determinant of teacher supply is the relative wage on offer. There is a large body of econometric evidence which finds that relative earnings of teachers are a major factor in individual's decisions to become a teacher or remain in the profession. There is considerable variability in what teachers are paid in different countries. In Fig. 28.7 we graph this in a comparable across countries in $US PPP terms. This shows that there are some countries where teachers earn 4—8 times (Luxembourg, Switzerland, and Germany) that in other countries, like former communist countries and some Latin American countries. In this graph, we also show how variable the teacher salary is for a new started and a teacher with 15 years' experience. It is noticeable is in some countries (Luxembourg, England, Belgium, Ireland, Netherlands and Israel) there is a much bigger range of earnings than in others where there is hardly any pay progression at all.

Fig. 28.8 shows how variable teacher's wages are across countries by graphing average teachers wage expressed as a proportion of GDP per head. This shows that there are some countries where teachers are earning appreciably more than the national average GDP per head (like Germany, Canada, Korea, Netherlands, Portugal and Spain). Most countries pay their teachers between 1 and 1.5 times the GDP per head,

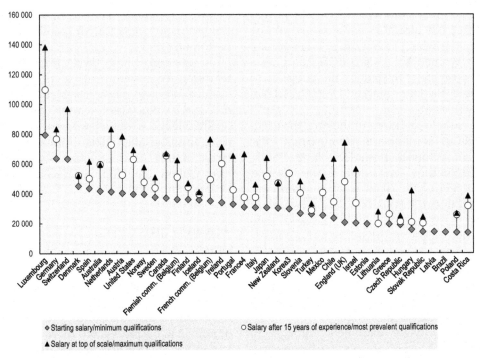

FIG. 28.7   Teachers' salaries in $US PPP, 2017. *Source: OECD (2018) (https://doi.org/10.1787/eag-2018-36-en).*

including most other European countries. Clearly in some countries being a teacher accords a much higher earnings status than in others. This will reflect on the caliber of the people doing the job in that country.

Tracking the relative pay of teachers over time in more detail is not straightforward in most countries. Dolton (2006) presents what has happened to relative teacher earnings over time in the UK and the USA Often the process of public sector wage settlement is subject to delays and lags. This is reflected in the process of declining real wages in teaching which may then be followed, as was the case in the UK, with periods of 'catch-up' following a decline in relative earnings.

Another important but neglected aspect of remuneration is what individuals are paid over their lifetime. There is good evidence for the UK (Dolton & Chung, 2004) that teachers fair badly in this regard over the course of their

whole working career and that the position has been getting worse. The earnings of male teachers were uniformly higher than earnings in the alternative occupation in 1975. But over time, the earnings profile in the alternative occupation has been shifting up while that of teachers has been moving down. By 2000, it is clear that the wage in the alternative occupation is almost uniformly above that of teaching.

There are many other areas in which our knowledge about teacher supply is scant. Although teacher shortage is widespread we know from empirical evidence that many young people still choose to be teachers despite the low pay. Clearly non-pecuniary factors matter in occupational choice but we know relatively little about this part of the process and how it operates. We know relatively little about the role of expected future lifetime earnings in the decision process and how people trade this off against a job which is rewarding. We also know little

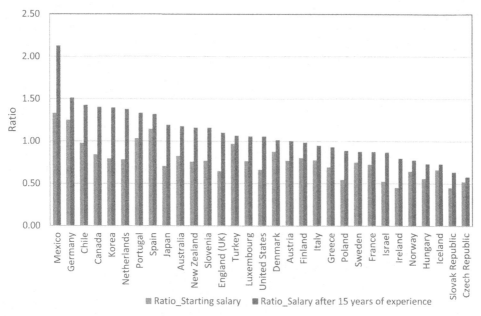

FIG. 28.8 Ratio of starting salary and salary after 15 years of experience to gross domestic product (GDP) per capita, lower secondary education, 2017. *Source: OECD.Stat (https://stats.oecd.org/) and Education at a Glance (2018), Table D3.1a, (https://doi.org/10.1787/eag-2018-en).*

about young people's perceptions of teaching as a career or their real relative perceptions of earnings in teaching. In some countries there are a sizable number of teachers who enter the profession in mid career after working in the private sector for some time. We need to know more about what motivates these individuals to make these choices and if they are more effective teachers due to their outside perspective on the real world.

Summary

Examining the pattern of evidence relating to teacher recruitment across OECD countries it is clear that there have been various trends. Teacher relative earnings have been declining and many countries have experienced teacher shortages particularly in subjects where graduates can earn a higher opportunity wage.

Countries can disguise these shortages in a number of ways including having more pupils taught by non-specialist teachers. These factors will compromise the quality of teaching delivered.

Many governments have tackled their problems with teachers by reforming the training of new teachers or the retraining of existing teachers with professional development schemes or trying to introduce teacher appraisal and various incentive schemes into teacher pay. Little is known about the effectiveness of these schemes compared to simply putting more government expenditure into education and teacher pay.

The overwhelming conclusion of research on the supply of teachers is that problems of teacher shortage could be alleviated with higher relative teacher salaries. If relative teacher salaries were higher than the problems of teacher recruitment, retention and duration would be alleviated.

It is clear in most countries that there are teacher supply problems. There is evidence from different states in the USA and from other countries around the world that there are persistent episodic shortages of teachers. This manifests itself in terms of not enough recruits entering the profession and too many leaving it prematurely. However, it is also clear that there is not a universal shortage of all categories of teacher. Specifically, teachers are in short supply in difficult schools in areas with inner city urban problems and in subjects which have a high opportunity wages for those with specific technical skills. The problems seem to be worst in scientific and mathematical subjects where the outside option is higher. Hence the real challenge of teacher supply is to get teachers into teaching the subjects and areas that are not appealing. The straightforward economic answer is to consider differential pay for those shortage categories. What is less clear are the long term consequences of having children taught by temporary, nonspecialist or low quality teachers.

The perennial challenge for governments and education administrators is to establish a high quality teacher labor force which is hard working and effective. Such problems could easily be solved by paying teachers higher wages. The problem of course is that governments are reluctant to throw more money at such problems and that even if they did it, is not clear what the outcome of increased expenditure is — precisely. Hence more research on the relationship between educational resource inputs, teacher quality and outcomes must inevitably have important lessons for the importance of teacher supply. For example, if we knew categorically that the size teacher pupil ratios had no effect on pupil outcomes then we could simply solve teacher shortage problems by having larger classes. In addition, we do not know in much detail, the effect of teacher working conditions on their relative effectiveness. There are many unanswered questions relating to teacher supply which deserve the attention of research in the future.

References

Chevalier, A., Dolton, P., & McIntosh, S. (2007). Recruiting and retaining teachers in the UK: An analysis of graduate occupation choice from the 1960s to the 1990s. *Economica, 74*, 69–96.

Dolton, P. (1990). The economics of UK teacher supply: The graduate's decision. *Economic Journal, 100*, 91–104.

Dolton, P. (2006). Teacher supply. In E. Hanushek, & F. Welch (Eds.), *Handbook of education economics*. North Holland.

Dolton, P. T., & Chung, T.-P. (2003). *Teacher supply and the economic cycle*. Report to the OECD.

Dolton, & Chung, T.-P. (2004). The Rate of return to teaching: How does it compare to other graduate jobs? *National Institute Economic Review, 190*, 89–103.

Dolton, P., & Makepeace, G. (1993). Female labour force participation and the choice of occupation: The supply of teachers. *European Economic Review, 37*, 1393–1411.

Dolton, P., & Marcenaro-Gutierrez, O. D. (2011). If you pay peanuts do you get monkeys? A cross-country analysis of teacher pay and pupil performance. *Economic Policy, 26*, 5–55.

Dolton, P., & Marcenaro-Gutierrez, O. D. (October 2013). *An international index of teacher status*. Varkey GEMS Foundation.

Dolton, P., Marcenaro-Gutierrez, O. D., DeVries, R., & She, P. (2018). *Global teacher status index 2018*. Varkey Foundation.

Dolton, P., McIntosh, S., & Chevalier, A. (2003). *Teacher pay and performance: A review of the literature'*. Bedford way papers. London: Institute of Education.

Dolton, P., & Newson, D. (2003). The relationship between teacher turnover and pupil performance. *London Review of Education, 1*(2), 133–140.

Dolton, P., & Van der Klaauw, W. (1995). Leaving teaching in the UK: A duration analysis. *Economic Journal, 105*, 431–444.

Further reading

Brookings Institution. (2007). Excellence in the classroom. *The Future of Children*. Princeton, Brookings.

Dolton, P., & Van der Klaauw, W. (1999). The turnover of UK teachers: A competing risks explanation. *Review of Economics and Statistics, 81*(3), 543–552.

Hanushek, E., & Rivkin, S. (2006). Teacher quality. In E. Hanushek, & F. Welch (Eds.), *Handbook of education economics*. North Holland.

Murnane, R. J., Singer, J. D., Willett, J. B., Kemple, J. J., & Olsen, R. J. (1991). *Who will teach? The Policies that matter*. Cambridge: Harvard University Press.

OECD. (2005). *Teachers matter: Attracting, developing and retaining effective teachers*. Paris.

OECD. (2018a). *Education at a glance*. Paris: OECD.

OECD. (2018b). *Effective teacher Policies: Insights from PISA*. Paris: OECD.

Economic approaches to teacher recruitment and retention

S. Loeb, J. Myung
Stanford University, Stanford, CA, United States

Introduction

The quality of teaching in a school results from a range of factors, including available resources, curriculum, and instructional leadership, but it is also driven by the individuals who teach in each classroom. The staffing of teachers in schools, in turn, is a product of both recruitment and retention practices. This article describes how the choices of teachers and the actions of schools and districts influence who enters the profession and who stays. It then identifies common policy approaches for advancing recruitment and retention goals and summarizes the current research, discussing the effectiveness of these policies. The article focuses on teacher labor markets in the United States (for information on teacher labor markets outside of the US, see Ladd (2007) and Vegas (2007)).

The supply and demand model provides a simple framework for considering recruitment and retention. Wages and nonpecuniary job attributes combine to determine the supply of individuals interested in teaching in a given school, district, or state. A large body of research

suggests that, like other workers, potential and current teachers respond to wage changes, although research on the degree of this response is not conclusive. Nonpecuniary components of teaching that influence the supply of teachers include working conditions, school location, and ease of entry into the occupation and the school. Feelings of success in the classroom also appear to be important for the retention of teachers already in the workforce.

The demand for teachers and the institutional constraints within which these demands are expressed also affect the teacher workforce. The number and characteristics of teachers demanded constitute a function of many factors, including student enrollment, teacher turnover, and the ability and willingness to pay for teachers. Institutional constraints, such as the skill and efficiency of hiring authorities, available information on the quality of individual teachers, budget timing, certification and licensure policies, tenure policies, and teacher contract provisions, can all affect the ability of districts to recruit and retain teachers.

In what follows, we address supply- and demand-side factors affecting this workforce in

The Economics of Education, Second Edition
https://doi.org/10.1016/B978-0-12-815391-8.00029-X

more detail, and conclude with a discussion of policies aimed at improving recruitment and retention.

The supply of teachers

The decisions of eligible individuals willing to teach aggregate to determine the teacher labor supply. Multiple factors affect the choices individual teachers make. Research has enumerated a few of these factors, including relative wages, working conditions, job location, and ease of entry into the occupation and into each job. Teacher self-efficacy also factors into teachers' decision of whether to remain in teaching.

Wages

A large body of literature suggests that individuals are more likely to choose to teach when starting teacher wages are high relative to wages in other occupations. Drawing upon multiple data sources, Bacolod (2007) found that highly qualified teachers are especially sensitive to changes in relative wages. Over the long run, trends in relative teacher pay have correlated with trends in teacher quality (Corcoran, Evans, & Schwab, 2004). Wages may also affect retention. Murnane and Olsen (1990) found that teachers who are paid more stay longer in teaching, but that wages influence retention less for teachers with high test scores than for teachers with lower scores. Approximately 15% of public school teachers who decided to move to another school in 2004–2005 reported having done so for better wage or benefits (Marvel, Lyter, Peltola, Strizek, & Morton, 2007). Wages are clearly associated with the retention decisions of teachers, although the causal analysis of this is less clear since high teacher wages in schools are often associated with a variety of other reasons for which teachers may choose to stay, such as better

working conditions or higher student achievement.

While teachers respond to wages, much of the variation in teacher wages is between districts, reflecting differences in alternative wages, not within labor markets. Thus, the differences that we see across schools in the supply of teachers are likely driven by nonpecuniary characteristics of the jobs (Loeb & Page, 2000).

Working conditions

Nonpecuniary job characteristics strongly affect the dynamics of the teacher labor market. While in some occupations additional wages compensate for adverse working conditions, in teaching, the single wage schedule at the district level in the United States, and in many countries at the national level, can lead to great variation in the appeal of teaching in different schools, driven by variation in nonwage characteristics of the job.

Multiple studies have documented a relationship between teachers' career choices and the school's student population: teachers, on average, prefer schools with high-achieving, high-income, and white students. Whether these preferences are driven by direct preferences for particular types of students or by differences in working conditions in the schools these students attend is less clear. As an example, Georgia elementary teachers move from schools with higher proportions of minority students and from low-performing schools, but the latter appears to be explained by teacher preferences for fewer minority students (Scafidi, Stinebrickner, & Sjoquist, 2003). Texas and New York data, on the other hand, found that teachers prefer higher achieving students even after controlling for student racial composition. Teachers, especially highly qualified teachers, are more likely to transfer or quit when teaching lower achieving students (Boyd, Lankford, Loeb, & Wyckoff, 2005b; Hanushek, Kain, & Rivkin,

2004). As further evidence of the weight some teachers put on student-body characteristics, when class size reduction in California increased the demand for teachers across the state, many teachers in schools with low-achieving students switched to schools with higher achieving students (Betts, Rueben, & Danenberg, 2000).

Student characteristics are not the only working condition that affects teachers' choices, in particular, school leadership also affect teachers' decisions. Approximately 37% of teachers move from their school due to dissatisfaction with their administrators (Marvel et al., 2007). Weiss (1999) found perceived school leadership to be among the strongest variables associated with first-year teachers' feeling that it is worthwhile to exert their best effort, commitment to career path, and intentions to stay in teaching. An effective principal may have the ability to create a positive working environment for teachers, in spite of attributes of schools typically associated with high turnover. Other school factors are also important. A study of California teachers found that among the strongest predictors of turnover in a school are teachers' ratings of their tangible school conditions, such as physical facilities and availability of textbooks and technology, as well as the quality of professional development, involvement of parents, and quality and appropriateness of tests teachers are required to administer (Loeb, Darling-Hammond, & Luczak, 2005). Buckley, Schneider, and Shang (2005) also found that facility quality is an important predictor of the decision of teachers to leave their current position, even after controlling for other contributing factors.

Psychic benefits and costs

Tangible working conditions are part of a job's appeal but teachers also respond to less-concrete job attributes.

Johnson and Birkeland (2003) found that new teachers who find that they cannot achieve a sense of success with students are less likely to find teaching a rewarding work and to remain in the classroom. Teachers who feel successful with students and whose schools were organized to support them in their teaching - providing collegial interaction, opportunities for growth, appropriate assignments, adequate resources, and school-wide structures supporting student learning - were less likely to leave their school than teachers in schools who were not organized to support them.

Farkas, Johnson, and Foleno (2000) similarly found the primary source of satisfaction among new teachers who planned to continue teaching was their confidence that they were making a difference in the lives of their students. In teachers' decisions to stay, leave, or transfer schools after the first year of teaching, more than anything else, teachers weighed whether they could be effective with their students. Difficult working conditions can affect a teacher's opportunity to teach well which, thus, affects his/her ability to succeed with students; however, it is this success that may ultimately determine whether or not the teacher chooses to stay.

School location

School location has a strong influence on the distribution of teachers. Of all public school teachers who chose to move from one school to another between 2003–2004 and 2004–2005, 26% cited proximity to home as a very or extremely important factor in their decision to move; and of those who left teaching, 11 % cited changing residence as very or extremely important (Marvel et al., 2007). Most teachers prefer to teach close to where they grew up or in districts that are similar to the districts they attended as high-school students. Sixty-one percent of teachers who entered public school teaching in New York State between 1999 and 2002 started teaching in a school district located within 15 miles of the district where they went to high school, and 85% of teachers started in teaching in schools within 40 miles of their high school (Boyd, Lankford, Loeb, & Wyckoff, 2005a). Reininger (2006) found that these results are consistent nationwide in the US; in comparison to college graduates in nearly 40 other occupations, teachers were significantly more likely to reside in their hometown 8 years after high-school graduation.

Teachers' preferences to teach close to home or in similar settings pose serious concerns for urban districts, since urban areas produce a lower proportion of college graduates, and thus potential teachers, than do suburban areas. Rural areas also often have a smaller pool of college-educated workers from which to recruit teachers. Schools with large minority enrolments and large percentages of students receiving free and reduced-price lunch have significantly lower percentages of students earning bachelor's degrees — a prerequisite for teaching. As a result, schools in these regions depend on hiring teachers from other regions. If they are unable to find qualified candidates, then they are forced to hire from a less-qualified pool of applicants or increase compensation.

Barriers to entry

Traditionally, teaching in public schools in the United States required at least a bachelor's degree and certification, which in turn specifies coursework requirements, student teaching experiences, and a passing score on at least one standardized certification test. In theory, these requirements improve teaching by ensuring a minimum standard of quality on all teachers. However, these requirements also impose costs on qualified prospective teachers, which may deter them from entering the profession, effectively reducing the supply of teachers.

Until recently, while in theory teachers were required to be certified, in practice, many large urban areas employed a substantial number of uncertified teachers. Potentially, as a response

to the Highly Qualified Teacher provision of the No Child Left Behind Act of 2001, schools and particularly schools serving a high proportion of students in poverty hire far fewer uncertified teachers. This tightened adherence to certification was accompanied by the creation of a number of alternative certification programs that reduced the entry requirements for teaching. Many states rely heavily on alternative routes for teachers. New Jersey, Texas, and California, for instance, obtain more than one-third of their new teachers from alternative routes. The reduced entry requirements in combination with substantial recruitment effort have substantially expanded the pool of individuals interested in becoming teachers. Furthermore, these new candidates often have stronger academic backgrounds than teachers entering from more traditional routes (Boyd, Grossman, Lankford, Loeb, & Wyckoff, 2006).

The demand for teachers

The supply of teachers determines the number of individuals willing to enter the profession and to teach in a given school, but the number of teachers actually hired and the characteristics of those teachers also depend on the demand. Important among demand factors are student enrolments, teacher retirement rates, class sizes, district hiring practices, and institutional constraints, which are described below.

Student enrollment and teacher retirement

Due to the post-World War II baby boom, student enrollment increased in the United States in the 1950s and 1960s. Student enrolments declined by approximately 5 million between 1970 and 1990, but have since been steadily increasing. The baby boom era triggered a dramatic increase in the demand for teachers. Since the baby-boom generation moved through school, student enrollment changes have not driven as substantial an increased demand for teachers. However, currently, the teachers hired in the baby-boom era are reaching retirement age. Approximately 31% of public school teachers were aged 50 years or more in 2004–2005 (Marvel et al., 2007). This segment of the teaching force is likely to retire over the next 10–15 years, which increases the demand for new teachers.

Reduction in student-to-teacher ratios

Student-to-teacher ratios, which also affect the demand for teachers, have declined substantially during the past half century. In 1955, the ratio was 26.9; by the fall of 1985, it was 17.9, and in 2005, the average student/teacher ratio was 16.2 across all regular public schools (Marvel et al., 2007). Federal policy has contributed to the decline of student-teacher ratios and the related increased demand in teachers since the 1970s. The Individuals with Disabilities Education Act (IDEA), implemented in 1975 and reauthorized in 2004, requires schools to provide accommodations for students with learning disabilities. Many schools have hired additional teachers to support students to comply with the act.

In a review of the research on class size effects, Hanushek (1998) attributed approximately a third of the decline in student–teacher ratios to special education accommodation. More recently, state policies such as the California Class Size Reduction Initiative of 1996, which paid schools to cap class sizes at 20 in grades K-3, have contributed to an increasing demand for teachers.

Hiring processes

School and district hiring processes also affect demand and the resulting teacher workforce. In a study documenting district hiring practices across New York State, Baiter and Duncombe (2008) found that most districts advertise openings in local newspapers and on the Internet; work with local colleges by supervising student teachers, posting job notices on campus, and contacting college faculty; attend at least one job fair; and use compensation for extracurricular activities and for outside teaching experience as recruitment incentives. Almost 90% of districts also use strategies to increase the local supply of teachers, such as recruiting substitute, alternatively certified, or retired teachers; or by providing assistance for parapro-fessionals to become teachers. In spite of the efforts of districts in recruitment and hiring, however, it is difficult to tell who will be a good teacher. Jacob and Lefgren (2006) show that while principals are able to identify the best and the worst teachers in their schools, they are not able to identify where the rest fall in the ability distribution. It is clearly even more difficult to tell who will be a good teacher during the hiring process. In a study of teacher hiring practices in New York State School Districts, districts most often chose candidates for interview on the basis of certification in the subject to be taught, major in the subject to be taught, and references or recommendations. A much smaller proportion of schools considered measures of a candidate's academic success such as his/her certification exam score, caliber of certifying institution, grade point average (GPA), and quality of teacher portfolio (Baiter & Duncombe, 2008).

Institutional constraints

The problem of suboptimal staffing is also driven by institutional constraints, outside the immediate control of schools and the district human resources department. In a study of district hiring patterns, the New Teacher Project uncovered three district-level policies contributing to the delays leading to suboptimal staffing patterns: lenient vacancy notification requirements, teachers' union transfer requirements, and late budget timetables (Levin, Mulhern, & Schunck, 2005).

Lenient vacancy notification requirements do not require resigning or retiring teachers to provide notification of their intention to leave until late in the summer before the next school year. Such late notification deadlines make it very difficult for administrators to know which posts will be available when the school year starts, typically in September. By the time some districts extend offers, many of the applicants have already accepted other offers and have withdrawn their outstanding applications. Applicants who withdraw from the process early to accept other positions tend to be significantly better qualified than new hires in terms of undergraduate GPAs, a degree in their teaching field and completion of educational coursework.

Union contract provisions leave room for experienced teachers to request last-minute transfers, which excesses less senior incumbent teachers. In response, many principals delay advertising vacancies for fear of being required to hire a transferring teacher they do not want. Finally, as a result of late state budget deadlines, administrators are unaware of which positions will be funded in their schools. In 46 states, the fiscal deadline is not until 30th June, and even then, states can get extensions. Although stringent union contracts can decrease hiring effectiveness, in a study of the legal and policy structures designed to place high-quality teachers in high-minority schools, Koski and Horng (2007) did not find persuasive evidence that the seniority preference rules associated with union contracts independently affect the distribution of teachers across schools or exacerbate the negative relationship between higher minority schools and noncredentialed and low-experience teachers.

Recruitment and retention policies to date

Districts that face difficulty in hiring or retaining the teachers that they want aim to increase the supply of teachers and/or to remove institutional constraints to facilitate more effective hiring. This section looks at the following policies addressing recruitment and retention of teachers in the United States: partnerships between districts and local colleges, monetary incentives, changes in entry requirements, teacher induction and mentoring, performance-based pay, career differentiation, improving hiring practices, and modifying teacher due-process procedures. A review of extant literature reveals a lack of research that convincingly identifies the effects of most of these policy approaches.

Partnerships between districts and local colleges

To recruit potential teachers into the teaching pipeline, some districts have created partnerships with local colleges to encourage students to enter teaching. In New York State, for example, the most common college recruitment strategies used by districts are supervision of student teachers, posting of job notices at the colleges, and contacting college faculty in local colleges (Baiter & Duncombe, 2008).

As a second example, the Urban Teacher Academy Program (UTAP) in Broward County Public Schools in Florida prepares high-school students for careers in urban education. This grow-your-own model provides successful program graduates with a scholarship at one of the district's higher education partners. While in college, these students major in education with opportunities for field experience in local schools. After finishing college, graduates are guaranteed a teaching job in the district. As of yet, no rigorous analyses of the effectiveness of such programs on teacher recruitment and retention have been conducted.

Monetary incentives

In recent years, a number of states have experimented with various ways to offer higher compensation to prospective teachers to aid in recruitment and retention. Signing bonuses or crediting teachers for their years of experience teaching in other districts are examples of monetary incentive bonuses for recruitment. Some bonuses are paid in increments over time to promote retention.

Research on the effectiveness of monetary incentive programs for recruitment and retention is not conclusive. One such program, the Signing Bonus Program, implemented in Massachusetts in 1998 combined heavy recruiting, and a 7-week fast-track certification program, and a $20000 bonus paid in increments to all participants who continued to teach for 4 years in the state. The program did not succeed in retaining its participants — 20% of the first cohort of bonus recipients left teaching after 1 year, and attrition was particularly high in state-designated, high-need districts. Furthermore, over 50% of its second cohort ended up teaching in schools outside of the state-designated, high-need school districts for which the program was intended (Fowler, 2003).

Conversely, Clotfelter, Glennie, Ladd, and Vigdor (2006) found positive effects of North Carolina's program that provided yearly $1800 bonuses to teachers of math, science, and special education in middle and high schools serving low-income or low-performing students. The authors estimate that this program reduced teacher attrition by approximately 14%, though, perhaps because school eligibility for the bonus for a given academic year was not usually announced until the year had started, the program was not an effective recruitment tool.

Changes in entry requirements

Many states, in an attempt to increase the supply of teachers without the high cost of monetary incentives, are expanding the pool of potential teachers by reducing the cost of entry for academically competent individuals. Forty-

seven states and the District of Columbia have some form of alternative-route program to recruit, train, and certify teachers. Many of these states rely heavily on alternative routes for teachers. Although alternative certification programs vary in size, scope, and competitiveness, the offer of alternative certification appears to be an effective recruitment strategy. Nearly 50% of those entering teaching through alternate routes say they would not have become a teacher if an alternate route to certification had not been available. Approximately one-third of entrants into teaching through alternate routes are nonwhite compared to 11 % of the current teaching force. In terms of retention, nearly two-thirds of the survey respondents entering teaching through alternate routes expect to be teaching K-12 about 5 years from now. States with the highest percentage of alternatively certified teachers report that 87% of them are still teaching after 5 years. (Feistritzer, 2005).

Teacher induction and mentoring

Beginning teacher induction and mentoring have grown in prominence in school districts as methods to support new teachers' transition into the profession and to increase teacher retention. Induction programs typically involve meetings, informal classes for new teachers, and the formation of new-teacher peer-support groups. The duration, intensity, and content of mentoring interactions can greatly vary across programs. Mentoring programs typically pair new teachers with experienced ones.

Studies of mentoring programs to date suggest that this may be a promising approach for increasing the retention of early career teachers. However, they are based on nonexperimental data and it is possible that districts or schools that implement high-quality mentoring differ from other districts, perhaps by being well run in other dimensions, and it is the other differences that drive the relationships that we see.

In a synthesis of 10 empirical studies, Ingersoll and Kralik (2004) found empirical support for the claim that mentoring programs have a positive impact on teachers and their retention. Similarly, Smith and Ingersoll (2004) found that the turnover rates among new teachers decrease as the number of induction components in addition to mentoring increased — such as planning time with other teachers in the same subject, regularly scheduled collaboration with other teachers, and being part of an external network of teachers. In addition, schools that provided teachers with more autonomy and administrative support had lower levels of teacher attrition and migration. These studies suggest that mentoring may be a useful tool for retaining early career teachers. In one of the more convincing studies, Reed, Rueben, and Barbour (2006) found that in California, Beginning Teacher Support and Assessment (BTSA) programs in the early 1990s reduced the probability of transfer and exit among new teachers.

Performance-based pay

Some policymakers believe that the traditional single-wage schedule based on teacher's years of experience and number of university units provides no incentive for teachers to increase academic performance of students, and thus discourages particularly effective teachers from entering the classroom. Performance-based pay is a form of flexible compensation in which a portion of teachers' compensation is based on estimates of their effectiveness at raising student achievement. The unit of analysis can be individual teachers, groups of teachers, or schools, and payment can be based on student test performance or principal or peer evaluation.

Proponents of performance-based pay structures posit that rewarding teachers on the basis of an established set of goals would improve the motivation of teachers and assist in the recruitment and retention of high-quality staff.

Critics of performance-based pay structures believe that teachers' output is too varied and difficult to observe. In addition, they worry that performance-based pay could distort incentives which could lead to suboptimal practices for long-term learning, such as teaching to the test. In addition, competition for merit awards could result in competitive behavior among faculty at the same school and even reduce the appeal of teaching, particularly for individuals who are averse to risk.

There is little research on the effect of performance-pay on recruitment and retention, although the empirical research on the programs implemented to date has not found consistently positive effects from these reforms on student learning. Kelley (1999) examined the ways in which school-based performance award programs motivated teachers to modify or improve teaching practice in Kentucky, North Carolina, Colorado, and Maryland and concluded that such programs motivated teachers largely by creating conditions that increased intrinsic rewards and focused teacher efforts. Ballou and Podgursky (1993) found that teachers in districts that used performance-based pay did not seem demoralized by the system or hostile toward it, and that teachers of disadvantaged and low-achieving students were generally supportive of the system.

Career differentiation through ladders

While the retention patterns of teachers are similar to that of other professions, such as nursing, social work, and accounting (Harris & Adams, 2007), some posit that teacher retention could be reduced by differentiating the profession, allowing paths for teacher promotion. Such promotions could provide the psychic benefits needed to improve retention. As an example, some career ladders divide the teaching career into stages by increasing responsibility and leadership, or by rewarding outstanding teaching practice. Career ladders have the potential to increase the job satisfaction of experienced teachers by diversifying their workday and skill set, thus increasing their likelihood of staying at the school, particularly because 20% of teachers leaving high-poverty urban schools report that more opportunities for advancement might induce them to stay (Ingersoll, 2004). Career ladders also have the built-in potential to increase retention among less-experienced teachers by presenting a challenging and rewarding future career prospect attainable without leaving the school. Brewer (1996) found evidence which suggests that later career opportunities affect quit decisions among teachers by examining the relationship between teaching and school administration. A study by Booker and Glazerman (2009) found that teachers in schools participating in the Missouri Career Ladder Program were less likely to leave the district as well as to leave teaching, as compared to those teachers in districts without career ladder programs, all else equal. However, the Missouri Career Ladder Program included bonuses with advancement, thus it is difficult to disentangle the impact of the monetary incentives on teacher retention from the impact of career differentiation itself.

Evidence of the effects of differentiation on teacher retention is mixed. Variations in the design and implementation of career ladders influence teacher experiences with career ladders. Rosenblatt (2001) found that conditional on holding leadership roles that are well matched to individuals' skills and offer skill variety, career ladder programs can decrease the likelihood of burnout and increase teachers' intention to stay in their schools. However, career ladder programs that do not successfully match teachers skills to the position or offer variety can induce additional anxiety and stress for some teachers due to extra responsibilities (Henson & Hall, 1993). Without reasonable teacher assignment or without quality administrator support, the implementation of a career ladder policy is unlikely to have any positive effect on teacher satisfaction or retention. As with most retention and recruitment policies, there is little convincing causal evidence on either the advantages or disadvantages of career differentiation.

Improving hiring practices

Hiring practices have received attention from researchers, but relatively little attention from school leaders and policymakers. Given the contractual constraints placed on principals during the hiring process, principals are often forced to hire teachers late, by which time many higher qualified teachers may have already taken positions. Consequently, many teachers are hired late — more than one-third of new teachers in California and Florida were hired after the school year has already started (Liu & Johnson, 2006). Loosening institutional constraints on administrators and district personnel may increase efficiency in the hiring process. Jacob (2007) recommends that urban districts should streamline the administrative procedures associated with hiring so that they can make job offers more quickly; improve their ability to identify effective teachers from the pool of candidates; and implement a more decentralized process would likely result in better matches between teachers and schools. Furthermore, in their study of teacher hiring processes, the New Teacher Project formulated the following recommendations to facilitate more effective teacher hiring: ensure that transfer and excess placements are based on the mutual consent of teacher and receiving school, permit the timely hiring of new teachers, and better protect novice teachers who are contributing to their school.

Reform of due process

Teacher tenure policies were initially implemented to protect teachers who have successfully completed a probationary period from arbitrary dismissal. The job security tenure offers may attract prospective teachers in the teaching force and keep teachers already in the classroom. While little research has been conducted on the effect of teacher tenure on recruitment and retention, a study by Brunner and Imazeki (2007) explored variation in probationary periods across districts and its relationship to variation in wage. The authors found evidence that districts compensate for longer probationary periods by offering higher wages. Wages for both beginning and experienced teachers are measurably higher in districts in states with longer probationary periods, which suggest that the offer of tenure may serve as a recruitment device, as teachers appear to value the prospect of an early tenure in their decision of where to teach. Clearly, tenure is a factor in a teacher's decision to remain teaching. After the probationary period, tenure creates a high level of job security and stability in the teaching profession, which could serve as an incentive for teachers to stay in the field, although no empirical work has been done to study the relationship between tenure with teacher recruitment or retention to date. Of course, tenure has the potentially negative effect of making it more difficult to dismiss less effective teachers and serves as a reminder that all teacher attrition may not be detrimental.

Conclusion

A growing body of research confirms the importance of teacher quality on student learning gains. These findings emerge at a time when policymakers and school leaders face growing concern about their ability to keep teachers currently in classrooms and how to replace teachers who leave. The teacher labor market is not all that different than other labor markets on average but the pool of available teachers is strikingly different across schools.

Some schools, usually those with high proportions on non-white and low-achieving students, face a far more difficulty recruiting and retaining high-quality teachers. This article described how teachers' choices and their related preferences affect the supply of teachers and how the actions of schools and districts affect the demand for teachers and how supply and demand come together to create the workforce that we see. The article also summarized policy approaches to advancing recruitment and retention and the current research estimating the effectiveness of these policies. What stands out, as stands out in much of education policy research, is how little we know about the effectiveness of different policy approaches. Teachers respond to wage incentives, but non-wage aspects of jobs are at least as important in their decision to stay. Leadership plays a critical role both in working conditions and in the hiring process but, the market for school leadership faces similar issues of recruitment and retention and is an area in which we know even less.

See Also

Teacher Incentives; Teacher Labor Markets: An Overview; Teacher Supply.

References

Bacolod, M. P. (2007). Do alternative opportunities matter? The role of female labor markets in the decline of teacher quality. *Review of Economics and Statistics, 89*(4), 737–751.

Baiter, D., & Duncombe, W. (2008). Recruiting highly qualified teachers do district recruitment practices matter? *Public Finance Review, 36*(1), 33–62.

Ballou, D., & Podgursky, M. (1993). Teacher attitudes towards merit pay: Examining the conventional wisdom. *Industrial and Labour Relations Review, 47*, 50–60.

Betts, J. R., Rueben, K. S., & Danenberg, A. (2000). *Equal resources, equal outcomes? The distribution of school resources and student achievement in California.* San Francisco: Public Policy Institute of California.

Booker, K., & Glazerman, S. (2009). *The effects of the Missouri career ladder program on teacher mobility and retention*

(MPR reference No. 6333-400). Washington, DC: Mathematica Policy Research.

Boyd, D., Grossman, P., Lankford, H., Loeb, S., & Wyckoff, J. (2006). How changes in entry requirements alter the teacher workforce and affect student achievement. *Journal of Education Finance and Policy, 1*(2), 176–216.

Boyd, D., Lankford, H., Loeb, S., & Wyckoff, J. (2005a). Explaining the short careers of high-achieving teachers in schools with low-performing students. *American Economic Review Proceedings, 95*(2), 166–171.

Boyd, D., Lankford, H., Loeb, S., & Wyckoff, J. (2005b). The draw of home: How teachers' preferences for proximity disadvantage urban schools. *Journal of Policy Analysis and Management, 24*(1), 113–132.

Brewer, D. J. (1996). Career paths and quit decisions: Evidence from teaching. *Journal of Labor Economics, 14*(2), 313–339.

Brunner, E. J., & Imazeki, J. (2007). Teacher tenure: Does length of probation matter?. In *Paper presented at American education finance association conference*.

Buckley, J., Schneider, M., & Shang, Y. (2005). Fix it and they might stay: School facility quality and teacher retention in Washington, D.C. *Teachers College Record, 107*(5), 1107–1123.

Clotfelter, C. T., Glennie, E., Ladd, H. F., & Vigdor, J. L. (2006). *Would higher salaries keep teachers in high-poverty schools? Evidence from a policy intervention in North Carolina*. Cambridge, MA: National Bureau of Economic Research.

Corcoran, S. P., Evans, W. N., & Schwab, R. M. (2004). Changing labor-market opportunities for women and the quality of teachers, 1957–2000. *American Economic Review Papers and Proceedings, 94*(2), 230–235.

Farkas, S., Johnson, J., & Foleno, T. (2000). *A sense of calling: Who teaches and why*. New York: Public Agenda.

Feistritzer, C. E. (2005). *Profile of alternate route teachers*. Washington, DC: National Center for Education Information.

Fowler, R. C. (2003). The Massachusetts signing bonus program for new teachers: A model of teacher preparation worth copying? *Education Policy Analysis Archives, 11*(13).

Hanushek, E. A. (1998). *The evidence on class size*. Rochester, NY: University of Rochester, W. Allen Wailis Institute of Political Economy.

Hanushek, E. A., Kain, J. F., & Rivkin, S. G. (2004). Why public schools lose teachers. *Journal of Human Resources, 39*(2), 326–354.

Harris, D. N., & Adams, S. J. (2007). Understanding the level and causes of teacher turnover: A comparison with other professions. *Economics of Education Review, 26*(3), 325–337.

Henson, B. E., & Hall, P. M. (1993). Linking performance evaluation and career ladder programs: Reactions of teachers and principals in one district. *Elementary School Journal, 93*(4), 323–353.

Ingersoll, R. M. (2004). *Why do high-poverty schools have difficulty staffing their classrooms with qualified teachers?* Washington, DC: Center for American Progress.

Ingersoll, R. M., & Kralik, J. (2004). *The impact of mentoring on teacher retention: What the research says*. Denver, CO: Education Commission of the States.

Jacob, B. (2007). The challenges of staffing urban schools with effective teachers. *Future of Children, 17*(1), 129–153.

Jacob, B., & Lefgren, L. (2006). When principals rate teachers. *Education Next, 6*(2), 59–69.

Johnson, S., & Birkeland, S. (2003). Pursuing a "sense of success": New teachers explain their career decisions. *American Educational Research Journal, 40*(3), 581–617.

Kelley, C. (1999). The motivational impact of school-based performance rewards. *Journal of Personnel Evaluation in Education, 12,* 309–326.

Koski, W. S., & Horng, E. L. (2007). Facilitating the teacher quality gap? Collective bargaining agreements, teacher hiring and transfer rules, and teacher assignment among schools in California. *Education Finance and Policy, 2*(3), 262–300.

Ladd, H. F. (2007). Teacher labor markets in developed countries. *Future of Children, 17*(1), 201–217.

Levin, J., Mulhern, J., & Schunck, J. (2005). *Unintended consequences: The case for reforming the staffing rules in urban teachers union contracts*. New York: The New Teacher Project.

Liu, E., & Johnson, S. M. (2006). New teachers' experiences of hiring: Late, rushed, and information-poor. *Educational Administration Quarterly, 42*(3), 324–360.

Loeb, S., Darling-Hammond, L., & Luczak, J. (2005). How teaching conditions predict teacher turnover in California schools. *Peabody Journal of Education, 80*(3), 44–70.

Loeb, S., & Page, M. E. (2000). Examining the link between teacher wages and student outcomes: The importance of alternative labor market opportunities and nonpecuniary variation. *Review of Economics and Statistics, 82*(3), 393–408.

Marvel, J., Lyter, D. M., Peltola, P., Strizek, G. A., & Morton, B. A. (2007). *Teacher attrition and mobility: Results from the 2004–05 teacher follow-up survey*. U.S. Department of Education, National Center for Education Statistics. Washington, DC: US Government Printing Office.

Murnane, R. J., & Olsen, R. (1990). The effects of salaries and opportunity costs on length of stay in teaching: Evidence from North Carolina. *Journal of Human Resources, 25*(1), 106–124.

Reed, D., Rueben, K. S., & Barbour, E. (2006). *Retention of new teachers in California*. San Francisco, CA: Public Policy Institute of California.

Reininger, M. (2006). *Teachers' location preferences and the implications for schools with different student populations*. Working Paper.

Rosenblatt, Z. (2001). Teachers' multiple roles and skill flexibility: Effects on work attitudes. *Educational Administration Quarterly, 37*(5), 684–708.

Scafidi, B., Stinebrickner, T., & Sjoquist, D. L. (2003). *The relationship between school characteristics and teacher mobility.* Working Paper. Atlanta, GA: Georgia State University.

Smith, T. M., & Ingersoll, R. M. (2004). What are the effects of induction and mentoring on beginning teacher turnover? *American Educational Research Journal, 41*(3), 681–714.

Vegas, E. (2007). Teacher labor markets in developing countries. *Future of Children, 17*(1), 219–230.

Weiss, E. M. (1999). Perceived workplace conditions and first-year teachers' morale, career choice commitment, and planned retention: A secondary analysis. *Teaching and Teacher Education, 15*(8), 861–879.

Further reading

Guarino, C. M., Santibanez, L., & Daley, G. A. (2006). Teacher recruitment and retention: A review of the recent empirical literature. *Review of Educational Research, 76*(2), 173–208.

Hanushek, E. A., Kain, J. F., & Rivkin, S. G. (1999). *Do higher salaries buy better teachers?*. NBER Working Paper 7082.

Jacob, B. (2007). The challenges of staffing urban schools with effective teachers. *Future of Children, 17*(1), 129–153.

Murnane, R. J., & Steele, J. L. (2007). What is the problem? The challenge of providing effective teachers for all children. *Future of Children, 17*(1), 15–43.

Rivkin, S. G., Hanushek, E. A., & Kain, J. F. (2005). Teachers, schools, and academic achievement. *Econometrica, 73*(2), 417–458.

Compensating differentials in teacher labor markets

Li Feng

Department of Finance and Economics, McCoy College of Business, Texas State University, San Marcos, TX, United States

The whole of the advantages and disadvantages of the different employments of labour and stock must, in the same neighbourhood, be either perfectly equal or continually tending to equality. If in the same neighbourhood, there was any employment evidently either more or less advantageous than the rest, so many people would crowd into it in the one case, and so many would desert it in the other, that its advantages would soon return to the level of other employments. This at least would be the case in a society where things were left to follow their natural course, where there was perfect liberty, and where every man was perfectly free both to choose what occupation he thought proper, and to change it as often as he thought proper. Every man's interest would prompt him to seek the advantageous, and to shun the disadvantageous employment. *Adam Smith (1776) the Wealth of Nations.*

In 1776, Adam Smith laid the groundwork for the compensating wage differentials that came to be widely used in labor economics literature to investigate why some jobs pay more than others. Rosen (1974) laid out the theoretical foundation. The main idea was that employees generally prefer to work in a safe environment and will need to be compensated more in terms of salary if the environment may put them in danger. For example, a construction worker driving a crane may require a higher wage premium. According to the Bureau of Labor Statistics, there were 220 total crane-related deaths from 2011 to 15. In equilibrium, different workers will be matched to different firms with different levels of job safety.

In labor economics, we usually employ hedonic wage regression, which regresses the log wage on these job characteristics such as fatal or non-fatal injury rates. In an oft-cited compensating wage differential review, Smith shows that the amount that employers are willing to pay for a 1/1000 reduction in risk of death per worker can range from $200-$3500 (Smith, 1978).

Teachers generally do not face life and death situations in their daily work environment. All teachers work in school settings that could differ in many dimensions such as geographical location, student characteristics, community characteristics, parental support, and administrative environment. Some schools may not have the best facilities with many portable classrooms, may be located in an unsafe neighborhood, may have many students with Limited English

Proficiency, or may face other challenges. Teachers working in these types of schools will need to be compensated more than teachers who are teaching in resource-rich suburban schools.

In research on the teacher labor market, the key question to be addressed by compensating wage differentials is: how much extra do we need to pay teachers in terms of salaries or bonuses to work in a school or school district that has a challenging student population? We can break down this major research question into three specific research questions:

1. Does the current teacher-pay schedule compensate teachers to teach in schools with a larger share of low-income and disadvantaged minority students' population? How much do we need to compensate teachers to teach in these schools?
2. How much additional money do we need to pay teachers for them to stay at a high-poverty and low-performing schools versus an average school?
3. What financial incentives, such as salary supplements or bonuses, have worked to retain teachers in these high-poverty, high-minority, low-performing, and/or chronically short-staffed schools?

Traditionally, compensating wage differentials are investigated using hedonic wage regression. We will review this line of empirical research literature (Boyd, Lankford, Loeb, & Wyckoff, 2003, 2013; Brunner & Imazeki, 2010; Goldhaber, Destler, & Player, 2010; Harris, 2006; Levinson, 1988; Martin, 2010; Player, 2009; Winters, 2011). As pointed out by Goldhaber et al. (2010), hedonic wage regression is not a good fit for analyzing teacher labor markets due to several reasons. First, teacher salaries are determined by the teacher-salary schedule that is generally negotiated between the school district and teachers' union. This implies that teachers' salaries do not equilibrate as suggested by the hedonic model. Second, there is lack of competition within the education labor market or between school districts and therefore, little incentive for any given school district to pay different salaries for teachers. Thirdly, average salary estimates may be biased upward if teachers in wealthier districts are getting paid efficiency wages.

In view of these shortcomings of hedonic wage regression, we will also review another line of literature that focuses on teacher retention outcomes. In these studies, researchers usually include explanatory variables such as student body characteristics and teacher wages. We can get at the question of how much we need to compensate teachers to teach in schools that serve low-income or disadvantaged minority students to ensure these schools have the same retention rate as an average school. In this section, we will rely on two recent studies (Borman & Dowling, 2008; Guarino, Santibanez, & Daley, 2006) that have collectively reviewed the literature on teacher retention from 1980 to 2005.

The last set of literature reviewed here approaches compensating wage differentials from a different angle. This line of research focuses on quasi-experimental literature. We review how labor supply responds to financial incentives. These studies provide evidence on loan forgiveness programs in Florida, additional salary supplements for high-poverty and low-performing schools in North Carolina, bonuses for being highly effective teachers in the Washington DC area or in the state of Tennessee, and salary supplements for teachers in short-staffed schools in Norway (C. Clotfelter, Glennie, Ladd, & Vigdor, 2008; Dee & Wyckoff, 2015; Falch, 2010, 2011; Feng & Sass, 2018; Springer, Swain, & Rodriguez, 2016).

Compensating wage differentials through empirical studies using hedonic wage regression

Method

Hedonic wage regression can be represented using the following equation. Teacher annual base salary W is the outcome of interest and it represents a teacher i working in school j and school district k located in community m. Control variables include teacher characteristics T_{ijkm}, school characteristics S_j, school district characteristics D_k, and community characteristics C_m. Most importantly, all the studies reviewed included some student body characteristics X_{ijkm}.

$$\log(W_{ijkm}) = \alpha + \beta_1 * T_{ijkm} + \beta_2 * S_j + \beta_3 * D_k$$
$$+ \beta_4 * C_m + \beta_5 * X_{ijkm} + \varepsilon_{ij}$$

(30.1)

According to the hedonic model, we can formulate hypotheses for β_5. If we include student poverty and share of disadvantaged minority students as student characteristics, we expect the coefficient in front of X_{ijkm} to be statistically significant and positive. We can predict that there will be positive compensating differentials. This will indicate that salaries need to be compensated for teachers that teach in a more challenging environment.

Data

Nearly all recent studies on compensating wage differentials employ the nationally representative dataset, the Schools and Staffing Surveys (SASS), which has been collected for various years (Gilpin, 2011; Goldhaber et al., 2010; Harris, 2006; Martin, 2010). SASS is one of the longest running surveys administered by the National Center on Education Statistics in the USA It consists of five different survey instruments on public and private school districts, schools, teachers, principals, and library media

centers. It is a cross-sectional survey and can be stacked for use as a synthetic panel, such as that used by Martin (2010). Unfortunately, the cross-sectional survey nature of the SASS limited our ability to obtain further insights that might be possible with a longitudinal survey.

In addition to studies directly related to the compensating wage differentials, other studies have used SASS to study teacher-salary schedules. For example, West and Mykerrezi examine the impact of teachers' unions on salary schedules (West & Mykerezi, 2011). Grissom and Strunk investigate whether front-loading salaries may be helpful in improving performance in student achievement tests (Grissom & Strunk, 2012). Bifulco examines whether urban districts located in strong performance-based accountability areas use front-load teacher-salary schedules to attract new entrants (Bifulco, 2010).

In addition to the SASS data, two studies have employed state-level data from the Michigan Department of Education and New York State Department of Education (Boyd et al., 2003; Levinson, 1988). Levinson uses cross-sectional data while Boyd et al. employ panel data.

In the last twenty years, different states in the US have developed various state-based longitudinal datasets that can potentially be used to investigate compensating wage differentials. Unfortunately, there is still only a limited amount of research utilizing these datasets to address compensating wage differentials. This is probably due to the limited amount of information collected in terms of teacher-related job or occupation characteristics.

Findings

Instead of examining the individual study's specific coefficients, we will combine these studies and examine both the statistical significance and magnitude of these estimates on compensating wage differentials. Table 30.1 summarizes recent empirical studies that directly test compensating wage differentials.

TABLE 30.1   Empirical studies on teachers wages from 2000.

Author	Year	Title	Journal	Data	Dependent variable	Unit of analysis and N	Key results
Arik Levinson	1988	Reexamining teacher preferences and compensating wages	Economics of education review	Michigan department of education HR data 1970	Log (teacher salary)	Teacher level, White teachers 5088, Non-white teachers 336	White versus non-white teachers % Poor students in a district -0.0304 (0.0355) -0.0702 (0.3278) % non-white students in a district 0.0829*** (0.0136) 0.1447 (0.0869)
Donald Boyd, Hamilton Lankford, Susanna Loeb, James Wyckoff	2003	Analyzing the determinants of the matching of public school teachers to jobs: Estimating compensating differentials in imperfect labor markets	NBER working paper series #9878 Later published in Journal of labor economics	New York state department of education data 1994–95 to 1999–2000	Log (wage)	5028 teachers, 2443 schools, 6 years, 5 MSA	% School minority student 1.37*** (0.10) % School students on FRL -1.12*** (0.09)
Debbi Harris	2006	Lowering the bar or moving the target: A wage decomposition of Michigan's charter and traditional public school teachers	Educational administration quarterly	1999–2000 schools and staffing survey (SASS) Michigan subsample	Log (teacher salary)	Teacher level, 723 public school teachers, 468 charter school teachers	Traditional public schools % Students of color -0.001** (0.000) % Students on FRL -0.005 (0.000) Charter schools % Students of color 0.001** (0.000) % Students on FRL 0.0001 (0.000)
Eric Brunner and Jennifer Imazeki	2010	Probation length and teacher salaries: Does Waiting pay off?	Industrial and labor relations review	1999–2000 schools and staffing survey (SASS)	Log (beginning teacher salary)	District level 4145 and 2615	All sample versus only CBA districts Fraction poverty 0.116** (0.055) 0.115 (0.083) Fraction non-shite 0.078** (0.025) 0.111** (0.035)
Stephanie Martin	2010	Are public school teacher salaries paid compensating wage differentials for student	Education economics	1990–2000 and 1999–2000 schools and	Log (teacher salary)	Teacher level Baseline: 17,959 MSA FE:	Cross-sectional versus longitudinal model

TABLE 30.1 Empirical studies on teachers wages from 2000.—cont'd

Author	Year	Title	Journal	Data	Dependent variable	Unit of analysis and N	Key results
		racial and ethnic characteristics?		staffing survey (SASS)		11,420 Longitudinal: 34,957	School % black -0.00021*** (0.00003) -0.00007 (0.00028) District % black 0.00018*** (0.00002) 0.00277*** (0.00047) District % Latino -0.00107*** (0.00002) 0.00250*** (0.00045) School % free lunch -0.00016*** (8.41E-06)
Dan Goldhaber, Katharine Destler, Daniel Player	2010	Teacher labor markets and the perils of using hedonics to estimate compensation differentials in the public sector	Economics of education review	1990–2000 and 1999–2000 schools and staffing survey (SASS)	Log (teacher salary)	Teacher level, 56,354 teachers in 5465 public schools, 10,706 teachers in 3558 private schools	Challenging student population: Public schools OLS versus FE 0.026** (0.011) 0.011** (0.003) Private schools OLS versus FE 0.078** (0.031) 0.067** (0.031) Disaggregated analysis Top quartile % asian 0.037** (0.021) 0.030** (0.012) % FRL 0.011 (0.011) -0.003 (0.010)
John Winters	2011	Teacher salaries and teacher unions: A spatial econometric approach	Industrial and labor relations review	1999–2000 schools and staffing survey (SASS)	Log (teacher salary with MA degree and 20-year experience) Log (teacher salary with	District level 4237	Log (MA20) OLS versus spatial model Share of white students -0.0150 (0.0109) -0.0286*** (0.0089) {ME-0.0314} Share of low-

(Continued)

TABLE 30.1 Empirical studies on teachers wages from 2000.—cont'd

Author	Year	Title	Journal	Data	Dependent variable	Unit of analysis and N	Key results
					BA degree and no experience)		income students -0.0505*** (0.0114) -0.0115 (0.0087) Log (BA0) OLS versus spatial model Share of white students -0.0381***(0.0079) -0.0294***(0.0062) {ME-0.0330} Share of low-income students -0.0278***(0.0083) -0.0068(0.0060)
Daniel Player	2009	Monetary returns to academic ability in the public teacher labor market	Economics of education review	Schools and staffing surveys 1999/2000	Log (total annual income)	Teacher level 33,285	Models with or without median house value School % minority enrollment 0.1411*** (0.0106) 0.0987*** (0.0098) School % subsidized lunch eligible -0.1146*** (0.0128) -0.0051 (0.0132)

At 0.01 level

**At 0.05 level*

*** *Statistically significant at 0.01 level.*

Student Poverty: Looking across various studies, we discover that there is no consensus on whether there are compensating wage differentials for the share of students eligible for the Free or Reduced Lunch program in general. There are seven regression specifications that have zero coefficients (Brunner & Imazeki, 2010; Goldhaber et al., 2010; Harris, 2006; Levinson, 1988), four negative coefficients (Boyd et al., 2003; Martin, 2010; Winters, 2011), and one positive coefficient (Brunner & Imazeki, 2010). Judging from the large number of zero and negative coefficients, we can conclude that teachers are not paid compensating differentials to teach low-income students.

Minority Student: All of the empirical studies examined have found that there are compensating wage differentials for teaching minority students, with the exception of one study. We will discuss this small sample size study first before we discuss the other studies on the fraction of minority students.

Using only the Michigan teachers' sample data from the SASS 1999—2000, Harris (2006) compared teachers' salaries in public schools and charter schools. She found that on average, charter school teachers make $15,000 less than their counterparts in public schools. This wage difference can be partly explained by their differences in experience and certification.

In the log wage regression, Harris included student characteristics such as share of students of color in school and share of students eligible for free/reduced lunch. There was a negative compensating wage differential for students of color in traditional public schools. However, there was a positive compensating wage differential for students of color in charter schools. Due to the small sample size of a few hundred public school teachers, we are conservative about the negative compensating wage differentials found in the public school sample.

All of the following studies have shown some positive compensating wage differentials for the share of minority students in one or more of their empirical specifications. To summarize, these past studies appear to point out positive compensating differentials, of magnitudes ranging from 0.00,277 in Martins (2010) to 0.115 in Brunner and Imazeki (2010). We will discuss these studies in detail in the following paragraphs.

Levinson (1988) used data from 1970s Michigan Department of Education. Levinson regressed first-year teachers' starting salaries based on district-level characteristics such as high school indicator, student-teacher ratio, percentage of students whose family income is below poverty line, and percentage of non-white students. Levinson reexamined a question posed by Antos and Rosen (1975) "How much is required to induce white teachers to teach in black schools?" He concluded that a 0.08% per percentage-point increase in the share of minority students will require $500 in additional salary.

Martin (2010) employed the Schools and Staffing Survey (SASS) 1999/2000 data matched with the 2000 Census Special School District Tabulation. For part of the longitudinal data analysis, she also used SASS 1990/91 and 1990 Census data. She created a dissimilarity index that

measures the share of racial and ethnic student population in the school relative to the district average. There are three main specifications. The first one is a cross-sectional analysis of all teachers. The second is a cross-sectional analysis with Metropolitan Statistical Areas (MSA)-fixed effects. The last one is a longitudinal analysis of teachers who taught in both SASS waves. Interestingly, she found that there are conflicting results in terms of compensating wage differentials. For example, the district's share of black students is statistically significant and positive. This means that teachers working in these types of districts command a higher salary, and thereby supports the compensating wage theory. However, she also found that when the share of black students in the district is held constant, the share of black students in a school is associated with lower salary. This indicates that there are negative compensating wage differentials. Even across three specifications, there are conflicting results. For example, the district share of Latino population is negative in cross-sectional analysis and turns positive in the longitudinal model. District shares of black students are consistently positive in two of the three specifications. School shares of Hispanic students are also consistently positive in two of the three specifications. These suggest evidence of compensating wage differentials for working with minority students.

Brunner and Imazeki (2010) also found that the fraction of non-white students are statistically positive in two regression models. The first regression included all districts, and the second included only districts with Collective Bargaining Agreements. For every one percentage-point increase in non-white students, the salary increased by 7.8% or 11.1%. Boyd et al. (2003) used a two-sided matching model in their analysis of compensating differentials instead of the traditionally employed hedonic regression analysis. Though their results also show statistically positive compensating wage differentials related to the share of school minority students, it is hard to interpret the impact because teacher quality index was included in their model.

Goldhaber et al. (2010) have provided many convincing arguments against using the hedonic wage regression in the context of public school teachers. They proposed to estimate both public and private school teachers in two separate regressions and compare the coefficients associated with the percent minority and percent students eligible for Free or Reduced Lunch (FRL) programs. Unlike much of the previous literature, Goldhaber et al. (2010) included seven dummy indicators in one of the disaggregated student characteristics: top quartile indicators for %FRL, % African-American, % Hispanic, % Asian-American, % American Indian, % Limited English Proficient (LEP), and % Individual Education Plan (IEP). Interestingly, there was only one variable that displayed consistent patterns across sample and specifications. The share of Asian-American students seems to be statistically significant and positive. This seems to suggest that teachers need to be compensated for teaching in schools with a larger share of Asian-American students. This confirms earlier literature in that teachers need compensating wage differentials to teach minority students.

Using factor analysis and four demographic variables such as % LEP, % IEP, % minority students (African-American and Hispanic), and % FRL, they also include one composite measure of student characteristics called "challenging student population." They find that in both public and private schools, this variable is statistically significant and positive. They also find that private school teachers command a higher pay to teach similarly challenging student populations.

Accounting for possible spatial spillover impacts on neighboring district salaries, Winters (2011) applied a spatial econometric model to estimate the effect of teachers' unions on salaries for beginning teachers and more experienced teachers. They also included district-level shares of white students in their four main specifications. For teachers with at least a master's degree and 20 years of experience, the OLS coefficient is not statistically significant. The spatial model coefficient is negative and significant. Though this is different from all other model specifications included in this analysis, we can think of the share of white students as the inverse of the share of non-white students. For example, if the share of white students is 0.80 then the share of non-white students will be 1−0.80 or 0.20. Winters found that there are negative compensating wage differentials for white students (or positive compensating wage differentials for non-white students). All of the magnitudes estimated were around 2.86–3.81% points.

Unlike previous studies, Player used the same information from the SASS dataset but focused on the total income earned by teachers, including base salary and any extra remuneration from extracurricular assignments (Player, 2009). He focused on the returns to teachers who graduated from a set of selective colleges. The selective college premium is around 5.83 to 13.23% points in terms of log points in total income. He also included school share of minority enrollment and found positive compensating wage differentials of a magnitude of around 9.87 to 14.11% points.

To summarize, literature on compensating wage differentials points out that there are positive compensating wage differentials in terms of minority student enrollments. The magnitude of the compensating wage differentials that are required ranges from a few percentage points to 14% points. In terms of students on FRL programs, a majority of the literature points out that there is a precisely estimated zero effect. These two findings seem to be either conflicting with each other or paradoxical.

One of the shortcomings of current literature is that all of these studies on compensating wage differentials include only the salary. It is quite possible that teachers in high-poverty schools are rewarded according to different compensation schemes. For example, teachers who have taught in Title I schools continuously for five years are eligible for federal loan forgiveness programs for any remaining undergraduate college debts. Another potential limitation is that nearly all of the studies reviewed use a cross-sectional dataset. In a review of cross-sectional studies, Brown (1980) attributed the lack of support for compensating wage differentials to "the omission of important worker abilities, biasing the coefficients of job characteristics" (Brown, 1980). If high-ability teachers all gravitate toward better working conditions, i.e., small share of students on the free and reduced lunch program, this may cause a downward bias in the estimated coefficients and could be why we observe many zero coefficients. Individual fixed effects in a longitudinal panel setting may address this omitted ability bias in future studies.

Compensating wage differentials through empirical studies of teacher attrition and retention

In one recent meta-analysis of the teacher attrition and retention, Borman and Dowling provided a detailed analysis of all previous empirical studies on the topics (Borman & Dowling, 2008). In one table of their paper (Table 30.1), they listed the outcomes reported and related these outcomes to teachers' salary and school student body characteristics such as socioeconomic composition and racial/ethnic composition. We can potentially answer the compensating wage differentials question: how much do you need to pay teachers to teach in schools with a larger share of minority students or students from disadvantaged backgrounds?

Essentially, we could examine the coefficients associated with teacher salaries and the share of minority students to see how much of a salary increase is necessary to induce teachers to stay in these challenging schools. In these type of studies, authors often use odds ratio to indicate the impact of the program on teacher retention. Odds ratios are centered on one. Odds ratio less than one indicates teachers in these groups are less likely to depart when compared with baseline group while odds ratio more than one

indicates teachers in these groups are more likely to depart.

According to Borman and Dowling, the odds ratio associated with salary for teachers with 0—5 years of experience is 0.98 (z = -2.76**) from six studies with six effect sizes (Borman & Dowling, 2008, p. 392). The odds ratio associated with salary for teachers with 6—30 years of experience is 0.66 (z = -3.44**) from five studies with five effect sizes. Many of these studies reviewed also included the percentage of students eligible for a free lunch. The odds ratio is 1.01 (z = 3.19**) from eight studies with eight effect sizes. In addition, the odds ratio for percentage of minority students is 1.03 (z = 5.53**). Judging from these estimates, a one percentage-point increase in salary for teachers with fewer than five years of experience would be enough to neutralize the effect of teaching in schools with a one percentage-point increase in the share of students in poverty. Interestingly, a two percentage-point increase in salary may be necessary to neutralize a one percentage-point increase in the share of minority students.

Though these two lines of research are very distinct from the methodologies used, these studies seem to agree on the conclusion that a larger salary increase or another type of bonus is necessary to compensate teachers for teaching at a more diverse school than at a school with more students in poverty.

Compensating wage differentials using policy interventions

Despite the evidence that we found from these two strands of literature, the challenge of answering the question of how much salary or another financial incentive is needed to induce teachers to teach and stay in these hard-to-staff schools remains unanswered. The biases from omitted variables will be minimized by the recent wave of policy intervention studies using quasi-experimental and random assignment research design.

The rigid salary schedule and the lack of evidence for compensating wage differentials from these cross-sectional studies lead us to investigate one alternative channel to examine compensating wage differentials. If teachers' salaries do not properly account for the challenges of teaching in certain schools, teachers will "vote with their feet" and transfer within the same district or move to a nearby district. This partly creates the problem of chronically short-staffed schools. These schools usually have trouble recruiting and retaining their teachers. Many states have tried to use salary or bonus incentives as levers to counterbalance the churning of teachers in these schools. In this section, we will focus our attention on these types of studies to find out whether these policy interventions are effective at "leveling the playing field" (C. T. Clotfelter, Ladd, & Vigdor, 2011).

One illustration of this idea is on page 37 where the probability of teachers remaining in their initial placement is plotted against their base salaries for a mix of low poverty/minority, middle poverty/minority, and high-poverty/minority schools (L. Feng, 2014). According to this study, "to achieve the same teacher retention rate as middle poverty and minority schools, schools with high poverty and minority rates must increase salaries by least $18,000 or two standard deviations." The same article also mentions that former classroom teachers will make $14,000 more annually if they move to other education sectors. These former teachers can earn $20,000 more annually if they change into editing, writing, or performing industries. In another related article, Feng (2009) showed that in the context of the state of Florida, a salary differential of $10,000 is necessary to improve teacher retention rate in hard-to-staff schools to bring it to the same level as in an average school (L. Feng, 2009).

One important consequence of rigid wage schedule is its inability to compensate for teaching in more challenging schools. Another consequence is that it is also unable to properly account for the fact that subject-area teachers may require different salaries because their opportunity cost of teaching is different. Walsh and colleagues find that the opportunity cost of teaching is much higher for teachers with higher math abilities (SAT math score) than for teachers with higher verbal abilities (SAT verbal score) (Walsh, 2014).

Quasi-experimental evidence

We will review several recent policy interventions to see if we can have a better understanding of compensating wage differentials in different contexts. These six studies cover North Carolina, Florida, Tennessee, District of Columbia, ten unidentified school districts in the US, Washington, and Norway (C. Clotfelter et al., 2008; Cowan & Goldhaber, 2018; Dee & Wyckoff, 2015; Falch, 2010, 2011; L. Feng & Sass, 2018; Protik, Glazerman, Bruch, & Teh, 2015; Springer et al., 2016).

Table 30.2 provides a summary of these studies reviewed and their important eligibility rules. These programs have many similar features such as targeting shortage subject areas (North Carolina and Florida), targeting shortage schools (Norway), targeting schools with high poverty rate (North Carolina, 10 anonymous school districts, DC, Washington), targeting low-performing schools (North Carolina and Tennessee), targeting teachers who will obtain National Board Certification (Washington DC), and targeting effective teachers (Tennessee, 10 anonymous school districts, DC). We will analyze each of these studies in detail.

One analysis identified that a retention bonus of $1800 per year was paid to existing North Carolina teachers (Clotfelter et al., 2008). The North Carolina program was a combination of subject-area and school-type differential pay. To qualify, teachers had to be certified in math, science, or special education, and had to be working in

TABLE 30.2 Eligibility rules for empirical studies using policy interventions.

Study	Student poverty (share of students eligible for free or reduced lunch program)	Student test score	Teacher subject areas	Teacher certification	Teacher VAM	Shortage designation
Feng and Sass(Florida)			Secondary math and science, special education, foreign languages, secondary English, reading, ESOL, technology education/Industrial arts	Certified in above areas		Designated shortage subject areas
Clotfelter, Glennie, Ladd, and Vigdor (North Carolina)	80% above	50% failure rate in algebra or biology exam	Secondary math and science, special education	Certified in above areas		
Springer, Swain, Rodriguez (Tennessee)		Bottom 5% on a composite proficiency rate			Level 5 in effectiveness	
Protik, et al. (10 US school districts)	70% above (70% receiving vs. 55% sending)				Top 20% of the VAM in subject, grade, district	
Dee and Wyckoff (DC)	Higher poverty school: 60% or higher; lower poverty school: Below 60%				Highly effective: Bonuses; ineffective: Dismissal	
Falch 2010 and 2011 (Norway)						List of schools with 20% or more shortage
Cowan and Goldhaber (Washington)	70% above elementary; 60% above middle; 50% above			National Board-certified teachers		

middle and high schools that were serving primarily low-performing or low-income students. The $1800 bonus was equivalent to about 4–5% of the average pay of teachers in North Carolina. Clotfelter et al. (2008) adopted a difference-in-difference-in-difference strategy to compare teachers before and after the implementation of the program, eligible teachers with ineligible teachers, and teachers in eligible schools with those in ineligible schools. Despite some problems in making teachers aware of the program, the targeted salary increases were sufficient to reduce turnover rates by 17%. The labor elasticity thus calculated was around -3 to -4.

In another study, we evaluated the impact of the Florida Critical Teacher Shortage Program that was established in 1984 to increase the labor supply of teachers in designated shortage areas. One primary component of the program was to provide loan forgiveness for up to $10,000 ($2500 per year for up to four years) for teachers who are both certified and who taught in a set of pre-determined shortage subject areas, e.g., middle and high school math and science, special education, foreign languages, and reading. This program continued for over 20 years and was terminated in 2011. There was also a one-time bonus program of $1200 offered to teachers of these subject areas in secondary schools. Our study employed intertemporal and exogenous designation of subject areas to estimate the causal impact of these programs on retention of teachers in Florida public schools (L. Feng & Sass, 2018). On average, teachers received a modest loan forgiveness amount ($1203), equivalent to 3.44% of the base salary of $35,000. The program impact was an approximately ten percentage-point reduction in turnover rate. The labor elasticity in our study was around -2 to -3 for middle and high school science and math teachers.

Falch (2010, 2011) studied a decade-long bonus program for Norwegian teachers. The program paid a wage premium of about 10% to teachers in schools with chronic staffing shortages. The program was effective, reducing the likelihood of voluntary departures by about six percentage points. Falch calculated the short-run labor elasticity to be around -1 and long-run elasticity to be around -3.5, which are closely aligned with the North Carolina study and our study in Florida.

Cowan and Goldhaber (2018) evaluated a teacher bonus program, i.e., the Challenging School Bonus program, in the state of Washington. Teachers who obtain the National Board Certification and teach in an elementary school with at least 70% students on FRL program are eligible for a bonus of $5000. Cowan and Goldhaber found a reduction of 3.2–4.2% points, corresponding to a 31–41% lower turnover rate. They also report that the $5000 bonus is equivalent to a 7.2% increase in salary. The labor elasticity thus calculated was around -4.3 and -5.7.

Springer, Swain, and Rodriguez evaluated a teacher bonus program in the state of Tennessee (Springer et al., 2016). This program targeted the bottom 5% of schools in terms of their composite proficiency rate for students. Highly effective teachers in these schools were able to secure a $5000 bonus. Using the regression discontinuity method, the authors found that the retention bonus did not have any statistically significant effect on the full sample but found that the retention bonus reduced turnover rate by 21% points for teachers in tested subject areas. Given the base salary of $52,414, the bonus amount of $5000 corresponds to approximately 9.54% of base pay. We can conclude that the labor elasticity is around -2.2.

Dee and Wyckoff evaluated a high-stakes teacher evaluation system implemented in the District of Columbia (DC) (Dee & Wyckoff, 2015). Teachers who were rated as highly effective were eligible to receive bonus pay. Bonus pay was structured at $5000 in lower poverty schools (less than 60% students on FRL program). An additional $5000 bonus was offered to teachers in tested subject areas and another additional $2500 for teachers in special education, bilingual education, and English as a second language as well as secondary math and science. For teachers in high-poverty schools, all bonuses were doubled.

The eligibility rules appear to be quite complicated. The intent of the bonuses is to address all three challenges: (1) retaining effective teachers ($5000 in lower poverty schools and $10,000 in high-poverty schools); (2) compensating teachers in group 1, i.e., those teachers who add value individually ($5000 in lower poverty schools and $10,000 in high-poverty schools); (3) compensating teachers in high-need subject areas such as special education, secondary math and science ($2500 in lower poverty schools and $5000 in high-poverty schools).

Though DC IMPACT offers the largest bonus program, the authors found that bonuses have zero effect on the retention rate. We can surmise that this may be due to a couple of reasons. First, DC is a large metropolitan area and may require additional compensating wage differentials. Another reason might stem from the threat of being dismissed. Indeed, they find that the strongest effect of the program is at the low-end of the value-addition scale. The DC IMPACT program effects mainly arise from dismissing the least effective teachers.

Table 30.3 provides a summary of all these studies, bonus amounts offered, their impact on retention rate reduction, and calculated labor elasticity. The bonus amounts range from a couple of thousands of dollars in Florida and North Carolina to $5000 in Tennessee and all the way up to $10,000 in the talent transfer program and $25,000 in the IMPACT program in DC In terms of program impact, reduction in teacher turnover is around 8–22%. On average, labor elasticity is between one and three. Ultimately, we are not interested in the program impact on retention. We are interested in finding out how much additional bonus or pay is needed to compensate teachers to teach in more challenging environments. We will use the labor elasticity results we obtained and one recent random assignment study to tackle that question.

The challenge is how to separate the bonuses used to reduce retention rate from the bonuses used to compensate the challenging work environment. We will carry out a simple back-of-the-envelope calculation using research findings from prior analyses to understand the elusive compensating wage differentials for teachers.

TABLE 30.3 Major findings for empirical studies using policy interventions.

Study	BONUS amount	Base salary high	% BONUS as base pay	% reduction in turnover or quit	Labor elasticity
Feng and Sass	$1,203	$35,000	3.44	10.4	3.03
Feng and Sass	$1,203	$35,000	3.44	8.9	2.59
Clotfelter, Glennie, Ladd, and Vigdor	$1,800	$40,000	4.50	17	3.78
Feng and Sass	$2,000	$35,000	5.71	10	1.75
Springer, Swain, Rodriguez	$5,000	$52,414	9.54	21	2.20
Cowan and Goldhaber	$5,000	$69,374	7.21	31	4.30
Protik, Glazerman, Bruch, The	$10,000	$50,740	19.71	22	1.12
Dee and Wyckoff	$12,500				
Dee and Wyckoff	$25,000				
Falch 2010	Unknown	Unknown	10.00		1.02
Falch 2011	Unknown	Unknown	10.00		3.50

Random assignment evidence

In an effort to address the equitable distribution of highly effective teachers across schools with different student body characteristics, Glazerman et al. (2013) conducted an experimental analysis of the "Teacher Transfer Initiative," a federally funded initiative that offered $20,000 in incentives for high-quality teachers to teach in low-achieving schools for two years. Researchers found much lower turnover rates among teachers when the incentive of $20,000 ($10,000 per year) was in place during the two-year program (Protik et al., 2015).

According to one online report by Mathematica, the retention rate was 93 versus 71% between control and treatment groups. This is a 22-percentage-point reduction in retention rate. If we use the most recent labor supply elasticity measure around -3 (Clotfelter et al., 2008; Falch, 2010, 2011; Feng & Sass, 2018), we can conclude that to induce a 22-percentage-point increase in retention rate, a salary increase of about 7.3% (22% divided by labor supply elasticity 3) is necessary. According to the authors, the average teachers' salary is around $50,000, so this corresponds to a salary increase of approximately $3650 (=50,000*7.3%).

We also gathered that receiving schools generally have a minority student share of 15% points more (76.3% vs. 91.3%) than that of sending schools. Receiving schools on average have 24.4% points more students on FRL program (68.1% in sending vs. 92.6% in receiving). Given the total amount of bonus is $10,000 per year; we are left with $6,350, i.e., $10,000-$3650. This bonus amount ($6350) can be considered as combat bonuses for teaching in a more challenging school. This may be the compensating wage differential that is necessary to compensate teachers to teach in schools with 15% points more minority students and 24.4% points more students on FRL.

Findings and future directions

After reviewing these three different strands of research literature, we discover that there is some evidence of positive compensating wage differentials from both hedonic wage literature and meta-analysis evidence. As the demographics in the US and around the world become more diverse, the resources necessary and challenges associated with educating a more diverse student body will be more acutely felt by schools and school districts.

With the improvement of data availability, more research using longitudinal datasets are necessary to resolve some of the conflicting results found in this review. Moreover, additional data collection efforts pertaining to the teachers' working environment are necessary. Currently, the share of disadvantaged and minority students is used to represent working conditions. This is a poor proxy for general working conditions faced by teachers. Moreover, conflicting results for the share of minority students and the share of students in poverty uncovered in hedonic wage regression makes it paramount to uncover new model specifications or better data. More studies using a quasi-experimental or random assignment research design are needed to answer the question of how much additional compensation is needed for teachers to teach in schools with more challenging environments or to teach subject areas that face chronic shortages.

References

Adam, S. (2000). *The wealth of nations / Adam Smith; Introduction by Robert Reich; edited, with notes, Marginal summary, and enlarged index by Edwin Cannan* (pp. 1723–1790). New York: Modern Library.

Antos, J. R., & Rosen, S. (1975). Discrimination in the market for public school teachers. *Journal of Econometrics, 3*(2), 123–150.

Bifulco, R. (2010). The influence of performance-based accountability on the distribution of teacher salary increases. *Education Finance and Policy, 5*(2), 177–199. https://doi.org/10.1162/edfp.2010.5.2.5203.

Borman, G. D., & Dowling, N. M. (2008). Teacher attrition and retention: A meta-analytic and narrative review of the research. *Review of Educational Research, 78*(3), 367–409. https://doi.org/10.3102/0034654308321455.

Boyd, D., Lankford, H., Loeb, S., & Wyckoff, J. (2003). *Analyzing the determinants of the matching of public school teachers to jobs: Estimating compensating differentials in imperfect labor markets.* NBER Working Paper Series No. 9878.

Boyd, D., Lankford, H., Loeb, S., & Wyckoff, J. (2013). Analyzing the determinants of the matching of public school teachers to jobs: Disentangling the preferences of teachers and employers. *Journal of Labor Economics, 31*(1), 83–117. https://doi.org/10.1086/666725.

Brown, C. (1980). Equalizing differences in the labor market. *The Quarterly Journal of Economics, 94*(1), 113–134.

Brunner, E., & Imazeki, J. (2010). Probation length and teacher salaries : Does waiting pay off ? *Industrial and Labor Relations Review, 64*(1), 164–180.

Clotfelter, C., Glennie, E., Ladd, H., & Vigdor, J. (2008). Would higher salaries keep teachers in high-poverty schools? Evidence from a policy intervention in North Carolina. *Journal of Public Economics, 92*(5–6), 1352–1370. https://doi.org/10.1016/j.jpubeco.2007.07.003.

Clotfelter, C. T., Ladd, H. F., & Vigdor, J. L. (2011). Teacher mobility, school segregation, and pay-based policies to level the playing field. *Education Finance and Policy, 6*(3), 399–438. https://doi.org/10.1162/EDFPa00040.

Cowan, J., & Goldhaber, D. (2018). Do bonuses affect teacher staffing and student achievement in high poverty schools? Evidence from an incentive for national board certified teachers in Washington state. *Economics of Education Review, 65,* 138–152. https://doi.org/10.1016/j.econedurev.2018.06.010.

Dee, T. S., & Wyckoff, J. (2015). Incentives, selection, and teacher performance: Evidence from IMPACT. *Journal of Policy Analysis and Management, 34*(2), 267–297. https://doi.org/10.1002/pam.

Falch, T. (2010). The elasticity of labor supply at the establishment level. *Journal of Labor Economics, 28*(2), 237–266. https://doi.org/10.1086/649905.

Falch, T. (2011). Teacher mobility responses to wage Changes : Evidence from a quasi-natural experiment. *American Economic Review: Papers and Proceedings, 101*(3).

Feng, L. (2009). Opportunity wages, classroom characteristics, and teacher mobility. *Southern Economic Journal, 75*(4).

Feng, L. (2014). Teacher placement, mobility, and occupational choices after teaching. *Education Economics, 22*(1). https://doi.org/10.1080/09645292.2010.511841.

Feng, L., & Sass, T. R. (2018a). The impact of incentives to recruit and retain teachers in "Hard-to-Staff" subjects. *Journal of Policy Analysis and Management, 37*(1), 112–135. https://doi.org/10.1002/pam.22037.

Feng, L., & Sass, T. R. (2018b). The impact of incentives to recruit and retain teachers in "Hard-to-Staff" subjects. *Journal of Policy Analysis and Management, 37*(1). https://doi.org/10.1002/pam.22037.

Gilpin, G. A. (2011). Reevaluating the effect of non-teaching wages on teacher attrition. *Economics of Education Review, 30*(4), 598–616. https://doi.org/10.1016/j.econedurev.2011.03.003.

Glazerman, S., Protik, A., Teh, B. R., Bruch, J., & Max, J. (2013). In *Transfer incentives for high-performing teachers: Final results from a multisite randomized experiment.* NCEE 2014–4004, National Center for Education Evaluation and Regional Assistance.

Goldhaber, D., Destler, K., & Player, D. (2010). Teacher labor markets and the perils of using hedonics to estimate compensating differentials in the public sector. *Economics of Education Review, 29*(1), 1–17. https://doi.org/10.1016/j.econedurev.2009.07.010.

Grissom, J. A., & Strunk, K. O. (2012). How should school districts shape teacher salary schedules? Linking school performance to pay structure in traditional compensation schemes. *Educational Policy, 26*(5), 663–695. https://doi.org/10.1177/0895904811417583.

Guarino, C., Santibanez, L., & Daley, G. (2006). Teacher recruitment and retention. *Review of Educational Research, 76*(2), 173–208. https://doi.org/10.1083/jcb.50.2.432.

Harris, D. C. (2006). Lowering the bar or moving the target: A wage decomposition of Michigan's charter and traditional public school teachers. *Educational Administration Quarterly, 42*(3), 424–460. https://doi.org/10.1177/0013161X05282612.

Levinson, A. M. (1988). Reexamining teacher preferences and compensating wages. *Economics of Education Review, 7*(3), 357–364. https://doi.org/10.1016/0272-7757(88)90007-6.

Martin, S. M. (2010). Are public school teacher salaries paid compensating wage differentials for student racial and ethnic characteristics? *Education Economics, 18*(3), 349–370. https://doi.org/10.1080/09645290802470228.

Player, D. (2009). Monetary returns to academic ability in the public teacher labor market. *Economics of Education Review, 28*(2), 277–285. https://doi.org/10.1016/j.econedurev.2008.06.002.

Protik, A., Glazerman, S., Bruch, J., & Teh, B. R. (2015). Staffing a low-performing school: Behavioral responses to selective teacher transfer incentives. *Education Finance and Policy, 10*(4), 573–610. https://doi.org/10.1162/EDFPa00174.

Rosen, S. (1974). Hedonic Prices and implicit markets: Product differentiation in pure competition. *The Journal of Political Economy, 82*(1), 34–55.

Smith, R. S. (1978). Compensating wage differentials and public policy: A review. *Industrial and Labor Relations Review, 32*(3), 339. Retrieved from http://heinonline.org/HOL/Page?handle=hein.journals/ialrr32&id=341&div=&collection=journals.

Springer, M. G., Swain, W. A., & Rodriguez, L. A. (2016). Effective teacher retention bonuses: Evidence from Tennessee. *Educational Evaluation and Policy Analysis, 38*(2), 199–221. https://doi.org/10.3102/0162373715609687.

Walsh, P. (2014). When unified teacher pay scales meet differential alternative returns. *Education Finance and Policy, 9*(3), 304–333. https://doi.org/10.1162/EDFPa00135.

West, K. L., & Mykerezi, E. (2011). Teachers' unions and compensation: The impact of collective bargaining on salary schedules and performance pay schemes. *Economics of Education Review, 30*(1), 99–108. https://doi.org/10.1016/j.econedurev.2010.07.007.

Winters, J. V. (2011). Teacher salaries and teacher unions : A spatial econometric approach. *Industrial and Labor Relations Review, 64*(4), 747–764.

Teacher incentives

L. Santibañez

Fundación IDEA, México City, México

Recent evidence suggests that teachers matter for student learning (OECD, 2005). Consequently, education systems around the world strive to recruit and retain high-quality teachers. To ensure qualified teachers get to the classroom (and remain there), salaries must be set accordingly. Because education is a labor-intensive endeavor, in many countries teacher salaries account for 60–95% of educational spending. The traditional way of paying teachers, however, using education- and seniority-based salary schedules is not designed to reward or encourage superior performance (Hanushek, 1996; Lavy, 2007; Mumane & Cohen, 1986). To tackle this problem, the use of targeted incentives or pay-for-performance has often been proposed.

The rationale behind using incentives to promote changes in individual behavior was first explored in the economics and business literature. Salary-incentive programs are designed to solve the employer's problem of motivating workers to perform well when individual effort and ability is not readily measured or observed (Asch, 2005). In other words, incentives are useful when a principal and an agent (i.e., an individual performing work for an employer) have differing objectives in a context of asymmetric information, when the employer cannot or does not want to dictate a particular procedure for attaining the outcome.

The school presents employers with a similar kind of principal—agent problem. School administrators, parents, and policymakers all want teachers to achieve certain outcomes (e.g., improve learning, develop well-adjusted adults, and build citizenship), but cannot monitor teachers' daily activities. To address this situation in a way that improves educational outcomes, incentive programs in education are being increasingly favored.

This article presents an overview of teacher incentive programs implemented in various countries. It begins with a brief background section on the kinds of incentive programs that have been put in practice. Second, it discusses the advantages of incentive programs and some of the positive results reported in the literature. These results are divided into individual and group incentives. Within these categories, the discussion is organized by type of outcome: efficiency and productivity, and the recruitment and retention of qualified teachers. Third, it explores some of the main disadvantages and criticisms of incentive programs as well as some of their unintended or adverse consequences. The last section concludes.

Background on incentive programs

Teacher incentive programs come in different flavors. They can be targeted to the individual or be designed to reward the group as a whole (a group of teachers, a school, or a school district). Incentives can be structured as rewards only, or as a system of rewards and sanctions. It can be a one-time event or an ongoing reward. They can be based on a relative criterion (value-added) or an absolute one (Lavy, 2007).

Most incentive programs reward teachers with salary-bonuses, but some offer nonmonetary rewards. Incentives can be offered to teachers in the form of improved working conditions, in-kind contributions (e.g., educational materials), job stability, pensions, and the like (Vegas & Umansky, 2005). Other common examples of nonmonetary incentives are promotion-based (where promotions to higher grades in a career schedule are based on performance assessed over several time periods) and seniority-based incentives (when employers offer a reward later in an employee's career contingent on current levels of effort) (Asch, 2005). Both of these can be effective in improving worker productivity, but they are of limited use in educational systems. (Obviously, the first kind of incentives only works in an organization with a vertical hierarchy (e.g., workers promoted to managers). The second approach suffers from the problem of workers not wanting to retire when they are senior employees because they are being paid more than their productivity (Lazear, 1979, 1983). In addition, this approach is in some ways reflected by current salary schedules that are based on seniority. Research has found that more senior teachers are not necessarily more competent than junior teachers who have been teaching for at least 2—3 years (Hanushek, 1997). However, senior teachers receive higher salaries than novices do on all salary schedules.)

Mumane and Cohen (1986) discussed merit pay and concluded that most plans fail because the microeconomic framework under which most plans are based is not entirely appropriate for compensating teachers' work. For example, school administrators were rarely in a position to accurately explain why some teachers received merit pay and others did not, and what the latter group could due to receive merit pay in the future.

However, most recent incentive programs are merit-pay style programs focusing on student test scores as the main measure of teacher performance. Focusing on test scores is an attractive choice because they provide observable measures of student learning. In addition, there is evidence to suggest that they are correlated with other longer-term outcomes such as lifelong earnings (Klerman, 2005). Next we discuss the main advantages of incentive programs. To illustrate these, a brief discussion of recent experiences is included. By design, most of the positive effects are on standardized student test scores. Whenever appropriate, however, we discuss effects on other outcomes of interest such as teacher attendance.

Advantages of incentive programs

This section discusses positive results reported by incentive programs implemented in various countries. It is organized in two main categories: incentives targeted to the individual teacher and group incentives. Within these two categories, the discussion is divided into efficiency and productivity results, and effects on recruitment and retention of qualified teachers.

Individual incentives *Efficiency and productivity*

In theory, the main advantage of incentive programs is that basing some part of a teacher's compensation (or offering incremental payments) on a common objective (learning, test scores, and graduation rates) enables the alignment of incentives directed to teachers or schools with those directed to students (Lavy, 2007). This could generate efficiency gains because teachers focus their efforts on those objectives that are valued most by parents and policymakers. Individual merit-pay schemes of this type help correct potential distortions in a teachers' effort that might result from gaps between her (work) preferences and those of her students (Lavy, 2007). In other words, incentives could produce better educational outcomes at lower or equal cost than traditional across-the- board salary raises.

There are some recent experiences that suggest the alignment of teacher and student objectives through incentives produces positive results. In India, Duflo, Hanna, and Ryan (2007) evaluated an intervention to reduce teacher absenteeism in rural areas through the use of teacher monitoring and incentives. An experiment of 57 randomly selected treatment schools (out of 113 schools) was conducted to explore if financial incentives would motivate teachers to have fewer absences (the baseline data suggested an absence rate of 42%). Teachers in the treatment schools were given a tamper-proof date and time camera to record their attendance at the beginning and end of the school day. Teacher salaries were calculated on the basis of valid school days. Tying salary to teacher attendance not only resulted in a drastic decline in teacher absence (to 21 % in treatment schools over a period of two years) (the proper evaluation phase lasted only 10 months; therefore, the positive effects on attendance lasted well beyond the experiment), but it also positively improved student achievement levels. A year after the program began, student test scores in treatment schools were higher (0.17 standard deviations) than test scores in comparison schools (Duflo et al., 2007).

Other countries have experimented with incentives to improve teacher attendance in rural areas with less encouraging results. In Bolivia, teacher incentives were used to attract teachers

to rural areas. The size of the incentive was small (between 0.3% and 1.1% of monthly salary) and was not successful in attracting teachers to these hard-to-staff areas. Furthermore, because of urbanization and demographic growth, some areas classified as rural were in fact borderline urban. The authors found that the test scores and other educational outcomes of students of urban- and rural-classified teachers with the same background and characteristics were not significantly different (Urquiola & Vegas, 2005).

In Mexico as part of the Programa para Abatir el Rezago Educativo (PARE) (this program was implemented in Mexico from 1992 to 1996 as part of a World Bank initiative to provide additional resources to very disadvantaged students, primarily those in rural areas and indigenous communities), teachers were offered monetary bonuses if they demonstrated they attended school regularly. A novel feature of PARE was that it was the parent associations who were in charge of teacher attendance records and monitoring. A qualitative evaluation of PARE, conducted in nine schools in two Mexican states, found incentives effectively reduced teacher absenteeism only in schools that had strong school principals and parent associations or had lower levels of teacher absenteeism (comparatively) before PARE was implemented (Ezpeleta & Weiss, 1996).

In Mexico, an evaluation of the national teacher incentive program *Carrera Magisterial* (teachers' career) showed slight positive effects of the monetary incentives on a small group of secondary school teachers, but virtually no effect on primary teachers (McEwan & Santibañez, 2005; Santibañez et al, 2007). This program, unique in the world for its size and scope (implemented in 1992, the program is national in scope; hundreds of thousands of teachers and millions of students are tested every year as part of its yearly evaluations), awards bonuses beginning at 25% of base salary, up to 200% to teachers who consent to an evaluation of several factors including teacher knowledge (measured using a standardized teacher test) and student achievement (using a standardized student test). To evaluate the program and try to circumvent the fact that no natural comparison group exists, the authors used regression discontinuity design which compared teachers with strong incentives to those with weaker incentives during the evaluation year. (To obtain the bonus (get incorporated into the program) teachers must obtain a minimum of 70 out of a total 100 points in the yearly evaluation. Up to 80 points of the total can be thought of as exogenous, because they either increase automatically every year or remain the same (the case of points given for seniority and highest degree earned, respectively), have virtually no variation (the case of the peer review component), or are within the control of the teacher (points given for obtaining professional development or the teacher test). Teachers with exogenous point scores below 50 or above 70 are in the weak incentive group. Teachers with exogenous point scores between 50 and 70 have a high incentive to improve student achievement, which is worth 20 points and could get them above the minimum cutoff for incorporation (McEwan & Santibañez, 2005).) Results suggest that students of teachers in the strong incentive group who were competing for the bonus did exhibit slightly higher test results than teachers in the weak incentive group. This effect, however, was only observed for a very small group of secondary school teachers and not for primary teachers (McEwan & Santibañez, 2005; Santibañez et al., 2007).

Using various data sources including the National Education Longitudinal Survey (NELS), Figlio and Kenny (2006) found that a strong positive association between the presence of merit pay in teacher compensation and student test scores in the United States. The authors were not able to conclude whether this positive association was the result of the incentives *per se* or of some unobserved measure of school quality not captured by the model.

Dee and Keys (2004) analyze the Career Ladder Evaluation System. This program was implemented in the state of Tennessee to improve student achievement through a blend of salary rewards with nonmonetary benefits such as more teacher autonomy and released time from teaching.

Using results from the Tennessee STAR class-size experiment, the authors found that the Career Ladder Evaluation System program had only mixed success in targeting rewards to the more meritorious teachers. They concluded that assignment to a career ladder teacher significantly increased mathematics scores by roughly three percentile points. However, most career-ladder teachers were not significantly more effective at promoting reading achievement. Furthermore, assignment to a teacher who had advanced further up the career ladder was not uniformly associated with significantly higher achievement (Dee & Keys, 2004). The authors acknowledge that one important caveat to their analysis stems from the fact that it uses an assessment system that was specifically designed to evaluate class size and not the effects of the incentive program.

Incentive programs could also encourage teachers to improve their practice or engage in professional development activities. One such study is the evaluation of the National Board Certification Pilot Project in Iowa. This project offers teachers' monetary incentives in exchange for obtaining advanced teacher certification. The evaluation found that teachers involved in the certification process with the monetary incentives engaged in more professional development activities than teachers not targeted by the incentives (Dethlefs, Trent, Boody, & et al, 2001). In Mexico, Ornelas (2002), in his study of CM, concluded that one of the major successes of the program's monetary incentives was to emphasize professional development. (However, it is not difficult to make the case that professional development should not be a goal in and of itself, but should be an intermediate objective to improving student learning. While it is important for teachers to receive continuous training, it is more important that training results in improvements in teaching that have ultimate beneficial consequences in the classroom.) A caveat to these programs is that teacher professional development or certification might not be an objective in and of itself. This is particularly true if these activities do not lead to better student learning. In this case, the incentive program could not lead to improvement in the bottom line goal of higher education quality.

Recruitment and retention of qualified teachers

If incentive programs correctly identify teacher productivity they will help recruit and retain more productive teachers. In theory, if the incentive program is well designed, it will tend to discourage teachers who are not as productive from remaining in the system and will tend to encourage more productive teachers to do so.

On the issue of how incentives affect teacher recruitment and retention, there is considerable US-based evidence suggesting that increasing teacher salaries affects who chooses to enter and remain in teaching. In the United States numerous studies suggest a link between higher teacher salaries and higher retention (Brewer, 1996; Gritz & Theobald, 1996; Kirby, Berends, & Naftel, 1999; Podgursky, Monroe, & Watson, 2004; Stockard & Lehman, 2004). Incentives used to attract teachers to less desirable schools may not work as well, however.

Group incentives *Efficiency and productivity*

Some of the gains in productivity discussed above are not only derived from individual incentive programs. Incentive programs

designed to target a group of teachers or the school as a whole can help foster collaboration among teachers by getting them to work for a unified goal. This could have the dual positive effect of producing higher learning and overcome some of the potential negative effects of targeting individual teachers (Dee & Keys, 2004; Mumane & Cohen, 1986).

Glewwe, Ilias, and Kremer (2003) examine a teacher incentive program in Kenya which provided teachers with bonuses based on student performance and attendance. Teachers in 50 rural schools were randomly selected (out of 100) for the incentive program based on the average test score of students already enrolled in school at the start of the program. Each year the program provided prizes valued at up to 43% of typical monthly salary to grade 4–8 teachers. The incentives were given to all teachers in the winning schools (regardless of their own individual performance), based on the performance of the school (relative to other schools) on the Kenyan government's districtwide exams.

The authors found that during the life of the program, students in treatment schools were more likely to score higher, at least on some exams, than students in the comparison group. This effect, however, tended to be short-lived. In addition, a closer examination of the channels through which this effect took place, suggested that teachers might have been teaching to the test. The authors did not find strong evidence to support that the program had induced greater teacher effort or that it would be able to reach longer term outcomes: student dropout rates did not fall, teacher attendance did not improve, the amount of homework assigned did not increase, and pedagogy did not change. There is, however, evidence that teachers' increased efforts to increase the number of pupils taking tests and to raise short-run test scores (by focusing instruction on the test). In addition, the authors found evidence that teachers adjusted to the program over time by offering more test preparation sessions (Glewwe et al., 2003).

Lavy (2002) examined a small-scale program in Israel that provided incentives to teachers in 62 nonrandomly selected schools. He used a regression discontinuity approach to compare student outcomes in these schools with those of schools that just missed treatment because of eligibility rules. The program offered combined incentives to schools in the form of performance awards. These awards included merit pay for teachers and improvements in working conditions. Awards were based on student test scores and reduced dropout rates. This type of incentive program is of the rank order type, which awards prizes based on the rank order of the winners.

An interesting feature of the Lavy (2002) paper is that it compares an incentive intervention with what he calls a resource intervention. That was a separate program awarding additional (and identical) resources, such as teacher training, to schools showing improvements. A comparison group of schools not admitted into the resource program serves as the basis for identification of programmatic effects. Lavy evaluates the effect of this parallel program and compares its effectiveness and cost to the teachers' incentives intervention.

Lavy's results suggest that monetary incentives had some effect in the first year of implementation in some schools and caused significant gains in many dimensions of students' outcomes in the second year in all schools. The program led to an increase in average test scores and a higher proportion of students who gained the high school matriculation certificate (especially among those from a disadvantaged background). It also appears to have contributed to a decrease in the dropout rate in the transition from middle to high school. The results regarding the resource program suggest that it also led to significant improvements in student performance. However, the comparison of the programs based on cost equivalency suggests that the teachers' incentive intervention is more cost-effective (Lavy, 2002).

In Chile, the *Sistema Nacional de Evaluación del Desempeño de los Establecimientos Educacionales* (SNED) or National System of School Performance Assessment, offers monetary bonuses to schools that show high student-achievement marks. This program was implemented in 1990 and preliminary evidence shows a cumulative positive effect on student achievement for schools which had a relatively high probability of winning the award (Mizala & Romaguera, 2003).

Summary of key findings

Table 31.1 provides a summary of key findings from more recent studies, divided by type of intervention (individual or group incentives).

As the table suggests, most of the teacher incentive interventions that showed positive results on student achievement and other outcomes, were carefully designed, small-scale interventions with sizable benefits for teachers and schools.

Disadvantages and criticisms

The theory behind incentive programs is appealing in its simplicity. It is intuitive that individuals will tend to work harder if they know they will be rewarded for their efforts. As the evidence from the business field shows, this logic often tends to work. In practice, however, many incentive programs in education often fail to reach their intended goals. Most authors attribute these failures to both design and implementation factors.

First, incentive program design assumes that there is a clear and known definition of performance (Klerman, 2005). This implies a common agreement about outputs. In most examples from the economics and business literature, the output is well defined and has a readily available measure for performance. For example, papers

TABLE 31.1 Summary of key findings from recent studies, by type of intervention.

Study	Country	Scale	Description	Intervention design	Results
Individual incentives					
Santibañez et al. (2007)	Mexico	National scale	Provides monthly salary bonus (beginning at 25% of base salary) to teachers who pass a national evaluation including tests of their knowledge and their students' knowledge	Nonrandomized intervention, voluntary participation. Most teachers in the country in the program enrolled in program. Evaluation used regression discontinuity to identify a strong incentive group	Students of teachers in strong incentive group had slightly higher results in secondary schools. No significant results in primary schools
Duflo et al., (2007)	India	Small pilot program	Provide financial incentives to teachers who could demonstrate regular attendance through the use of tamper-proof cameras	Experiment randomly selected 120 treatment schools and 60 comparison schools	Tying salary to attendance and using rigorous monitoring (cameras) significantly and drastically decreased teacher absence and improved student achievement
Urquiola and Vegas (2005)	Bolivia	National	Offered salary bonuses to teachers who taught at less desirable (i.e., rural) schools	Nonrandomized intervention, used regression discontinuity to identify effect of bonus	Rural pay differential was not successful in attracting more effective teachers to rural areas. The bonus had no effect on student test scores
Group incentives					
Glewwe et al. (2003)	Kenya	Small pilot program	Provide teachers with bonuses (prized at 43% monthly salary) based on student performance and attendance. All teachers in winning school get the incentive	100 rural schools, teachers in 50 randomly selected schools get treatment	Students in treatment schools scored higher in exams, only during life of the program
Lavy (2002)	Israel	Small-scale	Offered schools combined awards (salary bonuses for teachers and improvements in school working conditions) for improvements in student test scores and reduced dropout rates	Used regression discontinuity approach to evaluate results in 62 nonrandomly selected schools	The program had positive and significant effects on student test scores and dropout rates during its 2-year duration
Mizala and Romaguera (2003)	Chile	National scale	Offers monetary bonuses to schools that show high student- achievement marks	Nonrandom selection of schools. Descriptive and qualitative analysis	Preliminary evidence shows cumulative and positive results on student achievement for schools with high probability of winning the award

in the business literature have shown incentives improved the productivity of workers installing car windshields (Lazear, 2000) and planting trees (Paarsch & Shearer, 2000).

Working toward achieving or producing a well-defined output is not usually the case in education. Teachers and schools have multiple and complex objectives which include, but are not limited, to student learning. Self-esteem, citizenship building, development of core values, and social skills are all outputs valued to varying degrees by teachers, parents, and policymakers. Even when all of us could agree that student learning is the top priority, it is not clear that a standardized test can capture learning in a way that satisfies a common definition. In addition, the objectives of teachers and their employers (principals, school boards, and education authorities) could compete with one another and even be mutually exclusive. For example, government agents might be interested in ensuring an equitable education for all its citizens, while teachers or school administrators might want to keep difficult or at-risk students out of the classroom (Vegas & Umansky, 2005).

Second, incentive schemes assume workers know the best way to improve their work. In other words, workers know the technology and have the means to implement it. Research on accountability in education, however, suggests that teachers could need assistance to figure out how to best improve student achievement (Hamilton, 2005). Hamilton (2005) argues that accountability reforms are often accompanied by technical assistance to schools, but that this technical assistance might not be enough to compensate for insufficient capacity problems (e.g., insufficient material and financial resources), or, for the broader context in which some schools must operate. Aside from some well-documented findings, there is a general lack of knowledge about how to improve teacher practice (Hamilton, 2005).

Third, incentive programs assume that the benefit of obtaining a desired outcome outweighs the costs of measuring performance. This is less of a problem when simple tasks are involved, but when performance is multidimensional and involves a series of complex tasks (as is the case in education), measurement costs might outweigh the benefits (Asch, 2005). This is related to the premise (on which incentive programs are based) that there is an operational (and commonly agreed to) definition of performance (Klerman, 2005). The more precise and operational this definition, the easier it will be to design a system of incentives to reach it.

Fourth, because education is a multidimensional task, focusing on a single dimension (e.g., student test scores) is problematic. Some have criticized these programs for curtailing creative thinking or teaching to the test (Hannaway, 1992; Holmstrom & Milgrom, 1991). Programs could design ways to reduce these unintended responses, for example, by combining the use of outcome measures (e.g., student tests) and practice measures (e.g., classroom observations, interviews, and supervisor ratings).

Because there is certain to be some level of noise affecting each period's evaluation, rewarding the worker for performance during a single period might expose him to considerable risk (Prendergast, 1999). For example, the program could reward teachers whose performance during the evaluation period improved due to a positive shock in working conditions rather than increased efforts in a given year. Using repeated incentives could reduce this noise and improve the quality of the performance measure. However, the costs and feasibility of using more precise measures of performance needs to be weighed against its potential benefits.

Fifth, some argue that explicit incentives (e.g., salary incentives) can reduce productivity by eliminating intrinsic desire. Most of the incentives literature in business and economics assumes that effort is costly for the worker, but other research argues that in some cases the pride or sense of mission workers derive from their work makes carrying out their tasks an enjoyable activity.

Teaching might just be such a job. Teachers often cite a desire to work with young people and contribute to society as important reasons to enter the teaching profession (Guarino, Santibañez, & Daley, 2006). Some authors have found that incentive programs demoralize teachers and lead to lower effort (Fehr & Schmidt, 2004 cited in; Duflo et al., 2007) or harm their motivation and sense of duty and enjoyment (Kreps, 1997 cited in; Duflo et al., 2007).

Adverse and unintended consequences of teacher incentive programs

Other critiques of using targeted incentives to improve teacher quality center on the unintended, even adverse consequences of these kinds of programs. Upon deeper analysis of why some incentive plans improved student achievement, for example, it was found that teacher cheating (Jacob & Levitt, 2003), exclusion of low achieving students (Cullen & Reback, 2002; Figllo & Getzler, 2002), focus on the tested subjects in detriment of others (Hamilton, Stecher, & Klein, 2002), teaching to the test (Koretz, 2002), or even increasing students' caloric intake on the day of the test (Figllo & Winicki, 2005) were largely behind the observed results.

Group incentives can also have adverse consequences by exacerbating the potential for free-riding of teachers. Research has shown that if an employee's share of the reward is small relative to the difficulty of the work, and if the effort of all team members is difficult to observe by the employer, an individual on the team will have an incentive to shirk his or her work while benefiting from the teams' work or free-riding on the effort of others. This phenomenon weakens the power of group incentives (Asch, 2005; Asch & Karoly, 1993; Prendergast, 1999).

Conclusions

The evidence regarding the impact of programs that offer teachers monetary incentives to improve student achievement is mixed. Some small-scale programs have found that incentives are effective at improving student learning, although in most cases these results are short-lived and not always the product of increased teacher effort or improved teacher practice. Some programs (notably the India case) have found positive effects of financial teacher incentives on attendance, but this has not always been the case in other countries. Individual financial teacher incentives used to improve recruitment and retention or increasing professional development, seem to have positive effects, but those used for other purposes, such as increasing teacher attendance, have demonstrated mixed results. Still, even if their positive results are modest, targeted incentives are more cost-effective than traditional salary increases (which have also not shown consistent positive results on student learning) and are thus more likely to remain an attractive policy tool.

Years of incentive program design and implementation have yielded programs of very different forms and shapes. All the programs reviewed here used monetary incentives to encourage teachers, but some of the programs showing positive results mix individual and group (or school-based) incentives. None of the programs discussed here had sanctions for poor performance. Some were national in scale, some targeted only a few schools. Some rewarded student achievement only, some included other dimensions of a teachers' work.

In all cases and to improve its potential for positive effects the program should have a well-defined measure of teacher performance covering all outcomes of interest and including short- and long-term measures (Lavy, 2007). Value-added measures are preferred to absolute measures that can confound context and other factors (Lavy, 2007; McEwan & Santibañez, 2005). Perhaps a mix of group and individual incentives in addition to subjective (peer or supervisor review) with objective measures can be used to counterbalance criticisms about hindering teacher collaboration and the limited scope of standardized tests, respectively (Lavy, 2007).

See also

Economic Approaches to Teacher Recruitment and Retention; Teacher Labor Markets: An Overview; Teacher Supply; The Economics of School Accountability.

References

Asch, B. J. (2005). The economic complexities of incentive reforms. In R. Klitgaard, & P. C. Light (Eds.), *High-performance government: Structure, leadership, incentives* (pp. 309–342). Santa Monica, CA: RAND Corporation, MG-256-PRGS.

Asch, B. J., & Karoly, L. (1993). *The role of the job counselor in the military enlistment process.* Santa Monica, CA: RAND National Security Research Division, RAND.

Brewer, D. J. (1996). Career paths and quit decisions: Evidence from teaching. *Journal of Labor Economics, 14*(2), 313–339.

Cullen, J. B., & Reback, R. (2002). *Tinkering toward accolades: School gaming under a performance accountability system.* Unpublished Manuscript. University of Michigan.

Dee, T. S., & Keys, B. J. (2004). Does merit pay reward good teachers? Evidence from a randomized experiment. *Journal of Policy Analysis and Management, 23*(3), 471–488.

Dethlefs, T. M., Trent, V., Boody, R. M., et al. (2001). *Impact study of the national board certification pilot project in Iowa. Report.* Des Moines: Iowa State Department of Education.

Duflo, E., Hanna, R., & Ryan, S. (2007). *Monitoring works: Getting teachers to come to school.* Cambridge, MA: Poverty Action Lab.

Ezpeleta, J., & Weiss, E. (1996). Las escuelas rurales en zonas de pobreza y sus maestros: Tramas preexistentes y políticas innovadoras. *Revista Mexicana de Investigación Educativa, 1*(1), 53–69.

Fehr, E., & Schmidt, K. (2004). Fairness and incentives in a multi-task principal-agent model. *Scandinavian Journal of Economics, 106*(3), 453–474.

Figlio, D. N., & Kenny, L. (2006). *Individual teacher incentives and student performance.* Working Paper No. 12627. Cambridge, MA: National Bureau of Economic Research.

Figlio, D. N., & Getzler, L. S. (2002). *Accountability, ability, and disability: Gaming the system.* Working Paper No. 9307. Cambridge, MA: National Bureau of Economic Research.

Figlio, D. N., & Winicki, J. (2005). Food for thought: The effects of school accountability plans on school nutrition. *Journal of Public Economics, 89,* 381–394.

Glewwe, P., Ilias, N., & Kremer, M. (2003). *Teacher incentives.* Working Paper No. 9671. Cambridge, MA: National Bureau of Economic Research.

Gritz, R., & Theobald, N. (1996). The effects of school district spending priorities on length of stay in teaching. *Journal of Human Resources, 31*(3), 477–512.

Guarino, C., Santibañez, L., & Daley, G. A. (2006). Teacher recruitment and retention: A review of the recent empirical literature. *Review of Education Research, 76*(2), 173–208.

Hamilton, L. (2005). Lessons from performance measurement in education. In R. Klitgaard, & P. C. Light (Eds.), *High-performance government: Structure, leadership, incentives.* Santa Monica, CA: RAND Corporation, MG-256-PRGS.

Hamilton, L., Stecher, B., & Klein, S. (2002). *Making sense of test-based accountability in education.* Santa Monica, CA: RAND Corporation.

Hannaway, J. (1992). Higher order skills, job design, and incentives: An analysis and proposal. *American Educational Research Journal, 29*(1), 3–21.

Hanushek, E. A. (1996). Outcomes, costs, and incentives in schools. In E. A. Hanushek, & D. W. Jorgenson (Eds.), *Improving America's schools: The role of incentives* (pp. 29–52). Washington, DC: National Academy Press.

Hanushek, E. A. (1997). Assessing the effects of school resources on student performance: An update. *Educational Evaluation and Policy Analysis, 19*(2), 141–164.

Holmstrom, B., & Milgrom, P. (1991). Special issue: Multitask principal-agent analyses: Incentive contracts, asset ownership, and job design. *Journal of Law, Economics, and Organization, 7,* 24–52.

Jacob, B. A., & Levitt, S. D. (2003). Rotten apples: An investigation of the prevalence and predictors of teacher cheating. *Quarterly Journal of Economics, 118,* 843–878.

Kirby, S., Berends, M., & Naftel, S. (1999). Supply and demand of minority teachers in Texas: Problems and prospects. *Educational Evaluation and Policy Analysis, 21*(1), 47–66.

Klerman, J. A. (2005). Measuring performance. In R. Klitgaard, & P. C. Light (Eds.), *High-performance government: Structure, leadership, incentives* (pp. 343–380). Santa Monica, CA: RAND Corporation, MG-256-PRGS.

Koretz, D. (2002). Limitations in the use of achievement tests as measures of educators' productivity. *Journal of Human Resources, 37*(4), 752–777.

Kreps, D. (1997). Intrinsic motivation and extrinsic incentives. *American Economic Review, 872*(2), 359−364.

Lavy, V. (2002). Evaluating the effect of teachers' group performance incentives on pupil achievement. *Journal of Political Economy, 110*, 1286−1317.

Lavy, V. (2007). Using performance based pay to improve the quality of teachers. *Future of Children, 17*(1), 87−109.

Lazear, E. (1979). Why is there mandatory retirement? *Journal of Political Economy, 87*, 1261−1264.

Lazear, E. (1983). Pensions as severance pay. In Z. Bodie, & J. Shoven (Eds.), *Financial aspects of the United States pension system* (pp. 57−89). Chicago, IL: University of Chicago Press.

Lazear, E. P. (2000). Performance pay and productivity. *American Economic Review, 90*(5), 1346−1361.

McEwan, P. J., & Santibañez, L. (2005). Teacher incentives in Mexico. In E. Vegas (Ed.), *Beyond pay: Motivating teachers to raise student learning. Lessons from Latin America* (pp. 213−254). Washington, DC: The World Bank.

Mizala, A., & Romaguera, P. (2003). Regulación, incentivos y remuneraciones de los profesores en Chile. In C. Cox (Ed.), *Políticas educacionales en el cambio de siglo: La reforma del sistema escolar de Chile*. Santiago: Editorial Universitaria.

Mumane, R. J., & Cohen, D. K. (1986). Merit pay and the evaluation problem: Why most merit pay plans fail and a few survive. *Harvard Educational Review, 56*(1), 1−17.

OECD. (2005). *Teachers matter: Attracting, developing and retaining effective teachers*. Paris: Organisation for Economic Co-operation and Development.

Ornelas, C. (2002). Incentivos a los maestros: La paradoja mexicana. In C. Ornelas (Ed.), *Valores, calidad y educación* (pp. 137−161). Santillana/Aula XXI: México.

Paarsch, H. J., & Shearer, B. (2000). Piece rates, fixed wages, and incentive effects: Statistical evidence from payroll records. *International Economic Review, 41*(1), 59−92. Department of Economics, University of Pennsylvania and Osaka University Institute of Social and Economic Research Association.

Podgursky, M., Monroe, R., & Watson, D. (2004). The academic quality of public school teachers: An analysis of entry and exit behavior. *Economics of Education Review, 23*, 507−518.

Prendergast, C. (1999). The provision of incentives in firms. *Journal of Economic Literature, 37*(1), 7−63.

Santibañez, L., Martínez, J. F., Datar, A., et al. (2007). *Breaking ground: Analysis of the assessments and impact of the camera magisterial program in Mexico*. Santa Monica, CA: RAND/MG-141 (Also available in Spanish.).

Stockard, J., & Lehman, M. B. (2004). Influences on the satisfaction and retention of 1 st-year teachers: The importance of effective school management. *Educational Administration Quarterly, 40*(5), 742−771.

Urquiola, M., & Vegas, E. (2005). Arbitrary variation in teacher salaries: An analysis of teacher pay in Bolivia. In E. Vegas (Ed.), *Incentives to improve teaching: Lessons from Latin America* (pp. 187−211). Washington, DC: The World Bank.

Vegas, E., & Umansky, I. (2005). Improving teaching and learning through effective incentives. Lessons from Latin America. In E. Vegas (Ed.), *Incentives to improve teaching: Lessons from Latin America* (pp. 1−15). Washington, DC: The World Bank.

Further reading

Figlio, D. N. (2002). Can public schools buy better teachers? *Industrial and Labor Relations Review, 55*, 686−699.

Hanushek, E. A., & Raymond, M. E. (2002). Improving educational quality: How best to evaluate our schools? In Y. K. Kodrzycki (Ed.), *Education in the 21st century: Meeting the challenges of a changing world* (pp. 193−224). Boston, MA: Federal Reserve Bank of Boston.

Kane, T. J., & Douglas, O. S. (2002). The promise and pitfalls of using imprecise school accountability measures. *Journal of Economic Perspectives, 16*(4), 91−114.

Podgursky, M. J., & Springer, M. G. (2007). Teacher performance pay: A review. *Journal of Policy Analysis and Management, 26*(4), 909−949.

Rivkin, S. G., Hanushek, E. A., & Kain, J. F. (2005). Teachers, schools, and academic achievement. *Econometrica, 73*(2), 417−458.

PART V

Education markets, choice and incentives

The economic role of the state in education

D.N. Plank[a], T.E. Davis[b]

[a]Stanford University, Stanford, CA, United States; [b]University of Maryland, Baltimore, MD, United States

Glossary

Actuarially fair insurance An insurance policy is actuarially fair if the expected payout is equal to the premium

Asymmetric information When one party to a transaction has more or better information than another, there is asymmetric information. The field of information economics identifies various manifestations of asymmetric information, such as adverse selection, moral hazard, hidden action, screening, and signaling

Division of labor By breaking down industrial production into simple, repetitive tasks, each worker is able to specialize and become more productive. The division of labor increases economic efficiency

Externalities When the private actions of one individual or firm affect others, there exist either positive or negative externalities

Government failure When government action leads to an inefficient allocation of resources, there is a government failure. Government failure is a common focus of public-choice economists

Market failure There is a market failure when certain characteristics of the market lead to an inefficient allocation of resources. These characteristics may include the existence of a monopoly, asymmetric information, externalities, transactions costs, or poorly defined property rights

Private In economics, private refers to individual consumers and firms as opposed to government

Public choice Neoclassical economics is often criticized for giving short shrift to the role of government. Public choice is an area of economics that focuses on government by looking at the private motivations of bureaucrats and politicians in the public sector

Public spending Economists refer to government expenditure as public spending

Rent-seeking Rent-seeking occurs when economic actors manipulate the regulatory, economic, or political situation for their own benefit instead of earning a profit through production and trade

Risk aversion The unwillingness to accept an uncertain future payoff instead of a certain payoff with a lower value

State monopoly When a government agency is the sole provider of a good or service, economists call it a state monopoly

The economic and political importance of education has increased dramatically over the course of the past century. Education is the largest item of public expenditure in countries around the world, and formal schooling consumes an ever-larger quantity of young people's time. The centrality of education in modern societies is mainly a consequence of state action. The state has built and expanded national education systems, encouraged and sometimes compelled young people to attend school, and fostered rewards systems that make adult success increasingly contingent on academic persistence and performance. In this article we question why this should be so, and discuss the economic factors that help to explain why the state finances and often provides schools.

Constructing education systems

Modern states constructed national education systems in the service of political, economic, and military goals (Archer, 1982). In France, for example, the state extended the public school system to all corners of the nation in order to foster a sense of national identity by encouraging fluency and literacy in French and familiarity with canonical knowledge and civic traditions (Weber, 1976). Following the opening of japan in 1853, the state created a new education system, modeled on those in Prussia and the United States, in an effort to keep up economically and militarily with its Western rivals (Passin, 1965). In the US, state action supported the expansion, integration, and standardization of previously local educational systems (Tyack, 1974). More recently, the United Nations and the World Bank have encouraged and financed the construction and expansion of national education systems in countries around the world, in an effort to guarantee the right to education and to achieve the goal of education for all by 2015 (UNICEF, 2000).

National education systems grew inexorably in the 19th and 20th centuries, in two distinct ways. On the one hand, the state worked systematically to extend educational opportunities both socially and geographically, to incorporate previously excluded groups including rural children, girls, linguistic and ethnic minorities, and the disabled. On the other hand, the state sponsored and supported policies that required young people to spend an ever-increasing share of their time within the education system. These have evolved from the introduction and enforcement of child labor and compulsory education laws (which at first typically required 4 years of schooling, and now often require 12 or more) to current initiatives aimed at ensuring universal access to preschool and postsecondary education.

As in nineteenth-century Japan, state action to expand and improve national education systems has been and continues to be justified by reference to the imperatives of economic and military competitiveness. In the United States, for example, successive waves of state-sponsored educational reform have gained their impetus from public anxieties about keeping up with the Germans, the Russians, the Japanese, the Chinese, and the Finns (e.g., Marshall & Tucker, 1993; Reich, 1992). The competition among states for positional advantage in the global economy has spawned an educational arms race; the putative need for more and better education is called upon to justify increased state involvement in the education of its citizens.

Economics and the State's role

Is education a public good?

One generally acknowledged role for the state in the economy is the provision of public goods (Musgrave & Musgrave, 1980; Stiglitz, 2000). Consumption of these goods is nonrival: the amount consumed by one person has no effect on the amounts available for consumption by others. For example, adding more listeners to a radio broadcast does not diminish the value of the service to any of the existing listeners. Consumption of public goods is also nonexcludable: once a radio signal is broadcast there is no practical way to exclude additional listeners.

Private goods are both rival and excludable. The gallon of gas that a driver puts in his/her car is not available to other drivers, and the owner of the service station is readily able to exclude prospective consumers by demanding payment in advance. Private goods are efficiently provided through the familiar institutions of the market. Buyers and sellers have powerful incentives to reveal their true preferences, and their interactions determine how much of the good will be produced and sold.

Pure public goods must be financed by the state, as the price mechanism on which markets rely fails when goods are nonrival and nonexcludable. When consumption of a good is nonrival, it is not scarce to consumers; allocation of the good no longer depends on who has a stronger preference for it. When consumption of a good is nonexcludable, it is impossible to prevent consumers from making use of the good, whether they have paid for it or not. Under these circumstances, consumers will not reveal their true preferences. The incentives they face instead push them to become free riders, consuming as much as they like of the good while paying little or nothing to support its provision (Olson, 1971). As a result, reliance on markets to produce public goods will result in too little (or no) production of these goods.

Stiglitz (2000) classifies education as a publicly provided private good because there is a large marginal cost associated with educating each additional child, which makes education rival. Education is also excludable, as can be readily observed in private schools or in tuition-funded colleges and universities. Since education does not satisfy the economist's definition of a public good, it could in principle be bought and sold in a market much the same as other private goods. The argument for public provision must therefore be sought elsewhere, in the failure of markets to produce an optimal level of educational output or an equitable distribution of educational opportunities and outcomes.

Market failure in the market for education

Competitive markets may fail to deliver the optimal level of a good or service for a variety of reasons, including the presence of positive or negative externalities, information asymmetries between buyers and sellers, economies of scale, and risk aversion. Defenders of a strong state role in funding and providing schools argue that significant market failures in the market for education justify the state's involvement in the education system.

Externalities

Externalities exist when the private actions of one individual or firm affect others, either positively or negatively. For example, a farmer at the headwaters of a river decides how much water and fertilizer to use based on a private calculation of costs and benefits, without regard to the costs his/her decisions impose on fishermen and municipal water systems downstream. These external costs may be substantial, and state action may be the best way to ensure that they are taken into account (Coase, 1960).

Private decisions about education produce a number of mostly positive externalities for the broader society, above and beyond the benefits that the individual student receives. In considering how much education to consume, however, individuals base their decisions on their own private calculation of costs and benefits, taking no account of external benefits that may accrue to others. In consequence, leaving choices about education to individuals in a private market may result in a suboptimal level of educational investment for the society as a whole.

Economists have long recognized a number of positive externalities associated with an educated citizenry. In the *Wealth of Nations*, for example, Smith (1937) described two external benefits of education. First, he argued that education is a necessary antidote to the mind-numbing repetition that results from the division of labor into the narrowly specialized tasks performed by each worker. Workers lacking in education would eventually become unable to converse, formulate emotional sentiments, or perform the normal duties of private life, rendering them unable to defend the country in a time of war. In addition, Smith argued that modern education, including science and mathematics, would provide a constant source of innovation in the production process.

More recent work has identified a wide variety of additional external benefits to educational investment. In general, a literate society functions more smoothly, with reduced communications costs, stronger democratic institutions, and a higher degree of social cohesion (Belfield, 2000; Stiglitz, 2000). Education also has a strong positive impact on health and fertility, both within and across generations. Educated mothers have fewer, healthier children, and the children of educated mothers are more likely to enroll and remain in school (Becker, 1991; Colclough, 1993; Schultz, 1988). Barnett (1985, 1996) has documented the effect of education on reducing crime and welfare payments.

There is a vast macroeconomic literature that suggests that education is a key input that drives technological change and economic growth (Barro, 1997; Hall & Jones, 1999; Krueger & Lindahl, 2001; Mankiw, Romer, & Weil, 1992; Romer, 1990). To the extent that this is so, state action to expand and improve the education that citizens receive and thereby raise the rate of economic growth may be fully justified (and even financed) by the increased productivity and gross domestic product (GDP) growth produced by educational investments (Hanushek & Kimko, 2000).

Realizing the external benefits of education may require state action; the economic and social gains produced by an educated citizenry and workforce may justify the state in encouraging individuals to acquire more education than they might otherwise prefer. In a contrasting view, however, increasingly powerful private incentives to invest in education may be sufficiently strong to produce high levels of external benefit even in the absence of state action. The fundamental question with regard to externalities is therefore the extent to which they are extra-marginal: Does state subsidy or state provision produce external benefits in addition to those that would be produced through private action alone?

Information asymmetry

One of the conditions for the efficient operation of markets is complete information. In a perfectly competitive market, buyers and sellers are on equal footing; both have full information on the quality and price of the product.

In some markets, however, including for instance the market for used cars, sellers have more and better information about the product than prospective buyers. Markets in which the distribution of information is asymmetric may produce inefficient outcomes (Akerlof, 1970; Stiglitz, 1996).

The education system is clearly characterized by asymmetric information between the consumers of education services (parents) and the producers (schools). Education is a complex bundle of services that involves a large commitment of time, a cumulative instructional process, and uncertain future payoffs. The production process is poorly understood and output measures are ambiguous, which makes interschool comparisons difficult. As a result, parents face great difficulties in accurately assessing the quality of the education services provided by the various schools available to their children.

There are two main ways to address the problem of asymmetric information in the education system. On the one hand, the state may provide schools itself, seeking to standardize educational services and guarantee minimum quality standards across schools. For example, the state may regulate curricula, require certification for teachers, or equalize funding across schools or school districts (Brown, 1992). On the other hand, the state may seek to increase the information available to parents by publishing data on the character and performance of different schools. Recent advances in assessment and information technology make the latter choice increasingly feasible (Gintis, 1995).

Uncertainty and risk aversion

Brown (1992) applies the economics of uncertainty and information to education to show why the public provision of education is so widespread and why schools are so similar. Parents face uncertainty about their children's abilities and the future payoffs to investments in their education. Schools are better able to shoulder risk than their more risk-averse students, enabling them to offer actuarially fair insurance (Kreps, 1990; Mas-Colell, Whinston, & Green, 1995). There are two components to this insurance. First, the vast majority of schools offer a comprehensive and broadly similar curriculum, giving all students access to a wide array of courses and programs. In addition, schools generally allow their students to accumulate a diversified portfolio of educational experiences, rather than requiring them to specialize in a specific course of study. Private and charter schools must compete with public schools in providing this form of insurance, which results in the observed similarity between curricula in state and other schools.

More fundamentally, parents and students may not fully know their own preferences for education due to the complex and cumulative process of schooling. Students' consumption of education services often relies critically on the goodwill and competence of the parents, which cannot be assumed (Gintis, 1995; Stiglitz, 2000).

As it is difficult to collateralize loans for primary and secondary schooling, parents may face credit constraints as well. In light of these circumstances, public provision may be warranted as a protection against the long-term private and social costs of bad choices or constrained resources.

Economies of scale

Economies of scale arise when producers' average total cost falls as output increases (Mankiw, 1998). In education, this suggests that larger schools and districts may face a lower per-pupil cost. For example, larger schools have a greater ability to provide science laboratories and libraries by spreading the cost over more taxpaying households. There are also potential scale economies in information gathering, organization, and in the development of a curriculum (Belfield, 2000). To the extent that there are economies of scale in the delivery of education services, market forces may result in a monopoly, as smaller schools are driven out of business by established state schools. Faced with this tendency for the market to drive out small schools, the state has two options: either run large schools as state monopolies, or actively encourage competition by leveling the playing field for smaller schools.

Equity and equal opportunity

The state may also have an interest in making the distribution of educational opportunities and attainments more equitable. State actions to advance equity goals may take either of two forms. On the one hand, the state may seek to ensure that all young people are provided with an education of sufficient duration and quality to equip them for productive citizenship and protect them from poverty (e.g., Colclough, 1993). On the other hand, the state may seek to alter the distribution of wealth and status in favor of previously disadvantaged groups through the provision of targeted subsidies or other forms of affirmative action (e.g., Fiske & Ladd, 2004).

The state can in principle pursue equity objectives through public financing rather than public provision, by targeting subsidies to specific groups. As Davis (1998) points out, however, the government may be more effective than private markets at ensuring the fair allocation and distribution of resources, equal access to services, nonprofit decision making in the best interest of consumers, appropriate personnel policies, and cooperative labor relations (Belfield, 2000).

In the US, education is primarily a local responsibility, which has led to large differences in the resources devoted to education. Where these differences solely related to consumer preferences for education, there would be very little need for government intervention. In fact, however, a number of state supreme courts have ruled that reliance on local property taxes to finance education violates the provisions of state constitutions that guarantee equal access to public education (Odden & Picus, 2004; Stiglitz, 2000).

Critique of state provision

The claim that the state should finance the education of its citizens is rarely subject to argument. Controversy arises over whether the state should provide schools itself, or underwrite the provision of schools by other actors including for-profit firms. The argument turns on questions of the relative efficiency and equity effects of state and private provision.

Friedman (1962) revived the libertarian argument against government provision of education, which dates back to Thomas Paine (West, 1964) and Smith (1937). Friedman acknowledged two justifications for government involvement in education. First, he described the positive externalities produced by schools, which include the basic skills and core values required for social stability. Second, he noted the state's paternalistic concern for the welfare of children, whose parents may not always act in their best interest. Friedman argued that these concerns warrant state funding and minimal regulation in the education system, but not a government monopoly in the provision of schooling.

Public choice and government failure

In the decades since the publication of Friedman's seminal essay, economists and others have developed a comprehensive critique of state provision, closely associated with a call for greater reliance on markets in the education

system (e.g., Chubb & Moe, 1990). Just as the case for state provision relies on claims of market failure, the case against state provision relies on claims of government failure (Tullock, Seldon, & Brady, 2002), including inefficiency in production, inequity in provision, the institutionalization of low expectations, and rent-seeking by educators who exploit positions of authority and trust to increase their own utility at the expense of their students.

Inefficiency in production

State provision of schools may be less efficient than market provision for two main reasons. First, the absence of competition in the state education system undermines incentives for innovation and improvement. In a market where schools are obliged to compete with one another for the patronage of parents, in contrast, schools receive meaningful market signals about quality from consumers. The attendant challenge to compete for students should drive schools to lower costs, improve quality, and innovate (West, 1997). In the short run, competition might be expected to induce educators to work harder, to allocate resources more efficiently, and to make better staffing decisions. In the long run, a competitive market for education could make schools more receptive to parental involvement, give them incentives to provide better student achievement information, reward more productive teachers with higher wages, lead schools to abandon unproductive pedagogical techniques, and ultimately affect the size and number of schools (Hoxby, 2003).

To the extent that state action in the provision of education replaces private production, consumers of education must rely on political institutions to voice their preferences. With the specification of the educational production function uncertain, the use of resources is determined through political interaction, according to criteria that bear no necessary connection to valued outcomes including student learning

(Downs, 1957; Hanushek, 1986). The interplay of interests in the political system can easily lead to allocations of resources that are suboptimal from the standpoint of economic efficiency. For example, the free-rider problem may become a tax avoidance problem, as taxpayers seek to minimize the cost of educating other people's children (Tullock et al., 2002). At the same time, the state's obligation to exercise strict control over the use of public resources may result in excessive regulation and high administrative costs, without commensurate gains in productivity (Hanushek, 1986; Stiglitz, 2000).

Inequity in opportunities and outcomes

Advocates of market-based policies in education argue that greater reliance on markets could also improve the overall equity of the education system (Coons, Clune, & Sugarman, 1970; Howell & Peterson, 2002). Wealthy parents are able to choose the schools that their children attend, either by moving to a desirable school district or by sending their children to private schools. It is only the children of the poor who are deprived of choice under the current system of state provision, and these children are often obliged to attend the least-salubrious and lowest-performing schools (Ladd, 2002; McEwan, 2000). Opening up the system to additional providers would serve to increase the number and variety of schools available to poor households (e.g., Tooley & Dixon, 2005), giving parents more and better choices about the schools their children attend and increasing the chances of educational and subsequent economic success for poor children (West, 1997).

Standardization and enforced mediocrity

State efforts to standardize educational services and guarantee minimum educational standards for all students may reduce the quality of instruction for young people attending state schools (Finn, 1993; Ravitch, 1985). The state's obligation

to protect parents from risk and to ensure at least minimally equitable opportunities for students may prevent schools from accomplishing or even.

Seeking ambitious goals, preferring instead to institutionalize low expectations and low standards in an effort to ensure success for all of the children under their care. For example, the performance of American students on international assessments of reading and mathematics is often adduced as evidence of the disadvantages of state provision, to be remedied by the introduction of more choices and increased competition in the education system (e.g., Chubb & Moe, 1990; Walberg, 2007).

Rent-seeking and corruption

In the education system, as elsewhere in the public sector, individuals and groups may have opportunities to divert public resources to their own private benefit. Examples of rent-seeking may include widespread absenteeism among educators, who regard their jobs as sinecures and frequently fail to show up to teach their students or run their schools (Banerjee & Duflo, 2006; Castro & Fletcher, 1986). Transfer programs can be used to solicit political patronage rather than to improve the access to education of those in need (Plank, 1995). In similar fashion, unions may be more concerned with protecting the interests of their adult members than with the education of the children in their charge (Hess, 2004; Moe, 2001). Under some circumstances rent-seeking may give way to corruption, as educators employed by the state offer private instruction, passing grades, and diplomas for sale to students and households that are able to pay (Hallak & Poisson, 2007).

A role for the state?

Under some circumstances, the state may supply education more efficiently than private markets (Belfield, 2000). First, it can bundle other services with education, such as health screening for vision and hearing. As the government offers unemployment insurance and welfare benefits, public provision of education that reduces these fiscal obligations could also be seen as bundling education and social services. Second, if people perceive the state as having a long-term commitment to the education of its citizens, then the state may be trusted more than private firms that come and go in a competitive market. As Shleifer (1998) has argued, if consumers have a difficult time identifying quality then producers will struggle to build their reputations and be unable to increase demand for their services. Third, economies of scale could lead to an education monopoly, which might be better run by the state than by a profit-seeking firm. Fourth, government providers can mediate the asymmetry of information and bargaining power between schools and individuals.

Gintis (1995) acknowledges that markets may be more efficient and more responsive to parents' preferences. He simultaneously argues that extensive state action may be required to ensure that markets work efficiently and fairly.

He proposes some regulatory interventions aimed at expanding school choice while mitigating market failures caused by violations of five fundamental assumptions:

Many producers. First, the state could subsidize student transportation costs. Second, it could either offer low-interest loans to new schools or construct the buildings and rent them to providers. Third, the state could force schools to share classrooms, athletic facilities, or other resources in order to decrease the minimum feasible school size.

Product quality is known. In order to be accredited to accept public tuition, schools could be required to provide standardized measures of school performance such as test scores, retention rates, and graduation rates. Schools could also be required to provide data on teacher accreditation, building safety and instructional techniques.

Consumers know their preferences. A guardian should be appointed when parents are found legally incapable of making sound decisions for their children. Unscrupulous schools that mislead parents should be sanctioned and schools should be prohibited from pandering to selfish parents who place their personal interests before the best interests of their children (e.g., by accepting kickbacks).

The price is set so that supply equals demand. The price of schooling is the tuition fee, which is set and paid by the government. Economists worry that because parents do not pay for education, they may consume more than they would in the absence of a government subsidy. In the presence of positive externalities, however, it is widely assumed that parents consume too little education on behalf of their children, rather than too much.

Education is a private good. As education confers both private and social benefits, some worry that parents will focus exclusively on the private benefits when making schooling decisions. Regulation can increase the social benefits to education by requiring schools to develop a curriculum that reflects social values and providing incentives to schools that encourage a diverse student body.

Education and the shrinking state

After more than a century of steady growth, there are signs that the state's role in national education systems may have begun to shrink. As ever, there is little dissent from the idea that the state should finance the educational opportunities available to its citizens, but the benefits traditionally ascribed to state provision have been subjected to increasingly overt challenge. This is especially visible in higher education, where reduced public support for universities and their students has been matched by dramatic increases in the number and variety of private and for-profit higher education institutions (e.g., Altbach & Levy, 2005). Strong political pressures bolstered by arguments and evidence from economists (e.g., Barnett, 1985; Heckman & Masterov, 2007) to expand the state's role in early childhood and preschool education have run into significant opposition, based in part on resistance to increased taxes and public spending, and in part on aversion to the idea that very young children should be placed under the care of the state rather than their families and communities (Fuller, 2007). In Europe and elsewhere, groups defined by communal, religious, and linguistic affinities have begun to demand increased control over the education of their own children, including the right to establish their own schools (Plank, 2006). Whether this marks a genuine turning point in the history of education or a brief pause in the steady expansion of the state's role in the education system remains to be seen.

See also

Competition and Student Performance; Educational Privatization; Human Capital; The Economics of Catholic Schools; The Economics of Charter Schools; The Economics of Parental Choice; The Economics of School Accountability; The Efficacy of Educational Vouchers; The External Benefits of Education; Tiebout Sorting and Competition.

References

Akerlof, G. (1970). The market for 'lemons': Quality uncertainty and the market mechanism. *Quarterly Journal of Economics, 84*(3), 488–500.

Altbach, P., & Levy, D. (2005). *Private higher education: A global revolution.* Rotterdam: Sense Publishers.

Archer, M. (1982). *The sociology of educational expansion: Take-off, growth, and inflation in educational systems.* New York: Sage.

Banerjee, A., & Duflo, E. (2006). Addressing absence. *Journal of Economic Perspectives, 20*(1), 117–132.

Barnett, S. (1985). Benefit-cost analysis of the Perry preschool program and its policy implications. *Educational Evaluation and Policy Analysis, 7*(4), 333–342.

Barnett, S. (1996). *Lives in the balance: Age-27 benefit-cost analysis of the high/scope perry preschool program.* Ypsilanti, Ml: The High/Scope Press.

Barro, R. J. (1997). *Determinants of economic growth: A cross-country empirical study, lionel robbins lectures.* Cambridge, MA: MIT Press.

Becker, G. (1991). *A treatise on the family: Enlarged edition.* Cambridge, MA: Harvard University Press.

Belfield, C. (2000). *Economic principles for education: Theory and evidence.* Northhampton, MA: Edward Elgar Publishing.

Brown, B. (1992). Why governments run schools. *Economics of Education Review, 11*(4), 287–300.

Castro, C., & Fletcher, P. (1986). *A Escola que os Brasileiros Freqüentaram em 1985.* Brasilia: IPEA/IPLAN.

Chubb, J., & Moe, T. (1990). *Politics, markets, and America's schools.* Washington, DC: Brookings Institution.

Coase, R. (1960). The problem of social cost. *Journal of Law and Economics, 3*, 1–44.

Colclough, C. (1993). *Educating all the children: Strategies for primary schooling in the south.* Oxford: Clarendon Press.

Coons, J., Clune, W., & Sugarman, S. (1970). *Private wealth and public education.* Cambridge, MA: Harvard University Press.

Davis, E. (1998). *Public spending.* Harmondsworth, UK: Penguin.

Downs, A. (1957). *An economic theory of democracy.* New York: Harper Collins.

Finn, C. (1993). *We must take charge: Our schools and our future.* New York: Free Press.

Fiske, E., & Ladd, H. (2004). *Elusive equity: Education reform in post- apartheid South Africa.* Washington, DC: Brookings Institution Press.

Friedman, M. (1962). *Capitalism and freedom.* Chicago, IL: University of Chicago Press.

Fuller, B. (2007). *Standardized childhood: The political and cultural struggle over early education.* Stanford, CA: Stanford University Press.

Gintis, H. (1995). The political economy of school choice. *Teachers College Record, 96*(3), 1–20.

Hallak, J., & Poisson, M. (2007). *Corrupt schools, corrupt universities: What can Be done?* Paris: UNESCO.

Hall, R., & Jones, C. (1999). Why do some countries produce so much more output per worker than others? *Quarterly Journal of Economics, 114*(1), 83–116.

Hanushek, E. (1986). The economics of schooling: Production and efficiency in public schools. *Journal of Economic Literature, 24*, 1141–1177.

Hanushek, E., & Kimko, D. (2000). Schooling, labor-force quality, and the growth of nations. *American Economic Review, 90*(5), 1184–1208.

Heckman, J., & Masterov, D. (2007). *The productivity argument for investing in young children.* NBER Working Paper No.

13016. Cambridge, MA: National Bureau of Economic Research.

Hess, F. (2004). *Teacher quality, teacher pay.* Washington, DC: American Enterprise Institute. http://www.aei.org/publicatlons/filter. all,publD.20326/pub_detail.asp.

Howell, W., & Peterson, P. (2002). *The education gap: Vouchers and urban schools.* Washington, DC: Brookings Institution.

Hoxby, C. (2003). School choice and school productivity: Could school choice be a tide that lifts all boats? In C. Hoxby (Ed.), *The economics of school choice* (pp. 287–342). Chicago, IL: The University of Chicago Press.

Kreps, D. (1990). *A course in microeconomic theory.* Princeton, NJ: Princeton University Press.

Krueger, A., & Lindahl, M. (2001). Education for growth: Why and for whom? *Journal of Economic Literature, 39,* 1101–1136.

Ladd, H. (2002). School vouchers: A critical view. *Journal of Economic Perspectives, 16*(4), 3–24.

Mankiw, N. (1998). *Principles of microeconomics.* Orlando, FL: Dryden Press.

Mankiw, N., Romer, D., & Weil, D. (1992). A contribution to the empirics of economic growth. *Quarterly Journal of Economics, 107*(2), 407–437.

Marshall, R., & Tucker, M. (1993). *Thinking for a living: Education and the wealth of nations.* New York: Basic Books.

Mas-Colell, A., Whinston, M., & Green, J. (1995). *Microeconomic theory.* New York: Oxford University Press.

McEwan, P. (2000). The potential impact of large-scale voucher programs. Occasional Paper No. 2. In *The occasional paper series of the national center for the study of privatization in education.* New York: Teachers College, Columbia University.

Moe, T. (2001). Teachers unions and the public schools. In T. Moe (Ed.), *A primer on America's schools* (pp. 151–184). Stanford, CA: Hoover Institution Press.

Musgrave, R., & Musgrave, P. (1980). *Public finance in theory and practice* (3rd ed.). New York: McGraw-Hill.

Odden, A., & Picus, L. (2004). *School finance: A policy perspective* (3rd ed.). New York: McGraw-Hill.

Olson, M. (1971). *The logic of collective action: Public goods and the theory of groups.* Cambridge, MA: Harvard University Press.

Passin, H. (1965). *Society and education in Japan.* New York: Columbia University Press.

Plank, D. (1995). *TheMeansof our salvation: Public education in Brazil, 1930–1995.* Denver: Westview Press.

Plank, D. (2006). Unsettling the state: How 'demand' challenges the education system in the US. *European Journal of Education, 41*(1), 13–27.

Ravitch, D. (1985). *The troubled crusade: American education, 1945–1980.* New York: Basic Books.

Reich, R. (1992). *The work of nations: Preparing ourselves for 21st century capitalism.* New York: Vintage Press.

Romer, P. M. (1990). Endogenous technological change. *Journal of Political Economy, 98*(5 part 2), S71–S102.

Schultz, T. P. (1988). Educational investments and returns. In H. Chenery, & T. N. Srinivasan (Eds.), *Handbook of development economics* (Vol. 1, pp. 543–630). Amsterdam: North-Holland Press. Sections 2-S.

Shleifer, A. (1998). State versus private ownership. *Journal of Economic Perspectives, 12*(4), 133–150.

Smith, A. (1937). *An inquiry into the nature and causes of the wealth of nations* (Originally Published in 1776). New York: The Modern Library.

Stiglitz, J. (1996). *Whither socialism?* Cambridge, MA: MIT Press.

Stiglitz, J. (2000). *Economics of the public sector* (3rd ed.). New York: WW Norton.

Tooley, J., & Dixon, P. (2005). *Private education is good for the poor: A study of private schools serving the poor in low-income countries.* Washington, DC: Cato Institute.

Tullock, G., Seldon, A., & Brady, G. (2002). *Government failure: A primer in public choice.* Washington, DC: Cato Institute.

Tyack, D. (1974). *The one best system: A history of American urban education.* Cambridge, MA: Harvard University Press.

UNICEF. (2000). *Education for all: No excuses.* New York: UNICEF.

Walberg, H. (2007). *School choice: The findings.* Washington, DC: Cato Institute.

Weber, E. (1976). *Peasants into frenchmen: The modernization of rural France, 1870–1914.* Stanford, CA: Stanford University Press.

West, E. (1964). Private versus public education: A classical economic dispute. *Journal of Political Economy, 72*(5), 465–475.

West, E. (1997). Education vouchers in principle and practice: A survey. *World Bank Research Observer, 12,* 83–103.

CHAPTER

33

Quasi-markets in education: the case of England

Steve Bradley

Department of Economics, Lancaster University Management School, Lancaster, England

Introduction

It is several decades since a number of governments around the world began to increase the role of market forces in education. Several reasons can be put forward for such a radical transformation of education provision, particularly in the provision of primary and secondary sectors. First, the view that educational outcomes had plateaued, in the UK case starting from the early 1970s and continuing to the mid-1980s. Too many young people, it was argued, left compulsory schooling with few or no qualifications — the so-called 'long tail of low achievement', giving rise also to problems of illiteracy and innumeracy, truancy and high drop-out rates from secondary school, with subsequent links to juvenile crime. Furthermore, and second, too few young people progressed to further and then higher education (See Machin & Vignoles, 2004; Prais, 1995). A further manifestation of the performance of compulsory schooling was that the UK began to fall behind in international league tables with respect to maths and science test scores. The combined effect of the comparatively poor performance of compulsory schooling was

a relatively lower rate of vocational skills acquisition, creating a 'skills gap', which impeded productivity growth and, it was argued, comparatively lower economic growth rates. Similar arguments and reasoning prevailed in the US and elsewhere. Of course, a third reason for the radical transformation of compulsory schooling in the UK was undoubtedly political, insofar as right wing Conservative governments sought to roll back the influence of the state in the provision of education, thereby allowing market forces to flourish.

Prior to the introduction of market forces into primary and secondary education, governments typically regulated the content of provision through regulation of curricular and testing, the demand for education through compulsory attendance laws, and educational provision through funding. Proponents of market-based provision of compulsory education argued that state provision by local education districts and schools could, and had, reflected some of the worse features of monopolies that operated in the private sector. Therefore, although education districts did provide a range of educational services, and although some parents could sort between districts based on the quality of provision and parental incomes, it was still the case that, because all pupils were essentially 'allocated' to schools, the consequence was to ' … remove the incentive to provide the amount of output consistent with making consumers as well off as possible' (Betts, 2005, p. 21). In this case output refers to the quantity and quality of education and consumers are parents and, more directly, pupils. Furthermore, the lack of competition for students meant that schools often compromised by seeking to serve the needs of diverse groups of pupils, hence reducing innovation in the curriculum, accompanied by lower student educational outcomes. Local school districts also had to gather substantial information, and employ bureaucracies, in order to try to meet the needs of parents and pupils in delivering a 'quality' education. Such costs were deemed to be too high, and did not deliver 'value for money'. From an economic perspective, the provision of education was inefficient in both an allocative and productive (use) sense.

In sum, State financing and provision of compulsory education was seen to be failing in many countries.

The debate about the most appropriate way of organizing the education system has been ongoing for some time, but most recently can be traced back to the work of Friedman (1962) and West (1965, 1991). Friedman in particular advocated a market-based approach, in which decision-making on resource use, curriculum design and school choice, for instance, was decentralized leading to highly diversified educational provision. The objective was to drive efficiencies, in terms of resource allocation and use, increasing educational outcomes for all, including disadvantaged groups, while also trying to stimulate schools to innovate in their teaching practices and curriculum design.

The introduction of market forces into education has typically involved the decentralization of decision-making, reducing the power of 'local' bureaucracies and increasing the role of parents

and pupils — the consumers — and schools — the producers of slightly differentiated products sub-groups of the pupil population (Betts, 2005). Imperfect competition between schools for pupils drives efficiency gains at the school level and the costs of education district bureaucracies are reduced. Note that schools in a locality can be clustered within a hierarchy (Bagley, 2006), into non-competing groups, where competition occurs within a cluster, but cooperation can occur between schools in different clusters on a wide range of issues. Competition is also dynamic and Bagley (2006) provides detailed case study evidence for these views of competition between schools. Ultimately, educational outcomes were expected to improve. However, increasing the role of markets often comes at a price — in the case of educational provision - inequality of educational opportunity and educational outcomes. Thus, at the heart of the debate about the merit, or otherwise, of introducing market forces into education is the so-called 'efficiency-equity' trade-off in terms of outcomes.

In this chapter, we focus on the effect of introducing market forces into compulsory education in England. This is because countries differ with respect to the institutional arrangements that determine the 'rules of the game' with respect to the conduct and performance of agents, be they businesses, consumers or other types of agencies. It is no different for education markets, especially when the introduction of market forces into the provision of compulsory education is still, relatively speaking, still in its infancy, and when compared to the operation of markets in other sectors. Evaluating the effects of market forces in education have to, in some sense, 'control' for the institutional setting within which schools compete and parents and pupils make choices. This is more easily achieved by focusing upon a country where the institutional setting is more homogenous, and the 'rules of the game' are similar. Of course, there may be local variations in the application and interpretation of those 'rules' but these are more easily identified and understood in a single country context. Since England has experienced systemic educational reforms, it can be regarded as a 'laboratory' for testing and understanding whether the introduction of market forces delivered improvements in educational outcomes, in an efficient way, while avoiding increasing educational inequality.

We start by reviewing the reforms that led to the creation of a so-called quasi-market in compulsory education. This section seeks to address the question: how could the various educational reforms introduce market forces? We refer in this chapter to markets in the education context as quasi-markets following Le Grand (1991), Glennerster (1991) and Le Grand and Bartlett (1993). In the next section, analyze the empirical evidence on the effects of introducing quasi-markets, in terms of educational outcomes where we consider efficiency and equity perspectives. Since the introduction of market forces in 1988, the UK has seen different political parties in power, which have had different priorities for educational policy. In section 3, we investigate whether the introduction of other educational initiatives, or policies, have complemented or contradicted the attempt to create markets in education. Specifically, we identify policies which attempted to create greater collaboration, rather than competition, between schools, and it is necessary to understand the effects on educational outcomes. We end with our conclusions. The focus throughout is on primary and secondary education markets.

How could markets in education operate?

Alternative approaches

Market forces have been introduced in many English-speaking countries, such as New Zealand, the US and the UK, as well as countries as diverse as Sweden, Tanzania and Pakistan. Federal, state and national governments have created a wide range of mechanisms and policies in which to stimulate the introduction of market forces into the provision, and in some cases financing of, compulsory schooling. These range from the introduction of choice-based mechanisms, which also seek to stimulate competition for students between schools, through to what may be termed quasi-markets in education, in some senses a more complete market approach. Choice-based mechanisms include the provision of educational vouchers, which can be geared toward disadvantaged groups in society with a view to reducing segregation and closing ethnic and socio-economic 'ability gaps', as in the case of the US and Chile, for example, to the introduction of 'private' schools, such as Charter schools in the US, the purpose of which is to compete with public schools. In the case of the US, for instance, State level implementation of such choice-based mechanisms have varied, making comparison of their effects more difficult. In the UK context, the approach has been to introduce market forces into education provision, with central government providing the funding, which has given rise to a quasi-market solution.

Regardless of the approach to introducing market forces, school choice is inextricably linked with a wide range of other decisions that households, schools, education districts and governments might take. These include in the case of households their residential location decisions, which is itself partly a function of the quality of local schooling and local tax rates. Schools can still operate admissions policies, either explicitly in the case of faith and grammar schools in the case of the UK, or covertly when faced with excess demand for places, which gives rise to the phenomenon of 'cream skimming'. Administrators and policymakers within education districts can support the merger of schools, as well as the closure and re-location of a school, so changing the competitive landscape within an education market, or they can replace the leadership within a school. Governments also impact school choices when they implement policies on public transportation or housing construction. These decisions and policies interact with policies to introduce market forces into education provision, making the task of understanding how markets in education operate and their impact on educational outcomes — equity and efficiency broadly defined — very difficult. This is further reason for focusing on a single country.

Quasi-markets in England

In the UK, an educational reform program began in the early 1980s, however, perhaps the most important piece of legislation was the 1988 Education Reform Act. According to Kenneth Baker, then Secretary of State for Education (cited in Lawton, 1989), the Act sought to '... inject a new vitality into that system ...' and to '... create a new framework, which will raise standards, extend choice and produce a better informed Britain'. The Act simultaneously created a new framework for the provision of compulsory education based on the concept of the market, but also reduced the power of education districts, known in the UK as Local Education Authorities (LEA). Glennerster (1991) and Le Grand (1991) explain why the Education Reform Act of 1988 was not a full market solution, nevertheless, it did bring in sweeping changes to the operation of education districts, schools, parents and pupils. The reduction in the powers of education districts came with greater centralized control over the curriculum in terms of the introduction of a National Curriculum, which specified which subjects and the curriculum that schools should teach.

There have been a number of subsequent 'revisions' to the provision of primary and secondary education since the 1988 Education Reform Act. Table 33.1 shows the measures that were introduced by the 1988 Act and the subsequent policy interventions in the market up to the present day. In the remainder of this section we seek to explain how these policy reforms may have led to the creation of a market.

Table 33.1 attempts to show how each policy intervention, or reform, has contributed to the creation of a quasi-market.

Below, we distinguish here between the demand-side and the supply-side.

The supply side

On the supply side, three major changes eroded the power of education districts to control the provision of primary and secondary education. These were the introduction of *formula funding*, which was based on age-weighted pupil numbers at a school, Local Management of Schools (LMS), and the opportunity for schools to opt-out of education district (LEA) control completely in order to create a *Grant Maintained School*. This type of school was funded directly from central government rather than via the education district.

Levacic and Hardman (1998) investigate the impact of formula funding on school budgets for 300 secondary schools during 1991–96, and showed that changes in the school roll accounted for 60% of the average annual rate of change of a school's share of an education districts budget. Consequently, formula funding had a substantial year-on-year effect with respect to changes in school resourcing arising from the changes in school rolls (Whitty, Power, & Halpin, 1998). The opportunity to opt-out of education district control led to an increasing number of schools choosing to become grant-maintained, rising from 216 in 1992 to 638 in 1998. Alongside the reduction of education district control over education provision came increased school site governance, on the grounds that de-centralized decision-making would be more optimal with respect to the allocation of resources within the school (Levin, 1991a). The role and powers of school governors increased and, in collaboration with head teachers, took decisions regarding staffing, both promotion and redundancy and, subject to the school budget constraint, the

TABLE 33.1 Educational reforms, educational policies and the evolution of the Quasi-market in England.

Educational reform	Date	Pre-conditions for Quasi-markets:						
		Decentralized decision-making	Responsiveness	Incentives	Information	Choice	Voice	Co-operation
Formula funding	1988	x	x	—	—	—	—	—
Local management of schools	1988	x	—	—				
Open enrollment	1980s	—	x	x		x		
Opting-out/Grant maintained schools	1988	x	?		x	x		
School initiatives and policies:								
City technology colleges	1986					x		
Specialist schools	1993					x		
New grammar schools	1996					x		
Excellence in cities	1997				—		—	x
Academies	2010	x	?			x		x
Free schools	2010	x	?			x		
National curriculum/testing	1988							
School-site governance	1988	x					x	
School performance tables	1992		x	x	x			
Regulation/Ofsted publication of reports	1992		x	x	x			

This table uses some data from The Institute of Government (2012) report.

recruitment of additional staff (DES, 1988). Schools became far more accountable for resource use and for educational outcomes.

The introduction of 'open enrollment' of pupils removed the limit on the number of places available at a school, and when combined with formula funding, these reforms provided the necessary incentives for schools to recruit more pupils. Successful schools were expected to grow and increased resources would permit their expansion, whereas less successful schools had to improve to compete for pupils. Of course, in the short run schools did face capacity constraints arising from their physical space, however, over time schools could seek ways to increase their physical infrastructure.

The demand side

Waslander, Pater, and van der Weide (2010) refer to demand-side mechanisms which are fundamentally about parent and student choice of school. In the UK context, this means that in theory parents were free to choose a school for their child, rather than being allocated by the local education district, however, there are clearly constraints on that choice. The government guidance at the time stated that: '… no child should be refused admission to a school unless it is genuinely full' (DES, 1988). In practice, where schools were over-subscribed, or faced excess demand, then proximity to the school, the presence of siblings at the school and other admissions criteria could be applied. The consequences were likely to be cream-skimming by popular schools of the most able students.

The introduction of school site governance also meant that school decision-making was brought closer to the preferences of parents, which suggests that parents could, and do, have a greater say in curricular and co-curricular decisions (Levin, 1991b). Over time, even though a National Curriculum was in place, the content of the curriculum did become more varied between schools. The Specialist

school's initiative meant that schools could also specialize in particular subjects, such as languages, IT or science, helping to further differentiate themselves from competitor schools, and so giving more information to parents and students in exercising choice. Furthermore, in the absence of price differences between schools, if parents were to make informed choices, then information on all schools was needed on a consistent basis to allow comparisons to be made. The most explicit way in which this has been provided is through the annual publication of the School Performance Tables, which inevitably led to the publication of school league tables. One measure of school performance published in the performance tables was, and still is, the percentage of pupils achieving 5 or more GCSEs grades A*-C, although value added measures were subsequently included in the Tables.

For markets to function it is important that incentive structures exist and function effectively. The 1988 reforms ushered in a series of reforms which sought to change incentives for all agents operating in the education market. It was expected that parents would seek the best education for their children, and so they would respond in making a choice of school to the signals about school quality published in the Performance Tables. The incentives facing schools as a result of the reforms are more complex. Primarily, they have a greater incentive to provide a 'quality' education for their pupils to compete to attract students. Popular, or successful, schools were expected to attract more pupils, and financial resources then followed. Less popular schools, with relatively lower exam performance, must seek ways to improve their exam performance, or differentiate themselves in other ways, in order to maintain pupil numbers. Overall, average exam performance should increase. In terms of the objectives of local education districts under the reformed system of provision, it is clear that they must take a strategic view of education provision in their area. They clearly wish to see educational standards rise, however, competition between schools may create a real threat of closure for *failing* schools and the local education district must be centrally involved in decisions to rejuvenate by changing the leadership, merge or close such schools (DES, 1988).

The quasi-market may, however, have a 'self-adjusting mechanism', insofar as schools that become too big may jeopardize their educational standards, which in turn leads to falling applications. Schools may therefore face a trade-off between the number of pupils taught and performance in exams. Popular schools can manage this trade-off by becoming more selective in their recruitment of new pupils (West, Pennell, & Noden, 1998), given the physical capacity of a school. This behavior could lead to the education system becoming 'polarised', exhibiting greater segregation with respect to ability, socio-economic background or ethnic origin.

Regulation and monitoring of schools

While UK governments have increased the role of the market in the provision of education, they have also sought to regulate that provision. OfSTED is the UK body which periodically reviews each school's performance on a rolling 5–7 year cycle, and where schools are deemed to be 'failing' they do make interventions, including the removal of the school's management team. Moreover, OfSTED also publish the findings of their inspections of each school on the web, including a summative statement of performance ranging from 'outstanding' to 'unsatisfactory'. These findings assist parents in making a choice of school, however, they also impact the reputation of the school in the local education market, consequently affecting pupil recruitment. Indeed, Hussein (2016) finds that changes in inspection ratings impact on house prices, as well as school choice decisions by parents, and also relate to 'underlying school productivity'.

Test score outcomes

Fig. 33.1 shows, at a descriptive level, how education outcomes at secondary school level have improved since the 1988 Educational Reform Act, and is derived from data in Smithers (2014). There has been a dramatic increase in educational outcomes, but the question is, to what extent, if any, is this due to the introduction of market forces into secondary. Similar arguments apply to the primary school sector. A large literature now exists which tries to explain the contribution of aspects of the quasi-market on test score outcomes, however, as Bayer and MacMillan (2005) note it is important to evaluate the "… overall impact of increased choice on school performance [which] depends on demand and supply factors …" This means assessing the effect of increased choice of school on the competitiveness of the local education market, which impacts what they call the 'residual elasticity of demand for schools', and the effect of increased competition (the supply-side) on school performance. Many empirical studies investigate either

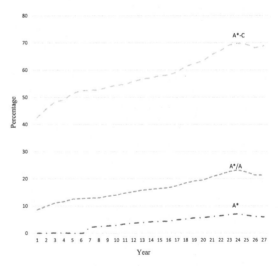

FIG. 33.1 Trends in GCSE passes. *Source:Derived from Smithers, A. (August 2014) GCSE trends 1988-2014, center for education and employment research: University of Buckingham.*

the demand side or the supply side which, according to Bayer and MacMillan provides 'indirect guidance' on the impact of increased choice, or market forces, on school performance and pupil test scores. With this caveat in mind, below we review in the next section those empirical studies of the quasi-market in primary and secondary sectors in England.

Evaluating the effects of Quasi-markets on educational outcomes

Most of the previous research in this area is based on the US, with very little evidence for the UK Nevertheless, we focus here on the evidence for the UK, whereas the chapter in this volume by Foliano and Silva (2019) discusses the broader literature on the effects of competition on pupil and school level educational outcomes. Their chapter also discusses the statistical problems that arise when trying to measure and identify causal effects of competition on educational outcomes.

Does the market operate?

Before we consider the effects of competition between schools on educational outcomes, or assess whether parents and pupils actually exercise choice of primary and/or secondary school, it is necessary to ask the more fundamental question of whether the reforms above actually succeeded in introducing market forces.

Bradley, Crouchley, Millington, and Taylor (2000) test to see whether quasi-market forces were present in the early stages of the education market in secondary education. They looked at the impact of competition between schools on test scores and the effect of competition on social segregation of pupils (see below), however, they examined changes in school enrollments and changes in the physical size of schools (i.e. capacity). They find, using school-level data for a short time period (1992—98) that new admissions to a school is positively related to a school's test score

performance and negatively related to that of competing schools in the same market, and these effects got stronger over time. The impact of competition was small, however, schools with relatively better test score performance did grow faster, including an increase in physical capacity. They conclude that these results suggested that a market in secondary education was operating.

Other research investigated the impact of changes in school governance i.e. the possibility for schools to opt out of education district control and become Grant Maintained. The objective of this reform was to simultaneously improve a school's performance, while also increasing competitive pressure on other schools in the expectation that they would also improve and/or opt-out. Clark (2009) shows that of the 2500 secondary schools in England around one-third of mainly high performing schools, chose to opt out between 1988 and 1998, which is a significant number. His results suggest that there were 'dramatic gains in student achievement' for schools that opted-out. This improvement emerged soon after the school had opted out (year 2) and persisted for at least 8 years. The gain in performance equated to 0.25 of a standard deviation in examination pass rates. Schools which opted out also witnessed increases in enrollments, albeit modest (5% per annum on an average base average enrollment of 176 pupils), and the effect of improvements in test score performance on enrollments was positive but also modest.

The effect of competition between schools

The effects of competition between schools on education outcomes has been investigated at the pupil and school level for both primary and secondary schools. Allen and Burgess (2014) provide a review the evidence for four countries (Chile, England, the US and Sweden). In contrast to the US and Sweden, where the evidence is mixed, they note that in the case of England there is limited evidence of an effect of competition from neighboring schools on pupil performance in a particular school. They also note the difficulty of identifying causal effects of competition on pupil test scores.

In a series of school level analyses for England, the impact of competition between schools on school outcomes - the percentage of pupils obtaining five or more GCSEs at grades A* to C has been investigated (Bradley et al. 2000, 2001; Bradley & Taylor, 2002). The data refer to over 3000 publicly funded secondary schools in England observed annually between 1992 and 2006. Bradley et al. (2000) and Bradley and Taylor (2002) focus on the impact of the quality of rival schools' output (i.e. exam performance) on a school's own exam performance. They show that an improvement of 3% points in the exam performance of a school's competitors is followed by an improvement of 1% point in the school's own exam performance. Thus, competition between schools does appear to improve the exam performance of pupils, but these effects are small in magnitude.

Gibbons, Machin, and Silva (2008a) use secondary school pupil-level, and show that educational progress is faster in more densely populated areas (with an elasticity of only +0.02). As Allen and Burgess (2014) note, this '... positive cross-sectional effect falls somewhere between the positive estimate of Bradley et al. (2001) and the null finding of Levačić (2004)'. Gibbons, Machin, and Silva (2008b) investigate the relationship between population density, competition and test scores for London. In an attempt to identify a causal relationship, they use the distance of a school from its nearest education district boundary as an instrumental variable to predict the amount of competition it faces. Competition between schools has no effect on a school's own performance, although a positive effect of competition from religious schools is found. Burgess and Slater (200?) find similar evidence in the case of Berkshire which in 1998 was split into six separate educational districts, implying a fall in the level of competition.

However, a more in-depth study of faith schools by Allen and Vignoles (2009) finds no evidence that proximity to a faith school induces an increase in educational outcomes in neighboring schools.

Many of the above studies explicitly, or implicitly, define an education market as an education district. However, it is perhaps inappropriate to adopt this definition of a market if pupils can cross education district boundaries to attend a school of their choice. Alternatively, competition may occur between sub-sets of schools within an education district. Bradley et al. (2001) adopt a different approach. The former study models of 'spatial' competition between schools by constructing a set of overlapping education markets, which enables them to examine whether the effect of competition decays with distance. The effect of competition between schools is then reflected by a) the number of non-selective schools in each spatially delimited education market, and also by b) the number of selective schools. A school's exam performance is found to be positively related to the intensity of local competition. This approach is taken further Bradley et al. (2001), who first obtain school 'efficiency' scores for all secondary schools, based on multiple school outcomes — test scores and the attendance rate -, and then show that the degree of competition is found to be an important determinant of the *change* in technical efficiency over time. This study also found evidence that less efficient schools had improved by more than the most efficient schools over the study period.

Do parents actually exercise choice and does this make a difference to test score outcomes?

Do parents value schools and their performance? Are parents actually sensitive to differences in school performance? If parents are able to exercise their choice of preferred school, are test score outcomes of their offspring improved? Researchers have sought to answer these questions by investigating the impact of school quality on house prices, controlling for other neighborhood, amenity and housing characteristics.

As suggested above, housing decisions are often made partly on the basis of the quality of the schools in a neighborhood. In the absence of more direct, system-wide, information on parental choice of school, some researchers have used house prices as an indirect indicator. For instance, Black (1999) uses house prices to infer the value parents place on school quality, the latter proxied by test scores. She finds a strong relationship between house prices and test scores insofar as a 5% increase in test scores leads to a 2.1% rise in house prices. Cheshire and Sheppard (2004) estimate a house price differential of 19% between a location in the vicinity of the worst performing secondary school and the location of the best performing school. Machin (2011) reviews the evidence on the relationship between housing valuations and school quality, and shows that for a number of countries there is a strong preference by parents for good schools. Focusing on studies that identify causality, and hence address the problems of endogenous school quality and omitted variable bias, it is shown that a consensus estimate is a 3–4% house price premium for a one standard deviation increase in school quality.

For England, Gibbons and Machin (2003) investigate the relationship between property prices and primary school attainment for London, using regression discontinuity techniques at education district boundaries, and show that a 1% increase in test scores at age 7 leads to a 2.8% increase in the log of house prices, whereas a 1% increase in the value-added score between the ages of 7 and 11 lead to a 3.7% increase in log house prices. Parents do value good schools.

In responding to claims made in the 2005 White Paper (Higher Standards, Better Schools for All), which argued that the majority of parents wanted a real choice of school, Exley (2012) uses the British Social Attitudes Survey (2010) which directly asks parents about their views on school choice. It is shown that 67% of 1870 respondents, believed that they have a '... basic right to choose their school ...', however, it is also shown that parents want schools to ensure that all pupils are helped by schools to 'do the best they can', and there was a strong view that pupils should go to their local school, especially where they could not afford to travel to more distant schools. Nevertheless, 40% of pupils avoided the nearest state school because of poorer exam performance. This suggests that there is mixed evidence on the desire for choice.

In a series of papers, Allen and Burgess have investigated the impact of School Performance Tables (SPTs) on school choice, as well as the consequences of actual school choice. Allen and Burgess (2011 and 2013) address the question: Can school league tables help parents choose schools? They show that about 50% of pupils/parents say they use the SPTs, and in particular school outcomes measures, such as the percentage of pupils achieving 5+A-C GCSE scores, and to a lesser extent value added by the school. Based on a single cohort of pupils (500,000) making a choice of secondary school, they show that SPTs do not score well on all three of the criteria by which they judge them - 'functionality', 'relevance' (informs about similar local children) and 'comprehensibility' (provides a useful information metric). None of the main performance measures score well on all three. The SPT are shown to be functional in helping parents make school choices. They are limited with respect to comprehensibility and relevance. Consequently, they conclude that current items to facilitate choice in the SPT are deficient in one way or another. However, using the SPTs is 'strongly better than choosing at random' (Allen & Burgess, 2013).

Allen and Burgess (2014) reports on earlier research where they ask 'what if' a pupil had been re-assigned to a higher performing school, hence addressing the outcomes of choices?

They note that between 5 and 10% of secondary and primary school pupils could have gone to a better school, and this is particularly the case for disadvantaged and black pupils. Indeed, in some education districts, there could have been, on average, gains of between 10 and 20% of a pupil standard deviation of GCSE points score if they gone to a higher performing school. For primary schools this effect rises to 30–40% of a standard deviation, and reallocation to a better performing school would have benefited pupils from disadvantaged backgrounds.

Do market forces lead to inequality or segregation?

Research shows that the segregation of pupils between high performing and low performing schools based on some form of disadvantage (i.e. a pupil's social background, ethnicity or immigrant status) does lead to lower overall test scores from the school system, and serves to exacerbate the so-called 'achievement gap' between the advantaged and disadvantaged pupils, for example (Gorard, 2016).

A reasonably extensive literature now exists on the effects of the market on educational inequality, or more precisely the effect of markets on the segregation of pupils between schools based on social, ethnic or ability lines. Gorard (2016) describe trends in segregation between schools within education markets over the long-term (1989–2014), and reveals similar trends for primary and secondary schools. At the national level, Gorard shows that there is a persistent minimum level of pupil segregation of 30%, when based on Free School Meal (FSM) eligibility or take-up (i.e. measures of poverty). However, this level of segregation is unlikely to be due to market forces but more likely to be the result of the business cycle — as household income falls in recessions, more pupils are caught by the FSM net. At the local level, however, Gorard argues the strongest correlations are between pupil segregation and local school types, where segregation is lowest where there are more schools controlled by a local education district with comprehensives. Other factors, such as residential segregation patterns and the quality of transport links also contribute to pupil segregation but are less amenable to change via educational policy whereas the school mix can be changed. Gorard, Hardosy and Huat-See (2013) also show that there is variation in the level of pupil segregation over time with respect to ethnicity and second language status, and this has fallen between 1998 and 2011 possibly due to the relaxation of school admission policies, following government intervention during the period 2003–07.

Burgess, Propper, Slater, and Wilson (2005) show for England that schools tend to be more segregated than neighborhoods, implying substantial intra-neighborhood sorting of pupils, which is greatest in more densely populated areas with a larger number of 'autonomous' schools. Similarly, voluntary-aided, faith, schools tend to select pupils from higher socio-economic groups (Allen & West, 2010). Gorard, Hardosy, and See (2013) describe trends in segregation in terms of socio-economic and ethnic groups, for instance, and suggest that it is not school choice, or more generally the market, that is the cause of increased segregation. They argue that the cause is the diversity of the schooling provision in education markets, reflected in the mix of faith, grammar and other types of school.

The effects of complementary and contradictory educational policies

The 1988 Education Reform Act introduced a number of educational reforms that attempted to create markets in the provision of primary and secondary education markets. We have explored how these different policy initiatives individually and collectively worked to determine test score outcomes, parental choice and social segregation. However, the policy stance on markets in education has not always been entirely consistent over time between governments of different political persuasions. True, there has been no attempt to 're-nationalize' education provision, however, some have identified phases over the last 30 years where collaboration, rather than competition, between schools has been dominant (The Institute for Government (2012).

Various policies have encouraged a mixture of collaboration between schools (e.g. Excellence in Cities initiative, EiC), or they have sought to differentiate schools in terms of their offer to pupils and parents (e.g. Specialist Schools Program, SSP), although often there was a mixture of the two. More recent initiatives have been the Academies Program, initially designed to support 'failing' schools precluded from participation in the SSP, and the proposal to expand Grammar Schools which are highly selective with respect to academic ability. We review the evidence on the effects of these initiatives on pupil and school performance, while also answering the question as to whether they complemented or contradicted the thrust to increase market forces in education.

The Specialist Schools policy was introduced in 1993, building on the City Technology Colleges, with the aim of differentiating secondary schools with respect to curriculum specialization, hopefully improving allocative efficiency by better matching of pupil's skills and the expertize of schools. Schools could seek to specialize in subjects such as, IT, business, maths or languages. Those maintained schools that were admitted to the program had to raise £50,000 in private funding, which was matched by £100,000 from central government plus £130 per pupil for 4 years. Schools had autonomy on how these extra funds could be used. Differentiation through specialization implies greater parental choice and hence could be seen as a way of enhancing the role of the market, however, specialist schools were also expected to share good practice with other schools, implying co-operation.

Bradley, Migali, and Taylor (2012) evaluate the effect of the SSP on pupil test scores, and also seek to disaggregate the funding from the specialization effects. They show that specialist schools have a small causal effect on test scores of around 0.4−0.9 GCSE points, while also showing that the duration of participation in the SSP was important. This finding is consistent with that of Schagen and Goldstein (2002), who show that the program increased GCSE points by between 0.2−0.11. Pupils from poorer backgrounds benefited most from attending schools in the program. The specialization effect, which could be regarded as a market-orientated effect, accounted for between 20 and 50% of the total test score effect, which is imprecize but indicative. There have been no attempts to evaluate the effect of introducing a specialist school into a local education market on the performance of competing schools.

As a response to the plight of disadvantaged secondary school pupils mainly in poorer urban areas, the Labor Government introduced its EiC policy with a view to creating Education Action Zones, which was launched in 1999 for secondary schools and extended to primary schools in 2001. The policy sought to develop different learning and teaching approaches for low and high ability pupils in selected schools, including learning mentors, learning support units and a Gifted and Talented Program. Extra resources for schools followed from central government to support these initiatives. However, since all schools in poorer education districts were included in the initiative, Machin, McNally, and Meghir (2004) also note that '... cooperation between schools [was expected] in the dissemination of knowledge ...' There have been two major evaluations of the impact of the EiC policy on pupil test score outcomes. The first by Machin et al. (2004) who, using matching methods coupled with difference-in- difference techniques, evaluated the pilot phase of the program and shows that the policy improved test scores at age 14 (i.e. Key Stage 3) by 0.3 of a level in Maths, or put differently, the EiC policy increased the number of pupils moving up a level by 3%. Weak effects were observed for English, but the effect on truancy was large and negative. A second study by Machin, McNally, and Meghir (2010) evaluated the different phases of the EiC covering the period 1999–2001. The outcome of interest was whether pupils achieved the government target of level 5 in Maths and English in KS3 by age 14. The policy increased the probability of a pupil achieving level 5 Maths by 1.9% points, and duration of time a school was in the program mattered. For instance, schools in the first phase of the program (starting September 1999) witnessed a 2.9pp increase in the probability of level 5 Maths attainment, which fell to 1.5pp for phase 2 schools (2000) with little effect for phase 3 (2001) schools. The effects of the policy were higher for medium-high ability pupils. No effects were observed for attainment in English. Bradley and Taylor (2010), using a panel of English schools in for the period 1992–2006, find that only around a third of the increase in test scores could be attributed to the effects of increased competition between schools, the EiC and specialist school policies.

Nevertheless, these studies show that increasing resources to schools does make a difference, especially for medium-high ability disadvantaged pupils, however, what is less certain is the impact of cooperation between schools. As far as we know, there have been no quantitative studies that have sought to measure the impact of cooperation, versus competition, on pupil or school performance. Furthermore, these two approaches to improving school performance are not always incompatible. For example, one secondary school head responded: "We have been heavily involved in the Excellence in Cities initiative and were part of an Excellence Cluster, but if you are not full on your first choices and the school down the road is taking them, then you can talk about collaboration all you want, but what you are actually doing is competing." (cited in Bagley, 2006).

A small but growing literature has developed which evaluates the Academies Schools policy (see Machin & Vernoit, 2010 and, 2011; Eyles & Machin, 2019), which increased school autonomy, and the evolution of this policy is discussed in Foliano and Silva (2019) in this volume, hence we do not review this initiative here. They also review the empirical evidence on the causal effects of this policy on test score outcomes, whereas Gorard and his co-authors provide more descriptive evidence. See also Eyles, Hupkau, and Machin (2016) who compare the effects on educational outcomes of academies, charter and free schools.

Conclusions and future research

This chapter has reviewed the evolution of the quasi-market in primary and secondary education in England. The evidence suggests that the intention of governments to introduce market forces into education has materialized, at least in part. In terms of the effects of these market forces on test score outcomes, it has been shown that competition for pupils between schools has had a small positive effect, however, this has come at a cost of increased segregation of pupils based on social class. Research on both of these themes continues.

Allen and Burgess (2014) review the obstacles to the operation of a quasi-market and suggest several reforms to the operation of the market to help improve it. Poorly performing schools, it is argued are under insufficient pressure to improve because not all parents get their first choice thus admissions to poor schools are maintained. Perhaps in response to this finding, the 2006 Education and Inspections Act for England was supposed to mitigate some of limitations of the quasi-market by enhancing competition between schools. One measure introduced by the Act was increased government funding of school transport costs for pupils from disadvantaged backgrounds, thereby extending the choice set of schools. A second measure was the introduction of school choice advisers to boost the know-how of parents and pupils vis-à-vis school performance, again focused on disadvantaged families. To control the practice of cream skimming by schools, the Act introduced a stricter mandatory admissions code. Le Grande also notes a further change in the form of a 'positive discriminating voucher', including fairer funding of disadvantaged pupils, which was designed to encourage schools to admit these pupils. See Allen and Burgess (2014) for further discussion of this issue.

Further research should consider the long-term effects of the quasi-market on educational outcomes, which has been only partly considered in the context of trends in social segregation, whereas more could be done with respect to test score outcomes. Similarly, there has been no attempt that we are aware of which attempts to compare the impact of markets in primary versus secondary school sectors. Both would be useful in order to further evolve the role of markets in education.

References

Allen, R., & Burgess, S. (2011). Can school league tables help parents choose schools? *Fiscal Studies, 32*, 245–262.

Allen, R., & Burgess, S. (2013). Evaluating the provision of school performance information for school choice. *Economics of Education Review, 34*, 175–190.

Allen, R., & Burgess, S. (January 2014). *School performance and parental choice of school: Secondary data analysis, Research Report*. Department for Education.

Allen, R., & Vignoles, A. (2009). *Can school competition improve standards? The case of faith schools in England*. DoQSS Working Paper No. 09/04.

Allen, R., & West, A. (2010). *Why do faith secondary schools have advantaged intakes? The relative importance of neighbourhood characteristics, social background and religious identification amongst parents*. Mimeo.

Bagley, C. (2006). School choice and competition: A public-market in education revisited. *Oxford Review of Education, 32*, 347–362.

Bayer, P., & MacMillan, R. (2005). *Choice and competition in local education markets*. Working Paper 11802. Cambridge MA: NBER.

Betts, J. R. (2005). The economic theory of school choice, Chapter 2. In J. R. Betts, & T. Loveless (Eds.), *Getting choice right: Ensuring equity and efficiency in education policy*. Washington DC: Brookings Institute Press.

Black, S. E. (1999). Do better schools matter? Parental valuation of elementary education. *Quarterly Journal of Economics, 114*, 578–599.

Bradley, S., Crouchley, R., Millington, J., & Taylor, J. (2000). Testing for quasi-market forces in secondary education. *Oxford Bulletin of Economics and Statistics, 62*, 357–390.

Bradley, S., Johnes, G., & Millington, G. (2001). The effect of competition on the efficiency of secondary schools in England'. *European Journal of Operational Research, 135/3*, 99–122.

Bradley, S., Migali, G., & Taylor, J. (2012). An evaluation of the impact of funding and school specialisation and student performance using matching models. *Journal of Human Capital, 7*, 76–106.

Bradley, S., & Taylor, J. (2002). Quasi-market forces and the efficiency-equity trade-off'. *Bulletin of Economic Research, 54*, 295–314.

Bradley, S., & Taylor, J. (2010). Diversity, choice and the quasi-market: An empirical analysis of secondary education policy in England. *Oxford Bulletin of Economics and Statistics, 72*, 1–26.

Burgess, S., Propper, C., Slater, H., & Wilson, D. (2005). *Who wins and who loses from school accountability?*. CMPO Discussion Paper 05/128.

Cheshire, P., & Sheppard, S. (2004). Capitalising the value of free schools: The impact of supply characteristics and uncertainty. *Economic Journal, 114*, F397–F424.

Clark, D. (2009). The performance and competitive effects of school autonomy. *Journal of Political Economy, 117*, 1262–1289.

Department of Education and Science. (1988). *Education reform: The government's proposals for schools*. London: HMSO.

Exley, S. (2012). *Are quasi-markets in education what the British public wants?*. Don't quote.

Eyles, A., Hupkau, C., & Machin, S. (2016). Academies, Charter and Free school: Do new school types deliver better outcomes? *Economic Policy, 31*, 453–501.

Eyles, A., & Machin, S. (2019). The introduction of academy schools to England's education. *Journal of the European Economic Association, 17(4)*, 1107–1146.

Foliano, F., & Silva, O. (2019). School competition and educational standards. In S. Bradley, & C. P. Green (Eds.), *Economics of education* (2nd ed.). Amsterdam: Elsevier.

Friedman, M. (1962). *Capitalism and freedom*. Chicago: Chicago University Press.

Gibbons, S., & Machin, S. (2003). Valuing English primary schools. *Journal of Urban Economics, 53*, 197–219.

Gibbons, S., Machin, S., & Silva, O. (2008a). Competition, choice and pupil achievement. *Journal of the European Economic Association, 6*, 912–947.

Gibbons, S., Machin, S., & Silva, O. (2008b). *Does additional spending help urban schools? An evaluation using boundary discontinuities?*. CEE Discussion Paper. No. 128. London School of Economics.

Glennerster, H. (1991). Quasi-markets for education. *Economic Journal, 101*, 1268–1276.

Gorard, S. (2016). The complex determinants of school intake characteristics and segregation, England 1989—2014. *Cambridge Journal of Education, 46,* 131—146.

Gorard, S., Hardosy, R., & See, B. H. (2013). Narrowing the determinants of segregation between schools 1996—2011. *Journal of School Choice, 7,* 182—195.

Hussein, I. (July 23, 2016). *Do consumers respond to short-term innovations in school productivity? Evidence from the housing market and parents' school choices.* Working Paper, Department of Economics, University of Sussex.

Institute for Government. (2012). *The development of quasi-markets in secondary education.* London: England.

Lawton, D. (1989). *The Education Reform Act: Choice and Control.* London: Hodder and Stoughton.

Le Grand, J. (1991). Quasi-markets and social policy. *Economic Journal, 101,* 1256—1267.

Le Grand, J., & Bartlett, W. (1993). The theory of Quasi-markets, Chapter 2. In J. LeGrand, & W. Bartlett (Eds.), *Quasi-markets and social policy.* London: Macmillan.

Levačić, R. (2004). Competition and the performance of English secondary schools: further evidence. *Education Economics, 12*(2), 177—193.

Levacic, R., & Hardman, J. (1998). Competing for resources: The impact of social disadvantage and other factors on English secondary schools' financial performance. *Oxford Review of Education, 24,* 303—328.

Levin, H. (1991a). The economics of educational choice. *Economics of Education Review, 10,* 137—158.

Levin, H. (1991b). Views on the economics of educational choice: A reply to west. *Economics of Education Review, 10,* 171—175.

Machin, S. (2011). Houses and schools: Valuation of school quality through the housing market. *Labour Economics, 18,* 723—729.

Machin, S., McNally, S., & Meghir, C. (2004). Improving pupil performance in English secondary schools: Excellence in cities. *Journal of the European Economic Association, 2,* 396—405.

Machin, S., McNally, S., & Meghir, C. (2010). Resources and standards in urban schools. *Journal of Human Capital, 4,* 365—93.

Machin, S., & Vernoit, J. (2010). *A note on academy school policy.* http://cep.lse.ac.uk/pubs/download/pa011.pdf.

Machin, S., & Vernoit, J. (2011). *Changing school autonomy: Academy schools and their introduction to England's education.* London School of Economics. CEE Discussion Paper. No. 123.

Machin, S., & Vignoles, A. (2004). Educational inequality: The widening socio-economic gap. *Fiscal Studies, 25,* 107—128.

Prais, S. J. (1995). *Productivity, education and training.* Cambridge: Cambridge University Press.

Schagen, I., & Goldstein, H. (2002). Do specialist schools add value? Some methodological problems. *Research Intelligence, 80,* 12—15.

Smithers, A. (August 2014). *GCSE trends 1988—2014, centre for education and employment research.* University of Buckingham.

Waslander, S., Pater, C., & van der Weide, M. (2010). *Markets in education: An analytical review of empirical research on market mechanisms in education".* OECD Education Working Papers, No. 52. OECD Publishing.

West, E. G. (1965). *Education and the state.* Institute for Economic Affairs.

West, E. G. (1991). Public schools and excess burdens. *Economics of Education Review, 10,* 159—69.

West, A., Pennell, H., & Noden, P. (1998). School admissions: Increasing equity, accountability and transparency. *British Journal of Educational Studies, 46,* 188—200.

Whitty, G., Power, S., & Halpin, D. (1998). *Devolution and choice in education: The school, the state and the market.* Open University Press Buckingham.

Tiebout sorting and competition

Thomas J. Nechyba

Duke University, Durham, NC, United States

Over 60 years ago, Charles Tiebout hypothesized that decentralized provision of public services (such as public schools) through local governments can result in efficient levels of such services (Tiebout, 1956). His key insight was that residential mobility of households might provide a disciplining force analogous to typical market forces under perfect competition in private goods markets. Local communities are viewed as analogous to competing shopping malls (that offer different mixes of services and stores) which compete with one another while at the same time appealing to somewhat different clienteles. By considering the mix of local taxes and public services much as they consider the mix of services and goods at malls, households in effect "vote with their feet", choosing locations that best meet their needs while making it difficult for local governments to engage in excessive rent-seeking.

Such Tiebout competition has three essential features: First, in the presence of heterogeneous demands for public services, decentralization permits the emergence of heterogeneous packages of such services and taxes across communities, providing opportunities for households to match to communities that are optimal from their perspective. Second, the resulting competition between communities for residents reduces the scope for local governments to focus on inefficient behavior that is not aimed directly at meeting the needs of their "customers". These two features combine to form the Tiebout hypothesis that competition between communities can provide a sufficient array of choices to satisfy heterogeneous household needs in a productively efficient manner. At the same time, however, demand is determined in part by ability-to-pay — which implies a third feature of such Tiebout competition: sorting will occur at least in part on the basis of household income.

Since Tiebout's original article, it has become clear that his insights have considerable empirical support. In the area of public education, however, it is far from clear that the results from Tiebout competition are as unambiguously desirable as might have been originally assumed. This is in large part due to the nature of education production that involves financial and non-financial scarce resources which are rationed through the same Tiebout forces that cause households to sort across communities. While such sorting indeed occurs along the lines suggested by Tiebout, much of it is related to household income and race — and this implies an equilibrium public school system in which public school quality invariably becomes highly correlated with these household characteristics

The Economics of Education, Second Edition
https://doi.org/10.1016/B978-0-12-815391-8.00034-3

even when higher level governments equalize financial resources available to local public schools. The equity concerns that arise from residential Tiebout segregation (and the resulting sorting of non-financial inputs into schools) may then need to be balanced with any efficiency gains from sorting and from competitive pressures on school producers.

Residential mobility, capitalization and household preferences for education

The earliest empirical tests of the Tiebout Hypothesis (that decentralized provision results in efficiency) were, in many ways, only tests of the underlying Tiebout *assumption* of residential mobility. These tests, beginning with Oates (1969), took the form of tests for the capitalization of inter-jurisdictional differences in local service and tax levels into house prices. The only mechanism that would give rise to such capitalization is precisely the one that arises from Tiebout's assumption of residential mobility. If households indeed consider local service and tax levels as they determine their optimal residential location, it was argued, then identical houses in different jurisdictions will be priced differently depending on these jurisdictional variables. At the same time, as was first pointed out by Edel and Sclar (1974) in a response to Oates, the presence of such capitalization can be interpreted as evidence against Tiebout's larger efficiency hypothesis. This is because capitalization of public service and tax levels suggests there is room in the "market" for additional communities to form — with the increased supply of housing attached to such service and tax levels driving capitalization to zero under free entry of new communities. The presence of capitalization therefore suggests a violation of free entry of new providers — a central feature required for efficiency to emerge in competitive markets. A more careful theoretical exploration of capitalization under Tiebout competition, reviewed in more detail by Epple and Nechyba (2004), then clarified some of the initial confusion over the relationship between empirical findings of capitalization and the validity of the larger Tiebout hypothesis.

The empirical literature on capitalization of local services in general, and of school quality in particular, is substantial and has increased in sophistication since Oates' original paper. Black (1999), for instance, introduced a particularly useful innovation by considering housing price differences immediately around district boundaries rather than comparing housing across districts more generally — thus limiting the analysis to houses that arguably differ primarily in terms of the access they provide to local schools. This boundary discontinuity design has since been generalized in more structural models that attempt to directly estimate household preferences for school and neighborhood characteristics rather than merely identifying the magnitude of capitalization into housing prices (Bayer, Ferreira, & McMillan, 2007). Although magnitudes differ, the qualitative finding of school capitalization effects has been robust across all research designs and across countries (Black & Machin, 2011). More importantly, however, the most recent literature directly confirms the importance of household preferences for both schools and neighbors, a result that has important implications for Tiebout sorting when access to public schools is based on household residence.

Tiebout sorting and the rationing of school inputs

Equity concerns that arise from Tiebout sorting are then closely linked to an understanding of the mechanism that gives rise to school quality. If financial inputs, such as per pupil spending which in turn is closely linked to teacher student ratios, fully characterized the education production process, such concerns could easily be addressed through higher-level government redistribution of financial resources. In many ways, this was precisely the focus of policy for a number of decades following a wave of state court decisions that found excessively decentralized public school funding mechanisms to violate the equal protection clauses in state constitutions. Beginning with the famous California *Serrano* decisions in California in the 1970's, states have responded with a variety of state interventions ranging from mandating essentially equal per pupil spending across all districts to different state aid formulas that assist poorer districts in raising per pupil spending levels. It is now well understood, however, that there is a limit to which such policies can address the inequities in a Tiebout-based system of public education (Nechyba, 2004). The reason for this is that financial inputs represent only one category of inputs essential for public school quality, with a number of different non-financial inputs likely playing a significantly more important role.

These non-financial inputs have typically been modeled as "peer effects" (Epple & Romano, 2011). Models begin with the assumption that students are endowed with some innate "ability" level, and a given student's performance is dependent on the ability levels of students who attend the same school or class. When such ability levels are correlated with household income, the residential Tiebout sorting of households then implies a sorting of non-financial inputs into schools — which in turn implies that equalization of financial inputs cannot be expected to equalize educational opportunities within a system in which residential Tiebout competition sorts students into schools.

More generally, the same applies to other non-financial inputs that can be modeled in ways similar to such peer effects. For instance, teacher quality, long recognized as both an important input into school production and at best weakly correlated with measurable characteristics of teachers (Hanushk & Rivkin, 2006),

is similarly allocated across schools — especially in systems that do not permit differential pricing of teacher salaries. In particular, when high quality teachers cannot be adequately compensated through salary differentiation, they either leave the teaching profession or are compensated through assignments to more desirable schools in higher income districts (Loeb & Page, 2001). This mechanism then gives rise to a differential sorting of teachers that is correlated with the residential sorting of higher income households. It is similarly recognized that parents themselves are an important input into school production — both because of the home production of education (that results in different levels of child "ability") and because of the role they play in monitoring schools. And both these features of parental inputs into education are also correlated with parental income — once again implying a differential allocation of non-financial inputs that arises from residential Tiebout sorting.

When incorporated explicitly into Tiebout models of residential location choices, this understanding of school production as emerging from both financial and non-financial inputs has given rise to empirically grounded simulation models that can be used to investigate the potential for policy to address equity concerns from Tiebout sorting. Such models begin with a characterization of the underlying housing market within and across jurisdictional boundaries. While early attempts modeled housing as differing primarily or solely between jurisdictions, it has been documented that housing quality varies both within and across districts — which in turn has led to different approaches for introducing within-jurisdiction heterogeneity in the housing stock. In some such approaches, this heterogeneity emerges from multi-dimensional differences in household tastes across education and housing quality — with housing supply responding to such differences (Epple & Sieg, 1999). Alternatively, the distribution of housing quality can be modeled as exogenously given and calibrated to empirical distributions of such quality within and across districts, with housing prices adjusting to equilibrate supply and demand at each location (Nechyba, 2000).[1] School production is then modeled as a function of both financial and non-financial inputs, with the latter assumed to be correlated with aspects of the income distribution of the households whose children attend local public schools. Such Tiebout models that combine housing markets with realistic school production processes are considerably richer than earlier versions because of the endogenous emergence of school inputs that result from residential location choices that in turn are linked to more realistic models of housing markets. In addition, while non-financial inputs emerge from the residential sorting patterns that result from households "voting with their feet", financial inputs are often also modeled as emerging endogenously through a political process in which households vote in the more traditional sense.

The complexity of such theoretical models then precludes an analysis that is purely analytic — there are simply too many competing forces that depend on the underlying primitives in the models. These primitives include the characteristics of housing markets and the nature of jurisdictional boundaries, the relative weight that school production functions place on financial and non-financial inputs, the underlying income distribution and the parameters that characterize household tastes for consumption, schooling and housing quality. It therefore becomes necessary to find ways of allowing data to inform these underlying primitives — to in essence convert a rich theoretical model into one that is empirically grounded to the extent that it can replicate important features of local education and housing markets. Initial attempts relied heavily on calibration of these primitives while more recent attempts rely on structural estimation of underlying parameters of the models.

A series of papers emerging from Nechyba (2000), reviewed in greater detail by Epple and Nechyba (2004) and Nechyba (2006), relied solely on calibration techniques to give rise to computational models that could replicate the salient features of local school and housing markets while providing a platform for simulating alternative policy regimes. Several insights have emerged from such simulations: First, while they suggest that the move toward less reliance on local sources of funding for public schools has resulted in a narrowing of education quality differences under Tiebout competition, they also provide evidence that substantial inequities persist precisely because of the rationing of non-financial resources that emerges from sorting across housing markets (Nechyba, 2004). This sorting appears to be largely immune to school finance policy. Second, by introducing private (or charter) school markets that do not explicitly rely on Tiebout sorting in admitting students, the simulations suggest that the de-coupling of residential location from school choices has profound impacts on residential location patterns and that Tiebout-sorting across public schools cannot be analyzed fully without taking the impact of private school markets into account (Nechyba, 2003). This becomes particularly important in light of increasing efforts to de-couple location from schooling within the public sector through non-traditional public schools (such as charter schools) and through explicit formulations of public school choice policies (involving lotteries) in many cities. And third, simulations of different types of private (or charter) school competition — ranging from horizontal competition through targeted curricula to vertical competition through "cream skimming" of the best students from the public system — suggest that the systemic effect of new innovations on public school quality within a framework of residential Tiebout sorting

---

[1] These approaches are discussed in greater detail in Epple and Nechyba (2004) and Nechyba (2006).

differs widely depending on the precise nature of the competitive forces unleashed through such innovations (Nechyba, 2000).

Alongside this emergence of calibrated Tiebout models of education markets, more recent attempts have focused on developing new methodologies for using econometric techniques to estimate (rather than calibrate) an increasingly rich set of underlying theoretical models. Three different strains have emerged in this literature. First, Ferreyra (2007) builds an estimation framework directly on the Nechyba (2000) model while introducing explicit channels for horizontal differentiation of schools. Second, Epple and Sieg (1999) estimate an alternative framework based on the theoretical model of Epple and Platt (1998) that more directly endogenizes the housing stock within and across jurisdictions. Finally, Bayer and McMillan (2007, 2012) develop a more flexible and computationally tractable approach grounded in methodological innovations from industrial organization and focus more directly on the link between household income and race in Tiebout sorting.[2]

Each of these empirical methodologies has provided independent evidence for the importance of Tiebout's insights that households indeed "vote with their feet" within local economies and that this leads to complex patterns of residential sorting which in turn forms the basis for admission to traditional public schools. Ferreyra's approach again highlights both the limits of traditional school finance policies as well as the potential role for policy to inhibit or foster horizontal competition through policy innovations that introduce non-residence based competition. And Bayer and McMillan demonstrate that the inclusion of race into Tiebout models of residential and school choice adds an important and previously neglected level of complexity. Not only does ability-to-pay determine residential sorting

patterns, but race is independently important as members of different racial groups exhibit a desire to live in communities in which their racial group is represented (Bayer, Fang, & McMillan, 2014). For middle-income black households in particular this often results in a difficult set of trade-offs in many cities — with better public schools located in primarily non-black communities and large representations of black households primarily located in communities with poor public schools.

Tiebout competition to enhance productive efficiency

The literature highlighted above has concentrated on sorting patterns that emerge from Tiebout competition linked to education markets. As such, it has focused heavily on the first of the two primary features of Tiebout competition — the sorting of households as households match with communities. At the same time, this literature has remained largely disconnected from the second primary feature of Tiebout competition — the potential for a disciplining market-like force that restrains rent-seeking and thus enhances efficiency. This force has been most notably highlighted by Hoxby (2000) who finds that increased public school competition (as represented by a higher concentration of local school districts within an education market) leads to lower costs and better educational outcomes. While the result has not been uncontroversial, it relates directly to one of the central arguments in favor of decentralized provision of public schooling envisioned by Tiebout.

The empirical question is whether allocating non-financial inputs that are linked to households is in essence a zero-sum game or whether more competitive mechanisms for achieving such an allocation result in more efficient

---

[2] Bayer, Casey, Ferreira, and McMillan (2016) also offer innovative new empirical ways of introducing dynamic elements into estimating demand for neighborhoods.

production of school quality. Simulations emerging from the Nechyba (2000) model suggest that, if such competitive forces are sufficiently strong, the introduction of more competition through non-traditional school markets can *in principle* overcome equity concerns that emerge from increased vertical sorting across schools, but that — in the absence of sufficient efficiency gains, the reverse would hold as competition leads to lower non-financial inputs in some public schools. Put differently, sufficiently strong disciplining forces through competition can give rise to school reforms that result in a positive sum game, but whether they do depends ultimately on the nature of such reforms and the degree to which such forces are empirically important.

A partial divorce between competition and tiebout

When confined to the traditional Tiebout setting in which residential location patterns directly determine the allocation of students (and thus the distribution of non-financial inputs) into public schools, an inherent tension therefore emerges between the equity concerns from income (and race) based rationing of non-financial inputs and the potential for productive efficiency gains from decentralized competition. A major thrust in school finance policy, however, introduces an added element that emerges from deliberate attempts on the part of policy-makers to partially disconnect residential location choices from school assignments (Greene et al., 2010). Such policies, whether they take the form of non-residence based public school competition (with lotteries) or increased private school activity subsidized through some form of school voucher, essentially introduce new channels of competition that operate alongside the traditional Tiebout competition through housing markets. The challenge for researchers and policy makers alike lies in identifying

potential channels through which such new forces can operate alongside traditional forces to address both efficiency and equity concerns that emerge under Tiebout competition.

The nature of the underlying issue can be put into focus by considering explicitly how different policies would ration access to the scarce resource of seats within good schools. In the traditional Tiebout mechanism, such rationing occurs solely through housing markets that indirectly price access to schools in the public sector. In traditional private schools, on the other hand, this rationing arises both from explicit tuition pricing and from admissions policies defined by private schools. As greater non-residence based choice is introduced into the public sector, neither the implicit pricing through housing markets nor the explicit pricing through tuition levels is available as such public "choice" schools explicitly reject residential location as a main determinant for admission while at the same time being constrained to offer seats for "free" to those who are admitted. This has resulted in some role for lotteries to determine allocations of students to public "choice" schools when such schools are oversubscribed. In charter schools, such lotteries are simply designed for each school independently, but an increasing number of cities have turned toward a greater role for lotteries in their assignment mechanisms for all public schools (Abdulkadiroglu, 2013) — both those that emerge from the traditional Tiebout-based system and those that have formed more recently as charter schools.

Such districts typically do not rely solely on lotteries to determine where children are assigned. Rather, a Tiebout element is retained as "walk-zones" are defined around public schools — with households that reside within these zones given preference. Similarly, preference is typically given to siblings of children who are already enrolled in a particular school. Households provide school districts with rankings for schools to indicate their preferences, and assignments then proceed with both these rankings and the priority classes in mind. The resulting "assignment mechanisms" are therefore structured in tiers that define priority classes, with ties within classes broken through lotteries. Early incarnations of such mechanisms, however, had the unfortunate feature that they were not what economists call "strategy proof" in that they contained incentives for households to misrepresent their true preferences in attempts to alter the outcomes. For instance, households might not rank their most preferred school if they viewed their chance of being assigned to that school as low, choosing instead to list less preferred schools to which they were more likely to be assigned.

Economists have played an important role in refining these assignment mechanisms in large urban districts as such districts move toward increasing non-Tiebout choice within their public systems. In particular, strategy proof mechanisms built on the same common priority classes have been developed and implemented, with such mechanisms designed to remove the incentives for households to strategically misrepresent their true preferences (Abdulkadiroglu, 2013; Abdulkadiroglu & Sönmez, 2003). Such mechanisms can now be viewed as filling in the gap between the extremes of relying solely on Tiebout competition or relying solely on lotteries. They also provide potential opportunities for the public and private school systems to partially merge into a single system if public funding is extended to private schools to the extent to which private schools accept student assignments through the same mechanism (thereby foregoing the ability to explicitly "cream-skim" students from public schools).

The challenge of such attempts to foster non-traditional channels of competition within an environment of Tiebout completion lies in finding ways of minimizing the undesirable features of competition from vertical sorting while maximizing the desirable features from horizontal sorting and from gains in productive efficiency. As the literature that we have reviewed

illustrates, vertical sorting emerges naturally under Tiebout competition as ability-to-pay determines where households will locate in equilibrium and where the non-financial inputs that accompany households are located. Such vertical sorting plays a similar role in private schools that rely on tuition pricing to ration access, with explicit attempts by private schools to cream-skim the "best" students from public schools reinforcing such sorting further. The introduction of non-traditional competition through mechanisms that reduce the role of residential location in school assignments reduces the vertical sorting that emerges in Tiebout-based school assignments, and, to the extent to which private schools are included in such assignment mechanisms in exchange for public funding, such vertical sorting into private schools is similarly ameliorated. At the same time, such new forms of competition open the door to more desirable channels of competition — i.e. those that provide incentives for schools to compete by targeting students through pedagogical or curricula innovations and those that reward productive efficiency.

Conclusion

A rich literature on Tiebout competition in education markets has moved increasingly in the direction of developing empirical computational models that in turn have shed light on both the positive and negative aspects of a system that relies on residential location as the primary vehicle for assigning students to public schools. By incorporating non-traditional schools into the analysis, these models have also demonstrated alternative channels of school competition that can play a role within local economies in which Tiebout forces that are closely linked to household income and race play an important role. The challenge for researchers now emerges directly from new policy innovations that emphasize new channels through which competition operates, with the current literature offering hints as to how the resulting competitive forces might change the availability and distribution of educational opportunities.

References

Abdulkadiroglu, A. (2013). School choice. In N. Vulkan, A. Roth, & Z. Neeman (Eds.), *The handbook of market design* (pp. 138–169). Oxford University Press.

Abdulkadiroglu, A., & Sönmez, T. (2003). School choice: A mechanism design approach. *American Economic Review, 93*, 729–747.

Bayer, Casey, P. M., Ferreira, F., & McMillan, R. (2016). A dynamic model of demand for housing and neighborhoods. *Econometrica, 84*(3), 893–942.

Bayer, P., Fang, H., & McMillan, R. (2014). Separate when equal? Racial inequality and segregation. *Journal of Urban Economics, 82*, 32–48.

Bayer, P., Ferreira, F., & McMillan, R. (2007). A unified framework for measuring preferences for schools and neighborhood. *Journal of Political Economy, 115*(4), 588–638.

Bayer, P., & McMillan, R. (2012). Tiebout sorting and neighborhood stratification. *Journal of Public Economics, 1129*, 43.

Black, S. (1999). Do better schools matter? Parental valuations of elementary education. *Quarterly Journal of Economics, 114*, 577–599.

Black, S., & Machin, S. (2011). Housing valuations of school performance. In *Handbook of economics of education* (pp. 485–519). Amsterdam: North Holland.

Edel, M., & Sclar, E. (1974). Taxes, spending and property values: Supply adjustment in a tiebout-oates model. *Journal of Political Economy, 82*(5), 941–954.

Epple, D., & Nechyba, T. (2004). Fiscal decentralization. In V. Henderson, & J. Thisse (Eds.), *Handbook of regional and urban economics* (Vol. 4, pp. 2426–2480). Amsterdam: North Holland.

Epple, D., & Romano, R. (2011). Peer effects in education: A survey of the theory and evidence. In J. Benhabib, A. Bisin, & M. Jackson (Eds.), *Handbook of social economics* (pp. 1053–1063). Amsterdam: North Holland.

Epple, D., & Platt, G. J. (1998). Equilibrium and local redistribution in an urban economy when households differ in both preferences and incomes. *Journal of Urban Economics, 43*(1), 23–51.

Ferreyra, M. (2007). Estimating the effects of private school vouchers in multi-district economies. *American Economic Review, 97*, 789–817.

Greene, J., Loveless, T., McLeod, B., Nechyba, T., Peterson, P., Rosenthal, M., et al. (2010). Expanding choice in elementary and secondary education: A report on rethinking the federal role in education. In *Brown center on education policy*. Brookings Institution.

Hanushk, E., & Rivkin, S. (2006). Teacher quality. In *Handbook of the economics of education* (pp. 1052–1078). Amsterdam: North Holland.

Hoxby, C. (2000). Does competition among public schools benefit students and taxpayers? *American Economic Review, 90*, 1209–1238.

Loeb, S., & Page, M. (2001). Examining the link between teacher wages and student outcomes: The importance of alternative labor market opportunities and nonpecuniary variation. *Review of Economic Studies, 82*, 393–408.

Nechyba, T. (2000). Mobility, targeting and private school vouchers. *American Economic Review, 90*, 130–146.

Nechyba, T. (2003). School finance, spatial income segregation and the nature of communities. *Journal of Urban Economics, 54*(1), 61–88.

Nechyba, T. (2004). Prospects for achieving equity or adequacy in education: The limits of state aid in general equilibrium. In J. Yinger (Ed.), *Helping children left behind: State aid and the Pursuit of educational equity* (pp. 111–145). MIT Press.

Nechyba, T. (2006). Income and peer quality sorting in public and private schools. In E. Hanushek, & F. Welch (Eds.), *Handbook of economics of education* (Vol. 2, pp. 1327–1368). Amsterdam: North Holland.

Oates, W. (1969). The effects of property taxes and local public spending on property values: An empirical study of tax capitalization and the Tiebout hypothesis. *Journal of Political Economy, 77*, 957–971.

Tiebout, C. M. (1956). A pure theory of local expenditures. *Journal of Political Economy, 64*, 416–424.

Economic approaches to school efficiency

Geraint Johnes

Lancaster University Management School, United Kingdom

Introduction

The study of efficiency has a long history in economics. Farrell (1957) famously developed elementary methods whereby the conceptual work of Debreu (1951) and Koopmans (1951, p. 61), building in turn on the work of Pareto (1909, p. 355), could be confronted by data. Later literature bifurcated, with one strand following the parametric, statistical approach of stochastic frontier analysis (Aigner, Lovell, & Schmidt, 1977) while the other took a non-parametric approach, underpinned by linear programming, and known as data envelopment analysis - DEA (Boles, 1971; Charnes, Cooper, & Rhodes, 1978, 1979). In both cases, inefficiency is measured as a residual indicating the distance between observed outcomes and a frontier of best practice. This frontier may be the production function or (in a dual representation) a cost curve, either of which is effectively an envelope defined by efficient provision. Both the statistical and non-parametric approaches have allowed emphasis to be placed on the distinction, raised by Leibenstein (1966) between allocative and x-efficiency — loosely defined, respectively, as producing the right things and producing things right.

The focus on managerial efficiency, or x-efficiency, doing things right, has received renewed attention in recent years following the work of Bloom and Van Reenen (2007) who demonstrate wide variation across businesses and countries in economic performance due to differences in the quality of management. Bloom, Lemos, Sadun, and Van Reenen (2015) show that differences in the performance of educational institutions are likewise explained in large measure by differences in managerial efficiency. Specifically in the context of education, efficiency matters.

This is particularly so, since the disciplines of a perfect market are conspicuously absent in most education contexts. Competition is muted, with students often being assigned to schools rather than acting as decision-making, utility-maximizing consumers. Even where quasi-markets have been introduced to allow elements of choice, this choice is often restricted by the presence of oversubscribed (full) schools. And the objective functions of schools' decision-makers are typically complex; schools do not respond to a straightforward profit motive. In education, market forces cannot necessarily be relied upon therefore to generate efficiency.

The Economics of Education, Second Edition
https://doi.org/10.1016/B978-0-12-815391-8.00035-5

Meanwhile the funders of education — typically governments operating on behalf of taxpayers — are keen to ensure that outputs are maximized for any given level of input (or that inputs are minimized for any given level of output — a distinction that is dealt with later in this chapter).

This being the case, there has been widespread interest in the evaluation of efficiency in education. Several surveys have been published in recent years covering research in this area. Johnes (2004) is an early example. Thanassoulis et al. (2016) and parts of Johnes (2015) provide more recent overviews, and De Witte and López-Torres (2017) review numerous papers, offering an exhaustive bibliography. Blackburn, Brennan, and Ruggiero (2014) offer a book-length treatment of DEA in the education context, with SAS code provided for many non-standard DEA models not commonly available in specialist software. Our approach in the present chapter is more selective, focusing on a selection of major developments in the methodology and, in particular, on the insights that these have allowed in our understanding of problems in the sphere of education.

In the next section, we review the basic models of data envelopment analysis (DEA) and stochastic frontier analysis (SFA), giving examples of their use in the education context. This is followed by discussion of various refinements of the basic models and their application to education. The final section of the chapter offers conclusions and suggestions for the future direction of travel for research in this area.

Models of efficiency

Data envelopment analysis

Consider n firms, each of which is a decision-making unit (DMU) that produces s different types of output using m different types of input. The efficiency of the kth DMU may be expressed as the ratio of (weighted sum of) outputs to (weighted sum of) inputs. A conventional interpretation of the weights used in this calculation is that they are prices. But this interpretation may be inappropriate in the context of a non-market sector such as education; while, in a competitive setting, prices faced by all producers are the same and are thus parameters, there is no reason to suppose that producers of education all weight their outputs and inputs similarly. Indeed, different producers are likely to have distinct missions, with some attaching more weight to certain outputs (or inputs) than do others. For example, one university might attach particular importance to the caliber of its graduates while another emphasizes its role in widening participation. This being the case, each DMU is, subject to certain constraints, able to choose its own vectors of input weights, v, and output weights, u, so as to maximize a measure of its efficiency

$$\sum_{r=1}^{s} u_r y_{rk} / \sum_{i=1}^{m} v_i x_{ik}$$

where y_{rk} and x_{ik} respectively denote the kth DMU's output of type r and input of type i. The constraints are that

$$\sum_{r=1}^{s} u_r y_{rj} / \sum_{i=1}^{m} v_i x_{ij} \leq 1 \forall j$$

so that the weights adopted by the kth DMU cannot, for any of the DMUs, result in the ratio of weighted outputs to weighted inputs exceeding one, and

$$u_r, v_i > 0 \forall r, i$$

This can be reformulated as a straight forward linear programming (LP) problem. A LP is solved for each of the n DMUs simultaneously;

for the kth DMU weighted outputs are maximized subject to a constant weighted input:

$$\text{Max} \sum_{r=1}^{s} v_i x_{ik} \text{ s.t.} \sum_{i=1}^{m} v_i x_{ij} - \sum_{r=1}^{s} u_r y_{rj}$$

$$\geq 0 \forall j, \sum_{r=1}^{s} u_r y_{rk} = 1, u_r, v_i > 0 \forall r, i$$

An alternative approach, which yields identical results in the simple case considered here, is to minimize the weighted input subject to given weighted output. The distinction between these two approaches is that of input orientation versus output orientation. In more refined models, such as those that accommodate variable returns to scale, input orientation and output orientation generally produce different results.

Given the constraints in this problem, the ratio of weighted output to weighted input lies in the unit interval and may be interpreted as an efficiency score. If a given DMU has an efficiency score of one, then no other DMU (or linear combination of other DMUs) outperforms it.

The flexibility that this model affords is appealing in a number of respects. It allows a multiplicity of inputs and of outputs, thereby reflecting the complexity of much productive activity. The non-parametric nature of the model, which allows different DMUs to attach different weights to their inputs and outputs, reflects the heterogeneity of missions that is characteristic of DMUs in non-market activities such as education. That said, the simple model outlined here may be regarded as too flexible in that it might allow weights to be attached to inputs or outputs that are at variance with those deemed acceptable by policy-makers. This observation has led to the construction of models in which restrictions may be placed on the weights (Dyson & Thanassoulis, 1988). After its developers (Charnes et al., 1978), the original DEA model has come to be known as the CCR model.

An important variant of this simple DEA model relaxes the implicit assumption that returns to scale are constant. Banker, Charnes, and Cooper (1984) add a further constraint to the linear programs of the CCR model, allowing the computation of efficiency scores both under constant and variable returns to scale. Again in honor of its developers, this has come to be known as the BCC model.

Application of the DEA methodology in the context of education came soon after the development of the technique. Indeed Charnes et al. (1978) refer to the analysis of school districts as a potential application. Bessent and Bessent (1980) provide an early application of a CCR model in a study comparing the efficiency of 55 elementary schools in a single school district in Houston. Their model has two outputs (measuring performance in reading and in mathematics at year t) and some 13 inputs (measuring performance in reading in mathematics at year t-1, measures of socio-economic conditions, school resources, school organizational climate, and an indicator of the extent to which teaching is oriented to the needs of the individual student). Some 31 schools achieve an efficiency score of unity; most of the remainder have efficiency scores above 0.90, but the least efficient school has a score of 0.78. Comparison of this school with its more efficient peers allows areas where improvements can be made to generate 'quick wins'. A more recent application to school data is that of Bradley, Johnes, and Millington (2001) who examine around 1500 secondary schools in England and use the results to demonstrate the impact on efficiency of the prevalence of local competition.

A more recent application is that of Veiderpass and McKelvey (2016) who compare 944 higher education institutions across 17 countries within Europe using the Eumida data set. The EUropean MicroDAta (Eumida) project piloted the collection of comparable data on higher education institutions throughout Europe (Niederl et al., 2014). Further information on Eumida (and its later incarnation, the European Tertiary Education Register (ETER) is available at https://www.eter-project.com/about/faq-s, where data are available for download. The model used by Viederpass and McKelvey is a BCC analysis using five output variables (headcounts of graduates at different levels) and eleven inputs (total income, non-personnel expenditures, and headcounts of different categories of staff). They report average efficiency of institutions within each country, with Slovakia being the most efficient and Denmark the least; only 6 out of 28 higher education institutions in Denmark are listed in the Eumida database.

While instructive, this type of analysis has a drawback that is very obvious to those familiar with applied economic analysis. It is descriptive rather than analytical — it does not follow the conventional route of formulating and then testing hypotheses, and this limits what it can teach us about underlying principles. While DEA is not a statistical tool, the efficiency scores can be bootstrapped to provide confidence intervals and hence allow statistical inference. Following Efron (1979), Simar and Wilson (1998) developed the bootstrapping tool for use in this context. Many recent applications of DEA in education, including Veiderpass and McKelvey (2016), report bootstrapped efficiency scores. Nevertheless, a methodological framework that offers the full toolkit of statistical inference, and with which many economists are therefore more comfortable, is provided by the statistical method of stochastic frontier analysis, and we now turn to consider this approach.

Stochastic frontier analysis

Statistical approaches built on the foundation of least squares regression involve finding the parameters of an equation describing a line of best fit through a scatter of data points. The essential nature of a frontier, however, is that it should not be a line of best fit. Rather, it should provide an envelope defined only by the observations corresponding to efficient DMUs. To estimate such a frontier using the statistical approach, an assumption is made about the nature of inefficiency. Specifically, inefficiency is assumed to follow a distribution across DMUs that is not Gaussian — typically it is assumed to be half-normal, truncated normal, exponential or gamma. This inefficiency can then be separated out from the usual (normal) distribution of regression residuals.

Consider a cost function that takes the form

$$C_i = \mathbf{X_i}\boldsymbol{\beta} + v_i + u_i$$

where C_i denotes the costs of the ith DMU associated with the production of output vector $\mathbf{X_i}$. The terms v_i and u_i denote, respectively, a normal error term and an asymmetric residual. As demonstrated by Aigner et al. (1977), the coefficient vector, $\boldsymbol{\beta}$, can be estimated by maximum likelihood methods. Jondrow, Lovell, Materou, and Schmidt (1982) show how the DMU-specific values of u_i can be retrieved; these can then be expressed as efficiency scores that, in a similar fashion to those obtained from DEA, lie in the unit interval.

A typical example of the application of SFA in the context of education involves estimation of a cost function for higher education institutions. Following early work in this field that did not use frontier approaches (see, for example, Cohn, Rhine, & Santos, 1989), cost functions for such complex institutions should recognize the multiproduct nature of production, and so should be consistent with the desiderata identified by Baumol, Panzar, and Willig (1982). This has led many researchers to use the quadratic functional form, enabling the analysis to yield significant insights into economies of scale and scope (and hence allocative efficiency) as well as into technical efficiency. An early example of such an exercise is provided by Izadi, Johnes,

Ozkrochi, and Crouchley (2002). Using data on British universities, the researchers find (in line with both intuition and more recent studies) that average incremental costs are lower for tuition in arts than in science, and lower for undergraduate than for postgraduate tuition. They also confirm that product-specific returns to scale are unexhausted for several output types, particularly for postgraduate and research activity, suggesting that further concentration of these activities would be globally optimal. This observation has led researchers to study the link between cost functions estimated using frontier methods, on the one hand, and merger activity in education, on the other. See, for example, Green and Johnes (2009) and Johnes and Tsionas (2018). The findings of typical studies in this area suggest that most universities have quite high levels of technical efficiency — In the Izadi et al. (2002) paper, for example, 87 of 99 institutions studied have efficiency scores of 0.8 or above. Two institutions, both of which were small and have since (interestingly) merged with other institutions, have efficiency scores below 0.5.

The parametric nature of SFA also allows the full toolkit of statistical inference to be applied, arguably making the technique more attractive to economists than the non-parametric DEA. SFA has some disadvantages, however. In particular, while many public sector organizations are characterized by having multiple inputs and multiple outputs, SFA is capable of investigating only a single input (costs) if there are multiple outputs — or a single output if there are multiple inputs (the production function case). That said, Johnes (2014) provides an interesting mechanism for generalizing the SFA model to the case of multiple inputs and multiple outputs. The relative strengths and weaknesses of DEA and SFA have ensured that both methods have remained in common use. Where both methods have been applied to the same data (as, for example, in Johnes, 1999) a reasonable measure of positive correlation is typically

observed, though the distribution of efficiencies differs markedly across methods.

Many refinements have been made to the basic models, and some of these form the subject of the next section.

More advanced models

Non-parametric models

Metafrontiers

Systems of education are complex. Performance depends on the mapping of inputs onto outputs at a multiplicity of levels. For instance, students come from families, mix with peers from their neighborhood, and attend schools — and they learn from each of these. The schools, in turn, are typically organized into school districts, and the way in which these districts run their affairs can likewise have an impact on student learning. This multilayered structure has been well understood by specialists in educational research for many years, and has motivated the appeal of multilevel modeling in this arena (see, for example, Goldstein, 1986).

DEA models have accommodated similar concerns, leading to the adoption of a 'metafrontier' approach (Charnes, Cooper, & Rhodes, 1981; Portela & Thanassoulis, 2001). This involves executing multiple DEA exercises — first evaluating the efficiency scores for each DMU when compared with other units in their own locale (to provide a 'unit-within-locale' measure of efficiency), and then evaluating the scores for each DMU when compared with *all* other units; the ratio of the former efficiency score to the latter, averaged across all DMUs within a given locale, provides a 'locale-within-all-locales' measure of efficiency. Metafrontier analyses of this kind have been adopted widely in the area of education. Examples include Johnes (2006), Waldo (2007), De Witte, Thanassoulis, Simpson, Battisti, and Charlesworth-May (2010), Thieme, Prior, and

Tortosa-Ausina (2013), Johnes (2018a), and Johnes and Virmani (2019).

An early application is due to Johnes (2006) who examines student performance at university, hence obtaining student-within-university and university-within-all-universities measures of efficiency. She shows that a considerable proportion of the variation in efficiency scores derived at aggregate (university) level is due to variation at individual student level. This provides important insight into the source of good performance, and allows institutions of higher education more precisely to indentify what they need to due to enhance their efficiency — and what must be left to the students themselves.

Malmquist indices

The metafrontier approach allows investigation of a sample of DMUs drawn from a wider cross-section. More generally, data for a sample of DMUs might be drawn from a universe of data that allows those DMUs to be compared across time. An influential paper by Färe, Grosskopf, Norris, and Zhang (1994), drawing on earlier work by Malmquist (1953), introduced the methods that have become standard for comparing whereby efficiency scores obtained from a DEA across time. The key insight is that, as time passes, a given DMU's efficiency can change relative to the period-specific frontier, and the position of the frontier itself is likely also to shift over time. This suggests an instructive decomposition between the change in efficiency between two periods, on the one hand, and the change in production technology (that is, a change in the position of the frontier between two periods).

The Malmquist index used to operationalize this decomposition is defined as

$$\frac{D_t/D_t^t}{D_q/D_q^q} \sqrt{\left[\frac{D_t/D_t^q}{D_t/D_t^t} \cdot \frac{D_q/D_q^q}{D_q/D_q^t}\right]}$$

where D_a denotes observed output at time a and D_a^b denotes the maximum output that could possibly be produced at time a given the technology available at time b (in each case given inputs). The first term on the right hand side measures the change in efficiency, while the second (using a geometric mean) measures the change in production technology.

An example of the application of Malmquist indices to education is provided by Thanassoulis, Kortelainen, Johnes, and Johnes (2011) who investigate changes in the performance of higher education institutions in England in the early years of this millennium. They find evidence to support the hypothesis that, specifically for institutions that were granted university status after 1992, the efficiency frontier shifted out over the time period considered, thereby allowing productivity gains in this part of the sector. Elsewhere the researchers found little change.

Revenue efficiency models

Most applications of DEA, including those considered above, focus on the mapping between inputs and outputs without consideration of prices. Given inputs, an increase in output is deemed sufficient to raise efficiency. Where DMUs act as price takers, this is eminently reasonable. Under conditions of imperfect competition, however, a change in output brings about a change in price, and in these situations it is appropriate to consider the impact of output decisions on revenue.

With this in mind, Johnson and Ruggiero (2011) have developed a DEA model in which prices are endogenous. To be specific, they consider the case of monopolistic competition. In their model, total revenue (defined by the sum, across all output types, of prices multiplied by output) replaces the optimand in the dual linear programs used in solving the problem. Moreover, prices are endogenized in this model by assuming a downward sloping demand function linking prices to output.

This model has been applied by Johnes and Ruggiero (2017) to data drawn from universities in England in academic year 2012−13. This was an interesting period to study owing to the substantial increase in tuition fees charged to domestic undergraduate students around that time. Information on the responsiveness of student demand to prices, and specifically on the demand elasticity, is taken from the received literature (see, for example, Wolgemuth, 2013). In response to the hike in fees, the researchers find that the revenue-efficient level of recruitment of domestic undergraduates implied that certain universities − specifically smaller research-intensive universities − would likely wish to expand their student intakes considerably. The same is not true for their larger counterparts or for less research-intensive institutions. Interestingly, changes in recruitment to universities over the subsequent period appear broadly in line with this finding.

Network DEA models

Early work by Färe (1991) and Färe and Grosskopf (1996), subsequently refined by Tone and Tsutsui (2009), shows how the standard DEA model can be adapted to provide information about the efficiency with which different nodes in a network perform their operations. A network may be a supply chain, or may be different departments within a single system. Using information about the architecture of the network, about the inputs and outputs of the system as a whole, and about intermediate outputs (that is, outputs from one node of the network that become inputs into other nodes), the efficiency of different parts of the network can be evaluated.

It took some time for network DEA models to gain common currency in the literature, owing largely to the difficulties inherent in devising software for such flexible models. With the appearance of MaxDEA (www.maxdea.cn) this constraint has been removed. Early applications

of network DEA models in education include Rayeni and Saljooghi (2010) and Johnes (2013).

In the sphere of education, an obvious application for network DEA models concerns student progression, for example between lower and upper secondary school. Johnes (2018b) investigates this using data from the schools performance tables for England, focusing on those students whose potential transit from lower to higher secondary education occurred in academic year 2013−14 (so that results of upper secondary education, obtained in 2015−16, are available). The network is constructed with data on teacher numbers, numbers of students (disaggregated by socio-economic status), and financial information as inputs. At upper secondary level, student entrants from other schools serve as a further input. The outputs at lower secondary level include academic results in the GCSE examinations (these serving as an intermediate output − that is, they become an input into the production process at upper secondary level); final outputs from lower secondary education comprise numbers of students progressing to further education outside the school itself, and numbers transferring into apprenticeships. Efficiency scores at lower secondary education level are high throughout England, though the reasons for this differ across geographies. Meanwhile, efficiency scores at upper secondary level vary significantly across the country, and are significantly lower than elsewhere in areas where the local unemployment rate is relatively high, and also in the Northern Powerhouse. (The Northern Powerhouse is an urban region of northern England that has been targeted for future infrastructure investments with the aim of stimulating growth through agglommeration economies. It has also been identified in various studies as an educational 'cold spot' - see http://www.hefce.ac.uk/analysis/maps/employment/).

We now turn to review some recent developments in the parametric modeling of efficiency using variants of the stochastic frontier model.

Parametric models

Causality

The vast bulk of applied microeconometric work in recent years has concerned the identification of causal relationships between variables. An early review of this work, as applied to education, is provided by Card (2001). In efficiency studies, however, owing to the focus on the residual rather than on parameter estimates, the issue of causality has been largely neglected. Recent work addresses this shortcoming.

One area in which regression discontinuity designs, of the type pioneered (coincidentally in the field of education) by Thistlethwaite and Cambpell (1960), have been commonly used concerns the issue of class size and student performance. The research of Angrist and Lavy (1999) which exploits Maimonides' rule — whereby an institutional maximum on class size generates discontinuities — has been particularly influential. Piketty (2004) and Gary-Bobo and Mahjoub (2013) are two examples of subsequent work. But most research in this area ignores the fact that the educational production function is a frontier — that is, that inefficiencies typically exist and that this should be allowed for in the estimation strategy. Johnes and Tsionas (2018) develop methods for conducting a regression discontinuity design within the framework of a stochastic frontier, and illustrate this using data on class size and student performance from Texas, where a form of the Maimonides rule operates. With a maximum class size of 22, there are discontinuities when the size of the year group passes this number and multiples of this number. The researchers show that there is a clear improvement in performance at the discontinuities, as class size falls. This is accompanied, however, by a rise in inefficiency. The conflation of these two effects may explain, in part at least, the ambiguous results across many analyses of class size surveyed by Hanushek and Woessmann (2017).

Panel data models

Early work on educational cost functions suffered the drawback that it could at best take very limited account of unobserved heterogeneity across the units of observation. The advent of panel data has allowed such concerns to be mitigated. In the context of frontier analysis this is due to random parameter and latent class[1] methods developed by Tsionas (2002) and Greene (2005). While often used with panel data (see, for example, Agasisti & Johnes, 2015), the latent class model does not require the data set to be longitudinal. The essence of the latent class model is that DMUs are divided into two (or more) groups — the latent classes — and separate parameters are estimated for each class, with the allocation of DMUs into one class or the other being determined, alongside the parameter values, by maximum likelihood. An example of this technique being applied to a *cross-section* of higher education data is provided by Johnes and Johnes (2016).

These developments have led to a large number of papers using frontier methods to evaluate efficiency and estimate the parameters of cost functions in education. The random parameter frontier model, in particular, is of interest because it allows statistical estimation of a model that has many of the appealing characteristics of a DEA — specifically it allows the weights attached to various outputs to vary across DMUs, reflecting heterogeneity of mission. An early application is that of Johnes and Johnes (2009). In common with many subsequent studies, this finds that — once allowance is made for unobserved heterogeneity — levels of efficiency in higher education are typically high.

Transitory and permanent inefficiencies

Panel data afford opportunities to evaluate efficiencies under a range of assumptions. Efficiencies may be constrained to be constant over time, or may vary over time — freely or according to some prescribed mechanism (Cornwell, Schmidt, & Sickles, 1990; Pitt & Lee, 1981). This observation has led to further developments in the stochastic frontier model, one of which has proved to be of particular interest in the field of education. Tsionas and Kumbhakar (2014) separate out the asymmetric residual into two components, the first reflecting persistent inefficiency (relating to long-term or structural issues) and the second reflecting transient inefficiency (due to short-term fluctuations). Their model has been applied to data on education by Papadimitrou and Johnes (2016), Gralka (2016) and Agasisti and Gralka (2019). These studies respectively analyze the nature of efficiency in English, German and Italian universities, and in all three cases inefficiency is found to be more the consequence of structural problems rather than short-term issues. Hence improvements in efficiency call for change in, for example, deep-rooted management practices of government regulations.

Network SFA

Just as it is possible to analyze efficiencies in a network DEA, the methods of SFA can be applied to a network, though such work remains in its infancy. Johnes, Tsionas, and Izzeldin (2018) develop the statistical methodology, and illustrate its operation with an application in an education context. Using a short panel of data on universities in England, they investigate a network in which the final outputs are graduate employability and student satisfaction. Degree results are an intermediate output that, along with research reputation, affect employability. The quality of student intake, the student:faculty ratio, and per student expenditure all serve as inputs, influencing degree results. While the average efficiency of universities at each node of the model is high (in excess of 0.9), universities appear to be somewhat less efficient in their production of employability than they are in producing good degree results and high student satisfaction. These results tally with findings from an earlier study by Johnes (2013) that used network DEA to evaluate efficiencies in a similar network.

Conclusions

The advances that have been made in the evaluation of efficiency in education are considerable. In concluding this chapter, however, an important caveat is in order. Either by identifying a uniform set of weights (as in the parametric approach) or by allowing flexibility in weights (as in the non-parametric methods), the tools of analysis discussed above enable the evaluation of efficiency scores. Yet these scores are unlikely to be uncontentious. Different stakeholders are likely to have different views, not least about the range of weights that is acceptable. Where quantitative methods identify apparent inefficiencies, there remains merit in supporting such analysis with qualitative investigation designed to uncover the source of slack.

References

Agasisti, Tommaso, & Gralka, Sabine (2019). The transient and persistent efficiency of Italian and German universities: a stochastic frontier analysis. *Applied Economics*, 51(46), 5012–5030.

Agasisti, T., & Johnes, G. (2015). Efficiency, costs, rankings and heterogeneity: The case of US higher education. *Studies in Higher Education, 40*, 60–82.

Aigner, D., Lovell, C. A. K., & Schmidt, P. (1977). Formulation and estimation of stochastic production function models. *Journal of Econometrics, 6*, 21–37.

Angrist, J. D., & Lavy, V. (1999). Using Maimonides' rule to estimate the effect of class size on scholastic achievement. *Quarterly Journal of Economics, 114*, 533–575.

Banker, R., Charnes, A., & Cooper, W. W. (1984). Some models for estimating technical and scale efficiencies in data envelopment analysis. *Management Science, 30*, 1078–1092.

Baumol, W. J., Panzar, J. C., & Willig, R. D. (1982). *Contestable markets and the theory of industry structure*. San Diego: Harcourt Brace Jovanovich.

Bessent, A. M., & Bessent, E. W. (1980). Determining the comparative efficiency of schools through data envelopment analysis. *Educational Administration Quarterly, 16*, 57–75.

Blackburn, V., Brennan, S., & Ruggiero, J. (2014). *Nonparametric estimation of educational production and costs using data envelopment analysis*. New York: Springer.

Bloom, N., Lemos, R., Sadun, R., & Van Reenen, J. (2015). Does management matter in schools? *Economic Journal, 125*, 647–674.

Bloom, N., & Van Reenen, J. (2007). Measuring and explaining management practices across firms and countries. *Quarterly Journal of Economics, 122*, 1341–1408.

Boles, J. N. (1971). *The 1130 Farrell efficiency system: Multiple products, multiple factors*. Berkeley: Giannini Foundation of Agricultural Economics, University of California.

Bradley, S., Johnes, G., & Millington, J. (2001). The effect of competition on the efficiency of secondary schools in England. *European Journal of Operational Research, 135*, 545–568.

Card, D. (2001). Estimating the return to schooling: Progress on some persistent econometric problems. *Econometrica, 69*, 1127–1160.

Charnes, A., Cooper, W. W., & Rhodes, E. (1978). Measuring the efficiency of decision making units. *European Journal of Operational Research, 2*, 429–444.

Charnes, A., Cooper, W. W., & Rhodes, E. (1979). Measuring the efficiency of decision making units: A short communication. *European Journal of Operational Research, 3*, 339.

Charnes, A., Cooper, W., & Rhodes, E. (1981). Evaluating program and managerial efficiency: An application of data envelopment analysis to program follow through. *Management Science, 27*, 668–697.

Cohn, E., Rhine, S. L. W., & Santos, M. C. (1989). Institutions of higher education as multiproduct firms: Economies of scale and scope. *The Review of Economics and Statistics, 71*, 284–290.

Cornwell, C., Schmidt, P., & Sickles, R. C. (1990). Production frontiers with cross-sectional and time-series variation in efficiency levels. *Journal of Econometrics, 46*, 185–200.

De Witte, K., Thanassoulis, E., Simpson, G., Battisti, G., & Charlesworth-May, A. (2010). Assessing pupil and school performance by non-parametric and parametric techniques. *Journal of the Operational Research Society, 61*, 1224–1237.

De Witte, K., & López-Torres, L. (2017). Efficiency in education: A review of literature and a way forward. *Journal of the Operational Research Society*, 339–363.

Debreu, G. (1951). The coefficient of resource utilization. *Econometrica, 19*, 273–292.

Dyson, R. G., & Thanassoulis, E. (1988). Reducing weight flexibility in data envelopment analysis. *Journal of the Operational Research Society, 39*, 563–576.

Efron, B. (1979). Bootstrap methods: Another look at the jackknife. *Annals of Statistics, 7*, 1–26.

Färe, R. (1991). Measuring Farrell efficiency for a firm with intermediate inputs. *Academia Economic Papers, 19*, 329–340.

Färe, R., & Grosskopf, S. (1996). Productivity and intermediate products: A frontier approach. *Economics Letters, 50*, 65–70.

Färe, R., Grosskopf, S., Norris, M., & Zhang, Z. (1994). Productivity growth, technical progress, and efficiency change in industrialized countries. *The American Economic Review, 84*, 66–83.

Farrell, M. (1957). The measurement of productive efficiency. *Journal of the Royal Statistical Society A, 12*, 253–281.

Gary-Bobo, R., & Mahjoub, M.-B. (2013). Estimation of class size effects, using Maimonides' rule and other instruments: The case of French junior high schools. *Annals of Economics and Statistics, 111/112*, 193–225.

Goldstein, H. (1986). Multilevel mixed linear model analysis using iterative generalized least squares. *Biometrika, 73*, 43–56.

Gralka, S. (2016). *Persistent effects in the efficiency of the higher education sector*. https://bit.ly/2Hs8SgF.

Greene, W. (2005). Reconsidering heterogeneity in panel data estimators of the stochastic frontier model. *Journal of Econometrics, 126*, 269–303.

Green, C., & Johnes, G. (2009). Economies of scale and mergers in higher education. In T. Malcolm, M. Ka Ho, J. Huisman, & C. Morphew (Eds.), *The routledge international handbook of higher education* (pp. 369–380). New York: Routledge.

Hanushek, E. A., & Woessmann, L. (2017). School resources and student achievement: A review of cross-country economic research. In M. Rosén, K. Y. Hansen, & U. Wolff (Eds.), *Cognitive abilities and educational outcomes* (pp. 149–171). New York: Springer.

Izadi, H., Johnes, G., Ozkrochi, R., & Crouchley, R. (2002). Stochastic frontier estimation of a CES cost function: The case of higher education in Britain. *Economics of Education Review, 21*, 63–71.

Johnes, G. (1999). The management of universities, president's lecture delivered at annual meeting of the Scottish economic Society. *Scottish Journal of Political Economy, 46*, 505–522.

Johnes, J. (2004). Efficiency measurement. In G. Johnes, & J. Johnes (Eds.), *International handbook on the economics of education* (pp. 613–742). Cheltenham: Edward Elgar.

Johnes, J. (2006). Measuring teaching efficiency in higher education: An application of data envelopment analysis to economics graduates from UK universities, 1993. *European Journal of Operational Research, 174*, 443–456.

Johnes, G. (2013). Efficiency in higher education institutions revisited: A network approach. *Economics Bulletin, 33*, 2698–2706.

Johnes, J. (2014). In *Efficiency and input substitutability in English higher education, 1996/97 to 2008/09, paper presented at the INFORMS conference, San Francisco, 9–12 November*.

Johnes, J. (2015). Operational research in education. *European Journal of Operational Research, 243*, 683–696.

Johnes, G. (2018a). Planning v competition in education: Outcomes and efficiency. *Welsh Economic Review, 26*, 57–66.

Johnes, G. (2018b). Efficiency in lower and upper secondary education as a network: Implications for the northern

Powerhouse. *Investigaciones de economía de la educación, 12,* 303−314. http://repec.economicsofeducation.com/2017murcia/murcia2017.pdf.

Johnes, G., & Johnes, J. (2009). Higher education institutions' costs and efficiency: Taking the decomposition a further step. *Economics of Education Review, 28,* 107−113.

Johnes, G., & Johnes, J. (2016). Costs, efficiency and economies of scale and scope in the English higher education sector. *Oxford Review of Economic Policy, 32,* 596−614.

Johnes, G., & Ruggiero, J. (2017). Revenue efficiency in higher education institutions under perfect competition. *Public Policy and Administration, 32,* 282−295.

Johnes, G., & Tsionas, M. (2018). *A regression discontinuity stochastic frontier model with an application to educational attainment.* mimeo.

Johnes, J., & Tsionas, M. (2018). *An analysis of the efficiency effects of merger using Bayesian methods: The case of English universities.* Manchester School. forthcoming.

Johnes, G., Tsionas, M., & Izzeldin, M. (2018). *Network stochastic frontier analysis: A Bayesian approach.* mimeo.

Johnes, G., & Virmani, S. (2019). The efficiency of private and public schools in urban and rural areas: Moving beyond the development goals. *International Transactions in Operational Research* (forthcoming).

Johnson, A., & Ruggiero, J. (2011). Allocative efficiency measurement with endogenous prices. *Economics Letters, 111,* 81−83.

Jondrow, J., Lovell, C. A. K., Materou, I. S., & Schmidt, P. (1982). On the estimation of technical inefficiency in the stochastic frontier production function model. *Journal of Econometrics, 19,* 233−238.

Koopmans, T. C. (1951). Analysis of production as an efficient combination of activities. In T. Koopmans (Ed.), *Activity analysis of production and allocation* (pp. 33−97). New York: Wiley. https://bit.ly/2vy5DPc.

Leibenstein, H. (1966). Allocative efficiency versus x-efficiency. *The American Economic Review, 56,* 392−415.

Malmquist, S. (1953). Index numbers and indifference surfaces. *Trabados de Estatistica y de Investigación Operativa, 4,* 209−242.

Niederl, A., Bonaccorsi, A., Lepori, B., Brandt, T., De Filippo, D., & Ulrich, S. (2014). Mapping the European higher education landscape: New insights from the EUMIDA project. In A. Bonaccorsi (Ed.), *Knowledge, diversity and performance in European higher education.* Cheltenham: Edward Elgar.

Papadimitrou, M., & Johnes, J. (2016). Persistent and transient cost inefficiency in the English higher education sector: A generalised true random effects model. In *Paper presented at the OR58 conference, operational research Society, Portsmouth, 6 September.*

Pareto, V. (1909). *Manuel d'économie politique* (p. 355). Paris: Giard et Brière. https://bit.ly/2qOCVnA.

Piketty, T. (2004). *L'impact de la taille des classes et de la ségrégation sociale sur la réussite scolaire dans les écoles françaises: Une estimation à partir du panel primaire 1997.* http://piketty.pse.ens.fr/files/Piketty2004b.pdf.

Pitt, M. M., & Lee, L.-F. (1981). Measurement and sources of technical inefficiency in the Indonesian weaving industry. *Journal of Development Economics, 9,* 43−64.

Portela, M. C. A. S., & Thanassoulis, E. (2001). Decomposing school and school-type efficiency. *European Journal of Operational Research, 132,* 357−373.

Rayeni, M. M., & Saljooghi, F. H. (2010). *Journal of Computer Science, 6,* 1252−1257.

Simar, L., & Wilson, P. (1998). Sensitivity analysis of efficiency scores: How to bootstrap in nonparametric frontier models. *Management Science, 44,* 49−61.

Thanassoulis, E., Kortelainen, M., Johnes, G., & Johnes, J. (2011). Costs and efficiency of higher education institutions in England: A DEA analysis. *Journal of the Operational Research Society, 62,* 1282−1297.

Thanassoulis, E., Witte, K. De, Johnes, J., Johnes, G., Karagiannis, G., Concericao, S., et al. (2016). Applications of data envelopment analysis in education. In J. Zhu (Ed.), *Data envelopment analysis: A handbook of empirical studies and applications* (pp. 367−438). New York: Springer.

Thieme, C., Prior, D., & Tortosa-Ausina, E. (2013). A multilevel decomposition of school performance using robust nonparametric frontier techniques. *Economics of Education Review, 32,* 104−121.

Thistlethwaite, D. L., & Cambpell, D. T. (1960). Regression discontinuity analysis: An alternative to the ex post facto experiment. *Journal of Educational Psychology, 51,* 309−317.

Tone, K., & Tsutsui, M. (2009). Network DEA: A slacks-based measure approach. *European Journal of Operational Research, 197,* 243−252.

Tsionas, M. E. G. (2002). Stochastic frontier models with random coefficients. *Journal of Applied Econometrics, 17,* 127−147.

Tsionas, M. E. G., & Kumbhakar, S. C. (2014). Firm heterogeneity, persistent and transient technical inefficiency: A generalised true random effects model. *Journal of Applied Econometrics, 29,* 110−132.

Veiderpass, A., & McKelvey, M. (2016). Evaluating the performance of higher education institutions in Europe: a nonparametric efficiency analysis of 944 institutions. *Applied Economics, 48(16),* 1504−1514.

Waldo, S. (2007). On the use of student data in efficiency analysis: Technical efficiency in Swedish upper secondary school. *Economics of Education Review, 26,* 173−185.

Wolgemuth, D. (2013). Estimating the market demand and elasticity for enrollment at an institution. *Strategic Enrollment Management Quarterly, 1,* 67−74.

School competition and the quality of education

Francesca Foliano[a], Olmo Silva[b]

[a]Institute of Education, University College London, London, United Kingdom; [b]Department of Geography and Environment and Centre for Economic Performance, London School of Economics, London, United Kingdom

Glossary

Academies state-funded, non-fee charging English schools, which are directly funded by the Department for Education but are independent of local authority control. There are two main types of academies. Sponsored academies are schools that have been converted as part of a government remedial-education intervention strategy and are run by a Government-approved sponsor. Converter academies instead are schools that voluntarily convert to academy status and do not need a sponsor

Charter schools non-fee charging US schools that are subject to fewer rules and regulations than traditional state schools. They are typically funded through a fixed amount per pupil — a 'charter fee' — and can operate both not-for-profit and for-profit. Charter schools are authorized to operate once they receive a 'charter', that is a mandatory performance contract detailing the school's mission, goals, students served, methods of assessment, and ways to measure success. Charters are usually approved for 3–5 years and renewal depends on the school serving its 'charter' contract

Performance or League tables publicly-available rankings of schools compiled on the basis of centrally administered and externally marked SATs (standard assessment tests). Most tables provide information on school average 'raw scores' — i.e., levels of achievements — and/or shares of students attaining centrally determined performance targets. Progressively, league/performance tables have published metrics that tract student progress — for example, school average 'value added' — and school demographics

Free schools privately run Swedish schools that receive public funding based on their pupil numbers though the national voucher system. Free schools do not charge fees and are not academically selective. They are often part of school networks (chains) which can be run for-profit. Their pedagogical approaches and teaching methods can vary widely

Voucher system or education/school voucher system. A system in which government funding is portable and attached to students, and schools receive funding on the basis of their capacity to attract students via the process of school choice. Per-pupil funding is usually granted for one year, and mainly used to fund public schools. In some instances, private school can opt into the voucher system, though they might need to adapt admission practices, stop charging fees and/or set-up scholarship scheme for students from disadvantaged backgrounds

Introduction

Spurred by mixed evidence on the effectiveness of resource-based interventions (Hanushek, 2003), policy makers around the world have come to promote reforms that aim to improve

The Economics of Education, Second Edition
https://doi.org/10.1016/B978-0-12-815391-8.00036-7

standards by injecting into the education system elements of school choice, autonomy and market-type incentives.

The idea that systems centered on these principles can improve standards is predicated on some core mechanisms (already discussed in the seminal work by Milton Friedman (1962). First, autonomy provides schools with an opportunity to differentiate their offer by changing management, teaching and recruitment practices and serve 'consumers' — i.e., parents and their children — with different needs and preferences. A diversified market allows for a better match between pupils and schools, raising the efficiency of the education provision and improving standards. A second channel runs through teachers and leadership teams: autonomy in the system allows schools to diversify their character; this attracts workers who subscribe to the school mission and are motivated to 'work hard' to achieve the organization goals — including high quality (see Besley & Ghatak, 2005). However, the most often discussed idea is that autonomy 'works best' when coupled with the quasi-market incentives generated by the process of school choice: it is the combination of choice — with parents ready to abandon unsatisfactory providers — and autonomy — with schools responding to demand pressures to retain market shares — that can creates competitive incentives for schools to 'up their games' or risk closure.

The validity of these arguments requires four building blocks to be part of systems centered on quasi-markets in education. First, an accountability framework must provide parents with standardized and accessible information on quality. This is commonly achieved through the publication of league tables that allow comparisons of schools on the basis of uniform metrics. This is often coupled with additional inspection regimes by autonomous 'gatekeepers' that provide further (sometimes simplified) information on aspects of school quality that league tables can hardly capture (e.g., managerial talent; student wellbeing). Accountability alone can improve standards — for

example, via 'name-and-shame' dynamics to which motivated principals respond by improving standards. However, accountability most often comes as part of reform packages that provide choice to parents — and thus sharpen its possibly beneficial effects. Two key elements should characterize choice in education for it to be effective. First, choice should have financial implications for schools that fail to attract students because 'money follows pupils'. This can be achieved directly by providing students/parents with a voucher that can be spent on the schools they like; or indirectly by creating a clear link between school funding and pupil roll. However, choice would not improve education standards if parents did not value them — so a second prerequisite is that parent demand school attributes that are linked to better attainments, be these the composition of peers or the proficiency of teachers. Needless to say, for choice to be meaningful, schools should be able to differentiate and respond to changes in demand. This is why operational autonomy is a key ingredient of market-oriented education reforms. Finally, the education market should be allowed to 'play out' its effects so that school competition can leverage the other elements of the system (accountability, choice and autonomy) to improve standards. In simple terms, this means: allowing bad schools to fail and exit the market; allowing successful schools to expand their market share and provide them with incentives to do so (e.g., in the form of extra resources); and promote entry to attract new quality providers to the education market (Brunello & Rocco, 2008; McMillan, 2004 put forward some countervailing arguments on the possible downsides of quasi-markets in education. Both studies suggest that schools can lower their standards in competitive environment either by specializing in educating 'high effort cost' students who would not thrive in more demanding schools, or by going 'down the market' to serve families with little preference for high education standards — and save on the costs of providing them).

In this chapter, we review evidence that sheds light on the impact of competition on educational standards. Conversely, we do not review papers that focus on the effects of accountability per se (e.g., Burgess, Wilson, & Worth, 2013; Figlio & Rouse, 2006 on the abolition of league tables in Wales); on the determinants of school choice (e.g., Bertoni, Gibbons, & Silva, 2017; Burgess, Greaves, Vignoles, & Wilson, 2015; Hastings, Kane, & Staiger, 2005); on its effects (e.g., Cullen, Jacob, & Levitt, 2006); or on autonomy (e.g., Abdulkadiroğlu et al., 2011, 2016, 2017; Eyles & Machin, 2018; Eyles, Hupkau, & Machin, 2016). A discussion of some of these issues in the UK context is also provided by Bradley in Chapter 32 of this book.

Furthermore, we do not review all types of evidence. Instead, we chose articles that take a quantitative approach and that score three or above on the Maryland 'Scientific Method Scores' (SMS). The SMS is a five-point scale that ranks the methodological quality used (mainly) in social science studies developed by Sherman et al. (1997) with the aim of communicating effectively to practitioners and policy makers that empirical studies differ in their methodological quality. This means we include studies that have a well-defined 'treatment' and 'control' structure and that account for unobservables by either exploiting panel variation in the data (e.g., a difference-in-difference approaches), or by exploiting quasi-random variation in competition (e.g., quasi-randomness in policy interventions). Finally, we focus on studies from economics and closely related disciplines (e.g., social and public policy) because these are the fields that have pioneered the idea of promoting markets in education and empirically assessed its validity. It is also the literature we have contributed to, and the field we are mostly familiar with by background training.

In terms of geographical coverage, we focus on evidence from four countries: the United Kingdom; the United States; Sweden; and Chile. Several reasons dictate this choice. First, these four nations have been experimenting with market-oriented education systems for some decades — and a relatively established core of evidence on the effects of competition exists by now. Furthermore, all countries moved in the direction of injecting choice, autonomy and market elements in education because of a strong political impetus — which lead to the implementation of fairly radical ideas and policies. Finally, all four countries embody to varying degrees the four building blocks discussed above which should allow school competition to exert its effects and potentially lead to the improvement of standards. Before moving to our review of the evidence, we briefly discuss the system of each of the four nations.

We start by discussing the institutional framework that characterizes the biggest nation of the UK, namely England. Reforms that brought choice, autonomy and competition to state-sector education were ushered in by the Education Reform Act of 1988. According to Kenneth Baker — then the Education Secretary — the reform package aimed to increase attainments by overhauling the system and leveraging quasi-market incentives in education. A number of radical changes were introduced. First, a new funding formula was introduced linking resources to pupil numbers — in essence creating a (quasi-)voucher system with portable funds following students through the process of school choice. Second, more autonomy was given to schools — which were empowered with more decision making. Some of them — e.g., Grant Maintained schools — were also given a chance to 'opt out' of the Local Authority (LA) control and manage their operations independently. Third, the process of choice was enshrined in the legislation that led to these changes and caps imposed on school size by the central government were lifted — giving good schools a chance to expand. Finally, parental choice was assisted through the publication of yearly performance tables that ranked schools on the basis of centrally administered and externally marked exams. Although these core principles have remained essentially unchanged over time, their details have evolved. Performance tables have over time published not only percentages of students achieving national targets set on the basis of final exams, but also been enriched with information on school size and composition — including percentages of students with different ethnicities or eligible for free meals (a proxy for low income). Recent government initiatives have moved the emphasis toward measures that capture 'value added' and thus represent quality in terms of progress. Additionally, ratings by the school inspectorate (OFSTED) have been published over time — further assisting the process of school choice by providing a simplified assessment of quality overall and on aspects that performance tables do not capture (e.g., student safety, behavior and wellbeing). A 'pupil premium' was also introduced in 2011 providing more funds to educate disadvantaged pupils. This reduced incentives for schools to 'cream skim' and opened the possibility to create a market for schools interested in specializing in hard-to-teach students. However, the latest major educational policy initiative was the introduction of academy schools which brought unprecedented degrees of school autonomy to the education landscape. Academies are schools that, despite being state-funded, non-selective and non-fee-charging, fall outside the control of the local government in terms of key strategic decisions and management. They were introduced by the Labor Government in 2002 as a remedial intervention aimed at failing schools, forcing organizational change under the guidance of a sponsor willing to invest in the school (usually an entity from the private/charitable sector). However, from 2010 the Conservative/ Liberal Democrat Coalition Government dramatically expanded the academy program and changed its nature by allowing high-performing schools to become academies and acquire operational autonomy. At present, approximately 27% of primary schools and

more than 70% of secondaries operate as academies. A smaller program — the 'free school' initiative — also allowed completely new schools founded by parents or charitable groups to enter the market and operate with substantial autonomy (at the time of writing there are approximately 150 and 170 primary and secondary free schools, respectively). While the system seems geared toward producing competition-like incentives that could lead to higher standards, some drawbacks remain. First, choice (conditional on place of residence) is in fact limited: when schools are oversubscribed, priority is given to pupils living nearby. As a result, living close to good schools attract a high house-price premium (see Gibbons, Machin, & Silva, 2013) limiting choice for the less well-off who cannot afford to live close to good schools. Furthermore, students who cannot be assigned to a school of their choice because of capacity constraints are allocated to the closest school with spare capacity — artificially boosting the roll of underperforming and under subscribed schools. This blunts the link between quality and market 'exit threat' — decreasing the sharpness of the competition forces. Similarly, expansions of highly performing schools are not incentivized: the reputation (and the salaries) of the head-teachers and other key figures on the school managerial team depends on the school's reputation — and its link to a large school size is far from obvious. Furthermore, expansions at good — generally already at-capacity — schools is also not easy because of planning restrictions and institutional constraints — mainly the unavailability of suitable sites, which are tightly controlled by the LA.

The US education system is characterized by a much more fragmented reality that varies from state to state, and across local jurisdictions. Historically, school admissions have been organized around catchment areas — meaning that school choice has mainly been exercised through residential relocation and school competition materialized as competition between local administrative authorities in the sense of Tiebout (1956). Nevertheless, choice programmes have existed locally (e.g., the Chicago Public School (CPS) system guarantees students admission to their neighborhood school, but also allows them to apply for any other school in the system). However, the two most commonly discussed initiatives that have expanded choice in the US are voucher programmes and charter schools. Political support for voucher programmes dates back to the late 1980s and one of the most high profile early example was the program introduced in Milwaukee in 1990 — currently used by approximately 15,000 students. The details of voucher programmes vary substantially across the US, but broadly speaking they are publicly funded resources used by students to attend a public school of their choice — though private schools can be part of voucher systems. Similarly, the charter school movement started in the early 1990s and has now become a mainstream feature of the US education system — counting 6900 schools and enrolling more than 3 million pupils in 2016. Charter policies are not radically different from voucher programmes: charter schools are 'chartered' by the local government to educate pupils in exchange for a publicly funded fee — a form of voucher. However, charter schools tend to be new market entrants; are not allowed to practice positive discrimination; and are reassessed at regular times to evaluate whether certain government-determined criteria are met and the charter (i.e., the mission) of the school has been accomplished (e.g., educating the poor and disadvantaged). Besides charter fees and the vouchers, schools in the US are mainly funded from local property and income taxes — implying that resources are unequally distributed across space. While this type of funding is not directly portable, the high degree of mobility in the US means that parents 'vote' for bundles of taxation and school quality by sorting across communities — creating a link between quality, school popularity and available resources.

Remarkably, until the 2001 No Child Left Behind Act (NCLB), there was little in the way of a standardized accountability framework. NCLB supported standards-based education reforms and required states to set up standardized and centrally administer tests to receive federal funding (though it did not enforce nation-wide uniform standards and allowed states to develop their own tests). In conclusion, when considering the possible effects of competition on education standards in the US, local details matter substantially. Nevertheless, a general perception is that voucher programs and charter schools are likely to have introduced significant market oriented forces and incentives to which public schools might have reacted. We will therefore review the literature on vouchers and charter schools that tries to isolate the 'competition' effect that they might have had on attainments by causing system-wide responses. On the other hand, we will not cover the literature that focuses on the effect of attending a charter school; Epple, Romano, and Zimmer (2015) provides a comprehensive survey of this strand of research.

Sweden started sweeping reforms in the late 1980s/early 1990s which saw the introduction of choice and a significant decentralization of its education system. In particular, the centre-right government elected in 1991 passed legislation in 1992 that enshrined a universal voucher system, allowed private 'free schools' (sometimes for-profit institutions linked in chains) to receive public funding and forced local municipal schools to depend on the voucher system for their funding. These changes significantly lowered the entry barriers for private, autonomous educators — which saw a rapid expansion from approximately 1% of pupils in 1992 to around 15% in the 2015. Although the Swedish system is often regarded as an ideal setting for competition to manifest its effects, drawbacks are evident. First, choice is constrained (as is in England) because over-subscribed schools prioritize local students. Second, until the mid-1990s 'free schools' received less funding than municipal ones and − even after legislation was passed to equalize funding − disparities persist in favor of local state schools because of the way compensations for administrative costs and tax deductions for educational activities are treated in the two sectors. However, the biggest drawback lies with the fact that Sweden lacks a proper accountability framework. Performance tables to assess school quality are underdeveloped and mainly publish average GPA scores (though since 2000 some corrections are made for students' demographics). More importantly, GPAs do not come from centrally administered and marked tests, rather from teacher-assessed exams managed at the school level. This greatly reduces the effectiveness of choice and the power of school competition in driving education standards and introduces the risk of 'grade inflation' as a response to competitive pressures (see discussions in Shalgren, 2011 and some evidence in Hinnerich & Vlachos, 2017).

Lastly, we briefly describe the Chilean education market. Following large-scale interventions in 1981, more competition, choice and autonomy were injected in the system. Control of local public schools was devolved to municipalities; a system of vouchers was introduced to make per-pupil spending portable and allow choice; and private non-fee charging schools were allowed to operate in the same market as municipal ones and to receive voucher funding (at a later stage fee-charging schools were allowed in the voucher system if they set some of the received funds aside to sponsor scholarships for less affluent pupils). Further reforms were introduced in the 1990s to strengthen the functioning of the education quasi-market. To begin with, employment contract at municipal schools were made less 'rigid', helping public schools to deploy their workforce more effectively (and shed the ineffective teachers). The nominal value of vouchers was also increased, and a 50% premium was introduced for less well-off and difficult-to-teach students. These changes helped meet the costs of delivering quality teaching

(Chilean professionals hold a consensus that the initial level of the voucher was too low for this purpose) and reduced the incentives for schools to 'cream skim' and select only the best and easy-to-teach students. The latter issue was further addressed by more recent reforms which banned schools from selecting students on ability until sixth grade. Nevertheless, two significant problems remain in what is arguably the oldest 'market for schools'. First, municipal schools still operate under (relatively) soft budget constraints. This means that public underperforming schools remain in the market blunting competition effects that work through the threat of 'market exit'. Second, the level of information provided to parents to guide their choice is insufficient. Although standardized and centrally market tests (the SIMCE) were introduced in 1991, most of the published data relates to raw scores − as opposed to value-added measures or assessment of quality net of student composition. Changes were introduced in the 2000s with more information presented to parents on school inputs − such as class size and teacher evaluations − as well as outputs. Nevertheless, there remains some opacity in terms of simple cross-school comparisons of like-for-like quality proxies.

We next move to a review of the available evidence. This will be organized country by country and with some attention to the methodological approach taken by the studies. We will then conclude with a brief discussion of possible mechanisms that might hold back competition from exerting its positive effects.

Empirical evidence

England

Research based on pupil and school level administrative data on England finds either limited or no effects of competition in education markets on education standards.

Gibbons and Silva (2008) investigate this issue indirectly by studying the effect of urban density on achievement. Using administrative data on several cohorts of pupils in state schools in England, the authors estimate an education production function in value-added form with school fixed effects, and focus on three measures of urban density: density of schools, amount of developed land and residential population density. Identification comes from variation in density around schools attended by pupils during the compulsory transition from primary to secondary school. Their evidence shows that pupils experience an improvement in attainment between age 11 and age 16 when they move from low to high density locations to attend secondary schools: an additional school within 2 km is associated with a rise in attainment of 0.08−0.1 percentiles. Digging deeper, the estimates show that changes in school density − rather than in urbanization or population − lead to a positive change in attainment, and that differences in school resources or policies implemented in the more dense locations are unlikely to explain this finding. In fact, the measure of school density has a positive and statistically significant effect only when measured in terms of secondary schools available to pupils − leading the authors to conclude that competition or (less likely) cooperation between schools must be the driving forces behind their effects. While important, this analysis is limited by the inability to distinguish between the effect of cooperation and competition − and to disentangle the impact of competition from the effect of choice (i.e., the effect stemming from a better school-to-pupil matching).

More indirect evidence is added by Allen and Vignoles (2016) who assess the 'total' effect of the presence of secondary Catholic schools on the attainment of pupils enrolled in neighboring schools. If more advantaged parents seek a place in religious schools (as in England; see Gibbons & Silva, 2011), then the presence of Catholic schools may have three effects on students in non-religious schools: it may produce a spillover effect in the local educational market because of potential competition that triggers greater efforts in other schools; it may affect peer composition through sorting; and finally it may give pupils more choice − and allow a better match with education providers. Importantly, the supply of places in Catholic schools can be endogenous to the quality of pupils in the market. Therefore, to identify the causal effect of competition induced by Catholic schools, Allen and Vignoles use an instrumental variable (IV) strategy that predicts the variation in the current proportion of available places in local Catholic schools using historic proportions of Catholics living in the areas. This strategy finds no association between Catholic school presence and the academic performance of pupils in neighboring schools. One important limitation of this research design is that it is based on one single cross section of pupils in England and cannot exploit any change in the supply of Catholic school places. This raises the question of whether historical instruments truly by-pass school and market-wide unobservables that could bias the association between religious school density and students' outcomes. Furthermore, the work provides a limited discussion about whether lack of positive effects comes from lack of competition-driven responses − as opposed to positive quasi-market effects counterbalanced by negative factors (such as differential peer composition in the religious vs. non-religious sector).

More robust evidence comes from Clark (2009) who examines the effects of a reform that introduced a shock in the local supply of autonomous schools: in 1988, state schools were given the possibility of opting out of the control of the district and gain unprecedented independence while being funded directly by the central government. The autonomy included ownership of the school premises and complete control of staffing. Schools wishing to gain this autonomy had to win a majority vote among the parents of current students. Clark therefore uses a regression discontinuity (RD) strategy that compares schools that narrowly won and narrowly lost the vote to estimate the effect of this increased autonomy on the achievement of pupils at these autonomous institutions, as well as on the performance of surrounding schools — under the assumption that spill-overs could happen because of competitive pressure (or increased support by local authorities for schools that do not 'opt out' of their control). The findings show a positive effect of increased autonomy on current pupil achievement — but no spill-overs on neighboring schools. While more robust to school and local unobservable shocks, this analysis still cannot disentangle whether the lack of evidence on competition effects stems from a lack of school reactions to quasi-market forces or other counter-balancing impacts.

Burgess and Slater (2006) exploit a different shock in the supply of local schools. They base their research design on a feature of the education system in England: almost all pupils outside London attend a school in the district (Local Authority) where they reside because of administrative barriers that make it difficult to apply for schools in other districts. In a quasi-experiment setting, they exploit a change in boundaries that split a single district into six different authorities (the split occurred in 1998). This reduced the competition faced by certain schools as some local alternatives suddenly become no longer available, allowing the authors to focus on the effect of a reduction in competitive pressure. Using two cohorts of students — one that concluded secondary school before the change and one that finished after — the authors conduct a difference-in-difference study using schools in similar areas that did not experience boundary changes as a control group. Their estimates are negative but not statistically different from zero.

A significant innovation in the study of competition is introduced by Gibbons, Machin, and Silva (2008) who empirically separate the effect of choice on attainment from the impact of competition, and use an IV strategy based on district boundary impediments to by-pass selection

biases due to unobservable shocks. Their work focuses on the primary education market in an urban area in England and is based on administrative microdata on pupils attending schools in this location. Detailed information on pupil residence postcodes and school postcodes allows the authors to create a measure of school choice available for each pupil, and a measure of competition faced by each school in the data. As the authors argue, choice is a property of residential location of the pupils so a meaningful choice index can be defined as the number of school 'accessible' to each pupil from home — i.e., those within a reasonable travel distance. On the other hand, competition is a property of school that depends on how many alternative its pupils had — so an intuitive competition index can be defined by considering the average number of alternatives available to enrolled pupils. As families choose where to live partly on the basis of available schools and their characteristics (i.e., schools drive residential sorting), these indices could be endogenous to the production of attainment. The authors therefore use an IV strategy based on the intuition that pupils living near the boundary of a school district will face on average longer distances to attend a school other than their closest one — so choice is restricted — and consequently schools near the district's boundaries face less competition than schools located further away. Their results show that school choice does not have any effect on pupil achievement — neither positive nor negative — whereas competition is positively linked to achievement but only among schools that have more autonomy in governance: one additional competitor increases the growth in achievement by almost 0.20 of a standard deviation in the achievement distribution (hereafter σ).

To conclude this section, we note that at present no evidence has been collected on the possible competition effects of the mass 'academization' of the English system on students' outcomes. This is an important area for future research.

US

As discussed, in the US a common form of competition between schools is driven by Tiebout choice — i.e., households making their residential choices among school districts. However, the widespread presence of private schools and state-specific voucher and charter programmes has provided parents with wider school choice — and thereby increased competition faced by schools — even conditional on place of residence.

Hoxby (2000) evaluates the effect of Tiebout choice and inter-district competition in metropolitan areas on education outcomes by using repeated observations for a sample of students. In her analysis, Hoxby measures competition at metropolitan area-level and based on the concentration of pupils across school districts within the area (i.e., a Herfindahl index based on student shares). Big and small cities differ in the cost households incur in exercising their choice: the more districts are within the reach of most households' residences, the lower the cost of choosing for households. In turn, this can have a positive effect on achievement if choice pushes districts to compete on the quality of education they provide to attract students. Obviously, simple estimation of an education production function that includes such a measure of choice is complicated by the possibility that the district concentration is endogenous to the quality of the education provided. To by-pass the problem, Hoxby devises an innovative instrument based on the extent of natural barriers that prevent districts from merging with each other — in particular, the number of streams within the metropolitan area. IV estimates show that Tiebout choice raises productivity of school districts by increasing achievement and lowering per-pupil costs: an increase by 10 percentage points in the choice index implies reading scores that are 0.3–0.57 points higher (up to 0.05σ) and 0.76% decrease in per-pupil spending. Furthermore, Hoxby finds that where households have more Tiebout choice they are less likely to choose

private schools as competition raises the quality of public schools. An important finding of this study is that not accounting for endogeneity biases toward zero the effect of competition induced by choice.

In another seminal study, Hoxby (1994) examines the effect of competitive pressure from private school enrollment on public school outcomes using student survey data. Endogeneity of private enrollment is accounted for with an IV estimation strategy where current county shares of population with different religious denominations — in particular the incidence of Catholics — are used to predict variation in private school enrollment (as most private schools are religious). As religious shares are historically determined, Hoxby makes the argument that they are not correlated to the quality of the current provision of education. Her findings indicate a positive effect of competition from private schools on public school outcomes: a 10% points increase in the share of enrollment in Catholic schools causes an extra 0.33 years of education for public school students. The author performs an extensive set of checks to rule out possible alternative explanations — for example, that Catholics simply perform better on average or that greater religious homogeneity of the population is linked to higher achievement because it allows public schools to perform better. All of these confirm her baseline estimates showing a strong and significant impact of competition on outcomes.

State-specific voucher programmes have also given US researchers the possibility to exploit 'shocks' to the local supply of schools and estimate short and mid-term effects of choice programmes — and the competition among schools they trigger. Targeted vouchers for poor students were introduced in Milwaukee in the early 1990s. Hoxby (2003) assesses the competitive effect of this program on the productivity of local public schools using data around 1998, when she argues the scale of participation was likely to have generated competition effects. In her analysis, the author compares three types of schools before and after 1998: schools that were more heavily treated (i.e., where at least two-thirds of students were eligible for vouchers), schools that were less intensely treated (i.e., where less than two-thirds of students were eligible) and control schools (i.e., those located in the rest of Wisconsin that were unaffected by the reform). Estimates obtained with this difference-in-difference strategy and using school-level data show that public schools responded to competition from private schools with a sharp increase in productivity. Furthermore, the stronger was the degree of competition faced by schools, the greater was the effect on public school performance.

While important, these early estimates obtained using school-level data cannot disentangle the effect of endogenous movement of pupils across sectors once choice is introduced from the direct effect of school competition. This issue is rigorously addressed by Figlio and Hart (2014) in their evaluation of a means-tested voucher program that was announced in Florida in 2001 and implemented one year later. The intervention provided scholarships to disadvantaged students who wanted to attend private schools and initially focused on a very small share of public school students (less than 1%). Despite the small targeted population, the authors argue that the vouchers created an incentive for schools to compete on performance because educators were simply aware of the existence of the program rather than of its scale. In order to estimate the (short-term) impact of the increased competitive pressure generated by the program, Figlio and Hart use a difference-in-difference strategy and administrative data for all students in Florida covering the year pre-reform and several years post-reform. The identification strategy exploits the geographical variation in the potential for private school competition measured by the number and diversity of pre-reform private education alternatives. Their estimates indicate that competition from

private schools has a small positive effect on achievement of pupils: adding 10 nearby private schools increases test scores by 0.02σ. An analysis of the heterogeneity of the results shows that gains in achievement are greater in schools that are at the margin of receiving additional funding for disadvantaged pupils and so face bigger financial consequence as a result of competition.

As the charter school sector has rapidly emerged and spread across US states, several studies have also investigated the 'competition' effect of this new type of school on traditional public school outcomes. We consider four studies that identify credible causal estimates for the effect of charter competition by either exploiting the variation in the timing and number of entry of charter schools (Booker, Gilpatric, Gronberg, & Jansen, 2008; Cordes, 2017); or by finding exogenous sources of variation in the location of charter schools (Bettinger, 2005; Imberman, 2011).

Booker et al. (2008) test for the existence of competitive effects of charter schools in Texas by using panel data covering all students enrolled in public schools. The authors measure charter competition as the number of charter schools or charter students within a fixed radius from each public school and estimate a value added model with student/school spell fixed effects. The coefficients of interest are identified by pupils who stay in the same school for more than a year. Estimates show a positive but small effect of charter school entry and penetration on nearby public school attainments. Similarly, Cordes (2017) uses a difference-in-difference strategy that exploits the variation in the timing of entry of charters within one mile radius from a public school, as well as the distance from the closest charter school, to estimate the effect of charter competition on traditional public schools in the densely populated area of New York City. While this study accounts for the endogenous movement of pupils across public schools (with an intention-to-treat approach where pupils are fixed in the school where they are first observed), it does not fully tackle the issue of the sorting of pupils into/out of the public school sector. Nonetheless, the results show that charter schools have a small positive effect on the attainment of public school students: attending a public school located within 1 mile from a charter school increases achievement by 0.015σ; this effect monotonically increases with the proximity of charters. Overall, these estimates are comparable in size to the ones found by Booker et al. (2008) in Texas and by Figlio and Hart (2014) in Florida.

Studies that use difference-in-difference identification strategies however cannot fully control for the endogeneity of charter location. Researchers have therefore looked for potential research strategies that use instruments associated with the location of charters but otherwise uncorrelated with the education outcomes of pupils in public schools. One such study is Bettinger (2005) which exploits a unique characteristic of charter legislation in Michigan: the governing boards of universities can authorize charter schools — and the ten universities where the state governor appointed the board approved all the university-authorized charters. This was most likely the result of political pressure exerted by the governor which is unlikely to be related to the outcomes of students in specific public schools. Bettinger thus estimates a value-added model for achievement and uses the distance of public schools from the closest of one of these ten universities as an instrument for the number of local charters. The author finds no effect of charter competition on the achievement of public school students. A limitation of this study is that it uses school level data and therefore cannot account for the selection of pupils in public schools.

The issues of sample selection and endogenous location of charters are jointly considered by Imberman (2011). To identify the effect of charter competition on nearby public schools in the presence of endogenous entry of charters, Imberman proposes an IV strategy where charter penetration is instrumented with the number of sizable non-residential buildings in the proximity of each public school. The intuition behind this instrument is that charter schools open where appropriately sized buildings are available to rent. To take into account pupils' self-selection into public schools, the empirical model further includes pupil fixed effect. Results show small negative effects of charter competition on the achievement of public primary school students: a 10% points increase in the penetration index is linked to a drop in achievement by $0.06-0.07\sigma$. The author also finds that an increase in charter school competition corresponds to a reduction in disciplinary infractions for middle and high school pupils. The author argues that the joint sorting of pupils with worst behavior and teachers with the highest 'impact' toward charters could explain these results.

The latter hypothesis is partly supported by Jackson (2012) who investigates the effect of charter entry on teacher labor market in North Carolina. The author finds that schools with more difficult students and located in the proximity of charter schools hire fewer new teachers and experience a decline in the quality of their staff. In addition, Jackson finds that schools that face charter competition pay higher salaries, possibly to retain and attract better teachers. This result is confirmed by Terrier and Ridley (2018) who assess the effects of a reform that lifted the cap on charter schools in Massachusetts and find that traditional public schools that face increased charter competition increases their per-pupil expenditure in salaries and instruction-related activities.

Sweden

As discussed, Sweden implemented sweeping reforms in the early 1990s that led to increased choice and sharpened competition — in particular between municipality schools and private 'free schools'. In our review, we focus on studies that explicitly investigate the competition-like effects of these reforms.

The first is Sandström and Bergström (2005) who use data for a cross section of pupils enrolled in public schools in 1997/98 and estimate an achievement production function where student performance is a function of individual and school characteristics as well as the share of private school enrollment in the municipality where the student lives. The authors argue that the latter variable is a measure of the market-like pressures on public schools exerted in each market/municipality by private competitors in the aftermath of the 1990s reforms. This measure could be endogenous to the quality of public schools in the municipality or to unobserved characteristics of the population that are correlated with achievement. To deal with the problem, Sandström and Bergström select a set of political features of the municipalities in their sample as instruments for the share of private enrollment (in particular, they use measures of the attitude of the municipalities toward the establishment of private schools as proxied by the share of non-school public sector activities contracted out to non-state agents). However, the authors face a second challenge when conducting their analysis — namely the sorting of students between private and public schools. In order to address the issue, they use a Heckman-correction approach to take into account the non-random selection of pupils into public schools with variables capturing political orientations as 'excluded instruments' (i.e. variable that only enters the selection equation). While it is reasonable to assume that their instruments for the share of local private schools do not affect outcomes directly — and so the exclusion restriction holds — the argument that political preferences only affect outcomes via the choice of school sector (public/private) is more dubious. Nevertheless, the authors' final estimates indicate that competitive pressures improve the scores of pupils enrolled in public schools.

More recently, Böhlmark and Lindahl (2015) use administrative data for all Swedish students who finished compulsory school between 1988 and 2009 and investigate the effect of the 1990s reform on student achievement at the end of compulsory schooling, as well as long-term outcomes such as university attendance and years of schooling. Given the problems faced by Sandström and Bergström (2005) in dealing with selection into private or public schooling, the authors focus on the market-wide effect of the reform — i.e., pooling students in both sectors. Their empirical strategy exploits the long time-series dimension available and identifies the impact of the policy by focusing on long differences. In particular, the authors study how changes in students' outcomes aggregated at the municipal level between the last available post-reform cohort and the last available pre-reform cohort relate to the corresponding changes in the share of private enrollment (thus differencing out all municipal time-fixed unobservables). To probe the robustness of their approach, Böhlmark and Lindhal use additional data for several years before the implementation of the reform to test whether pre-reform trends in several municipality characteristics can predict post-reform private enrollment. Their evidence shows no clear associations — and in particular rejects the possibility that the share of private school enrollment increased substantially in municipalities where public schools where failing before the reform. Overall, the authors find a positive association between the incidence of private schools and achievement both at the end of compulsory schooling and on long-run outcomes. Once again, it is however difficult to understand whether these stems from competition effects or better matching between pupils and schools once choice is extended to the private sector.

Finally, an interesting related study is Hensvik (2012) who looks at the effect of the reform on the teacher market by using a panel of teachers matched to schools. The author finds that the expanding private sector after the reform attracted teachers from the upper part of the skill distribution. Furthermore, his evidence suggests that competition between schools resulted in an increase in teacher salaries across all schools (in line with Jackson, 2012). This finding is interesting for two reasons. First, given that teacher quality has been identified as one of the main determinants of student outcomes, these results suggest that the reform might have detrimental long-run effects on state schools by pushing more effective teachers into the private sector. Second, these patterns support the idea that public schools have faced competitive pressure from private schools located in the same municipality and have reacted to it by raising salaries to (try to) retain good teachers and to compete on quality.

Chile

The first education reform that widened choice and increased the competitive pressure faced by municipal schools in Chile was introduced in 1981. This reform determined a sharp increase in the number of private schools — particularly in urban and wealthier neighbourhoods.

Hsieh and Urquiola (2006) evaluate the overall effect of this reform on educational outcomes by using a panel of municipalities and comparing the change in aggregate achievement in urban and rural areas with the change in private school shares. Like most previous studies, the authors make no attempt to disentangle between the effect of choice and the effect of competition. Furthermore, they assume that the differential entry of private schools in different areas was driven by time-invariant characteristics of the communities living in these areas, and that these time-persistent aspects can be differenced out by looking at pre/post-policy differences in outcomes. As a robustness check, Hsieh and Urquiola supplement their approach

with an IV strategy that uses pre-reform characteristics of the municipalities as instruments for the share of students enrolled in private schools — under the assumption that these are not correlated to unobservable municipality shocks that could directly affect changes in achievement following the reform. The authors find no evidence of an effect of the reform on achievement and propose two possible explanations. First, it is possible that post-reform enrollment in private schools expanded where there were pre-existing negative trend in achievement; these offset the improvement in educational outcomes determined by wider choice and reallocation of pupils toward better schools. Second, parents choose schools with better peers rather than better quality and schools responded to quasi-market pressures by trying to attract better pupils — instead of competing on productivity. However, better peers alone might not necessarily improve average achievement (Lavy, Silva, & Weinhardt, 2012). This hypothesis is supported by empirical evidence of pupil sorting across schools: Hsieh and Urquiola find that an increase in private enrollment is associated to a decrease in the relative income of public school parents and a decline in the relative academic performance of public schools. These findings suggest that the sorting component driven by increased school choice is likely to dominate the effect of competition on public school quality.

Gallego (2005) similarly studies whether the competition from private voucher-schools improve attainments but adopts an IV strategy similar to the one used by Allen and Vignoles (2016) for England. The author argues that interaction of the number of Catholic priests in different areas in 1950 and the institution of the voucher system in 1981 is a valid instrument for the potentially endogenous incidence of private schools. Using this approach, Gallego finds that private voucher-school market entries have a positive effect on tests scores — and that this effect is similar for students attending public and private schools. The latter finding especially should be taken with caution: to deal with the problem of sorting of students across sectors, Gallego uses a Heckman-type sample-selection correction with parents' views on the importance of 'teaching of values' (mainly religious/Catholic) as an instrument for private school choice. While it is reasonable to assume that this variable influences school choice (i.e., there is a first stage), it is far from obvious that the proxy only affects achievement through the chosen school sector — and not directly via the ethos that such families have (i.e., the exclusion restriction is unlikely to hold).

Last, we discussed the work by Neilson (2013) who focuses on a recent policy change (in 2008) that introduced a targeted voucher program transferring more resources to schools — either public or private — that matriculated pupils in the poorest 40% of the population (schools were not allowed to charge additional fees to eligible pupils). Neilson evaluates the impact of this policy by distinguishing two mechanisms through which achievement of poor pupils could improve: the wider and better choice of schools given to them — i.e., a 'matching' effect; and the incentive for schools to improve quality and compete for the enrollment of these pupils — i.e., a market competition effect. The author estimates the parameters of an empirical structural model of school choice which allows the identification of the demand and supply side effects of the policy. In particular, he finds that the choices of disadvantaged families are more affected by distance and prices — and less by quality of schools — than the choices of the better off. Therefore schools in poor neighbourhoods face a demand that is less sensitive to changes in quality before the introduction of the voucher. However, the targeted voucher program lowers the price of better schools and so it decreases the market power of schools in poorer neighbourhoods — giving them an incentive to improve standards. Overall, Neilson finds that the intervention raised test scores of the poorest 40% of students by 0.2σ and that two-thirds of

this aggregate policy effect can be explained by inter-school competition and the remaining third by choice. Alongside Gibbons et al. (2008), this paper is the only one that makes an effort at distinguishing 'choice' from 'competition' and estimating the relative contributions of these components — albeit with a radically different approach.

Conclusions

Our review suggests that the evidence on the impact of competition on pupil attainment is mixed. Studies that use school- and municipal-level data tend to find larger effects than studies that rely on pupil-level data. However, the latter are probably better at identifying the impact of competition alone — net of any possible effects stemming from the sorting of students across schools/sectors when choice is extended or introduced.

What could lie behind such dismal findings? Some common feature could explain the failure of competition to improve standards — some of which we discussed above. First, across the four countries (albeit with varying degrees), market forces are still not allowed to fully 'play their role' and thus manifest their effects. Primarily this is because 'bad' schools are not forced to close, and 'good' schools not incentivized to expand. Indeed, underperforming schools under the control of the local authorities are often 'protected' from the full force of the quasi-markets — either because admission systems top up their roll with students that cannot be seated at other schools, or because their funding is somewhat decoupled from their (in-)ability to attract students. Although controversial, evidence suggests that closing underperforming schools improves outcomes of reassigned students — with negative spill-over effects in receiving schools that are too modest to justify the 'status quo' (see among other Brummet, 2014). At the opposite end, outstanding schools have limited incentives to expand and captures market shares — if anything complicated regulations tend to constrain expansion plans — and fairly steep entry barriers prevent new providers from coming to the market. As in many other settings, these constraints are likely to dampen the potential for competition to raise productivity.

A second problem lies with the structure of the accountability frameworks characterizing the four countries we investigated. Broadly speaking, too much emphasis is placed on final grades in the league tables than on value-added — implying that schools might not have incentives to improve their effectiveness. In fact, such systems might create incentives for schools to attract easy-to-teach students with advantageous backgrounds — as they are more likely to perform well in final exams. Reforms — like those promoted in Chile and England — that attach more funding to disadvantaged students while at the same time moving toward metrics that more explicitly focus on progress are a step in the direction: they push schools to focus on effectiveness and potentially provide them with incentives to 'specialize' in difficult-to-teach students.

More fundamentally, however, the choice element that is at the core of such systems often remains a notional idea — especially for disadvantaged families. This is so for two reasons. First, 'navigating' the system and 'digesting' the extensive amounts of information on school quality produced by the accountability regimes is not straight forward — especially for worse-off individuals and for those who have not experienced the system first-hand (e.g., migrants). On the positive side, available evidence suggests that information campaign targeting parents of deprived pupils are a cost-effective way of addressing this issue (see Avvisati, Gurgand, Guyon, & Maurin, 2014). Second, too often good — and therefore oversubscribed — schools prioritize student admission by distance or by catchment areas. Because of the capitalization of school quality into house prices (see Black &

Machin, 2010 for a survey), this means that the less affluent have fewer chances of gaining admission to better schools because of 'selection' in the housing market. This potentially concentrates the benefits of good schooling on better-off students who might do well in any case — while depriving pupils who would benefit the most from an outstanding education.

Indeed, besides efficiency considerations, the biggest concern with systems centered on choice, autonomy and quasi-markets is that they might lead to increased segregation of pupils of different background across schools of different quality. While we have not surveyed the literature that focuses on these aspects, such evidence can be found in all four countries we have considered (see for example Gibbons & Silva, 2006 for England and Bölhmark et al., 2016 for Sweden). When considering whether school competition is a 'good' or 'bad' way of organizing education systems, we believe both efficiency and equity considerations should play an equally important role in arriving at an answer and formulating the best policy advice.

References

Allen, R., & Vignoles, A. (2016). Can school competition improve standards? The case of faith schools in England. *Empirical Economics, 50*(3), 959–973.

Abdulkadiroğlu, A., Angrist, J. D., Dynarski, S. M., Kane, T. J., & Pathak, P. A. (2011). Accountability and flexibility in public schools: Evidence from Boston's charters and pilots. *The Quarterly Journal of Economics, 126*(2), 699–748.

Abdulkadiroğlu, A., Angrist, J. D., Hull, P. D., & Pathak, P. A. (2016). Charters without lotteries: Testing takeovers in New Orleans and Boston. *American Economic Review, 106*(7), 1878–1920.

Abdulkadiroğlu, A., Angrist, J. D., Narita, Y., & Pathak, P. A. (2017). Research design meets market design: Using centralized assignment for impact evaluation. *Econometrica, 85*(5), 1373–1432.

Avvisati, F., Gurgand, M., Guyon, N., & Maurin, E. (2014). Getting parents involved: A field experiment in deprived schools. *Review of Economic Studies, 81*(1), 57–83.

Bertoni, M., Gibbons, S., & Silva, O. (2017). *School choice during a period of radical reform. Evidence from the academy programme*. IZA Discussion Paper 11162.

Besley, T., & Ghatak, M. (2005). Competition and incentives with motivated agents. *American Economic Review, 95*(3), 616–636.

Bettinger, E. P. (2005). The effect of charter schools on charter students and public schools. *Economics of Education Review, 24*(2), 133–147.

Black, S., & Machin, S. (2010). Housing valuations of school performance. In E. Hanushek, S. Machin, & L. Woessmann (Eds.), *Handbook of the economics of education* (Vol. 3). North Holland.

Böhlmark, A., Holmlund, H., & Lindahl, M. (2016). Parental choice, neighbourhood segregation or cream skimming? An analysis of school segregation after a generalized choice reform. *Journal of Population Economics, 29*(4), 1155–1190.

Böhlmark, A., & Lindahl, M. (2015). "Independent schools and long-run educational outcomes: Evidence from Sweden's large-scale voucher reform". *Economica, 82*(327), 508–551.

Booker, K., Gilpatric, S. M., Gronberg, T., & Jansen, D. (2008). The effect of charter schools on traditional public school students in Texas: Are children who stay behind left behind? *Journal of Urban Economics, 64*(1), 123–145.

Brummet, Q. (2014). The effect of school closings on student achievement. *Journal of Public Economics, 119*, 108–124.

Brunello, G., & Rocco, L. (2008). Educational standards in public and privates schools. *Economic Journal, 118*(533), 1866–1887.

Burgess, S., Greaves, E., Vignoles, A., & Wilson, D. (2015). What parents want: School preferences and school choice. *Economic Journal, 125*, 1262–1289.

Burgess, S. M., & Slater, H. (2006). *Using boundary changes to estimate the impact of school competition on test scores*. Mimeo, Centre for Market and Public Organisation, University of Bristol.

Burgess, S., Wilson, D., & Worth, J. (2013). A natural experiment in school accountability: The impact of school performance information on pupil progress. *Journal of Public Economics, 106*(2013), 57–67.

Clark, D. (2009). The performance and competitive effects of school autonomy. *Journal of Political Economy, 117*(4), 745–783.

Cordes, S. A. (2017). In pursuit of the common good: The spillover effects of charter schools on public school students in New York City. *Education Finance and Policy*, 1–49 (Just Accepted).

Cullen, J., Jacob, B., & Levitt, S. (2006). The effect of school choice on participants: Evidence from randomized lotteries. *Econometrica, 74*(5), 1191–1230.

Epple, D., Romano, R., & Zimmer, R. (2015). *Charter school: A survey of research on their characteristics and effectiveness*. NBER Working Paper 21256.

Eyles, A., Hupkau, C., & Machin, S. (2016). Academies, charter and free schools: Do new school types deliver better outcomes? *Economic Policy, 31*(87), 453–501.

Eyles, A., & Machin, S. (2019). The introduction of academy schools to England's education. *Journal of the European Economic Association, 17*(4), 1107–1146.

Figlio, D., & Hart, C. (2014). Competitive effects of means-tested school vouchers. *American Economic Journal: Applied Economics, 6*(1), 133–156.

Figlio, D., & Rouse, C. (2006). Do accountability and voucher threats improve low-performing schools? *Journal of Public Economics, 90*(1–2), 239–255.

Friedman, M. (1962). *Capitalism and freedom*. Chicago-IL: University of Chicago Press.

Gallego, F. (2005). *Voucher-school competition, incentives, and outcomes: Evidence from Chile*. Boston (MA): Job-Market Paper, Department of Economics, MIT.

Gibbons, S., Machin, S., & Silva, O. (2008). Choice, competition, and pupil achievement. *Journal of the European Economic Association, 6*(4), 912–947.

Gibbons, S., Machin, S., & Silva, O. (2013). Valuing school quality using boundary discontinuities. *Journal of Urban Economics, 75*(1), 15–28.

Gibbons, S., & Silva, O. (2006). Competition and accessibility in school markets: Empirical analysis using boundary discontinuities. In T. J. Gronberg, & D. W. Jansen (Eds.), *Improving school accountability: Check-ups or choice?, advances in applied microeconomics* (Vol. 14). Elsevier.

Gibbons, S., & Silva, O. (2008). Urban density and pupil attainment. *Journal of Urban Economics, 63*(2), 631–650.

Gibbons, S., & Silva, O. (2011). Faith primary schools: Better schools or better pupils? *Journal of Labor Economics, 29*(3), 589–635.

Hanushek, E. (2003). The failure of input-based policies. *Economic Journal, 113*(485), F64–F98.

Hastings, J., Kane, T., & Staiger, D. (2005). *Parental preferences and school competition: Evidence from a public school choice program*. NBER Working Paper 11805.

Hensvik, L. (2012). Competition, wages and teacher sorting: Lessons learned from a voucher reform. *Economic Journal, 122*(561), 799–824.

Hinnerich, B. T., & Vlachos, J. (2017). The impact of upper-secondary voucher school attendance on student achievement. Swedish evidence using external and internal evaluations. *Labour Economics, 47*, 1–14.

Hoxby, C. M. (1994). *Do private schools provide competition for public schools?*. National Bureau of Economic Research Working Paper 4978.

Hoxby, C. M. (2003). School choice and school productivity. Could school choice be a tide that lifts all boats?. In *The economics of school choice* (pp. 287–342). University of Chicago Press.

Hoxby, C. M. (2000). Does competition among public schools benefit students and taxpayers? *American Economic Review, 90*(5), 1209–1238.

Hsieh, C. T., & Urquiola, M. (2006). The effects of generalized school choice on achievement and stratification: Evidence from Chile's voucher program. *Journal of Public Economics, 90*(8–9), 1477–1503.

Imberman, S. A. (2011). The effect of charter schools on achievement and behavior of public school students. *Journal of Public Economics, 95*(7–8), 850–863.

Jackson, C. K. (2012). School competition and teacher labor markets: Evidence from charter school entry in North Carolina. *Journal of Public Economics, 96*(5–6), 431–448.

Lavy, V., Silva, O., & Weinhardt, F. (2012). The good, the bad and the average: Evidence on ability peer effects in schools. *Journal of Labor Economics, 30*(2), 367–414.

McMillan, R. (2004). Competition, incentives, and public school productivity. *Journal of Public Economics, 88*(9-10), 1871–1892.

Neilson, C. (2013). *Targeted vouchers, competition among schools, and the academic achievement of poor students.* Mimeo, Yale University.

Ridley, M., & Terrier, C. (2018). *Fiscal and education spillovers from charter school expansion.* National Bureau of Economic Research. Working Paper 25070.

Sahlgren, G. H. (2011). Schooling for money: Swedish education reform and the role of the profit motive. *Economic Affairs, 31*(3), 28–35.

Sandström, F. M., & Bergström, F. (2005). School vouchers in practice: Competition will not hurt you. *Journal of Public Economics, 89*(2–3), 351–380.

Sherman, L. W., Gottfredson, D. C., MacKenzie, D. L., Eck, J., Reuter, P., & Bushway, S. (1997). *Preventing crime: What works, what doesn't, what's promising: A report to the United States Congress.* Washington, DC: US Department of Justice, Office of Justice Programs.

Tiebout, C. M. (1956). A pure theory of local expenditures. *Journal of political economy, 64*(5), 416–424.

The economics of catholic schools

W. Sander[a], D. Cohen-Zada[b]

[a]DePaul University, Chicago, IL, United States; [b]Ben-Gurion University, Beer-Sheva, Israel

Glossary

Error term A variable that is created when the model does not fully represent the actual relationship between the independent variable(s) and the dependent variable

Exogenous variable A factor in a causal model or causal system whose value is independent from the states of other variables in the system

Instrumental variable A method that is used to estimate causal relationships when controlled experiments are not feasible

Self-selection A term that is used to indicate that individuals select themselves into a group causing a biased sample

Standard deviation A measure of variability or dispersion

Introduction

This article examines Catholic schooling in the United States. The article is organized as follows. First, an overview of Catholic schooling in the United States is given. Second, the determinants of the demand for Catholic schools are reviewed. Third, literature on the effects of Catholic schooling is presented. Although the focus of this article is on Catholic schooling in the United States, some attention is also given to Catholic schooling in other countries.

Overview

History and enrollment

The establishment of Catholic schools in the United States was partly a result of the nature of public schooling in the nineteenth century. At that time, many public schools promoted Protestantism and some were overtly anti-Catholic. This resulted in Catholics establishing their own parochial schools. In 1884, Catholic bishops in the United States asked Catholic parishes to support at least one Catholic school and Catholic parents to send their children to them. By 1900, about 5000 Catholic schools had been established serving around 1 million students. The increase in enrollment in Catholic schools was also due to the massive waves of immigration of Catholics to the United States. According to Finke and Stark (2005), between 1890 and 1906, the Catholic population increased from 7 million Catholics (12% of the population) to more than 14 million Catholics (17% of the population). Catholic schools continued to increase both in number and the percentage of the population served until about 1960. By 1960, there were almost 13 000 Catholics schools serving

The Economics of Education, Second Edition
https://doi.org/10.1016/B978-0-12-815391-8.00037-9

over 5 million students. Catholic schools at that time accounted for about 90% of private-school enrollment. Since 1960, Catholic schools have declined in number and the percentage of the population served. Many Catholic schools especially in big cities in the East and Midwest regions have closed. For example, about half of the Catholic schools in Chicago have closed over the past three decades. Enrollment has declined even more from about 132 000 in 1976–77 to 52 000 in 2004–05 (McDonald, 2007).

By 2000, about 11% of elementary and secondary school students attended private schools. Although the percentage attending private schools has not changed too much since 1960, only about half of this population is now in the Catholic school sector. Other religious schools and nonsectarian private schools account for the rest of the private school sector. The most recent data indicate that there are 7498 Catholic elementary and secondary schools that serve over 2 million students. Although Catholic schools have declined overall, there has been some growth in demand in the West and Southeast. This is a result of high rates of economic growth in these areas that has resulted in more Catholics living in these regions (McDonald, 2007).

Teachers

If one goes back in time, most of the teachers in Catholic schools were in religious orders. For example, in 1960 about three out of four Catholic school teachers were members of a Catholic religious order. Over time, this percentage has declined markedly. Recent data indicate that only about 5% of Catholic school teachers are members of a Catholic religious order (McDonald, 2007).

Students

Part of the decline in the Catholic school population is a result of a decline in the demand for a Catholic education by Catholics. For Catholics born before 1950, at least half of them attended a Catholic school for at least 1 year. By 1991, only about one in five Catholic children of elementary school age attended a Catholic school (Youniss and Convey, 2000).

The decline in the demand for a Catholic education by Catholics has been partially offset by an increase in the demand for a Catholic education by non-Catholics. In 1970, only about 3% of Catholic school students were not Catholic. By 2007, the percentage of non-Catholics in Catholic schools increased to about 14%. Part of the increase in non-Catholics attending Catholic schools is a result of more non-Catholic African-Americans in big cities attending Catholic schools. For example, in Chicago about three out of four blacks in Catholic schools are not Catholic (McDonald, 2007; Sander, 2001).

Although most students in Catholic schools are non- Hispanic whites, the percentage of minorities in Catholic schools has increased over time to about one in four students in 2007. About 7% of Catholic school students are black, 6% are Hispanic, 3% are Asian, and 2% are multiracial (McDonald, 2007).

Location

Catholic schools are concentrated in urban areas and in the East and Midwest regions.

Over 40% of Catholic schools are located in big cities while about one in three are located in suburbs of cities. The rest are located in rural areas. Further, over 50% of Catholic schools are located in the East or Midwest regions where the Catholic population is more concentrated. The ten largest Catholic school systems are as follows: (1) New York, (2) Chicago, (3) Philadelphia, (4) Los Angeles, (5) Brooklyn, (6) Cleveland, (7) St. Louis, (8) Cincinnati, (9) Boston, and (10) Newark (McDonald, 2007).

Some metropolitan areas are served by more than one Catholic school system such as New York and Chicago. The reason for this is that the boundaries of the school system are defined by the Catholic archdioceses rather than census boundaries.

Tuition and costs

The average tuition at Catholic schools in 2007 was US $2607 at parish-based elementary schools and US$6906 at secondary schools although the per-pupil cost was higher - US$4268 at grade schools and US$8743 at high schools. The difference between tuition and cost is a result of many factors such as parish subsidies and fund raising. This is below the average per-pupil expenditures at public schools. One of the reasons for relatively low costs at Catholic schools is the relatively low teacher salaries. Further, subsidies from parishes and elsewhere help keep tuition below costs. Recent data indicate that the tuition at Catholic grades schools covers 61.7% of the actual cost per pupil while 80% of the cost per pupil is covered by tuition at Catholic high schools (Harris, 1996; McDonald, 2007).

Hoxby (1994) shows that higher Catholic-population densities have several important implications for tuition and per-pupil cost. First, the number of Catholic schools and Catholic school places per person increase as density goes up. Second, subsidies as a percentage of Catholic school income increase substantially as the Catholic share in the population grows. Third, tuition per pupil decreases as the Catholic share in the population increases.

Market served

Although Catholic schools were established to serve all Catholics and did so for many decades, higher costs and tuition are resulting in Catholic schools serving fewer low-income students and more high-income students. Still, many Catholic school systems try to reach out to students who cannot afford them. For example, in Chicago many Catholic schools are designated as Big Shoulders schools — schools that mostly serve low-income minority students. The dropout rate in these schools is only 1%, while the high school graduation rate is 97%. The dropout rate for public schools in Chicago is markedly higher (Sander, 2001, 2006).

School practices

It is possible that Catholic schools are more effective than public schools due to differences in school practices (Figiio & Ludwlg, 2000). It has been reported that the proportion of students in Catholic schools who report that their school is excellent or good in effectiveness and of discipline is substantially higher than what is reported by public school students (72% vs. 42%). They report similar differences between Catholic and public schools in fairness and discipline (46% vs. 36%).

Vouchers

Vouchers that would enable more students to attend Catholic schools have been a controversial political issue in the United States. Several voucher programs are now ongoing in several states. In the New York voucher experiment, Howell and Peterson (2002) compare the achievement of voucher recipients relative to a similar control group, where the voucher amount was applied mainly to tuition at low-cost Catholic schools. They find that there are positive gains from using educational vouchers only for African-Americans. However, these gains are not consistent across the years of the trial. They have been challenged on methodological grounds by Krueger and Zhu (2004) who find that the difference in test scores between the treatment group and the control group is not significant.

Catholic schools in other countries

Catholic schools are also present in many other countries. In fact, the Catholic school system is the world's largest faith-based educational network with 120 000 schools and over 1000 colleges and universities (Grace and O'Keefe, 2007). In Australia, Catholic schools form the second largest sector after government schools (Wikipedia). As of the early 1990s, private schools accounted for about 25% of enrollment with approximately 75% attending Catholic schools (Vella, 1999). In Canada, seven of the 13 provinces and territories fund faith-based Catholic schools (Wikipedia).

In England and Wales, 2300 Catholic schools educate around 840 000 pupils each year. In Scotland, Catholic schools are all fully funded by the government. In Northern Ireland, about half of all students attend Catholic schools (Wikipedia).

In Italy, Catholic schools are relatively expensive and therefore tend to serve high-income families. In 1998, approximately 10.3% of high school graduates attended private schools in Italy. Of these, about one-third were Catholic (Di Pietro & Cutillo, 2006). In the Netherlands, about one in five primary schools are Catholic (Levin, 2002). In Chile, about one in ten grade school students is enrolled in a Catholic school (McEwan, 2001).

Demand

Many factors affect the probability that parents send their children to Catholic schools. The most recent study that estimates the relative importance of these factors finds that the probability of attending a Catholic school is higher for Catholics, especially more religious Catholics. Catholics who attend church at least weekly have about a 50% likelihood of sending their children to Catholic schools; Catholics who attend church once a month only have about a 25% likelihood of sending their children to Catholic schools; and Catholics who attend church less than once a month have an even lower probability of sending their children to Catholic schools. Non-Catholics have a very low probability of sending their children to Catholic

schools regardless of their level of religiosity (Cohen-Zada & Sander, 2007).

Over time, Catholic religiosity as measured by church attendance has declined for Catholics aged less than 65 years. About 50% of Catholics 35—44 years attended church almost every week or more often during the 1970s. Regular church attendance declined for this age group to about 25% by the 1990s. If church attendance by adults is a determinant of the demand for a Catholic education, declines in Catholic religiosity is a plausible reason for some of the decline in the demand for a Catholic education for children (Sander, 2005).

Other factors that have been found to affect the demand for Catholics schools include family income, parents' education, location, and race. Families who have very low incomes are less likely to send their children to Catholic schools. Parents with some college are more likely to send their children to Catholic schools relative to parents with a college degree and parents with a high school diploma. Parents with less than a high school education were the least likely to send their children to a Catholic school. Also, African-American has a positive effect on the demand for Catholic schools. Although blacks are disproportionately Protestant, a likely reason that they have a higher demand for Catholic schooling is that they are concentrated in big cities where the quality of public schooling is problematic (Cohen-Zada & Sander, 2007).

Another important factor that affects the demand for Catholic schooling is price. Large declines in the number of teachers in religious orders have forced Catholic schools to hire lay teachers who are more costly. Further, declines in subsidies from Catholic parishes have resulted in large increases in tuition. This is partly a result of declines in Catholic Church contributions over time. If one goes back to the 1960s, Catholics contributed over 2 % of their income to the church. This declined to about 1% by the 1980s (Harris, 1996; Zech, 2000).

Further, the quality of public schools in a locality affects the demand for Catholic schools. In inner-city areas where the quality of public schooling is often perceived as low, the demand for a Catholic education is higher. For example, in Chicago about half of the children of non-Hispanic whites attend private schools. Most of these schools are Catholic. In the suburbs of Chicago, the demand for Catholic schools is much lower because the quality of public education is higher. Catholic parents are less willing to pay for both public schools and Catholic schools in such areas (Sander, 2006).

At the aggregate level, several factors affect the share of students in a county that attend Catholic schools (Cohen-Zada, 2006). The variable that has the most substantial effect is the Catholic share in the population. A one standard deviation increase in the Catholic share in the population increases the county Catholic-enrolment rate by more than 2% points. This variable has a concave effect on the Catholic-enrolment rate. It has been shown that in places where Catholics are a lower share of the population, a higher percentage of them send their children to Catholic schools. One possible reason for this is that in these places where they are a minority, they have a stronger need to send their children to Catholics schools in order to preserve their religious identity. A higher Catholic-enrolment rate is also associated with a higher population density, higher mean income of the population, higher share of African-Americans in the population, and a lower share living in a rural area. Finally, for a given Catholic share in the population, a higher share of Hispanics implies a lower-Catholic enrollment rate.

Effects

Academic achievement and educational attainment

Students who attend Catholic high schools are more likely to graduate and go on to college relative to their public school counterparts. Recent data put the high school graduation rate in Catholic schools at 99.1%. The public high school graduation rate is only 71.0% if general educational development (GED) certificates are excluded. It is 86.5% if they are included. Further, students in Catholic schools have higher test scores on the average than students in public school. Data from the National Assessment of Education Progress (NAEP), the nation's report card, indicate that students in Catholic grade schools and high schools have higher test scores on the average than students in public schools (McDonald, 2007).

Higher graduation rates and test scores do not necessarily indicate that Catholic schools provide superior schooling. It could be the case that Catholic schools simply select better students. This so-called selection issue has received considerable attention by researchers.

There are a large number of studies on the effect of Catholic schools on various measures of educational attainment and academic achievement that try to control for selectivity bias. Important studies in the early 1980s by James Coleman and others at the University of Chicago indicated that Catholic high schools had positive effects on test scores and high school graduation rates (Coleman, Hoffer, & Kilgore, 1982; Coleman & Hoffer, 1987). The results in these studies were considered problematic by some because they did not control for selection into Catholic schools, especially on unobserved variables like unobserved aspects of family background.

A number of studies over the past two decades have tried to statistically control for the possibility of positive selection into Catholic schools (Neal, 1997; Perie & Goldstein, 2005; Sander, 2001). The idea is that if Catholic school attendance is correlated with any determinant of students' outcome that is missing in the estimation, one is likely to obtain biased estimates of Catholic school attendance on educational outcomes. The bias is a result of the estimated coefficient of Catholic school attendance capturing the effect of the missing variable on the outcome. For example, Cohen-Zada and Sander (2007) show that religiosity is positively correlated with Catholic school attendance and student outcomes. Thus, if religiosity is not taken into account, one tends to overestimate the effect of Catholic school attendance on educational outcomes.

Most studies try to control for selection into Catholic schools by using instrumental variables that causally affect Catholic school attendance, but do not have a direct effect on educational outcomes. Using this strategy, one estimates the effect of Catholic school attendance on outcomes using a two-stage approach. In the first stage, Catholic school attendance is regressed on the instruments and all of the other exogenous variables in the model. Assuming the instruments are exogenous, the predicted Catholic school attendance that one obtains from the first stage is also exogenous. This allows one to tease out the exogenous component of the variation in Catholic school attendance. In the second stage, the outcome equation is estimated by replacing Catholic school attendance with its exogenous approximation obtained from the first stage. This identification strategy is valid only if there is no unobserved determinant of the educational outcome that is correlated with the instrumental variable.

The results of many of the studies on the effect of Catholic schooling are somewhat problematic because the instruments that are used are not valid. That is, they have a direct effect on the outcome and are thus likely to be correlated with the error term. For example, Cohen-Zada and Sander (2007) show that Catholic religion and density of Catholic schools, which are often used as instruments for Catholic school attendance, are correlated with religiosity which is often missing in estimations of the treatment effect of Catholic schools. Altonji, Elder, and Taber (2005b) examined the validity of religious affiliation and the proximity to Catholic schools as instruments for Catholic school attendance and found that none of them were useful sources of identification of the Catholic school effect.

Perhaps the best study to date on Catholic high school effects finds that they have a positive effect on high school graduation rates and on attending college but no effect on test scores. This study acknowledges that none of the previously used instruments for Catholic school attendance is valid and thus develops a new estimation method for obtaining a lower bound for the causal effect of Catholic school attendance on outcomes based on the assumption that the amount of selection on the unobservables is not more than the amount of selection on the observables (Altonji, Elder, & Taber, 2005a). Recently, Cohen-Zada (2007) shows that the Catholic share in a county in 1890 is a valid instrument for private school competition and a potentially valid instrument for Catholic school attendance.

Another important study on Catholic high schools finds that the benefits of a Catholic education are particularly high for minorities in big cities where the quality of public schooling is low (Neal, 1997). Although most of the studies on Catholic schools have tended to focus on Catholic high schools, studies on Catholic grade schools indicate that the effects on academic achievement are modest at best (Jepsen, 2003; Sander, 2001).

Bad behavior

A recent study uses a propensity score matching method to control for positive selection into Catholic schools and finds that Catholic school attendance reduces the propensity that female students use cocaine and have sex. However, it increases the propensity that male students use and sell drugs (Mocan & Tekin, 2006). Other studies provide evidence that Catholic schools are not more effective than public schools in reducing marijuana use, alcohol abuse, or smoking although Catholic school attendance may reduce some risky youth behaviors including sexual activity, criminal behavior, and the use of hard drugs (Figiio & Ludwlg, 2000).

Civic participation and altruism

A number of studies have examined the effect of Catholic and other private schooling on civic participation and altruism. Some results from this literature are as follows. A study on the effect of vouchers on students' altruistic behavior finds that students attending private (mostly Catholic) schools in Ohio, after being randomly assigned to these schools through a lottery, gave more to charitable organizations but not more to their peers (other children attending the experiment) (Bettinger & Sionim, 2006). Another study using data from the National Household Education Survey of 1999 finds that Catholic school attendance is positively associated with community service participation, civic skills, political knowledge, and tolerance (Belfield, 2004). Greeley and Rossi (1966) found similar results regarding tolerance of civic liberties; on the other hand, they did not find that Catholic school attendance was related to community involvement. Other findings include Catholic schools increasing racial tolerance and voting (Dee, 2005; Greene, 1998).

Economic effects

One of the few studies that considers the effects of Catholic schooling on economic outcomes finds that attending a Catholic high school increases earnings both directly and indirectly for young black and Hispanic men. Catholic schooling directly increases wages after controlling for educational attainment and indirectly increases wages by increasing the probability of graduating from high school and college. In this study, no effect is discerned for non- Hispanic white men (Neal, 1997).

Other effects

Although studies on Catholic schools have focused on academic effects, other effects have been considered as well. One line of research focuses on the effect of Catholic and other private schooling on the quality of public education. One of the issues of interest is whether competitive pressures from private schools could increase the quality of public schools. The findings from research on this topic are not conclusive (Hoxby, 1994).

Catholic schools exist in part to provide a religious value-based education. The data indicate that Catholics who attend Catholic schools are more religious Catholics. They tend to pray more, attend church more often, retain a Catholic identity as an adult, and have Catholic beliefs. Statistical analysis of the effects of Catholic schools on religiosity indicates that Catholic schools have a positive causal effect on all of these outcomes except church attendance (Sander, 2001).

The effect of catholic school attendance in other countries

In the last decade, researches have examined whether the substantial effect reported for attending Catholic schools in the United States, also exists for students in Catholic schools in other countries. A study on Catholic schooling in Australia indicates that attending a Catholic school increases the probability of completing high school, attending college, and being employed (Vella, 1999).

A recent study on Catholic schooling in Italy finds that attending a Catholic school increases the probability of attending a university, but it does not affect the probability of dropping out of college (Di Pietro & Cutillo, 2006).

A study on Catholic schooling in the Netherlands finds significantly higher achievement scores for fourth-, sixth-, and eighth-grade students in Catholic schools (Levin, 2002). The Dutch experience is of particular interest because Dutch law mandates equal public financing across all schools, regardless of their religious affiliation.

Conclusions

Catholic schools have made important contributions to education in the United States and elsewhere. However, the effects of Catholic schooling have been difficult to nail down conclusively. Further, little attention has been given to the changing nature of Catholic schooling by location and over time. Similarly, very little attention has been given to the effects of different types of Catholic schools such as parish-based schools or schools sponsored by religious orders. This is the grist for future research.

See also

Education and Civic Engagement; Educational Privatization; Empirical Research Methods in the Economics of Education; The Efficacy of Educational Vouchers.

References

Altonji, J. G., Elder, T. E., & Taber, C. R. (2005a). Selection on observed and unobserved variables: Assessing the effectiveness of catholic schools. *Journal of Political Economy, 113*, 151−184.

Altonji, J. G., Elder, T. E., & Taber, C. R. (2005b). An evaluation of instrumental variable strategies for estimating the effects of catholic schools. *Journal of Human Resources, 40*, 791−821.

Belfield, C. R. (2004). Democratic education across school types: Evidence for the U.S. from NHES99. *Education Policy Analysis Archives, 12*(43). http://epaa.asu.edu/epaa/v12n43.

Bettinger, E., & Sionim, R. (2006). Using experimental economics to measure the effects of a natural educational experiment on altruism. *Journal of Public Economics, 90*, 1625−1648.

Cohen-Zada, D. (2006). Preserving religious values through education: Economic analysis and evidence from the US. *Journal of Urban Economics, 60*, 372−398.

Cohen-Zada, D. (2007). An alternative instrument for private school competition. *Economics of Education Review, 28*, 29−37.

Cohen-Zada, D., & Sander, W. (2007). Religion, religiosity, and private school choice: Implications for estimating the effectiveness of private schools. *Journal of Urban Economics, 64*, 85−100.

Coleman, J., & Hoffer, T. (1987). *Public and private high schools.* New York: Basic Books.

Coleman, J., Hoffer, T., & Kilgore, S. (1982). *High school achievement: Public, catholic and private schools compared.* New York: Basic Books.

Dee, T. (2005). The effects of Catholic schooling on civic participation. *International Tax and Public Finance, 12*, 1−21.

Di Pietro, G., & Cutillo, A. (2006). Does attending a catholic school make a difference? Evidence from Italy. *Bulletin of Economic Research, 58*, 193−234.

Figiio, D., & Ludwlg, J. (2000). *Sex, drugs and Catholic schools: Private schooling and non-market adolescent behaviors.* NBER Working Paper Number 7990.

Finke, R., & Stark, R. (2005). *The churching of America, 1776-2005: Winners and losers in our religious economy.* Piscataway, NJ: Rutgers University Press.

Grace, G., & O'Keefe, J. (Eds.). (2007). *International handbook of catholic education.* Dordrecht: Springer.

Greeley, A. M., & Rossi, P. H. (1966). *The education of American Catholics.* Chicago, IL: Aldine.

Greene, J. P. (1998). Civic values in public and private schools. In P. E. Peterson, & B. C. Hassel (Eds.), *Learning from school choice* (pp. 335−356). Washington, DC: Brookings Institution Press.

Harris, J. C. (1996). *The cost of catholic parishes and schools.* Kansas City, MO: Sheed and Ward.

Howell, W., & Peterson, P. (2002). *The education gap.* Washington, DC: Brookings Institution.

Hoxby, C. M. (1994). *Do private schools provide competition for public schools?* National Bureau of Economic Research. Working Paper No. 4978.

Jepsen, C. (2003). The effects of catholic primary schools. *Journal of Human Resources, 38*, 928−941.

Krueger, A., & Zhu, P. (2004). Another look at the New York city school voucher experiment. *American Behavioral Scientist, 47*, 658−698.

Levin, J. (2002). *Essays in the economics of education.* Amsterdam: Tinbergen Institute.

McDonald, D. (2007). *United States catholic elementary and secondary schools 2006−2007.* Washington, DC: National Catholic Educational Association.

McEwan, P. (2001). The effectiveness of public, catholic, and non-religion private schools in chile's voucher system. *Education Economics, 9*, 103−128.

Mocan, N., & Tekin, E. (2006). Catholic schools and bad behavior: A propensity score matching analysis. *Contributions to Economic Analysis and Policy, 5*(1), 1403.

Neal, D. (1997). The effects of catholic secondary schooling on educational attainment. *Journal of Labor Economics, 15*, 98−123.

Perie, M., & Goldstein, A. (2005). *Student achievement in private schools: Results from NAEP 2000−2005.* Washington, DC: US Government Printing Office.

Sander, W. (2001). *Catholic schools: Private and social effects.* Boston, MA: Kluwer Academic Press.

Sander, W. (2005). Catholics and catholic schooling. *Education Economics, 13*, 257–268.

Sander, W. (2006). *Private schools and school enrollment in Chicago. Chicago fed letter number 231.* The Federal Reserve Bank of Chicago.

Vella, F. (1999). Do catholic schools make a difference? Evidence from Australia. *Journal of Human Resources, 34,* 208–224.

Wikipedia. (2007). The free encyclopedia. In J. Youniss, & J. J. Convey (Eds.), *Catholic schools at the crossroads.* New York: Teachers College, Columbia University.

Youniss, J., & Convey, J. J. (2000). *Catholic schools at the crossroads: survival and transformation.* New York: Teachers College Press.

Zech, C. E. (2000). *Why Catholics don't give.* Huntington: Our Sunday Visitor Publishing Division.

Evans, W. N., & Schwab, R. M. (1995). Finishing high school and starting college: Do Catholic schools make a difference? *Quarterly Journal of Economics, 110,* 941–974.

Greeley, A. M., McCready, W. C., & McCourt, D. (1976). *Catholic schools in a declining church.* Kansas City, MO: Sheed and Ward.

Grogger, J., & Neal, D. (2000). Further evidence on the effects of catholic secondary schooling. In W. G. Gale, & J. R. Pack (Eds.), *Brookings-wharton papers on urban affairs* (pp. 151–193). Washington, DC: The Brookings Institution.

Sander, W., & Krautmann, A. (1995). Catholic schools, dropout rates, and educational attainment. *Economic Inquiry, 33,* 217–233.

Wikepedia 'Catholic education in Australia', https://en.wikipedia.org/wiki/Catholic_education_in_Australia

Further reading

Bryk, A. S., Lee, V. S., & Holland, P. B. (1993). *Catholic schools and the common good.* Cambridge: Harvard University Press.

Cohen-Zada, D., & Justman, M. (2005). The religious factor in private education. *Journal of Urban Economics, 57,* 391–18.

Relevant websites

http://www.ncea.org - National Catholic Educational Association.

http://www.ncspe.org - National Center for the Study of Privatization in Education.

http://nces.ed.gov - The National Center for Education Statistics (NCES).

Private schools: choice and effects

Francis Green

UCL Institute of Education, London, United Kingdom

Introduction

'Public' or 'state' schooling is ubiquitous, but in most countries there exists also a sector of private schools alongside those funded and governed by government. Although this sector educates, in most countries, only a small proportion of children, there is widespread interest in what private schools do that might be different from state schools, and in what their effect might be on other schools, on the education system as a whole, and on society. This interest stems, on one hand, from concerns with social mobility and with educational inequality. If, as is common though not universal, the schools are socially exclusive, and if the schools prove to be gateways to economically-rewarding jobs and positions in society, then private schools may play a role in limiting social mobility. On the other hand, private schools are also of interest if they use their independence to offer diversity and an escape from constraints in the state sector; they might find innovative and effective ways to teach, from which other schools could benefit; innovation might theoretically stem from being less regulated if the regulations are ill-considered, or from market competition.

In line with much of the literature, I define a private school as a fee-paying school, that is, as one where fees are payable by most students. Private schools nevertheless normally receive subsidies from governments. Moreover, this definition of private is quite separate from the concept of a 'privately managed' school, defined by the OECD as a school that is 'managed directly or indirectly by a non-government organization; e.g. a church, trade union, business, or other private institution'. Some studies of 'private school' use this term as a short-hand for 'privately-managed' school, but this is not the intended meaning here. Privately managed schools may be funded largely by the government; some state schools, charging no fees, are privately managed. To add to the terminological confusion, in Britain fee-paying secondary schools have, for reasons bound up with 19th century history, been called 'public schools', and this usage sometimes lingers on in public discourse; yet 'public school' in other countries is synonymous with 'state school', the term to be used hereafter in this article.

Participation in private schooling, using the proper definition of fee-paying schooling, ranges from the relatively small — for example, 15% of school pupils in France — to below 1% or virtually non-existent, as in Sweden and Finland. Participation is about 6% in Germany, 6% in the United Kingdom, 7% in Ireland, 10% in the

The Economics of Education, Second Edition
https://doi.org/10.1016/B978-0-12-815391-8.00038-0

United States, and 12% in Denmark (Andersen, 2008; Green, Anders, Henderson, & Henseke, 2017; Snyder, de Brey, & Dillow, 2018; Courtois, 2018).

The nature of private schools varies much between countries, depending on the degree of public subsidy they receive, their resources, and the extent to which the schools are regulated and autonomously governed. In some countries private schools serve heterogeneous needs, including religious preferences and desires for boarding education; in the United States this heterogeneity results in distinct religious (mainly Catholic) and non-sectarian private sectors. A widespread growing demand is for internationally-oriented education, often in English or some other world language, typically not following the national curriculum of the host country. The role of private schools also depends on the alternatives offered by the state. As a general rule, the lower is the quality of education available for free in the state sector, the greater is the likelihood for private providers to succeed in attracting students.

Private schools' effects may also vary across countries. A particularly relevant factor is the level of fees, and the resources available to the schools. Average fees are especially high, for example, in Britain (average £14,500 in 2018 for day schools, £33,700 for boarding), somewhat lower in the United States ($11,250 tuition in 2012 in 2015 prices) and very much lower — typically, less than €2500 in France where private school teachers' pay is met by government funds (ISC 2018; Snyder et al., 2018). High fees, supplemented by endowed assets, lead to resource gaps between private and state schools. In Britain, the resource gap is estimated to be very approximately three, including a teacher pupil ratio that is twice as high in the private sector as in the state sector (Green & Kynaston, 2019); in the United States, the teacher-pupil ratio is about 50% higher in non-sectarian schools than in state schools, but lower than the state sector in the Catholic private schools (National Center

for Education Statistics, 2003). In Germany, the far-from-socially-exclusive private schools have 15% fewer resources per pupil than the average state school (DESTATIS, 2016).

For all these reasons — the variability in their type of governance, in their degree of state subsidy, in their quality and resources, and in the quality of state education — considerable caution needs to be exercised when comparing private education across countries. One should not, for example, come to general conclusions about the effects of private education on pupil progress, when those effects could arise for a diversity of reasons which are not common across countries. In this article I will first briefly describe the theoretical framework for considering the role of private schooling in any country, before considering evidence on private school choice and effects in a range of environments.

Theory

The theory and evidence surrounding the role of private schools concern two related issues – parental choice and private schools' effects on individuals — which are subsets of the more general agenda of education economics, when it considers choice and the effects of resources, peer groups, competition and autonomy on school or pupil outcomes.

Parents' choice of the private or a state school sector can be framed in economic terms as a maximization problem. Taking the family as the unit, it decides whether the expected discounted future benefits are sufficient to exceed the extra costs of paying for private school. The maximization is constrained, however, by current family resources and borrowing limitations. From this it can be concluded that key explanatory variables are (in addition to the magnitude of the future benefits) family income, wealth, price and families' rates of time preference. Nevertheless, it must be accepted that such forward-looking behavior is far from universal.

Interestingly, a common finding in studies of parental choice in Britain has been that those choosing the private sector typically do show signs of long-term and strategic planning; partly this is stimulated by the need for financial planning to manage the expense (Green, Anders et al., 2017).

Expected benefits comprise both educational, and potential long-term economic and social outcomes; the latter include a pay premium, higher occupational status, and marrying a higher-earning spouse (reflecting positive educational and school-type assortative mating (Green, Henseke, Parsons, Sullivan, & Wiggins, 2018)). Potential non-economic gains can include improved health behaviors and life satisfaction. The educational outcomes need not be confined to the purely academic. Many parents make choices and express direct preferences for schools which have broader visions than simply better test results. Some also express preferences for particular peer groups or forms of instruction. For example, some prefer religious schools and this is especially relevant if not available in the state sector; others might prefer especially expensive schools precisely because they have a socially exclusive student body; yet others state the opposite, that a high quality education entails growing up in a cross-section of society. The study of the choice of school-type, therefore, is somewhat complex. Sociological studies typically indicate a mix of motives and ambivalent attitudes, both rational and moral. (e.g. Ball, 1997; Fox, 1985).

What might be the source of private schools' advantage in delivering benefits, if any? The impact of going to a private school on individuals depends on the character of the schools. Positive effects on academic outcomes, relative to attending a state school, can be expected on average in a country if the private schools have more resources than the state schools, if the social composition of its pupils make for beneficial peer groups in the classroom, or if they are distinctly better managed. I consider each of these three factors in turn.

Where present, such as in several Anglophone countries, large resource gaps between the private and state school sectors are sufficient reason to expect there to be effects on performance. While the impact of resources on outcomes has been controversial for a long time, recent influential studies using a range of quasi-experimental methodologies show both short and long term effects of superior resources (sometimes, in particular, lower class sizes) on performance (e.g. Krueger & Whitmore, 2001; Fredriksson, Oeckert, & Oosterbeek, 2013; Jackson, Johnson, & Persico, 2016). This finding should hardly be surprising for a discipline such as economics, where the production function is a central concept. The relationship between inputs and outputs breaks down only under conditions of substantive inefficiency. In Britain, where the private/state resource gap is very large (approximately a factor of three), there is accordingly an expectation of a substantive performance gap.

Peer groups have also been shown, using both quasi-experimental and observational methodologies, to have significant effects on individuals' outcomes (Sacerdote, 2011). In many countries, with pupil composition both price-rationed and culturally selective, private schools recruit relatively few students from significantly disadvantaged families. In some countries, academic selection adds a positive bias to the peer group in private schools. Where, therefore, the pupil composition has a disproportionate concentration of academically bright pupils, and at the same time fewer pupils with behavioral challenges, one can again expect a positive effect of private schools on individuals — though in this case the effect derives, not directly from the schools, but from their pupil composition. Academic peer effects provide an incentive, alongside reputational advantages, for private schools to become academically selective in student recruitment, and to offer academic scholarships — i.e. reduced fees for more able students (Walton, 2010).

Whether private schools are likely to be better managed, by contrast, is an open question. If competitive forces are especially strong, private schools, to survive, must improve their methods and deliver for their customers; this external pressure applies whether or not the schools are for-profit or whether they are constituted as not-for-profit charities. External pressures may, however, be weak, where schools rely on tradition and on brand name reputations, affording quasi-rental returns in the market; state schools may also be subject to competitive pressures. In practice, management efficiency is not found to differ significantly between the two sectors in most countries for which there is data. Bloom et al. (2015) find that efficient management practices are more prevalent in Brazil's private sector than in its state sector, but that this is not true elsewhere where they looked: in each of five OECD countries (namely Canada, Germany, Italy, the United Kingdom and the United States), private schools' management practices are no more efficient than those in non-autonomous government schools. In India, also, private schools' management practices do not differ between the private and state schools, once school characteristics (including resources) are controlled for. The same story is found in Uganda (Crawfurd, 2017). Bryson and Green (2018) find that, if anything, Britain's private schools utilize fewer beneficial human resource management practices than its state schools.

Private schools' broader role within the education system and society in general should also be considered. To the extent that education is a positional good (Adnett & Davies, 2002), a private school education that delivers better exam results, which become the gateway to higher ranking colleges or jobs, has positive private benefits for private school pupils, but negative external benefits and uncertain overall social benefits. Where private schools are socially exclusive in their pupil composition, and where they constitute more than a tiny minority of the school population and their private effects on individuals are substantive, the consequences for low social mobility can be considerable, though hard to quantify. On the other hand, privately educated pupils might have external benefits for society if the mission of that private education was to intensively stimulate a propensity toward altruistic and community-oriented behavior; or the private schools themselves might have positive external benefits, if they discover and diffuse to other schools some innovative methods of teaching and learning. Again, whether private schools have these broader effects, and whether they are harmful or beneficial, is likely to depend on the particular characteristics of the private and state school sectors of each country.

Evidence on choice

Economists and sociologists have sought evidence on private school choice using complementary methodologies. Survey methods, and semi-structured interviews, reveal a range of private school preferences. The modal stated reason for choosing private schooling in the British context is usually for better teaching and academic performance. However, other factors can also be important, such as the desire or need for a boarding school education, or religious preferences. The latter are likely to be much more relevant in countries where state-funded schools are constrained to be secular. Another common reason is a preference for particular peer groups; however, this motive is almost certainly under-estimated by direct methods of preference reporting, since some interview respondents are reluctant to report their social preferences and prejudices (Green, Anders et al., 2017). Racial discriminatory preferences that are not shown up by direct statements of preferences may be evidenced in other ways: 'white flight', for example, is revealed by parents in areas with low proportions of white students in schools choosing private education (Fairlie & Resch, 2002). In India, caste has been shown to be a factor (Azam, 2017), and there is a gender gap which is rising over time (Sahoo, 2017).

Given families' preferences and financial constraints, a key variable determining private school choice is income. The concept of income to be used in research is, however, important: this should be long-term or permanent income (Henseke, 2018). The reason is partly that, other than where private school is especially cheap, a private education constitutes a major investment in children over a long period. In addition, switching schools is costly; hence, educational investment is less likely to respond to transitory variations in income. Physical and financial wealth are also likely to be important: even if a large gain were to be identified from a private school investment, parents' ability to borrow against their children's future income is constrained by uncertainty and the impossibility of writing contracts secured against another's future income (that of their child). A family's assets enable high private school investments to be made without excessive sacrifices of current consumption. In this case, the family may need to be defined broadly, to include grandparents and other extended family members who may take an interest in children's futures. Valatheeswaran and Khan (2018) find, for example, remittances from family members abroad are positively associated with private school enrollments in Kerala, India.

Private schooling is sensitive to price, but evidence on this is quite scarce. It is rarely straightforward to estimate demand price elasticities, owing to endogenous variations in price. One estimate from the United States exploits sibling discounts as a means of identifying price effects: Dynarski, Gruber, and Li (2009) find that the average price elasticity of attendance at Catholic elementary schools is -0.19; however, they also find that the price elasticity is greater for those on low incomes, and becomes virtually zero for those on high incomes. Blundell, Dearden, and Sibieta (2010) estimate the price elasticity of demand in Britain to be 0.26. There may be several reasons why price elasticity is so low, especially for upper income groups. First, there are substantial variations in the resources available in schools, so that where price is higher, so too is quality. Second, a higher price produces a more socially exclusive population. Even the direct evidence suggests that an affluent social composition is a desirable factor in a private school which parents are prepared to pay more for. A third, related, reason is that a high price also delivers an element of conspicuous consumption, at least for some parent groups. Fourth, for high-income families the income effect of a price rise is smaller than it is for low-income families. There has also been some evidence of cartel-like behavior by British schools, but in the only proven case, where schools were fined by competition authorities, collusive action was not found to be a significant long-term factor in price formation (Elliott, Konara, & Wei, 2016).

Price rationing leads to social exclusivity in the social composition of private school student population. Other factors, however, can also lead to social exclusivity, such as religious affiliation, where this is part of the reason for private school choice. In the large majority of countries (notable exceptions are the Netherlands, South Korea and Indonesia), there is a social stratification between privately and publicly managed schools, indicating that it is commonly the better-off families who make use of the diversity afforded by autonomy from government (OECD, 2012). The social gradation — the gap between the socio-economic background of students in privately and publicly managed schools — is especially high in Mexico, Greece, the United States, the United Kingdom and New Zealand; in all three countries the privately managed schools are private schools funded largely through fees. Murnane and Reardon (2018) find that in the three decades up to 2013, places at private schools (both Catholic and non-sectarian) were increasingly occupied by students from high-income families. Henseke (2018) finds no strong trends in Britain, with private school concentration among top-decile families remaining unchanged from the mid-1990s through to 2015.

Evidence on effects

Methods

Evidence on the impact of attending a private school, as opposed to a state school, might be sought either for policy purposes — owing to the above-noted associations with social mobility — or for the purposes of informing parents (the investors) considering whether to choose private schooling. For parents, it is not sufficient to demonstrate an effect: the magnitude of the effect on someone's pay throughout a career and beyond needs to be set against the fees. The standard investment calculus balancing discounted lifetime earnings against up-front costs determines if, from the rational actor's perspective, private schooling is worth it.

Both the heterogeneity of private schools within and between countries, and the multiplicity of mechanisms through which effects are generated, imply that it is not possible to reach *generalized* conclusions about whether private schools have positive, neutral or negative effects on pupils. Where, for example, a positive effect is found, it could in principle arise from any of the three mechanisms noted earlier — superior resources, peer groups or better management. The policy implications, and the advice to be given to parents, therefore depend on which among these factors is driving the effect. Localized studies in particular countries or regions, where the private schools' characteristics are known, can be useful for both parents and policy makers. But in general the significance of evidence on private school effects is indeterminate, unless one is able to utilize additional information on which factors are involved in producing the beneficial effects.

Another source of potential variation in findings lies in the data and the methodology. Effects would be expected to differ according to the length of time that students spend in private schools. In many studies, private school treatment is proxied by whether they participated in private schooling in one particular year, sometimes at primary, others at secondary level. While typically most students will spend their whole childhood in either private or state schools, many will switch between the private and state sectors. Such transitions might be dictated by financial resources, or by parents' interventions in the light of their children's experiences and academic performance; in either case, switchers might differ systematically but in unobserved ways from those who remain in their sector. Educational and other outcomes also need to be carefully specified. Academic outcomes could be high-stakes examinations that determine students' futures or low-stakes tests like the PISA program; they could be narrowly focused on core topics of language and numeracy, or cover a broad range of achievements including the arts and humanities, or other outcomes such as religious observances or beliefs, cultural activities and sport. Because private schools may focus their energies on a different portfolio of outcomes from state schools, good studies of private school effects may need to establish their robustness with respect to multiple outcome measures where possible.

While the gold standard of a Randomized Control Trial would be hard or impossible to manage for a representative sample of a country's population, a favored methodology in private school studies is to make use of lotteries, where they exist. In some countries, children, typically from eligible low-income groups, can be selected by lottery to attend private schools; their progress can then be compared with that of peers who fail to win the lottery. This quasi-experimental methodology can be used, if the circumstances are right, to produce causal estimates of the impact of 'treating' students with private school participation. However, the conditions of lotteries may not generate truly random assignment. Private schools may choose whether to participate in admissions lotteries, and if that choice is materially affected by their quality the findings of effects on students may be biased. Schools' behavior might change because of the lottery program's existence. And small-scale voucher programs might not capture the full effects of introducing a system-wide lottery for private school attendance.

Alternatively, studies may use observational data. By far the most common investigative strategy is some kind of single-equation regression on the outcome of interest; alternative, supplementary approaches may make use of propensity score methods; others have used structural equation methods which simultaneously estimate the correlations between prior socio-economic and human capital variables, private school selection and subsequent outcomes (Sullivan, Parsons, Green, Ploubidis, & Wiggins, 2017). Whatever the modeling strategy, however, the quality of the longitudinal controls is paramount. In most situations, family background will affect educational and long-term labor market outcomes directly, as well as the likelihood of attending a private school. Thus, good observational studies of private school 'effects' have rich control variables covering parental socio-economic data; the best come from longitudinal studies — for example, cohort studies — where contemporaneous data is collected from different stages of childhood prior to the treatment of attending a private school. Moreover, since it is often the case that prior attainment or ability affect selection into private schooling, it is imperative for observational studies to have some measure of that prior attainment for each observational unit. Since prior attainment is a strong predictor of subsequent attainment, any study of private school effects which does not include prior attainment risks generating biased estimates. Where

students are positively selected on ability, the estimates of the effects of private schooling will be upward biased.

The socio-economic characteristics of school peers are control variables of some interest. In most studies, where sampling is from a population of individual students, the peer characteristics are not collected. Then, any estimated private school effects incorporate peer effects alongside the other mechanisms. Where peer characteristics are known, however, — for example, where the sampling of students is via schools rather than households — these can be additionally controlled for, thus enabling researchers to drill down further to any further effects from the resources or management efficiency of the schools. In such cases care needs to be taken in the interpretation of findings: even where private schools, after allowing for peer effects, are found to be no better managed or resourced that state schools, those schools may still be attractive to parents precisely because going private is their means of choosing what they see as a desirable peer group for their children.

Even in those studies where good controls are used for both socio-economic background and for prior attainments or ability, it can be suspected that unobserved factors may influence both participation and attainment, implying potentially biased estimates. In this instance, one recourse is to derive estimate bounds, based on assumptions about the relationships between the observed and unobserved control variables (Sakellariou, 2017). Fully credible instruments or other identifying strategies have not yet been seen, though future possibilities might emerge. Nevertheless, where substantive effects are found, and where there are clear causal mechanisms at work which can be externally validated, it is reasonable to interpret well-controlled observational estimates of private school effects as consistent with those mechanisms, even if the causation has not been proved. Conversely, where an observational study with good controls produces null findings, with private schools having no conditional correlations with outcomes, it is normally safe to conclude cautiously that private schools have no causal effects (Pianta and Ansari, 2018).

Findings

Estimates of private school effects on academic outcomes around the world vary considerably. While some of this variation may be due to methodological differences between studies — for example, between lottery-based and observational studies — it is likely that the differences are largely down to the heterogeneous character of private and state schools across countries, noted earlier.

In the United States, results from both quasi-experimental and observational studies are mixed. For example, a study of the New York City voucher program uncovered positive effects for African American students, though not for Latino students; while other lottery-based studies show negative or null effects (Dynarski, 2016). Using observational longitudinal data, Pianta and Ansari (2018) are able to broaden the outcomes examined to beyond the narrow academic tests typically captured in lottery evaluations; they find that private schooling in the US had no effects on either academic or other, social and psychological outcomes, once students' social and economic backgrounds are controlled for. No positive influence on test scores from attending a private Catholic primary school has been found among pupils with similar prior cognitive attainment and socio-economic background (Carbonaro, 2006; Elder & Jepsen, 2014; Jepsen, 2003; Lubienski, Crane, & Lubienski, 2008).

Statistically insignificant effects from private schools are also found in a number of other developed countries. In Denmark, for example, voucher-financed private schooling is reported to have no significant impact on final examination scores on average (Andersen, 2008); however, private school students perform better than in state schools where the other students in the school are of higher socio-economic status, and worse than in state schools where the other students are of lower socio-economic status — a finding which the author considers to be probably due to peer effects. Agasisti, Murtinu, and Sibiano (2016) find a positive effect of private primary schools on standardized test scores for immigrants and for disadvantaged families, but no significant overall effect, in Italy; Nghiem, Nguyen, Khanam, and Connelly (2015) report no significant effects from private primary schooling in Australia.

In contrast to these findings, several studies in Britain show positive effects of private schooling on educational outcomes. For those educated before 2000, several studies reveal positive effects at various stages of education (O'Donoghue, Thomas, Goldstein, & Knight, 1997; Dearden, Ferri, & Meghir, 2002; Sullivan and Heath (2003); Feinstein and Symons, 1999; Sullivan, Parsons, Wiggins, Heath, & Green, 2014). Green et al. (2017) also shows effects on non-cognitive outcomes – 'locus of control', aspirations, access to networks. Heterogeneity within the private sector is reflected in there being better performance by students at the richer schools (Graddy & Stevens, 2005). A further notable observation about Britain's private schools is that they have been substantially modernized in the last three decades, with new management practices introduced, proper forms of regulation, and an enormous influx of resources (with fees trebling in real terms since 1980). All studies covering those at school since 2000 again indicate positive effects (Henderson, 2018; Malacova, 2007; Ndaji, Little, & Coe, 2016; Parsons, Green, Ploubidis, Sullivan, & Wiggins, 2017; Smith-Woolley et al., 2018). In addition, while Sakellariou (2017) finds that in many countries there is no significant effect of private schooling on PISA scores, after controlling for pupil background and school characteristics such as class size and peer effects, in the UK there remains a statistically-significant positive effect. Most of these studies, though not all, control in some way for prior attainment, and show modest but significant effects at all three main stages of schooling: primary, lower secondary and upper secondary. Collectively, therefore, they show a picture of cumulative gain from private education, which is reflected in beneficial access to higher-ranking universities. The unusually large private/state resources gap in Britain, noted earlier, provides one explanation for these effects. Indeed, the high quality of Britain's private schools illustrates what can be achieved with a very large infusion of resources — even though some of the resources are expended on luxuries for the wealthy clientele rather than educational requirements. The impact of peer groups is another explanation, there being evidence that Britain's private school students have higher levels of prior attainment, and fewer psychological and behavioral challenges (Green & Kynaston, 2019).

Britain's private schools also deliver long-term positive outcomes in the labor market: even after controlling for socio-economic background, privately educated alumni are more likely to reach high-status occupations than their state-educated peers; they will on average gain a substantial wage premium and disproportionately occupy places at the top of professions and in public life (Crawford, Gregg, Macmillan, Vignoles, & Wyness, 2016; Crawford & Vignoles, 2014; Dearden et al., 2002; Green et al., 2011, 2017b; Kirby, 2016; Macmillan, Tyler, & Vignoles, 2015; McKnight, 2015; Sullivan et al. 2018). While much of this premium is accounted for by the educational outcomes just described, especially in the case of women, for men there remains a private-school premium over and above what could be predicted by their educational achievements. This 'direct' premium for men, it is hypothesized, might derive from privileged access to job networks or from social and cultural capital, but there are as yet no quantitative studies that confirm these conjectures (Green et al., 2017).

Finally, several studies from less developed countries, where private schools have been growing rapidly in recent decades, find positive effects on academic outcomes. Azam, Kingdon, and Wu (2016), for example, report robust positive effects from private schooling in India, while Amjad and MacLeod (2014) show the same for Pakistan. However, the picture is by no means universally positive. Singh (2015) finds very mixed results in India's Andrha Pradesh state, with private schools raising scores in English but not in Maths, while Chudgar and Quin (2012) found no significant private school effects across India, once all socio-economic controls are introduced, using propensity score matching. In these cases, the comparator of state schooling may typically be lower quality than is available, through superior resources, in developed countries; the resources gap between private and state schooling is often unclear. Equally, the private/state contrast between the extent and quality of regulation and the degree of central control can be more stark than in developed countries.

Conclusion

In all these studies of private school effects, the framework is essentially microeconomic, trying to estimate 'effects' for an individual, by comparing outcomes for a 'treated' individual who participates in private education with the counterfactual outcomes if the individual did not participate. These estimates do not necessarily give an accurate guide, however, where system-wide policy changes are proposed. In a system-wide policy — such as, for example, a proposal to strongly constrain private schooling — the comparison might be between the status quo and a counterfactual education system with only a few private schools. Included in this assessment should be the implications for the performance of state schools of having less private school competition, and the role of parental pressures for school improvement which would be transferred to state schools. A standard way of finding system-wide evidence is through international comparisons, a methodology that characterizes some of the OECD's work using its PISA and PIAAC data bases. In this topic of private schooling, however, the possibilities for this kind of inference are limited by the variable nature of private schools between countries.

Research on private schooling should strive to be relevant for policy purposes, as well as for describing the realities faced by school leaders and by parents deciding about their children's schooling. Yet there are substantial gaps in our research knowledge. Where private school effects are found, we do not adequately understand the mechanisms. In many countries, we do not have much evidence of how much difference, if any, a private schooling makes for individuals. Scarcer still are estimates of rates of return, taking into account both the fees and expected lifetime earnings. Most strikingly, there is little quantitative evidence on the extent to which private schools are genuinely innovative in their teaching and learning, as implied by their autonomy from government and their ability to offer diverse educational services. Nor do we have estimates of any influence such innovativeness might have had on state schools' practices. Finally, there are whole areas of the private provision of education that are underresearched. The growth of private tuition is a long-standing issue, especially in some East Asian countries. And international schools, one of the fastest-growing sectors of education even if from a small base, have so far attracted little scientific interest.

References

Adnett, N., & Davies, P. (2002). Education as a positional good: Implications for market-based reforms of state schooling. *British Journal of Educational Studies, 50*(2), 189–205.

Agasisti, T., Murtinu, S., & Sibiano, P. (2016). The heterogeneity of the 'private school effect' in Italian primary education. *CESifo Economic Studies, 62*(1), 126–147.

Amjad, R., & MacLeod, G. (2014). Academic effectiveness of private, public and private-public partnership schools in Pakistan. *International Journal of Educational Development, 37*, 22–31.

Andersen, S. C. (2008). Private schools and the parents that choose them: Empirical evidence from the Danish School Voucher System. *Scandinavian Political Studies, 31*(1), 44–68.

Azam, M. (2017). Explaining caste differences in private school attendance. *Review of Development Economics, 21*(4), 1191–1204.

Azam, M., Kingdon, G., & Wu, K. B. (2016). Impact of private secondary schooling on cognitive skills: Evidence from India. *Education Economics, 24*(5), 465–480.

Ball, S. J. (1997). On the cusp: Parents choosing between state and private schools in the UK: Action within an economy of symbolic goods. *International Journal of Inclusive Education, 1*(1), 1–17.

Bloom, N., Lemos, R., Sadun, R., & Van Reenen, J. (2015). Does management matter in schools? *Economic Journal, 125*(584), 647–674.

Blundell, R., Dearden, L., & Sibieta, L. (2010). *The demand for private schooling: The impact of price and quality*. London: Institute of Fiscal Studies.

Bryson, A., & Green, F. (2018). Do private schools manage better? *National Institute Economic Review, 243* (February).

Carbonaro, W. (2006). Public–private differences in achievement among kindergarten students: Differences in learning opportunities and student outcomes. *American Journal of Education, 113*(1), 31–66.

Chudgar, A., & Quin, E. (2012). Relationship between private schooling and achievement: Results from rural and urban India. *Economics of Education Review, 31*(4), 376–390.

Courtois, A. (2018). *Elite schooling and social inequality: Privilege and power in Ireland's top private schools*. London: Palgrave Macmillan.

Crawford, C., Gregg, P., Macmillan, L., Vignoles, A., & Wyness, G. (2016). Higher education, career opportunities, and intergenerational inequality. *Oxford Review of Economic Policy, 32*(4), 553–575.

Crawford, C., & Vignoles, A. (2014). Heterogeneity in graduate earnings by socio-economic background. *IFS Working Paper(W14/30)*, 1–20. https://doi.org/10.1920/wp.ifs.2014.1430.

Crawfurd, L. (2017). School management and public-private partnerships in Uganda. *Journal of African Economies, 26*(5), 539–560.

Dearden, L., Ferri, J., & Meghir, C. (2002). The effect of school quality on educational attainment and wages. *The Review of Economics and Statistics, 84*(1), 1–20.

Destatis. (2016). *Finanzen der Schulen. Schulen in freier Trägerschaft und Schulen des Gesundheitswesens 2013*. Wiesbaden: Statistisches Bundesamt. Available at: www.destatis.de.

Dynarski, M. (2016). *On negative effects of vouchers*. Washington, DC: Brookings Institution.

Dynarski, S., Gruber, J., & Li, D. (2009). *Cheaper by the dozen: Sibling discounts at Catholic schools to estimate the price elasticity of private school attendance*. National Bureau of Economic Research, Working Paper 15461. Cambridge, MA: NBER.

Elder, T., & Jepsen, C. (2014). Are Catholic primary schools more effective than public primary schools? *Journal of Urban Economics, 80*(1), 28–38.

Elliott, C., Konara, P., & Wei, Y. (2016). Competition, cooperation and regulatory intervention impacts on independent school fees. *International Journal of the Economics of Business, 23*(2), 243–262.

Fairlie, R. W., & Resch, A. M. (2002). "Is there "white flight" into private schools? Evidence from the national educational longitudinal survey. *The Review of Economics and Statistics, 84*(1), 21–33.

Feinstein, L., & Symons, J. (1999). Attainment in secondary school. *Oxford Economic Papers, 51*, 300–321.

Fox, I. (1985). *Private schools and public issues. The parents' view.* London: Macmillan.

Fredriksson, P., Oeckert, B., & Oosterbeek, H. (2013). Long-term effects of class size. *Quarterly Journal of Economics, 128*(1), 249–285.

Graddy, K., & Stevens, M. (2005). The impact of school inputs on student performance: A study of private schools in the United Kingdom. *Industrial and Labor Relations Review, 58*(3), 435–451.

Green, F., Anders, J., Henderson, M., & Henseke, G. (2017). *Who chooses private schooling in Britain and why?* London: Centre for Research on Learning and Life Chances (LLAKES). Research Paper 62.

Green, F., Henseke, G., Parsons, S., Sullivan, A., & Wiggins, R. (2018). Do private school girls marry rich? *Longitudinal and Life Course Studies Journal, 9*(3), 327–350.

Green, F., Henseke, G., & Vignoles, A. (2017). Private schooling and labour market outcomes. *British Educational Research Journal, 43*(1), 7–28.

Green, F., & Kynaston, D. (2019). *Engines of privilege: Britain's private school problem*. London: Bloomsbury.

Green, F., Machin, S., Murphy, R., & Zhu, Y. (2008). Competition for private and state school teachers. *Journal of Education and Work, 21*(5), 383–404.

Green, F., Machin, S., Murphy, R., & Zhu, Y. (2011). The changing economic advantage from private schools. *Economica, 79*, 658–679.

Green, F., Parsons, S., Sullivan, A., & Wiggins, R. (2017). Dreaming big? Self-valuations, aspirations, networks and the private-school earnings premium. *Cambridge Journal of Economics, 42*(3), 757–778.

Henderson. (2018). Private schooling, subject choice and upper secondary academic attainment in England. In *Workshop on Britain's private schools in the 21st century, UCL Institute of Education, 17th December 2018.* https://www.llakes.ac.uk/event/workshop-britain%27s-private-schools-21st-century.

Henseke, G. (2018). The income and wealth concentration of private school attendance in Britain.. In *Workshop on Britain's private schools in the 21st century, UCL Institute of Education, 17th December 2018.* https://www.llakes.ac.uk/event/workshop-britain's-private-schools-21st-century.

Jackson, C. K., Johnson, R. C., & Persico, C. (2016). The effects of school spending on educational and economic outcomes: Evidence from school finance reforms. *Quarterly Journal of Economics, 131*(1), 157–218.

Jepsen, C. (2003). The effectiveness of Catholic primary schooling. *Journal of Human Resources, 38*(4), 928–941.

Kirby, P. (2016). *Leading people 2016*. London: The Sutton Trust.

Krueger, A. B., & Whitmore, D. M. (2001). The effect of attending a small class in the early grades on college-test taking and middle school test results: Evidence from Project STAR. *Economic Journal, 111*(468), 1–28.

Li, M. L. (2009). Is there "white flight" into private schools? New evidence from high school and beyond. *Economics of Education Review, 28*(3), 382–392.

Lubienski, C., Crane, C., & Lubienski, S. T. (2008). What do we know about school effectiveness? Academic gains in public and private schools. *Phi Delta Kappan, 89*(9), 689–695.

Macmillan, L., Tyler, C., & Vignoles, A. (2015). Who gets the top jobs? The role of family background and networks in recent graduates' access to high-status professions. *Journal of Social Policy, 44*(3), 487–515.

Malacova, E. (2007). Effect of single sex education on progress in GCSE. *Oxford Review of Education, 33*(2), 233–259.

McKnight, A. (2015). *Downward mobility, opportunity hoarding and the 'glass floor'.* London: Social Mobility and Child Poverty Commission.

Murnane, R. J., & Reardon, S. F. (2018). Long-term trends in private school enrollments by family income. *AERA Open, 4*(1), 1–24. January-March.

National Center for Education Statistics. (2003). *A brief profile of America's private schools*. NCES 2003–417. Washington, DC: Project Officer: Barbara Holton.

Ndaji, F., Little, J., & Coe, R. (2016). *A comparison of academic achievement in INdependent and state schools, centre for evaluation and monitoring*. Durham University.

Nghiem, H. S., Nguyen, H. T., Khanam, R., & Connelly, L. B. (2015). Does school type affect cognitive and non-cognitive development in children? Evidence from Australian primary schools. *Labour Economics, 33*, 55–65.

OECD. (2012). *Public and private schools: How management and funding relate to their socio-economic profile*. OECD Publishing. https://doi.org/10.1787/9789264175006-en.

O'Donoghue, C., Thomas, S., Goldstein, H., & Knight, T. (1997). *1996 study on value added for 16–18 Year olds in England*. DfEE Research Study RS52. http://www.bristol.ac.uk/media-library/sites/cmm/migrated/documents/alevdfee.pdf.

Parsons, S., Green, F., Ploubidis, G. B., Sullivan, A., & Wiggins, R. D. (2017). The influence of private primary schooling on children's learning: Evidence from three generations of children. *British Educational Research Journal, 43*(5), 823–847.

Pianta, R. C., & Ansari, A. (2018). Does attendance in private schools predict student outcomes at age 15? evidence from a longitudinal study. *Educational Researcher, 47*(7), 419–434.

Sacerdote, B. (2011). Peer effects in c: How might they work, how big are they and how much do we know thus far?. In E. A. Hanushek, S. Machin, & L. Woessmann (Eds.), *Handbook of the economics of education* (Vol. 3, pp. 249–277).

Sahoo, S. (2017). Intra-household gender disparity in school choice: Evidence from private schooling in India. *Journal of Development Studies, 53*(10), 1714–1730.

Sakellariou, C. (2017). Private or public school advantage? Evidence from 40 countries using PISA 2012-mathematics. *Applied Economics, 49*(29), 2875–2892.

Singh, A. (2015). Private school effects in urban and rural India: Panel estimates at primary and secondary school ages. *Journal of Development Economics, 113*, 16–32.

Smith-Woolley, E., Pingault, J. B., Selzam, S., Rimfeld, K., Krapohl, E., von Stumm, S., et al. (2018). Differences in exam performance between pupils attending selective and non-selective schools mirror the genetic differences between them. *NPJ Science of Learning, 3*, 1–7.

Snyder, T. D., de Brey, C., & Dillow, S. A. (2018). *Digest of education Statistics 2016* (NCES 2017-094).

Sullivan, A., & Heath, A. (2003). Intakes and examination results at state and private schools. In G. Walford (Ed.), *British private schools: Research on policy and practice* (pp. 77–104). London: Woburn Press.

Sullivan, A. L., Parsons, S., Green, F., Wiggins, R. D., & Ploubidis, G. (2017). The path from social origins to top jobs: social reproduction via education. *British Journal of Sociology, 69*(3), 776–798.

Sullivan, A., Parsons, S., Green, F., Wiggins, R. D., Ploubidis, G., & Huynh, T. (2018). Educational attainment in the short and long term: Was there an advantage to attending faith, private, and selective schools for pupils in the 1980s? *Oxford Review of Education*, 1–17.

Sullivan, A., Parsons, S., Wiggins, R. D., Heath, A., & Green, F. (2014). Social origins, school type and higher education destinations. *Oxford Review of Education, 40*(6), 739–763.

Valatheeswaran, C., & Khan, M. I. (2018). International remittances and private schooling: Evidence from Kerala, India. *International Migration, 56*(1), 127–145.

Walton, N. (2010). The price of admission: Who gets into private school, and how much do they pay? *Economics of Education Review, 29*(5), 738–750.

The economics of charter schools

Adam Kho[a], Ron Zimmer[b], Richard Buddin[c]

[a]University of Southern California, Los Angeles, CA, USA; [b]University of Kentucky, Lexington, KY, USA; [c]University of Virginia, Charlottesville, VA, USA

Glossary

Charter schools Schools that receive public funding under a contract, or charter, with a public entity (e.g., school district, state, and universities), and are given greater autonomy than other public schools over curriculum, instruction, and operations

External validity An estimate of an effect that is valid beyond the sample of observations included in the analysis

Fixed effects Econometric method of estimating time-invariant factors in panel data analysis

Internal validity An estimate of an effect that is valid only to the sample of observations included in the analysis

Selection bias Estimated effect of programs could be biased because participants have chosen to participate, which is not captured by the econometric model

Introduction

Charter schools are an educational reform in the United States that provide more school alternatives to parents and more local autonomy for individual schools. Individual charter schools receive public funding under a contract, or charter, with a public entity, also known as the charter authorizer (e.g., school district, state, or university). Charter schools are given greater autonomy than traditional public schools over curriculum, instruction, and operations in exchange for greater accountability for results — charters of charter schools who fail to meet expectations can be non-renewed, effectively closing the school.

The first US charter school opened in Minnesota in 1992. The scale of the charter movement has grown to nearly 7000 schools and three million students in 43 states plus the District of Columbia as of the 2016-17 school year. Charter enrollments constitute about 6% of annual public school enrollments in the United States with enrollment shares as high as 16% and 43% for Arizona and the District of Columbia, respectively.

Charter reform has been a contentious education and public policy issue. Proponents argue that traditional public schools are burdened by excessive centralized control and regulation and greater school autonomy under charter reform allows schools to innovate and improve (Finn, Manno, & Vanourek, 2000). School choice is heralded as a key component of charter success — charters must compete for students with traditional public schools, and their survival is predicated on their ability to implement programs that attract students. Students and parents are afforded more options which creates healthy competition for nearby schools to also improve.

The Economics of Education, Second Edition
https://doi.org/10.1016/B978-0-12-815391-8.00039-2

Critics see charters as drawing resources away from traditional public schools and distracting them from internal reforms and innovation. These opponents argue that charter schools are no more effective than traditional public schools, that they create fiscal strains for school districts, that too many of them are unreliably operated, and that they would fail to serve all populations of students, possibly exacerbating racial segregation (Wells et al., 1998). Charter competition is seen as inconsequential in many cases or as counterproductive when traditional public schools placate parents with programs that do little to enhance student learning.

The emergence of charter schools in the United States has paralleled movements in other countries that enacted legislation to create foundation or independent schools that operate much like charter schools in the United States — that is, they receive substantial public funding and have independent authority over curriculum and governance (Brewer & Hentschke, 2008). A key difference between these independent schools and traditional public schools is that enrollment is generally tied to parental choice. As with charter schools, the choice aspect of these schools means that their existence is directly tied to their ability to serve parents and their children.

Policy questions

The extant literature has examined the comprehensive effects of charter schools on the educational system in the United States. Much of the research has narrowly focused on how charter schools affect achievement for students who attend these schools. However, it is important to consider the possible impact charter schools are having more broadly, including their cost effectiveness, systemic effects (e.g., effects on students who choose not to attend traditional public schools), distributional effects, both by ability and race, and any operational differences

between charter and traditional public schools, which may lead to broader educational innovations. This article primarily focuses on four issues:

1. What are the demographic profiles of students entering charter schools? How do charter schools affect the mix of students in traditional public schools by race/ethnicity and academic ability?
2. Are charter schools and traditional public schools receiving comparable funding? Do charters have the same public resources to educate students as traditional public schools?
3. What is the effect of charter schools on the achievement of their students?
4. Do charters promote improved achievement in traditional public schools by introducing competition, or do they harm the performance of traditional public schools?

When summarizing the literature across these questions, we highlight why these questions are important and synthesize the findings across the literature, bearing in mind the quality of the research.

What types of students do charter schools serve?

As charter schools are schools of choice, it is important to examine whether they are serving the full range of the student population. Table 39.1 provides a snapshot of selected characteristics of students served in traditional public schools and charter schools in the 2015—16 school year (USDOE, 2017). On average, charter schools serve more black and Hispanic students than traditional public schools and tend to serve students on further ends of the income distribution than traditional public schools. Over half of the nation's charter schools are located in urban settings as compared to about a quarter of traditional public schools.

TABLE 39.1 Characteristics of traditional public school and charter school students, 2015−16.

	Traditional public schools	Charter schools
Race/Ethnicity		
White	49.9%	33.1%
Black	14.7%	26.8%
Hispanic	25.6%	31.7%
Asian/Pacific Islander	5.4%	4.3%
American Indian/Alaska Native	1.0%	0.7%
Two or more races	3.4%	3.4%
Percent of students eligible for free or reduced-price lunch program		
0%−25.0%	19.6%	22.2%
25.1%−50.0%	27.4%	18.0%
50.1%−75.0%	26.9%	18.6%
75.1%−100%	23.9%	32.6%
Locale		
City	24.9%	56.5%
Suburban	32.1%	25.9%
Town	14.1%	6.7%
Rural	28.9%	10.9%

Source: United States Department of Education, National Center for Education Statistics (2017).

Charter school critics argue that charter success might be illusory if they further stratify an already ethnically or racially stratified system (Cobb & Glass, 1999; Wells et al., 1998). In general, these critics fear that charter schools may not only have negative consequences for the charter students who attend these schools, but may also have social and academic consequences for students in affected traditional public schools. However, proponents of charter schools argue that charter schools will improve racial integration by letting families choose schools outside of neighborhoods where housing may be racially segregated (Finn et al., 2000; Nathan, 1998).

Several studies have examined the racial/ethnic makeup of charter schools relative to the average racial/ethnic makeup of their surrounding districts and states (Frankenberg & Lee, 2003; Miron & Nelson, 2002; International, 2000; Powell, Blackorby, Marsh, Finnegan, & Anderson, 1997; RPP). While this research has provided some insights, it uses cross-sectional, snapshots of schools' enrollments, which do not permit examination of students moving between schools. Understanding how charter schools affect the mix of students requires a dynamic model that uses longitudinal data to examine the characteristics of students who migrate from a traditional public school to a charter school and compares the students' characteristics with the distribution of students at the old and new schools.

Several studies have examined the migration patterns of students of different race/ethnicity between traditional and charter schools. Bifulco and Ladd (2007) found that black students in North Carolina were likely to switch to charter schools with higher concentrations of black students than the traditional public schools they left. This charter school migration increased the racial isolation of black students. Booker, Zimmer, and Buddin (2005) also found that in California and Texas, black students generally transferred to charter schools with higher concentrations of black students. In contrast, Hispanic students in both states are likely to transfer to charter schools with a lower concentration of Hispanics than in the traditional public schools they left. These patterns have been echoed in a study by Zimmer et al. (2009) across two states and five urban districts across the United States. In Texas, Weiher and Tedin (2002) found that students of white, black, and Hispanic races all transferred into charter schools with greater proportions of their own race than the traditional public schools they left.

Using similar or more rigorous strategies, researchers have also investigated another critique of charter schools – that any success of charter schools is driven by selectively enrolling students through cream skimming high ability students from traditional public schools or pushing out lower-performing students (Ravitch, 2012). Using data from California and Texas, Booker et al. (2005) compare the prior performance levels of students who move into charter schools with the students at the traditional public schools they leave and find that those moving into charters are generally lower-performing than their previous peers. Similar analyses in a study examining charter schools in Ohio, Texas, and five other major US cities revealed similar conclusions (Zimmer et al., 2009). Zimmer and Guarino (2013) investigate the claim of pushing out low-performing students in an anonymous major urban school district. They find no evidence consistent with this practice. Two other

studies (Kho & McEachin, 2017; Kho & Zimmer, 2017) investigate both claims of cream skimming and pushout in Tennessee and North Carolina's charter schools. Neither studies find evidence consistent with such selective enrollment strategies according to student performance level. However, both find some evidence consistent with charter schools' pushout behaviors based on students' disciplinary records. Overall, claims regarding systematic selective enrollment of students, at least according to academic ability, have been unsubstantiated. It is possible that individual charter schools may participate in such practices, but the evidence shows that this would not appear to be a systemwide behavior.

Are charter and traditional schools receiving comparable funding?

Charter schools are nominally entitled to funding comparable with traditional public schools, but some evidence suggests that charter school funding is lagging behind in many states (Batdorff et al., 2014; Osberg, 2006; Schneider & Tice, 2007). A recent study (Batdorff et al., 2014) compares the average funding per pupil for traditional public schools and charter schools in 30 states and the District of Columbia and finds that average funding per pupil is about 28.4% lower for charter students, with discrepancies over 40% in some states. In only one state observed is funding comparable across the two sectors – Tennessee. The extent of these funding gaps is largely a function of state policies, including whether the state provides funding for facilities (or requires districts to provide facilities), whether state funds are supplemented by local resources to pay for education, and whether the state paperwork limited charter access to a large array of categorical funds.

In many states, charter schools are expected to pay for facilities out of the operating revenue, which creates large funding gaps (Krop & Zimmer, 2005). In addition, when states rely heavily upon local tax revenue to pay for education, charter schools are less likely to gain a share of these revenues — again creating large funding gaps (Osberg, 2006). Finally, some states require education agencies to complete complex forms to receive categorical funding. In school districts, the cost of completing forms is spread over a large enrollment, but autonomous charter schools must complete comparable paperwork to receive funding for small numbers of students. This diseconomy of scale for charters reduces their access to categorical programs compared with traditional public schools and contributes to the reduced funding level of charter schools (Zimmer et al., 2003).

The challenges of these funding gaps are gradually being recognized by states and some new policies have been introduced to address these issues. However, some argue that since one of the objectives of charter schools is greater efficiency, charter schools should prove they can provide similar or better results with fewer resources.

How do charter schools affect the performance of charter students?

Over the last two decades, a series of papers has emerged examining student achievement in charter schools in various states and cities throughout the U.S. In addition, several studies have examined student achievement in charter schools nationally (Carnoy et al., 2005; CREDO, 2009; Cremata et al., 2013; Gleason, Clark, Tuttle, & Dwoyer, 2010; Hoxby, 2004; Nelson, Rosenberg, & Van Meter, 2004). Some of this research has relied upon school-level data (Greene, Forster, & Winters, 2003; LOEO, 2003; Miron, Nelson, & Risley, 2002; Rogosa, 2003; Russo, 2005) or cross-sectional comparisons of achievement in charter schools and traditional public schools at a single point in time.

A key weakness of a school-level analysis is the high degree of aggregation, which masks changes over time in the school's population of students, and variation of performance across different subjects and grades. In essence, school-level data may not pick up the nuances of school characteristics and can only provide an incomplete picture of why outcomes vary across schools. Meanwhile, point-in-time data, even at the student level, cannot account for the amount of time spent in different schools and cannot factor out the various non-school forces at work.

Both school-level and point-in-time studies are likely to provide misleading indications of charter effectiveness due to a selection bias in charter-school enrollment. Parents choose charter alternatives because the traditional schools are not meeting their learning objectives. This parent selection process means that charter students are not representative of the pool of traditional school students, so the average difference in the performance of charter and traditional school students is a misleading indication of the effectiveness of charter schools. For example, if a charter school focuses on low-achieving students that are struggling in traditional schools, then the charter's average test score is likely to reflect the weak preparation of its incoming students. Alternatively, if a high school charter's curriculum is built around college preparation, then the average charter test score may reflect the stronger preparation of its incoming students than that of a nearby traditional high school serving a broader mix of students. The danger is that charter effectiveness measures are easily confounded by the mix of student background and non-school factors that lead parents to choose charter schools for their students.

Reliable measures of charter performance must assess the additional gain or value-add from charter enrollment and not the historical background of students choosing charter schools. Researchers have dealt with the selection bias in charter enrollment in two ways: randomized experiments and longitudinal analyses. Both methods allow researchers to account for the amount of time a student has spent in a particular school, and both methods address differences among student populations served. Randomized experiments are often considered the gold standard in research, because, by assigning subjects randomly to the treatment condition or control condition, they ensure that differences observed later are the result of treatment rather than the result of background differences between the subject groups.

Several studies examine oversubscribed charter schools that randomly admit students through lotteries. For instance, Hoxby and Rockoff (2005) examined four charter schools in Chicago, which provided evidence that this set of charter schools is outperforming traditional public schools. Later, Hoxby and Murarka (2007) used a similar design to evaluate 47 charter schools in New York City and found a small positive achievement effect for students attending charter schools. More recent studies using lotteries in Boston, Washington DC, and New York City (Abdulkadiroglu et al., 2011; Curto & Fryer, 2014; Dobbie & Fryer, 2011) have all found positive effects for oversubscribed charter schools.

These studies have strong internal validity — in other words, the results have strong implications for schools included in the evaluation. One drawback of this randomized-design approach is that while it produces valid and reliable results for the set of charter schools examined, it may have limited implications for charter schools that are not part of the analysis. In other words, these studies have weak external validity. In order to conduct a randomized experiment of charter schools, researchers have relied upon randomly assigning students for schools that are oversubscribed with substantial wait lists. Therefore, these studies may have limited implications for those schools that do not have wait lists. In fact, one would expect schools with wait lists to be the best schools and it would be surprising if they had the same results as other charter schools.

When randomized designs have not been possible, or when researchers wanted to be more inclusive in their analysis of charter schools, researchers have often used a student fixed-effect approach to deal with the selection bias, which requires longitudinal student-level data. Student fixed-effect approaches minimize the problem of selection bias by examining the academic gains made by individual students over time, factoring out those students' baseline achievement levels. Moreover, they permit within-student comparisons of achievement gains, examining changes in the achievement trajectories of individual students who move from traditional public schools to charter schools, or vice versa.

To date, a handful of studies have used this approach across a select number of states. In North Carolina, Bifulco and Ladd (2006) used the fixed-effect approach and found negative reading and math effects for its charter schools. These results were supported in later research by Carruthers (2012) after including an additional five years of data. In California, Zimmer and colleagues (2003) examined student-level data from six large districts and found that charter schools were performing on par with traditional public schools. In addition, Betts, Rice, Zau, Tang, and Koedel (2006) examined charter schools exclusively in San Diego and similarly found that charter schools were performing on par with traditional public schools. A cross-state study (Zimmer et al., 2009) looked at charter schools in two states and five major cities in the US and found a mix of negative effects (in Chicago and Texas) and effects comparable between charter schools and traditional public schools (in Denver, Milwaukee, Philadelphia, San Diego, and Ohio).

Three separate studies using similar approaches found mixed results in Texas. Gronberg and Jansen (2001) found that charter schools that focus on at-risk students provided slightly more value-add than traditional public schools while non-at-risk charters provided slightly less value-add than traditional schools. Hanushek, Kain, and Rivkin (2002) found negative achievement effects for Texas charter schools that were in the first few years of their operation, however, and no significant effect in reading and small positive effect in math in the long run. In a more recent study, Booker, Gilpatric, Gronberg, and Jansen (2007) found that in the first year of attending charter schools, student test scores dropped, but the students' performance became comparable with students in traditional public schools by the second and third year in reading and math, respectively. In Florida, Sass (2006) found that charter schools initially had lower performance than traditional public schools, but eventually produced similar educational gains over time and by the fifth year, these schools were generally producing small positive effects. Similarly, in Arizona, Solmon, Paark, and Garcia (2001) found that students initially had lower scores, but students who remained 2–3 years in charter schools outperformed traditional public school students in reading and performed at least as well as public school students in math and possibly better (depending upon the model). In Milwaukee and Indianapolis, Witte, Weimer, Shober, and Schlomer (2007) and Nicotera, Mendiburo, and Berends (2009), respectively, found positive effects for charter schools in math. Finally, in an anonymous district, Imberman (2011) found mixed results for charter schools with a small positive effect in math and a small negative effect in reading.

While the fixed-effect approach can be a strong control for selection bias, there are drawbacks to the fixed-effect approach as well. One of the greatest drawbacks is that the fixed-effect approach provides an estimate of student achievement only for students who switch from a traditional public school to a charter school or vice versa (switchers). Students who remain in either charter or traditional public schools for the duration of the analysis do not contribute to the estimate because the analysis does not compare their results in both contexts (charter schools and traditional public schools).

Work by Ballou, Teasley, and Zeidner (2007) shows how the reliance on switchers can create two problems. First, charter schools that have high turnover rates (which may he associated with poor performance) will disproportionately contribute to the fixed-effect estimate. Second, Ballou et al. (2007) note that switchers may differ from nonswitchers in important ways, possibly biasing results that rely exclusively on switchers. They explore these issues by examining charter schools in Idaho using both a longitudinal student fixed-effect model, which only uses switchers, and by estimating the impact using all tested charter and noncharter students. Exploring both approaches, they find conflicting results. The authors argue that the bias from only examining switching students in a student fixed-effect model may be greater than the self-selection bias the model attempts to correct and may imply that researchers should not exclusively rely upon fixed-effect models. However, in an interesting counterexample, Betts et al. (2006), using data from San Diego, found that a fixed-effect approach produces math results much closer to the result of a randomized-design approach than other nonexperimental designs. In reading, random-effects models produced the best results.

A third empirical strategy researchers have used recently for charter school evaluation is matching. In this approach, charter school students are matched and compared to students in traditional public schools who look similar on observable characteristics and may have the same propensity to attend a charter school. This approach addresses the problem of student fixed-effect models in that students who have always been enrolled in charter schools or traditional public schools can be included in the estimation, not just switchers. Miron, Cullen, Applegate, and Farrell (2007) use a matching strategy to evaluate charter schools in Delaware and find negative effects for elementary schools but positive effects for middle and high schools. The Center for Research on Educational Outcomes (CREDO) has released multi-state studies also using a matching strategy (CREDO, 2009; Cremata et al., 2013), finding mixed results that vary by state. In the earlier study, which includes 15 states and the District of Columbia, they find overall negative results. In the latter study, which includes 27 states and the District of Columbia, they find overall positive results.

Several studies have incorporated matching strategies with other methods. Dobbie and Fryer (2016) examine charter schools in Texas using matched samples in combination with fixed effects to evaluate charter schools in Texas. They find that charter schools perform on par with traditional public schools. Berends, Watral, Teasley, and Nicotera (2008) use matching with random effects in a study in an anonymous urban school district and find that charter schools perform worse than traditional public schools in initial years of enrollment, but those effects become positive as the number of years enrolled in the charter school increases.

Matching also has its drawbacks, most commonly discussed is that students are only matched based on observable characteristics. Other characteristics for which data is not available, like motivation, may actually drive students' decisions to enroll in charter schools and be highly correlated with their achievement. By omitting this factor in the matching process, it is unclear whether the matched charter and traditional public school students are truly comparable. Overall, no methodology is perfect. The concerns with each approach suggests that researchers need to be explicit about the types of students the model is examining and what possible bias is remaining when examining charter schools.

Overall, the best of the current research has found that the student achievement results charter schools vary greatly across settings. However, much of this research has shown that charter schools do improve over time, which implies that we may have to wait longer to draw definitive conclusions about the performance of charter schools.

Is charter school competition improving the performance of traditional public schools?

While much of the existing research on charter school has focused on student achievement effects for students who choose to attend charter schools, we argue that this focus may be too narrow. Supporters hope that charter schools can exert healthy competitive pressure on the existing K-12 educational system by giving families alternatives to traditional public schools. In fact, given that charter schools will probably never educate a substantial portion of the nation's student population, charter advocates argue that these schools may have their greatest impact through systemic effects — the competitive effects of charter schools could improve the performance of traditional public schools and enhance the performance of students who do not attend charter schools.

The challenge in evaluating possible competitive effects is in knowing when district or school personnel will perceive a competitive threat. Do charter schools create competitive pressure when they are located near a traditional public school or when they first appear in a district? Do charter schools only create competitive pressure when they start recruiting students away from a particular school, or do they exert pressure when they capture a certain portion of students within a marketplace? In addition, the local environment may influence the competitive pressure that charter schools create. For instance, some districts may have well-developed, preexisting choice programs, including magnet schools or open enrollment policies. Moreover, some districts may be experiencing significant growth or already have overcrowded schools, in which case charter schools may act more like a release valve than a source of competitive pressure.

Nevertheless, research is developing around this issue and has made critical assumptions about the competitive process, which could affect conclusions made about the competitive effects. For example, Hoxby (2002) defines competition as where there is minimum market penetration of charter schools within a district and finds substantial positive competitive effects in Arizona and Michigan. However, Bettinger (2005), using an instrumental variable strategy, also examines competitive effects in Michigan as measured by distance and finds no effects. Using school-level data in North Carolina, Holmes, DeSimone, and Rupp (2003) also used distance as a proxy for competition and found substantial competitive effects. In contrast, Bifulco and Ladd (2006) use student-level data in North Carolina and map out the distances of students exiting public schools to enter charter schools. Using this mapping, they analyze the effect charter schools have on traditional public schools within concentric distances of charter schools. Their analysis finds no competitive effects. Sass (2006) and Booker, Gilpatric, Gronberg, and Jansen (2008) also use student-level data in Florida and Texas, respectively, to examine competitive effects. Similar to Bifulco and Ladd, Sass uses concentric circles around public schools and measures whether a charter school is within these concentric circles and what proportion of total students are enrolled in charter schools. Using these approaches, Sass (2006) finds small positive competitive effects in Florida. Booker et al. (2008) uses two approaches, which find consistent competitive effects. First, like Hoxby, the authors use market-penetration measure at the district level. Second, they also use a campus-level market-penetration measure, which is defined by the percentage of students at a particular campus that exits the school to go to a charter school. They find competitive effects across both measures.

In a more recent paper, Buddin and Zimmer (2009) examine the competitive effects of charter schools using both survey and longitudinal student-level data in California. Examining survey responses from traditional public school principals about the changes in school operations, the analysis by the authors suggests that charter schools have no measurable impact on the performance or operation of traditional public schools. The authors go on to examine the student achievement data, in which they use metrics of distance to the nearest charter schools along with the number of charter schools and the share of students attending a charter school within 2.5 miles of a traditional public school, while controlling for the level of preexisting competition and also using various measures of competition. Again, the authors found no evidence that charter schools create a competitive effect. Across these studies, the authors generally found limited evidence of a competitive effect from charter schools. However, that could be explained by the fact that charter schools generally represent a low share of students in districts or states or by the fact that charter schools, at least in growing districts, may act as a release valve rather than a competitive pressure. It is possible that a broader implementation of charters would exert pressure on traditional public schools to improve their performance.

Conclusion

The charter movement grew out of a hope that by providing greater autonomy to schools, charter schools would be able to cut through bureaucratic frustrations and offer innovative, efficient, and effective educational programs, provide new options to families, and promote healthy competition for traditional public schools. However, critics feared that charter schools would drain scarce resources from the existing public education system, create greater stratification both by ability and race/ethnicity, and provide no real academic advantages to students attending these schools.

The current research has not shown charter schools to be a panacea for challenges facing the educational system that advocates hoped for, but expanding charter numbers and enrollments indicate that these schools may be meeting other academic and/or other nonacademic needs without requiring as many public resources. As the sector continues to grow and charters enter into new facets of the education system, their effects may become more prominent. Researchers should continue to assess and evaluate the charter movement with a greater focus on what particular innovations are and are not driving results for students.

References

Abdulkadiroğlu, A., Angrist, J. D., Dynarski, S. M., Kane, T. J., & Pathak, P. A. (2011). Accountability and flexibility in public schools: Evidence from Boston's charters and pilots. *The Quarterly Journal of Economics, 126*(2), 699–748.

Ballou, D., Teasley, B., & Zeidner, T. (2007). Charter schools in Idaho. In M. Berends, M. G. Springer, & H. Walberg (Eds.), *Charter school outcomes* (pp. 221–241). New York: Erlbaum.

Batdorff, M., Maloney, L., May, J. F., Speakman, S. T., Wolf, P. J., & Cheng, A. (2014). *Charter school funding: Inequity expands. University of Arkansas – Department of education reform: School choice demonstration project.* Retrieved from http://www.uaedreform.org/wp-content/uploads/charter-funding-inequity-expands.pdf.

Berends, M., Watral, C., Teasley, B., & Nicotera, A. (2008). Charter school effects on achievement: Where we are and where we're going. *Charter School Outcomes, 243–266.*

Bettinger, E. P. (2005). The effect of charter schools on charter students and public schools. *Economics of Education Review, 24,* 133–147.

Betts, J. R., Rice, L. A., Zau, A. C., Tang, E., & Koedel, C. R. (2006). *Does school choice work? Effects on student integration and achievement.* San Francisco, CA: Public Policy Institute of California.

Bifulco, R., & Ladd, H. (2006). The impact of charter schools on student achievement: Evidence from North Carolina. *Journal of Education Finance and Policy, 1,* 778–820.

Bifulco, R., & Ladd, H. (2007). Race and charter schools: Evidence from North Carolina. *Journal of Policy Analysis and Management, 26*(1), 31–56.

Booker, K., Gilpatric, S., Gronberg, T. J., & Jansen, D. W. (2007). Charter school performance in Texas. *Journal of Public Economics, 91,* 849–876.

Booker, K., Gilpatric, S., Gronberg, T. J., & Jansen, D. W. (2008). The effect of charter schools on traditional public students in Texas: Are children who stay behind left behind? *Journal of Urban Economics, 64*(1), 123–145.

Booker, K., Zimmer, R., & Buddin, R. (2005). *The effect of charter schools on school peer composition.* Santa Monica, CA: RAND Corporation.

Brewer, D., & Hentschke, G. (2008). The global phenomenon of publicly-financed, privately-operated schools. In M. Berends, M. Spnnger, D. Ballou, & H. Walberg (Eds.), *Handbook of research on school choice* (pp. 227–246). New York: Erlbaum.

Buddin, R., & Zimmer, R. W. (2009). Is charter school competition in California improving the performance of traditional public schools? *Public Administration Review, 69*(5), 831–845.

Camoy, M., Jacobsen, R., Mishel, L., & Rothstein, R. (2005). *The charter school dust-up: Examining the evidence on enrollment and achievement.* Washington, DC: Economic Policy Institute.

Carruthers, C. K. (2012). New schools, new students, new teachers: Evaluating the effectiveness of charter schools. *Economics of Education Review, 31*(2), 280–292.

Center for Research on Education Outcomes [CREDO]. (2009). *Multiple choice: Charter school performance in 16 states.*

Cobb, C. D., & Glass, G. V. (1999). Ethnic segregation in Arizona charter schools. *Education Policy Analysis Archives, 7,* 1–36.

Cremata, E., Davis, D., Dickey, K., Lawyer, K., Negassi, Y., Raymond, M., et al. (2013). *National charter school study.* Center for Research on Education Outcomes, Stanford University.

Curto, V. E., & Fryer, R. G., Jr. (2014). The potential of urban boarding schools for the poor: Evidence from SEED. *Journal of Labor Economics, 32*(1), 65–93.

Dobbie, W., & Fryer, R. G. (2011). Are high-quality schools enough to increase achievement among the poor? Evidence from the Harlem Children's zone. *American Economic Journal: Applied Economics, 3*(3), 158–187.

Dobbie, W. S., & Fryer, R. G. (2016). *Charter schools and labor market outcomes (No. w22502).* National Bureau of Economic Research.

Finn, C. E., Manno, B. V., & Vanourek, G. (2000). *Charter schools in action: Renewing public education.* Princeton, NJ: Princeton University Press.

Frankenberg, E., & Lee, C. (2003). *Charter schools and race: A lost opportunity for integrated education.* Cambridge, MA: Harvard Civil Rights Project. Retrieved from https://files.eric.ed.gov/fulltext/ED478410.pdf.

Gleason, P., Clark, M., Tuttle, C. C., & Dwoyer, E. (2010). *The evaluation of charter school impacts: Final report (NCEE 2010-4029)*. Washington, DC: National Center for Education Evaluation and Regional Assistance, Institute of Education Sciences, U.S. Department of Education.

Greene, J. P., Forster, G., & Winters, M. A. (2003). *Apples to Apples: An evaluation of charter schools serving general student populations*. Center for Civic Innovation. Education Working Paper No. 1.

Gronberg, T. J., & Jansen, D. W. (2001). *Navigating newly chartered waters: An analysis of Texas charter school performance*. Austin, TX: Texas Public Policy Foundation.

Hanushek, E. A., Kain, J. F., & Rivkin, S. G. (2002). *The impact of charter schools on academic achievement*. Stanford, CA: Hoover Institute.

Holmes, G. M., DeSimone, J., & Rupp, N. (2003). *Does school choice increase school quality?*. Working Paper 9683. Cambridge, MA: National Bureau of Economic Research.

Hoxby, C. M. (2002). How school choice affects the achievement of public school students. In H. Paul (Ed.), *Choice with equity* (pp. 141–177). Stanford, CA: Hoover Press.

Hoxby, C. M. (2004). *A straightforward comparison of charter schools and regular public schools in the United States*. NBER Working Paper. Cambridge, MA: National Bureau of Economic Research.

Hoxby, C. M., & Murarka, S. (2007). *Charter schools in New York city: Who enrolls and how they affect their students' achievement*. Cambridge, MA: National Bureau of Economic Research.

Hoxby, C. M., & Rockoff, J. E. (2005). *The impact of charter schools on student achievement*. Working Paper. Cambridge, MA: Harvard University.

Imberman, S. A. (2011). Achievement and behavior in charter schools: Drawing a more complete picture. *The Review of Economics and Statistics, 93*(2), 416–435.

International, R. P. P. (2000). *The state of charter schools' national study of charter schools fourth-year report*. Washington, DC: Office of Educational Research and Improvement, US Department of Education.

Kho, A., & McEachin, A. (November 2017). Investigating selective enrollment practices in North Carolina's schools of choice. In *Paper presented at the meeting of the Association for Public Policy and Management, Chicago, IL*.

Kho, A., & Zimmer, R. (March 2017). A comprehensive examination of the performance levels of students served by Tennessee's charter schools. In *Paper presented at the meeting for the Association for Education Finance and Policy, Washington, DC*.

Krop, C., & Zimmer, R. (2005). Charter school type matters when examining funding and facilities: Evidence from California. *Education Policy Analysis Archives, 13*, 50.

Legislative Office of Education Oversight [LOEO]. (2003). *Community schools in Ohio: Final report on student performance, parent satisfaction, and accountability*. Columbus, OH: Legislative Office of Education Oversight.

Miron, G., Cullen, A., Applegate, B., & Farrell, P. (2007). *Evaluation of the Delaware charter school reform: Final report*. Kalamazoo, MI: The Evaluation Center of Western Michigan University.

Miron, G. N., & Nelson, C. (2002). *What's public about charter schools?* Thousand Oaks, CA: Corwin Press.

Miron, G., Nelson, C., & Risley, J. (2002). *Strengthening Pennsylvania's charter school reform: Findings from the statewide evaluation and discussion of relevant policy issues*. Kalamazoo, MI: The Evaluation Center/Western Michigan University.

Nathan, J. (1998). *Controversy: Charters and choice*. The American Prospect. November-December. Retrieved from http://prospect.org/article/controversy-charters-and-choice.

Nelson, F. H., Rosenberg, B., & Van Meter, N. (2004). *Charter school achievement on the 2003 national Assessment of educational progress*. Washington, DC: American Federation of Teachers.

Nicotera, A., Mendiburo, M., & Berends, M. (2009). Charter school effects in an urban school district: An analysis of student achievement gains in Indianapolis. In *Prepared for school choice and school improvement: Research in state, district and community contexts*. Vanderbilt University.

Osberg, E. (2006). Charter school funding. In T. H. Paul (Ed.), *Charter schools against the odds: An assessment of the Koret task force on K-12 education* (pp. 45–69). Stanford, CA: Hoover Institution Press.

Powell, J., Blackorby, J., Marsh, J., Finnegan, K., & Anderson, L. (1997). *Evaluation of charter school effectiveness*. Menlo Park, CA: SRI International.

Ravitch, D. (2012). CON: Say 'no thanks' to charter schools. In *Montgomery advertiser*. Retrieved from http://groups.yahoo.com/group/nyceducationnews/message/43167.

Rogosa, D. (2003). *Student progress in California charter schools, 1999–2002*. Stanford, CA: Stanford University Working Paper.

Russo, A. (2005). *A tough nut to crack in Ohio: Charter schooling in the Buckeye state*. Washington, DC: Progressive Policy Institute.

Sass, T. R. (2006). Charter schools and student achievement in Florida. *Journal of Education Finance and Policy, 1*, 91–122.

Schneider, M., & Tice, P. (2007). School choice what the NOES can and cannot tell us. In M. Berends, M. G. Springer, & H. Walberg (Eds.), *Charter school outcomes* (pp. 267–281). New York: Erlbaum.

Solmon, L., Paark, K., & Garcia, D. (2001). *Does charter school attendance improve test scores? The Arizona results*. Phoenix, AZ: Goldwater Institute Center for Market-Based Education.

United States Department of Education, National Center for Education Statistics [USDOE]. (2017). Table 216.30: Number and percentage distribution of public elementary and secondary students and schools, by traditional or charter school status and selected characteristics: Selected years, 2000-01 through 2015-16. In U.S. Department of Education, & National Center for Education Statistics (Eds.), *Digest of Education Statistics*. Retrieved from https://nces.ed.gov/programs/digest/d17/tables/dt17_216.30.asp?current=yes.

Weiher, G. R., & Tedin, K. L. (2002). Does choice lead to racially distinctive schools? Charter schools and household preferences. *Journal of Policy Analysis and Management, 21*, 79–92.

Wells, A. S., Artiles, L., Carnochan, S., et al. (1998). *Beyond the rhetoric of charter school reform: A study of ten California school districts*. Los Angeles, CA: UCLA Charter School Study.

Witte, J. F., Weimer, D., Shober, A., & Schlomer, P. (2007). The performance of charter schools in Wisconsin. *Journal of Policy Analysis and Management, 26*, 574–575.

Zimmer, R., Buddin, R., Chau, D., et al. (2003). *Charter school operations and performance: Evidence from California*. Santa Monica, CA: RAND Corporation.

Zimmer, R., Gill, B., Booker, K., Lavertu, S., Sass, T. R., & Witte, J. (2009). *Charter schools in eight states: Effects on achievement, attainment, integration, and competition*. Santa Monica, CA: RAND Corporation.

Zimmer, R., & Guarino, C. (2013). Is there empirical evidence consistent with the claim that charter schools "push out" low performing students? *Educational Evaluation and Policy Analysis, 35*(4), 461–480.

40

The economics of vocational training

Samuel Muehlemann[a,b], Stefan C. Wolter[b,c,d]

[a]LMU Munich, Munich, Germany; [b]IZA Bonn, Bonn, Germany; [c]University of Bern, Bern, Switzerland; [d]CESifo Munich, Munich, Germany

Introduction

This chapter focuses on the economics of vocational training, and apprenticeship training in particular. Apprenticeship training is a particular type of vocational training, where a significant fraction of the education takes place in the training firm and another part takes place in vocational school. For that reason, the literature typically refers to the *dual* form of apprenticeship training, even though a coherent definition remains difficult due to the heterogeneity of such programmes across different countries (Wolter & Ryan, 2011). A further distinctive feature of apprenticeship programmes is that apprentices typically receive a wage and also participate in a firm's production process. Thus, apprenticeships differ substantially from programmes in countries where all the education takes place in vocational school, and the trainees only spend a few weeks as (often unpaid) interns in a work placement to gain work experience. Conversely, school-based vocational training, which takes on an important role in many countries, is more similar to a general (college) education. From an economic perspective, apprenticeship training is of particular interest, for at least two reasons: first, as firms participate in an apprenticeship system voluntarily, it is important to understand the economics behind a firm's decision to offer apprenticeship positions, because a large and successful apprenticeship system can only exist as long as a sufficient number of firms are willing to take on apprentices. The second reason is because apprenticeships include not only either certified occupation or industry-specific skills but also firm-specific skills that are only valuable to the training firm. In a world where people are increasingly expected to be mobile across firms and to change not only jobs but also occupations during their working career, it is therefore interesting to know whether apprentices are locked-in with the training firm and in the trained occupation or are, instead, free to move to an outside firm after graduation and change occupations as easily as do students graduating from general education (e.g., Acemoglu & Pischke, 1998; Mueller and Schweri, 2015).

For these two reasons, this chapter addresses two main questions: first whether and under what economic conditions firms are willing to provide training positions, and, second, whether apprentices following this type of training can expect similar, worse, or better labor market outcomes than can students following programmes of general education. The two questions are interlinked, because, if firms try to improve the cost-effectiveness of their training by simply lowering the apprentices' wages, then the private rates of return of apprentices would decrease. Similarly, if apprentices' wages are set by either law or social partner agreement, firms could try to lower their training investments because the quality of apprenticeship training is difficult to contract, and training firms could then exploit apprentices as cheap labor (De la Croix, Doepke, & Mokyr, 2017). Thus, to ensure high-quality training, successful apprenticeship systems typically include a monitoring system that involves different stakeholders, including employer associations, unions, and state representatives. However, this topic will not be addressed in detail in this chapter.

The structure of this chapter is as follows: we first discuss the benefits of apprenticeship training for firms and discuss the empirical evidence on the costs and benefits of apprenticeship training, with a focus on countries with a dual apprenticeship system. Second, we discuss the benefits of apprenticeship training for individuals and the problems associated with estimating rates of returns to apprenticeship training. Third, we provide a brief discussion of fiscal returns to apprenticeship training. The last section concludes and discusses a few still under-researched topics of the economics of vocational education and either training or apprenticeship.

Costs and benefits of training investments for firms

Why firms pay for general training

Firms make substantial investments in training activities, and, consequently, they expect to generate a return on their investment. In competitive labor markets, the classical human capital theory (Becker, 1962) predicts that individuals must pay for their own investments in skills that are useful in other firms as well (*general skills*). Consequently, firms would never pay for general training, because competition on the labor market ensures that workers are paid according to their marginal productivity, implying zero returns to training for a firm. If firms provide instead only firm-specific skills, the classical human capital theory predicts that firms and workers share costs and benefits. In this situation only, firms would be ready to bear a part of the training costs. However, in most traditional apprenticeship countries, the skills acquired through apprenticeship are mainly general, in order to guarantee labor market mobility after training (Mueller & Schweri, 2015). Therefore, one would expect that training firms will not bear substantial net costs when training apprentices. Contrary to this prediction, a number of empirical observations clearly show otherwise. A famous example is the case of German apprenticeship training, where training firms make substantial net investments of several thousand Euros per apprentice (Jansen, Pfeifer, Schönfeld, & Wenzelmann, 2005, Jansen, Strupler Leiser, Wenzelmann, & Wolter, 2005). In trying to explain this puzzle, Acemoglu and Pischke (1999) introduced labor market frictions in their analysis of a firm's training decision. In a labor market with frictions, contrary to competitive labor markets, firms can pay wages below the marginal productivity of a worker because of either mobility costs or information asymmetries. Thus, a firm will find it profitable to invest in general training as long as the training-related increase in productivity exceeds the corresponding wage-increase and the costs of training. Acemoglu and Pischke refer to such a situation as a labor market with a *compressed wage structure*. There is, however, a paucity of empirical studies that analyze how a firm's training investments increase subsequent wages and productivity while also accounting for training costs. A notable exception is the study by Konings and Vanormelingen (2015), who used Belgian linked-employer-employee data that includes information on further training costs, as well as subsequent wage and productivity increases of individual workers in a particular firm. They found that a marginal hour of firm-sponsored training increases productivity by 0.76%, whereas wages increase only by 0.44%, where a firm's return to training is the difference between the productivity and the wage increase.

There are also other potential benefits for a firm from providing training. For instance, after spending a number of years in the training firm, apprentices accumulate not only valuable general or occupation-specific human capital but also relevant firm-specific knowledge. Retaining apprentices as skilled workers after training can, therefore, be beneficial for the training firm, because it can save on future hiring costs for skilled workers that would arise in the absence of apprenticeship training (Soskice, 1994; Stevens, 1994). Blatter, Muehlemann, Schenker, and Wolter (2016) provided empirical evidence that Swiss firms who face high external hiring costs offer more apprenticeship training positions and are also more likely to retain the apprentices as skilled workers after training. Moreover, the number of training positions increases as hiring costs increase relative to the (net) costs of providing apprenticeship training. In addition, Muehlemann and Strupler Leiser (2018) showed that hiring costs, and search cost in particular, increase when labor markets are tight. Thus, the benefit of being able to retain graduated apprentices is particularly important in times of tight labor markets.

Costs and benefits of apprenticeship training

Despite the theoretical advances in the training literature in the past two decades, empirical evidence on the benefits (and the costs)

of apprenticeship training is scarce. Evaluating apprenticeship training is more demanding compared to evaluating short training spells, as apprenticeships typically last two to four years, rather than only a few days or weeks. Most of the empirical evidence on the returns to apprenticeship training for firms is based on cost-benefit-surveys on apprenticeship training that were regularly carried out in Germany, Switzerland, and, on some occasions, in Austria, the United Kingdom, and Australia.[1] These surveys show that the costs of providing apprenticeship training consist mainly of wage costs for apprentices, costs for training instructors, and, to a much smaller extent, other costs, such as training materials, infrastructure, or exam fees. Training benefits are calculated as opportunity costs: costs that would arise for the firm if it had to pay either skilled or unskilled workers to carry out the tasks that are allocated to apprentices. Thus, calculating the short-term benefits for firms takes into account the savings in wage costs for the time that apprentices spend with productive tasks in the company. Cost-benefit surveys typically distinguish between simple tasks that can be carried out by workers without any qualification and skilled tasks that require a vocational qualification (adjusted for the initially lower productivity of apprentices in such tasks). The total benefit for the firm from having an apprentice carry out productive tasks depends on the absolute and the relative wages of skilled and unskilled workers, the shares of skilled and unskilled work performed by apprentices, and, finally, on the relative productivity of apprentices, compared to average experienced workers in the training firm.

Table 40.1 shows the benefit-cost ratios of apprenticeship training programmes in Austria, Switzerland, and Germany, three countries with a long tradition of apprenticeship training

---

[1] For recent survey articles, including detailed descriptions of the methodology of cost-benefit-surveys, see Muehlemann (2016), Muehleman and Wolter (2014), or Wolter and Ryan (2011).

TABLE 40.1 Benefit-cost ratio of dual apprenticeship training for the training firm (per apprentice).

Country	1st year	2nd year	3rd year	4th year	Total
Austria	0.87	0.86	0.83	0.76	0.83
Germany (3 year programmes)	0.68	0.78	0.89		0.79
Germany (3.5 year programmes)	0.35	0.49	0.64	0.60	0.51
Switzerland (3 year programmes)	0.99	1.12	1.18		1.10
Switzerland (4 year programmes)	0.79	0.95	1.13	1.35	1.07

Source: Adapted from Strupler, M., & Wolter, S. C. (2012). Die duale Lehre: eine Erfolgsgeschichte-auch für Betriebe. Ergebnisse der dritten Kosten-Nutzen-Erhebung der Lehrlingsausbildung aus Sicht der Betrieb. Chur/Zurich: Rüegger, Jansen, A., Pfeifer, H., Schönfeld, G., & Wenzelmann, F. (2015). Ausbildung in Deutschland weiterhin investitionsorientiert—Ergebnisse der BIBB-Kosten-Nutzen-Erhebung 2012/13. BIBB-Report, 1(2015), 1—15, and Schlögl, P., & Mayerl, M. (2016). Betriebsbefragung Zu Kosten Und Nutzen Der Lehrausbildung in Österreich: Endbericht. Vienna: Österreichisches Institut für Berufsbildungsforschung.

by year of training and in total. It becomes apparent that there are large differences even between these three countries that feature a dual apprenticeship system. The benefits never outweigh the costs in Austria and Germany, where a training firm, on average, bears net training costs by the end of the training period. Conversely, the training benefits exceed the training costs in Switzerland, yielding an average return on a firm's training investment of 7—10%. The next subsection discusses the main factors that explain why such different outcomes in training costs and benefits in similar systems can arise.

Cross-country comparisons

While analyzing the costs and benefits of apprenticeship training in a particular country can yield valuable information per se, comparing costs and benefits across countries generates additional important insights into the functioning of dual apprenticeship systems. The isolation of the factors that explain the large differences between firms operating in similar training systems can also provide important information for countries that are currently taking measures to either expand their apprenticeship systems or create one.

The first detailed comparative analysis of the German and the Swiss dual apprenticeship training system was provided by Dionisius et al. (2009). Advantages of this study are that it analyzed data that came from almost identical survey questionnaires and, furthermore, that both surveys were carried out in the two countries in the same year (2000). The results show a striking difference in the cost-benefit outcomes between the two apprenticeship systems in three-year apprenticeship programmes. Although the study confirmed earlier results obtained for Germany showing that apprenticeship training resulted in a considerable net investment for a training firm, the results for Swiss firms showed that apprenticeship training can, in fact, be provided without having to make a net investment. In other words, apprentices paid for their own training by accepting sufficiently low pay during the training period to allow their productive contribution to cover the firm's training expenses. The study revealed, however, that a combination of several factors explains why Swiss firms were able to provide training profitably. The following two factors explain most of the differences in the net cost of training between similar German and Swiss firms:

- *Allocation of productive tasks*: German apprentices spent much more of their time at the firm on tasks that yielded no direct value to the company, such as doing simulations and exercises (57% in the first year of training). Conversely, Swiss apprentices spent most of their time (79% in the first year of training) carrying out productive work, including a substantial fraction of skilled work. Thus, the Swiss firm's benefits from training apprentices were higher because they allocated a higher volume of work to their apprentices.

- *Apprentice, unskilled, and skilled worker wages*: While lower apprentice wages imply a direct reduction in net training costs, higher levels of unskilled and skilled worker wages increase the value of an apprentice's productive work (as a firm would have to pay more to hire other workers to carry out their tasks instead), but also wage costs for training personnel. Interestingly, the level of apprentice wage costs was almost identical in Switzerland and Germany when taking into account the exchange rate at the time (between 660 and 690 Euros per month). However, because both unskilled and skilled worker wages were much lower in Germany than in Switzerland, the average apprentice wage during a three-year program *relative* to the average wage of a skilled worker in the corresponding occupation was considerably higher in Germany (33%) compared to Switzerland (20%).

A possible drawback of the Swiss model could have been a slower increase in skills because apprentices spent most of their time with productive tasks. However, the study found no empirical evidence to support such a claim. In fact, the productivity of Swiss apprentices in skilled tasks in relation to a worker with a vocational qualification was found to be very similar to German apprentices both in the first year (Germany: 30%, Switzerland: 36%) and in the last year of training (Germany: 68%, Switzerland: 75%). This observation, that the increase in skills does not suffer from a more production-oriented training approach,

is supported by additional evidence that apprentices receive approximately the same amount of formal instruction time while they are in the workplace. Thus, learning and practising new skills in the context of a firm's production process appears to be equally effective to practising skills in a training environment.

Summing up, the comparative study by Dionisius et al. (2009) shows that the business case of dual apprenticeship training can be very different, even when considering two neighboring countries that feature a large dual apprenticeship system with a long tradition that yields high-quality outcomes for apprentices. Therefore, an important question is why German firms — and, to a somewhat smaller extent, Austrian firms — are willing to make such a large net investment in apprenticeship training. A first answer to the question can be found in the share of apprentices that remains with the training firm after training. In Switzerland, on average, only 36% of apprentices were working as skilled workers with the training firm one year after completing their training (Strupler & Wolter, 2012). In Germany, however, the corresponding figure was 59% on average, and it was even 82% in large firms with more than 500 employees (Jansen, Pfeifer et al., 2015). Thus, it becomes apparent that much of the returns to training in German firms arise potentially after graduation, whereas this is clearly not the case for Swiss firms. To the extent that the stricter labor market regulations in Germany were an important reason why German firms were willing to make a large net investment in apprenticeship training, as argued by the theoretical literature (Acemoglu & Pischke, 1999), it was not clear how training firms would react to the substantial deregulation that took place in Germany since 2003 (that essentially reduced the post-training benefits for firms). Jansen, Strupler Leiser et al. (2015b) found that German training firms did not reduce their training activities but instead significantly reduced their net training costs by allocating a higher share of productive tasks to apprentices, thereby increasing the benefit from training apprentices. At the same time, the study found, after allocating more productive work to apprentices, training firms even reported higher levels of relative productivity than in the previous surveys. Therefore, Jansen et al. provide further indication that apprentices can improve their work skills more effectively by performing real work instead of doing exercises or simulations.

In a recent comparative study, Moretti, Mayerl, Muehlemann, Schlögl, and Wolter (2019) compared the costs and benefits, as well as post-training benefits of Swiss and Austrian training firms, following the methodology of Dionisius et al. (2009). Their study found that, while Austrian apprentices perform similar shares of productive and non-productive tasks as do Swiss apprentices, much of the differences in the benefit-cost ratio between the two countries could be explained by a higher wage for Austrian apprentices relative to the wage of skilled workers. However, Austrian firms retained a significantly higher fraction of apprentices after training, and the savings in hiring costs from not having to recruit from the external labor market were more substantial compared to Switzerland. Thus, even though Austrian firms initially make a net investment in apprenticeship training, Moretti et al. (2019) were able to show empirically that a training firm can recoup most of its training investment within a short time after training.

Given the findings, a factor that might prevent firms from participating and investing in apprenticeship training in countries where firms make a net investment during the training period is a high probability that apprentices will leave the training firm voluntarily after graduation. Only in the Swiss case, poaching is not an issue in general, because an average firm can already recoup their training expenses by the end of the apprenticeship program.

However, even in Switzerland, approximately one-third of all training firms report a negative benefit-cost ratio (i.e., net training costs). Through analyzing the factors that have made a considerable fraction of Swiss firms accept net training costs, Muehlemann and Wolter (2011) found that firms are more willing to offer training in local labor markets with a low concentration of competing firms that could eventually poach their graduates after training. Furthermore, Muehlemann, Ryan, and Wolter (2013) were able to show that firms with monopsony power in a local labor market were able to pay apprentices lower wages (relative to unskilled wages) than in comparable firms in more competitive local labor markets. For Germany, Mohrenweiser, Zwick, and Backes-Gellner (2019) found that poaching is not an issue for large training firms, as they are able to retain most of their apprentices after training due to the availability of an internal labor market. Although Mohrenweiser (2016) shows that most apprentices in Germany who leave their training firm after graduation are employed subsequently by other training firms that also train apprentices, and not (as could be expected) by non-training firms, the share of small German firms that participate in apprenticeship training has decreased in recent years, which might be a sign that, in a situation of expected net training costs, poaching is a still a relevant factor determining the willingness of firms to provide training.

Benefits of apprenticeships for individuals

Although a firm's willingness to train is the necessary precondition for a firm-based training model like apprenticeship, a firm cannot and will not uphold such a training model if there is not sufficient interest from potential trainees. These, in turn, must be convinced that the individual rates of return on this type of education are sufficiently high to make it attractive in comparison to other educational pathways. Low individual rates of return on an apprenticeship qualification would affect potential training firms not only quantitatively, with an insufficient supply of trainees, but also qualitatively, in terms of both cognitive and non-cognitive skills of potential apprentices. Only those individuals who cannot get into the more prestigious and rewarding educational programmes would be interested in doing apprenticeships. Low-ability trainees, however, would increase training costs and thereby have a negative effect on the willingness of firms to offer training places. In other words, a successful and well-functioning apprenticeship training system is a product of a high quality, high return to training equilibrium of supply and demand.

Given the importance of the individual rates of return to education of apprenticeship training, one would expect abundant empirical literature on this subject. However, the contrary tends to be the case, and this not just because of a lack of interest but also because of different inherent difficulties in measuring individual rates of return to education in general, and to apprenticeships in particular. The six biggest obstacles — as already highlighted in Wolter and Ryan (2011, pp. 550) — are as follows: First, the search for an adequate counterfactual. The principal potential alternatives are either full-time school-based upper secondary education, general or vocational, or labor market experience, including various mixtures of employment, unemployment, and labor market programmes. The latter comparison is often done in developing countries, where the goal is to find out whether apprenticeships are effective in raising

the salaries of the trainees at all (e.g., Attanasio, Kugler, & Meghir, 2011). The reason for this comparison is that a massive number of people enter the labor market without any post-compulsory qualification because access to higher and general education is not only limited in terms of numbers but also not affordable for most people. In developed countries, however, calculating the rates of return to apprenticeships only provides valuable information if these rates are then compared to those of alternative post-compulsory educational programmes. When comparing apprenticeships or vocational education[2] to general education, an additional question is whether one compares rates of return to education per year of education, irrespective of the total number of years of education, or whether one compares the discounted earnings streams of different education types that can differ in length or of different educational programs that are all of comparable length. All approaches are observable in the empirical literature, and which one of the comparisons makes more sense depends not only on several assumptions but also on the goals of the analyses. Second, the allocation of young people to upper-secondary programmes is unlikely to be random. If either 'ability' or 'talent' represents unobserved individual attributes, then, in the absence of effective statistical controls for differences therein, estimates of the effect of apprenticeship will be downward-biased. Therefore, a meaningful analysis requires controls, whether experimental (natural or social experimentation) or statistical (econometric), for unobserved individual heterogeneity. Thirdly, appropriate outcomes have to be chosen. Besides employment

---

[2] Many statistics do not differentiate between school-based vocational education and training programmes and firm-based apprenticeships, which usually include a variable part of school-based training. Therefore, when comparing rates of return to education between general and vocational programmes, it is very often not entirely clear to what extent the latter were apprenticeships and either whether the median returns to vocational education are representative for apprenticeships or whether the returns to apprenticeships are in the lower or upper part of the distribution of the returns.

and pay, a potential benefit of apprenticeships may also be that they induce youngsters to remain in post-compulsory education, both during and after their training programmes. These benefits of an increase in educational attainment are captured only partly by labor market outcomes. However, where apprenticeship is, as observed in many countries, a form of training outside the formal education system, it may be educationally damaging, as it reduces educational attainment by those who would otherwise have remained in full-time schooling. Fourth, rates of return to education should involve a comparison of discounted costs and benefits. In practice, however, most empirical studies focus only on pay and employment probability, leaving aside the costs of training that the individual has to bear. In times of rising costs (tuition fees) of general and vocational education in many countries, failing to take into account the private costs of education is another element that biases the returns to apprenticeship downward.[3] Fifth, when calculating the discounted income streams of apprenticeships, the entire educational pathway should be taken into account. In countries, like the US or Canada, where a considerable share of apprentices are adults holding a high-school degree or even higher educational qualifications, the comparison group is distinctively different that in from continental European countries, where most apprentices are either aged below or around 20 and are doing an apprenticeship instead of following a high-school program in general education at upper secondary level. But there is a considerable heterogeneity, even within some of the traditional apprenticeship countries. For example, in Germany, some of the most demanding apprenticeships, such as in banking, are given mainly to older individuals who have already passed the general baccalaureate (*Abitur*) at upper-secondary level; meanwhile, in other occupations, mainly handicraft and related occupations, apprentices are compulsory school-leavers at approximately 16 years of age. Finally, firm-based training programmes like apprenticeships show a much higher diversity across countries than do programmes of general education. Some of these programmes include formal education at school, whereas others do not, some of them require formal education provided by firms, and, in others, firms only provide work-experience. In some countries, apprenticeships lead to nationally-recognized and certified diplomas, whereas, in other countries, they lead just to firm-specific certification that has limited portability across the industry. Therefore, the external validity of findings in one particular country is often rather limited.

Given these obstacles to empirical research, it is not surprising that most of the available literature only addresses parts of these problems and that a general statement on whether apprenticeships are a profitable investment relative to other educational alternatives for individuals is not possible. However, the existing literature tentatively provides two general insights. The first is that, if vocational education is replaced by general education at the system-level, the economic outcomes for the individuals do not change significantly. Two studies that illustrate such effects with a natural experiment are Malamud and Pop-Eleches (2010) and Zilic (2018). Both studies exploit the effects of a system-wide reform of the education system, the first in Romania and the second in Croatia. In both reforms, the vocational tracks existing prior to the reform were replaced by prolonged general education at the upper-secondary level. Contrary to widespread claims that students

---

[3] Cattaneo (2011) is one of the few studies that shows, in the context of tertiary-level vocational education (professional education), how crucial assumptions about the cost-sharing are when calculating the private rates of return to education.

attending vocational tracks will be less well prepared for technological changes compared to students with more general education, both studies — covering transformation countries that underwent radical changes of their economy after the fall of communism — show no differences in the labor market prospects between the cohorts both before and after the reform. Similar results were found for smaller reforms in the Netherlands (Oosterbeek & Webbink, 2007) and Sweden (Hall, 2012) finding no wage premium for more general education. Therefore, observed salary differences between people with vocational degrees and those with general education are attributable mainly to selection[4] effects and not to differences in the returns on education between vocational and general education. The limitation of these studies is that they compare school-based vocational programmes with general education and, therefore, do not tell us whether the same would hold for firm-based training (apprenticeships).

One study that tries to make this distinction is Hanushek, Schwerdt, Woessmann, and Zhang (2017). The authors compare the labor market outcomes (employment and wages) between countries with mainly general education, countries with vocational programmes, and, finally, countries where vocational programmes are predominantly apprenticeships. For the main part, the study uses data from the IALS (International Adult Literacy Survey of the OECD) assessment of adult competencies of the OECD. The study finds a trade-off of early advantages (in line with a well-established literature showing smoother transitions from school-to-work for

vocational students; see, e.g., Ryan (2001) for an early literature overview) in terms of employment and pay for students following vocational programmes (or apprenticeships) and later disadvantages compared to students taking general education. Such a trade-off is found also in other studies using either cohort data (Brunello & Rocco, 2017) or large administrative data (e.g., Golsteyn & Stenberg, 2017). If either apprenticeship or vocational training lead to early career gains at the cost of later losses, the question comes up as to whether, over the whole lifecycle, students in vocational education and training (VET) or more specifically apprenticeships are either better or worse off than are students in general education. Hanushek et al. (2017) present heterogeneous results on this question. Whereas VET students in Denmark are net losers, VET students are in Switzerland are net gainers, and Germany sits in the middle of these opposite cases.[5] Another observation that can be made based on the results of studies such as Hanushek et al. (2017) is that the disadvantages for VET students only become statistically significant relatively late in the career; in the non-linear specification of age, the difference is large only for workers aged 56–65. Although some argue that this is due to the fact that the occupation-specific skills learned through VET become obsolete at a faster rate, Hanushek et al. caution against this interpretation, as other explanations are possible: *"While there is a general presumption that the vast majority of males not employed — including those entering early retirement — in the later age groups do so involuntarily, it is possible that generous early-retirement schemes may*

[4] It is important to note that these selection effects comprise self-selection as well as selection by the educational authorities or schools, as in many countries students are assigned to vocational and general education tracks according to their ability.

[5] Besides heterogeneous results in country comparisons, most studies also find rather large differences in the rates of return to apprenticeship programmes between women and men, and between different occupations and programmes with different skill requirements (see, e.g., Cavaglia, McNally, and Ventura (2018) for recent results on early labor market outcomes for apprentices in England).

be differentially available to workers with vocational and general education. In this case, the detected age-employment pattern may not necessarily be driven by differential adaptability to changing economic conditions, but rather by specifics of the existing retirement policies." (pp. 67 + 69).

One can summarize the rather scarce literature existing on private rates of return on either vocational education or apprenticeship training in four points: First, natural experiments based on educational system reforms reveal that replacing vocational education by general training does not cause an improvement in labor market outcomes. Observable differences in labor market outcomes between students of vocational programmes and general education are, therefore, attributable to selection effects. Second, several studies show a trade-off between early gains and later disadvantages for students of vocational programmes relative to students of general education over the life cycle. However, whether the trade-off leads to a net disadvantage for students of vocational education depends on the country and the programmes and is also a question of interpretation, as the disadvantages later in life may be driven by factors other than the form of education chosen initially. Third, most empirical analyses show considerable heterogeneity of outcomes between women and men and between different occupations and different levels of skill requirements of vocational programmes or apprenticeships. Last but not least, vocational programmes and apprenticeships are extremely time- and country-specific; therefore, the external validity of findings in one context to another country or time is rather limited.

Fiscal returns to apprenticeship training

When analyzing the returns to education, focusing on firms and individuals provides an incomplete picture, as apprenticeships also differ from either school-based general or vocational education in relation to the fiscal costs and benefits of education. This aspect of apprenticeship training has generally been neglected in the economics of vocational training, and empirical results are even less prevalent than are studies on the private rates of return to education. This is an interesting gap in the literature, given that many governments still struggle to sustain the costs of education in the aftermath of the financial and fiscal crisis of the last decade. Whereas the comparison of school-based VET and general education is difficult to make, as both lead to very different occupations and jobs, Switzerland provides an interesting case to compare the fiscal rates of return between firm-based apprenticeship and school-based vocational programmes as both lead to the same occupational qualifications. Although robust comparisons for the individual rates of return for both programmes are missing because of the small number of students following the school-based versions, one can assume that both types will lead to similar labor market outcomes and, therefore, similar tax benefits for the state. On the cost side, however, the differences are enormous, both in terms of levels and of the adaptability to fluctuations in the number of students. Comparisons between Swiss cantons show that the public costs for a VET student doubled if half of the apprenticeships were replaced by school-based programmes (see SCCRE, 2018). This is mainly due to the necessity for the government to buy expensive machinery and tools for educational purposes in the context of the school-based programmes, whereas, in the apprenticeships, the same machinery and tools are provided by firms, which use them not only for training but also for production.

In the light of potentially significant differences in the public costs for different types of education, including the fiscal costs and benefits as well as the social costs and benefits would certainly lead to a more comprehensive view of the economics of vocational education and apprenticeships.

Conclusions

This chapter provided a brief summary of the empirical evidence with regard to the return to apprenticeship training programmes for firms, individuals, and the state. Although apprenticeship training has a long tradition in Austria, Germany, and Switzerland, cost-benefit studies highlight clearly that there are substantial differences in the returns to apprenticeship training for firms. In Switzerland, a country with few regulations in the labor market, firms organize apprenticeship training in a cost-efficient way so that they do not need to rely on post-training benefits to cover their initial training investments. Swiss apprentices are willing to accept a relatively low pay during training because they can expect substantial returns to training after graduation. Post-training mobility is rather high, as the large majority of Swiss apprentices leave the training firm within one year after training. Conversely, labor markets are more rigid in Austria and Germany, where unions are more widespread and employment protection legislation is more pronounced. Cost-benefit studies reveal that German and Austrian firms are willing to make rather large net investments in training because they are able to retain most of their apprenticeship graduates as skilled workers, thereby generating substantial savings on external hiring costs that would arise in the absence of providing apprenticeship training.

However, even though the business case for apprenticeship training has been the focus of a number of recent policy initiatives, empirical evidence about a firm's return to apprenticeship training is still based largely on cross-sectional cost-benefit-surveys. Although such studies yield important insights about the level of a firm's return to training at a particular time, little is known about how an individual firm's cost-benefit ratio changes over time, for instance, due to policy measures, such as either the introduction or the increase of minimum wages for apprentices, business cycle effects, supply shocks due to demographic change, or changes in technology and corresponding adjustments in a firm's production processes. Panel data with information about a firm's return to training for several periods would be required to identify such interesting effects. Moreover, to account for heterogeneity in the ability of individual apprentices, the use of linked employer–employee data would better identify the effects of training in the workplace on future labor market outcomes for individuals, such as employability, wages, job satisfaction, and subsequent career developments.

References

Acemoglu, D., & Pischke, J. S. (1998). Why do firms train? Theory and evidence. *Quarterly Journal of Economics, 113*(1), 79–119.

Acemoglu, D., & Pischke, J.-S. (1999). Beyond Becker: Training in imperfect labour markets. *Economic Journal, 109*, F112–F142.

Attanasio, O., Kugler, A., & Meghir, C. (2011). Subsidizing vocational training for disadvantaged youth in Colombia: Evidence from a randomized trial. *American Economic Journal: Applied Economics, 3*(3), 188–220.

Becker, G. (1962). Investment in human capital: A theoretical analysis. *Journal of Political Economy, 70*(5), 9–49.

Blatter, M., Muehlemann, S., Schenker, S., & Wolter, S. C. (2016). Hiring costs for skilled workers and the supply of firm-provided training. *Oxford Economic Papers, 68*(1), 238–257.

Brunello, G., & Rocco, L. (2017). The labour market effects of vocational and academic education over the life cycle. Evidence based on a British cohort. *Journal of Human Capital, 11*(2), 106–166.

Cattaneo, M. A. (2011). New estimation of private returns to higher professional education and training. *Empirical Research in Vocational Education and Training, 3*(2), 71–84.

Cavaglia, C., McNally, S., & Ventura, G. (2018). *Do apprenticeships pay? Evidence for England.* CEP Industrial Strategy Paper IS03.

De la Croix, D., Doepke, M., & Mokyr, J. (2017). Clans, guilds, and markets: Apprenticeship institutions and growth in the preindustrial economy. *The Quarterly Journal of Economics, 133*(1), 1–70.

Dionisius, R., Muehlemann, S., Pfeifer, H., Walden, G., Wenzelmann, F., & Wolter, S. C. (2009). Costs and benefits of apprenticeship training. A comparison of Germany and Switzerland. *Applied Economics Quarterly, 55*(1), 7−37.

Golsteyn, B. H. H., & Stenberg, A. (2017). Earnings over the life course: General versus vocational education. *Journal of Human Capital, 11*(2), 167−212.

Hall, C. (2012). The effects of reducing tracking in upper secondary school evidence from a large-scale pilot scheme. *Journal of Human Resources, 47*(1), 237−269.

Hanushek, E. A., Schwerdt, G., Woessmann, L., & Zhang, L. (2017). General education, vocational education, and labor-market outcomes over the lifecycle. *Journal of Human Resources, 52*(1), 58−87.

Jansen, A., Pfeifer, H., Schönfeld, G., & Wenzelmann, F. (2015). Ausbildung in Deutschland weiterhin investitionsorientiert−Ergebnisse der BIBB-Kosten-Nutzen-Erhebung 2012/13. *BIBB-Report, 1*(2015), 1−15.

Jansen, A., Strupler Leiser, M., Wenzelmann, F., & Wolter, S. C. (2015). Labour market deregulation and apprenticeship training: A comparison of German and Swiss employers. *European Journal of Industrial Relations, 21*(4), 353−368.

Konings, J., & Vanormelingen, S. (2015). The impact of training on productivity and wages: Firm-level evidence. *Review of Economics and Statistics, 97*(2), 485−497.

Malamud, O., & Pop-Eleches, C. (2010). General education versus vocational training: Evidence from an economy in transition. *Review of Economics and Statistics, 92*(1), 43−60.

Mohrenweiser, J. (2016). Recruitment and apprenticeship training. *Industrielle Beziehungen/The German Journal of Industrial Relations*, 6−24.

Mohrenweiser, J., Zwick, T., & Backes-Gellner, U. (2019). Poaching and firm sponsored training. *British Journal of Industrial Relations, 57*(1), 143−181.

Moretti, L., Muehlemann, S., Mayerl, M., Schlögl, P., & ad Wolter, S. (2019). So similar and yet so different: A comparative analysis of a firm's cost and benefits of apprenticeship training in Austria and Switzerland. *Evidence Based HRM, 7*(2), 229−246.

Muehlemann, S. (2016). *The cost and benefits of work-based learning*. OECD Education Working Papers, No. 143. Paris: OECD Publishing.

Muehlemann, S., & Leiser Strupler, M. (2018). Hiring costs and labor market tightness. *Labour Economics, 52*, 122−131.

Muehlemann, S., Ryan, P., & Wolter, S. C. (2013). Monopsony power, pay structure, and training. *ILR Review, 66*(5), 1095−1112.

Muehlemann, S., & Wolter, S. C. (2011). Firm-sponsored training and poaching externalities in regional labor markets. *Regional Science and Urban Economics, 41*(6), 560−570.

Muehlemann, S., & Wolter, S. C. (2014). Return on investment of apprenticeship systems for enterprises: Evidence from cost-benefit analyses. *IZA Journal of Labor Policy, 3*(1), 25.

Mueller, B., & Schweri, J. (2015). How specific is apprenticeship training? Evidence from inter-firm and occupational mobility after graduation. *Oxford Economic Papers, 67*(4), 1057−1077.

Oosterbeek, H., & Webbink, D. (2007). Wage effects of an extra year of basic vocational education. *Economics of Education Review, 26*(4), 408−419.

Ryan, P. (2001). The school-to-work transition: A cross-national perspective. *Journal of Economic Literature, 39*(1), 34−92.

SCCRE. (2018). *Swiss education report 2018*. Aarau: Swiss Coordination Centre for Research in Education.

Schlögl, P., & Mayerl, M. (2016). *Betriebsbefragung Zu Kosten Und Nutzen Der Lehrausbildung in Österreich: Endbericht*. Vienna: Österreichisches Institut für Berufsbildungsforschung.

Soskice, D. (1994). Reconciling markets and institutions: The German apprenticeship system. In Lynch (Ed.), *Training and the private sector, 1994*. Chicago: University of Chicago Press.

Stevens, M. (1994). An investment model for the supply of training by employers. *The Economic Journal*, 556−570.

Strupler, M., & Wolter, S. C. (2012). *Die duale Lehre: eine Erfolgsgeschichte-auch für Betriebe. Ergebnisse der dritten Kosten-Nutzen-Erhebung der Lehrlingsausbildung aus Sicht der Betrieb*. Chur/Zurich: Rüegger.

Wolter, S. C., & Ryan, P. (2011). Apprenticeship. In R. Hanushek, S. Machin, & L. Wössmann (Eds.), *Handbook of the economics of education* (Vol. 3). Amsterdam: Elsevier.

Zilic, I. (2018). General versus vocational education: Lessons from a quasi-experiment in Croatia. *Economics of Education Review, 62*, 1−11.

Student incentives

Eric R. Eide, Mark H. Showalter

Brigham Young University, Provo, UT, United States

Introduction

A basic tenet of economics is that people respond to incentives. They change their behavior to maximize their well-being as the conditions they face change. In recent years, numerous education policies have leveraged the fundamental economic principle of incentives to try to improve educational outcomes at both the K-12 and college levels and among both students and teachers. For example, some districts offer the opportunity of financial rewards to students who perform at benchmark levels of achievement on standardized tests (for example Bettinger, 2012). The notion is that when faced with the prospect of financial rewards for high performance, students (and possibly their teachers) will exert more focus and effort in order to obtain the rewards.

Recent years have seen a marked increase in the number of studies focused on better understanding the role of incentives in student behavior. A primary area of focus has been on incentives offered through randomized experiments in order to ascertain a causal effect of student incentives on student effort and outcomes. This article provides an overview of how incentives interact with students in multiple contexts, including incentives for students and

teachers in K-12 education, in developing countries, and in higher education. Because of the rapid growth in this area of research we focus most of our attention on more recent studies.

Student incentives in K-12 education

Financial incentives

Several relatively recent studies have evaluated the effect of offering monetary incentives to improve various educational outcomes. The following provides a sampling of the recent research on this topic.

The first example is a study designed to test a purely financial reward paid directly to students. Bettinger (2012) evaluates the outcomes from a randomized experiment in Coshocton, Ohio. Coshocton is a relatively poor community in eastern Ohio. The population was about 94% white and over 55% of students qualified for free or reduced price lunch. The school district in Coshocton made cash payments to students in grades 3 through 6 for attaining specified goals on annual standardized exams. Being eligible to receive the payments was based on a randomization strategy that allowed for causal inference. The program was structured such that the financial reward was directed at the student rather than the student's family. The experiment led to about a 0.15 standard deviation improvement in math test scores. However, there was no statistically discernible effect on reading, social science, or science test scores.

A second example focuses on the effects of cash incentives for low income families. Aber, Morris, Wolf, and Berg (2016) report on a randomized conditional cash transfer program for low income families in New York City in 2007. The program provided randomly selected, low-income families a cash payment based on a mixture of student outcomes (e.g. attainment of particular scores on standardized tests) and family or student inputs (school attendance, attending parent-teacher conference). The program also gave separate cash rewards for behaviors that improved health and employment. The experiment resulted in statistically significant increases in parental spending and saving on education for all students. It also showed a statistically significant increase in academic time use and achievement outcomes for academically prepared students.

A third example of the causal effect of cash incentives is List et al. (2018). This paper reports on a field experiment that takes a fixed payment for a student attaining a particular academic goal and varies the payoff to the student, their family, and a tutor. The study was done in Chicago Heights, Illinois, a suburb of Chicago. The district was relatively low income with 93% of students eligible for the free lunch program. Thirty eight percent of students were African American and 53% are Hispanic. Tutors were available in these schools and 23 of 27 tutors also participated in the experiment. The experiment paid $90 if a student attained a specified outcome on standardized tests. The experiment created various payoffs with some arms of the experiment paying the full $90 to the student, or the family, or the tutor, and other arms of the experiment splitting the $90 across the three groups. The study was designed to measure empirical complementarities across inputs for student achievement. The results suggest that a given level of financial resources have a far greater impact on student achievement when directed at just one input rather than being spread over multiple inputs.

Non-financial or mixed incentives

In addition to financial incentives, researchers have evaluated the effectiveness of a variety of other incentive mechanisms. For example, Carrell and Sacerdote (2017) report on an experiment using high school seniors in New Hampshire from 2009 to 2014. With help from participating high schools, the researchers identified students at risk of not applying to college. These students were randomly assigned to various treatments that included mentoring, information, and financial help in applications. Treatments that provide only financial incentives (help with application fees) or information had little statistically discernible effect. However, women who receive mentoring experienced a 15% point increase in the college-going rate. The effect was persistent, leading to a college completion rate that was similar to a control group of college enrollees. In contrast, the effect for men was statistically insignificant. The authors present additional evidence that the differential between males and females is in part due to differences in labor market expectations: men have higher expectations on labor market outcomes based on their high school degree than women. The authors also suggest that assigned mentoring acts as a substitute for mentoring from significant adults such as parents and teachers.

An earlier study focused on low-income youth more generally. Rodriguez-Plana (2012) reports on the long run results of a study begun in 1995 where students entering the ninth grade in 11 high schools across the US were randomly assigned to a treatment or a control group. During the next five years, the students in the treated group received both significant financial incentives to attain various educational goals, and a variety of support services including mentoring by multiple individuals (approximate cost of $25,000 per enrollee). The program was evaluated when the youths were 19, 21, and 24 years old. The results showed a significant increase in the female high school graduation rate, but the effect for males was statistically insignificant. Five years after the end of the program, there were no significant effects of the intervention on employment outcomes.

Martorell, Miller, Santibañez, and Augustine (2016) report on a field experiment to increase summer school attendance in an unidentified urban school district in 2011. The experimental group were students entering the first through the fifth grade in the fall and had three treatment branches: 1) small prizes for children who completed specified attendance goals and gift cards to parents whose children achieved the attendance goals; 2) just the reward to the children; and 3) a control group. The authors found that the combined treatment (branch 1) increased the daily attendance rate by 9% and the likelihood of having perfect attendance by 63%. The student-only incentives had a smaller and statistically insignificant effect on attendance. The authors also evaluated whether there was a measureable effect on standardized test scores during the following school year, but found little effect.

Another interesting example of non-financial incentives is Fryer (2016). This paper describes a field experiment in Oklahoma City Public Schools in which students were provided with either information, direct incentives, or both. Students were first provided with free cellular phones. Then one arm of the experiment provided students with daily information about the link between human capital and future outcomes via text message (information only). A second arm of the experiment provided the same text messages as in the first arm, but also offered additional minutes to talk/text by reading books outside of school (information and incentives). A third treatment arm just offered the additional minutes from reading books but not receiving the daily text messages (incentives only). Finally, there was a control group which received neither information nor incentives. Students were in the sixth and seventh grade in 2010–11. The experiment resulted in no statistically significant effects on student effort, attendance, suspensions, or state test scores. However, there is evidence that scores on college entrance exams four years later increased.

There have been an increasing number of studies that evaluate behavioral economic aspects of behavior. One example is Levitt et al. (2016) which investigated the role of the timing of rewards. They found a substantial impact on test scores from incentives when the rewards are delivered immediately. There was suggestive evidence that rewards framed as losses outperform those framed as gains. They also found that nonfinancial incentives can be considerably more cost-effective than financial incentives for younger students, but were less effective with older students. All motivating power of incentives vanished when rewards were handed out with a delay.

Incentives in developing countries

Work in developing countries provides unique opportunities to evaluate a variety of incentive mechanisms to increase human capital. We review a few recent examples.

Barrera-Osorio and Filmer (2015) evaluated a strategy comparing cash incentives based on poverty status and another based on merit. The programs operated in three Cambodian provinces where schools were randomly selected to offer either a poverty-based scholarship or a merit-based scholarship. Of those schools, about half were randomly assigned to begin in the first year and the remainder in the second year. All fourth graders in all of the selected schools were given a math and a language test the initial year (2008). All fourth graders in those schools were assessed for poverty status of their household at the same time. Schools that were assigned the poverty treatment arm then selected a set of students in their school to receive the poverty-based scholarship and schools in the merit-based treatment arm selected a set of students to receive merit-based scholarships. Scholarships had a value of US$20; annual household income in the area had a mean value of US$610. Scholarship recipients were required to stay enrolled, attend school regularly, and maintain passing grades. Both approaches increased enrollment: for example, one measure showed that merit-based recipients had a 13.7% higher probability of completing the sixth grade than the control group of fourth graders who were in schools not eligible for either scholarship; poverty-based scholarship recipients had a 19.1% higher probability of completing the sixth grade than the control group.

Another study that focused on cash incentives is Chaudhury and Parajuli (2010). This study evaluated the effectiveness of targeting cash incentives to increase female school enrollments in Punjab, Pakistan. School districts in the province were assigned to either a 'treated' or 'untreated' status. In treated districts, households with females eligible to enroll in grades 6 through 8 received a monthly payment if the girl enrolled in a public school and attained an attendance rate of at least 80%. The program began in February of 2004. Between 2003 and 2005, the authors estimated that female enrollment increased by 9%.

In a study that explores several aspects of the education production function, Behrman, Parker, Todd, and Wolpin (2015) report on an interesting experiment to increase performance on math test scores. In 2008, 88 Mexican high schools were randomly assigned to one of four treatment arms, with one of the treatment arms being a control with no incentives. Treatment

arm 1 offered students a cash prize for attaining a certain level on an end-of-year standardized math exam. Treatment arm 2 offered math teachers a cash prize based on the performance of the students in their classes. Treatment arm 3 offered cash awards to both teachers and students similar to those offered in arms 1 and 2, along with additional rewards to administrators. The research found the largest effects from treatment arm 3 that included incentives for students, teachers and administrators, increasing test scores by 0.3–0.6 standard deviations. Treatment arm 1 increased test scores by 0.2–0.3 standard deviations. There was also evidence that the student-incentives increased cheating, but accounting for that effect still indicated relatively large gains from treatment arms 1 and 3. The teacher-only incentives (treatment arm 2) did not result in statistically discernible effects. Costs of the three treatment arms also varied significantly, with treatment 3 (incentives for all groups) being about 50% more expensive than the student-only treatment, and treatment 2 (teacher-only) being about 1.5% of the cost of the student-only treatment.

In contrast to narrowly targeted cash payments, Wydick, Paul, and Rutledge (2013) studied the effect of private sponsorship programs on a variety of outcomes. Sponsorship programs allow households in wealthy countries to supplement a sponsored child's resources for education, health and other programs. Using data from a leading sponsorship organization, researchers used data on children receiving sponsorships in 1980–1992 in six countries (Bolivia, Guatemala, India, Kenya, Philippines, and Uganda) to evaluate the effectiveness of these programs. Average duration of sponsorship for a child was about 9 years. Identification of causal effects came from nonlinear program rules (limitation on number of children per household that could be sponsored, age restriction on children starting the program and distance from a given sponsor-provided project). Estimated impacts were quite large. Secondary school completion increased by 12—18% points over a baseline of 44.5%. Researchers also found positive and significant effects on the probability of adult employment.

A study by Berry (2015) reports on a field experiment in Gurgaon, India in 2007. The experiment compared the outcomes of various financial and non-financial rewards for meeting performance goals on a reading exam. One treatment offered a financial reward to parents if their child reached a specific performance goal on a reading test. A second treatment offered the cash award to the child. The third treatment offered the child one of four small toys, given to the child at school to minimize the probability of a parent expropriating it. The fourth treatment offered a voucher that the child could use to buy a toy. The primary goal of the study was to measure relative effectiveness of various reward strategies and so no control group was included in the experimental design. The authors did not find a statistically different effect in outcomes across the four treatment groups. However, there was evidence that children who scored relatively poorly on the pretest were more responsive to the toy rather than to the cash.

Blimpo (2014) reports on an experiment done in the West African country of Benin during 2008—09. One hundred secondary schools were randomly selected to be in one of three treatment groups or a control group. Within each school a set of 12—16 students were randomly chosen to be eligible to participate. Treatment 1 offered a cash prize to a student based on their own performance on a standardized end-of-year comprehensive test. Treatment 2 offered a cash prize based on team performance, where teams of four students were randomly assigned among the selected students. Treatment 3 had a tournament model where three teams of four students compete for three prizes based on the team score. All three treatments produced a large and similar average treatment effect, ranging from 0.27 to 0.34 standard deviations relative to the control group.

To summarize, there is a large and growing literature evaluating the effects of a variety of incentive mechanisms in developing countries. Countries vary significantly on the type of challenges they face in the effort to increase human capital formation and so it is unlikely that there will be a one-size-fits-all solution that works in all countries for all circumstances. The approach of most of these studies is to tailor an experiment to the local conditions and test what works and what does not in that particular area, and update policy accordingly. This is likely to be a fruitful approach moving forward.

Teacher incentives in K-12 education

Teachers are a critical input in the education production function. A sizable body of research has emerged which incentivizes teachers to improve student outcomes. Offering teachers pay bonuses for improved performance of their students could potentially lead to teachers exerting more effort which could lead to better student outcomes. Incentives can be targeted to individual teachers or toward a group of teachers. Individual incentive plans have the benefit that they connect individual performance to rewards thereby in principle rewarding teachers for effort and ability. However, they can also lead to a competitive environment that many teachers dislike, and can lead to unintended consequences such as teaching to the test and in the extreme case, teacher cheating. Group incentive plans provide an environment more conducive to collaboration and cooperation among teachers, but can also lead to free-riding behavior as the group size of teachers increases.

Individual teacher incentives

The Project on Incentives in Teaching (POINT), conducted by Springer et al. (2012), was a three-year study implemented in the Metropolitan Nashville School System from

2006 to 07 through 2008–09. Middle school mathematics teachers voluntarily participated in a controlled experiment to assess the effect of financial rewards for teachers whose students showed large gains on standardized tests. Participating teachers chose what they needed to do to improve student performance, including participate in more professional development, seek coaching, collaborate with other teachers, or simply reflect on their practices. The authors found for the most part the teacher incentives were ineffective. Students of teachers randomly assigned to the treatment group (eligible for bonuses) did not outperform students whose teachers were assigned to the control group (not eligible for bonuses).

Fryer, Levitt, List, and Sadoff (2012) conducted a study that illustrated the importance of program design in teacher incentive effectiveness. In one treatment, teachers were paid in advance and asked to return the money if their students did not improve sufficiently, hence assessing the role of loss aversion in treatment effectiveness. A second treatment, identical to the loss aversion treatment but implemented in the standard fashion with financial incentives in the form of bonuses at the end of the year linked to student achievement, yields smaller and statistically insignificant results. This suggests their findings were driven by loss aversion rather than other design features or the sampled population.

Some studies examined how female and male teachers respond differently to teacher incentive plans. Hill and Jones (2018) evaluated three performance pay programs in North Carolina and found that while male teachers' value-added remains flat before and after the introduction of performance pay, the value-added of female teachers declined. They also found suggestive evidence of a gender difference in retention, with men more likely to remain in schools with performance pay. Relatedly, Lavy (2012) studied how teachers' performance is affected by a competitive environment and its gender mix.

Teachers participated in a tournament that provided cash bonuses based on test performance of their classes. The author found no evidence of gender differences in performance under competition in any gender mix environment, or in teachers' knowledge of the program and in effort and teaching methods. Women, however, were more pessimistic about the effectiveness of teachers' performance pay and more realistic about their likelihood of winning bonuses.

Teacher incentive programs can be designed to directly change and measure teacher behavior. Yuan et al. (2013) examined teacher survey responses from randomized experiments exploring three different pay-for-performance programs to examine the extent to which these programs motivated teachers to improve student achievement and the impact of such programs on teachers' instruction, number of hours worked, job stress, and collegiality. They found that most teachers did not report their program as motivating, and that none of the three programs changed teachers' instruction, increased their number of hours worked or job stress, or damaged their collegiality.

Group incentives for teachers

Fryer (2013) conducted a school-based randomized trial in over 200 New York City public schools in order to better understand the impact of teacher incentives. He found that providing incentives to teachers based on the school's performance involving student achievement, improvement, and the learning environment did not increase student achievement in any statistically meaningful way. He found that teacher incentives may actually decrease student achievement particularly in larger schools. In another study using New York City data, Goodman and Turner (2013) examined a group-based teacher incentive program where they investigated whether specific features of the program contributed to its ineffectiveness. While overall the program had a negligible effect on student achievement, they show that in schools where incentives to free ride were lowest the program led to small increases in math achievement.

Imberman and Lovenheim (2015) used a group-based incentive pay program to estimate the impact of incentive strength on achievement. Their program design provided variation in the share of students in a subject-grade that a teacher instructed, which measured incentive strength because as the teacher share increased, a teacher's impact on the probability of award receipt grew. They found that achievement on incentivized exams, but not non-incentivized exams, improves when incentives strengthen. For the incentivized exams, they found that effects fade out monotonically as a teacher's portion of the group increases to between 20 and 30% and were larger for teachers with low-achieving students.

Teacher-student aligned incentives

Another design feature is to align incentives for both students and teachers to try to improve student outcomes. Jackson (2010) analyzed a program implemented in Texas schools serving underprivileged populations that pays both students and teachers for passing grades on Advanced Placement (AP) examinations. He found that program adoption was associated with increased AP course and exam taking, increases in the number of students with high SAT/ACT scores, and increases in college matriculation. In another study, Jackson (2012) examined the effects of paying both students and teachers for passing scores on Advanced Placement exams on college outcomes. He found that affected students of all ethnicities attend college in greater numbers, had improved college GPAs, and were more likely to remain in college beyond their freshman year.

Fryer, Devi, and Holden (2017) explored how aligning incentives among parents, teachers and

students can affect math achievement. The authors conducted randomized field experiments in 84 urban public schools in two cities. In Washington, DC, incentives were provided to students for various outputs including attendance, behavior, interim assessments, homework, and uniforms. In Houston, incentives were provided to parents, teachers, and students for math performance. On outcomes for which there were direct incentives, there were large and statistically significant effects from both treatments.

While overall the findings on teacher incentive pay plans are mixed, the alignment of incentives across teachers and students appear to be a promising design feature.

Higher education incentives

A variety of financial incentives are used to attempt to improve the outcomes of college students. Programs try to improve student outcomes and behavioral responses by offering scholarship or grant aid, cash payments, and student loans in order to reduce financial constraints faced by the student. Targeted outcomes include areas such as improved academic performance, increased enrollment, persistence and graduation rates, greater student effort, and borrowing behavior.

Scholarships, grants, and cash awards

Many scholarship incentive programs attempt to improve college enrollment, persistence, and graduation rates, particularly for low income students and those with traditionally low college attendance. Angrist, Autor, Hudson, and Pallais (2017) report initial findings from a randomized evaluation of a large privately-funded scholarship program for applicants to Nebraska's public colleges and universities. They found that the awards enabled groups with historically-low college attendance to 'level up,' largely equalizing enrollment and persistence rates with traditionally college-bound peers, particularly at four-year schools. Awards offered to prospective community college students had little effect on college enrollment or the type of college attended. Barrow, Richburg-Hayes, Rouse, and Brock (2014) explore whether a performance-based scholarship combined with counseling services affected the educational outcomes of low-income community college students. They found that eligibility for the performance-based scholarship increased persistence by increasing enrollment probability in the second semester after random assignment. After 2 years, program group students earned 3.7 credit hours more than the control group students, an advantage of 37%. They also found some evidence that the program may have affected academic performance and effort.

In fall 2006, Ohio adopted a new state financial aid policy that was significantly more generous than the previous plan. Bettinger (2015) exploits a natural experiment based on this change to estimate the effects of need-based aid policies on first-year college persistence rates. Students who benefited from the program received awards about $800 higher than they would have received under the prior program. These students' drop-out rates fell by 2% as a result of the program. The new program also increased the likelihood that students attend 4-year campuses and increased their first-year grade point averages.

Evidence on college students' responsiveness to incentives exists outside the US as well. Fack and Grenet (2015) used comprehensive administrative data on France's single largest financial aid program to provide evidence on the impact of large-scale need-based grant programs on the college enrollment decisions, persistence, and graduation rates of low-income students. They found that the provision of 1500 euros cash allowances to prospective undergraduate or graduate students increased their college enrollment rates by 5−7%. They also showed

that need-based grants have positive effects on student persistence and degree completion. Angrist and Lavy (2009) report on an experiment that used cash incentives to increase rates for the Israeli matriculation certification, a prerequisite for most postsecondary education, among low-achievers. The experiment used a school-based randomization design offering awards to all students who passed their exams in treated schools. As a result, certification rates increased for girls but not for boys. The increase in girls' matriculation rates led to a greater likelihood of college attendance. Angrist, Oreopoulos, and Williams (2014) evaluated the effects of academic achievement awards for students in their first two years of study at a Canadian commuter college. The award program offered cash incentives for course grades above 70. Program engagement was high but yielded small overall treatment effects. The intervention increased the number of courses graded above 70 and points earned above 70 for second-year students but generated no significant effect on overall GPA.

While the magnitude of responses differs across studies, the bulk of the evidence on college students' responsiveness to financial aid in the form scholarships, grants, and cash awards is largely positive and improves outcomes such as enrollment, persistence, and graduation, among others.

Student loans

Student loans are an important source of financial aid for college students, and researchers have examined how college students respond to various types of loan offers. Cadena and Keys (2013) set out to explain the borrowing phenomenon that one in six undergraduate students offered interest-free loans turns them down. Models of impulse control predict that students may optimally reject subsidized loans to avoid excessive consumption during school. The authors examine students' take-up decisions and identify a group of students for whom the loans create an especially appealing liquidity increase. Students who would receive the loan in cash are significantly more likely to turn it down, suggesting that consumers choose to limit their liquidity in economically meaningful situations.

Marx and Turner (2018) estimated the effect of grant aid on City University of New York (CUNY) students' borrowing and attainment using a regression discontinuity/kink design based on the federal Pell Grant formula. Each dollar of grant aid reduced loans by $1.80 among borrowers. They only found crowd-out of this magnitude in colleges that "offer" no loan aid and require students to opt into borrowing.

In another study by Marx and Turner (2019), the authors estimated the effect of student loan "nudges" on community college students' borrowing, and also provided experimental evidence of the effect of student loans on educational attainment. They found that students randomly assigned to receive a nonzero loan offer were 40% more likely to borrow than those who received a $0 loan offer. Nudge-induced borrowing increased both GPA and credits earned by roughly 30% in the year of the intervention, and in the following year, increased transfers to four-year colleges by 10% points (nearly 200%).

Conclusion

Much of education policy relies on incentives to induce greater student effort and performance. The policies reviewed in this article suggest some evidence that students and their teachers respond to changing incentive structures. At least in some cases, carefully designed studies, often involving randomized control trials, suggest evidence that students perform better when there is a reward attached to their performance. The evidence on teachers is somewhat more mixed, although when incentives are aligned for both students and teachers student outcomes appear to improve. The effectiveness of particular interventions depend on the structure of incentives and the context of the program. Taken together, the evidence to date suggests that the incorporation of appropriate incentive structures within education policy holds promise as a driver for improving student outcomes.

References

Aber, J. L., Morris, P., Wolf, S., & Berg, J. (2016). The impact of a holistic conditional cash transfer program in New York city on parental financial investment, student time use, and educational processes and outcomes. *Journal of Research on Educational Effectiveness, 9*(3), 334–363.

Angrist, J., Autor, D., Hudson, S., & Pallais, A. (2017). *Leveling up: Early results from a randomized evaluation of post-secondary aid.* NBER Working Paper No. 20800.

Angrist, J., & Lavy, V. (2009). The effects of high stakes high school achievement awards: Evidence from a randomized trial. *American Economic Review, 99*(4), 1384–1414.

Angrist, J., Oreopoulos, P., & Williams, T. (2014). When opportunity knocks, who answers? New evidence on college achievement awards. *The Journal of Human Resources, 49*(3), 572–610.

Barrera-Osorio, F., & Filmer, D. (2016). Incentivizing schooling for learning: Evidence on the impact of alternative targeting approaches. *Journal of Human Resources, 51*(2).

Barrow, L., Richburg-Hayes, L., Elena Rouse, C., & Brock, T. (2014). Paying for performance: The education impacts of a community college scholarship program for low-income adults. *Journal of Labor Economics, 32*(3).

Behrman, J. R., Parker, S. W., Todd, P. E., & Wolpin, K. I. (2015). Aligning learning incentives of students and teachers: Results from a social experiment in Mexican high schools. *Journal of Political Economy, 123*(2), 325–364.

Berry, J. (2015). Child control in education decisions: An evaluation of targeted incentives to learn in India. *The Journal of Human Resources, 50*(4), 1051–1080.

Bettinger, E. (2012). Paying to learn: The effect of financial incentives on elementary school test scores. *The Review of Economics and Statistics, 94*(3), 686–698.

Bettinger, E. (2015). Need-based aid and college persistence: The effects of the Ohio college opportunity grant. *Educational Evaluation and Policy Analysis, 37*(1S), 102S–119S.

Blimpo, M. P. (2014). Team incentives for education in developing countries: A randomized field experiment in Benin.

American Economic Journal: Applied Economics, 6(4), 90–109.

Cadena, B. C., & Keys, B. J. (2013). Can self-control explain avoiding free money? Evidence from interest-free student loans. *The Review of Economics and Statistics, 95*(4), 1117–1129.

Carrell, S., & Sacerdote, B. (2017). Why do college-going interventions work? *American Economic Journal: Applied Economics, 9*(3), 124–151.

Chaudhury, N., & Parajuli, D. (2010). Conditional cash transfers and female schooling: The impact of the female school stipend programme on public school enrolments in Punjab, Pakistan. *Applied Economics, 42*(28), 3565–3583.

Fack, G., & Grenet, J. (2015). Improving college access and success for low-income students: Evidence from a large need-based grant program. *American Economic Journal: Applied Economics, 7*(2), 1–34.

Fryer, R. G. (2013). Teacher incentives and student achievement: Evidence from New York city public schools. *Journal of Labor Economics, 31*(2), 373–427.

Fryer, R. G. (2016). Information, non-financial incentives, and student achievement: Evidence from a text messaging experiment. *Journal of Public Economics, 144*, 109–121.

Fryer, R. G., Devi, T., & Holden, R. T. (2017). *Vertical versus horizontal incentives in education: Evidence from randomized trials.* NBER Working Paper 17752.

Fryer, R. G., Levitt, S. D., List, J., & Sadoff, S. (2012). *Enhancing the efficacy of incentives through loss aversion: A field experiment.* NBER Working Paper 18237.

Goodman, S. F., & Turner, L. J. (2013). The design of teacher incentive pay and educational outcomes: Evidence from the New York city bonus program. *Journal of Labor Economics, 31*(2).

Hill, A. J., & Jones, D. B. (2018). The impacts of performance pay on teacher effectiveness and retention: Does teacher gender matter? *The Journal of Human Resources.* https://doi.org/10.3368/jhr.55.2.0216.7719R3.

Imberman, S. A., & Lovenheim, M. F. (2015). Incentive strength and teacher productivity: Evidence from a group based teacher incentive pay System. *Review of Economics and Statistics, 97*(2), 364–386.

Jackson, C. K. (2010). A little now for a lot later: A look at a Texas advanced placement incentive program. *The Journal of Human Resources, 45*(3), 591–639.

Jackson, C. K. (2012). *The effects of an incentive-based high school intervention on college outcomes.* NBER Working Paper No. 15722.

Lavy, V. (2012). Gender differences in market competitiveness in a real workplace: Evidence from performance-based pay tournaments among teachers. *The Economic Journal, 123*(569).

Levitt, S. D., List, J. A., Neckermann, S., & Sadoff, S. (2016). The behavioralist goes to school: Leveraging behavioral

economics to improve educational performance. *American Economic Journal: Economic Policy, 8*(4), 183–219.

List, J. A., Livingston, J. A., & Neckermann, S. (2018). *Harnessing complementarities in the education production function.* University of Chicago. unpublished mimeo.

Martorell, P., Miller, T., Santibañez, L., & Augustine, C. H. (2016). Can incentives for parents and students change educational inputs? Experimental evidence from summer school. *Economics of Education Review, 50*, 113–126.

Marx, B. M., & Turner, L. J. (2018). Borrowing trouble? Human capital investment with opt-in costs and implications for the effectiveness of grant aid. *American Economic Journal: Applied Economics, 10*(2), 163–201.

Marx, B. M., & Turner, L. J. (2019). Student loan nudges: Experimental evidence on borrowing and educational attainment. *American Economic Journal: Economic Policy, 11*(2), 108–141.

Rodríguez-Planas, N. (2012). Longer-term impacts of mentoring, educational services, and learning incentives: Evidence from a randomized trial in the United States. *American Economic Journal: Applied Economics, 4*(4), 121–139.

Springer, M. G., Ballou, D., Hamilton, L., Le V. Lockwood, J. R., McCaffrey, M. P., et al. (2012). *Final report: Experimental evidence from the Project on incentives in teaching.* Nashville, TN: National Center on Performance Incentives at Vanderbilt University.

Wydick, B., Glewwe, P., & Rutledge, L. (2013). Does international child sponsorship work? A six-country study of impacts on adult life outcomes. *Journal of Political Economy, 121*(2).

Yuan, K., Le, V., McCaffrey, D. F., Marsh, J. A., Hamilton, L. S., Stecher, B. M., et al. (2013). Incentive pay programs do not affect teacher motivation or reported practices: Results from three randomized studies. *Educational Evaluation and Policy Analysis, 35*(1), 3–22.

Further reading

Balch, R., & Springer, M. G. (2015). Performance pay, test scores, and student learning objectives. *Economics of Education Review, 44*, 114–125.

Barrow, L., & Rouse, C. E. (2018). Financial incentives and educational investment: The impact of performance-based scholarships on student time use. *Education Finance and Policy, 13*(4).

Bettinger, E., & Slonim, R. (2007). Patience among children. *Journal of Public Economics, 91*(1–2), 343–363.

Conger, D., & Turner, L. J. (2017). The effect of price shocks on undocumented students' college attainment and completion. *Journal of Public Economics, 148*, 92–114.

Cornwell, C., Mustard, D. B., & Sridhar, D. J. (2006). The enrollment effects of merit-based financial aid: Evidence from Georgia's HOPE program. *Journal of Labor Economics, 24*(4).

Denning, J. T., & Patrick, T. (2017). Was that smart? Institutional financial incentives and field of study. *The Journal of Human Resources, 52*(1), 152–186.

List, J. A., Livingston, J. A., & Neckermann, S. (2018). Do financial incentives crowd out intrinsic motivation to perform on standardized tests? *Economics of Education Review, 66*, 125–136.

Sojourner, A. J., Mykerezi, E., & West, K. L. (2014). Teacher pay reform and productivity panel data evidence from adoptions of Q-comp in Minnesota. *Journal of Human Resources, 49*, 945–981.

The economics of school accountability

D.N. Figlio[a], H.F. Ladd[b]

[a]Northwestern University, Evanston, IL, United States; [b]Duke University, Durham, NC, United States

Glossary

Growth model A measure of aggregate student test performance based on year-to-year changes in the test scores of individual students.

Principal-agent problem A circumstance in which one individual or group is entrusted to make decisions on behalf of other people who may not share the same objectives.

Status model A measure of aggregate student test performance based on the average level of student test scores.

Test-based school accountability The practice of identifying, rewarding, and sanctioning schools on the basis of aggregated student test performance.

Demands for more accountability and results-based incentive systems in K-12 education come from many directions and currently dominate much of the education policy discussion at both the state and federal levels in the United States (Ladd, 1996; Ladd & Hansen, 1999) and abroad (Burgess, Propper, Slater, & Wilson, 2005). Accountability in education is a broad concept that could be addressed in many ways: using political processes to assure democratic accountability, introducing market-based reforms to increase accountability to parents and children, developing peer-based accountability systems to increase the professional accountability of teachers, or using administrative accountability systems designed to drive the system toward higher student achievement. This article focuses on this last approach and pays particular attention to programs that focus on the individual school as the primary unit of accountability.

The use of school accountability programs in other countries notwithstanding, this article focuses exclusively on evidence and policies from the United States. The accountability systems of interest here operate within the traditional public school system and rely heavily on student testing (Hanushek & Raymond, 2003). Most emblematic is the federal No Child Left Behind Act (NCLB), which became law in 2002. NCLB requires states to test students in reading and mathematics in grades 3–8, as well as in one high school grade. In addition, it requires states to assess schools on the basis of whether their students (both in the aggregate and by subgroup) are making adequate yearly progress (AYP) toward the ultimate goal of 100% proficiency by 2014, and it imposes consequences on schools and districts that fail to make AYP. This law is the most recent incarnation of a bipartisan standards-based reform movement that emerged from a historic 1989 summit in Charlottesville, Virginia, between President George H. W Bush and the state governors. The meeting generated a set of national education goals that were subsequently embedded in the Clinton administration's 1994 Goals 2000: Educate America

The Economics of Education, Second Edition
https://doi.org/10.1016/B978-0-12-815391-8.00042-2

Act. NCLB differs from that act by its far heavier emphasis on accountability and its significantly greater federal intrusion into the operations of individual schools and districts.

School-based accountability programs preceded NCLB in many states. As of 2001, 45 states published report cards on schools, and 27 of them rated schools or identified low-performing ones (*Education Week, Quality Counts, 2001*). Several states (e.g., North and South Carolina, Texas, Kentucky, and Florida) as well as districts such as Chicago, Dallas, and Charlotte-Mecklenburg, also had full school-based accountability programs in which they rated schools based on their students' performance, provided rewards either to schools or to teachers for improved performance, and provided some combination of sanctions and assistance to low-performing schools.

The rationale for school-based accountability

The current school-based accountability efforts emerged from the broader standards-based reform movement that began in the 1980s. Standards-based reform involves the setting of clear, measurable, and ambitious performance standards in a set of core academic subjects for students at various ages, aligning curriculum to these standards, and establishing high expectations for students to meet them. Assessment of students is a key component of standards-based reform. These assessments are used to measure student progress toward mastery of the standards and also the effectiveness of the schools they attend. The goal is to provide incentives for schools to raise student achievement.

In the context of standards-based reform, accountability is only one part of a larger policy package. Accountability - whether for schools, students, teachers, or districts - can also be viewed as a stand-alone policy. One rationale

for such a policy comes from comparisons to the private sector where business firms focus attention on results and rely on benchmarking procedures to measure progress. Another rationale is provided by the economists' model of the principal—agent problem. In such a model, school administrators and teachers may underperform because the state policymakers do not have a good means of monitoring them. It follows that student achievement would improve if state policymakers could monitor the teachers and school administrators more effectively.

School accountability systems serve as a mechanism for counteracting this principal—agent problem. By assessing schools against a common metric, policymakers generate independent information about the performance of schools and school districts. This common yardstick then allows policymakers to compare each school's performance to that of another school or to an external standard. By measuring, reporting, and, in many cases, attaching positive consequences to strong school performance and negative consequences to weak performance, policymakers provide incentives for schools and school districts to focus attention on what is being measured and possibly to change the way in which they deliver education. Such information may also facilitate improved monitoring by another important set of stakeholders in the education system, namely parents. Whether by complaining about poor performance or by threatening to withdraw their child from the school, parents could potentially use the publicly provided information on school performance to induce their children's schools to improve.

Most administrative accountability systems measure only a very small fraction of the educational outcomes that parents and policymakers value. The outcomes in such systems typically include student achievement as measured by test scores in only the core subjects of math and reading, supplemented in some cases (as under NCLB) with some nontest-based measures such as student attendance or graduation rates. As documented by Rothstein and Jacobson (2008), educational stakeholders value a much broader range of academic outcomes as well as other outcomes such as citizenship. Some of these, according to Hanushek and Raymond (2003), are more highly related to student achievement than are others. However, the narrow focus of administrative accountability systems on test results in math and reading clearly privileges one narrow set of outcomes over others.

School accountability systems can also provide administrators with incentives to game the system. Some of these responses, which tend to increase the measured achievement of a school's students but not necessarily their true achievement, are described later in this article. A number of other factors may also keep an accountability system from generating better student outcomes. Outcomes might not improve, for example, if the extrinsic motivations imposed by the accountability system crowd out powerful intrinsic motivations for educating children.

(Frey, 2000). Perhaps, most important is that educators may lack the necessary skills, knowledge, or resources to meet the expectations of an accountability system. Thus, it could be that one of the major assumptions underlying stand-alone accountability programs — namely that teachers are underperforming because of insufficient monitoring of their behavior - is incorrect. In any case, greater learning gains associated with school accountability are by no means assured.

Designing school accountability systems

How a school accountability system is designed can have a significant impact on the nature of and the strength of the incentives that schools face to raise student achievement in the tested subjects. Moreover, the design can affect which students are likely to receive the most additional attention.

Broadly speaking, two main approaches have been used to measure school performance - status measures in which schools are judged based on their levels of performance, typically measured by average test scores or by the fraction of students attaining certain proficiency levels, and growth or value-added measures in which schools are rated on how much they improve individual students' performance from one year to the next (Hanushek & Raymond, 2003). The simplest way to measure achievement growth, or value added, is to use gains in student test scores from one year to the next. In some cases, those gains, averaged across all students in the school, are then compared to the gains in test scores that are predicted for that school given the achievement level of its students in the prior year. More refined measures of value added can be based on regression models, with or without additional statistical controls for student characteristics (Ladd & Walsh, 2002). States and local school districts have used variations of both the status and the growth approach (Hanushek & Raymond, 2003). Although NCLB requires that schools be evaluated in terms of their AYP toward the ultimate goal of 100% proficiency, such progress is measured based on comparisons of aggregate levels of student performance from one year to the next. Thus, the current iteration of NCLB is essentially a status model not a growth model, although the US Department of Education has recently given a few states the authority to introduce some growth elements into the basic approach.

The two types of measures have somewhat different goals and generate somewhat different incentives. Status-based systems that focus on the percent of students who achieve at proficient levels seek to encourage schools to raise performance at least to that level. This approach is appealing to many policymakers because it sets the same target for all groups of students and because it encourages schools to focus attention on the set of low-performing students who in the past may have received little attention. Status-based systems also have the advantage of being transparent.

The goal of the growth-model approach is to encourage schools to improve the performance of their students independently of the absolute level of that achievement. Such an approach is appealing to many people because of its perceived fairness. It explicitly takes into account the fact that where students end up is heavily dependent on where they start and the fact that the starting points tend to be highly correlated on average with family background. At the same time, the use of the growth-model approach may raise political concerns, both because the public may find the approach less transparent than the status approach and because some see it as a way of letting schools with low average performance off the hook.

Systems using status and growth models generate different incentives in part because they lead to different rankings of schools. Many schools deemed ineffective based on their aggregate performance levels may actually have quite high value added and vice versa (Kane & Staiger, 2002). Some accountability systems (e.g., Florida's and North Carolina's) encourage both high levels of performance and high test score growth, by focusing on both levels and gains (Ladd & Zelli, 2002; Rouse, Hannaway, Goldhaber, & Figlio, 2007).

In addition, the two approaches send different signals about which students deserve more attention. Under a status-based system designed to encourage schools to raise student performance to some threshold level, the position of the threshold matters. A challenging performance threshold - for example, one that would be consistent with the high aspirations of the standards-based reform movement — would provide incentives for schools to focus attention on a larger group of students than would be the case with a lower threshold. Evaluating schools on the basis of value added, by contrast, provides a stronger incentive for schools to expend effort on the entire student body. In such a system, however, schools may have an incentive to focus attention on the more-advantaged

students because the test score gains of those students are likely to exceed those of the less-advantaged students (Ladd & Walsh, 2002).

Under either approach, random errors in the measurement of student performance can generate inconsistent rankings of schools over time — a factor that weakens incentives for improvement. That is especially true for small schools because the smaller the number of students in the school, the larger the school-wide average measurement error, and hence less consistent the school's ranking is likely to be from 1 year to the next. Schools deemed to be improving at one point in time are often found to be declining the next year due to measurement error (Kane & Staiger, 2002). The problem of measurement error is exacerbated when schools are rated based on the growth model because it requires test scores for more than 1 year. The danger is that personnel in such schools may receive such inconsistent signals from 1 year to the next that they have little incentive to respond in a constructive way.

Measurement-error issues in accountability are particularly pronounced when an accountability system focuses attention on specific subgroups within a school, as is mandated by NCLB and some state accountability systems. A potential alternative to the subgroup requirement would be to focus special attention on the segment of the school's students that performed at a low level in the previous year and to track that group's growth. This segment would likely include a large fraction of the economically disadvantaged and racial minority students, and so might capture the spirit of the NCLB law without exacerbating the problem of measurement error.

Neither approach to measuring school performance captures what economists call school efficiency - the effectiveness with which schools use their resources to maximize student outcomes, given the students they serve. According to the economists' model of the education production function, student achievement is determined by the characteristics of the student and his or her classmates, the school's resources (including the quantity and qualifications of the teachers), and the efficiency with which those resources are used. Efficiency cannot be observed directly and therefore, it must be inferred from statistical analysis that controls both for the resources available to the school and the characteristics of the students being served (Stiefel, Schwartz, Rubinstein, & Zabel, 2005). If the goal of an accountability system is to induce schools to use the resources they have more effectively, then, in principle, schools should be rated on their efficiency, not simply on the level or growth of their students' achievement. The problem is that the data requirements for such efficiency measures are often daunting and the statistical techniques can be complex (Ladd & Walsh, 2002; Stiefel et al., 2005).

The evidence on student achievement

Measuring the effects of test-based accountability systems on student achievement is not a simple task. When such systems are part of a larger standards-based reform effort, it is difficult to separate the effects of the accountability system from those of other components of the reform package. In addition, researchers face the challenge of finding appropriate control groups to determine what would have happened to student achievement in the absence of the accountability system. In practice, researchers have used a variety of empirical strategies to address these challenges.

Due to the short time since NCLB was introduced and the lack of a counterfactual, the most compelling studies of how accountability affects student achievement are based on the state and local accountability systems that preceded NCLB. This research includes district- or state-specific studies as well as cross-state studies that measure achievement using the results from the National Assessment of Education Progress (NAEP). Researchers conducting district- and state-specific studies (e.g., Figlio & Rouse, 2006; Jacob, 2005; Krieg, 2007; Ladd, 1999; Neal & Schanzenbach, 2007; Rouse et al., 2007; West & Peterson, 2006) have used a combination of state- or district-wide trends in achievement, along with trends or patterns in school and student-level achievement in other comparable districts or states, to sort out how the specific accountability system in that district or state affected student achievement. The main advantages of district and state studies are that the analysis is firmly focused on a specific, well-defined accountability system. Some of the studies, particularly those for particular states, are hampered by the difficulty of predicting what would have happened to student achievement in the absence of the state's accountability system. However, it is possible to exploit idiosyncratic differences in state policy effects (e.g., Figlio & Rouse, 2006) or changes in accountability rules (e.g., Rouse et al., 2007) in order to make apples-to- apples comparisons within a state.

Cross-state studies (e.g., Carnoy and Loeb (2002) and Hanushek and Raymond (2005) make use of the variation across states in the nature or timing of accountability *systems*. Although the conclusions of cross-state studies are sensitive to how accountability policies are defined as well as to methodological considerations such as the determination of control groups, the findings of cross-state studies are likely to be less idiosyncratic and more generalizable than those that emerge from the analysis of a specific program.

Some researchers have found modest but meaningful gains in test scores associated with school accountability, though many studies find little or no effect. Although a few methodologically rigorous studies, including Jacob (2005), Rouse et al. (2007), and Neal and Schanzenbach (2007), find positive impacts on reading scores, positive achievement effects emerge far less frequently in reading than in math. Larger and more consistent effects for math are intuitively plausible and are consistent with findings from other policy interventions such as voucher programs and tax and expenditure limitations. Compared to reading skills, math skills are more likely to be learned in the classroom, the curriculum is well defined and sequenced, and there is less opportunity for parents to substitute for what goes on in the classroom (Cronin, 2005).

Some evidence from the district- or state-specific studies suggests that the schools at the bottom of the performance distributions exhibit the greatest gains under an accountability system. This conclusion emerges from both Chicago (Jacob, 2005) and Florida (Figlio & Rouse, 2006). Working in the other direction is the finding from national study that the effects of high stakes are greater for the higher-scoring students. As predicted theoretically, school accountability systems often lead schools to target attention to students at particular points in the ability distribution: Neal and Schanzenbach (2007) and Krieg (2007) show that the gains in achievement associated with a status-based system tend to be most concentrated in the bubble students near the margin of proficiency, and Rouse et al. (2007) find that when Florida moved away from a status-based system to one that incorporates gains in student test scores, the students at the ends of the distribution (away from the bubble) appear to have benefited the most.

Evidence on unintended consequences

In any monitoring situation, those being monitored face incentives to appear as effective as possible against the metric being assessed. Thus, the concern arises that teachers might teach so narrowly to high-stakes tests that little or no generalizable learning would take place (Koretz & Barron, 1998). Typically, however, as long as the high-stakes tests reflect material that policymakers and the public consider important, teaching to the test would still be expected to improve student learning in the tested

areas, at least to some extent. In a few cases, however, reported gains may be completely bogus. Jacob and Levitt (2004), convincingly demonstrate, for example, that a small fraction of Chicago teachers responded to accountability pressures in that city by engaging in outright cheating in order to boost measured student test performance.

Regardless of whether teacher cheating takes place, substantial evidence supports the conclusion that schools tend to concentrate their attention on the subjects tested and on the grades that have high-stakes tests (see, e.g., Deere & Strayer, 2001; Ladd & Zelli, 2002). Other studies (e.g., Hamilton, Berends, & Stecher, 2005; Stecher, Barron, Chun, & Ross, 2000) show that teachers and schools tend to narrow the curriculum and shift their instructional emphasis from nontested to tested subjects, while earlier work by Shepard and Dougherty (1991) and Romberg, Zarinia, and Williams (1989) suggest that teachers focus more on tested content areas within specific subjects. In related work, Chakrabarti (2005) presents evidence that schools may concentrate their energies on the most easily improved areas of instruction, rather than on subjects across the board.

A common way to examine whether student learning has increased is to measure achievement using a low-stakes test, that is, one with no specific consequences for schools. A natural test for that purpose is the NAEP, which has been administered to a nationally representative random sample of students since the early 1970s and to representative samples of students in grades 4 and 8 in most states since the 1990s. The downside to measuring achievement using scores from a test with no consequences for students or teachers is that students may not take the test sufficiently seriously to do their best work. Unless student effort differs from one administration of the low-stakes test to the next, however, changes in performance on the low-stakes test should provide a reasonable estimate of gains in student learning. In some cases, tests offer low stakes for schools but high stakes for students (e.g., for track placement or school choice); here, the low-stakes tests could potentially provide at least lower-bound estimates of the effects of accountability on genuine learning. In general, smaller estimates of accountability effects emerge when the researcher focuses on tests with lower stakes, although in some cases the lower-stakes test results approach the magnitudes of the high-stakes test results.

Schools may also engage in strategies that artificially improve test scores by changing the group of students subject to the test. The most widely studied behavior of this type is the selective assignment of students to special education programs. Many studies, including Cullen and Reback (2006) and Jacob (2005), show that schools tend to classify low achievers as learning disabled in the context of accountability systems. Though there may be some debate about whether the greater rates of classification are undesirable in all cases, nonetheless, they highlight the possibility that schools are manipulating the testing pool specifically to inflate measured school performance. Figlio's (2006) finding that some Florida schools changed their discipline and suspension patterns around the time of the testing in ways consistent with the goal of improving test-takers' average scores reinforces this concern.

Evidence suggests that schools engage in other types of strategic behavior as well. For example, Figlio and Winicki (2005) demonstrate that schools change their meal programs at the time of the tests in an apparent attempt to raise performance on high-stakes examinations, while Anderson and Butcher (2006) find that schools subject to accountability pressure are more apt than other schools to sell soft drinks and snacks through vending machines.

Many of these behaviors are less likely to occur in growth-based accountability systems than in status-based systems. The reason is that in the growth approach, the manipulative behavior that increases student achievement in one year would make it more difficult for the school to attain accountability goals the following year. No such trade-off arises in status-based accountability systems.

New evidence shows that Florida schools subject to accountability pressures in a system that includes both status and growth measures changed their instructional policies and practices in productive ways. Using detailed survey data collected from a census of public schools in Florida, Rouse et al. (2007) find that changes in educator practices account for a significant proportion of the realized test-score gains associated with the change in accountability systems. The results indicate that accountability systems not only provide educators with incentives to change their behavior but also that their design affects the mix of productive and unproductive responses.

In conclusion, school accountability systems have the potential to influence school behaviors in tangible ways. School accountability systems in the United States appear to have modestly increased measured student test performance, at least in mathematics, and have likely done so through a combination of substantive and artificial means. There remains much to learn on the subject, and the research on the mechanisms through which accountability influences student achievement — and the macro-consequences of these mechanisms - is still in its infancy. More work is needed to fully understand the relative benefits and costs of school accountability systems.

See also: Competition and Student Performance; Economic Approaches to School Efficiency; Empirical Research Methods in the Economics of Education; Student Incentives; Teacher Incentives; Tiebout Sorting and Competition.

References

Anderson, P., & Butcher, K. (2006). Reading, writing, and refreshments: Are school finances contributing to children's obesity? *Journal of Human Resources, 41*(3), 467–494.

Burgess, S., Propper, C., Slater, H., & Wilson, D. (2005). *Who wins and who loses from school accountability? The distribution of educational gain in English secondary schools*. Working Paper. University of Bristol.

Carnoy, M., & Loeb, S. (2002). Does external accountability affect student outcomes? A cross-state analysis. *Educational Evaluation and Policy Analysis, 24*(4), 305–331.

Chakrabarti, R. (2005). *Do public schools facing vouchers behave strategically?*. Working Paper. Harvard University.

Cronln, J. (2005). *The impact of the NCLB act on student achievement and growth: 2005 edition*. Lake Oswego, OR: Northwest Evaluation Association.

Cullen, J., & Reback, R. (2006). Tinkering towards accolades: School gaming under a performance accountability system. In T. Gronberg, & D. Jansen (Eds.), *Improving school accountability: Check-ups or choice, advances in microeconomics* (Vol. 14, pp. 1–34). Amsterdam: Elsevier Science.

Deere, D., & Strayer, W. (2001). *Putting schools to the test: School accountability, Incentives and behavior*. Working Paper. Texas A&M University.

Figlio, D. (2006). Testing, crime and punishment. *Journal of Public Economics, 90*(4–5), 837–851.

Figlio, D., & Rouse, C. (2006). Do accountability and voucher threats improve low-performing schools? *Journal of Public Economics, 90*(1–2), 239–255.

Figlio, D., & Winicki, J. (2005). Food for thought? The effects of school accountability plans on school nutrition. *Journal of Public Economics, 89*(2–3), 381–394.

Frey, B. (2000). Motivation and human behaviour. In P. Taylor-Gooby (Ed.), *Risk, Trust and Welfare* (pp. 31–50). Basingstoke: Macmillan.

Hamilton, L., Berends, M., & Stecher, B. (2005). *Teachers' responses to standards-based accountability*. Working Paper, RAND Corporation.

Hanushek, E., & Raymond, M. (2003). Lessons about the design of state accountability systems. In P. E. Peterson, & M. R. West (Eds.), *NCLB? The politics and practice of school accountability* (pp. 127–151). Washington, DC: Brookings Institution Press.

Hanushek, E., & Raymond, M. (2005). Does school accountability lead to improved school performance? *Journal of Policy Analysis and Management, 24*(2), 297–329.

Jacob, B. (2005). Accountability, incentives and behavior. *Journal of Public Economics, 89*(5–6), 761–796.

Jacob, B., & Levitt, S. (2004). Rotten apples. *Quarterly Journal of Economics, 118*(3), 843–878.

Kane, T., & Staiger, D. (2002). *Improving school accountability systems*. Working Paper. National Bureau of Economic Research.

Koretz, D., & Barron, S. (1998). *The validity of gains on the Kentucky instructional results information system (KIRIS)*. Working Paper. RAND Corporation.

Krieg, J. (2007). Are students left behind? The distributional effects of the no child left behind act. *Education Finance and Policy, 3*(2), 250–281.

Ladd, H. (1996). *Holding schools accountable: Performance based reform in education*. Washington, DC: Brookings Institution Press.

Ladd, H. (1999). The Dallas school accountability and incentive program: An evaluation of its impacts on student outcomes. *Economics of Education Review, 18*(1), 1–18.

Ladd, H. F., & Hansen, J. (1999). *Making money matter: Financing America's schools*. Washington, DC: National Academy Press.

Ladd, H., & Walsh, R. (2002). Implementing value-added measures of school effectiveness: Getting the incentives right. *Economics of Education Review, 21*(1), 1–17.

Ladd, H., & Zelli, F. (2002). School-based accountability in North Carolina: The responses of school principals. *Educational Administration Quarterly, 38*(4), 494–529.

Neal, D., & Schanzenbach, D. (2007). *Left behind by design: Proficiency counts and test-based accountability*. Working Paper. National Bureau of Economic Research.

Romberg, T., Zarinia, E., & Williams, S. (1989). *The influence of mandated testing on mathematics instruction: Grade 8 teachers' perceptions*. Madison, Wl: National Center for Research in Mathematical Science Education, University of Wisconsin-Madison.

Rothstein, R., & Jacobson, R. (2008). Educational goals: A public perspective. In H. F. Ladd, & E. B. Fiske (Eds.), *Handbook of research in education finance and policy* (pp. 78–86). New York: Routledge.

Rouse, C., Hannaway, J., Goldhaber, D., & Figlio, D. (2007). *Feeling the Florida heat? How low-performing schools respond to voucher and accountability pressure*. Working Paper. National Bureau of Economic Research.

Shepard, L., & Dougherty, K. (1991). *Effects of high-stakes testing on instruction*. Working Paper. ERIC.

Stecher, B., Barron, S., Chun, T., & Ross, K. (2000). *The effects of the Washington state education reform on schools and classrooms*.

Stiefel, L., Schwartz, A. E., Rubinstein, R., & Zabel, J. (Eds.). (2005). *Measuring school performance and efficiency: Implications for practice and research*. Larchmont, NY: American Education Finance Association 2005 Yearbook. Eye on Education.

West, M., & Peterson, P. (2006). The efficacy of choice threats within school accountability systems: Results from legislatively induced experiments. *Economic Journal, 116*(510), C46–C62.

Further reading

Amrein, A., & Berliner, D. (2002). March 28. High states testing, uncertainty and student learning. *Education Policy Analysis Archives, 10*(18). http://epaa.asu.edu/epaa/v10n18.

Clotfelter, C., & Ladd, H. (1996). Recognizing and rewarding success in public schools. In H. Ladd (Ed.), *Holding schools accountable: Performance-based reform in education* (pp. 23–64). Washington, DC: Brookings Institution Press.

Elmore, R., Abelmann, C. H., & Fuhrman, S. H. (1999). The new accountability in state education reform: From process to performance. In H. F. Ladd (Ed.), *Holding schools accountable: Performance-based reform in education* (pp. 65–98). Washington, DC: Brookings Institution Press.

Figlio, D., & Getzler, L. (2006). Accountability, ability and disability: Gaming the system? In T. Gronberg, & D. Jansen (Eds.), *Vol. 14. Improving school accountability: Check-ups or choice, advances in microeconomics* (pp. 35–50). Amsterdam: Elsevier.

Haney, W. (2000). The myth of the Texas miracle in education. *Education Policy Analysis Archives, 8*(41). http://epaa.asu.edu/epaa/v8n41.

Jones, G., Jones, B., Hardin, B., et al. (1998). The impact of high-stakes testing on teachers and students in North Carolina. *Phi Delta Kappan, 81*, 199–203.

Ladd, H. (2001). School-based educational accountability systems: The promise and the pitfalls. *National Tax Journal, 54*(2), 385–400.

O'Day, J. A., & Smith, M. S. (1993). Systemic reform and educational opportunity. In S. Fuhrman (Ed.), *Designing coherent education policy: Improving the system* (pp. 250–312). San Francisco, CA: Jossey-Bass.

Peterson, P. E., & West, M. R. (2003). *Nclb? The politics and practice of school accountability.* Washington, DC: Brookings Institution Press.

Richards, C., & Sheu, T. (1992). The South Carolina school incentive reward program: A policy analysis. *Economics of Education Review, 11*(1), 71–86.

Index

'*Note:* Page numbers followed by "f" indicate figures, "t" indicates tables.'

A

Academic achievement, 513–514
Academies, 493–494
Actuarially fair insurance, 449
Acute illnesses, 246
Altruism, 515
American higher education system, 345
  graduate and professional program, 350–351
  HOPE scholarship program, 346
  net tuition, 347
  rising
    private higher education, 347–349
    public higher education, 349–350
  tuition discount rate, 346–347, 349
Annual returns, 46–47
Apprenticeships, 548–552
Apprenticeship training, 544, 546t
Armed Forces Qualifying Test (AFQT), 141–142
Asthma, 245–246
Asymmetric information, 448
Averaged Freshman Graduation Rate (AFGR), 150

B

Behavioral economics
  biased beliefs, 23
  cognitive ability, 22
  deadlines, 26–27
  default bias, 22
  defaults, 25
  education interventions, 23–32
  framing, 25–26
  goal setting, 27–28
  identity activation, 31–32
  informational nudges, 28–30
  limited attention, 22
  loss aversion, 22
  mindset nudges, 31–32
  nudging, 23–32
  peer group manipulations, 26
  reminders, 28
  reminding students, 28
  self-control, 21–22
  skills to alleviate self-control problems, 30
  social belonging, 31–32
  social comparison nudges, 30–31
  social preferences, 23
Birth weight, 244
Black/white test-score gap, 142–143

C

Capitalization, 472
Cash awards, 561–562
Catholic school attendance, 515
Catholic schools
  academic achievement, 513–514
  altruism, 515
  bad behavior, 514
  catholic school attendance, 515
  civic participation, 515
  demand, 512–513
  economic effects, 515
  educational attainment, 513–514
  enrollment, 509–510
  error term, 514
  exogenous variable, 514
  history, 509–510
  instrumental variable, 514
  location, 510–511
  market served, 511
  in other countries, 511–512
  school practices, 511
  self-selection, 513
  standard deviation, 513
  students, 510
  teachers, 510
  tuition and costs, 511
  vouchers, 511
Charter reform, 531
Charter schools, 494–495
  charter reform, 531
  definition, 531

external validity, 536
fixed effects, 538
internal validity, 536
performance, 535–538
policy questions, 532
selection bias, 536
traditional public schools, 533t, 538–539
traditional schools, 534–535
types of students, 532–534
Child health
  developing countries, 99–100
  family background, 92
  immediate effects of education, 93
  implications, 100–101
  intergenerational effects of education, 93–94
  lifecycle, 94–99
  non-monetary returns to education, 92
  prenatal influences, 94–99
    in adolescence, 96–97
    in adulthood, 97–98
    at birth, 94–95
    in childhood, 95–96
    in late life, 98–99
  socio-economic differences, 92
Cincinnati Public Schools (CPS), 363–365
Civic engagement
  educational attainment
    additional schooling, 104–105
    responsibility, 104
    volunteering, 104
  public and private schools
    catholic schools, 106
    cognitive skills, 105–106
    externalities, 105
    selection biases, 106
    social capital, 106–107
    transaction costs, 107
    voting, 106
Civic participation, 515

Class size economics
  achievement results, 326–328
  additional caveats, 328–329
  empirical approaches, 322
  experimental research, 323–325
  nonexperimental research, 322–323
  policy-induced variation, 329–330
  quasi-experimental research, 329
  randomization checks, 325–326
  reducing impact, 321
Cognitive ability, 22, 61–62
Cognitive skills, 143
College premium, 79–83, 80f
Comparable Wage Index (CWI), 338
Computer-assisted learning, 374–375
Contract teachers, 207–208, 382,
  385–386
Control group, 4–5
Corruption, 451
Crime
  contemporaneous schooling,
    114–115
  educational attainment, 110–113
  education effects, 113
    arrest and incarceration, 115–116
    female crime, 113
    policies, 116
    school choice, 113–114
    school quality, 113–114
  measures, 115
  school quality, 110–115
Cross-section data, 137–139, 138f,
  138t
Current Population Survey (CPS),
  79–80

D
Decision-making unit (DMU),
  480–481
Deliberate random assignment,
  293–295
Developed countries
  ability bias, 42–45
    education system, 43–45
    proxy measures, 43
    regression discontinuity (RD)
      procedures, 45
    twin studies, 43
  annual returns, 46–47
  heterogeneous returns, 45–46
  hourly wages *vs.* measures, 41–42
  international evidence, 48–49
  measurement error, schooling, 42
  non-pecuniary benefits, 47

  omitted variables, 42–45
  schooling equations, 40–41
  selection bias, 42–45
  sheepskin effects, 46–47
  signaling, 46–47
  social benefits, 47
Developing countries
  causality, 60–61
    costs, 60–61
    estimated returns, 61t
    instrumental variables (IV),
      60–61
    ordinary least squares, 61
  cognitive ability, 61–62
  educational mismatch
    Brazil, 273, 282
    China, 274–276, 283
    consequences, 282–284
    degree of mismatch, 273
    economic growth, 284
    general findings, 272
    India, 274, 283
    informality, 278–280
    job satisfaction, 284
    low-income countries, 276–277,
      283–284
    measurement issues, 271–272
    overeducation, 284
    policy, 284–285
    quality of education, 280–281
    rates of overeducation, 273–277
    reflection, 284–285
    Russia, 273–274, 282–283
    STEP survey, 281
    underemployment, 270
    underutilisation, 270
  education production functions,
    183–188
    conditional cash transfers, 197
    definition, 188–194
    demand-side interventions,
      196–203
    empirical results, 189t–192t
    endogenous program placement
      bias, 195
    estimation, 194–196
    information-based interventions,
      203
    in-kind transfers, 202
    measurement error bias, 195
    merit-based scholarships, 199
    omitted variable bias, 194–195
    policy impacts, 196–210

    primary enrollment rates,
      185t–186t
    research, 210–211
    school fee reductions, 200
    secondary enrollment rates, 186t
    selection and attrition bias, 195
    supply-side policies, 203–210
    unconditional cash transfers, 196
    vouchers, 200
  Mincerian, 55
  returns to education
    age-earnings profiles, 54f
    causality, 60–61
    cognitive ability, 61–62
    educational level, 56t
    gender, 57t
    low-income countries, 56–57
    mean earnings, 58f
    preschool, 59–62
    vocational education, 57–59
  teachers
    categorization, 372
    computer-assisted learning,
      374–375
    contract teachers, 382, 385–386
    diagnostic feedback, 382–383,
      386
    educational outcomes, 372
    interventions analysis, 383–386
    learning inputs, 374–378
    literacy programs, 376–377
    literature selection, 372
    longer school days, 377
    materials/curriculum training,
      380–381
    multi-dimensional teacher
      interventions, 383, 386
    pedagogy interventions, 373, 384
    pupil-teacher ratio, 376
    remedial education, 378–379
    right level, 378–379
    school input interventions, 384
    school interventions time, 372–373
    teacher monitoring, 382–383, 386
    teacher performance pay, 381–382,
      384–385
    teacher-related governance
      interventions, 373–374
    tracking students, 379–380
    tutoring, 378–379
    unique interventions, 377–378
Diagnostic feedback, teachers,
  382–383, 386

Difference-in-differences (DiD)
    approaches, 13—15
District of Columbia Public Schools
    (DCPS), 361
Division of labor, 447

E

Early childhood interventions
    cognitive and academic outcomes,
        233—234
    economic rationale, 229—231
        equity, 230—231
        human capital formation, 231
        market failures, 230
        redistribution, 230—231
    economic returns, 236
    female labor supply, 235—236
    indirect effects, 235—236
    noncognitive outcomes, 234—235
    types, 231—233
Earnings function method, 55
Economic growth
    causality, 176—178
    cognitive skills, 174—176
    economic growth, 172—173
    economic institutions educational
        quality, 178
    educational reform, 178—180
    gross domestic product (GDP), 172
    quality of education, 173—174
    schooling quantity, 172—173
Economics education
    definition, 3
    standard approaches, 4
Economies of scale, 449
Educational attainment, 513—514
    earnings, 126f
Education outcomes, inequalities
    adults in employment, education
        level, 127f
    changes over time, 128—130
    economic outcomes, 125—130
    educational attainment earnings,
        126f
    ethnicity, 122—123
    gender, 123—125, 124f
    immigrant status, 122—123
    race, 122—123
    skill-biased technical change (SBTC),
        130
    social background, 119—122, 120f
Education production functions
    benefits, 168
    Coleman Report, 167—168

costs, 168
estimation approach, 167
human capital, 161—163
implications, 168
knowledge capital, 163
measuring skills, 161—163
overview, 161
school inputs, 164—165
statistical analysis, 164
study quality, 165—166
value-added analysis, 165, 168
Education systems, 446—447
Empirical estimation
    causation, 3—5
    endogeneity problem, 3—4
    research
        difference-in-differences
            approach, 13—15
        explicit randomization, 5—9
        fixed-effects approach, 15—17
        instrumental-variable approach,
            9—10
        lotteries of oversubscribed
            programs, 7—9
        panel data, 13—17
        randomized controlled
            experiments, 5—7
        regression-discontinuity
            approach, 10—13
    reverse causality, 3
Endogeneity problem, 3—4
Enforced mediocrity, 451
Environmental toxins, 246
Error term, 514
Ethnicity, 122—123
European Tertiary Education
    Register (ETER), 481—482
Evaluation systems, 316
Exogenous variable, 514
Externalities, 447—448
External validity, 7, 536

F

Families environment
    behavioral responses, 217—227
    education production, 218—220
    empirical findings, 221—225
    extensions, 219—220
    factors, 223—224
    input interactions, 218—220
    methodological approaches,
        220—221
    multiple inputs and agents,
        224—225

schooling inputs, 224—225
test score impacts, 225
Fetal origins hypothesis, 243
Fiscal returns, 552
Fixed-effects approach, 15—17
Formal training, 312—313
Free schools, 494—495
Full discounting method, 55

G

General Education Development
    (GED), 150
Geographic Cost of Education Index
    (GCEI), 338
Grossman health model, 240

H

Hedonic wage regression, 417—423
    data, 417
    findings, 417—423
    method, 417
    minority student, 420
    student poverty, 420
    teachers wages, 418t—420t
HE records (HESA), 82—83
Heterogeneity, higher education
    college premium, 79—83, 80f
    Current Population Survey (CPS),
        79—80
    definition, 83—89
    economic values, 78—89
    "exponential" discounters, 78—79
    HE records (HESA), 82—83
    Higher Education nstitutions (HEIs),
        76
    "hyperbolic", 78—79
    Longitudinal Education pportunities
        (LEO), 82—83, 83t
    OLS estimates, 81
    student choice, 83—89
Heterogeneous returns, 45—46
Higher education incentives
    cash awards, 561—562
    grants, 561—562
    scholarships, 561—562
    student loans, 562—563
Higher Education nstitutions (HEIs),
    76
High school dropouts
    Averaged Freshman Graduation
        Rate (AFGR), 150
    "college and career-ready" (CCR)
        diploma, 151
    comprehensive approaches, 155—156

High school dropouts (*Continued*)
consequences, 151–152
dropout rates, 149–150
General Education Development (GED), 150
indicators, 149
individual factors, 152–153
institutional factors, 153–155
community and peers, 154–155
families, 153
schools, 153–154
intervention strategies, 155–156
Organization for Economic and Cooperative Development (OECD), 151
students, 152–155
systemic approaches, 156
targeted approaches., 155
Hiring more teachers, 204
Hiring practices, 411
HOPE scholarship program, 346
Hourly wages, 41–42
Household preferences, 472

I
Immigrant status, 122–123
Induction, 409–410
Informational nudges
financial aid and assistance, 29–30
information about behavior and ability, 29
parental information, 28–29
returns to schooling, 29
Institutional constraints, 407–408
Instrumental-variable (IV) approach, 9–10, 60–61, 297–298, 514
Instrument exogeneity, 9
Instrument relevance, 9
Intergenerational effects of education, 93–94
Internal validity, 536
International evidence, 48–49
Interventions analysis, 383–386

K
Knowledge capital
causality, 176–178
cognitive skills, 174–176
economic growth, 172–173
economic institutions educational quality, 178
educational reform, 178–180
gross domestic product (GDP), 172

quality of education, 173–174
schooling quantity, 172–173
K-12 public education systems, 333

L
Labor market discrimination, 139, 144
Labor market variables, 313–315
teacher mobility, 315
teacher unions, 314–315
teacher wages, 313–314
teacher wage systems, 313–314
Linear programming (LP) problem, 480–481
Literacy programs, 376–377
Literature selection, 372
Local Education Authorities (LEA), 458
Local Management of Schools (LMS), 458
Longer school days, 204, 377
Longitudinal data, 144–145
Longitudinal Education pportunities (LEO), 82–83, 83t
Low-income countries, 56–57

M
Materials/curriculum training, 380–381
Measurement error, schooling, 42
Medical services, 209
Mentoring, 409–410
Mincerian, 55
Minority women, 139–140
Monetary incentives, 408–409
rewards, 252–253
sensitivity to cash size, 250–252
students' motivation, 252
Multi-dimensional teacher interventions, 383, 386

N
Narrow-social, 55
National Assessment of Educational Progress (NAEP), 336, 355
Net tuition, 347
No Child Left Behind Act (NCLB), 494–495
Noncognitive skills, 143
Nonexperimental research, 322–323
Nonlinearity, 300–302
Non-monetary incentives
categorization, 255t
effectiveness, 257–264
parents and teachers, 263–264

research, 259t–261t
selection, 254–257
social recognition, 256–257
students, 257–263
types, 253–254
Non-monetary returns to education, 92
Non-pecuniary benefits, 47
Nudging, 23–32

O
Ordinary least squares, 61
Organization for Economic and Cooperative Development (OECD), 151

P
Parental education
adolescence, 96–97
adulthood, 97–98
child health at birth, 94–95
childhood, 95–96
developing countries, 99–100
immediate effects, 93
implications, 100–101
intergenerational effects, 93–94
late life, 98–99
Parental information, 28–29
Parental socioeconomic status
acute illnesses, 246
asthma, 245–246
birth weight, 244
causation, 241–242
children's educational outcomes gaps, 247
correlation, 240–241
environmental toxins, 246
evidence, 243–246
external benefits, 240
fetal origins hypothesis, 243
Grossman health model, 240
mental health, 245
nutrition, 244–245
possible channels, 242–243
sibling fixed effects, 242
in utero, 243–244
Pedagogy interventions, 373, 384
Peer effects
deliberate random assignment, 293–295
fixed effect, 298–299
heterogeneity, 300–302
instrumental variable, 297–298
nonlinearity, 300–302

recent empirical evidence, 293–302

regression-discontinuity design, 295–297

variance restriction, 300

Peer group manipulations, 26

Performance-based pay, 410

Performance or league tables, 492, 505

Perry Preschool Program, 6

Policy-induced variation, 329–330

Pool of Inactive Teachers (PIT), 394

Pool of Recoverable Teachers (PRT), 394

Preschool, 59–62

Price rationing, 523–524

Private higher education, 347–349

Private schools

benefits, 521

economically-rewarding jobs, 519

evidence on choice, 522–524

findings, 526–527

methods, 524–526

nature, 520

parents' choice, 520–521

participation, 519–520

price rationing, 523–524

price sensitive, 523

quasi- experimental studies, 526

racial discriminatory preferences, 522–523

randomized control trial, 524–525

socio-economic characteristics, 525

theory, 520–522

Productive tasks allocation, 546–547

Provision of material inputs, 205

Psychic benefits, 405

Public higher education, 349–350

Public spending, 452–453

Pupil-teacher ratio, 376

Q

Quality studies

causal returns assessing, 67–68

high school quality, 68–70

labor market returns, 66t

middle school quality, 68–70

quasi-experimental research, 67–68, 70

returns to college, 70–71

Quasi-markets, England

alternative approaches, 457–458

competition between schools, 462–463

complementary, 465–467

contradictory educational policies, 465–467

demand side, 460–461

educational outcomes, 462–465

educational policies, 459t

educational reforms, 459t

inequality, 465

Local Education Authorities (LEA), 458

operation, 462

regulation and monitoring of schools, 461

research, 467–468

segregation, 465

state financing and provision, 456

supply side, 458–460

test score outcomes, 461–465

R

Race, 122–123

Race earnings differentials

ability differences, 137

ability/educational quality differences, 140–142

black/white test-score gap, 142–143

Brazil and Israel results, 145–146

changes, 143–145, 144t

cognitive skills, 143

cross-section data, 137–139, 138f, 138t

ethnic earnings, United States, 134–136, 135t

labor market discrimination, 139, 144

longitudinal data, 144–145

minority women, 139–140

model, 136–137

noncognitive skills, 143

Random assignment evidence, 428

Randomization checks, 325–326

Randomized controlled trials (RCTs), 5–7

Regression discontinuity (RD), 10–13, 45

design, 295–297

Remedial education, 378–379

Rent-seeking, 451

Residential mobility, 472

Risk aversion, 449

S

Scholarships, 561–562

School accountability

designing, 569–571

growth model, 569–570

principal-agent problem, 568

rationale, 568–569

status model, 569

student achievement evidence, 571–572

test-based school accountability, 567–568

unintended consequences evidence, 572–573

School competition

academies, 493–494

charter schools, 494–495

empirical evidence, 496–503

Chile, 503–504

England, 496–498

Sweden, 501–503

US, 499–501

free schools, 494–495

performance or league tables, 492, 505

voucher system, 493–495

School construction, 203–204

School efficiency

competition, 479–480

data envelopment analysis (DEA), 480

models, 480–483

data envelopment analysis, 480–482

stochastic frontier analysis, 482–483

non-parametric models, 483–485

malmquist indices, 484

metafrontiers, 483–484

network DEA models, 485

revenue efficiency models, 484–485

parametric models

causality, 486

network SFA, 487

panel data models, 486

transitory and permanent inefficiencies, 486–487

stochastic frontier analysis (SFA), 480

School finance

context, 333–335

classification, 335t

multiple and evolving roles, 335–337

distributing resources, 337–340

guaranteed tax base (GTB) programs, 337–338

School finance (*Continued*)
    litigation, 339
    mechanisms, 337—338
    state funding systems challenges,
       338—340
    non-government sources, 336
    utilization of resources
       educational services, 341
       teacher compensation, 340—341
Schooling equations, 40—41
School input interventions, 384
School inputs rationing, 472—475
School interventions time, 372—373
School location, 405—406
School meals, 209
School Performance Tables (SPTs),
    464
Selection bias, 536
Self-selection, 513
Sibling fixed effects, 242
Skill-biased technical change (SBTC),
    130
Skilled worker wages, 547
Social belonging, 31—32
Social benefits, 47
Social preferences, 23
Standard deviation, 513
State economic role
    actuarially fair insurance, 449
    asymmetric information, 448
    corruption, 451
    critique, 450
    division of labor, 447
    economies of scale, 449
    education, 452—453
    education systems, 446—447
    enforced mediocrity, 451
    equity, 449—450
    externalities, 447—448
    government failure, 450—451
    inefficiency, 450—451
    inequity, 451
    information asymmetry, 448
    market failure, 447—449
    private, 446
    public choice, 450—451
    public spending, 452—453
    rent-seeking, 451
    risk aversion, 449
    role, 451—452
    shrinking state, 452—453
    standardization, 451
    state monopoly, 449

    uncertainty, 449
Student enrollment, 406—407
Student incentives
    developing countries, 557—559
    K-12 education
       financial incentives, 555—556
       non- financial/mixed incentives,
         556—557
Student loans, 562—563
Student-to-teacher ratios reduction,
    407

T
Talent Transfer Initiative (TTI), 362
Teacher attendance, 205
Teacher incentives, 206—207
    advantages, 432
    adverse and unintended
       consequences, 439
    criticisms, 436—439
    disadvantages, 436—439
    group incentives
       efficiency, 435—436
       productivity, 435—436
    incentive programs, 432
    individual behavior, 431
    individual incentives
       efficiency, 432—435
       productivity, 432—435
    K-12 education, 559—561
       group incentives, 560—561
       individual teacher incentives,
         559—560
       teacher-student aligned incentives,
         561
    recruitment and retention, 435
Teacher labor markets
    compensating differentials
       empirical studies, 417—423
       findings and future directions, 428
       hedonic wage regression,
         417—423
       labor economics, 415
       policy interventions, 423—424
       quasi-experimental evidence,
         424—427
       random assignment evidence, 428
       teacher attrition and retention, 423
    constrained teacher labor markets,
       356—359
    demand and supply, 357f
    economic and racial segregation, 357
    measurement and distribution, 366
    methodological challenges, 359—360

    National Assessment of Educational
       Progress (NAEP), 355
    non-traditional measures, 361
    quality of leadership, 359—360
    randomized control trials (RCTs),
       359
    recruiting effective teachers, 360—363
    retaining effective teachers, 363—365
    socio-economic status, 357
    talent transfer initiative (TTI), 362
    teacher quality, 358—359
    teacher workforce, 365—366
    Teach for America (TFA), 363
Teacher monitoring, 382—383, 386
Teacher performance pay, 381—382,
    384—385
Teacher quality
    education, 312—313
    estimating, 307—311
    formal training, 312—313
    individual teacher characteristics,
       311—313
    labor market variables, 313—315
       teacher mobility, 315
       teacher unions, 314—315
       teacher wages, 313—314
       teacher wage systems, 313—314
    measures, 315—316
    subject approach, 310—311
    teacher skills, 312—313
    value added approach, 308—310
    variation, 311—315
Teacher retirement, 406—407
Teachers recruitment and retention
    barriers to entry, 406
    career differentiation through
       ladders, 410—411
    changes in entry requirements, 409
    demand for teachers, 406
    districts and local colleges, 408
    hiring practices, 411
    hiring processes, 407
    induction and mentoring, 409—410
    institutional constraints, 407—408
    monetary incentives, 408—409
    performance-based pay, 410
    psychic benefits, 405
    quality of teaching, 403
    recruitment, 408
    reform of due process, 411—412
    retention policies, 408
    school location, 405—406
    student enrollment, 406—407

student-to-teacher ratios reduction, 407
supply and demand model, 403
supply of teachers, 404
teacher retirement, 406–407
wages, 404
working conditions, 404–405
Teacher supply
demand, 393f, 394–401
occupational choice, 399
recruitment, 396–397, 399
retention, 396–397
teachers' salaries, 399–401, 400f
Initial Teacher Training (ITT), 394
labor market, 391–394, 392f
OECD countries, 391
pupil-teacher ratio (PTR), 391–394
Teachers wages, 404
Teach for America (TFA), 361, 363
Technology-enhance instruction, 206
Test-based school accountability, 567–568
Tiebout sorting and competition
capitalization, 472
"customers", 471

household preferences, 472
local communities, 471
partial divorce, 476–477
productive efficiency, 475–476
residential mobility, 472
school inputs rationing, 472–475
Time dimension, 17
Traditional public schools, 538–539
Tuition and fees
American higher education system, 345
graduate and professional program, 350–351
HOPE scholarship program, 346
net tuition, 347
rising
private higher education, 347–349
public higher education, 349–350
tuition discount rate, 346–347, 349
Tuition discount rate, 346–347, 349

U
Uncertainty, 449
Uniform Crime Reports (UCRs), 111

Unintended consequences evidence, 572–573
Unskilled, 547

V
Value added approach, 308–310
Variance restriction, 300
Vocational education, 57–59
Vocational training
apprenticeships, 548–552
fiscal returns, 552
apprenticeship training, 544, 546t
costs and benefits, 544–548
apprentice, 547
cross-country comparisons, 546–548
general training firms, 544–545
productive tasks allocation, 546–547
skilled worker wages, 547
unskilled, 547
economic conditions firms, 543–544
school-based vocational training, 543
Voucher system, 493–495, 511